SECOND EDITION

People and Politics in Urban America

SECOND EDITION

People and Politics in Urban America

Robert W. Kweit
University of North Dakota

Mary Grisez Kweit
University of North Dakota

Garland Publishing, Inc.
A member of the Taylor & Francis Group
New York & London
1999

Library of Congress Cataloging-in-Publication Data

Kweit, Robert W.
     People and politics in Urban America / Robert W. Kweit, Mary
Grisez Kweit. — 2nd. ed.
       p.   cm. — (Garland reference library of social science ;
v. 1147)
     Includes bibliographical references and index.
     ISBN 0-8153-2607-6 (case : alk. paper). — ISBN 0-8153-2606-8
(pbk. : alk. paper)
     1. Municipal government—United States—Citizen participa-
tion.   2. Urban policy—United States—Citizen participation.
3. Political participation—United States.   I. Kweit, Mary Grisez.
II. Title.   III. Series.
HT123.K9   1999
320.8'5'0973—dc21   98-6537
                                CIP

Cover design: Robert Vankeirsbilck
Cover photograph: Paul Simcock, "East 51st Street, New York City"
© The Image Bank, New York City

Printed on acid-free, 250-year-life paper
Manufactured in the United States of America

To our parents

Contents

Tables and Figures

Tables

Figures

Preface

America's cities are anomalies. On the one hand, they house some of the greatest human accomplishments: museums that are full of artistic masterpieces, symphony halls that showcase musicians, dancers, and other performers, buildings that are architectural and technological marvels. On the other hand, those same cities also are home to human despair and depravity. People live in decayed and rat-infested buildings. Many, living in a drug-fogged world, prey on others for money to support their habits. Approximately 75 percent of Americans live in our cities and surrounding suburbs, and the characteristics of those cities inescapably affect the quality of their lives. This book examines the extent to which these Americans use the political process to control the characteristics of life in their metropolises.

Some reviewers saw the draft of the first edition of *People and Politics in Urban America* as a heretical work when it was first reviewed in 1988. At a time when the dominant paradigm in the field of urban politics was based on the assumption that politics was subservient to the inexorable forces of economic imperatives, the draft asked the question, "How can citizens use the political process to affect the quality of life in today's American cities?" The authors, both political scientists, felt that

question was legitimate and found reason for its legitimacy in political science research that focused on the role of citizen participation in political processes at the urban level.

The final manuscript melded the political science literature on the impact of participation with the urban literature that focused on reasons why the impact of participation must be seriously constrained by economics. It attempted to use both literatures to provide a balanced assessment of the possibilities and the limitations citizens face in attempting to control the urban environment. As the manuscript went to press, others in the urban field were publishing books that proclaimed that "politics matters," and new research began to appear that lent support to that claim. Researchers have now developed a body of literature that examines variation among cities in the nature of governing coalitions—or "regimes"—and concomitant variations in the role that various interests in the city, including major economic interests, play in decision-making.

The discipline has now accepted the position that allows for a more thorough discussion of the interdependence of politics and economics. While this makes *People and Politics in Urban America* less unique, the authors believe that these developments vindicate the thrust of the initial book. The revision addresses two basic questions: How can leaders put together a successful governing coalition? How can citizens impact the political process?

Clearly both questions are important to an understanding of urban politics. This revision attacks both questions by dealing more thoroughly than the initial edition with the urban political process as an interaction between political leaders attempting to form governing coalitions and citizens who need access to those coalitions to achieve their goals. It relies upon the concept of agenda-setting to bridge the individual and systemic perspectives. Leaders want to assemble a governing coalition to advance their agenda issues, but also use issues as a means of appealing to potential coalition partners. Citizens want their concerns to be on the agenda, and use various means either to become part of the coalition or to become a force that the coalition must consider.

This revision places greater emphasis than the first book on the role of political leaders, but it recognizes the interdependence between those leaders and various interests in the city. It draws upon the recent research—especially that examining the formation and transformation of governing coalitions in various cities. It examines the resources that citizens can use to become part of the coalition.

This version, however, retains the focus on the theme of democracy in the city and the importance of it for the citizens of the city. These issues are concerned from both an empirical and a normative perspective. The book retains many of the subjects addressed in the original text, although slightly reorganized, updating them by discussing current research and current events. Two areas most affected by the impact of current events are the discussion of the ethnic composition of the city and the discussion of the political changes occurring at the national level.

The original text examined the impact of the immigrants of the late nineteenth and early twentieth centuries and the impact of the more recent immigrants, identified as "blacks and Hispanics." The revised text includes discussion of these groups and moves the discussion of the early immigrants to the second chapter. It also includes an expanded examination of the increasing heterogeneity among blacks and Latinos, as well as the increasing importance of Asian-Americans and Asian immigrants in many cities.

Several events at the national level have had substantial implications for cities. The push to "reinvent government" has loosened the federal regulatory strings on state and local government, supposedly producing greater efficiency and effectiveness at all levels of government. Such a change may also be expected to create greater variation across cities in the implementation of many policies. The new Republican majority in Congress has transformed many federal transfer payments from categorical to block grants, thereby allowing greater variation in the way cities implement policies, and also greater variation in the policy mix of various cities. Because of the increased importance of local government management and innovation, a new chapter highlighting new urban management reforms has been included.

Chapters are arranged in four sections. The first part focuses on the urban context in which policymaking occurs. Part Two examines how issues are raised and placed on the agenda and how policy to deal with the issues is formulated. The third part looks at policy adoption, implementation, and evaluation. The final part examines various policy areas within this framework that are important in the urban setting.

Throughout the book, literature from various fields and perspectives is surveyed. In particular, the historical development of America's metropolises and of the major policy areas affecting them is reviewed. As a result, this text is relevant for a variety of urban studies, urban history, and community development courses.

Acknowledgments

We owe many debts which we tried to acknowledge in the prior edition, so we will spare the readers of this revision a long recounting. However, some important past debts still bear acknowledgment. We have learned the discipline from several outstanding scholars, including Alan Campbell, Guthrie Birkhead, Morton Schussheim, Julian Wolpert, Stephen Elkin, and Oliver P. Williams. We continue to learn and depend on our students past and present for help and advice. They include Peggy Kuhn, Lu Hoover, Mike Dorsher, Sharon Kessler, Deb Peterson, Marci Conmy, Laurie Konsella, Rolland Scott, Cindy Solberg, Deb Moreno, and Marcia Larson. Further, we are indebted to our overworked and underpaid office manager, Karen Bowles, who saw to the details and helped us put some order into our otherwise chaotic existence. We wish to thank also our editor, David Estrin of Garland Publishing. We have worked with many fine editors, and some not so fine, but we think David is the best. He has good judgment, a sense of humor, patience, and gets the most constructive manuscript reviewers. Finally, we wish to thank the reviewers of both editions for their suggestions, three of whom signed on for the revision, Tim Mead of the University of North Carolina at Charlotte, Richard Rich of Virginia Polytech and State University, and Craig Rimmerman of Hobart and William Smith Colleges. They were critical, constructive, good humored, and supportive. This book is much improved because of their input, and the authors hold themselves alone responsible for any shortcomings in this work.

SECOND EDITION

People and Politics in Urban America

CHAPTER 1

Introduction

In the 1940s, the mayor of Atlanta, Georgia, was William B. Hartsfield, a traditional southerner who believed in racial segregation. In fact, in 1944 he asked the Un-American Activities Committee of the U.S. House of Representatives to investigate the National Association for the Advancement of Colored People (NAACP). The NAACP was at that time one of the most effective advocates for equality for African-Americans. The segregationist Hartsfield just assumed that any organization pushing for racial equality had to be un-American. He also opposed the creation of a Fair Employment Practices Commission at the national level, a commission whose goal would be to ensure that African-Americans would be treated equally in the job market. At the time, both formal law and informal norms enforced racial segregation in Atlanta. The creation of a biracial coalition between the African-American community, the mayor, and the downtown Atlanta business interests, his longtime allies, would seem unlikely in such an environment. But that is exactly what happened.

Why would a traditional southern segregationist reach out to the African-American community and meet with its leaders? Why would that meeting lead to a pattern of co-operation between the mayor and those leaders? The answer is simple: votes. Mayor Hartsfield and his business allies had ambitious plans for the city of Atlanta, but to succeed the mayor needed the votes necessary to stay in office. Business did not control the number of votes needed, and the mayor's traditional constituency was migrating from Atlanta to the newly developing suburbs. Meanwhile, Atlanta's African-American community had succeeded in increasing the percentage of registered voters among its ranks from 4 percent to 27 percent. So began a pattern of mutually beneficial cooperation among political leaders, downtown business interests, and the African-American community that—although altered by time and events—prevails to this day. Atlanta mayors since Hartsfield have looked to the African-American community for support for major urban development projects from which the business interests profited; in return, the African-American community sought an end to the policies of segregation and an opportunity to share in the profits of urban development.[1]

The civic center in Grand Forks, North Dakota, was built in the 1950s. In 1992, a loose coalition of civic leaders decided that the city needed to build a new facility that would enable Grand Forks to attract conventions as well as some concerts and sporting events. The coalition convinced the mayor to name a prominent businessman to lead the campaign to encourage voters to approve the local sales tax increase that would be necessary to build the new center. The businessman carried a model of the proposed building to neighborhood meetings, Rotary Clubs, Lions Clubs, and any other organization that would give him time to promote the idea of a new events center. The new president of the University of North Dakota threw his support behind the plan, and the business community was solidly supportive. The general public was not. The voters soundly defeated the increase in the sales tax on which the new facility depended.

Barely two years later, Mayor Mike Polovitz called a news conference to insist that the city needed a new events center. The *Grand Forks Herald* reported the reaction:

> "Again," some asked. "It's too soon," others whispered. But Polovitz said, "If the Russians and the Americans can come together and conquer space, surely this community can come together and provide for a facility."[2]

The mayor and six city council members volunteered to study the issues, calling themselves The Civic Center Process Committee. They proposed a citywide planning process to determine if a new events center was needed. The city hired a coordinator to seek ways of getting the greatest citizen input into determining what kind of facility the city needed, what kinds of events it should accommodate, and where it should be located. Grand Forks sponsored 11 forums at which cards were distributed to solicit citizen views. At various stages of the process, the local newspaper published ballots to enable citizens to comment. In the fall of 1995, citi-

zens approved the increase in the sales tax for a new events center by a vote of 7,306 to 4,898.

The goal of this book is to help you understand how decisions like those outlined above are made in urban areas in the United States. To do that, the book examines the process by which **policy** is made. Policy is what governments say and do about a particular issue.[3] A special focus of the book is the question of what role citizens play in the policy process. A basic assumption of this book is that the question of citizen control is a crucial one. Three-quarters of Americans live in **metropolitan areas**. A metropolis is an urban area with a large population and many local governments, including those for cities, suburbs, counties, and others. The policies of the governments of the metropolis determine the quality of residents' day-to-day lives in intimate and inescapable ways. The cleanliness and safety of streets, the quality of education, the kind of buildings permitted in the neighborhood are all examples of crucial issues over which local governments have substantial control. Citizens must influence such policies if this country can legitimately claim to be a democracy.

Although citizen influence is essential in a democracy, that does not necessarily mean that everyone will view the policies that result from democratic decision making as good ones. No one who has ever attended a contentious public hearing can believe that citizens are always wise and always choose the best policy options. Many times citizens are focused on their own self-interest and find it difficult to accept or even listen to other points of view. Often they lack necessary information. While citizens may not always be wise, other interests that seek to influence urban policy may also suffer from a limited perspective and lack of information. The strength of a democratic policy process is that it maximizes the information available to decision makers, making it possible for them to incorporate various viewpoints in the development of broadly acceptable policy.[4] While broadly acceptable, such policy may not be exactly what any one citizen or group might have wanted.

In examining the policy-making process in metropolitan America and the role that citizens play in that process, this book will explore three themes. Atlanta and Grand Forks do not have much in common, but both of the vignettes above illustrate these themes: (1) the importance of the political process, (2) the importance of private control of resources, and (3) the influence of citizens on policy decisions.[5]

The Importance of the Political Process

The mayors of Atlanta and Grand Forks played a major role in developing policy in the cases reviewed above. That observation might not seem remarkable. Presumably the job of elected officials is to make the decisions that provide leadership and direction to their communities. Yet some scholars have argued that the major economic interests completely control urban decision making, leaving political leaders with little to do but ratify and facilitate the decisions of those interests.[6] On the contrary, this book will argue that political leaders do make decisions that substantially affect the direction local governments take. Mayors, like all elected executives, have special advantages as leaders because of their visibility and centrality in the political process, but other elected officials such as councilors and appointed managers are also important.

Although officials are important in decision making, they lack adequate power or authority to control the destiny of local communities by themselves. Americans have always been stingy in the allocation of power and authority to government at all levels. The framers wrote the Constitution to minimize the possibility of government tyranny—state constitutions follow that model. The powers and authority of local governments are especially limited. Getting what powers and authority they have from the state, local governments are in a legally subordinate role. Politics in metropolitan areas, then, occurs in the context of decisions and limits established by other governments in a complex web of intergovernmental relations. Accordingly, political leaders must find informal ways to augment their limited legal powers if they are to succeed in achieving their policy goals. Not only do the actions of other governments limit all governments in the metropolis, so does the extent to which private interests control important resources, the second theme of the book.

The Importance of Private Control of Resources

The Constitution's framers wanted a limited government to ensure that the liberty of private citizens to hold and control resources would be substantially unfettered. Clearly, governments at all levels do establish some limits on citizen liberty, largely through taxation and regulation. Compared to other developed countries, the United States imposes minimal limits.[7] While cities exercise some control over use of the land within their borders through planning and zoning, for the most part private interests own the land and determine its use. Decisions by private interests about location and investment substantially affect the economic health of local communities.

Because of the importance of the resources held by private interests, many of those interests will be significant participants in the policy-making process in governments in the metropolis. Major businesses are the most common of these private interest participants. In both Atlanta and Grand Forks, mayors sought developments to enhance their cities; in both cities, the business communities not only supported the proposals because they would benefit from the development but also pushed for those proposals in the first place. The dependence of officials on business is not a one-way street, however. Elected and appointed officials have the authority to make decisions that affect business health. While officials want to help business because business success contributes to a healthy urban economy, business is not monolithic. Decisions that affect one business positively may affect another negatively. For example, tax advantages for the development of new business may raise the taxes on established firms. The various business interests will vie with each other to seek favorable political decisions. The relationship between private interests and urban officials is mutual dependence rather than control of one by the other. But even the combined resources of urban officials and private interests are not adequate to enable them to govern independently of other citizens in the community.

Citizen Influence on Policy Decisions

Mayor Hartsfield of Atlanta needed votes to stay in office to pursue his development agenda. Mayor Polovitz in Grand Forks needed votes to approve the increase in the sales tax that was essential if a new events center were to be built. In both cases, the citizens who controlled those votes used them to force an alteration to the **policy agenda**, which is the combination of issues that are the focus of public debate and decision.[8] Altering the agenda led to a change in policy.

In Atlanta, the African-American com-

munity used its electoral clout to force the beginning of the dismantling of legal segregation in Atlanta, even before the United States Supreme Court moved to end it by ruling segregation in public education illegal in 1954. Through the years, African-Americans achieved other policy goals ranging from expanded housing options, to improved public transportation, to affirmative action in city contracts and hiring as the increasing size of the African-American community led to increased electoral clout. In Grand Forks, the second drive to get approval of the sales tax increase consciously focused on giving citizens a role in the planning of the design and location of the proposed new facility. As a result, the design differed substantially from the initial proposal. Gone was the reflecting pool from the front of the building; in went a facility that could accommodate University of North Dakota football games. While the changes in Grand Forks were not nearly as significant as those achieved by the African-American community in Atlanta, at the time some business leaders in Grand Forks believed the decision process marked a turning point in the city, signaling a new attitude of pro-growth optimism.[9]

Putting the Pieces Together

The three themes fit together. This book describes the urban policy process as one in which leaders—government officials or private interests—are important, but neither can govern in isolation. Rather interdependence among leaders and other interests characterizes the urban policy process. Not only are government leaders and private leaders, especially those in business, interdependent, they also depend on resources that others control. In Atlanta and Grand Forks, the resources were votes. In other cases different resources may be important—for example, expertise, or legitimacy granted by the endorsement of a popular citizen group. In any event, leaders can only lead if they can put together a **governing coalition**, which is composed of those who control the requisite resources. The need for such a coalition makes leaders in part dependent on others, who are then in a position to bargain. As the African-American community in Atlanta exchanged votes for policies to achieve greater racial equality, so other interests can try to exchange one favor for another. Other groups might want to become part of the governing coalition or to have an influence on the decisions it makes. Success in achieving either goal varies according to such factors as the resources the group controls and the need of the governing coalition for those resources.

The composition of governing coalitions varies. In some cities, a relatively stable group may interact regularly in the making of governing decisions. Clarence Stone referred to such ongoing governing coalitions as **regimes**.[10] In other cities, coalitions may compete, or different political coalitions may control different policy areas. The resources that business controls make it a powerful partner in a governing coalition, but business cannot always control the urban agenda nor can it control all policy. While business may set the agenda for economic development, it may not want to or be able to control educational policy, for example.[11]

The ultimate prize for all in the process of assembling a governing coalition is the ability to set the public policy agenda—to determine which policies will be considered legitimate concerns of government—and to determine policy, which allocates government resources. Some policies are almost habitually on the policy agenda. For example, local government must ensure the health and safety of residents, so it establishes a police force or a fire department or contracts with other governments to provide those services. In addition to those basic policies, individual local governments must determine if they will devote resources to redevelop the downtown into a thriving mecca for business or if they will build low-cost housing for poor residents. Should they focus on brick-and-mortar kinds of efforts—such as building a new events center—or should they devote their efforts to policies that will directly benefit residents in their daily lives, for example, job training programs for the unemployed or subsidized tuition at a city university? Such programs are not necessarily mutually exclusive, but given the limited fiscal resources of many local governments, decision makers must often choose between competing claims for limited funds.

In summary, the political process is important because it sets the public policy agenda and determines the policy of an urban area. Different people have different visions of what local governments in a metropolis should do. All need the help of others to achieve their goals. Political leaders are important as they assemble a coalition to pursue their agenda issues, but their potential coalition partners can use their bargaining clout to get other issues on the agenda. The leaders of major businesses are important because they have resources that make them attractive as coalition partners, but other citizens may as well. The African-American community in Atlanta demonstrated how citizen participation could be transformed into political influence. Citizens, then, who want their concerns addressed, need to find ways to become part of a governing coalition or to force that coalition to listen to them.

Overview of the Book

This book will examine how various interests compete to set the agenda and policies of the many governments in the metropolis.

A primary concern will be the ability of citizens to influence the agenda and resulting policies. The organization of this book follows the stages of policy making. While in the "real world" the policy process does not follow a neat progression through distinct stages, those who study policy have identified stages that help to focus attention on the various components of the process. There are five steps in the making of policy: (1) problem formation and agenda setting, (2) formulation, (3) adoption, (4) implementation and service delivery, and (5) evaluation.[12] (See Figure 1-1.)

In the **problem formation and agenda setting** stage, some people recognize that a problem exists that the public sector should possibly address. Those individuals then need to call the attention of others to the situation and convince them both that it is a problem and that a public solution should be sought.

This stage is crucial. If they are unsuccessful in getting a problem or situation considered a legitimate component of the public agenda, they have been defeated, even though no vote has been cast.

In the **formulation** stage, people suggest and debate alternative options for addressing the problem. The government then **adopts** one of the proposals through its regular decision process. The administrative arm of government **implements** the new program, a process that often involves providing citizens with additional services. Finally, an **evaluation** of the effect of the new program will be made to determine whether it adequately addresses the situation that initially triggered the process. The evaluation may be a formal study of the program or it may simply be the informal reactions of various people.

In reality the stages are not so distinct, nor do they follow neatly in sequence. Policy

---

FIGURE 1–1

Model of the Urban Policy-making Process

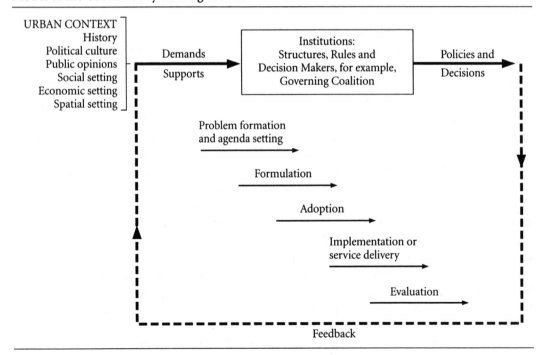

formulation may occur at the same stage as agenda setting, as discussions of whether a problem exists mingle with discussions of possible solutions. As governments consider adopting policy, they also often debate various formulations of policy options. Evaluation occurs as the program is implemented, or systematic evaluation may never occur. Nevertheless, identifying these stages helps analysts to think systematically about what occurs as policy is made and implemented.

The first part of this book recognizes the importance of the urban context in the policy process. Urban context affects what problems may arise that some people may see as requiring government action, and also affects the potential that citizens will be successful in influencing policy formulation to address the problems. The Introduction to Part I reviews the major factors that affect the urban context. **History** affects the current policies in urban areas because many policies change only incrementally over time. History is also a factor in the **political culture** of an area, which in turn influences the **public opinion** toward government and people's role in government. The **social setting** is important because interactions among people may lead to conflict, which may produce demands on government. Fiscal constraints resulting from the **economy** limit what local governments can do and the search for a healthy economy circumscribes many urban policies. The **spatial setting** also affects policy because location determines access to such things as transportation or job opportunities and creates different sets of demands, for example, snow removal in northern areas as opposed to senior citizen programs in the South.[13]

Part I of this book examines these contextual forces. Chapter 2 discusses the changes in social setting that resulted as the small towns of America grew into cities. The changes in social setting resulted in more issues being defined as public responsibilities, expanding the public agenda, and increasing the importance of politics and political leaders. Chapter 3 analyzes the historical development of cities and the economic implications of urban areas. Because of America's history and values, even though the political process has increased in importance, substantial resources have been left in private hands. Thus, private economic interests continue to play a major role in urban policy. Chapter 4 examines the social setting in greater depth by looking at the heterogeneity of the metropolitan population. Urban areas continue to receive new immigrants who become claimants on and participants in the urban policy process. The chapter looks at major groups of new urban immigrants and their ability to become parts of the governing coalitions to influence the policy process.

In the conflict among varying interests, multiple factors affect who will win and who will lose. One important factor is simply who is actively involved. If citizens are to affect the policy process, they must participate. The mobilization of people can change urban policy. Political activity has resulted in the incorporation of new groups into governing coalitions, as the Atlanta example illustrates. In some areas, African-Americans and Latinos have changed urban policy as they became significant parts of governing coalitions.[14] More recently, Asian-Americans have become an important political force in cities such as San Francisco and gays and lesbians have mobilized to fight against discrimination and for equal rights.

Part II of the book examines those groups that are most active in attempting to set the urban policy agenda, the variety of ways they attempt to influence the political process, and the reasons why participation does not always succeed in influencing policies. Chapter 5 discusses the groups that are usually the major actors in urban politics. Chapter 6 examines the ways those actors seek to gain influence.

Differing forms of citizen participation vary in their potential impact on decisions.

They also require differing amounts of citizen resources. Because of the need for resources, citizen participation does not always equal citizen control.

Individual citizen efforts and short-term protests rarely have an impact. To participate effectively, citizens must usually cooperate and form **voting blocs** or organizations that can communicate citizen demands to government. Because not all citizens possess equal resources, not all citizens can use the political process equally to attempt to influence the urban agenda and to seek policies that address issues of concern to them. The resources that the various interests in the city command and the skill with which they use those resources have a crucial impact on who wins and who loses in political conflicts. Some may decry the extent to which this demeans the political process and rewards those who are most effective at "bellying up to the bar," but the possession and use of resources affects success in competition nonetheless.[15] This means that politics does not guarantee equality, but may, in fact, aggravate the inequalities that already exist.

Part III examines the institutions of urban governments and considers how they affect the ability of citizens to influence policy adoption, implementation, and evaluation.. While involvement depends in part on individual citizen motivation, the governmental structure and the political process will also affect who becomes involved. For example, the election of city council members from electoral districts rather than citywide can affect whether minorities have any hope of winning election to the council because, although the votes of a minority may be diluted in a citywide election, they may constitute a majority in one or more neighborhood-based electoral districts. Institutional factors that affect the potential of success also affect individual motivations to participate in politics.

Chapter 7 examines the various organizational structures that comprise local governments. Chapter 8 looks at the roles, responsibilities, and powers of the officials in those structures. Chapters 9 and 10 review the fragmentation of power in the metropolis. Chapter 9 examines the horizontal fragmentation that occurs because at the local level power is shared among many different governments and special authorities. Chapter 10 investigates the vertical fragmentation that occurs because local governments have to contend with power exercised over them by different levels of government. Dillon's Rule in 1868 legally defined local units of government, such as city governments, as creatures of state governments, existing solely at the state's discretion and exercising only such powers as the state wished to grant them. The role of the national government in urban policy has exacerbated the vertical fragmentation of the urban political process. Chapter 11 looks more closely at the role of those who manage urban governments.

Part IV examines major policy areas and attempts to delineate the extent to which those policies have been affected by citizens. Local governments must attempt to enact policies that will make them attractive in the competition for residents and businesses. This requires providing services and amenities that they desire while keeping taxes low. The need to provide required services with low taxes while complying with the practical and legal limits created by the fragmented political process dominates the political process in urban areas today.[16]

The policies discussed in Part IV—education, crime control, transportation, community development, land use and planning, housing, and welfare—are among the most important issues facing local governments today. They are also areas of crucial concern to residents. Control by citizens over these basic areas of their lives is crucial if America is truly to call itself a democracy.

Notes

1. The definitive study of Atlanta and the source from which this short vignette was drawn is Clarence N. Stone, *Regime Politics: Governing Atlanta 1946–1988* (Lawrence: University of Kansas Press, 1989).

2. Kim Kozlowski, "Mapping a Victory," *Grand Forks Herald,* December 3, 1995, 1.

3. Randall B. Ripley and Grace A. Franklin, *Congress, the Bureaucracy, and Public Policy,* 5th ed. (Pacific Grove, California: Brooks/Cole, 1991), 1.

4. For an argument supporting the importance of democratic decision making, see Benjamin Barber, *Strong Democracy* (Berkeley: University of California Press, 1984); see also Peter Bachrach, *The Theory of Democratic Elitism* (Boston: Little, Brown, 1967).

5. The draft of this book was completed before the authors received a copy of Rufus P. Browning, Dale Rogers Marshall, and David H. Tabb, *Racial Politics in American Cities,* 2nd ed. (New York: Longman, 1997). The approach they take is very similar.

6. For an example, see Paul E. Peterson, *City Limits* (Chicago: University of Chicago Press, 1981).

7. John R. Logan and Harvey L. Molotch, *Urban Fortunes: The Political Economy of Place* (Berkeley: University of California Press, 1987), 2–3.

8. For a definition and discussion of public agendas, see Roger W. Cobb and Charles D. Elder, *Participation in American Politics: The Dynamic of Agenda-Building,* (Boston: Allyn and Bacon, 1972).

9. The great flood of April 1997 has put the plans for the new center on hold while the city turns to planning for its rebuilding.

10. Stone, *Regime Politics,* 4.

11. Clarence Stone, "The Politics of Urban School Reform: Civic Capacity, Social Capital, and the Intergroup Context." Paper prepared for presentation the Annual Meeting of the American Political Science Association, San Francisco, California, August 29–September 1, 1996, Appendix B, 14.

12. The general model, discussed in various places in this book, follows Charles S. Bullock III, James E. Anderson, and David W. Brady, *Public Policy in the Eighties* (Monterey, California: Brooks/Cole, 1983), 9–21.

13. Philip M. Hauser, "Urbanization: An Overview," in *The Study of Urbanization,* ed. Philip M. Hauser and Leo F. Schnore (New York: John Wiley, 1965), 1–47.

14. Rufus P. Browning, Dale Rogers Marshall, and David H. Tabb, *Protest Is Not Enough: The Struggle of Blacks and Hispanics for Equality in Urban Politics* (Berkeley: University of California Press, 1984); Raphael J. Sonenshein, *Politics in Black and White: Race and Power in Los Angeles* (Princeton: Princeton University Press, 1993); Browning, Marshall, and Tabb, *Racial Politics in American Cities.*

15. For such criticisms, see Stephen L. Elkin, *City and Regime in the American Republic* (Chicago: University of Chicago Press, 1987) and Theodore J. Lowi, *The End of Liberalism: The Second Republic of the United States* (New York: Norton, 1979).

16. The clearest statement of the sources of limits on urban politics is Paul E. Peterson, *City Limits.*

The Urban Environmental Context

Context for Urban Policy Making

Government programs do not exist in a vacuum. Policies depend on the needs and resources of those who make up the local community. Citizens attempt to define what will be on the public agenda by influencing how the government defines the needs of the community and the priorities that will govern the allocation of resources. Two important factors affect policy: the historical context and the current general context, which includes the political culture, public opinions, social setting, economy, and spatial patterns. Table I–1 (on page 14) provides a graphic summary of these factors.

Historical Context

The policy-making process does not start with a blank slate. Current public policies tend to reflect incremental changes from earlier policies. Sometimes cataclysmic factors force new issues onto the agenda, but this is the exception rather than the rule.

One example of the impact of history is preference for limited government and the importance of business interests. The United States has always left many resources in private hands and, even as the role of political leaders

increased as towns grew into cities, public decisions have often focused on protecting and augmenting those private resources. Indeed, the Colonial city was a **mercantile** city in which much public policy fostered trade, which benefited private interests. Economic elites traditionally demanded that the agenda of local government be minimized to keep costs down, even if doing so caused discomfort for the poor. Since then, government has assumed a more active role, but the extent of private control of resources and the resulting political influence of business represents continuity with the past.

The expansion of the role of government illustrates the importance of history as well as the impact of political leaders and of citizen demands on them. Chapter 2 examines the history of the expansion of America's small towns into cities and the impact of that growth on the social setting. The growth created an increased **impersonality, interdependence,** and **heterogeneity.** As a result of those changes, new problems arose that neither individuals nor private economic interests could solve. As the public agenda expanded, so did the role of political leaders. As Chapter 3 makes clear, however, substantial resources were left in private hands and major economic interests continued to play an important role in urban areas.

General Context

In addition to history, other factors affect public policy, including the following: (1) political culture; (2) public opinion; (3) social setting; (4) economic setting; and (5) spatial setting. The basic values and opinions of the public affect policy formation by determining the demands communicated to government, and the social, economic, and spatial contexts of urban areas help to shape those values and opinions.

Political culture refers to ". . . specifically political orientations—attitudes toward the political system and its various parts, and attitudes toward the role of the self in the system."[1] In essence, political culture refers to expectations regarding the role of government and its citizens. These political orientations substantially influence the public policy agenda, determining what issues are believed to be le-

gitimate for government consideration and how individuals may participate to press their preferences. Political culture thus affects what demands citizens make and how they make them.

Americans share many beliefs that affect public policy. They tend to be pragmatic as opposed to doctrinaire; to believe in equality, though usually in the abstract rather than in specific cases; to support basic political freedoms such as freedom of speech, religion, assembly; to desire efficiency; and to be optimistic about the future. Americans also value individualism and competition, both of which are at the heart of a capitalist economic system based on maximum private control of the economy. Government functioning reflects these values. On the one hand, the emphasis on political freedoms and individualism predisposes Americans to keep the role of gov-

TABLE I–1

Context for Urban Policy Making

Urban Context	Urban Factors
1. History	1a. Limited government
	1b. Support for business
	1c. Government—dependence on other levels of government
2. Urban Political Culture	2a. Estrangement from policy as basic decisions are made outside the city
	2b. Rising expectations about government services
	2c. Varying expectations about government services in different cities and regions
3. Public opinion	3a. Limited scope
	3b. Great intensity
4. Social setting	4a. Heterogeneity
	4b. Impersonality
	4c. Interdependence
	4d. Characteristics of people
5. Economic setting	5a. Fiscal constraints or wealth of community
	5b. Capitalist ideology
	5c. Conversion of economic power to political influence
6. Spatial setting	6a. Location
	6b. Climate

FIGURE I-1

Regional Political Cultures

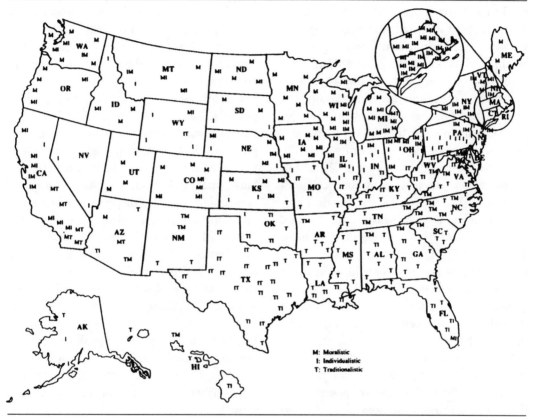

M: Moralistic
I: Individualistic
T: Traditionalistic

Source: Daniel Elazar, *American Federalism: A View from the States,* 3rd ed. (New York: Harper & Row, 1984), 106–107. Reprinted by permission of Addison-Wesley Educational Publishers, Inc.

ernment minimal and to leave many resources and decisions in private hands. Many government policies are designed to foster the growth of private wealth. Individuals are expected to be responsible for themselves. For example, prior to the New Deal, most Americans felt that government at all levels should play a minimal role in their lives. They believed, and many still do, that being poor was an individual responsibility. On the other hand, during the Great Depression many came to believe that individuals experienced want because of societal problems and only government could solve these problems. Hence the government agenda expanded.

Urban scholar Edward Banfield warns that the shift of responsibility from the individual to society and government is one of the main causes of what some call the "urban crisis."[2] While citizens may expect more services, they still prefer limited government and resist paying taxes. This makes it difficult for government to meet citizen expectations concerning services. Those expectations are now being reconsidered as fiscal problems are making it difficult for the national government to provide local governments with the financial resources necessary to respond to citizen demands.

Political culture varies in different parts of the country. Daniel Elazar has described three regional political cultures. Those in a **traditionalistic** culture, dominant in the South, support a limited government agenda, with the socially prominent assuming a leadership role. Those in the Midwest and West tend to have a **moralistic** political culture. The concept of community is important, and there exists "a greater commitment of active government intervention in the economic and social life of the community."[3] At the same time, the culture is very localistic and people resent intervention by "outside" governments.[4] The **individualistic** political culture dominates the Northeast. In this culture, "government action is to be restricted to those areas, primarily in the economic realm, which encourage private initiative and widespread access to the marketplace."[5] Figure I–1 (on page 15), which pictures the distribution of the cultures and beliefs in the country, demonstrates that while certain cultures are dominant in certain areas, a rich and diverse mix of cultures exists throughout the country.

These cultures affect the urban agenda. In the South and Southwest, urban areas tend to provide fewer public services and lower levels of benefits than do other areas of the country as a result of their traditional culture. Urban areas in New England with their moralistic–individualistic blend tend to be more active and generous in service delivery.

A political culture is dynamic. Values and beliefs change over time. Although these values affect policy, policy also influences these values. In addition, "common values and beliefs help determine the demands made upon policymakers and act to inform, guide, and limit their behavior,"[6] but they should not be viewed as rigidly determining action.

Another influence on policy is **public opinion**, which is a specific view of current issues based on more basic political values, that is, political culture. Charles S. Bullock and his colleagues express the general role of public

opinion: "Public opinion plays a part in mapping the broad boundaries and direction of public policy rather than the specific content of policies."[7] Just as public opinion may affect policy, government action may shape public opinion by "educating" the public or fostering situations where public reactions support government wishes.

Public opinion does not always affect public policy because some officials believe that they must make decisions based on the public's best interests, regardless of the will of the people. Further, it is often difficult to know what public opinion is. As V. O. Key observed: "to speak with precision of public opinion is a task not unlike coming to grips with the Holy Ghost."[8] Few Americans have opinions on all of the issues that government addresses and the opinions they do have can change often. Philip Converse estimates that less than 20 percent of the public hold stable, informed opinions on most issues despite the fact that a majority will generally express an opinion if asked.[9] Another reason why opinion does not always directly affect policy is that citizens do not communicate their views.[10]

People often tend to view local issues as less important than national issues, meaning that they are less likely to have opinions about issues on the local level and less likely to communicate their opinions. In addition, local media usually provide limited information for citizens to form opinions. The exception occurs, however, when an issue touches citizens directly; then they are likely to have intense opinions. Many local issues, for example, taxation, sewage lagoon location, the siting of public housing, can produce substantial public interest. People tend to feel strongly about such issues and are more likely to communicate their views clearly.

On a short-term basis, a one-to-one correspondence between public opinion and policy may be lacking, but over the long haul, if the decision makers do not follow public opinion or convert opinion to be supportive, they will probably be replaced. Public opinion thus sets the boundaries for policy, even if it is not always translated directly into policy. At any rate, Americans generally accept the legitimacy of individuals and organized interests seeking to influence policy goals to conform with their values and opinions. This is the reason why those who want to understand the urban policy process must consider the influence of citizens.

The role of political leaders is also important because political leaders are the ones who must react to the demands of individuals and organized interests. Those leaders may seek decisions that are a compromise among competing demands or they may merely rubber stamp the demands put forward by the dominant group. Different local governments will respond differently to groups and issues over time. The ability of citizens to develop resources that give them access to the political process is crucial.

A third contextual factor is **social setting**. As indicated above, this book focuses on the increasing **heterogeneity**, **interdependence**, and **impersonality** that characterize urban areas. The complex mix of people in urban areas creates heterogeneity. The United States is a pluralistic nation, made up of various ethnic and racial groups with many religious preferences. Nowhere is this heterogeneity more obvious than in urban areas. Starting early in the nineteenth century, large numbers of immigrants began settling in metropolitan America. These immigrants expanded the size and diversity of the areas where they settled. In the twentieth century, immigration into urban areas has continued, with African-Americans moving from the rural South into northern cities, Latinos moving into cities in the Southwest as well as other areas, and large numbers of people from Central and South America and Asia arriving in the metropolises of North America as a result of the reform of the immigration law in 1965. As they prepare

for the twenty-first century, America's urban areas are home to an incredibly heterogeneous population with vastly varying interests and needs.

This heterogeneous population is also interdependent. The density of most urban areas means that people are confronted with each other constantly; in addition, they are all potential claimants on the resources many other residents are also seeking. That leads to conflict. Because of the large numbers of people in the metropolis, people may not know many of their fellow residents. That impersonality means that the political process often must solve conflicts. Groups press demands and attempt to get issues of concern to them on the political agenda. Those who are not organized may mobilize and, because of the "transferability of resources," may use votes, or unity, or access to key policy actors to make their point.[11]

One role of government is to act as an umpire, setting the rules for groups to press their demands and seeing that the game is played fairly. Yet if governments do nothing but umpire the group struggle, policy may not reflect the needs and interests of all citizens, since the citizens who are politically active are likely to come from the middle and upper class. In this case the game is not a fair one. Some critics argue that government should not simply listen to organized interests, but should act on behalf of those who lack the resources or skills to communicate their demands.[12] Of course, discovering the desires of those who are not active is no easy task.

The fourth contextual factor is the **economic setting**. Governments cannot spend what they do not have. Indeed, local governments must maintain a current fund balance. Fiscal constraints are especially important at the local level as many economic factors are beyond local control. The national economic picture has a marked impact on local policy because a healthy economy often means new building, industrial expansion, and increased pollution. High inflation usually means increased wage demands by public employees. National trade policy may affect the well-being of a particular industry, such as automobile manufacturing, which in turn can profoundly affect local policies in places like Detroit.

Our economic beliefs also affect government policy. As noted above, our strong belief in capitalism and free market competition leads some to look to government activity only as a last resort, which limits the political agenda. Although the Great Depression and the New Deal changed some expectations, and the role of government as a result, Americans continue to have faith in the market system and many resources are left in private control. This means that government must work with the private sector. **Co-production**, or creating cooperative arrangements with citizens, private organizations, or other government units to help in the provision of urban services, is one path cash-strapped local governments have taken. This idea follows naturally from our basic economic values.

Respect for economic power allows such power to be translated into political power. A major firm's threat to relocate unless tax policy or environmental policy is reconsidered is likely to affect that policy both because of the status of business in a city's social structure and because of the role that taxes paid by business play in the economic livelihood of a city. The firm in this example may not get its way, but it most certainly will affect the policy process. While other interests may struggle to develop resources that would give them access to politics, business interests normally have adequate resources to guarantee they will "be at the table" if they desire. That does not always mean, however, that they will achieve everything they want.

The last contextual influence on policy is the **spatial setting**. Oliver Williams has argued that one of the key aspects of urban politics is the competition for space because physical location determines access to desired values, such as local services.[13] People who live near parks, for instance, may be less likely to want to allocate resources to develop additional parks than are those who live farther from a park. Encroachment into "one's space" by "undesirables" may create problems. Spatial boundaries limit the reach and responsibility of local governments to deal with problems.

Location has other far-reaching implications for urban policy. It affects access to various forms of transportation and markets, as well as availability of resources such as water supply. Different climatic conditions associated with location also affect the public agenda. For instance, Minneapolis can be expected to spend more on snow removal than Dallas. These factors, too, serve as constraints on local policy making. Land is an example of a resource that is substantially controlled by private interests. Conflicts over the use of urban land are a major component of the urban situation as governments try to exercise some control over land use through planning and zoning decisions.

Conclusion

Governments do not produce policies in a vacuum. History plays a role by affecting citizen values and demands. In addition, many current policies are only incrementally different from past policies. The culture is an important determinant of what goals people seek and whether they seek those goals through the political process. Freedom and individualism are fundamental American values. These values support the idea of limited government and a powerful economic system, leaving substantial resources in private hands. The culture also influences citizen opinions and whether those opinions will be translated into demands for political action. The metropolitan setting brings people with greatly differing goals into close proximity with each other, creating interdependence and conflict. In this setting, the political process plays an important role in resolving the conflicts that result. The spatial structure of the metropolis also contributes to the goals that people seek and the conflicts that arise because different locations provide differential access to various goods and services. Not everyone can own the same plot of prized land.

Notes

1. Gabriel Almond and Sidney Verba, *The Civic Culture* (Boston: Little, Brown, 1965), 12.

2. Edward C. Banfield, *The Unheavenly City Revisited* (Boston: Little, Brown, 1974), 76.

3. Daniel J. Elazar, *American Federalism: A View From the States,* 2nd Ed. (New York: Crowell, 1972), 98.

4. Ibid.

5. Ibid., 94.

6. Charles S. Bullock III, James E. Anderson, and David W. Brady, *Public Policy in the Eighties,* (Pacific Grove, California: Brooks/Cole, 1983), 12.

7. Ibid., 13.

8. V. O. Key, *Public Opinion and American Democracy* (New York: Knopf, 1961), 14.

9. Philip E. Converse, "Attitudes and Non-Attitudes: Continuation of a Dialogue," in *Quantitative Analysis of Social Problems,* ed. Edward Tufte (Reading, Massachusetts: Addison-Wesley, 1970).

10. Warren E. Miller and Donald E. Stokes, "Constituency Influence in Congress," *American Political Science Review* 57 (1963): 45–56.

11. Robert A. Dahl, *Who Governs?* (New Haven: Yale University Press, 1961).

12. See, for example, Theodore Lowi, *The End of Liberalism: The Second Republic of the United States,* 2nd ed. (New York: Norton, 1979).

13. Oliver P. Williams, *Metropolitan Political Analysis: A Social Access Approach* (New York: Free Press, 1971), 36 and passim.

CHAPTER 2

From Small Town to City

The goals that people seek from government are as varied as the people themselves. They want wrongs to be righted; recognition to be given; law and order to be guaranteed; schools, roads, housing to be built; and taxes to be reduced. In part, goals derive from fundamental hopes and ambitions of people, but they are also affected by context. For example, farmers have little need of zoning to protect their property values and city dwellers are hardly concerned about parity price supports for soybeans. Context also has an impact on which goals are seen as requiring government involvement and which are not. In other words, the context affects what issues are likely to appear on the public agenda as well as the potential that citizens will be successful in using the political process to place their issues on the agenda and to influence policy choices.

The focus of this chapter is on a characteristic that has a major impact on both the public agenda and the role of citizens: the size of a population concentration. As population size increases, it alters the social setting by increasing *impersonality, heterogeneity,* and *interdependence.* Those changes, in turn, lead to changes in the public agenda. More issues are defined as problems that need public solutions, and therefore the role of politics and political leaders expands.

This chapter will discuss the changes in social setting that occur as a community grows from a small town to a city. It also examines the contribution of the immigrants from the nineteenth and early-twentieth century to the rapid population increase in many American communities.

Effects of Increasing Size

The first obvious and fundamental way of defining an urban area is that it must have a concentration of people. On that there is agreement. Disagreement arises on the question of precisely how large a concentration of people constitutes an urban area. The Bureau of the Census currently defines an urban place as one with a population concentration of 2,500 or more residents. The problem with an absolute designation such as this is that numbers, while objectively reliable as criteria, actually are subject to relative and subjective interpretation. A community of 2,500 does not sound like an urban place to someone reared in New York City, yet to someone from Gackle, North Dakota (population 450), 2,500 does sound large.

Another problem with relying on size alone as a criterion for urbanness is that communities with small numbers of people with-

21

in their legal boundaries may be located so close to larger communities that the separate social and economic identities of each become blurred. Some suburbs on the fringes of large cities have small populations, but that is irrelevant because of the physical proximity of the two communities.

No attempt will be made here to specify an absolute limit for what constitutes an urban area. The relationship between size and urbanness is continuous: the greater the number of people, the more urban the place. New York City and Chicago are at one end of the continuum; Gackle, North Dakota, is at the other end. In between are communities like Charlottesville, Virginia; Portland, Oregon; and Austin, Texas—in which characteristics of small towns and big cities intermingle. In this text, most discussion will focus on large urban areas simply because more research is available on them.

Size is fundamental because quantitative differences often lead to qualitative differences.[1] As the number of people gathered together increases, the resulting population concentration produces economic, spatial, and social systems that grow in complexity. The effect of scale on complexity can perhaps be best understood by using an analogy. A model airplane is a representation of a jet airliner in much the same way a small town is a representation of a large city. Because the model is small, it lacks the complexity of the actual airplane.

Similarly, small towns do not have the complexity of cities. For example, cities are more *economically* complex than are small towns. The economy of small towns usually depends on a few stores or small businesses. As the population grows, stores begin to specialize in particular commodities. Other stores with similar specialties compete, adding their own unique appeals to attract customers. Similar specialization and expansion occur in other economic areas. Depending on the place, entrepreneurs start brokerage firms, computer companies, consulting agencies,

film companies, bathtub manufacturers, or auto body plants. No one city may have all of the possible range of economic concerns, but the range of businesses tends to expand as the population expands.

Increasing numbers of people also lead to increasing *spatial* complexity. Urban space is more densely occupied. A single block in Chicago may have more residents than many of the communities in South Dakota. In addition, urban space begins to become specialized, with particular areas serving unique functions, so the "downtown" commercial area becomes differentiated, with one area where the jewelry stores are located, another for antique shops, and other areas for boutique clothing stores, theaters, or X-rated bookstores. Residential areas also begin to display racial, socioeconomic, age-group, or ethnic residential uniqueness. Scholars who study the spatial patterning of urban areas refer to this as **segregation**.[2]

Space then begins to have meaning in social and economic terms. Location in the city affects access to jobs, shopping, recreation for individuals and to markets, raw materials, and eventually profits for business. Space in the city may also determine access to public services such as transportation, parks, and health centers. The advantages and disadvantages of place can be cumulative. For example, poor transportation can limit job opportunities, resulting in areas of high unemployment. Minorities are often denied access to certain sections of the city, inhibiting their social and economic integration into the community. Space, accordingly, has vast implications and is an important source of conflict among various groups in cities. Land is one of the important resources that is, to a large extent, privately controlled as much land is privately owned. But local governments do influence the use of space through regulations, primarily through planning and zoning decisions.[3] The conflict over use of space is a common item on the agenda of local governments. The use of space also often prompts citizen activity, especially when citizens are attempting to avoid or eliminate land use in their neighborhoods to which they are opposed, for example, public housing or a halfway house for criminals.[4]

Similarly, as the scale of population concentration grows, so does *social* complexity. This chapter will focus on three changes in the social setting that increase its complexity and that affect the content and scope of the public agenda: *impersonality, interdependence,* and *heterogeneity*.[5] These components do not suddenly emerge at a specific population size, rather they develop as the size increases. This chapter will examine how these dimensions distinguish the urban life-style from that in small towns and affect the public agenda and the policy-making process.

The Life-style of Small Towns

Americans seem to have a great nostalgia for small-town life. By 1990, only 1 in 16 Americans lived in places with fewer than 10,000 people, but one poll found that one-third of Americans wanted to live in a small town.[6] This nostalgia affects urban areas in many ways. For example, many citizens with the resources to do so seek to recreate small town life by moving to the suburban fringes. In 1995, the *New York Times* reported that the "fastest-growing residential communities in the nation" were small, planned communities that are designed to recreate the mythic small town.[7] In addition, much government policy tends to have an anti-urban bias, a fact that may be associated with the nostalgia for small town—as opposed to urban—life. Descriptions of small town life, however, present an image not quite as idyllic as the myth.

One of the most pervasive themes encountered in descriptions of small towns is their *personalism*. Arthur Vidich and Joseph Bensman give several examples of this personalism in their classic examination of

"Springdale," a small town in New York. For example, they explain the political power exercised by one resident, Lee, as follows:

> As editor and town clerk he has "social contacts" with a wide range of rural residents. The newspaper carried a social column for each of the rural areas ("Mrs. Smith and her daughter, Velma, went to Rockland on a shopping trip last Thursday," "Mr. and Mrs. Jones of Smithfield were the weekend guests of Mr. and Mrs. Rodney Alexander," "Peter Kloski has a new Farmall tractor"), a segment of the paper which serves as a communicator of important social facts for the rural readership. As town clerk he issues birth, marriage, and death certificates; dog, hunting and fishing licenses; and records all property assessments . . .
>
> In addition, however, as clerk of the board Lee is the supervisor of township elections. He sees to it that ballots are printed and distributed to each of the five voting districts in the township. He does these chores personally and in doing them comes in contact with those who officiate at the polls in each of the districts. He has known these people for a long time and has had a voice in their selection.[8]

Nor is Lee atypical. Another resident, Jones, owns a business that supplies farm implements, machinery repair, lumber, hardware, and similar commodities and services crucial to a rural community. The local farmers tend to use the store as a community center, gathering on rainy days to exchange information. As a result, Jones

> . . . has an intimate knowledge of the affairs of the farmers who are his customers. He knows what their indebtedness is, what their long-range expansion plans are, what their seasonal needs are and what their family life is like (i.e., whether the wife is a helpmate, which sons are interested in farming, what "quality" people they are).[9]

Another, more recent study, paints a similar picture of West Point, Virginia, where the mayor's political influence derived from his position as president of a local bank and was "augmented by the close ongoing relationship between the Citizens and Farmer's Bank and the Chesapeake Corporation, and the mayor's close personal association with the leadership of the corporation."[10]

Of course, urban dwellers also have networks of friends and relatives, but these networks represent a small proportion of the population of the city.[11] As a result, urban dwellers must frequently interact with those they do not know personally. A study of 50 communities in the San Francisco area found that more than half of the respondents living in small communities reported running into people they knew on a daily basis. The comparable number for those in metropolitan areas was less than a third.[12]

The personalism of small towns results from the constant and close interrelationship among the town's residents. Thus, on an individual level, the residents have much contact since they cannot avoid interacting. Similarly, people in small towns often voluntarily cooperate to help each other. Yet in another way there is significant *independence*, which is the second major characteristic of small town life. Independence in this context refers to the fact that in small towns there is minimal recognition of a collective, public responsibility for the town's affairs. In other words, the public agenda is limited and political leaders therefore play a minimal role.

Small towns usually offer few public services, leaving the provision of those services dependent on individual choice and resources. Individuals rely on themselves or perhaps on networks of friends and neighbors who voluntarily cooperate to achieve goals. Along with limited services goes limited formal regulation of individual behavior by statute, and, of course, lower taxes. Everett Ladd, in his description of the small town of Putnam, Connecticut, commented on this limited public agenda: "There is simply not much happening in the public sector in Putnam."[13]

Sam Warner has argued that the narrow definition of public purpose, which he calls *privatism*, has been part and parcel of the American tradition, especially at the local level. The essence of privatism, he argues, is:

> ... that the individual should seek happiness in personal independence and in the search for wealth; socially, privatism meant that the individual should see his first loyalty as his immediate family, and that a community should be a union of such money-making, accumulating families; politically, privatism meant that the community should keep the peace among individual money-makers, and, if possible, help to create an open and thriving setting where each citizen would have some substantial opportunity to prosper.[14]

In other words, substantial resources would be left in private hands and the limited role of government would be to help individuals augment their resources.

A final characteristic of small towns is the emphasis on *homogeneity*. Because of the small population size, the people may actually *be* homogeneous. Alternatively, even if there are differences, there are often strong pressures to submerge them. A study of a small town in New York reported:

> ... in nine situations out of ten the class structure is overshadowed by a basic social equality that results from the smallness of the community and the sense of common past. People who are thrown in constant contact over a long period of time learn to ignore distinctions that would make their relations difficult.[15]

A more recent study argued that in small towns there are "stronger incentives to conform to accepted political codes for behavior," and a "higher cost for political dissent," than in cities.[16]

BOX 2-1

Fisher Cafe, Community Keep Each Other Thriving

By Marsha Shoemaker

FISHER, Minn.—Bursts of laugher punctuate the lively midmorning chatter as six friends juggle conversations at their corner table.

It's not earthshaking news this combination of homemakers and downtown women exchange during their coffee hour at the Fisher Cafe, Ann Beiswenger says. "But oh, we hear some good stories."

The comment brings knowing nods and more hoots.

Someone says it's 11 o'clock. Amid murmurs about unmade beds and other unfinished business, the group scatters to home and office.

The morning ritual is played out most every morning at the Fisher Cafe, the gathering place the town midway between Grand Forks and Crookston built for itself.

Sometimes morning coffee is at someone's house, but this group feels just as much at home in the sundrenched restaurant wallpapered with blue pussy willows and brown wheat stems.

"We bought one of those chairs up at the counter," says Julie Rutherford, whose husband Herb was on the Fisher Chamber of Commerce committee that got the cafe going four years ago. Sure enough, their name is on a brass plaque nailed to the back of the swivel stool.

Most everyone in town donated to the cafe in one way or another, said Mayor Steve Williams. In 1984 the cafe committee got $15,000 in seed money from the Bremer Foundation, but the other $85,000 has come from residents in and around the little town.

"The fund raising continues," Williams says. The building has been paid for and turned over to the city for a year and a half, but each year around this time donations are solicited to keep it running in the black over the slow winter months.

It's clear this place is important to the farmers, businessmen and women, homemakers and students who frequent it—important enough to finance it.

"In my mind there's no question, the two most important assets of a small town are the cafe and the school," Williams says. "It brings people to town and together. It provides a meeting place."

"It's a lot like home here for them" says June Stevens, who manages the cafe for the four-member committee that represents the town's interest. "If they need anything, they can yell at me in the kitchen or help themselves. . . .They feel at home. And of course everybody knows everybody."

When the old Fisher Cafe, which was leased and operated by the Chamber of Commerce, was to be closed because of its unsafe building, the town rallied. "We had to have a cafe," Beiswenger says. "Everybody would miss it terribly."

From the time the cafe opens weekday mornings, at 6:30 during the summer and at 7 from November through the winter, the town and country residents take turns filling the tables.

First it's the farmers, who get the initial dose of this daily combination of socializing and group therapy. "This year they had a lot of problems," Rutherford says. "They spent a lot of time up here."

Later on the businessmen and the women come in, a rotating mixture of residents who know they don't need an invitation to join whoever is seated around the tables.

The men play serious cards, but they like their conversation light. They're sick of politics.

(continued on next page)

(continued)

"You just swear at everybody," Neil Volstad says about politicians.

"What else can you do?" says Ron Rutherford to Volstad, a former Fisherite visiting from Montana. "This election business . . . we'll be glad when it's over."

By 2:30 p.m., some of the women are usually back at their table for afternoon coffee. By the time they leave, school is out and the kids are in for sodas.

Even on Sundays the cafe is busy. When fall comes, Stevens stays open from 9 a.m. to 2 p.m. Parents sit and have coffee while they wait for their children to finish Sunday school so they can meet them for services. After church, folks are back for the Sunday dinner specials, usually roast beef or chicken.

Monday morning the weekday shuffle starts again at this haven where a piece of pumpkin pie this month is 47 cents and a friendly ear is free.

"It's sort of a livelihood in this town," says farmer Alton Tinkham. "If you don't have a cafe, you don't have nothing."

Source: *Grand Forks Herald* (November 6, 1988), 1A, 9A. Reprinted with permission.

The cafe in the small town of Fisher, Minnesota, illustrates the personalism, homogeneity, and independence of small town life. Everyone knows one another and, while the people have different occupations, they are similar enough to feel comfortable sharing a common meeting place. The cafe exists because of voluntary cooperation among community members rather than as a result of public policy.

The Role of Citizens in Small Towns

These three characteristics of small town lifestyle—personalism, independence, and homogeneity—have two implications for town politics. First, the personalism contributes to a minimal differentiation of roles. The two men described by Vidich and Bensman—Lee and Jones—illustrate this. Their responsibilities in government derive from and are part of their personal contacts with their fellow citizens. In other words, the distinction between "public" and "private" roles is blurred. For example, Lee's two roles as editor and board clerk were significantly interrelated. The town board met in the newspaper office and the minutes that Lee took at those meetings became the basis for the next issue of the paper.[17] In general, little distinction was made between his private economic role as editor and his public role as town clerk. Similarly, in West Point, Virginia, the mayor's role as bank president was the source of his political clout.[18] These examples also illustrate how easily economic power can be translated into political power.

Another illustration of the blurring of public and private roles is the fact that a position becomes a characteristic of an individual rather than a separate role. For instance, Lee inherited both his private role as editor and his public role as town clerk from his father. As a result, "The public records of town government have been in the Lee family for fifty years and the system of record keeping and the whereabouts of the records themselves are known only to Lee."[19] By and large, public officials in small towns are not nameless, faceless entities, but rather are next-door neighbors.

Second, all three characteristics contribute to the attempt to repress conflict. The emphasis on homogeneity, whether actually present or a result of pressure to conform, stifles urges to form groups based on distinctive interests. The absence of differentiated roles also retards the development of an "us versus them" mentality that would translate into political conflict. This is not to say there is never conflict, just that the homogeneity of small towns slows its development. Conflicts that do arise can be especially bitter, however, as those who are squaring off are people who must deal with each other in many contexts and on a daily basis. This personalism means that people attempt to suppress emergent conflicts to avoid resulting bitterness. As a study of West Point, Virginia, concluded, the search for political consensus derived in part from "the personal proximity of small town politics; public officials cannot escape, in a spatial sense, future daily interaction with those who have been the subject of their rebuff."[20]

The limited public agenda also contributes to the absence or minimization of conflict. Because few things are considered to be public responsibilities, there is no need to debate them publicly. As a result, those issues that are debated politically are "small, often petty, always limited."[21] A politics that deals with only minimal and mundane matters is unlikely to arouse much conflict. The only conflict that could arise would come from those who want the government to do something, and such demands would contradict the value of privatism.

The suppression of conflict undoubtedly is related to the tendency for small town politics to be dominated by a few people. For instance, in Springdale, Vidich and Bensman found that although the village had a potential electorate of 350–450 people, only 15 to 35 voted in village elections.[22] In fact the village board usually printed only 50 ballots. Candidates selected by the 3 men who composed what Vidich and Bensman called the "invisible government" (2 of whom were Lee and Jones) were never defeated because the only ones who had enough interest to vote were the village and party officials and their families. Other, more recent, studies produced similar findings. A study of two small towns

in Maryland found them both controlled by small cliques referred to by the citizens as "good-ole-boys" and the examination of West Point, Virginia, found that only 31 percent voted in municipal elections.[23]

Because the range of issues that are dealt with publicly is so narrow, the bulk of the population simply has no reason to be interested in politics. The few that are involved, are of course, aware of this, and there is evidence that they deliberately keep issues over which conflict might arise off the agenda to avoid the possibility of more people becoming interested and active in politics.[24] Another reason for the success of the elite is their ability and willingness to use their position to do favors for individuals. Everett Ladd characterized the politics of Putnam, Connecticut, as ". . . 'friends and neighbors' petty patronage politics."[25]

The decisions resulting from this limited, nonconflictual policy process tend to produce specific benefits for specific groups in the community rather than more generalized collective goods for the community as a whole. This might be considered to be the personalization of government policy. Such a political style fits comfortably with the personalism, independence, and homogeneity of the small town itself.

As the population of the community grows, the life-style begins to change. First, personalism decreases with the increase in population. No longer is it possible to know everyone, and people begin to see each other more as occupants of roles rather than as unique individuals. Second, as more people move in, homogeneity declines. The larger the population concentration, the greater the chance that a heterogeneous mix of values is represented. Finally, as towns grow into cities, interdependence increases among the residents. What total strangers do (for example, how loud the stereo is in the apartment next door) has an impact on the urban dweller's life. Because of the division of labor in cities, residents depend on others to provide them with necessary services. It becomes necessary to institutionalize the dependence on others by establishing government programs and policies. As a result, the public agenda expands—as does the role of political leaders.

Immigration and the Growth of Urban Areas

For many American communities, the growth from small town to city occurred in the nineteenth and early-twentieth centuries. In 1790, only 3.35 percent of Americans lived in communities with a population larger than 8,000; by the end of the nineteenth century, about 33 percent lived in such communities. Between 1800 and 1890, the U.S. population increased twelvefold, while the urban population increased eighty-sevenfold. While in 1800 only 6 cities had populations larger than 8,000, by 1890 there were 448 such communities. Six cities had more than half a million people by 1900, and 3 boasted populations larger than a million.[26]

Of course, some of this urban growth was attributable to movement from the farms. "Hundreds of thousands" of Americans flocked from the farms to the cities in the nineteenth century "when some new blight, or a change in climate, or, more frequently, a drop in prices resulting from overproduction brought disillusionment."[27] In many industrial cities, however, immigrants from outside the United States constituted a substantial proportion of the population. By 1890 in Fall River, Massachusetts, and 4 other New England textile towns, foreign-born immigrants represented between 40 and 50 percent of the residents. At the same time, the foreign-born residents were more than 40 percent of the populations of Chicago and San Francisco, and more than 33 percent of the populations of many other industrial cities.[28]

While immigration has occurred throughout America's history, the historical period that is most often identified with immigration is the late-nineteenth and early-twentieth centuries. Table 2–1 shows the numbers of people immigrating to this coun-

TABLE 2–1

Immigration to the United States 1820–1990

Years	Immigrants	Years	Immigrants
1820–1830	151,824	1911–1920	5,735,811
1831–1840	599,125	1921–1930	4,107,209
1841–1850	1,713,251	1931–1940	528,413
1851–1860	2,598,21	1941–1950	1,035,039
1861–1870	2,314,824	1951–1960	3,011,000
1871–1880	2,812,191	1961–1970	3,322,000
1881–1890	5,246,613	1971–1980	2,294,000
1891–1900	3,687,564	1981–1990	9,972,000
1901–1910	8,795,386		

Source: For the years 1820–1950, Marion T. Bennett, *American Immigration Policies: A History* (Washington, D.C.: Public Affairs Press, 1963). For the years 1961–1980, U.S. Bureau of the Census, *Statistical Abstract of the United States, 1988,* 108th ed. (Washington, D.C.: Government Printing Office, 1987), 10. For the years 1951–1960 and 1981–1990, Barry Edmonston and Jeffrey S. Passel, "Ethnic Demography, U.S. Immigration and Ethnic Variation," in Barry Edmonston and Jeffrey S. Passel, eds., *Immigration and Ethnicity: The Integration of America's New Arrivals* (Washington, D.C.: Urban Institute Press, 1994), 8.

try in each decade since records began to be kept in 1820. The numbers of people arriving increased steadily. In 1901–1910 almost nine million people arrived in America. From that time until the 1980s the numbers declined.

Especially in the early years of the nineteenth century, many of those people passed through the port cities on their way to a farm. But in the second half of the century, even though the Homestead Act of 1862 granted free farms of 160 acres to all applicants for citizenship as well as to citizens, many immigrants settled in the towns and cities because they could not afford the money for equipment and seed to go into farming. Those without such resources could have worked on farms, but the farm owners needed cheap labor, and "European peasants were hardly inclined to uproot themselves only to become serfs in America."[29]

Throughout time there have been two reasons why people leave the security of surroundings that are known and familiar and move to a new and strange land. One reason is the "pull" of the new land: the belief that the soil is richer, the pay is better, the life is freer. The second reason is the belief that conditions in the native land have become intolerable, a belief that "pushes" people away from their homeland.

After 1840, industrialization contributed to both the push and pull factors of immigration. Industrialization had contrary effects in Europe and America. In Europe, experiencing a population boom, industrialization meant a labor surplus both on the farm and in the factories. In the United States, industrialization created a demand for labor that was especially acute in urban factories.[30] Other products of the industrial revolution, the steamship and the railroad, contributed to increased immigration by making the trip from Europe to America cheaper and more palatable. As industrialization progressed, more and more Europeans poured into America.

So much did American business want the immigrants that many businesses began advertising campaigns in Europe to lure immigrants.

> Many businessmen, unwilling to leave matters entirely in the hands of a beneficent fate, actively expedited the immigrant traffic. Here the railroads played a key role, as they did throughout the economy. Railroads that pushed boldly into the empty West had a wilderness to settle. They needed immigrants not just for construction but to buy the great railroad land grants and to insure future revenues. Following the example set by the Illinois Central in the 1850's, the Burlington, the Northern Pacific, and other lines sent agents to blanket northern Europe with alluring propaganda.[31]

Drastic changes in life-style and politics could be expected to accompany the rapid growth. As many American cities in the nineteenth and twentieth centuries grew rapidly, impersonality increased. Since much of the population growth resulted from foreign immigrants, there was also a striking increase in heterogeneity. Prior to the nineteenth century, the American population—urban and rural—was predominantly of British ancestry. DeTocqueville underscored this homogeneity in his report of his travels in the United States in 1830:

> I do not know of any European nation, however small, that does not present less uniformity in its different provinces than the American people, which occupy a territory as extensive as one half of Europe. The distance from Maine to Georgia is about one thousand miles; but the difference between the civilization of Maine and that of Georgia is slighter than the difference between the habits of Normandy and those of Brittany.[32]

Almost as soon as deTocqueville wrote his description, America received the first of the waves of immigrants that were to end the homogeneity that had amazed him. Starting in 1830, large numbers of Germans immigrated to the United States, fleeing poor economic conditions, political instability, and rumblings of revolution. Fifteen years later thousands of Irish began pouring into the United States, fleeing famine caused by a blight of the potato, the staple of the Irish diet. In 1861, only 6 years after the flood of Irish had abated, large numbers of southern Italians began to arrive. Within another 10 years, larger numbers of Eastern Europeans, many of them Jewish, began to arrive in an attempt to escape both religious persecution and poor economic conditions.

To many "native" Americans, it seemed that as the century progressed the immigrants became more and more different. By 1880, of the 10,189,429 immigrants who had entered the country, 8,989,889 were from Europe. Of those 3,052,126 were from Germany and 2,829,206 were from Ireland. Some worried about the Germans. Even before the nineteenth century, Benjamin Franklin wrote:

Why should the Palatine boors be suffered to swarm into our settlements and, by herding together, establish their language and manners to the exclusion of ours?[33]

But there was grudging recognition that the Germans were industrious, and, after all, they were also usually Protestant, like the bulk of the population. The Irish, on the other hand, were predominantly Catholic, and their arrival following the potato blight in Ireland led to several states enacting laws that discriminated in various ways against Catholics. In North and South Carolina, for instance, Catholics were not allowed to hold office. In many places, job descriptions would carry the warning that "No Irish Need Apply."

The Germans and Irish—and other northern Europeans—who arrived in the early years of the nineteenth century were not nearly as threatening to the natives as were the immigrants who, lured by the jobs in the burgeoning factories, arrived in America's cities in the second half of the century. Unlike the old immigrants, the new arrivals tended to come from southern and eastern Europe. Table 2–2 shows the increase in southern and

TABLE 2–2

Sources of European Immigration 1820–1920

	Northern and Western Europe	Southern and Eastern Europe
	%	%
1820–1830	68.0	2.2
1831–1840	81.7	1.0
1841–1850	93.0	.3
1851–1860	93.6	.8
1861–1870	87.8	1.5
1871–1880	73.6	7.2
1881–1890	72.0	18.3
1891–1900	44.6	51.9
1901–1910	21.7	70.8
1911–1920	17.4	59.0

Source: Marion T. Bennett, *American Immigration Policies: A History* (Washington, D.C.: Public Affairs Press, 1963), 31.

BOX 2-2

Lower East Side, New York City, 1919

By Konrad Bercovic

NEW YORK—I strolled over Third Avenue into Mulberry Street. I was in Sicily at one end of the street and in Piedmont at the other end. The very same odor of fried fish I had tried to escape in Naples assailed my nostrils. The very same impudent cries of the Genoese fishseller greeted my ears. From one end of the street to the other not a word of English except the vilest curses. The signs over the doors in Italian. The clothes of the people, the litter on the streets, the colored shawls tied under the chins of the swarthy wrinkled faces of the prematurely aged women! It was all Italian. It was Italy, with separate provinces and dialects; and to my complete edification I witnessed knife play between a Sicilian fish-peddler and a Calabrese loafer. On the corner of the street stood a policeman. I was tempted to ask him "Please where is America?" But he scared me out of my wits.

I walked out of Mulberry Street and fell into the Greek Quarter. It looked more like some side street of Stamboul. Cafes every ten feet. Long-mustached, sleek fellows were playing cards and drinking coffee from small cups.

I soon came into the Jewish quarter. Here and there a sign in another language than Hebrew. I wandered into the Syrian quarter on Washington Street. Beautiful laces and heavy brocades in the store window. Goldsmiths working on the door sill with their legs crossed under them, and the little anvil between the knees. Sellers of sweets passing up and down the street. Vendors of lemonade in red fezes, and the whole atmosphere impregnated with the odor of the decomposing sugar from dates and figs. It was Smyrna or Jaffa or the Port of Athens. A young, barefooted boy sold a newspaper printed in the Arabic language which was eagerly bought by every one.

Source: Quoted from Konrad Bercovic, "In Quest of America in Foreign New York. Adventures of a Visitor from Rumania," *New York Times Magazine,* December 21, 1919. Copyright 1919 by The New York Times Company. Reprinted by permission.

eastern European immigrants, beginning in the 1860s and accelerating in 1890. These new immigrants were Italians, Serbs, Poles, Hungarians, and Russians. Not only did these people speak a different language, but they also differed in myriad ways from the white, Anglo-Saxon, English-speaking, Protestant majority. They were mostly Catholic, or Eastern Orthodox, or Jewish, and their holidays and festivals were different from those of the dominant Protestant population. These people settled overwhelmingly in industrial cities. Concentrated in the cities, their distinctiveness became even more visible.

In addition to the southern and eastern

Europeans, the Chinese and Japanese were also coming in large numbers in the second half of the nineteenth century to the West coast and along the rail routes in the West. Their differences from the Anglo-Saxon population were even more striking than those of southern and eastern Europeans.

Contributing to visible differences of the immigrants was the fact that, faced with the newness and strangeness of their new home, they often struggled to hold onto the traditions of the home they had left. For example, their religion often became more important to the immigrants than it had been in the old country.[34] Some have even argued that the sense of national identity only developed for many immigrants after they arrived in America and needed a way to identify themselves and others with whom they shared a culture.[35] The result was that "foreign travelers who wandered off Main Street had frequently to remind themselves that this was America and not some European country."[36]

The efforts of immigrants to preserve their old cultures were augmented by their tendency to huddle together in spatially segregated ethnic "towns" within the cities, increasing the spatial specialization. To a certain extent this segregation was voluntary. Immigrants sought out others like themselves who spoke their language, worshiped their God, and ate their food. In some instances, the recent immigrants even sought out people from their same village and desperately tried to recreate village life to lessen the shock of the new and unfamiliar and to ease the loneliness. In part, however, the segregation was due to discrimination and to the fact that the immigrants could only afford to live in poorer districts where the housing was cheap.

The observations of a visitor to New York City in 1919 illustrate its heterogeneous mix of people at that time and the spatial segregation that enabled them to preserve some of their culture and customs. (See Box 2–2 on page 31.)

As the waves of immigrants continued to arrive, the existing housing became unbelievably crowded. A building at 36 Cherry Street in New York was 5 stories high and 150 feet deep. In that building in 1853, 500 people were living without heat or indoor plumbing. Ten years later a row of privies had been put in the basement, but by then more than 800 people lived in the building.[37]

As the century wore on, builders settled on a form of building, called the dumbbell tenement, which made the maximum use of space on a real estate lot. The name came from the fact that the building was narrowed at the middle so that with two identical build-

ings adjacent to each other there was an airshaft 5 feet wide. The shaft could provide air and light to three rooms of an apartment so that only one room had to be on the street or the rear yard. Each apartment had 4 rooms with a total floor space of approximately 20 by 90 feet. Each building held up to 200 people and on a typical block there could be up to 4,000 people.

The obvious poverty of the immigrants also contributed to the heterogeneity of cities. In the early cities, class differences were not very great and the relationship between employer and employee tended to be personal. Employees were often young relatives of their employer and most businesses had only a few employees.[38] With industrialization, the class differences became stark. While the immigrants scratched out a living and huddled in tenements, the employers built mansions a few blocks away.

The concentration of the immigrants, their visibility, the squalid conditions in which they lived had numerous consequences, the first of which was an increase in prejudice against the newcomers. As one historian concluded, "At one time or another, immigrants of practically every non-English stock incurred the open hostility of earlier comers."[39] The result was increased conflict. Some businesses refused to hire the immigrants. More seriously, in some cities anti-foreign riots erupted.

As the greater heterogeneity of the city led to more conflict, the increasing size and density of the urban population also led to a growing discomfort with the interdependence of urban living. The tenements in the slums were unsightly, but the wealthy had other reasons for worrying about the conditions a few blocks from their mansions. The overcrowding and poor sanitary conditions in the tenements made epidemics common—epidemics that knew no social or geographical boundaries.

Social disorganization was also an issue. The crowded living conditions forced children into the streets to play, thus limiting the control their parents had over them. As a result, parents had less opportunity to teach their children the customs of the old country, and the children therefore quickly adopted the ways of America. The generations began to pull apart, weakening the family. Street gangs terrorized the immigrants because gangsters knew the newcomers were powerless.

The result of all of these dislocations was the first of America's "urban crises." The awareness of the interdependence of urban living led eventually to demands that urban governments expand their agendas to seek solutions for the crisis. While economic interests had often stimulated immigration, searching for cheap labor and more customers for their goods, the problems resulting from the concentration of immigrants in the city were relegated to city governments. Clearly changes in the life-style created new demands for government, changing the political process, expanding the public agenda, and increasing the importance of political leaders.

The Effects of Urban Life-style on Politics

The impersonality, heterogeneity, and interdependence that characterize urban living have important implications for the urban political process. First, because residents probably do not personally know public officials, the distinction between public and private roles becomes more sharply delineated.[40] This impersonality also encourages conflict to be expressed as it is now possible to vent one's spleen to a government official without having to worry about sitting next to that official in church next week.

Second, the urban life-style provides the milieu from which the problems arise that the political system must resolve. For ex-

ample, in a community where people know each other, crime tends to be less of a problem than in larger population concentrations. Per capita crime rates are higher in large cities than in small towns and rural areas.[41] Personal familiarity with people tends to depress crime. The old lady who might be a target to an anonymous mugger might not be such an easy mark to teenagers for whom she had babysat in the past and who are on a street populated by residents who could easily identify them during an escape attempt. In other words, impersonality reduces the social pressure to conform to the norms of society because it offers the possibility of anonymity to the person who decides to ignore the norms.

Heterogeneity may also cause the crime rate to increase because the complex mixture of values in a city may mean that it is not clear precisely what the accepted norms are. When this **anomie**—or sense of normlessness—is added to the absence of personal policing of these norms, the ease of engaging in criminal acts is likely to increase. Increased crime means increasing demands upon the political system, leading to an expansion in the urban agenda. Heterogeneity may also create other pressures on the political system because many people with different values, goals, interests, talents, and resources are forced to interact. Spatial patterning of people into neighborhoods composed of similar types of people may reduce the day-to-day interaction of people who differ. But even with spatial patterning, some interaction is unavoidable. While increased understanding and tolerance may result from such interaction, conflict is also likely.[42] Because spatial patterning has so many consequences, the control of land use is important. The attempts by urban governments to control land-use decisions creates conflict both with the private landowners and with other citizens who disagree about how land should be used.

The interdependence of urban life creates other demands on the urban political process. As the labor or work of residents of the city become more specialized, the residents need to rely more upon others to provide them with necessary services and to coordinate the delivery of these services. Because many of these resources or services are privately controlled, much of the coordination is accomplished by the economic system. The capitalist system provides incentives for people to produce goods to sell to others, making the division of labor in urban areas both possible and profitable.

The economic system, however, cannot handle all the problems of the interdependence of urban life. Economic solutions do not always equal what society would consider desirable solutions.[43] Two types of problems have devolved to the political system. One type is the provision of services that are not profitable for private business to supply, but that have been defined, normally by the political process, as necessities. For example, with few exceptions, urban mass transit systems have been economic failures since the dawn of the era of the private automobile. While no private company would for long engage in providing such an unprofitable service, urban areas have defined mass transit as a necessity. Many urban residents have no other means of transportation. Also, to the extent that people do use mass transit, the burden on other resources (for example, streets) is reduced.

A second kind of problem concerns externalities. An **externality** is a cost or benefit that is not reflected in (or is external to) market transactions. In essence, it is an unintended side effect. Private businesses produce goods they plan to sell in the marketplace for a profit. Yet the side effects of that production may be undesirable to others. A classic example of such an undesirable side effect is the smoke coming from a factory's smokestack. This smoke creates burdens for those who live around the factory.

Nothing in the economic system provides a means of making the factory either eliminate this externality or compensate those bearing the burden. Therefore, attempting to resolve the problems of the externalities becomes the responsibility of the urban political system. While externalities are not a unique characteristic of urban areas, the close proximity of people, industries, and businesses in the urban setting increases the likelihood of such externalities occurring and having consequences for other urban residents. What pours forth from the smokestack would not be as much a concern if the nearest neighbors lived miles away. In other words, the problem of externalities is aggravated by the interdependence inherent in the urban setting.

As a result of the failure of the economic system to address effectively the negative effects of the interdependence of people in urban areas, ideas of what constitutes public responsibility begin to change. The political agenda grows and the role of politics increases. A history of Springfield, Massachusetts, as it grew from town to city recorded an

> . . . emerging awareness of how dependent the public of an urban community were upon each other, and upon the institutions expressing that interdependence, precisely because the effects of any individual's weakness or irresponsibility now clearly extended well beyond the confines of his own life, necessarily if inadvertently touching all those around him.[44]

More issues were defined as public responsibilities, expanding the public agenda and increasing the role of public authorities in two ways. First, authorities regulated individual behavior to a greater degree. For example, in the town of Springfield the family pig could roam the town streets. Yet by 1865, following the population explosion of the Civil War years, the city deemed it necessary to ban pigs from the downtown business district. It is not hard to fathom why the pigs could be a menace both to traffic and to shoppers' noses if allowed to roam freely. Pig owners, though, faced a new intrusion on their liberty because their actions inevitably affected others. Once the political process produces such laws, public authorities are responsible for enforcing them.

Second, public authorities were expected to provide more services. In Springfield, a major step was made in expanding governmentally provided services by the construction of city water and sewage facilities. When the citizens were few in number and their houses were widely separated, there was little need to worry about the effect of one neighbor's privy on the water in another's well. But when the size and density of the population increased, it became clear that each resident's health depended on avoiding contamination from the neighbors. Thus Springfield realized that the city had to provide sanitary water and sewage treatment to all, regardless of ability to pay, because the health of the whole community depended on it.

> In this emerging urban society the kind of individualism that had been at the heart of the American myth, and the informal cooperation of individuals in the relatively intimate relationships of the town were simply inadequate for the management of life in large cities. . . . It became necessary for urban government to provide far more formal and elaborate arrangements for such functions as sanitation, fire service, law enforcement, transportation, health services, street maintenance, construction standards, parks, libraries, recreational services and education than in the towns of the earlier decades of the nineteenth century.[45]

People began to distinguish a *public* interest that was separate from private interests and to believe that the role of government was to serve the former. The differentiation of public and private roles contributed to this distinction. The definition of what should be the extent of public responsibility is constantly in dispute, and politics is the arena in which that dispute occurs. Urban residents line up on various sides of the debate concerning what should be regulated and what services should be provided, depending on the specific issue and their stake in it. The differentiation of roles produced distinctly political officials who had their own stake in how the debate was resolved.

To say there is conflict, however, is not to say there are not areas of agreement. Indeed, the study of Springfield found an emerging agreement that there was a public responsibility to encourage the development of the city. Such urban development benefited private economic interests in myriad ways. For one, private contractors reaped the profits from the paving of streets, building of sewers, and other construction projects that formed the backbone of urban development. For another, such capital improvement projects provided private business with the infrastructure necessary for operation. The use of public resources for private benefit was compatible with the value of privatism and represented a continuity with the focus of public policy in the mercantile cities of the colonial era.

Immigrants and Urban Politics

As the cities of the nineteenth century grew, the immigrant population began to play a major role in urban politics. For someone seeking both power and wealth, America's cities at that time must have looked like heaven. As the responsibilities of the city government expanded and cities developed, there were people to be hired, contracts to be granted, equipment to be bought. Each transaction had the possibility of lining the pockets not only of those hired or those who received the contracts, but also of a city official corrupt enough to accept kickbacks as part of the deal.

All that was necessary was to get elected, and the immigrants pouring into America's cities could help with that. The great majority of the immigrants desperately needed a friend. They had to find jobs and places to live. In general they required help in adjusting to a new, grim, and hostile world. An ambitious politician could supply that help and in return only asked that the immigrants remember their friend at election time.

Many politicians rode to power by striking such a deal. They were called **bosses** and the political organizations they controlled were called **political machines**. Political machines were very strong party organizations that developed a loyal following by distributing tangible material benefits such as jobs to potential supporters. The bosses were the leaders who controlled the hierarchically structured machines. Although political machines, which will be discussed more thoroughly in Chapter 7, existed in areas without large immigrant populations, in many cities such as New York, Chicago, and Jersey City, machines and immigrants had a symbiotic relationship.

The machines were instrumental in socializing immigrants to American society and politics, and some immigrant groups used them as a route of social mobility. Some observers argue this was especially true of the Irish, who controlled the machines—usually Democratic ones—in city after city.[46] Steven Erie has questioned the extent to which the machines did contribute to the economic advancement of the Irish, but agrees that they did dominate the political process in many northern and midwestern cities.[47] In fact, the identification of the Irish with machine politics led one writer to argue that "The function of the Irishman is to administer the affairs of the American city."[48]

While machines were certainly corrupt in some areas, the targeting of immigrants by political parties eager for power has a demo-cratic logic to it: It is a politics of numbers. Robert Dahl has pointed out in his study of New Haven that the emergence of immigrant groups and their descendants in the political process contributed to the dispersal of power from the patrician oligarchy that ruled that city until 1840.[49] He argues that the immigrants and their descendants became one component in the development of a **pluralistic** power structure. In such a structure, power is distributed among many—plural—sources.

This pluralistic power structure is related to the development of a style of politics aimed at placating major urban groups. This style recognizes the importance of groups in politics and attempts to distribute widely the benefits of politics so that all relevant groups can demonstrate to their members that they have received something. In some cases, the benefits distributed are material: a certain allocation of government patronage jobs going to each group or a park in each neighborhood. In some cases the benefits are purely symbolic. A St. Patrick's Day or a Columbus Day parade are good examples of symbolic rewards. Another good example is choosing a member of the group to be a candidate on the party ticket. When the immigrant groups or their descendants are involved in this process, it is referred to as **ethnic politics**.

There are several effects of a politics based upon the distribution of benefits among several ethnic groups. First, the groups get a sense of identification with the existing political process. In the past, this made it less likely that the early immigrants would turn to radical political movements, as so many feared. Second, the groups receive material benefits, for example, jobs that help at least some of a group's members to achieve social mobility and financial security. Finally, one observer argued that it is easier to govern in cities with an organized and active ethnic group structure.

From the viewpoint of those responsible for the larger social structure, these organizations are particularly convenient because the leadership is readily identifiable and is generally willing to negotiate for the advantage its own community members [sic] with an eye on the political realities in which it finds itself.[50]

Other observers have argued that ethnic politics has had negative effects. In an early statement, Raymond Wolfinger argued that the focus on placating ethnic groups has diverted attention from basic social and economic issues.[51] This in turn may impede the development of class politics. Similarly, Ira Katznelson argued that the division of the city spatially into homogeneous enclaves and the organization of the party system around those enclaves meant that the basic conflicts in the city were defined as the defense of ethnic turf rather than as basic issues of the allocation of wealth.[52]

While some fear the divisiveness of politics where the haves are pitted against the have-nots, others argue that by minimizing attention to economic and social issues the political process supports the status quo, thus maintaining the class differences that exist. The ethnics, then, rather than being a critical mass capable of assailing the power of economic interests, were **co-opted**, that is, invited to be part of the system so they would support it.

How persistent ethnic identification is among the descendants of the early immigrants is a matter of debate. In some areas it persisted even after the initial generation of immigrants had died, because voting loyalties were passed on to the children and grandchildren of the immigrants and because many people benefited from it. Jobs could still be found; the status of the group could still be recognized by having a candidate in a prominent location on the ballot, a process called **balancing the ticket**. The parties gained a

large and loyal constituency. And business—while at times disgruntled about kickbacks—still found the contracts and favors very profitable.

Ethnic identity flourished in the late 1960s and early 1970s, but later evidence points to the decline of ethnic politics. One reason is intermarriage among ethnic groups. In some places and in some ethnic groups, intermarriage is unacceptable, but for many Americans, answering a question about ethnic identity is difficult because their ancestry is an amalgam. Geographic mobility is also a factor in diluting ethnic politics. As ethnic groups become accepted and disperse throughout the urban landscape, the neighborhood and the ethnic identity become separated. In that case, some have argued that although ethnic identity may remain, the geographical community exerts a powerful pull on the voter choice—often more powerful than that of ethnicity.[53] But, the descendants of the early immigrants have now been joined by a new generation of immigrants. As Chapter 4 reviews, in the twentieth century many African-Americans and Latinos have moved into urban areas and a new wave of immigration from other countries has occured due to the immigration reform in 1965. While the strong party machines of the past are unlikely to be resurrected, the diverse ethnic mix in today's metropolis provides the possibility of continuing a political process based on distribution of benefits among organized blocs of ethnic voters.

Citizen Control in Cities

Although the future of ethnic politics may not be clear, the heterogeneity, impersonality, and interdependence of urban life continue to affect the ability of citizens to exert control in the urban policy process. These dimensions of the urban life-style make it difficult for citizens to organize to seek common goals. While single individuals can at times have an impact on political decision making, citizen input is more often effective when individuals organize. A large bloc of voters will be more likely to convince political leaders to include its concerns on the public agenda. More fundamentally, one researcher argues that an extensive network of associational memberships is related to participation in politics.[54] There are many ways in which the dimensions of the urban context make organizing difficult.

The heterogeneity of urban areas may make it difficult for individuals to see beyond their differences and unite for a common purpose. Racial antipathy is an obvious example of how differences between people impede their cooperation in other areas where their interests may coincide. Of course, heterogeneity may also mean that everyone can find at least a few like-minded others with whom to work. Yet that is likely to lead to a multiplication of the number of groups, making success for any one less likely.[55]

The impersonality of a city also makes political organization difficult. Organization requires communication and understanding. The segmented social networks of urban life may make such communication unlikely and difficult. The store clerk and the customer may actually want the same thing from the political process, but they may never know it since their conversation usually is limited to the matters at hand—selling a commodity.

The physical and political organization of cities aggravates this lack of communication. The separation of the city into a "mosaic pattern of ethnic settlement" and the resulting organization of parties and electoral districts around this mosaic pattern have made it impossible for the lower economic class to organize as a class. Ethnic and racial conflicts supplant class conflict as the focus of urban politics, leaving the economic status quo unchallenged.[56]

Finally, the interdependence of urban life

may also impede the cooperation among people that political organization requires. One aspect of interdependence is that different individuals and groups in the city are competing for the same finite resources. While cooperation might increase the amount of resources channeled their way, people often look on the political process as a **zero-sum** conflict in which resources going to others are resources that will not come to them, that is, if there are winners, there must be losers with the final total balancing out to zero. This often-accurate perception may aggravate hostility.

Interdependence has another potential effect on the political organization of citizens. Resources allocated to one will often automatically go to all members of a group. For example, if a crossing guard is posted on a busy intersection, the safety of all children in the neighborhood will be improved, those whose parents demanded it as well as those whose parents did not. Therefore, many citizens may shirk political activity because they feel sure others will do their work for them. Economists refer to this as the **"free rider"** problem.

One reason economic interests have been successful politically is the advantage they have in organizing. The business itself provides an existing organizational structure and communication channels. It is easy for those who earn a living from the business to see their own self-interest in the policies that benefit it. That may be the reason that economic interests have been particularly successful in defining their goals as the public good: The business of America is business. Warner argues this is especially true of local governments.[57] In competition over what issues deserve to be on the public agenda, other demands are often defined as coming from "special interests" while the demands from business represent the "public interest."[58]

The social context of urban areas can

make control by citizens over the political process more difficult because of the impediments it creates for citizen organization and cooperation. But it is not clear that such areas provide a significantly less-hospitable environment for citizen control than small towns. The pressure in small towns to submerge conflict and to keep the public sphere as limited as possible leaves few citizens with the interest or motivation to become politically active. Thus, a few people easily dominate the political process. For the few who do become active, a substantial blurring of their "public" and "private" roles occurs, making it easy for private interests to dominate the public policy process.

The impersonality, heterogeneity, and interdependence that characterize urban living provide fertile ground for the development of conflict and less informal pressure to submerge conflicts that develop. While the characteristics of urban life do create barriers to citizen control, they also result in an atmosphere that is tolerant of both the expression of and search for diverse values. Such activity is at the very core of the political process. The differentiation of roles also encourages political activity. Public officials who are not "friends and neighbors" and who are fulfilling a distinctly political role provide a clear target for citizens attempting to use politics as a means to achieve their goals. Those officials, in turn, need a supportive constituency to achieve their own goals, and therefore have an incentive to respond to citizen demands. At the same time the political leaders' responses will be tempered by the demand of economic interests because leaders rely on resources those interests control.

To say that incentive and motivation for citizen control exist in cities, perhaps to a greater degree than in small towns, is not to say that citizen control exists. The economic context of the city provides substantial barriers to meaningful popular control, as the next chapter explains.

Notes

1. G.W.F. Hegel, *Hegel's Philosophy of Right*, T.M. Knox, editor and translator (Clarendon, U.K.: Oxford University Press, 1965).

2. See, for example, F.D. McKenzie, "The Scope of Urban Ecology," in *The Urban Community*, ed. Ernest W. Burgess (Chicago: University of Chicago Press, 1987). For a fuller discussion of this term and other urban ecological terms, see Chapter Three of this book.

3. For an argument about the importance of land use in city politics, see Oliver P. Williams, *Urban Political Analysis* (New York: Free Press, 1971). For more recent arguments, see Stephen L. Elkin, *City and Regime in the American Republic* (Chicago: University of Chicago Press, 1987) and Clarence N. Stone and Heywood T. Sanders, *The Politics of Urban Development* (Lawrence: University of Kansas Press, 1987).

4. John R. Logan and Harvey L. Molotch, *Urban Fortunes: The Political Economy of Place* (Berkeley: University of California Press, 1987).

5. For a similar argument about the characteristics of urban areas, see Louis Wirth, "Urbanism as a Way of Life," *American Journal of Sociology* 44 (1938), 1–24. Wirth's belief that several negative consequences would inevitably follow from these characteristics has not been supported in research and is not implied here.

   Some argue that mass communication has eliminated the differences between small towns and cities. For a recent examination that concludes that differences remain, see Claude S. Fischer, *To Dwell Among Friends: Personal Networks in Town and City* (Chicago: University of Chicago Press, 1982).

   Meredith Ramsay questions the existence of an "urban-rural duality" by pointing to evidence that people in cities maintain social networks. The authors do not deny that, but argue that most urban dwellers—even those with extensive networks of friends and family—must deal more frequently with those whom they do not know than do the residents of small towns. (See Meredith Ramsay, *Community, Culture, and Economic Development: The Social Roots of Local Action* (Albany: State University of New York Press, 1996), 18–22.

6. Sam Roberts, "Yes, a Small Town Is Different," *New York Times*, August 27, 1995, Section E, 1; Michelle Seebach, "Small Towns Have a Rosy Image," *American Demographer* 14 (October 1992): 19.

7. Timothy Egan, "Many Seek Security in Private Communities," *New York Times*, September 3, 1995, 1.

8. Arthur J. Vidich and Joseph Bensman, *Small Town in Mass Society: Class, Power and Religion in a Rural Community* (Garden City, New York: Doubleday, 1960), 148–149.

9. Ibid., 51.

10. Nelson Wikstrom, *The Political World of a Small Town: A Mirror Image of American Politics* (Westport, Connecticut: Greenwood Press, 1993), 70.

11. See Ramsay, *Community, Culture, and Economic Development*, 18–22.

12. Fischer, *To Dwell Among Friends*, 60.

13. Everett Carll Ladd, *Ideology in America: Change and*

Response in a City, a Suburb and a Small Town (Ithaca, New York, and London: Cornell University Press, 1969), 139. See also, Wikstrom, *The Political World of a Small Town.*

14. Sam Bass Warner, Jr., *The Private City: Philadelphia in Three Periods of Its Growth* (Philadelphia: University of Pennsylvania Press, 1968), 3–4.

15. Granville Hicks, *Small Town* (New York: Macmillan, 1947), 97–98.

16. Bert E. Swanson, Richard A. Cohen, and Edith P. Swanson, *Small Towns and Small Towners: Framework for Survival and Growth* (Beverly Hills, California: Sage Library of Social Research, 1979), 170.

17. Vidich and Bensman, *Small Town in Mass Society,* 147.

18. Wikstrom, *The Political World of a Small Town,* 70.

19. Ibid.

20. Ibid., 144.

21. Ladd, *Ideology in America,* 140.

22. Vidich and Bensman, *Small Town in Mass Society,* 123.

23. Ramsay, *Community, Culture, and Economic Development,* 59, 96–97; Wikstrom, *The Political World of a Small Town,* 74.

24. Vidich and Bensman, *Small Town in Mass Society,* 130.

25. Ladd, *Ideology in America,* 138. See also, Vidich and Bensman, *Small Town in Mass Society,* 127, and Hicks, *Small Town,* 190.

26. John M. Blum, Bruce Catton, Edmund S. Morgan, Arthur Schlesinger, Jr., Kenneth M. Stampp, C. Van Woodward, *The National Experience* (New York: Harcourt, Brace & World, 1963), 442.

27. Blake McKelvey, *The Urbanization of America 1860–1915* (New Brunswick, New Jersey: Rutgers University Press, 1963), 62.

28. Ibid., 64.

29. Stephen Steinberg, *The Ethnic Myth: Race, Ethnicity, and Class in America* (New York: Atheneum, 1981), 26.

30. Ibid., 33–36.

31. John Higham, *Strangers in the Land: Patterns of American Nativism 1860–1925* (New York: Atheneum, 1965), 16.

32. Alexis deTocqueville, *Democracy in America,* in Peter Woll, *American Government: Readings and Cases,* 8th ed. (Boston: Little, Brown, 1984), 84.

33. Quoted in Marion T. Bennett, *American Immigration Policies,* 4.

34. Oscar Handlin, *The Uprooted: The Epic Story of the Great Migration That Made the American People* (Boston: Little, Brown, 1951), 117.

35. Ibid., 186.

36. McKelvey, *The Urbanization of America,* 67.

37. Handlin, *The Uprooted,* 148.

38. Peter R. Gluck and Richard J. Meister, *Cities in Transition: Social Changes and Institutional Responses in Urban Development* (New York: New Viewpoints, 1979), 39.

39. Steinberg, *The Ethnic Myth,* 11.

40. Fischer, *To Dwell Among Friends,* Chapter 18.

41. See Chapter 12 for a discussion of crime rates in cities.

42. Peter K. Eisinger, "Understanding Urban Politics: A Comparative Perspective on Urban Political Conflict," *Polity* 9 (Winter 1977): 218–240.

43. For a review of the argument that economic answers may not achieve the public interest, see Theodore J. Lowi, *The End of Liberalism: The Second Republic of the United States,* 2nd ed. (New York: Norton, 1979). See also Elkin, *City and Regime in the American Republic.*

44. Michael H. Frisch, *Town into City: Springfield, Massachusetts and the Meaning of Community 1840–1880* (Cambridge, Massachusetts: Harvard University Press, 1972), 236–237.

45. Terry L. Cooper, *An Ethic of Citizenship for Public Administration,* (Englewood Cliffs, New Jersey: Prentice-Hall, 1991), p. 100.

46. Robert A. Dahl, *Who Governs? Democracy and Power in an American City* (New Haven: Yale University Press, 1961), 40–42.

47. Steven P. Erie, *Rainbow's End: Irish-Americans and the Dilemmas of Urban Machine Politics, 1840–1985* (Berkeley: University of California Press, 1988), 240–241.

48. Quoted in Blum, et al., *The National Experience,* 451.

49. Dahl, *Who Governs?,* 20–24.

50. Andrew M. Greeley, *Why Can't They Be Like Us?: Facts and Fallacies about Ethnic Differences and Group Conflicts in America* (New York: Institute of Human Relations Press, 1969), 26, 43.

51. Raymond E. Wolfinger, *The Politics of Progress* (Englewood Cliffs, New Jersey: Prentice-Hall, 1974), 61.

52. Ira Katznelson, *City Trenches: Urban Politics and the Patterning of Class in the United States* (Chicago: University of Chicago Press, 1981).

53. Joseph Zikmund II, "Mayoral Voting and Ethnic Politics in the Daley-Bilendic-Byrne Era," in Samuel K. Gove and Louis H. Massotti, *After Daley: Chicago Politics in Transition* (Urbana: University of Illinois Press, 1982), 29.

54. Robert D. Putnam, "Bowling Alone: America's Declining Social Capital," *Current* (June 1995): 4–5. See Chapter 5 for a discussion of the role of organizations in citizen participation.

55. See Douglas Yates, *The Ungovernable City: The Politics of Urban Problems and Policy Making* (Cambridge, Massachusetts: MIT Press, 1977).

56. Katznelson, *City Trenches,* Chapter 3.

57. Warner, *The Private City,* 4.

58. Several authors have made this observation. For a recent and convincing example, see Elkin, *City and Regime in the American Republic,* especially Chapter 7.

The Development of Cities

Even though many Americans have a value system that is rooted in small town America and seem to be disdainful of cities, America is an urban nation. This chapter will focus on the **political economy** of cities, that is, the interrelationship between economic factors and government policy. The chapter examines how economic and technological forces influence the development of cities and how urban citizens organize their social and political relations to cope with the changing environment. Although the public agenda expanded as small towns grew into cities, the chapter will discuss how the resources held privately are still important to political leaders. That means that private interests have substantial effects on the urban political process and on the ways in which cities develop.

Economic and technological forces affect how people and businesses are attracted to and sort themselves out in the city. Because these forces are generated at a national and even international level, local governments are constrained in dealing with them. In addition, local governments occupy subordinate political positions to state and federal government, which limits their prerogatives further. Local political leaders must live with these constraints and must make choices within those limits. It is important, however, to realize that the decisions of local political leaders do have an effect on the fate of economic interests and on urban development. Michael Pagano and Ann Bowman concluded in a recent study of urban economic development in 10 cities: "Politics matters in explaining the path and direction a city chooses, because local officials perceive a relevant orbit and then try to mobilize public capital in a manner intended to keep their city in (or move it to) that orbit."[1]

Economic and Technological Influences on Development

Economic factors are important in understanding urban areas for a number of reasons. The control of land is an important economic resource. Urban areas act as marketplaces that increase productivity by bringing together people and resources. Economic groups tend to sort themselves spatially by class or business and the spatial pattern then affects social interactions. These groups sometimes organize around their common work in the form of professional organizations or unions.

What often remains unrecognized is that economic forces are prime determinants of the physical and ecological structure of cities. Directly or indirectly these forces influence the pattern of living as well as the social and governmental institutions of urban complexes. Changes in the mode of production or economic organization are inevitably reflected in the urban scene.[2]

Economics is intertwined with technology. Changes in technology affect the demand for skills and the value of land. As production changed from individual artisans in homes to mass production in factories, there were not only changes in the skills workers needed, but also spatial complexity increased and land values changed. Changes in transportation also affected access of workers to their jobs, and the value of land was reflected in the access it provided. First the seaport, then the railhead, and now the highway interchange are highly valued because of the access they provide.

The economic base of the city affects its character. Cities such as Palm Springs, California, which depends on the tourist trade, will have a different mix of businesses and require a different mix of services and skills than an industrial city such as Gary, Indiana. Different key industries attract different supporting businesses. The economic base also determines the vitality of the community. Both public and private decisions are constrained by the necessity of maintaining a strong economic base. Indeed, it is argued the most important determinant of urban policy is the need to maintain or create economic productivity in the city.[3] Major private interests can make decisions that affect the economic prosperity of urban areas and, for that reason, are usually guaranteed consideration by the governing coalition that determines urban policy and are often part of that coalition.

One way of looking at the economic influences on urban areas is through location theory. "Land . . . has use value, in a qualitative sense; and its use value as a place of residence or as a neighborhood setting to one group may come into conflict with its commodity value to another group that is more concerned about speculative profits or investment opportunities."[4] The underlying assumption of classical economics is that the land will be allocated most efficiently because those who derive the most benefit from a certain location can afford to bid the most. That assumption underlies the decision to leave land and land-use decisions substantially in private hands. But not everyone will be satisfied with the land use that such a process produces. Those already "using" a neighborhood for a residence may oppose neighborhood change that might be economically beneficial for the city as a whole. By the same token, speculators may wish to intensify or change land use to maximize profits even if it has detrimental impacts on the residents of a neighborhood.[5]

Individuals and businesses compete for locations that maximize access to something of value, be it a natural resource, rich farmland, or a harbor. Cities grow and change as people and industry compete for favorable locations. The settlement patterns of business and industry are often determined by factors such as minimizing transportation costs or having access to concentrations of consumers.* This explains why Colonial American cities grew up around harbors (the colonists depended on the sea for shipping) and why warehouses, processors, and traders competed

---

*Langdon White, Edwin J. Foscue, and Tom L. McKnight, *Regional Geography of Anglo-America* (Englewood Cliffs, New Jersey: Prentice-Hall, 1964), 23–29, identify 13 characteristics that make sites attractive: (1) proximity to markets; (2) proximity to raw materials; (3) proximity to power; (4) proximity to skilled manpower; (5) access to transportation; (6) climate; (7) water supply; (8) capital; (9) availability and cost of land; (10) human factors, that is, individual idiosyncrasies; (11) taxation; (12) cost of living; and (13) disposal of wastes.

for land by the wharves while the citizenry clustered around these businesses for employment and access to commodities.

The distribution of economic resources affects a city's spatial distribution because those groups with the greatest wealth have the most locational options. America's preindustrial cities developed as follows:

> The city's elite tended to live in the center of the community near their places of business and the center of government. The poor were on the fringe of the city, especially along the waterfront.[6]

In the industrial city, the housing pattern changed as the rich could afford to travel some distance from the factory. Although the pattern changed, it was still determined by the economic use of and competition for space. In the modern city, economic pressures still predominate in determining land-use decisions and most of the decisions are made privately, although affected by public decisions. Those decisions that take the form of restrictions, such as zoning or pollution control laws, or incentives, such as tax abatements and the location of public improvements, however, can alter the impact of the economics of location. One of the most important powers of local government is its ability to affect land use.

The economics of location tends to change over time as technology, social, and political conditions change. F.D. McKenzie noted that certain patterns tend to characterize the evolution of all cities. He used the perspective of **human ecology**, which examines the processes that determine the settlement and spatial distribution of people and institutions over time. He identified seven ecological processes that affect urban development: (1) concentration, (2) dispersion, (3) centralization, (4) decentralization, (5) segregation, (6) invasion, and (7) succession.[7]

Each of these processes describes changes

in the spatial patterning of urban settlements and their "natural" consequences. Favorable access to something valued makes some locations attractive to settlers. People and businesses with the most resources are able to *concentrate* at such sites. As the concentration continues, density and size increase. While changes in technology and beliefs mean that the limits of the modern city differ from those of ancient cities, urban concentration does have a practical limit.

As cities grow and become denser, *dispersion* becomes necessary. Land values change as density makes land more valuable for business and less valuable for residences. To make residences economically feasible, many families may be crowded into one house. Those with adequate resources can seek cheaper land elsewhere, which often leads to movement to the periphery of the city and eventually the founding of new towns or "suburbs." The well-to-do were the first to exercise this option. The advent of the streetcar and trolley during the latter part of the nineteenth century in the United States increased the ability of less affluent people to disperse and the residential mobility of cities' residents.

Within the settlement, some areas become focal points for certain activities; there is a tendency for *centralization*. Characteristics of the land or its access may lead to the development of distinct land uses such as offices and retailing in the Central Business District (CBD), or industrial usage, or residential neighborhoods. Another developmental tendency is *decentralization*, or movement away from the central location. For example, as new neighborhoods are established, stores in the CBD may start branches to be nearer their customers. Shopping malls exemplify the decentralization process in the United States.

Along with the centralization and decentralization processes, a *segregation* of specific groups and businesses develops in certain areas. Within residential areas, population groups tend to cluster by race, ethnic group, or class. This clustering may occur for reasons such as protection or necessity. Business also segregates into specialized areas such as a jewelry district, a red light district, or a restaurant row. Because consumers want a certain commodity, locating similar businesses together will lure more buyers. A customer who wants a pair of earrings can maximize selection and presumably minimize price by walking between stores located in the same area. Business gains because of the volume of consumers.

As cities develop and change, *invasion* takes place. As trade gives way to industry, unskilled workers rapidly move to the city and seek housing close to their jobs. Those with adequate means respond to this invasion by fleeing outward. Eventually the areas around the initial settlement are taken over by newcomers. In New York City's SoHo district, for example, land use changed from industrial to residential because the old loft buildings were no longer economical for industry, but their location was valuable for residences. When one group replaces another or when land use changes, *succession* occurs.

These ecological processes are constantly occurring in different parts of various cities. For instance, although a business may open stores in various areas (decentralization), the accounting, purchasing, and management of the business may be brought into or kept in the main downtown store (centralization). Other areas may be being invaded by yuppies (the sometimes pejorative term used to identify young upwardly mobile urban professionals) trying to change run-down areas into upper-class residential neighborhoods. As areas of the city pass from one stage to the next, conflicts may occur between the old inhabitants and those trying to change the neighborhood. It is necessary to go beyond ecological processes to develop a more complete understanding of urban development because these conflicts are apt to spill over into the political realm. "A more thoroughly man-made city

heightens our awareness of choice and responsibility and requires a political process that is more than simply permissive."[8]

Relationship of Economic and Political Factors

Although economic processes help shape urban growth and competing private economic interests may influence politics, these factors do not occur in a vacuum. Economic forces provide constraints for political decision makers, but these forces are not the sole determinant of urban development.[9] Urban development can best be understood as the interaction of economic and political forces or **political economy**.

Political economy affects urban development in three major ways. First, much urban development is controlled by private developers. This is an example of the privatism discussed in the last chapter. Second, those who demonstrate prowess in the marketplace are more likely to be accorded privileged access in the political arena and are able to play a larger role in shaping public decisions, resulting in public actions to boost the private market. Third, much of the political conflict in urban America results from the competition between the haves and the have-nots in the economic system—this competition often plays itself out in the political arena.

America has a long tradition of reliance on private market values rather than public, collective values to determine the distribution of urban land and resources.[10] Ted Gurr and Desmond King state:

> The prevailing American view is that the market is the primary shaper of cities and that policy intervention should aim at relieving its undesirable consequences, not at intentionally redirecting market activities.[11]

They argue, however, that the state is playing an ever-increasing role in shaping and reshaping the future city in postindustrial society, a point with which a recent study of economic development in 10 cities agrees.[12]

Many have argued that urban areas can only maintain their viability as communities if they are able to attract economic resources. To do this, government leaders must make decisions acceptable to major economic interests.[13] As public resources are invariably limited, political leaders must rely on the private sector to produce "necessary" development. They will often form coalitions with business leaders to assure that the city grows. This aids business by creating opportunities to increase profits and it aids politicians by expanding the tax base, which, in turn, makes it possible for political leaders to provide desired services to residents. At the same time, political officials are constrained by the need to build an electoral coalition or the desire to achieve policy goals other than those supported by business.[14]

Political decision making or non–decision making (that is, the decision not to make a decision and rely on the private market) interacts with economic factors to shape a city.[15] Former New York City Mayor Edward Koch made very clear that politics can influence economic choice. Two months after taking office he stated that "the main job of municipal government is to create a climate in which private business can expand in the city, to provide jobs and profit."[16] From the first urban settlements in the New World to the modern American city, the pattern of government action or inaction has been aimed primarily at the goal defined by Koch: creating a positive business environment.[17]

The American political culture supports such views. Belief in values such as individualism, competition, equality, and progress translates into strong support for both democracy and capitalism.[18] Much of the history of urban development is the result of the interplay of those political and economic beliefs. The assumption is that an economically healthy community is a good community.

Government "should keep the peace among individual money makers" and create an atmosphere where everyone could prosper.[19]

But the melding of economic and political goals is not total. While the goals of individualism and competition are central to both capitalism and democracy, the societal goal of equality is contradictory to the economic goals of capitalism. Some question whether following a privatist, market-oriented philosophy can result in desired goals for everyone. Capitalist principles may guarantee maximum production and minimum prices but "that says nothing about the society except that its average members will probably enjoy improved comforts and choices."[20] In other words, inaction can lead to inequity. Even when government acts, it may not do so to rectify inequities. It has been argued that though government activity has increased, it has often been used for individual interests not collective interests. The government does not rule but instead parcels out public authority to private interests.[21]

Warner sums up the impact of the privatist ideology on urban development.

> The tradition of privatism has meant that the cities of the United States depended for their wages, employment, and general prosperity upon the aggregate successes and failures of thousands of individual enterprises, not upon community action. It has also meant that the physical forms of American cities, their lots, houses, factories, and streets have been the outcome of a real estate market of profit-seeking builders, land speculators, and large investors. Finally, the tradition of privatism has meant that the local politics of American cities have depended for their actors, and for a good deal of their subject matter, on the changing focus of men's private economic activities.[22]

This points to a second important aspect of the political economy of the city and its impact on ordinary citizens. Economic power quickly becomes political power. Those successful in the economic sphere will sometimes seek political office, either elected or appointed. Or they may seek to use their economic resources to alter public decisions. Those who fail economically have, in essence, demonstrated their unworthiness. Although private decisions often have public impacts, there is no forum for the general public to participate in those decisions. For example, a decision by one firm to locate a factory producing noxious odors affects adjoining landowners. The noxious odors are viewed as negative externalities.

Under the ideology of privatism, government has tended to minimize its restraints on business in the interests of individual freedom and market competition. Government has often been most active in advancing business in the name of economic progress. Business enjoys a great deal of legitimacy when it participates in government; however, business still has an effect even when it does not play a role because its values predominate.[23] This does not mean, however, that economic interests always win.

> Since political and economic resources are unequally distributed, political entrepreneurs have a strong incentive to give greater weight to powerful interests whether or not they participate directly in politics. It is less obvious, but equally true, that powerful interests cannot count on having their way, can be frustrated by inertia of government practices, and that government can (at least at times) operate independently of them, and can even reorganize the constellation of private interests.[24]

Political leaders must maintain the confidence of the business community to be assured of the economic resources necessary to run the city; at the same time, they must try to balance this with efforts to maintain the support of the citizenry and to get re-elected.[25] The fact that political leaders must win popu-

lar election means that economic power does not always prevail. Other groups have other resources that affect the political system. To build winning coalitions, political leaders design policies that will be appealing to groups within the electorate beyond the economic elite.[26] In some cities that are seen as very desirable places to live, such as San Francisco, alliances among diverse groups of citizens can often be a successful counterpoint to the established economic elites.[27] Traditionally, those coalitions excluded the economic lower classes and minorities; however, as more and more center cities are being left to these groups, their political clout increases.

The third reason for the importance of understanding political economy is that many problems and conflicts in modern cities are rooted in the division of society into the haves and the have-nots. Because those with the most resources have a greater say in the shape of development through the marketplace and through political influence, the poor are often relegated to the old and decaying parts of the city. Cities are finding it increasingly difficult to maintain a middle class. Those who are wealthy can afford the cost to be near the jobs and entertainment that are concentrated in the center city. They can use their wealth to help insulate them from the discomforts that sometimes come with urban living. They sometimes create physical barriers to separate themselves from the have-nots. Many live in large apartment or condominium complexes with many self-contained amenities and elaborate security. An example is Presidential Towers in Chicago.

> The buildings are joined at the third floor into a roofed area that covers two city blocks and is entered at a single lobby that opens up onto an atrium, bar, cafe, grocery store, newsstand, restaurant, and escalator that routes residents to a single security station where both an entry card and phone-up system screen entrants through a second entrance. House staff wear recognizable uni-

TABLE 3–1

Epochs of Urbanization

Mercantile city	Colonial times–1840
Industrial city	1840–1920
Metropolitan city	1920–present

forms. Two-way radios cackle in the background. A health club occupies much of the fourth floor and the roof provides a jogging track and regulation-size basketball court.[28]

This and other similar developments were dubbed "communities under glass."[29]

The poor are often left behind, unable to move to the suburbs or follow jobs that have migrated out of the center city. Historically, these poor were immigrants who remained until they were assimilated into the mainstream of society. In addition to the most recent immigrants, the have-nots in the city are disproportionately African-Americans and Latinos. Many American cities offer stark contrasts between great wealth and great poverty. The differences in wealth and race often create conflicts that must be managed by the political system. Cities must determine whose needs will be met, and, as previously argued, American values and economic necessity give businesses and the haves in the society an upper hand.

While generally urban governments have tended to facilitate business interests, the exact relation between politics and economics has varied over time. To understand how the interplay between economic and political forces has shaped the modern urban landscape, we must examine the stages of urban development.

Stages of Development

The urbanization of America can be roughly divided into three epochs (Table 3–1). The first epoch, from colonial times until about 1840, can be characterized as the mercantile city. The period from 1840 through about 1930 saw the development of the industrial city. The period since 1920 can be termed the metropolitan city. The 1920s was a period of transition as various cities entered the metropolitan city era at different rates. The city was shaped by the economic and technological forces that were at work in each time period.

The Mercantile City

Although in Colonial times less than 10 percent of the population lived in urban areas, those communities had major social and economic influences on the hinterland.[30] One historian notes that, "Colonial America, though certainly 90 percent agricultural in an occupational sense, may also be described as 90 percent urban in a cultural sense."[31] For example, it was in the cities that the elites began to identify more as Americans than as Englishmen.[32]

The primary purpose of these cities, though, was economic. The Colonial city was a trading center for goods from across the ocean and a place for artisans to set up shop.[33] City government was primarily concerned with establishing a viable community so that trade and industry could flourish. As a result, the government's main function was to regulate and promote commerce, that is, to provide an environment that would ensure economic justice and prosperity.[34]

Not only was the purpose of city government defined in economic terms, participation in that government was determined by economic qualifications. Not surprisingly, as voting was based on economic circumstance, those with economic resources were disproportionately represented within the political leadership. For example, in New York City between 1675 and 1725, two-thirds of the aldermen were merchants and 30 percent were artisans and innkeepers.[35]

The functions of the government, which were limited and centered on economic well-being, included setting prices and wages, controlling entry into various occupations, fixing standard weights and measures, and establishing public markets. There was much less concern with education and poor relief. Warner uses Philadelphia as an example of the general role of government in Colonial America and its tie to privatist economic values.

> Urban problems that required direct and substantial reallocation of scarce resources . . . brought failure after failure to the future city. No urban, economic democracy emerged with time because the popular goal of Philadelphia was the individual race for wealth. This was to be the essence of the American, urban experience.[36]

Technology has also played a major role in the size and shape of cities. The size of settlements is dependent upon an adequate supply of potable water and sanitation to dispose of waste. Often these essential collective needs led to the establishment of a government or the expansion of an existing one.

Each of America's commercial centers was a compact settlement in which residents could easily walk from one side of town to the other.[37] Although some sorting of classes and occupational groups occurred, they lived near each other. Land uses were mixed as artisans often set up shop in their residences.

> The real secret of peace and order of the eighteenth-century town lay not in its government but in the informal structure of its community. . . . Graded by wealth and

divided by class though it was, it functioned as a single community. The community had been created out of a remarkably inclusive network of business and economic relationships and it was maintained by the daily interactions of trade and sociability.[38]

The mercantile city can be characterized in much the same way as today's small town. Decision making tended to be dominated by the economic elite. In many instances, only they could make decisions as members of the board of municipal corporations or as voters. Only white, male, property owners were allowed to vote. The primary function of municipal government was to further the economic development of the community; health and welfare programs came only in response to crises. Sharing space and values minimized conflict just as in small towns.

Nevertheless, conflict did occur from time to time. In some instances, demands arose for a greater government role in social issues. The inequality in the mercantile city generated popular protests. The increasing wealth of commercial interests generated increasing demands for economic and political equality.[39] In the 1730s and 1740s "concerns of health, safety, streets, and lighting outweighed those of monopolies, markets, price-fixing and commercial chicanery."[40] This resulted in demands for a shift in the public role from economic concerns to social welfare issues. On the other hand, the American Revolution, which represented a fight against central authority and support for the laissez-faire economics espoused by Adam Smith's *The Wealth of Nations,* led to even greater demands for limiting public regulation of economic activity.[41]

After the Revolution, municipal charters, which were seen as "perpetuating entrenched economic interests rather than as protecting freedom or being effective mechanisms for responding to the needs of the entire urban population," were nullified by state legislatures.[42] Meanwhile, changes in the economic base from commerce in the mercantile city to manufacturing in the industrial city brought changes in the structure and leadership of the urban community.

The Industrial City

Several changes occurred in the industrial city. The factory system, coupled with changes in transportation, altered the class structure and the physical form of urban America. Technological change acted as a centrifugal force pushing people off the farm as mechanization replaced workers. Centripetal forces acted to pull workers to the city—from rural areas and from abroad to work in the new factories. Much of the relative simplicity of the mercantile city was lost.

Diversity grew within and between cities in the industrial era. Some cities flourished, while others foundered. The mercantile cities grew up around waterways because most of the world's trade was conducted by barge and ship. The introduction of the railroad opened up new areas for urban development. Cities that became transfer points between water and rail transportation nodes prospered.

Within the city, the influx of newcomers increased the heterogeneity of the city's population. Industrialization meant a change in production from individual, dispersed artisans to a system dependent on concentrations of populations to staff factories. Division of labor increased the interdependence, and the factory system bred impersonality. The industrial city created new strains for local governments, such as providing the infrastructure for industry and addressing social problems created by unacculturated rural migrants and foreign immigrants.

In 1810 only a small percentage of workers were employed in industry, generally in small family-owned textile mills, smelting plants, and so on. The foundations of the economy were the tanners, coopers, blacksmiths, millers, and other craftsmen serving the community. Class differences were minimal.

After the Civil War, class and income distinctions increased and a new middle class was created. Blocks that had been a mixture of shops and residences were sorted out into specialized business and residential districts.[43]

> The increasingly well-defined class differences became replicated on the urban map of segregated residential patterns. Immigrant working-class tenement districts crowded around the Central Business District and were, in turn, surrounded by a middle-class ring. The wealthy class claimed exclusive urban areas such as Park Avenue or Beacon Hill or lived on estates beyond the middle-class sections.[44]

This is just one of the common configurations that cities take. Various urbanologists have posited theoretical models of urban form. The models do not fit any city perfectly because each has a different history, industrial mix, and physical characteristics (for example, rivers, hills). The models are useful because, despite unique aspects of any city, they point to commonalities such as spatial specialization by classes and land uses and are helpful in understanding why cities grew and developed as they did.

The concentric zone model was developed in the 1920s by the Chicago School of Urban Ecologists: Earnest Burgess, Robert Park, and F.D. McKenzie.[45] It contained a central business district (CBD) surrounded by relatively homogeneous, specialized rings based on the distance from the CBD.

This model is a relatively accurate description of many older cities. In the center is the *central business district,* which is filled with offices, stores, theaters, banks, and so on. Surrounding the CBD is an old area where the original settlers lived when they "commuted" on foot. Known as the *zone of transition,* this area is composed of apartment buildings and rooming houses, which have known better days, and perhaps warehouses and light industry. The zone of transition is often the first home for new immigrants and migrants and has often been the target of attempts at urban redevelopment.

Beyond the zone of transition is the *zone of workers' homes*. Because this model and most cities fitting this pattern were developed before automobile ownership was widespread, a worker could not easily live too far from the center city. The introduction of the car meant the more well-to-do residents could move farther from the urban hubbub in the CBD to homes where there was more room. Workers

gladly took over the older residences left behind. This class succession in housing is known as *filtering down*. Second-generation immigrants escaped to this area.

The fourth zone from the center, the *zone of better residences*, contained the newer homes. The furthest zone was the *commuter zone*, populated by those willing and able to trade off time for space. Figure 3–1 applies the concentric zone model to Chicago in 1920, just before it entered the modern era. The spatial structure of the city has not changed much since then. It should be noted that the model is not entirely circular and that the rings need

---

FIGURE 3–1

Concentric Zone Model of Chicago, Circa 1925

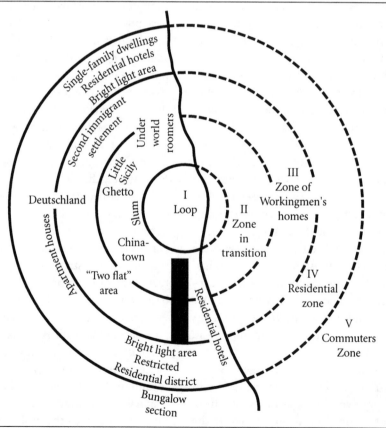

not be equal size or smooth. In the real world, geographic features such as lakes, rivers, and hills may create irregularities to this general pattern.

The shape of cities was affected by transportation innovation. The omnibus, a horse-drawn coach carrying about a dozen people was introduced in 1828. Other innovations followed, such as horsepowered trolleys that could carry more people at faster speeds for lower fares. In city after city, private entrepreneurs introduced "mass transit." As early as the late 1830s, Boston had introduced steam railroad lines that were relatively costly but quite speedy.[46] In the 1870s New York City introduced steam-powered elevated trains. In 1888, electric streetcars started running in Richmond, Virginia. In the 1890s New York City replaced its steam-powered trains with electric-powered elevated trains and subways.

These changes in transportation technology brought many consequences. The shape of the city altered with the beginning of the phenomenon of suburbanization. Residents with adequate means could be transported from the din of the industrial city to new areas at the end of the streetcar lines. The new technology also encouraged class segregation. "The rich moved farther away from the middle classes, who in turn moved away from the poor. Increasingly, areas of poverty became contained and segregated at the center of the city."[47]

Transportation also fostered economic specialization. Prior to 1870, warehouses dominated downtown areas. Financial and retailing districts were located near wholesaling and storage facilities. Between 1870 and 1900, downtown business districts developed into shopping and financial centers.[48] Strip shopping areas grew along trolley and streetcar lines. While some cities were developing in concentric zones, others were developing along strips defined by transportation routes.

Homer Hoyt developed the sector model to portray the dynamics of urban growth and

FIGURE 3–2

Sector Model

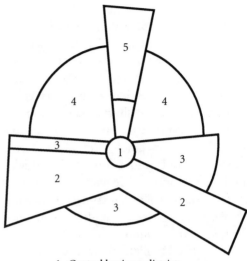

1. Central business district
2. Zone in transition
3. Zone of workers' homes
4. Zone of better residences
5. Commuter zone

spatial patterning during this period.[49] He argued that cities grew along transportation corridors superimposed on the concentric circles. The physical form of Philadelphia loosely fits this model (see Figure 3–2). The zone in transition lies along the Delaware River with factories, warehouses, the airport, and so on. Radiating north of the CBD, along Broad Street and west along South Street are other zones in transition. Toward the south and northeast are the workers' homes. "Better" apartment residences radiate out along Benjamin Franklin Parkway. Along the "main line," the former main track of the Pennsylvania Railroad, are the better residences and the commuter zone.

Transportation technology and the Industrial Revolution not only affected the internal structure of cities but also the national network of cities. The first cities of the "West" were outposts for trade that depended on water transportation. Pittsburgh was established at the confluence of the Monongahela, Allegheny, and Ohio Rivers. Louisville was founded further down the Ohio.

With the beginning of the Industrial Revolution, Pittsburgh, Louisville, and other successful cities began to diversify. In Pittsburgh, those who had amassed fortunes in commerce began to invest in new industrial enterprises.[50] By 1830, Pittsburgh had been transformed into America's "Iron City."[51] Lexington, Kentucky, and Cincinnati, Ohio, also industrialized. St. Louis and Louisville, Kentucky, used their locations to remain as commercial centers. The cities of Cincinnati, Louisville, and Lexington, which had always competed for river traffic, found they had to compete for the railroad to maintain their positions, as river trade was about to give up its dominance to the "iron horse."

This economic development of cities was largely influenced by private speculators, with government playing a limited but increasing role. Two important economic factors developed out of this tradition. One factor, which directly affected the physical form of the city, was the attempt by private speculators to influence public decisions about the location of colleges, hospitals, and county seats; the speculators hoped that increased land values would result from placement of these facilities. The speculators hoped they would reap benefits from the public actions. Economists call this a **positive externality**. As indicated previously, an externality is an effect of a decision on those who do not make the decision. In the example above, the externality is considered positive because the speculators' land would increase in value because of decisions made by political leaders. The other factor, which had an indirect effect, was adherence to the capitalist ideology, which legitimized the concentration of public power in private hands.[52]

The role of the common person was limited. Despite the immense possibility for democratic control through a variety of political channels, the scale of the city overwhelmed average citizens and they saw "themselves as men and women coping with the city and not participants in its building."[53] They worried about their homes and jobs, not the future of the city.

However, some middle- and upper-class social reformers did play a role. They felt that "the problems of irresponsible wealth and devastating poverty were juxtaposed in such glaring contrast, and the ethnic, cultural, and moral divisions were so sharply drawn" that some action was necessary.[54] Some reformers, such as Stanton Coit and Jane Addams, set up private settlement houses to aid the poor in achieving middle-class values and to lobby on their behalf. Others, such as Lawrence Veiller, fought for public sector regulation of housing conditions.[55]

Industrialization had brought new people with diverse values and traditions to the city. The personalism, homogeneity, and independence of the small town and mercantile city had eroded. Law and order were frequently threatened, and increased crowding created other problems. As these changes occurred, public decision making was also forced to change. Formal governmental structures were often inadequate and informal structures, such as political machines, developed to deal with the economic and social change.* The decision makers also changed, especially in the larger cities. The economic elites and those of Anglo-Saxon Protestant stock were forced, at least in some communities and in some policy arenas, to share or even relinquish power. The economic elites generally maintained influence in urban development, even if they lost some control over social issues.

---

*A political machine is a political organization that seeks to monopolize governmental control through the allocation of personal favors. This will be discussed in Chapter 7 .

Changing conditions and increasing complexity led to an expanded public agenda and necessitated a more professional government. During most of the nineteenth century, cities functioned primarily to promote individual economic activity. Only when clear threats to social order and public safety were perceived did government provide social services.[56] The services provided were generally inadequate because, "municipal authorities, loath to increase taxes, usually shouldered new responsibilities only at the prod of grim necessity."[57] As noted above, private, not-for-profit social reformers stepped in to fill the void.

As services grew, so did the complexity of government. Many specialized boards and commissions were created. This complexity made participation difficult for those, like the factory workers, who lacked time and education. Concurrently, "increased taxation encouraged more citizens to become aware of what was going on in city hall, leading to a greater interest in politics among the growing middle class."[58]

The Metropolitan City

The central city reached its apex in many respects in the 1920s. For the first time, urban dwellers composed more than 50 percent of the population. Radio, movies, and the automobile served to undermine agrarian values, while at the same time agricultural mechanization and economic depression drove migrants to the city. These migrants were being drawn not only to traditional industries such as iron and steel, but also to those emerging to produce automobiles, appliances, and the like.[59]

As cars permitted citizens and businesses to disperse, the industrial city gave way to the metropolitan city. Development sprouted beyond the legal boundaries of the initial urban concentration. Suburban communities proliferated outside the boundaries of the traditional city and competed with the central city

for resources. Sometimes those new communities were brought into an existing city through annexation, but other times they maintained their independence. The sorting out by race and class that became evident in the industrial city became more problematic in the metropolitan city because political boundaries often separated the problems in the city from the resources needed to address those problems. As a result, cities became more dependent on other levels of government to address their problems. The central city not only had to compete with other center cities for development, as had occurred in the industrial city era, it now was also in competition with other communities in the metropolitan area. After World War II, American cities also found themselves in competition with other world cities as changes in technology and transportation increased the mobility of business and capital. This mobility increased the influence of the economic elite on urban development because the elite could threaten to abandon the city if they were dissatisfied with public policy.

As cities grew, local government continued to encourage private development because a growing city meant a growing tax base. The role of local government also became more complex. In the metropolitan era, annexation of surrounding land became more difficult in many areas, especially in the Northeast and Midwest. This engendered competition between communities within metropolitan areas to encourage the migration of business and taxpayers to their confines and to discourage migration of those who would need government services.[60] Complexity increased because of the proliferation of governments in the metropolitan area and the expectation that they would provide a higher level of services.

During this era, local government regulation of the private sector in the area of land use increased with the introduction of zoning (see Chapter 12). Governments use zoning to control land use—to affect directly the physical location of various kinds of development and the kinds of residents and businesses that could locate in the community. Through zoning, communities could keep out the poor by not allowing low-income housing to be built. They could encourage or discourage various types of commercial or industrial development. Many battles have been fought over land-use regulation.

As a result of the Great Depression, the federal government increased its role in urban areas in two ways. The 1937 Housing Act provided direct aid to local governments. The federal government instituted an urban renewal program to help rebuild distressed areas within cities and to provide housing. This program also created jobs for those involved in the rebuilding. The second program, Social Security helped cities indirectly by providing benefits to individuals, thus easing the pressure on local governments. The issue of whether aid should go directly to individuals or be channeled through local governments is often a source of conflict in federal policy making.*

While local governments were trying to make the city more hospitable for middle- and upper-class individuals and businesses and trying to serve the needs of the poor, the federal government was instituting other programs that dispersed residents outside the center city. For example, the Interstate Highway Act of 1954 resulted in the construction of highways, which enabled people to move out to the suburbs and still have easy access to jobs in the city. In addition, the federal government created mortgage programs that discouraged investment in cities while fostering suburban growth.†

Another reason for the dispersion from the center city was technology. In the industrial city, streetcars and subways had allowed some

to flee along the path of mass transit; in like manner, the automobile allowed for a new style of growth and suburbanization. "In pursuit of social and ethnic separatism, Americans had abandoned the old single-nucleus city and created instead a cluster of cities, an amorphous mass with a scattering of nuclei."[61] This created a new model of urban form, the multiple nuclei city.[62] (See Figure 3–3.)

Many of those with the resources to do so moved out of the city into suburbs. Suburbanization is consistent with the American nostalgia for small towns.[63] The suburbs provided a place "where people could escape from the social, economic, and racial heterogeneity of the central city"[64] and return to the homogeneous environment of the small town. It allowed people to "live among those of similar income, lifestyles, and complexion, enjoying the neighborliness of persons who thought, acted, and looked alike."[65]

Although many left the center city, some remained because they liked the life-style of the city and could afford to insulate themselves against some of the problems of urban life. Certain neighborhoods in some cities have managed to maintain their cachet, for example, the Gold Coast in Chicago, Beacon Hill in Boston, New York's Upper East Side, San Francisco's Nob Hill, and Philadelphia's Rittenhouse Square. While many of the elite have fled the older cities, others remain because they enjoy the stimuli and diversions found only in the urban core. They are joined in the city by those who want to be close to the action.

But only a handful of larger metropolitan areas like New York, Chicago, Boston, Philadelphia, and Washington have truly cosmopolitan cores. As part of the redevelopment of downtowns, a growing number of medium-sized cities like Milwaukee and Bal-

---

*Part IV of this book will discuss a variety of programs that aid citizens directly, as well as programs where aid is funneled through local governments.
†See Chapter 14.

FIGURE 3–3

Multiple Nuclei Model

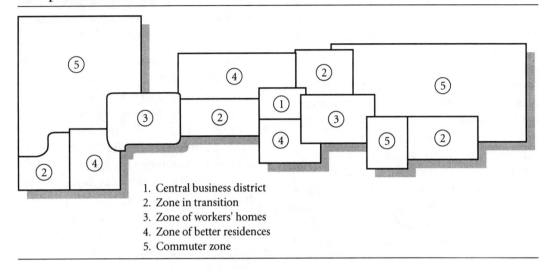

1. Central business district
2. Zone in transition
3. Zone of workers' homes
4. Zone of better residences
5. Commuter zone

timore have created pockets of "luxury" housing aimed at this market. In general, however, the smaller the metropolitan area, the more limited the number of homes occupied by elite and young professional households in the center city. That leaves the poor, by far the most robust segment of the market for inner city housing.[66]

The transportation technology extant at the time a city developed has a major impact on its internal structure, thus the cities of the Northeast (the Frost Belt*) tend to be relatively compact and are more densely populated along commuter bus or subway lines. This is because their major development occurred prior to the automobile age. The newer cities of the South, Southwest, and West, often considered the "Sun Belt," which have flourished since the advent of the automobile, tended to be more sprawling and with many "centers" rather than a main central business district complex. It might be said that:

Metropolitan areas constitute the true cities of the United States. The places that most people think of as the nation's important municipalities such as Los Angeles, San Antonio, Baltimore, or Boston, for example, are only the *central cities* of their much larger, but organically unified metropolitan complexes.[67]

Highways replaced railways in importance in shipping merchandise. Industry no longer needed to remain in the crowded downtown by the railhead but could now move out along the highway. As automobile congestion increased the difficulty of transportation in the older cities, movement to the suburbs or to the Sun Belt became a more attractive option for businesses as well as individuals. The older cities, many of which make up what we now call the Frost Belt or Rust Belt, were plagued with an outmoded infrastructure (for example, roads, sanitary systems, etc.) making them less attractive to heavy industry.

*Frost Belt states are considered in this work to be those in the Northeast, Mid-Atlantic, and Midwest. The Sun Belt is considered to be the states of the Southeast, Southwest, and West Coast.

Manufacturing technology was also transformed. The old loft system in which manufacturing took place in a vertical, multistory, compact setting gave way to the assembly line, which required large horizontal space. Large spaces in the downtown were not readily available or were in areas now zoned for residences. Even if space could be found, land costs were high. This made the suburbanization of industry more attractive. Industry fled to the suburbs for five reasons: (1) the search for space; (2) changes in transportation technology; (3) the movement of labor; (4) the availability of external economies of scale or economies of agglomeration, for example, an industrial park with one cafeteria or enough volume to get daily shipments; and (5) the flight from taxes.[68] These same factors (and others) made the Sun Belt appealing for new investment.

The transformation of America after World War II from an industrial into a post-industrial society also reinforced the movement of people and businesses outside the city. The base of the economy shifted from primarily manufacturing and processing to the provision of services. Increasingly the city lost manufacturing jobs, which were replaced by jobs in trade, finance, insurance, real estate, government, health, and research. Energy technology became less important than information technology.[69] The revolutionary communication and computer technology of the information age along with the availability of jet aircraft allowed corporations to locate different functions in different communities and even in different countries.

> A growing number of large organizations have moved routine operations to lower-cost quarters not only in the suburbs but as far away as South Dakota, Puerto Rico, Hong Kong, and Ireland. . . . Intensifying this decentralization is that the product of many enterprises is some form of information rather than physical objects or personal services. . . . Proximity is no longer neces-

sary. When it is, the increasing use of automobiles and air transportation has facilitated it. *The centrality of central cities has lost a lot of its importance for maintaining economic efficiency.*[70] [italics added]

The corporate headquarters could remain in the center city where it is visible and has access to financial and legal services; warehousing could be away from the city, perhaps near an airport; and product assembly could be done in a low-wage rural area or developing country because robotics has lessened the skill levels needed. As a result, blue collar manufacturing jobs became less plentiful as companies moved offshore to find cheaper workers. White collar services and information-related activities became the employment base for the new metropolis.

In the post–World War II period, the pace and scope of decentralization and deconcentration increased. Between 1930 and 1990 the number of metropolitan areas increased from 96 to 284[71], and the population of those in metropolitan areas went from less than 50 percent to almost 80 percent. In 1966, for the first time more people lived in the suburban circles that surrounded the core cities than lived in the core cities themselves. The 1990 census indicates that the movement of people to the suburban fringes continues.

Retail sales in the center city declined during the metropolitan era. Although large cities often have a strong retail commercial district, retail trade generally has been moving to the suburbs and suburban shopping malls. The first suburban shopping mall was built in 1923 in the Country Club district of Kansas City, Missouri. At that time, about 95 percent of all retail trade occurred in the central city. By 1977, in 12 of the 15 largest United States metropolitan areas, more than half of all retail sales occurred outside the center city.[72]

Center cities have tried to develop commercial districts in the CBD by copying the amenities offered by suburban malls. Many cities offer "vertical" or multistory malls to compete with the horizontal malls in the suburbs and maintain some vital areas for retail trade. Water Tower Place in Chicago, the Crown Center in Kansas City, Missouri, Liberty Place in Philadelphia, Harbor Place in Baltimore, and Pioneer Square in Portland, Oregon, are a few examples. Old downtown buildings are often refurbished into malls like the Terminal Tower in Cleveland, the Old Post Office in Washington, D.C., the Bourse in Philadelphia, or Union Station in St. Louis. Often old buildings are strung together as retail and entertainment centers as in Ghiradelli Square in San Francisco, Pike Street Market in Seattle, and Underground Atlanta. Whether vertical or horizontal, the keys to malls' success is that they provide a pedestrian scale and feelings of safety.

The changing economic base and the movement of residents, industry, and commerce has altered the shape of the city. Cities like Phoenix, Arizona; Charlotte, North Carolina; and Los Angeles, California tend to have small CBDs and a variety of business and commercial districts scattered around major highway intersections. Likewise, class-differentiated residential concentrations are widely distributed. Older cities were also influenced by the automobile as beltways surrounding the old center cities led to the development of dispersed concentrations. According to the 1990 census, 22 of the 29 communities whose populations increased to more than 100,000 between 1980 and 1990 are "suburban cities" in metropolitan areas.[73]

The growth in size of suburban communities is part of a phenomenon that one author calls "**post-suburbia**,"[74] a new pattern of development that blends the characteristics of suburbia and the central city in "**edge cities**."[75] New edge cities, which may or may not have political boundaries, combine jobs, shopping and entertainment. They can be categorized as: (1) having at least 5,000,000 square feet of leasable office space; (2) having

at least 600,000 square feet of retail space; (3) having more jobs than bedrooms; (4) being seen as a mixed-use destination; and (5) having developed from next to nothing in the last 30 years.[76] The Atlanta metropolitan area has several edge cities. These include the Midtown area, Buckhead (The Lenox Square Mall area), the Cumberland Mall–Galleria area, Perimeter Center area, the Gwinnett Place mall area, the Perimeter and I-85 area, and the Hartsfield International Airport area.[77]

Residents of these edge cities still value the small, intimate, and homogenous suburban life-style but recognize that economic development in their communities could bring benefits.

> They sought to preserve the green open space and clear waters of the rural past and longed nostalgically for the fields and forests that had first drawn them from the city. The people of post-suburban America remained resolutely anti-urban even as their world became increasingly urbanized. Yet at the same time they recognized the merits of the changes transforming their counties. Eager for lower tax rates, they could not help but welcome tax-paying businesses. As long as a tax-rich office tower was not visible from their patios and the employees did not jam their streets, then such development might prove a boon.[78]

Not only did development ease the tax burden, it also provided convenient shopping and shorter commutes to work. Life necessitated a delicate balance between the suburban ideal and "useful urban realities."[79] Post-suburban development can be seen in virtually every major metropolitan area. People who are leaving the central city are no longer as dependent on the central core cities as were the first suburbanites.

A spatial model of this type of development might be called the metroplex. It is similar to the multiple nuclei model but with more multipurpose and concentrated points.

FIGURE 3–4

Washington, D.C. Edge Cities

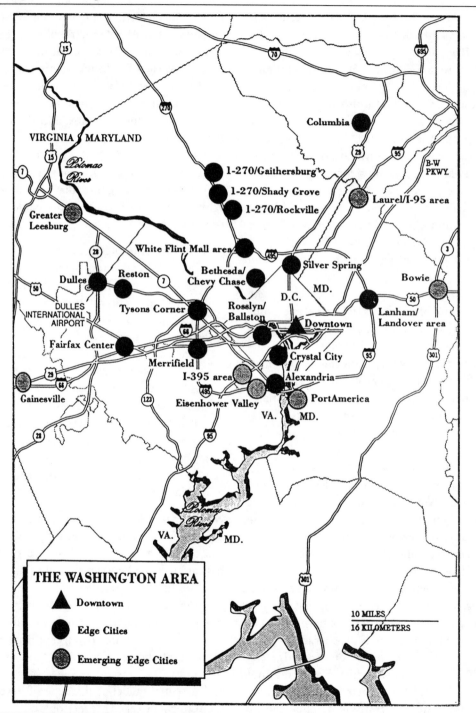

Source: From *Edge City* by Joel Garreau. Copyright 1991 by Joel Garreau. Used by permission of Bantam Doubleday Dell Publishing Group, Inc.

TABLE 3–2

Employment Changes (in Thousands) in Nine U.S. Cities, by Sector, 1987–1992 and 1967–1992

City	Period	Manufacturing[a]	Wholesale[b]	Retail	Selected Service	Total
Boston						
Boston, MA-NH,	1987–1992	−18.4	−1.9	−.6	+53.0	+32.1
PMSA[c] 1987, 1992	1967–1992	−462.7	−4.2	+98.0	+488.3	+119.4
SMSA[d] 1967						
New York						
New York, NY	1987–1992	−97.6	−22.6	−49.1	+58.2	−111.1
PMSA 1987, 1992	1967-1992	−683.2	−192.6	−168.5	+428.8	−615.6
SMSA 1967						
St. Louis						
St. Louis, MO-IL,	1987-1992	−12.8	−1.2	+8.7	+46.9	+41.5
MSA[e] 1987, 1992	1967-1992	−96.0	−4.8	−86.4	+256.1	+68.9
SMSA 1967						
Baltimore						
Baltimore, MD	1987–1992	−25.5	+2.1	−10.2	+43.8	+10.2
PMSA 1987, 1992	1967–1992	−93.8	+10.0	+74.5	+258.9	+249.7
SMSA 1967						
Philadelphia						
Philadelphia,PA-NJ,	1987–1992	−60.2	−6.4	−14.8	+78.6	−2.9
PMSA 1987, 1992	1967–1992	−268.1	−9.8	+108.5	+536.3	+366.8
SMSA 1967						
San Francisco						
San Francisco, County,	1987–1992	−8.6	−7.3	−5.2	−4.0	−25.2
1992,1987, 1967	1967–1992	−16.9	−12.4	+16.8	+89.1	+76.6
Atlanta						
Atlanta, GA	1987–1992	+4.0	+4.5	+18.4	+78.0	+104.8
MSA 1987, 1992	1967–1992	+64.0	+24.7	+192.4	+360.4	+641.5
SMSA 1967						
Denver						
Denver, CO	1987–1992	−7.0	+2.3	n/a	+38.2	+33.5
PMSA 1987, 1992	1967–1992	+11.7	+11.0	n/a	+205.2	+227.8
SMSA 1967						
Houston						
Houston, TX	1987–1992	+23.1	+7.2	+26.0	+145.7	+202.0
PMSA 1987, 1992	1967–1992	+33.3	+29.8	+167.2	+430.8	+661.0
SMSA 1967						

[a]Defined as Operating Manufacturing Establishments; [b]Includes proprietorships; [c]PMSA = Primary Statistical Area; [d]SMSA = Standard Metropolitan Statistical Area; [e]MSA = Metropolitan Distributed Area.

Source: U.S. Bureau of the Census, *Census of Manufacturing, Census of Retail Trade, Census of Wholesale Trade, and Census of Selected Services,* Geographic Area Series, selected years (Washington D.C.: Government Printing Office, 1970, 1990, and 1996).

Figure 3–4 shows the development of the Washington, D.C. metroplex. Most metropolitan areas exhibit similar layouts.[80]

Place or location is less important in the postindustrial economy. The result of this freedom of location is that, "the American population is no longer characterized by persistent agglomeration in relatively small numbers of large cities; rather, it has dispersed to increasing numbers of urban and non-metropolitan areas."[81] Such dispersal increased competition between communities to attract businesses and jobs. This means that local governments must not only consider the demands of private interests, but must also influence those interests through the public policies they adopt in their pursuit of the type of development the community desires.[82]

While manufacturing and retail trade have tended to move into the suburban fringes, other businesses have stayed in the city. Office buildings, financial institutions, government offices, and related services have tended to locate in the urban core. Professional services, such as law firms and health services, find the center city hospitable. The center city also provides the setting for many schools and universities.[83]

Those economic enterprises that have stayed in the city share a need for: (1) communication, (2) minimizing the cost of uncertainty, and (3) external economies of scale.[84] The financial district in New York illustrates these three incentives to locate in a central place. Financial analysts want to be part of the grapevine and need easy access to decision makers. Billions of dollars are often at stake, thus it is important to be "where the action is" to reduce uncertainty. In an information-based economy, quality information is crucial and face-to-face contact remains important. Center-city location facilitates this interaction.[85] External economies of scale are easily realized because banks, lawyers, and brokerage firms are in close proximity for transfers and can share service providers.

Some observers say we are entering the era of the global city where some cities dominate their region, becoming financial centers and providing corporate services.[86] New York, London, and Tokyo are but three examples. Increasing wealth is being concentrated in the global cities, and the differences between the haves and the have-nots is getting even starker.[87]

The changing economic base of the center city can be summarized by Table 3–2 (on page 59), which contains data on employment changes in nine cities. This table makes clear that manufacturing and wholesale jobs have declined while service jobs have increased. There is no clear pattern in retail jobs.

These changes have profound implications for the qualifications that people must have to find work in the city. As Table 3–3 illustrates, center-city job growth is occurring in jobs that are knowledge-intensive, that is, jobs that require more than a high school diploma.[88] Meanwhile, jobs that require less than a high school diploma are declining.

Box 3–1 (on page 62) discusses technological and economic change in New York City and its impact on the people and spatial arrangements as New York enters the twenty-first century. While New York City is always unique, the changes affect all urban areas to a greater or lesser extent.

The distribution of the urban workforce also changed, creating a mismatch between skills needed for success in the center city and the skills available. Movement to the suburbs, which began in the industrial city, exploded after World War II. While many well-educated middle- and upper-class residents moved out, the poor moved to the city looking for economic opportunity. Many of these new urban residents were African-American or Latino. Ironically, because of the changing economic function of the city, many of these people lacked the skills necessary to find jobs in the knowledge-intensive service and high-technology industries of the modern city. In almost all American cities, there is a mismatch between the labor pool and the availability of jobs.

Many less-knowledge-intensive retail and manufacturing jobs have moved outside the city, and the poor often lack the means to reach those jobs.[89] Public transportation does not, and perhaps cannot, provide easy access to all parts of the metropolitan area. The sprawl of businesses across the metropolis and

TABLE 3-3

Employment Changes, by Industry's Average Educational Requirements, for Nine U.S. Cities, 1970-1980

City and Industrial Categorization	Number of Jobs, 1980 (in Thousands)	Change, 1970–1980	
		Number (in Thousands)	Percent
New York			
Entry-level	+763	−472	−38.2
Knowledge-intensive	+462	+92	+24.9
Philadelphia			
Entry-level	+208	−102	−32.9
Knowledge-intensive	+91	+ 25	+37.8
Baltimore			
Entry-level	+108	−52	−32.4
Knowledge-intensive	+32	+5	+ 20.6
Boston (Suffolk County)			
Entry-level	+115	−34	−22.6
Knowledge-intensive	+75	+19	+33.3
St. Louis			
Entry-level	+103	−23	−18.2
Knowledge-intensive	+21	−8	−26.3
Atlanta (Fulton County)			
Entry-level	+136	−19	−12.1
Knowledge-intensive	+41	+11	+35.6
Houston (Harris County)			
Entry-level	+457	+194	+73.8
Knowledge-intensive	+152	+83	+119.4
Denver			
Entry-level	+110	+14	+14.5
Knowledge-intensive	+44	+21	+91.4
San Francisco			
Entry-level	+142	+13	−10.2
Knowledge-intensive	+65	+21	+46.8

Source: U.S. Bureau of the Census, *Current Population Survey* tape (March 1982) and *County Business Patterns* (1970, 1980). Figures are rounded in John D. Kasarda, "Urban Change and Minority Opportunities," in *The New Urban Reality*, ed. Paul E. Peterson (Washington, D.C.: The Brookings Institution, 1985), p. 50. Entry-level industries are those where mean schooling completed by employees is less than twelve years; knowledge-intensive industries are those where mean schooling completed is more than fourteen years.

the low density make public transportation impractical. Poor residents of the center cities may not have access to private transportation.

About one-half of all African-Americans and Latinos in Philadelphia and Boston and about one-third in New York City have access to an automobile or truck (see Table 3–4 on page 63). These figures represent all African-Americans and Latinos; needless to say the proportion of poor, inner city African-Americans and Latinos with private transportation would be much lower. A recent study in Chicago indicated that only 18 percent of unemployed ghetto residents had access to a car.[90] Without a car, commuting is often time-consuming and expensive. Those who might be able to purchase a car still need to consider operating costs, including insur-

BOX 3–1

The Postindustrial Transformation of New York City

The postindustrial transformation of New York City, like the prior Industrial Revolution, has been driven by changes in global capitalism, that is, rapid technological change, globalization of economic competition, increasing importance of finance relative to production, globalization and centralization of financial markets, and an international division of labor with third world migration to first-world core cities. Radical economic, social, and spatial changes led to political changes.

The city's population changed with "new immigrants"—black, Latino, and Asian—displacing native born of all races. Other demographic changes, such as increasing numbers of women in the workplace and nontraditional households along with the restructuring of the economy "worked to forge a new racial/ethnic/gender division of labor as well as new forms of inequality."

Up to the mid-1950s, the immigrants and their offspring constituted a base of blue collar ethnics. Few white, blue collar workers remain. New groups have replaced them, and office workers greatly outnumber production workers. Although women and blacks benefited from declining numbers of white workers, they were excluded from some positions. The overall poverty rate and income inequality grew during the 1980s. New York has been transformed from "a relatively well off, white, blue-collar city into a more economically divided, multiracial, white-collar city."

Concomitant with these changes were investment decisions that led to the construction of corporate office towers and zones of luxury housing and commerce while public infrastructure and ethnic neighborhoods crumpled, thus New York became a "phoenix in the ashes." New immigrants, and some upwardly mobile blacks, moved into former white working-class neighborhoods, prompting flight from the city. The growing number of poor blacks and Latinos reinforced the collapse of the ghettos.

Three political changes resulted from these trends. First, they created new interests with whom political entrepreneurs had to deal. Financial institutions, corporate law firms, real estate interests, and public service and nonprofit workers became more important while manufacturing firms and unions lost influence. As working- and middle-class ethnics and native-born blacks declined as a portion of the population, and the numbers of lower-class, youths, and non-English speakers increased, the electorate changed, resulting in shifts in the governing coalition.

"Second, these changes also exacerbated tensions along the characteristically postindustrial fault lines of race, nativity, ethnicity, gender, household form, and occupational sector."

Third, the unstable economy increased conflicts, and old patterns of accommodation gave way to new ones. This put the public sector on the defensive and provided increased public support for private sector investment. The result was an economic boom, increased government revenues and authority, and increased struggle over the "'stakes and prizes' of local government power."

The postindustrial transformation altered the social and economic order and, in the process, altered the claimants for political power, their respective influence, what they wanted from government and their strategies to gain power.

Source: Adapted from John Hull Mollenkopf, *A Phoenix in the Ashes: The Rise and Fall of the Koch Coalition in New York City* (Princeton: Princeton University Press, 1992), 46–49.

ance and parking, that are usually much higher in the city than in the suburbs. As a consequence, owning an automobile is often not cost-effective.[91]

The increasing racial and class segregation in the metropolis is occurring at a time when the job base is changing and those remaining in the city are at an increasing disadvantage in the competition for new jobs. Another problem of the African-American and Latino urban poor is that they are segregated into ghettos. Even before the ghettoization, "everyone who bothered to look at the lives of the poorest of the black poor, rural *and* urban, came away alarmed by deprivation, ignorance, ill health, and social disorganization they found."[92] [Italics in original.] One study documents the migration of African-Americans from the South to Chicago and the ensuing racial tensions that stymied any attempt to create integrated neighborhoods.[93] The invisible wall between white and black has had devastating consequences.

> The objective dimensions of the American urban ghettos are overcrowded and deteriorated housing, high infant mortality, crime, and disease. The subjective dimensions are resentment, hostility, despair, apathy, self-depreciation, and its ironic companion, compensatory grandiose behavior.[94]

William Tabb has made an analogy between American ghettoes and third-world nations. He found the following similarities:

1. Residents have low per capita income and high birth rates.
2. Most residents are unskilled.
3. Demand for unskilled workers, especially in the city, is decreasing, therefore unemployment is high.
4. Manufacturers lack capital and know-how.
5. Local markets are limited.
6. Credit default is high.
7. Little saving or local investment occurs.
8. Goods and services are imported.
9. Feelings of relative deprivation are common.
10. Residents depend on "foreign," that is, government, aid.
11. Business is owned by outsiders who spend profits outside the ghetto.
12. Important jobs are held by outsiders who impose their values and restrict the ability of residents to progress economically.[95]

These ghettoes do not have the economic resources to effect change and rarely do they possess the political resources to act in any way other than by creating turmoil for the "colonial master."

The dual migration, that is, business and white middle- and upper-class moving out and lower classes and minorities moving in, has had several consequences. One effect has been the declining density of the center city.[96] As Brian Berry observed, "the continuing centrifugal movement of urban population and

TABLE 3–4

Central City Minority Households With Access to an Automobile or Truck

Central City	African-American Households	Latino Households
Philadelphia	49.3%	52.1%
Boston	53.9%	52.0%
New York	36.3%	33.6%

Source: U.S. Bureau of the Census. 1990 Current Population and Housing Summary Tape File. (Washington, D.C.: U.S. Bureau of the Census, 1990).

urban institutions is leaving a widening core of obsolescent, deteriorated and abandoned buildings where once stood the richest sources of municipal revenues."[97]

William Julius Wilson chronicles the deterioration of the Chicago neighborhood of North Lawndale since 1960. Two large factories—the Hawthorne plant of Western Electric and International Harvester—have left, resulting in a loss of 57,000 jobs. Also gone is the world headquarters of Sears, Roebuck and Company and another 10,000 jobs, as well as Copenhagen Snuff, a Sunbeam factory, a Zenith factory, a Dell Farm food market, an Alden's catalog store, and a U.S. Post Office bulk mail station.

> The departure of the big plants triggered the demise or exodus of the smaller stores, the banks, and other businesses that relied on the wages paid by the large employers. . . . In 1986, North Lawndale, with a population of over 66,000, had only one bank and one supermarket; but it was also home to forty-eight state lottery agents, fifty currency exchanges, and ninety-nine licensed liquor stores and bars.[98]

As the populations of center cities declined, many slum areas thinned out as some were able to move into housing left behind by the middle and working class. This led to large-scale abandonment by landlords, who could no longer extort high rents for decaying buildings. In North Lawndale, for example, almost half of the housing stock has disappeared since 1960, and the remaining units are generally run-down or dilapidated.[99] Often the decrease was a result of arson as owners attempted to get an insurance settlement from an otherwise useless building or vandals torching buildings "just for the fun of it." These abandoned buildings fell prey to scavengers stealing copper plumbing and anything else of value, and often became "shooting galleries" for drug addicts. Virtually all groups left the center city as federal efforts led to decreased housing discrimination.

Urban residents are increasingly segregated by race and class. The differences between the groups remaining in the city are becoming starker as educated, middle-class African-Americans and Latinos move to the suburbs. This deprives those remaining in the ghetto of successful middle-class role models. Certain parts of major cities provide opulent life-styles, while other areas are desolate slums.

Because those with resources were moving to the suburbs, leaving the poor behind, substantial disparities developed between center cities and suburbs. These disparities are especially pronounced in the Frost Belt because annexation of suburbs was especially difficult in that area. As the wealthy moved out, the city could do nothing to try to capture them. As annexation was generally easier in Sun Belt cities, they were more able to capture the wealthy residents and their taxes. In those areas, which may have less city–suburb disparities, there is often a great deal of intracity disparity because Sun Belt cities have pockets of poverty along with wealthy enclaves.

Nathan and Associates developed indices to measure the urban condition of cities and the disparity between center city and suburbs in 25 cities in 1976–77. Variables considered included population decline, age of city, and degree of poverty, unemployment, dependency, education, income, crowded housing, and poverty.[100] Frost Belt cities like St. Louis, Newark, and Cleveland were found to be worst off. The cities that fared best were Dallas, Houston, and Phoenix, all Sun Belt cities. (See Table 3–5.)

More recent data indicate that Frost Belt cities continue to have greater income disparities, compared to their suburban neighbors than do Sun Belt cities, although disparities are increasing in both kinds of cities.[101] (See Table 3–6 on page 66)

Another kind of population movement is occurring at the same time as suburbanization: migration of both businesses and people out of cities in the Northeast and Midwest—

TABLE 3-5

Urban Conditions and Central City–Suburban Disparities in 25 Selected SMSAs by Region

	Urban Conditions Index[a]	Rank	Central City–Suburban Hardship Index[b]	Rank
Northeast				
Newark, NJ	321	3	422	1
Hartford, CT	223	9	317	3
Baltimore, MD	224	8	256	4
New York, NY	180	17	211	8.5
Philadelphia, PA	216	11	205	11
Boston, MA	257	6	198	12
Jersey City, NJ	226	7	129	17
Providence, RI	333	2	121	18
Syracuse, NY	210	12	103	21
North Central				
Cleveland, OH	291	4	331	2
Chicago, IL	201	13.5	245	5
St. Louis, MO	351	1	231	6
Dayton, OH	154	20	211	8
Detroit, MI	201	13.5	210	10
Youngstown, OH	220	10	180	13
Minneapolis, MN	174	18	131	16
South				
Atlanta, GA	118	21	226	7
New Orleans, LA	274	5	168	14
Louisville, KY	195	15	165	15
Dallas, TX	38	23	97	22
Houston, TX	36	24	93	23
West				
San Francisco, CA	188	16	105	19.5
Salt Lake City, UT	155	19	80	25
Los Angeles, CA	74	22	105	19.5
Phoenix, AZ	19	25	85	24

[a]100 represents an average score on the composite index. Above 100 indicates worse than average and below 100 indicates conditions better than average. [b]100 represents relatively equal socioeconomic conditions between central city and suburb. Above 100 indicates that the central city is poorer and below 100 indicates it is better off.

Source: Adapted from Richard P. Nathan and Paul Dommel, "The Cities," in *Setting National Priorities: The 1978 Budget*, ed. Joseph Pechman (Washington, D.C.: Brookings Institution, 1977), 290-291; and Richard P. Nathan and Charles Adams, "Understanding Central City Hardship," *Political Science Quarterly* (Spring 1976): 47-61.

the Frost Belt—to cities in the South and West—the Sun Belt. In 1950, only 4 of 14 metropolitan areas over 1 million people were located in the Sun Belt. By 1990, there were 37 metropolitan areas with over 1 million people and 20 were in the Sun Belt.[102] Between 1957 and 1990, cities with populations of over 300,000 declined from 21 to 17 in the Frost Belt while increasing from 15 to 34 in the Sun Belt.[103]

TABLE 3–6

City-Suburban Income Differentials By Region

Ratio of City Median Family Income to SMSA (Standard Metropolitan Statistical Area) Median

	1949	1959	1969	1979	1989
Frost Belt					
New York, NY–NJ	.95	.93	.89	.87	.75
Chicago, IL	.97	.93	.86	.77	.74
Philadelphia, PA–NJ	.96	.90	.85	.77	.72
Detroit, MI	.99	.89	.83	.69	.55
Washington, DC–MD–VA	.89	.79	.74	.69	.67
Sun Belt					
Los Angeles–Long Beach, CA[a]	.98	.98	.96	.92	.88
San Francisco–Oakland, CA[a]	1.00	.95	.89	.85	.84
Dallas–Fort Worth, TX[a]	1.03	1.01	.96	.90	.82
Houston, TX	1.02	.98	.97	.90	.82
Atlanta, GA	.91	.87	.79	.64	.61

[a]Ratios were calculated for Los Angeles, San Francisco, and Dallas.

Source: Adapted from Paul Kantor, *The Dependent City Revisited* (Boulder, Colorado: Westview, 1995), 89. Reprinted by permission of Westview Press.

As with suburbanization, Sun Belt growth exploded after World War II. While Frost Belt metropolitan areas were experiencing moderate growth or decline, Sun Belt cities sometimes grew at triple-digit rates. For example, the Anaheim, California area grew 226 percent between 1950 and 1960 and 102 percent between 1960 and 1970. It grew another 36 percent between 1970 and 1980 and 25 percent between 1980 and 1990. Phoenix has experienced growth rates of 100 percent, 46 percent, 55 percent, and 41 percent during those four decades.[104]

Employment also grew faster in the Sun Belt, accelerating especially since 1970. From 1970 to 1980, 78.2 percent of new jobs were created in the Sun Belt; in the last decade, 65.8 percent of the new jobs were created in the Sun Belt. In 1970, a majority of jobs, 54.7 percent, as still located in the Frost Belt. By 1989, only 45.6 percent of the jobs remained in this region.[105]

The Sun Belt has been attractive to businesses for many reasons. One reason is its traditional outlook on labor. There are more right-to-work laws and less unionization and activism in the Sun Belt. The lower cost of living means that employers can pay less and employees can still live better. Both businesses and individuals are attracted by lower land values and access to less expensive energy. They are also attracted to the Sun Belt because of the generally pleasant weather and access to the outdoors. In addition, Sun Belt cities are less congested because they were developed later than Frost Belt cities and have street systems designed for the automobile. A final appeal of the Sun Belt cities is lower taxes. Government services tend to be less developed in the Sun Belt due its generally conservative outlook.[106] The emphasis of the government is on maintaining order rather than on social welfare.[107] Sun Belt cities are more likely to have reformed government structures that emphasize businesslike decision making rather than political decision making.*

In the Sun Belt, strong local government and business coalitions developed to encourage growth. Where public money was spent, or taxes increased, it was often for the purpose of encouraging growth. For example, San Jose, California, more than quadrupled in population between 1950 and 1970. Beginning in 1944 a group of merchants, attorneys, industrialists, and major property owners organized the Progress Committee to elect candidates to local office and promote development.[108] "The combination of aggressive annexation, lenient zoning, eagerly supplied capital improvements, and the sewage monopoly sped growth on its way."[109] Once again economic advantage was enhanced by political decisions.

As with the movement of the middle class to the suburbs, the movement of business and individuals out of the Frost Belt has been facilitated by the actions of the federal government. The location of military bases and the awarding government contracts to Sun Belt firms helped to establish jobs.[110] In San Jose, defense contracts in electronics and aerospace provided jobs. Other federal policies also unintentionally encouraged the movement to San Jose and other Sun Belt cities. Federal programs that facilitated suburbanization also aided Sun Belt migration. Federal loans allowed people to buy homes near newly created jobs, and federal subsidies for highway construction made the homes and businesses accessible. Tax incentives such as tax credits and accelerated depreciation on new facilities made relocating easier for business. These programs lowered the costs for those who were predisposed to relocate. As the cost of living is generally lower in the Sun Belt, federal entitlement programs like Social Security, Medicare, and Medicaid supply a greater proportion of necessary resources for the population dependent on those programs.

The major reason for looking at the historical changes in America's cities is to realize that change is constant and inevitable. Some of the advantages of Sun Belt cities over Frost Belt cities are already beginning to decline. Federal contracts, especially in the defense industry, which helped fuel the Sun Belt expansion, have been cut back as a result of the end of the Cold War and fiscal austerity. This has led to severe recessions in some places. Also, as more people move to the Sun Belt, congestion increases. Growth creates environmental problems, leading to increasing political activism among professional and neighborhood groups in opposition to pro-growth regimes.[111] Minorities are also becoming more active in the political process.[112] In addition, migrants from Frost Belt cities expect more government services, necessitating higher taxes. As time goes on, workers are less likely to be satisfied with lower wages. Many of the older Sun Belt cities such as Atlanta, New Orleans, and Miami have social problems comparable to those of the Frost Belt. Some Frost Belt cities that were written off as dead or dying have made remarkable recoveries because of changes in their economic bases. Once a dirty town of dying steel mills, Pittsburgh has been revitalized through urban redevelopment and changes in its economic base. Downtown Pittsburgh has banks and office buildings as well as Three Rivers Stadium. The service economy, high-technology firms, and a boom in office construction have led to a revitalization of such cities as Boston.[113]

Similarly, the decline of neighborhoods in the central city may also be only one stage in a historical process of transition. Edgar Hoover and Raymond Vernon have developed a five-stage neighborhood life cycle that helps explain transitions in urban areas. The stages are: (1) new single-family subdivisions; (2) apartment development; (3) downgrading as single family homes are divided into apartments; (4) thinning out and abandonment; and (5) renewal.[114]

---

*These structures will be discussed in Chapter 7.

Many center-city neighborhoods—especially in the Frost Belt—are in stage four of the process, but the Hoover and Vernon model anticipates the renewal that has occurred in some other neighborhoods in those cities. In parts of many cities, decaying neighborhoods are being revitalized. In some cases, this revitalization involves efforts by current residents to upgrade their neighborhood. But the form of revitalization that has drawn the most attention, especially from the popular press, has been the movement of the upper and middle class into deteriorated neighborhoods. The process is referred to as **gentrification**, a term derived from the word gentry, meaning gentlemen or aristocracy.

The press has often identified gentrification as a "back to the city movement" and several causes have been suggested—the cost and time of commuting to suburbs, the cost of suburban housing, the desire to live close to the cultural and entertainment resources found in the city, and the investment potential. Other observers have argued it is due less to a "back to the city movement" than to movement of upper- and middle-class residents from other parts of the same city.[115] Renters from other neighborhoods buy dilapidated townhouses in a run-down section and, in renovating them, begin upgrading the neighborhood, which, in turn, attracts other similar people.

While gentrification is a hopeful sign for older cities, it has negative consequences. The major problem caused by gentrification is displacement of poor residents from their neighborhoods. A large part of the gentrification has been done through private development, thus good records on the amount of displacement are nonexistent. Some argue that the amount of displacement is not substantial, perhaps 4 percent of all moves in a year.[116] Others bitterly take issue with dismissing the problem in that way, pointing out that even if the number is "only" 4 percent, that represents a half million house-

holds, or one-half to two million people.[117]

Others have pointed out that the gentrification movement is small and likely to remain so.[118] Despite the renewal of some urban neighborhoods, George Sternlieb and James Hughes in 1983 concluded that "the nation's statistical ledgers document a faltering central city, characterized by heavy outmigration—particularly by the more affluent—absolute population losses, lagging incomes, and growing concentrations of poverty."[119]

Residents of the Tenderloin District of San Francisco faced the specter of gentrification. As shown in Box 3–2, they organized to try to protect their neighborhood.

Conclusion

This chapter has focused on economic and technological influences on American urbanization. It reviewed the importance of decisions made by private economic interests for the development of urban areas throughout history. The spatial patterning of cities can be understood through location theory, in which private individuals and firms compete for favored locations. In general, private economic decisions shaped the city, but local governments have also been important. Throughout history, public actions have been aimed at helping and protecting the property owner. By their use of mechanisms such as planning and zoning regulations and their use of public capital to support economic development, political leaders can also influence the pattern of development at the local level.

As noted earlier, the development of American cities follows some universal ecological patterns. *Concentrations* of population occur. As concentrations grow to an unwieldy size, *dispersion* follows. In the urbanized area there is a sorting out of similar functions into specific areas of the urban agglomeration; this is *centralization*. *Decentralization* occurs when

BOX 3–2

Gentrification and Resistance in San Francisco

While urban ecologists contribute to our understanding of the use of urban space by constructing models of cities, it is important to realize that there is nothing automatic about the development of cities. The uses of space do change over time, but that results from decisions made by both the public and the private sector. An example from San Francisco illustrates the ability of citizens to influence development decisions.

From the 1960s to the mid-1980s, the governing coalition in San Francisco was united on the vision of transforming the city into a major financial and commercial headquarters. To accomplish that, skyscrapers were built in the central business district. Along with the rebuilding in the central business district, blighted areas on its fringes were targeted for clearance to make way for more development and for the building of luxury housing. Residents uprooted by these developments increasingly clustered together in the one area of the city, called the Tenderloin, that still had low-cost housing available. The population density in the area increased, creating a severely blighted area. Surrounded by upscale developments, the Tenderloin became the target for developers who wanted to gentrify it, converting the land use to projects that would generate more profit than the run-down low-income residential hotels that provided much of the housing for the Tenderloin's residents.

In the 1970s, three major hotel chains announced plans to build tourist hotels on the edge of the Tenderloin. The city government was initially very "grateful" and supportive. But the Tenderloin residents were strongly opposed. Helped by a variety of local ministers, advocates, planners, the neighborhood organized a Luxury Hotel Task Force (LHTF). They staged protests, met with government officials, the press, and developers. They eventually asked that the zoning of the Tenderloin be changed to forbid the construction of high-rise buildings.

No one expected the protests to have an impact, but then the director of the Department of City Planning took a trip to Paris, where he was amazed to find lots of old buildings. He found out that there was a 50-foot height limit on buildings. Nothing taller than the existing buildings was permitted, so there was no economic incentive to tear down the existing buildings.

When he returned to San Francisco, the director committed his department to supporting the zoning change to permit no building taller than 80 feet. Faced with the organized neighborhood and the recommendation of the Department of City Planning, the supervisors approved the zoning change in the Tenderloin.

What had also changed in San Francisco was the unquestioned acceptance of the vision of the city held by the pro-growth coalition. People both in and outside of government developed a new sense of the importance of limiting growth and protecting neighborhoods. This case illustrates that neighborhood organization—even in a low-income neighborhood—can have an impact on political decisions that determine land use in the city.

Source: Adapted from Tony Robinson, "Gentrification and Grassroots Resistance in San Francisco's Tenderloin," *Urban Affairs Review* 30 (March 1995): 483–515.

some groups leave the central area and move outward. Then, as population groups or specific businesses settle in one section, *segregation* develops. Over time values change and new groups are attracted to areas of the metropolis already occupied by others; this is known as *invasion*. The stage when the new group supersedes the previous tenants is called *succession*. This process is continuous, with different parts of each city at different stages. These patterns occurred during each of the three developmental epochs discussed and continue today.

The first epoch was that of the mercantile city. The city's economy was based primarily on trading, craftsmen, and small manufacturing. Technological change wrought by the Industrial Revolution produced the industrial city. People from rural areas and abroad were attracted to the economic opportunities in America's cities. They brought new and different views, leading to heterogeneity and conflict. The growth in size and the nature of unskilled factory labor led to increasing impersonality. The specialization and division of labor accompanying the factory system bred interdependence, which bred conflict and stimulated government to become increasingly involved.

The introduction of the automobile led to the metropolitan city. The population of the center city peaked in the 1920s as annexation, which had kept up with urban spread, ceased to be a viable option in most areas of the country. As in the past, the wealthy found it easiest to escape; they moved to the suburbs, taking their resources with them. Federal policies after World War II facilitated the movement of the middle class and industry to the suburbs.

Economic factors have shaped the city, and economic factors continue to exert influence by affecting the demands placed on government and government's willingness and ability to respond. While the particular relationship between economic and political

forces has changed over time in America, the role of the private market continues to have a major effect on the allocation of resources in the city. Urban governments have, in general, seen their role as facilitating the private market system. At times, this has meant that the government kept its activities to a minimum, giving the market free rein. At other times, the government has entered the market to support the activities of private business, for example, by providing the infrastructure of roads and sewers necessary for development or by encouraging private business with tax breaks. But the guiding principle has tended to remain the same: The government should minimize its control over private business, leaving substantial resources in private hands.

This does not mean that the role of political leaders is inconsequential. Indeed, as Michael Pagano and Ann Bowman conclude:

> . . . it is government promotion of urban economic development projects that most profoundly alters a city's landscape; the critical elements in transforming the extant urban landscape into the cityscape of tomorrow are twofold: (1) the vision of a city's leaders, their determination and commitment to pursue their vision, and their capacity to mobilize public capital for the attainment of the vision and (2) the strengths, diversity, and resiliency of the local economic base.[120]

Since 1960 several trends have become apparent: (1) steady population shift from center city to the metropolitan area outside the city with concentration of minorities and immigrants in the inner city replacing working- and upper-class whites who moved to the suburbs; (2) migration of manufacturing and service sector jobs to outlying areas and growth within the city of knowledge-intensive jobs, especially in the areas of finance, insurance, and real estate; and (3) movement from the Frost Belt to the Sun Belt.

Economic issues continue to set the agenda. They affect who has access to the political system and who will be the decision makers. Economic factors impose limits on possible solutions. Economic beliefs help to circumscribe public and private responsibilities. While economic interests do not always get their way, politics in the city takes place in an economic context.

Some observers have questioned whether this degree of private power produces socially desirable results. One outcome has been the sometimes stark distinction between haves and have-nots. This chapter has referred to some of the reasons for the growing economic disparities in urban areas: government policies that facilitated the movement of the middle class to the suburbs; and technological changes that made industry, and thus jobs, move out of the cities.

Traditionally, cities were seen as places of economic opportunity. Changing economics has limited the ability of those moving to America's cities to find the economic advancement they seek. Local government is limited in its ability to respond because it must continue to attract businesses to maintain a solid economic base. In addition, because local government must compete with other governments in the metropolitan area, its policies have generally been aimed more to the haves of our society than to the have-nots. Cooperation between governments, always problematic, is more difficult because the development of the edge cities of post-suburbia has lessened the economic ties of the suburbanite to the city and the resulting community of interest. In addition, the urbanite is increasingly black, poor, and Democratic, while the suburban counterpart remains white, middle or upper class, and Republican.[121]

Further, legal limits on local governments make them dependent on higher levels for authority and resources. While the federal government has created several programs that have benefited cities and their residents, many programs have been detrimental. That fact will likely intensify the conflict between economic groups.

This chapter has discussed the economic context of urban areas, emphasizing the extent to which private economic interests control substantial and important resources. Because of their need for those resources, political leaders must look to private interests as potential partners in a governing coalition. The following chapter will continue examining the context of urban policy by discussing the social heterogeneity created by the mix of people in the metropolis.

Notes

1. Michael A. Pagano and Ann O'M. Bowman, *Cityscapes and Capital: The Politics of Urban Development* (Baltimore: Johns Hopkins University Press, 1995), 142.

2. John C. Bollens and Henry J. Schmandt, *The Metropolis*, 4th ed. (New York: Harper & Row, 1982), 62.

3. Paul E. Peterson, *City Limits* (Chicago: University of Chicago Press, 1981). For a fuller discussion of this argument, see Chapter 12 in this book.

4. Clarence N. Stone, "The Study of the Politics of Urban Development," in *The Politics of Urban Development*, ed. Clarence N. Stone and Heywood T. Sanders (Lawrence: University Press of Kansas, 1987), 9.

5. John Logan and Harvey L. Molotch, *Urban Fortunes* (Berkeley: University of California Press, 1987), 2 and passim.

6. Peter R. Gluck and Richard J. Meister, *Cities in Transition* (New York: New Viewpoints, 1979), 23.

7. F.D. McKenzie, "The Scope of Human Ecology," in *The Urban Community*, ed. Ernest W. Burgess (Chicago: University of Chicago Press, 1926), 172–177.

8. Gerald D. Suttles, *The Man-Made City: The Land-Use Confidence Game in Chicago* (Chicago: University of Chicago Press, 1990), 18.

9. Ted Robert Gurr and Desmond S. King, *The State and the City* (Chicago: University of Chicago Press, 1987), 9.

10. Sam Bass Warner, Jr., *The Private City: Philadelphia in Three Periods of Its Growth* (Philadelphia: University of Pennsylvania Press, 1968). See also Sam Bass Warner, Jr., *The Urban Wilderness* (New York: Harper & Row, 1972); Dennis R. Judd, *The Politics of American Cities* 3rd ed. (Boston: Little, Brown, 1988); Stephen L. Elkin, *City and Regime in the American Republic* (Chicago: University of Chicago Press, 1987).

11. Gurr and King, *The State and the City*, 8.

12. Ibid., 29; Pagano and Bowman, *Cityscapes and Capital.*

13. Peterson, *City Limits.* A large body of neo-Marxist literature argues that economic interests dominate public choices. See, for example, James R. O'Connor, *The Fiscal Crisis of the State* (New York: St. Martin's Press, 1973); Ralph Miliband, *The State in Capitalist Society: An Analysis of the Western System of Power* (New York: Basic Books, 1969); Manuel Castells, *The Urban Question: A Marxist Approach* (Cambridge, Massachusetts: MIT Press, 1977); and *Marxism and the Metropolis,* ed. William K. Tabb and Larry Sawers (New York: Oxford University Press, 1978).

14. See, for example, *The Politics of Urban Development,* ed. Stone and Sanders ; Clarence N. Stone, *Regime Politics: Governing Atlanta, 1946–1988* (Lawrence: University of Kansas Press, 1989); Gurr and King, *State and the City;* Elkin, *City and Regime in the American Republic;* and John Mollenkopf, *The Contested City* (Princeton: Princeton University Press, 1983).

15. Elkin, *City and Regime in the American Republic.*

16. Quoted in Ira Katznelson, *City Trenches: Urban Politics and the Patterning of Class in the United States* (Chicago: University of Chicago Press, 1981), 8.

17. Peterson, *City Limits.*

18. Louis Hartz, *The Liberal Tradition in America* (New York: Harcourt, Brace & World, 1955).

19. Warner, *The Private City,* 4.

20. Theodore J. Lowi, *The End of Liberalism: Ideology, Policy and the Crisis of Public Authority* (New York: Norton, 1969), 19.

21. Ibid.

22. Warner, Jr., *The Private City,* 4.

23. Ralph Miliband, *The State in Capitalist Society.*

24. Mollenkopf, *The Contested City,* 10.

25. Martin Shefter, *Political Crisis/Fiscal Crisis* (New York: Basic Books, 1985), 235.

26. Mollenkopf, *The Contested City.*

27. Richard Edward DeLeon, *Left Coast City: Progressive Politics in San Francisco, 1975–1991* (Lawrence: University of Kansas Press, 1992).

28. Suttles, *Man-Made City,* 168–169.

29. Paul Gapp in Ibid., 186.

30. Blake McKelvey, *American Urbanization* (Glenview, Illinois: Scott, Foresman, 1973), 6.

31. Julius Rubin, "Urban Growth and Regional Development," in *The Growth in Seaport Cities: 1790–1825,* ed. David L. Gilchrist (Charlottesville: University Press of Virginia, 1967), cited in Ibid.

32. Gluck and Meister, *Cities in Transition,* 23.

33. Jon Teaford, *The Municipal Revolution in America* (Chicago: University of Chicago Press, 1975), 17.

34. Gluck and Meister, *Cities in Transition,* 23.

35. Ibid., 27.

36. Warner, *The Private City,* 45.

37. Teaford, *Municipal Revolution,* 17.

38. Warner, *The Private City,* 11.

39. David M. Gordon, "Capitalist Development and the

History of American Cities," in *Marxism and the Metropolis,* ed. Tabb and Sawers, 36.

40. Teaford, *Municipal Revolution,* 47.

41. Dennis R. Judd, *The Politics of American Cities: Private Power and Public Policy,* 2nd Ed., (Boston: Little, Brown, 1984), 40.

42. Gluck and Meister, *Cities in Transition,* 31–32.

43. Warner, *Urban Wilderness,* 58.

44. Judd, *Politics in American Cities,* 2nd ed., 26.

45. Ernest W. Burgess, "The Growth of the City: An Introduction to a Research Report," in Robert E. Park and Ernest W. Burgess, eds., *The City* (Chicago: University of Chicago Press, 1925), 47–62.

46. Judd, *Politics in American Cities,* 2nd ed., 20–23.

47. Ibid., 22.

48. Ibid.

49. Homer Hoyt, *The Structure and Growth of Residential Neighborhoods in American Cities* (Washington, D.C.: Federal Housing Administration, 1939).

50. Richard C. Wade, *The Urban Frontier: Pioneer Life in Early Pittsburgh, Cincinnati, Lexington, Louisville, and St. Louis* (Cambridge, Massachusetts: Harvard University Press, 1959), 4.

51. Ibid., 47.

52. Warner, *Urban Wilderness,* 20.

53. Ibid., 55.

54. Jon C. Teaford, *The Twentieth-Century American City: Problem, Promise, and Reality* (Baltimore: Johns Hopkins University Press, 1986), 30.

55. Ibid., 30–31.

56. Judd, *Politics of American Cities,* 2nd ed., 33.

57. Arthur N. Schlesinger, "A Panoramic View: The City in American History," in Paul Kramer and Frederick L. Holborn, eds., *The City in American Life: From Colonial Times to the Present* (New York: Capricorn Books, 1970), 23.

58. Gluck and Meister, *Cities in Transition,* 42.

59. Ibid., 130–131.

60. Peterson, *City Limits.*

61. Teaford, *Twentieth-Century American City,* 153.

62. C.D. Harris and E.L. Ullman, "The Nature of Cities," *Annals of the Academy of Political and Social Science* 242 (November 1945): 7–17.

63. Robert C. Wood, *Suburbia: Its People & Their Politics* (Boston: Houghton, Mifflin, 1958), 16–17. This point is discussed more fully in Chapter 7.

64. Teaford, *The Twentieth-Century American City,* 104.

65. Ibid.

66. Peter D. Salins, "Metropolitan Areas: Cities, Suburbs, and the Ties that Bind," in Henry Cisneros, ed., *Interwoven Destinies* (New York: Norton, 1993), 153–154.

67. Ibid., 149.

68. Edgar M. Hoover and Raymond Vernon, *Anatomy of a Metropolis* (Garden City, New York: Anchor Books, 1959), Chapter 2.

69. Daniel Bell, *The Coming of Post-Industrial Society* (New York: Basic Books, 1973), 117 and passim.

70. Anthony Downs, *New Visions for Metropolitan*

America (Washington, D.C.: The Brookings Institution, 1994), 46.

71. Ibid.

72. Bollens and Schmandt, *The Metropolis,* 80–81.

73. Roberto Suro, "Where America Is Growing: Suburban Cities," *New York Times,* February 13, 1991, 16.

74. Jon C. Teaford, *Post-Suburbia: Government and Politics in the Edge Cities* (Baltimore: Johns Hopkins University Press, 1997).

75. Joel Garreau, *Edge City* (New York: Doubleday, 1988).

76. Ibid., 6–7.

77. Ibid., 426–427.

78. Teaford, *Post-Suburbia,* 6.

79. Ibid.

80. Gerreau, *Edge City.*

81. Paul Kantor, *The Dependent City Revisited: The Political Economy of Urban Development and Social Policy* (Boulder, Colorado: Westview Press, 1995), 97.

82. Pagano and Bowman, *Cityscapes and Capital.*

83. David L. Birch, *The Economic Future of City and Suburb* (New York: CED, 1970).

84. Hoover and Vernon, *Anatomy of a Metropolis,* Chapter 3.

85. Elliott D. Sclar and Walter Hook, "The Importance of Cities to the National Economy," in *Interwoven Destinies,* ed. Henry Cisneros (New York: Norton, 1993), 52.

86. Saskia Sassen, *The Global City* (Princeton: Princeton University Press, 1991).

87. The universality of the "global-city–dual-city" hypothesis is challenged by James W. White, "Old Wine, Cracked Bottle? Tokyo, Paris, and the Global City Hypothesis." Paper delivered at the Annual Meeting of the American Political Science Association, San Francisco, August 29–September 1, 1996.

88. John D. Kasarda, "Urban Change and Minority Opportunities," in *The New Urban Reality,* ed. Paul E. Peterson (Washington, D.C.: The Brookings Institution, 1985).

89. Nicholas Lemann, *The Promised Land: The Great Black Migration and How It Changed America* (New York: Vintage Books, 1991), 201.

90. William Julius Wilson, *When Work Disappears: The World of the New Urban Poor* (New York: Knopf, 1997), 39.

91. Ibid., 40–41.

92. Lemann, *The Promised Land,* 344.

93. Lemann, *The Promised Land.*

94. Kenneth B. Clark, *Dark Ghetto* (New York: Harper & Row, 1965), 11.

95. William K. Tabb, *The Political Economy of the Black Ghetto* (New York: Norton, 1970), 22–23.

96. Brian J.L. Berry, *The Human Consequences of Urbanization: Divergent Paths in the Urban Experience of the Twentieth Century* (New York: St. Martin's Press, 1973), 47–48.

97. Ibid., 48.

98. Wilson, *When Work Disappears,* 35.

99. Ibid., 34.

100. Richard P. Nathan and Charles Adams, "Understanding Central City Hardship," *Political Science Quarterly* (Spring 1976): 47–61; Richard P. Nathan and Paul R. Dommel, "The Cities," in *Setting National Priorities: The 1978 Budget,* ed. Joseph A. Pechman (Washington, D.C.: The Brookings Institution, 1977), 283–292.

101. Kantor, *The Dependent City Revisited,* 88.

102. William H. Frey, "Metropolitan America: Beyond Transition," *Population Bulletin* 45 (July 1990), 14.

103. Paul E. Peterson, "The Changing Fiscal Place of Big Cities in the Federal System," in *Interwoven Destinies,* ed. Henry Cisneros(New York: Norton, 1993), 188–189.

104. Dennis R. Judd and Todd Swanstrom, *City Politics: Private Power and Public Policy* (New York: Harper Collins, 1993), 248.

105. Ibid., 249.

106. Roland J. Liebert, *Disintegration and Political Action: The Changing Functions of City Government in America* (New York: Academic Press, 1976), 177–188.

107. Daniel J. Elazar, *American Federalism,* 2nd ed., (New York: Crowell, 1972), Chapter 4.

108. Philip J. Troustine and Terry Christensen, *Movers and Shakers: The Study of Community Power* (New York: St. Martin's Press, 1982), 87.

109. Ibid., p. 97.

110. Richard M. Barnard and Bradley Rice, "Introduction" in *Sunbelt Cities: Politics and Growth Since World War II,* ed. Richard M. Barnard and Bradley Rice (Austin: University of Texas Press, 1983), 12; and Richard S. Morris, *Bum Rap on America's Cities,* (Englewood Cliffs, New Jersey: Prentice-Hall, 1980).

111. Hank V. Savitch and John Clayton Thomas, *Big City Politics in Transition* (Newbury Park, California: Sage, 1991); Amy Bridges, "Politics and Growth in Sunbelt Cities," in *Searching for the Sunbelt,* ed. R.A. Mohl (Knoxville: University of Tennessee Press, 1990), 85–104; and Robert Kerstein, "Growth Politics in Tampa and Hillsborough County: Strains in the Privatistic Regimes," *Journal of Urban Affairs* 13 (1991): 55–75.

112. Michael F. Logan, *Fighting Sprawl and City Hall: Resistance to Urban Growth in the Southwest* (Tucson: University of Arizona Press, 1995).

113. Alexander Ganz, "Where Has the Urban Crisis Gone? How Boston and Other Large Cities Have Stemmed Economic Decline," *Urban Affairs Quarterly* 20 (June 1985): 449–468.

114. Hoover and Vernon, *Anatomy of a Metropolis,* 198.

115. Bruce London, "Gentrification as Urban Reinvasion: Some Preliminary Definitional and Theoretical Considerations" in *Back to the City: Issues in Neighborhood Renovation,* ed. Shirley Bradway Laska and Daphne Spain (New York: Pergamon Press, 1980), 79. Dennis E. Gale, "Neighborhood Resettlement: Washington, D.C.," in Ibid., 100.

116. Howard J. Sumka, "Neighborhood Revitalization and Displacement: A Review of the Evidence," *Journal of the American Planning Association* 45 (October 1979): 482.

117. Chester Hartman, "Comment on 'Neighborhood Revitalization and Displacement: A Review of the Evidence,'" *Journal of the American Planning Association* 45 (October 1979): 488.

118. Phillip G. Clay, *Neighborhood Renewal* (Lexington, Massachusetts: Lexington Books, 1979), 61; Brian J.L. Berry, "Islands of Renewal in Seas of Decay," in Peterson, ed., *The New Urban Reality*, 69–96.

119. George Sternlieb and James W. Hughes, "The Uncertain Future of the Central City," *Urban Affairs Quarterly* 18 (June 1983): 462.

120. Pagano and Bowman, *Cityscapes and Capital*, 137.

121. Teaford, *Post-Suburbia*, 208.

CHAPTER 4

The New Immigration

Many American cities grew from small town to city in the nineteenth century in part because of the immigration of large numbers of people from other countries seeking the promise of economic success or relief from political persecution.* Urban residents, most of whom were themselves the children or grandchildren of immigrants, viewed the invasion with alarm. Their concern led in 1924 to a strict immigration law that restricted the flow of immigrants by imposing an annual quota of people permitted to enter from each country and barred people from Asia, who had been declared ineligible for citizenship.

Immigration reform did not stop the influx of newcomers into America's urban areas. While foreign immigration was slowing at the start of the twentieth century, African-Americans from the South began to move in large numbers into northern cities.[1] Beginning in the early 1930s, Latinos also began moving into cities.† In 1965, another immigration reform permitted a new wave of foreign immi-

grants to arrive in the United States. The 1965 law eliminated both the country-specific quotas and the ban on Asian immigration. The result was a dramatic increase in the number of immigrants. While 3,011,000 people moved to the United States from other countries in the decade from 1950 to 1960, 9,972,000 arrived in the period 1980 to 1990.[2] Unlike the older immigrants, few of these newcomers came from Europe. The largest group were Asians including Chinese coming from Hong Kong, Taiwan, China, and Singapore; Filipinos; South Asians from India, Bangladesh, Sri Lanka, and Pakistan; Koreans; and Indo-Chinese from Vietnam, Cambodia, Laos, and Thailand. The second largest group of new immigrants came from Latin America, including Mexicans; from Central America, especially from El Salvador and Guatemala; and from South America, especially Colombia. Smaller numbers have arrived from the Caribbean and from Africa.[3] As was the case at the beginning of the twentieth century, many

---

*See Chapter 2 for a discussion of this immigration and its effect on urban politics.

†The term Latinos as used here refers generally to people of Spanish origin. The use of this single name by no means is meant to imply that Latinos are a homogeneous group. In fact, three main components of people of Spanish origin will be discussed here: Puerto Ricans, Cubans, and Mexican-Americans. Each differs substantially from the others. In addition, the arrival of immigrants from Central and South America is increasing the diversity of the Latino population.

of these immigrants settled in urban areas and the descendants of America's earliest immigrants—those of northern or western European ancestry—are seeing their communities changed by new groups seeking "the American dream."

As with the immigration in the nineteenth century, the new immigration is changing the social context of many urban areas. In many cities, those of northern or western European ancestry are a minority. Yet the increasing numbers of blacks, Latinos, and Asians in America's metropolises has not always been translated into political power. As in the past, the numbers of the new immigrants to the city creates the possibility of using votes to try to gain access to the governing coalition and to influence the policies of city governments. That possibility is not always realized. Differences among the groups often make it difficult to form political coalitions that would create a critical mass of votes to ensure that officials would hear the demands of the groups. For example, blacks in Miami have clashed with the Cuban population; in many other areas blacks have had confrontations with Asians. In addition, differences within each group may mean that it is impossible to assume that African-Americans will vote the same way, or that Latinos or Asians will. In New York City, the blacks from the Caribbean often fight to distinguish themselves from African-Americans, believing that their status in America would be higher as Caribbean immigrants than as African-Americans.[4] Some Asians accuse the Chinese and Japanese of attempting to dominate the other groups.[5]

Like earlier immigrants, these new urban residents came seeking economic advancement through jobs in factories and businesses. These urban newcomers differ in easily identifiable ways from their neighbors, and these differences are used as a basis for discrimination. While the new immigrants must face problems similar to those the older immigrants once faced, in some ways the new groups are confronting different and more difficult challenges. The ability of blacks, Latinos, and Asians to follow the earlier immigrants into the mainstream of urban politics is the most visible current challenge to the existence of democracy in America's cities.

The Problems Faced by Newcomers

The problems faced by the newcomers can be divided into four categories: individual, social, economic, and political. At the individual level, unlike previous immigrants, many of the new urban dwellers have little commitment to their new home. Modern transportation and communication technology make it easy for them to maintain contacts with their former homes. While those contacts provide emotional support to help them deal with the problems of adapting to their new environment, in many cases they also retard development of a commitment to that environment. Until such an attachment emerges, people are unlikely to become involved in organizations and activities to alter their lot. As a result, political activity is delayed. That is changing. Blacks, Latinos, and Asians are becoming increasingly committed to their new homes, resulting in an increase in political activity.

At the social level, skin color has been a major barrier for many newcomers. Americans have always had distinct problems with race relations. The incompatibility between America's egalitarian ideology and the prejudice white Americans often feel toward different races constitutes "an American dilemma."[6] Although progress has occurred, color discrimination remains. Earlier immigrants could and did change their names or their language, but it is impossible to change one's color to facilitate absorption into the mainstream. This fact of racial discrimination aggravates other problems that these groups face, such as finding housing and jobs.

Further, these groups face an economic system significantly different from those into which the former immigrants moved. Groups arriving in the nineteenth and early-twentieth centuries faced resistance and employment discrimination, but jobs were still available for unskilled laborers. These immigrant laborers did vital work that no one else wanted to do. The cities still were the major site of industry, and, except at times of economic depression, jobs were ample.

By the 1990s, industry had either moved to the suburbs searching for cheap land and low taxes or had closed for good.[7] As the last chapter indicated, the economic base of the modern metropolis is increasingly oriented to services, such as insurance and banking, and high technology, such as genetic and computer research. Employment in these fields requires education and training that many of the new immigrants do not have. In addition, many have difficulty following the jobs to the suburbs. Housing discrimination in many outlying areas makes it difficult for blacks and Latinos to move close to suburban jobs. Many cannot afford a car and the public transportation systems often do not extend to the suburban factories. As Terry Rosenberg writes, "In short, jobs are moving beyond the geographic reach of those who need them most."[8]

Members of the older immigrant groups used small businesses that catered to the ethnic market as a route of mobility. Such businesses are more difficult to start now because the amount of capital required to start a business is so great. In addition, raising such capital is difficult because the newer immigrants' own groups are unlikely to have it and bankers are unwilling to lend it because of stereotypes about what makes a good business risk.[9] On the other hand, some groups such as the Koreans have their own financing system.

Those stereotypes are not entirely inaccu-

rate. Even if a business is started, its chances of success and expansion are less now than in the past:

> For everyone, the growing advantages of bigness put the small and new competitor at a disadvantage. Suburban shopping centers remote from the center of town make expansion difficult for entrepreneurs who begin with the limited patronage of a neighborhood ethnic group.[10]

The metropolis does not provide the same source of economic opportunity as it did in the past, and the urban political system is also less hospitable. The political machines of the late nineteenth and early-twentieth century also provided some ethnic groups with a route of social mobility.* The local precinct captain was a neighbor to whom one could appeal on a personal basis for help. The efforts of reformers to eliminate what they believed to be a corrupt system succeeded in destroying the machines in many cities. Even where the remnants of the machines remained, they often were unwilling to reach out to the newcomers.[11]

In place of the machines, "good government" structures, as the reformers referred to them, were established. These structures substituted professional, "apolitical," rational standards for the administration of city services. The bureaucrat replaced the precinct captain. While the white middle class may see the elimination of personalism as good government, the poor who are increasingly dependent on government services often came to see the impersonal bureaucrat as the enemy and the personification of an uncaring system. Often a "veritable state of war" results between clients and bureaucrats.[12] Unionization of public bureaucrats aggravates the problem by specifying an increasing number of policies in contracts, reducing the ability of bureaucrats to respond in a personal way to client problems.[13]

---

*Political machines were briefly discussed in Chapter 2 and will be reviewed in greater depth in Chapter 7, along with the reformed structures that often replaced them.

Finally, a combination of economic and political factors also makes the problems faced by new groups more difficult. Local politics is always limited politics. One reason is that state governments establish legal limits on what local governments can do,* for example, on the kinds of taxes that can be levied. At times, local governments are left in a tenuous fiscal condition, dependent on other levels of government. Cutbacks in federal aid have made local government more dependent on state aid to respond to demands of residents.[14]

Practical limits exist because cities need to attract or maintain businesses to assure economic viability. The limits are greater now than before because businesses are more mobile. Mass communication means that many businesses no longer have to locate in central cities to maintain contacts with customers and suppliers. The development of assembly line technology, which requires space, usually makes it more economical for industry to locate outside a center city, where land values are lower. The increased mobility of business makes it more difficult for cities to maintain their economic bases. There is more pressure to devote efforts and resources to maintaining economic health. As a result, fewer resources can be redistributed to poor neighborhoods.

Nevertheless, blacks, Latinos, and Asians have become more politically active, and their activity has had an effect on urban policy. The emergence of each group as a force in urban politics will be examined in this chapter.

Blacks in the City

Until the beginning of the twentieth century, the African-American population lived primarily in the rural South. While legally free to move after the Civil War, few went far. The South's economy depended on cotton and cotton production depended on African-Americans. After the Civil War,

FIGURE 4–1

Black Population Distribution by Metropolitan and Non-metropolitan Residence, 1990

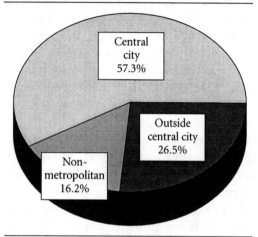

Source: Bureau of the Census, *General Population Characteristics,* (Washington, D.C.: U.S. Government Printing Office, issued November 1992), 260)

some southern plantation owners tried to lure European immigrants to work in the South, but few of the immigrants wanted to do the backbreaking work. The North also had an interest in the southern cotton crop because cotton was an essential raw material for northern textile mills and accounted for more than half of the U.S. export trade.

North and South cooperated in keeping African-Americans in the cotton fields. Some northern states passed laws forbidding African-American immigration. The Freedmen's Bureau, ostensibly created to help the newly freed slaves, coerced blacks into signing labor contracts with the plantation owners by cutting back on government rations to refugee blacks and providing funds only to help them to return to their former owners. Mostly illiterate and penniless, African-Americans had little option but to sign the contracts, which left them in a state of total dependency. The former slaves borrowed money from plantation owners for seed and equipment, but by charging exorbitant in-

---

*See Chapter 10 for a discussion of the limits.

terest rates and requiring a large share of the crop grown be given to them, the owners could be sure African-Americans would never make enough money to leave the plantation.[15] This sharecropping system, as it was called, took the place of slavery, placed African-Americans in a condition of permanent indebtedness, and, in many cases, meant that their role had simply changed from slave to serf.

Not until the beginning of the twentieth century did African-Americans start to move out of the rural south. The movement occurred because legislation and World War I had drastically reduced the number of European immigrants arriving in the country at the same time that an economic boom increased the need for labor in northern factories. In the search for cheap labor, employers lowered color barriers previously erected against African-American workers.[16]

The African-American laborers settled in a relatively small number of large cities, resulting in an explosion in the black population of those cities. For example, the African-American population of Chicago grew from 30,000 to more than 110,000 between 1900 and 1920.[17] The Great Depression slowed the migration, but the mechanization of cotton farming, World War II,

and the economic expansion that occurred afterward increased the movement from the rural South to the cities in both the North and South. In 1940, 77 percent of African-Americans lived in the South, with 49 percent in the rural South. Five million moved to the North after 1940.

In 1970, when the migration ended, black America was only half Southern, and less than a quarter rural; "urban" had become a euphemism for "black." The black migration was one of the largest and most rapid mass internal movements of people in history— perhaps *the* greatest not caused by the immediate threat of execution or starvation.[18]

The massive African-American influx to urban areas and to the North had another important consequence. It made race one of the key national issues in the second half of the twentieth century. "Race relations stood out nearly everywhere as the one thing most plainly wrong in America, the flawed portion of the great tableau, the chief generator of doubt about how essentially noble the whole national enterprise was."[19]

By 1990, 83.8 percent of all African-Americans lived in metropolitan areas. (See Figure 4–1) Table 4–1 presents the African-

TABLE 4–1

Black Population in Ten Largest Cities, 1990

Rank	City	Total Population	Black Population	% Black
1	New York	7,322,564	2,102,512	28.7
2	Los Angeles	3,485,398	487,674	14.0
3	Chicago	2,783,726	1,087,711	39.0
4	Houston	1,630,553	457,990	28.1
5	Philadelphia	1,585,577	631,936	39.9
6	San Diego	1,110,549	104,261	9.4
7	Detroit	1,027,974	777,916	75.7
8	Dallas	1,006,877	296,994	29.5
9	Phoenix	983,403	51,053	5.2
10	San Antonio	935,933	65,884	7.0

Source: U.S. Bureau of the Census, *General Population Statistics,* Census, 1990 (Washington, D.C.: U.S. Government Printing Office, issued November 1992).

American population in America's 10 largest cities according to 1990 census data. Among those cities, only Detroit has an African-American majority, but Table 4–2 indicates that 14 cities with populations over 100,000 had African-American majorities according to the 1990 census. Many cities have large black concentrations; in addition, blacks tend to cluster in certain urban areas, often called **ghettos**.

Four factors have contributed to the ghettoization of blacks. First, whites tend to leave areas into which blacks have moved, moving to suburbs. Second, public policies facilitated this so-called "white flight." One example is Federal Housing Administration loans that spurred development of the suburbs. These suburban developments often had restrictive covenants that prohibited blacks from living in the area. Such covenants are no longer legal.

Third, discrimination in the housing market contributes to the ghettoization of blacks. Research has demonstrated that blacks seeking housing are steered into predominantly black areas or are required to invest much more time and effort in finding housing than are whites. Finally, African-American attitudes also play a role. The ghetto provides a setting to develop group identity and start an organizational base. The ghetto has also begun to be the basis for political organization in many cities.[20]

The physical segregation of blacks had many implications. For one, it often resulted in seriously overcrowded housing. Because the housing stock relegated to African-Americans tended to be deteriorating, overcrowding simply accelerated the process. At a more basic level, the ghetto provided the mechanism for more general discrimination against African-Americans in the distribution of resources.

Ira Katznelson believes that the ghettoization of African-Americans perpetuated the tendency to define conflicts in the city in spatial rather than class terms. This limited the extent to which African-American demands could change the distribution of resources in any substantial way. He writes: "The racial challenge was transformed into an ethnic politics of a traditional kind even as the activities of city governments allowed militant nationalist black leaders to claim substantial victories."[21]

The opposite side of the coin, however, was the potential for political action that the ghettos provided. Many Americans first realized that potential in the 1960s. The early part of the decade was marked by efforts by both African-Americans and whites to end segregation in the South. One hundred years after the country had been torn apart by a civil war, precipitated in part by the issue of slavery, bus

TABLE 4–2

Cities over 100,000 Population with Black Majorities, 1990

City	% Black	City	% Black
Gary, IN	80.6	Newark, NJ	58.5
Detroit, MI	75.5	Jackson, MS	55.7
Atlanta, GA	67.1	Richmond, VA	55.2
Washington, DC	65.8	Memphis, TN	54.8
Birmingham, AL	63.3	Macon, GA	52.2
New Orleans, LA	61.9	Inglewood, CA	51.9
Baltimore, MD	59.2	Santa Rosa, CA	51.3

Source: US. Bureau of the Census, *Statistical Abstract of the United States,* 115th ed. (Washington, D.C.: U.S. Government Printing Office, 1995).

loads of freedom fighters rolled into the deep South to end the racial segregation that encompassed everything from separate black and white schools to separate toilets and drinking fountains. The efforts, dominated by Dr. Martin Luther King's philosophy of nonviolence, stirred the American conscience and produced some significant successes. For example, by the end of 1961, segregation in all interstate travel had been ended.[22] The changes in the South were followed by changes of a different sort in the ghettos of northern and western cities.

Adam Clayton Powell, Jr., an African-American Congressman from New York City, predicted that what he called the "black revolution" would have two phases. The one that was occurring in the South was concerned with such "middle-class matters" as school desegregation, and seating on buses and at lunch counters. But Powell predicted that the second phase would be in the North and would be concerned with what he called the "gut issue of who gets the money." It would, said Powell, be "rough."[23]

Powell was a true prophet. In 1964, an African-American teenager in New York City attacked, with a knife, a janitor who had impulsively turned a hose on him while hosing a sidewalk. An off-duty police lieutenant arrived and ordered the teenager to drop his knife. When the teenager attacked him, the policeman fired a warning shot and then shot the teenager, killing him instantly. Three days later, a group of African-Americans marched to the precinct station to demand the lieutenant's suspension. When no suspension was forthcoming, the group began throwing bottles and debris at the police, setting off a five-day riot. When the riot subsided in its point of origin in the Harlem section of Manhattan, it began anew in the Bedford-Stuyvesant section of Brooklyn. It was followed by riots in Rochester, New York; Jersey City, Paterson, and Elizabeth, New Jersey; Dixmoor, Illinois; and Philadelphia, Pennsylvania.[24]

That summer began a cycle of northern urban riots. The following year the Watts district of Los Angeles erupted for six days, resulting in 34 deaths, 898 injuries, over 4,000 arrests, and $45 million in damages. As bad as the Watts riot was, it was relatively isolated. In 1966 rioting was widespread. In 1966 riots began again in Los Angeles, followed by riots in Washington, D.C., Cleveland, Omaha, Des Moines, Chicago, Brooklyn, Baltimore, Perth Amboy (N.J.), Providence, Minneapolis, Milwaukee, Detroit, Dayton (Ohio), Atlanta, San Francisco, St. Louis, and numerous smaller communities. The summer's toll was 7 deaths, over 400 injuries, over 3,000 arrests, and over $5 million in damages.[25]

The pattern was repeated in 1967. By the end of 1967, 114 cities had experienced riots, accompanied by 88 deaths. It was beginning to appear that black militant H. Rap Brown was right when he observed that "violence is as American as cherry pie."[26]

The last *widespread* outbreak of urban riots occurred in 1968 following the assassination of Dr. Martin Luther King in April. In the month following the assassination, riots erupted in 168 cities and 27,000 people were arrested.[27] Despite predictions that the summer of 1968 would be the worst yet, the cities' ghettos were remarkably calm. Although there were 19 deaths in urban riots, half as many riots occurred as expected, and Cleveland was the only major city involved.[28] Since then, the two most serious riots occurred in the Liberty section of Miami in 1980 and in Los Angeles in 1992. While there have been few riots recently, one study of the 1992 Los Angeles riot concluded that it was ". . . among the most violent, destructive and frightening episodes in twentieth-century American urban history."[29]

At the time of the riots of the 1960s, a variety of theories were offered to explain what caused the violence. Joe Feagin and Harlen Hahn classified these theories into three broad groups: the conservative view, the liberal view, and the radical view.[30] The **conservative view** saw violence as pathological behavior engaged in by deviant people, who were often spurred to action by outside agitators seeking to disrupt American society. For example, Edward Banfield, a proponent of this view, discussed rioting in a book chapter entitled "Rioting Mainly for Fun and Profit." He argued that the riots were mainly an expression of youthful spirits by adolescent members of the lower class.[31]

The **liberal view** was that violence is the result of social conditions. The conditions believed to give rise to the urban riots of the 1960s were the deprived conditions of blacks in America—especially problems of unemployment and underemployment—and the remaining impact of slavery on Africa-American attitudes and family structures. Some proponents of this view also pointed to white racism as a fundamental explanation. As the *Report of the National Advisory Commission on Civil Disorders* summarized: "Race prejudice has shaped our history decisively; it now threatens to affect our future. White racism is essentially responsible for the explosive mixture which has been accumulating in our cities since the end of World War II."[32]

The **radical approach** saw the riots as a rebellion against a political and economic system that left blacks in a position of subjugation. According to this view, those at fault were not the rioters themselves, but those who systematically excluded African-Americans from economic and political power. The riot was seen as a rational and purposive response to conditions that had not been changed by more conventional strategies.*

Initially, government responses to the riots of the 1960s were based on liberal and even some radical premises about violence. These responses were limited and transitory.[33] As the riots continued, despite money being spent in the ghetto, the view of both the public and the government became more conser-

vative and funds were increasingly channeled into riot control rather than into social programs. The riots, however, demonstrated the potential power that the large urban concentrations of African-Americans could wield. As the 1960s drew to a close, and blacks began to focus their energies increasingly on electoral politics, that potential began to be translated into political power. Dr. Hiawatha Harris, a Watts psychiatrist, said, "the rioting phase, where we burn down businesses in our own areas, is over. The whole movement is in another direction—toward implementing black power and finding our dignity as a people."[34] The term "Black Power" became a slogan and a symbol of the efforts of many African-Americans to create both economic and political power for themselves, rather than having to rely upon the good will of whites.

In the midst of the riots, other developments occurred that were to aid African-Americans in translating their numbers into political power. The initiatives for these developments came from the national level and, in part, can be seen as a continuation of attempts by the Democratic Party to maintain an electoral majority by sponsoring policies favorable to center city residents, many of whom were black.[35] The Civil Rights Act of 1964 and the Voting Rights Act of 1965 effectively ended barriers to African-American voter registration. Especially significant were provisions in the 1965 Act that authorized the Justice Department to appoint voting examiners to register voters in areas that required a literacy test for registration or that had less than 50 percent of the voting age population registered in 1964.

Some believe that such structural barriers in the electoral system were the major reason for the traditionally lower rates of electoral participation among African-Americans.[36] Evidence for this belief can be found in the rapid increase in African-American voting that occurred in the South after the Voting

---

*A more thorough discussion of rioting as a form of participation appears in Chapter 6.

Rights Act of 1965 reduced the incidence of discrimination in the registration of African-American voters. Registration increased as much as 65 percent in some counties in Alabama, Louisiana, and Mississippi on the first registration day after the passage of the Voting Rights Act of 1965.[37]

As registration and voting became easier, many areas relied on other tactics to dilute the African-American vote.

> Seemingly the move has been from using registration and voting procedures as a means to diminish and halt the black voter in the late sixties and early seventies to the new techniques of dilution of concentrated black voting power which emerged because of patterns of residential segregation.[38]

For example, annexation of property adjacent to the city could help keep African-Americans, and other groups, a permanent minority. At-large or citywide, rather than district, elections can help ensure that the minority never has electoral clout.

In 1975, the Voting Rights Act required that electoral changes be submitted to the attorney general or to the District Court of the District of Columbia to ensure that the changes would not have negative effects on minority populations. While that prohibited officials from manipulating current structures for discriminatory purposes, existing structures that could have discriminatory effects, such as at-large elections, were left intact. In 1982, the 1975 Act was "altered to prohibit any electoral arrangement that denied or abridged the voting rights of citizens on the basis of race or color or language."[39] This change helped minorities attack electoral structures that had kept them electorally impotent.

In addition, various parts of President Lyndon Johnson's Great Society programs in the 1960s had an effect on African-American political power. Perhaps most significant was the War on Poverty, directed by the Office of Economic Opportunity. The legislation that authorized this program required that community action agencies be organized in local target areas to devise programs to address poverty. It further specified that these agencies had to have "maximum feasible participation" of the population in those target areas. While the programs devised by these local agencies were often considered failures, many times the agencies themselves did succeed in creating an organizational base in poor neighborhoods.

The agencies also often succeeded in recruiting and providing training to indigenous leaders, many of whom used the community action agencies as a political base. As Daniel Patrick Moynihan wrote in the early 1970s:

> Very possibly, the most important long run impact of the community action programs of the 1960s will prove to have been the formation of an urban Negro leadership echelon at just the time when the Negro masses and other minorities were verging towards extensive commitments to urban politics. Tammany at its best (or worst) would have envied the political apprenticeship provided the neighborhood coordinators of the antipoverty program.[40]

By the 1980s, Moynihan's prediction appeared to have been realized. African-Americans had used their voting clout effectively and had become part of the governing coalition in many cities. African-American mayors headed four of the nation's six largest cities: Philadelphia, Chicago, Los Angeles, and Detroit. Thirteen other big cities, including Washington, D.C., and Atlanta, also had black mayors. The fact that by the late 1990s Philadelphia, Chicago, and Los Angeles no longer have African-American mayors and New York City's first black mayor was defeated after only one term is an indicator of the numerous obstacles African-Americans face in retaining political power and in using that power as a route of social mobility.

One problem that African-Americans face is a lack of cohesion. At times they have effectively coalesced to cast their votes together and have won political power as a result. For instance, W. Wilson Goode was re-elected mayor in Philadelphia in 1987 based largely on 98 percent of the black voters. Such unity is not necessarily permanent. Race is only one factor affecting urban voters. William Nelson, who chronicled the rise and fall of African-American political power in Cleveland under the tutelage of former Mayor Carl Stokes, argues that black leaders are only fleetingly unified.

> In reality, the issues and emotional circumstances that create unity among black leaders are transitory. The more normal condition is one in which powerful centrifugal forces create tension and conflict among Black leaders that renders impossible the maintenance of unity and the promotion of collective activity.[41]

One centrifugal force in the black community is its increasing diversity. In some cities, especially New York City and Miami, black immigrants from countries such as Trinidad, Haiti, the Bahamas, and Nigeria have joined African-American communities. While others may categorize them all simply as blacks, "they have remarkably little in common in terms of language, culture, ethnic traditions, rituals, and religious affiliations."[42] Consequences of the diversification of the black community are discussed in Box 4–1.

Another source of diversity is class. The 1990 census revealed that the black community was increasingly polarized into one group living in extreme poverty and another rising into affluence. The affluent blacks often follow whites out of the center city and its problems and into outlying areas.[43] While all blacks may value the election of a black to office as a symbol, it is difficult for black leaders to define an issue agenda that appeals to such a divergent population. In fact, former New York City mayor Edward Koch managed to get a sizable minority of black votes by his emphasis on middle-class issues even though he was opposed by African-American leaders.[44]

Even in those cities where African-Americans have won election to major political office, barriers still exist to using those positions to alter the circumstances of their fellow blacks. First, problems often arise in attempting to unify the cities after the election. This is especially difficult in cities where the voters are polarized racially. For example, the election of Harold Washington as the first African-American mayor of Chicago split the city's Democratic machine into two factions—one black and one white. Only in 1986, one year before his death, did the mayor succeed in getting control of the city council.

Second, African-American political leaders must satisfy the expectations of their black constituents, and having a black mayor does not end the problem of blacks in cities. Political leaders alone cannot control the political process. City mayors have limited control over the kinds of decisions that affect the distribution of resources. Those decisions are controlled by other levels of government and by private business. An African-American mayor cannot single-handedly revitalize the economic base of a declining city to increase black employment.

Private businesses control decisions about business location and investment—issues that determine the economic health of cities. Attempts by African-American mayors to encourage business investment can at times lead to the impression that the mayor is "selling out" to the white upper-class.[45] Decisions made by the national government significantly affect urban conditions. For example, the recent reform of welfare that reduces the role of the national government in providing a federally financed "safety net" for the poor will affect all urban areas because of the large number of urban poor. Local governments will have to find ways to replace the national

BOX 4–1

Good Black/Bad Black?

The number of West Indians in New York City area has recently increased to 500,000. Although they share the skin color of African Americans, they tend to make substantially more money, live in better neighborhoods, and have stronger families. Not having been raised in a culture where skin color carries the stigma it does in the United States, the West Indians tend to ignore racial slights and to assume that they can compete successfully with whites for jobs and housing. Employers see West Indians as "good" blacks and are willing to hire them when they will not hire African-Americans.

The distinction between "good" blacks and "bad" blacks has serious implications. For the employers, it legitimizes negative stereotypes of African-Americans. They can say they are not racist because the issue is not skin color but individual capabilities. For African-Americans, it means that one other immigrant group is moving ahead while they stay behind. The fact that the new group shares their skin color makes the differential success all that more difficult.

The West Indians recognize that their success comes with a price. They feel guilty because their success derives from differentiating themselves from African-Americans and that differentiation has reinforced white racism. They also know that as they lose the accents that enable them to differentiate themselves, they will also lose their advantage and will soon be lumped together with African-Americans as simply blacks.

The influx of West Indians increases the diversity in the black community. At least in the short run, the interests of the immigrants differ from those of African-Americans. Those differences make political cooperation between the two groups very unlikely.

Source: Adapted from Malcolm Gladwell, "Black Like Them," *The New Yorker,* April 29 and May 6, 1996, 74–81.

resources, find jobs for those who once were on welfare, or face the consequences of increasing numbers of homeless and hungry people. All mayors will have to wrestle with this issue, but the impact may be greatest on African-American mayors because of the hopes that may have been raised among blacks by their attainment of political power in the cities.

Fiscal strains in many local governments have serious consequences for African-Americans. One analysis of New York City indicated that minority influence declined as a result of that city's fiscal crisis in the 1970s. Candidates for city office, including Democratic Mayor Edward Koch, did not find it necessary to include minorities, including blacks, in an electoral coalition, a fact that had "visible results in the distribution of benefits."[46] The financial crisis also contributed to the reduction of support for community programs aimed at incorporating minority interests. While Democrat David Dinkins managed to assemble a broad coalition of minorities in 1989 to become the first African-American mayor of New York, he could not hold the coalition together and lost the position four years later to Republican Rudolph Giuliani.

The long-term impact of the African-American focus on electoral politics is not known. The number of registered African-

American voters has increased from 6.3 million in 1966 to 13.4 million in 1992.[47] With the increase in numbers of black voters has come an increase in black officials, especially in cities. The National Conference of Black Mayors reports that as of October 1996, there were 412 black mayors.[48] The voting power of African-Americans has not only gained them a position in the governing coalition of many local governments, it has also enabled them to influence the policy process. U.S. Representative John Lewis (Democrat), a veteran civil rights activist, has observed that the behavior of white officials also changed with the increase in African-American voters: ". . . white Southern politicians changed their tune. They started going all out and appealing to the black voter. . . . They started paving roads, building bridges and paving streets in the black community."[49]

Many blacks are becoming upwardly mobile. The civil rights movement and resulting legal and social changes have opened doors to blacks unimaginable even 30 years ago. Yet discrimination persists and the growing number of middle- and upper-class African-Americans is counterbalanced by a growing number in extreme poverty. While blacks as a whole have gained in education, political representation, and white collar employment, they still lag in employment and jobs.[50] In 1992, the unemployment rate for blacks was 14 percent, compared to 6 percent for whites.[51] The percentage of blacks below the poverty line is much higher for blacks than for whites. Table 4–3 summarizes some social and economic characteristics of blacks. Many would undoubtedly still agree with the way Hazel Mangle Rivers—a participant in the 1963 March on Washington to protest racial discrimination—summed up the progress of blacks in the 20 years following: "We made it a little better for our grandchildren, . . . but there's a lot to be done. Our people need jobs and really need somewhere to stay. It's a little better than it was in '63, but we got a long way to travel."[52]

TABLE 4–3

Social and Economic Characteristics of the Black Population Compared to Whites, 1990[a]

Years of School Completed	% Black	% White	Family Income	% Black	% White
Elementary			Less than $5,000	10.7	2.5
0–8 years	10.3	8.4	$5,000–$9,999	15.1	4.8
			$10,000–$14,999	11.4	6.6
High school			$15,000–$24,999	18.6	15.1
1–3 years	16.8	9.5	$25,000–$49,999	26.7	33.9
4 years	36.2	34.5	$50,000 or more	17.6	37.2
College			Persons below		
1–3 years	23.8	24.6	poverty level	33.1	12.2
4 years or more	12.9	22.9			

[a]for persons 25 years and over.

Source: U.S. Bureau of the Census, *General Population Statistics*, Census, 1990 (Washington, D.C.: U.S. Government Printing Office, Washington, D.C., issued November 1992).

TABLE 4–4

Persons of Spanish Origin in the United States, 1990

Type of Spanish Origin	Number	Percent
Persons of Spanish Origin	22,354,059	100.0%
Mexican	13,495,938	60.4%
Puerto Rican	2,727,754	12.2%
Cuban	1,043,932	4.7%
Other Spanish (for example, Caribbean, Central American)	5,086,435	22.8%

Source: U.S. Bureau of the Census, *General Population Statistics*, Census, 1990 (Washington, D.C.: U.S. Government Printing Office, issued November 1992.).

An analysis of the causes of the 1992 Los Angeles riot pointed to the poverty of many blacks and the continued effects of racism. Many blacks are still living in poverty with no hope of improved living conditions. Both institutional and personal racism still exist, although often less openly expressed than in the past. The analysis listed the final cause to be the changing economic base of the metropolis discussed above and the impact of foreign immigration—both of which lead to conflict among various ethnic groups for scarce economic resources.[53]

In sum, disadvantaged blacks were joined in their inner city neighborhoods by Hispanic immigrants, who were also experiencing prejudice and discrimination. Asian immigrants replaced the whites as business and store owners in economically depressed neighborhoods. The economic restructuring of cities led to job losses, adding to the competitions and tensions. The results were growing inter-ethnic hostilities taking the form of local conflicts and disputes between blacks and Hispanics, blacks and Asians, and Asians and Hispanics.[54]

This chapter will turn next to examinations of the other two major ethnic groups in metropolitan America.

Latinos

As immigration is creating greater diversity within the black community, so too is the Latino community becoming increasingly heterogeneous due to the large number of legal and illegal immigrants arriving from Latin America. The one thing that Latinos share is a common Spanish-speaking origin. Beyond that, the distinctions are great. Rodolfo de la Garza, and his colleagues, even found that many respondents in the Latino National Political Survey do not identify themselves as part of a broader Hispanic or Latino community, but rather identify themselves in terms of national origin.[55]

This section will briefly examine three of the most numerous groups of Latinos in the U.S.—Puerto Ricans, Cubans, and Mexican-Americans—and discuss the effects of the newer immigrants on the Latino community. As with the black community, the ability of Latinos to forge effective political coalitions is affected by the diversity among the Latino groups. In fact, de la Garza, et al., conclude: "Overall, these groups do not constitute a political community."[56]

Table 4–4 provides numbers of Latinos in the United States. These groups originated from different locations and arrived in this country at various times. They also tended to settle in distinct regions of the country, al-

FIGURE 4–2

Hispanic Population Distribution by Metropolitan and Non-metropolitan Residence, 1990

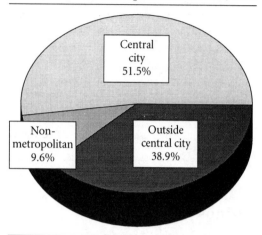

Central
city
51.5%

Non-
metropolitan
9.6%

Outside
central city
38.9%

Source: US. Bureau of the Census, *General Population Characteristics,* 1990 (Washington, D.C.: U.S. Government Printing Office, issued November 1992), 29

though all have tended to concentrate in the cities of those regions, as Figure 4–2 indicates. Table 4–5 indicates the percentage of Latinos in our largest cities and Table 4–6 illustrates the concentration of Latinos in 12 large cities.

Latinos have unique national identities and cultures and different levels of preparedness to deal with life here. Economically, Mexican-Americans and Cubans have significantly higher median incomes than Puerto Ricans or the newly arrived immigrants from Latin America. With the exception of Cubans, Latino immigrants tend to have low rates of naturalization, with Mexicans having the lowest level among Latinos.[57] Latinos also tend to have lower educational levels than other immigrant groups. The more recent immigrants have the fewest years of schooling.[58] They also have different racial backgrounds; Mexican-Americans tend to be of mixed Indian–Spanish heritage, while Cubans and Puerto Ricans tend to be a mixture of black–Spanish ancestry.

Puerto Ricans

In 1910, New York City had 500 people of Puerto Rican birth. By 1940, the number of Puerto Ricans had grown to 70,000. World War II cut off the migration because normal passenger shipping came to a halt. But after the war, the influx began again in great numbers.[59] To a large extent, Puerto Ricans stayed in the New York area. Only relatively recently has there been sizable movement to other areas such as Chicago and Boston.

Puerto Rican migration differed from that of European immigrants. Early in the twentieth century, the Puerto Rican legislature had explicitly rejected granting United States citizenship to Puerto Ricans. Despite that, the Jones Act in 1917 imposed citizenship on residents of the island. James Jennings argues that this was done only to make it easier for Puerto Ricans to migrate to the mainland and "provide cheap labor for industries in New York City during periods of waning European immigration."[60] The Puerto Ricans did not want citizenship, and when they arrived on the mainland they saw themselves not as a people searching for a new home, but only as migrant workers.

As a result, Puerto Ricans had little reason to organize themselves, to adapt to the dominant American culture, or to become politically active.

> The political organizations found in the European immigrant communities have been absent from Puerto Rican communities because the Puerto Rican, for a long time, felt that one day he would be returning to Puerto Rico. . . . Why should one put time and effort into cold cities like New York only to return home one day?[61]

Because they saw themselves as only temporary U.S. residents, Puerto Ricans did not even think the city government had a responsibility to them. As Jennings continues,

... Puerto Ricans would not feel slighted on seeing other groups favored by the government because all governments had the right to protect their own citizens before protecting strangers. Puerto Rican migrants saw themselves in the latter role.[62]

Attitudes such as these meant Puerto Ricans were slow to acculturate themselves to life on the mainland and remained essentially uninvolved in politics.

Even if they wanted to adapt to American culture, Puerto Ricans faced barriers. One major problem was something new in their experience: discrimination due to their color. Many Puerto Ricans are of mixed racial ancestry and, therefore, have varying skin color. The Puerto Rican immigrants soon became aware of what skin color meant on the mainland and adopted various strategies for coping with the discrimination. Those with light skin "passed" as whites and, in the process, lost their self-identification as Puerto Ricans. Those with darker skins, on the other hand, recognizing the discrimination against blacks, tried desperately to distinguish themselves as Puerto Ricans, not as blacks.[63] Lawrence Chenault claimed that ". . . the darker the

TABLE 4–5

Hispanic Population in Ten Largest Cities, 1990

Rank	City	Total Population	% Hispanic
1	New York	7,322,564	24.4
2	Los Angeles	3,485,398	39.9
3	Chicago	2,783,726	19.6
4	Houston	1,630,553	27.6
5	Philadelphia	1,585,577	5.6
6	San Diego	1,110,549	20.7
7	Detroit	1,027,974	2.8
8	Dallas	1,006,877	20.9
9	Phoenix	983,403	20.0
10	San Antonio	935,933	55.6

Source: U.S. Bureau of the Census, *General Population Statistics*, Census, 1990, (Washington, D.C.: U.S. Government Printing Office, Washington, D.C., issued November 1992).

TABLE 4–6

Cities Over 100,000 with Latino Majority, 1990

City	% Latino	City	% Latino
Laredo, TX	93.9	Miami, FL	62.5
Brownsville, TX	90.1	San Antonio, TX	55.6
Hialeah, FL	87.6	Oxnard, CA	54.4
El Monte, CA	72.5	Pomona, CA	51.3
El Paso, TX	69.0	Salinas, CA	50.6
Santa Ana, CA	65.2	Corpus Cristi, TX	50.4

Source: U.S. Bureau of the Census, *Statistical Abstract of the United States: 1995*, 115th ed. (Washington, D.C.: U.S. Government Printing Office, 1995).

person from the West Indies is, the more intense his desire to speak only Spanish, and to do so in a louder voice."[64]

In both cases, the coping strategies caused problems. The "passing" Puerto Ricans did nothing to ameliorate the problems of Puerto Ricans as a group. The darker Puerto Ricans used their language to distinguish themselves from African-Americans, but that language in turn was a barrier to their success in school and in the job market.

Other aspects of the environment were also singularly inhospitable. Puerto Ricans arrived after the large influx of African-Americans. Because the blacks had occupied the available low-cost housing, Puerto Ricans found the housing market limited or nonexistent.[65] Slum clearance made the housing market even tighter, and the resulting relocation of Puerto Ricans meant they were dispersed into various parts of the metropolitan area, which made maintaining a community as a basis for organization and political action difficult.[66] Their late arrival also meant that institutions that might have provided a basis for developing organizational strength (for example, churches and unions) were already in place and controlled by others. The Puerto Ricans in essence "inherited" them, but did not control them. Finally, the changing economic base of the city made finding jobs difficult for Puerto Ricans. In particular, the collapse of the garment industry in New York City between 1960 and 1980 left many Puerto Rican women out of work, and their inability to speak English made it impossible to find new jobs.[67]

Two other factors slowed the entry of Puerto Ricans into politics. One was the neglect by New York City's political parties. The Democratic Party, traditionally the party of immigrants and workers, might have been expected to attempt to mobilize Puerto Ricans. Sherrie Baver claims the Democrats did not reach out to Puerto Ricans in part because, like the churches and unions, the party was

controlled by white ethnics who saw the Puerto Ricans as "nonwhite and hence a threat to the city's white population."[68]

The second factor that retarded the political activity of Puerto Ricans was the "paternalism" of the government of Puerto Rico. In 1948, the Puerto Rican Department of Labor established a Migration Office in New York, which helped find jobs for migrants and interceded for them in acquiring needed social services. While intended to help Puerto Ricans adjust to the mainland, the office actually slowed that adjustment. By acting as their spokesperson, the Migration Office made it unnecessary for Puerto Ricans to develop their own local leadership. Puerto Ricans wanting to assume leadership positions in the community were ignored by New York City officials.[69]

Another factor, undoubtedly, was their economic condition. In 1984, Herman Badillo, a Puerto Rican who had been a congressman and had held several New York City offices, explained the fact that Puerto Ricans had the lowest voter registration rate in New York City by saying, "From my experience, the main concern in the Puerto Rican community is the overwhelming poverty, the struggle for day-to-day existence."[70]

Despite the barriers, Puerto Ricans are becoming politically active. One observer notes that there has been a "political explosion" in Puerto Rican communities of many cities.[71] Part of the explosion is seen in the increasing number of organizations that can provide a base for political action. The community in New York City has its own newspaper, *El Diario de Nuevo York*. There are Puerto Rican professional, athletic, cultural, and social organizations. In addition, increasing numbers of political clubs and organizations are attempting to play a major role in the electoral politics of many cities. Puerto Ricans have also managed to play an increasingly important role in Democratic Party politics. The emergence in 1970 of a Puerto Rican political party in New York City, the Young Lords, was the "symbolic death knell" of political quiescence for the group. The Young Lords Party used a combination of confrontation and community service to attempt to improve conditions for New York City's Puerto Ricans.

> The Young Lords signaled a new era in the politics of Puerto Ricans in urban America. This party was in effect the coup d' grace [sic] to the electorally passive, nonorganized Puerto Rican community, which previously was more interested in the politics of Puerto Rico than in the politics of the barrio.[72]

Puerto Ricans have become more politically active for many reasons. The major one apparently is a change in attitudes. Many Puerto Ricans have stopped thinking of themselves as transient migrant workers in America. They have begun to realize that Puerto Rico is not, and probably will not be, a separate country. In addition, their economic status on the mainland makes it impossible for them to make enough money to return to Puerto Rico and live comfortably. They have begun to think of themselves as citizens and to organize to demand their rights as citizens.[73]

Other factors helped Puerto Ricans in their political awakening. The elimination of literacy tests made it easier for Puerto Ricans to vote because, for many, English is a difficult second language. The civil rights activity of blacks helped crystallize Puerto Rican outrage over racial discrimination. Finally, many of the programs of the War on Poverty that helped African-Americans develop politically also helped mobilize Puerto Ricans.

Their political activity has produced some results. Puerto Ricans have managed to use Democratic Party organizations in many New York City neighborhoods to build a political base.[74] In 1990 eight Puerto Ricans were on the New York city council, a Puerto Rican borough president was serving in the Bronx, and Puerto Ricans represented the city in Congress and the state legislature.[75] In other cities, where the Puerto Rican population is smaller, they have been less successful in electoral politics. But in those cities Puerto Ricans have been appointed to city administration offices by Democratic mayors. While some argue such appointments will merely keep Puerto Ricans dependent on the dominant political leaders, others see them as recognition of the growing political power of Puerto Ricans.[76] Other Puerto Ricans are bypassing the traditional party mechanisms and are attempting to build independent power bases at the grass roots level.[77]

In any event, the emerging political activity of Puerto Ricans will inevitably have an effect on many American cities, especially New York, Chicago, and Boston. Some observers believe that as they become more active, the main goal will move from gaining influence to gaining power. Rather than attempting to gain access to a governing coalition to win limited concessions, Puerto Ricans will focus on becoming part of that coalition as a means of altering favorably their position in American society.[78] As Box 4–2 (on page 92) points out, however, many Puerto Ricans and other Latinos are still not always integrated into political activities because of ties to the homeland.

In New York City, where Puerto Ricans constitute approximately half of the Latino population, the Puerto Rican community is becoming more economically diverse. Families with two parents who have good educations are increasingly economically prosperous. Between 1980 and 1990, the number of Puerto Rican men in professional and managerial positions increased by 25 percent. In the same time period, Puerto Rican women in such positions increased by 137 percent. But those families with a single parent with little education are, for the most part, living below the poverty level.[79] As with blacks, increasing diversity may make it more difficult for leaders of the Puerto Rican community to define a political agenda on which the community can agree.

BOX 4–2

PRESSURES ON NEW IMMIGRANTS

The new immigrants face an entirely different experience than did most of the European immigrants who arrived in the United States in the nineteenth century. An immigrant who left France in the 1830s to escape constant political unrest or a Jew who left Russia in the 1890s to escape persecution knew he or she was leaving the past behind and was moving from one life to another. Today, immigrants live in two worlds because of communication and transportation technology.

An example is the young Puerto Rican couple, Lety and David Hernandez. Lety spent part of her childhood in Bridgeport, Connecticut. She returned to Caguas, Puerto Rico, and met David. When she became pregnant, the couple decided to return to Bridgeport because she would qualify for free maternity care and David expected to find work. But the Bridgeport they found was not the Bridgeport that Lety had left years before. The industries that had once fueled Bridgeport's economy had moved, leaving a decaying and bankrupt city. They were in danger of succumbing to the "peculiar Puerto Rican cyclical vortex": moving from the mainland, back to the island, and then back to the mainland, with the children becoming increasingly disoriented and farther behind in school.

Puerto Ricans constitute at least one-quarter of the population of Bridgeport, but they have not yet found a way to make their numbers count in the political process. Bridgeport resident Willie Matos explains the problem: "As long as Puerto Rico continues being and not being, we'll never solve anything. It's our fundamental problem, here and on the island. We have to decide who we are." David Hernandez has a shorter answer. When asked if he is angry that the Puerto Ricans on the island cannot vote, he replies: "Vote? Why bother?"

For many, this dual culture is not seen as a problem. They see the maintenance of a dual culture as a form of strength. Many Mexicans maintain their Spanish language long after moving to the United States and work to maintain their ties to their Mexican homeland and relatives. They cross the border between Mexico and the United States on a regular basis, and as one researcher observed: "They never thought of themselves as having left totally. I think one of the most remarkable things I see is the number of people to whom the border has become artificial."

Indeed, some who have moved to the States want to learn English, but have found it impossible because they do not come into contact with English speakers.

Source: Adapted from Alan Weisman, "Unsettled, Unseen, Unspoken For: A Puerto Rican Community Finds Its Dreams Stranded in a Yankee Town," *New York Times Magazine,* April 28, 1991; and Seth Mydans, "They're in a New Home, But Feel Tied to the Old," *New York Times,* June 28, 1991.

Cubans

In 1960, the year after Fidel Castro came to power in Cuba, 8,283 Cubans immigrated to the United States. By the following year the number had climbed to 14,287. For the next five years, the numbers of Cubans arriving per year ranged from 10,587 to 19,760. At the end of 1965, the United States and Cuba began a program, referred to as Freedom Flights. Under this program, the U.S. government sponsored two airline flights a day to bring Cubans to America. In 1967, the number of Cubans arriving climbed to 33,321 and, in 1968, jumped to 99,312. While the number entering subsided in 1969, 67,708 Cubans arrived in another dramatic wave in 1977. A huge torrent occurred in the spring of 1980 when an estimated 125,000 Cubans arrived in what is referred to as the Mariel Boat Lift. Castro announced that Cubans who wanted to emigrate could leave, and thousands of Cubans in Florida sailed to Cuba to pick up friends and relatives, only to be forced by Cuban officials to take prisoners released from jails, individuals ejected from mental institutions, and a variety of other people whom the Castro government felt were undesirable or were burdens.[80]

What is significant is the large numbers of people arriving during very short periods. Those increases become especially important when noting that 6 out of 10 Cubans are concentrated in two metropolitan areas: Miami and Union City–West New York in New Jersey. In 1960, only 5 percent of the population of Dade County, which is a Miami metropolitan area, was Latino. By 1990 the Latino population of the area had grown to 49 percent, and 59 percent of them were Cuban.[81]

When Cubans first began arriving after Castro's takeover, they were received with more tolerance and respect than any other recent immigrant group.[82] The fact that they were fleeing from a Communist regime meant that not only were they accorded special political refugee status by the American government (which meant generous federal help), but they also were viewed with understanding and sympathy by Americans. The fact that these early refugees tended to be well-educated and wealthy professionals probably contributed to the warm welcome.

As immigration continued, however, the warmth of the welcome cooled somewhat. One reason for the change in attitude was the numbers of the immigrants and their concentration in a few communities, factors that made them very visible. As one Miami resi-

dent complained, "I feel like a stranger in a foreign land. But it's not a foreign land, it's my own hometown."[83] Another reason is the fact that the newer immigrants have not had the same social status as the early refugees from Castro's rule. At a time when "natives" are worried about unemployment, economic refugees are often unwelcome. Finally, the Mariel Boat Lift also contributed to opposition to Cuban immigrants because it resulted in an influx of criminals, and mentally ill, elderly, and disabled people who were clearly going to require social services from the government.

The Cuban influx has had especially negative effects on Miami's black population. For one, the Cubans competed for jobs with blacks. Many of the refugees were highly educated; thus they were often able to edge out blacks. In addition, as the number of Cubans increased, it became increasingly important for employees who dealt with people—clerks, bank tellers, for example—to be bilingual. This also made it more difficult for blacks to find jobs.

The Cuban population is having a distinct and increasing impact on politics, especially in Miami. The early Cuban refugees hoped and believed they would return to their former homes. Their political efforts were focused almost entirely on encouraging American efforts, such as the Bay of Pigs invasion, aimed at overthrowing the Castro regime. However, as length of residence in America increases, Cubans are less likely to say they would return to Cuba even if Castro were out of power.[84]

As the numbers wanting to return decrease, the numbers of Cubans becoming American citizens increase. Once they become citizens, the political behavior of Cubans can be characterized as "participatory, personal, anti-communist, and conservative."[85] It is participatory because of the large percentage of Cubans who register and vote. Cubans are increasingly mobilizing for competition in the electoral arena. While they represent only about 15 percent of the national electorate, they are very active and were considered a force in the 1992 presidential election.[86] Their numbers and concentration in Union City–West New York and Miami, combined with their high levels of voting, guarantee they will have an impact in those areas. They made a first big push in Miami in 1981 in an attempt to unseat the mayor of Miami. Maurice Ferre, a Puerto Rican, had been elected previously with Cuban support, but in 1981 he was challenged by Manolo Reboso, a Cuban who had been a member of the Bay of Pigs invasion brigade. The challenge failed, but in 1985 Cubans succeeded in electing a Cuban-born mayor, Xavier Suarez. The current mayor of Dade County is Alex Pinelas, born in America but of Cuban descent. In the Miami area, Cuban-Americans have higher voter registration rates than other Latinos and, as a result, most of the elected Latino officials in the area are Cuban or of Cuban descent.[87]

Cuban politics is personal in the sense that Cubans do not feel comfortable dealing with an impersonal, bureaucratic, unsympathetic government. They prefer a government in which it is possible to receive favors as a result of personal contacts with people in positions of power. Some report that Cubans have succeeded in transplanting the style of politics they prefer to Miami, a fact that may help explain the high levels of political activity. The *Economist* has painted a somewhat extreme, but colorful, picture of the politics of *personalismo*.

> The scene has all the flavor of a banana republic. Politicians rail in Spanish against communism. Commando groups are courted. Palace friendships and favours are the negotiable currency. *Padrinos*, or godfathers, huddle with politicians over cups of expresso. Neighborhood bosses, called *sargento politicos*—their wrists and necks festooned with gold jewelry, the pockets of their guayabera shirts stuffed with fat cigars—backslap their way into city hall, looking for pay-offs.[88]

While increasing their focus on American politics, Cubans still retain a violent anticommunism. In addition, they tend to espouse conservative views. As a result, unlike blacks and fellow Latinos, Cubans are most likely to identify with the Republican Party. One report estimated that 90 percent of Cubans in the Miami metropolitan area voted for Ronald Reagan in 1980.[89] The Cuban influence transformed Miami from a liberal enclave in a conservative state to a conservative bastion.

While Cubans still are the dominant Latino group in the Miami area, their proportion of the Latino population has dropped from 91 percent in 1970 to 59 percent in 1990. New immigrants from Colombia, Nicaragua, Peru, Honduras, the Dominican Republic, and Haiti are creating diversity in the Latino population. Not all are as staunchly Republican as the Cubans. Some are beginning to complain about the Cuban political dominance. Organizations representing some of the other Latino groups have begun combining to give Latino groups a larger voice. While such diversity may make it difficult for the Latino population to coalesce to form an effective electoral coalition, one sociologist believes that "little by little, when the population becomes more American and less immigrant, they'll develop more of a sense of being Hispanic or Latino and will develop more unity."[90]

Mexicans

Mexican-Americans are among the earliest as well as the most recent immigrants to America. The latest group came, in part, because the division between Mexico and the United States is merely a fence that stretches across thousands of desolate miles. Despite concerted efforts by U.S. authorities that often result in both legal and illegal migrants being deported, it appears impossible to stop Mexicans from simply walking from one country to another. No one has an exact count of the number of these illegal aliens, but it is large. Nor is all immigration illegal. Because of lobbying by Southwest employers, the 1924 Immigration Act excluded Mexicans from its quota system.[91] Large numbers of Mexicans entered this country in the beginning of this century, and they continue to come. The Bureau of the Census reports that in 1990 there were approximately 13.5 million people of Mexican origin in the U.S., or 60 percent of the 22.3 million people of Spanish origin in the country.[92]

Some Mexican-Americans are different from any other group discussed here in the sense that they did not come to the United States; the United States came to them. As a result of the Mexican-American War in 1846–1848, the United States annexed territory in what are now the states of Texas, Arizona, California, New Mexico, Utah, and part of Colorado. Mexicans living in those territories were suddenly separated from their country; many of their descendants still resent what they see as occupation and colonization.[93]

Both early and recent immigrants harbor some ambivalence about the United States and the American dream. This ambivalence is compounded by "hostility, mistrust, and suspicion" by others in the society.[94] Ironically, however, demographers indicate that there may well be a "reconquista" of part of the Southwest by Latinos, due to their numbers. In 1990, Latinos constituted 39.9 percent of the population of Los Angeles, the largest single ethnic group in the city.[95] The growth of the Latino population throughout the country is expected to make it the largest minority group in the country by 2005.[96]

Prior to World War II, organizations formed by Mexican-Americans tended to downplay political activities. Early organizations were designed to encourage mutual self-help, education, and loyalty to the United States. Examples include the Order of the Sons of America and the League of United Latin American Citizens (LULAC).[97]

After World War II, several organizations emerged with the goal of increasing political activity among Mexican-Americans. Some focused on increasing involvement in electoral activity by encouraging voter registration, endorsing candidates, and helping in campaigns. Such groups included the American G.I. Forum, Mexican American Political Association in California, and the Political Association of Spanish Speaking Organizations in Texas. In the 1960s, Mexican-Americans organized a political party, *La Raza Unida,* to contest elections throughout the Southwest. The Southwest Voter Registration Project, founded in 1975, focuses on encouraging voter registration and electoral participation.

Several factors are contributing to change in the Mexican-American community. Rapid population growth is creating an important electoral base. The urbanization of Mexican-Americans is bringing them into close contact with each other, making collective action easier and therefore more likely.[98]

Traditionally, Mexican-American voting rates were believed to be substantially lower than those of Anglos.* The disparity is probably due in part to the failure by researchers to distinguish between citizens and noncitizens in the Mexican-American community.[99] Hence electoral participation might not be as low as it appears on the surface.

Another reason for lower turnout may be lower levels of **political efficacy** among Mexican-Americans.[100] Political efficacy is the personal feeling that it is possible to have an influence on the political process. Mexican-Americans in Phoenix, San Antonio, and East Los Angeles were found to be less efficacious than were Los Angeles Anglos. At the same time, it is important to note that Mexican-

---

*The term "Anglo" is used especially in the Southwest and West to distinguish non-Hispanic Caucasians, despite the extent to which that group may itself be heterogeneous.

Americans differ among themselves (as do other Americans) in political efficacy.

The differences appear to be related to differences in the characteristics of the local political systems rather than to characteristics of individuals. Mexican-Americans living in San Antonio, a city that has had single-member electoral districts for more than a decade, had substantially higher levels of political efficacy than did those in East Los Angeles and Phoenix, which had at-large district systems when the study was done.[101] In general, such characteristics of the political system as at-large or gerrymandered districts, poll taxes, and literacy tests have frequently been used in the past intentionally to depress the political activity of Mexican-Americans, as well as other minorities. Under such conditions, low levels of political efficacy should not be surprising.

Changes in laws, discussed previously, that were designed to help blacks have also had an impact on Mexican-American participation. The 1982 Voting Rights Act prohibited electoral structures that discriminate against minority groups, regardless of whether or not they were intentionally designed to do so. Armed with that provision, organizations such as the Mexican American Legal Defense and Education Fund, Texas Rural Legal Aid, and the Southwest Voter Registration Project have succeeded in instituting single-member district electoral systems in many Southwest communities.[102] Another helpful change was a 1975 amendment to the Voting Rights Act that guaranteed bilingual election materials.[103] As a result, Mexican-American participation in elections has increased.

One study documented the narrowing of the turnout gap. An examination of voting in school board elections concluded that Mexican-Americans were registering and voting at levels almost equal to those of Anglos when the election was for school board members. But in a school bond election, the gap between Mexican-American and Anglo turnout was large.

Thus it appears that the content of the vote is a critical variable in explaining Anglo–Mexican American turnout differentials. Mexican American turnout rates are more nearly equal to Anglo turnout rates in candidate-based, rather than issue-based, elections.[104]

The authors also examined both candidacy and candidacy success gaps between Mexican-American and Anglos in school board and city elections over a 14-year period. They found that "a significant gap still exists but that the gap has narrowed considerably between 1970 and 1983."[105]

The increase in political activity has produced some significant results. In 1982 the Democratic candidate for governor of Texas, Mark White, upset the incumbent, William Clements, due largely to the votes of Mexican-Americans, who had an 86 percent turnout. There have been increases in political office-holding by Latinos in the Southwest, ". . . most noticeably in local office holding, especially city councils and school boards."[106] In addition to Miami, both San Antonio, Texas, and Denver, Colorado, have had Latino mayors.

Clearly, Latinos are far from homogeneous. Puerto Ricans, Cubans, and Mexican-Americans at times seem to share little more than a Spanish-speaking origin. These three groups are being joined by immigrants from Central and South America. That heterogeneity, combined with their geographical dispersion, makes organizing Latinos into a single political force difficult. Yet the concentration of Latinos in urban areas means that their impact on urban politics is likely to increase. The Bureau of the Census reported that 82.4 percent of Hispanics are urban dwellers.[107] As more of the recent immigrants become citizens, the possibility of using their votes to alter the urban agenda increases. In 1992, only 35 percent of Latinos were registered to vote.[108] Even with that small number, the Bureau of the Census reported there were 5,459 Latino elected officials in 1994.[109]

Asians

The change in immigration law in 1965 that removed the prohibition on immigration of Asians to the United States has resulted in a huge increase in the numbers of Asians in American urban areas. Asians are now the fastest growing ethnic minority in the United States. The size of the Asian population doubled between 1980 and 1990, due largely to immigration, and it is expected that immigration will continue to enlarge the number of Asians in the United States.[110] While they now account for 4 percent of the U.S. population, they are estimated to be 10 percent of the population by 2050.

As with blacks and Latinos, the Asian population is diverse. The most common country of origin is China, followed by the Philippines and Japan. But there are also large numbers of Indians, Koreans, Vietnamese, and other Indo-Chinese. (See Table 4–7.) Like Latinos, Asians live primarily in America's metropolitan areas. The Bureau of the Census reports that 95 percent of Asians are urban

FIGURE 4–3

Asian/Pacific Islander Population Distribution

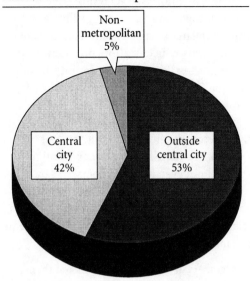

Source: U.S. Bureau of the Census, *General Population Statistics,* Current Population Survey, March 1994, (Washington, D.C.: U.S. Government Printing Office).

dwellers.[111] (See Figure 4–3.) While they are not as residentially segregated as blacks and

TABLE 4–7

Persons of Asian Origin in America

Type of Asian Origin	Number	Percent
Persons of Asian Origin	6,876,394	100%
Chinese	1,648,696	24.0%
Filipino	1,419,711	20.7%
Japanese	866,160	12.6%
Asian Indian	786,694	11.4%
Korean	797,304	11.6%
Vietnamese	593,213	8.6%
Cambodian	149,047	2.2%
Hmong	94,439	1.4%
Laotian	147,375	2.1%
Thai	91,360	1.3%
Other	282,395	4.1%

Source: U.S. Bureau of the Census, *Social and Economic Characteristics*, 1990 Census of Population, (Washington, D.C.: U.S. Government Printing Office, issued November 1993), 4.

Latinos,[112] almost half live in one of six metropolitan areas: Honolulu, Los Angeles–Long Beach, San Francisco–Oakland, New York City, Chicago, and San Jose.[113] Table 4–8 lists cities with large Asian or Pacific Islander populations. This concentration provides an opportunity for the Asian community to organize and to influence the political agenda in those areas.

Asian immigrants to the United States in the nineteenth century did not think of themselves as "Asians."[114] Like other immigrants, they did not even identify themselves by a national origin but rather by a locality, such as a community in a particular province or district. These early Asian immigrants sought to distance themselves from other Asians.

> Members of each group considered themselves culturally and politically distinct. Historical enmities between their mother countries further separated the groups even after their arrival in the United States.[115]

Such distancing was also a way of trying to avoid the prejudice they saw being directed at other Asians. As a result, before World War II

Asians were isolated in separated ethnic communities. After the war, these formerly homogeneous communities began to house other Asians. The increasing interaction permitted Asians to become aware of common problems, such as employment discrimination.[116] In the 1960s, Asian college students began to follow the example of the black power movement and founded pan-Asian organizations. In doing so, they rejected the term then used to refer to Asians—Orientals—and replaced it with the term Asian-American.

> In their attempt to forge a pan-Asian identity, Asian American activists first had to coin a composite term that would unify and encompass constituent groups. Filipino Americans' rejection of the term "yellow" and the activists' objection to the cliche-ridden *Oriental* forced the group to change its name to Asian American.[117]

The use of the term Asian-American quickly became widespread, and scores of Asian-American organizations developed. But that did not mean that the community was unified. The pan-Asian movement was domi-

TABLE 4–8

Ten U.S. Cities with the Largest Asian or Pacific Islander Population

Rank	City	Total Population	1990 Population	% Asian/Pacific Islander
1	New York, NY	7,322,564	512,700	7.0
2	Los Angeles, CA	3,485,398	341,800	9.8
3	Honolulu, HI	365,272	257,600	70.5
4	San Francisco, CA	723,959	210,900	29.1
5	San Jose, CA	782,248	152,800	19.5
6	San Diego, CA	1,110,549	131,000	11.0
7	Chicago, IL	2,783,726	104,100	3.7
8	Houston, TX	1,630,553	67,100	4.1
9	Seattle, WA	516,259	60,100	11.6
10	Long Beach, CA	429,433	58,300	13.6

Source: U.S. Bureau of the Census, *General Population Statistics,* 1990 Census (Washington, D.C.: U.S. Government Printing Office).

TABLE 4–9

Social and Economic Characteristics of the Asian Population Compared to Whites[a]

Years of School Completed	% Asian	% White	Family Income	% Asian	% White
Elementary	12.9	8.4	Less than $5,000	4.5	2.5
			$5,000–$9,999	4.8	4.8
High school	18.5	34.5	$10,000–$14,999	6.3	6.6
			$15,000–$24,999	13.0	15.1
College	36.6	22.9	$25,000–$49,999	31.7	33.9
4 years			$50,000 or more	39.7	37.2
or more					

[a]for persons 25 years and over.

Source: U.S. Bureau of the Census, *General Population Statistics, Census, 1990* (Washington, D.C.: U.S. Government Printing Office, issued November,1992).

nated by middle-class, educated Asians and was viewed with antagonism and hostility by other Asian-Americans.[118] Ethnic and class divisions in the Asian-American community still hamper cooperation, and those divisions are being exacerbated by the large numbers of new Asian immigrants. The divisions within the community derive from national origin, socioeconomic status, and generation.

The diversity and lack of unity affect the ability of Asian-Americans to be effective politically. Also limiting the impact of the community is its low levels of voting participation. One major reason for the low participation is the large number of recent immigrants who have not yet become citizens. But those immigrants are increasingly becoming naturalized, and community organizations are beginning to engage the community in the political process. Because of the large number with no party affiliation, both the Republican and Democratic Parties are courting the Asian-American vote.

Yvonne Lau reports increased Asian-American political activity of various kinds, including grass roots organizing, electoral activity, and fund raising, in Chicago.[119] While they have not yet been electorally successful, the Asian-American community has succeeded in getting members appointed to many city boards and commissions. Former Mayor Harold Washington appointed an Advisory Committee on Asian American Affairs, but that sparked ethnic and class rivalries because of the representation on the committee. One member complained:

Is it right that the Chinese get extra representation because they want to count Taiwan, and the PRC and Hong Kong? I think it's because those guys gave big donations so they want to come here and introduce their foreign agenda and mess things up. They should have representation on the basis of population ratios here so we can get our fair share. The new immigrants shouldn't think they're better than anyone else and try to dominate the Asian American political movement."[120]

The Asian-American community has been one of the most successful immigrant groups. The median family income of Asian-Americans is about the same as that of whites. The quote above demonstrates that economic clout can be translated into political clout, and some believe that Asian-Americans are second only to Jewish-Americans in campaign contributions.[121] The general success of Asian-Americans is apparent in Table 4–9.

TABLE 4–10

Social and Economic Characteristics of Latinos and Anglos

	% Anglos	% Mexican-American	% Puerto Rican	% Cuban	% Central and South American
Years of School Completed					
High school or higher	80.13	46.2	59.8	62.1	62.9
Bachelor's degree or higher	19.82	5.9	8.0	16.5	15.1
Family Income					
Below $10,000	29.0	52.3	60.1	41.0	51.6
$25,000 or more	71.1	47.7	40.0	58.9	47.0

Source: U.S. Bureau of the Census, *Statistical Abstract of the United States*, 115th ed. (Washington, D.C.: U.S. Government Printing Office, 1995), 48 and 51.

At the same time, the poverty level among Asian-Americans is almost twice that of whites, and for some groups the poverty rate is over one-third.[122] For example, 31.5 percent of Hmongs, 26.9 percent of Cambodians, and 18.9 percent of Laotians have family incomes below $10,000.[123] There is some evidence that the influx of new Asian immigrants has resulted in an increase in joblessness, school dropouts, and crime in Asian communities. This, in turn, has led to an increase in prejudice directed toward Asians. The small numbers of Asian-Americans means that to be effective politically they need to form alliances with others. Prejudice will make that task more difficult.

Conclusion

As did the earlier immigrants, the new immigrants are greatly increasing the heterogeneity of cities. All bring with them distinctive cultures, even African-Americans who had been in the country for generations. But these groups, to a greater degree than did earlier immigrant groups, found a city that is less hospitable to their goals and dreams. Urban areas are still places of opportunity, but primarily only for those with education and

training. Table 4–3 indicated that blacks tend to lag behind whites in levels of both education and income. Table 4–10 makes clear the same can be said for Latinos. This is not the case for many Asian immigrants as noted in Table 4–9. Some of the newer Asian immigrant groups, however, also lag behind whites.

Smokestack industries are closing or moving to the suburbs. The jobs open now to those with few skills are low paying and tend to offer little or no hope of advancement. Urban reformers have managed to remove or weaken urban political machines that could attempt to deal personally with problems faced by their constituents in return for votes. In their place "good government" structures that administer policy according to impersonal criteria have appeared. While all immigrants have had to face discrimination and prejudice, the skin color of many of the new immigrants exacerbates the problems of finding housing, jobs—and acceptance.

While many among these groups have followed older immigrants in moving up the social ladder, many appear at the moment to be stuck at the bottom. Some have feared that, for the first time, America is seeing the creation of a permanent underclass. If true, the clustering of that underclass in the metropolis will have serious implications.

To deal with the conditions facing them, many of the new immigrants are becoming increasingly politically active. They are voting in greater numbers. But the diversity of each of the groups may make it difficult to form a cohesive voting bloc that would convince a governing coalition that it must respond to the group's demands. In some cases, though, groups have formed such a bloc. African-Americans have become part of the governing coalition in cities where they managed to win elections. That may have an impact on policy because there is some indication that minority mayors are more likely to support increased spending for social programs. The point is that numbers alone do not guarantee power. For those numbers to be translated into political power, the group must compete effectively with the other major urban actors seeking to be part of the governing coalition or seeking to influence that coalition. Many of the other actors have advantages in the political process that new immigrants lack. The next part of the book will examine the major actors in urban politics and the means they have to attempt to influence the urban policy process.

Notes

1. David R. Goldfield, *Cotton Fields and Skyscrapers: Southern City and Region, 1607–1980* (Baton Rouge: Louisiana State University Press, 1982), 103–104, 165; and Lowell W. Culver, "Changing Settlement Patterns of Black Americans, 1970–1980," *Journal of Urban Affairs* 5, no. 4 (Fall 1982): 29–48.

2. Barry Edmonston and Jeffrey S. Passel, "Ethnic Demography: U.S. Immigration and Ethnic Variations" in *Immigration and Ethnicity: The Integration of America's Newest Arrivals*. ed. Barry Edmonston and Jeffrey S. Passel. (Washington, D.C.: Urban Institute, 1994), 8.

3. Ibid., 13.

4. Philip Kasinitz, *Caribbean New York: Black Immigrants and the Politics of Race* (Ithaca, New York, and London: Cornell University Press, 1992), 36.

5. Yen Le Espiritu, *Asian American Panethnicity: Bridging Institutions and Identities* (Philadelphia: Temple University Press, 1992), 171.

6. Gunner Myrdal with Richard Sterner and Arnold

7. George Sternlieb and James W. Hughes, "The Changing Demography of the Central City," *Scientific American* 243 (1980): 50.

8. Terry J. Rosenberg, *Residence, Employment, and Mobility of Puerto Ricans in New York City*, Research Paper No. 151 (Chicago: University of Chicago Department of Geography, 1974), 41.

9. Oscar Handlin, *The Newcomers: Negroes and Puerto Ricans in a Changing Metropolis* (Garden City, New York: Anchor Books, 1962), 76.

10. Ibid.

11. Ira Katznelson, *City Trenches: Urban Politics and the Patterning of Class in the United States* (Chicago: University of Chicago Press, 1981), Chapter 6; Steven P. Erie, *Rainbow's End: Irish-Americans and the Dilemmas of Urban Machine Politics, 1840–1985* (Berkeley: University of California Press, 1988), 245.

12. Douglas G. Glasgow, *The Black Underclass: Poverty, Unemployment, and Entrapment of Ghetto Youth* (San Francisco: Jossey-Bass, 1980), 12; see also Michael Lipsky, *Street-Level Bureaucracy: Dilemmas of the Individual in Public Service* (New York: Russell Sage Foundation, 1980), 151–156; and Norman I. Fainstein and Susan S. Fainstein, *Urban Political Movements* (Englewood Cliffs, New Jersey: Prentice-Hall, 1974).

13. Ibid.

14. George E. Peterson and Carol W. Lewis, "Introduction" in *Reagan and the Cities*, ed. George E. Peterson and Carol W. Lewis (Washington, D.C.: Urban Institute, 1986), 9.

15. Stephen Steinberg, *The Ethnic Myth: Race, Ethnicity, and Class in America* (New York: Atheneum, 1981), 191–199.

16. Ibid., 204.

17. Halford H. Fairchild and W. Belinda Tucker, "Black Residential Mobility: Trends and Characteristics," *Journal of Social Issues* 38 (1982): 54.

18. Nicholas Lemann, *The Promised Land: The Great Black Migration and How It Changed America* (New York: Vintage Books, 1991), 4.

19. Ibid., 7.

20. Fairchild and Tucker, "Black Residential Mobility," 56–59.

21. Katznelson, *City Trenches*, 177.

22. William Manchester, *The Glory and the Dream: A Narrative History of America, 1932–1972* (Boston: Little, Brown, 1974), 1155.

23. Ibid., 1250–1251.

24. Ibid., 1249–1251.

25. Ibid., 1305.

26. Ibid., 1322–1325.

27. Joe R. Feagin and Harlan Hahn, *Ghetto Revolts: The Politics of Violence in American Cities* (New York: Macmillan, 1965), 105.

28. Manchester, *The Glory and the Dream*, 1409.

29. Mark Baldassare, "Introduction" in *The Los Angeles Riots: Lessons for the Urban Future*, ed. Mark Baldassare (Boulder, Colorado: Westview Press, 1994), 1.

Rose, *An American Dilemma* (New York: Harper, 1944).

30. Feagin and Hahn, *Ghetto Revolts*, 202–204.

31. Edward C. Banfield, *The Unheavenly City Revisited* (Boston: Little, Brown, 1974), Chapter 9.

32. The National Advisory Commission on Civil Disorders, *Report of the National Advisory Commission on Civil Disorders* (New York: Bantam, 1968), 10.

33. James W. Button, *Black Violence: Political Impact of the 1960s Riots* (Princeton: Princeton University Press, 1978), 157.

34. Manchester, *The Glory and the Dream*, 1410.

35. John H. Mollenkopf, *The Contested City* (Princeton: Princeton University Press, 1983).

36. Hanes Walton, Jr., *Invisible Politics: Black Political Behavior* (Albany: State University of New York Press, 1985), 125–127.

37. Henry J. Abraham, *Freedom and the Court* (New York: Oxford University Press, 1967), 292–293.

38. Walton, *Invisible Politics*, 127.

39. Cited in Rodolfo O. de la Garza and Janet Weaver, "New Participants, Old Issues: Mexican-American Urban Policy Priorities" in *The Egalitarian City: Issues of Rights, Distribution, Access, and Power*, ed. Janet K. Boles (New York: Praeger, 1986), 76.

40. Daniel Patrick Moynihan, "Community Action Loses," in *The New Urban Politics: Cities and the Federal Government*, ed. Douglas M. Fox (Pacific Palisades, California: Goodyear, 1972), 173.

41. William E. Nelson, Jr., "Cleveland: The Rise and Fall of the New Black Politics" in *The New Black Politics: The Search for Political Power*, ed. Michael B. Preston, Lenneal J. Henderson, Jr., and Paul Puryear (New York: Longman, 1982), 204.

42. Manning Marable, "Building Coalitions among Communities of Color: Beyond Racial Identity Politics," in *Blacks, Latinos and Asians in Urban America: Status and Prospects for Politics and Activism*, ed. James Jennings (Westport, Connecticut: Praeger, 1994), 30.

43. Ibid.

44. John Hull Mollenkopf, *A Phoenix in the Ashes: The Rise and Fall of the Koch Coalition in New York City Politics* (Princeton: Princeton University Press, 1992), 222.

45. Peter K. Eisinger, "Black Mayors and the Politics of Racial Economic Advancement" in *Culture, Ethnicity, and Identity*, ed. William C. McCready (New York: Academic Press, 1983), 95–109.

46. John Mollenkopf, "New York: The Great Anomaly," *PS* 19 no. 3 (Summer 1986): 592.

47. U.S. Bureau of the Census, *Voting and Registration in Elections of November 1992*, Current Population Reports (Washington, D.C.: U.S. Department of Commerce, April 1993) 5.

48. Information received from a phone call to the National Conference of Black Mayors, October 1996.

49. Sharon Cohen, "Black Politicians Have Come Far in 20 Years," *Grand Forks Herald*, March 27, 1988, section C.

50. *New York Times*, Sunday, August 28, 1983.

51. U.S. Bureau of the Census, *Statistical Brief*, U.S. Department of Commerce (Washington, D.C.: U.S. Government Printing Office, May 1994).

52. E.R. Shipp, "'63 Marcher Sees Gains But a 'Long Way to Travel,'" *New York Times*, Sunday, August 28, 1983.

53. Baldassare, "Introduction," 3.

54. Ibid., 5.

55. Rodolfo O. de la Garza, Louis De Sipio, F. Chris Garcia, John Garcia, and Angel Falcon, *Latino Voices: Mexican, Puerto Rican and Cuban Perspectives on American Politics* (Boulder, Colorado: Westview Press, 1992), 13.

56. Ibid., 16.

57. Frank D. Bean, Jorge Chapa, Ruth R. Berg, and Kathryn A. Sowards, "Educational and Sociodemographic Incorporation Among Hispanic Immigrants to the United States" in *Immigration and Ethnicity*, ed. Barry Edmonston and Jeffrey S. Passel, 83.

58. Ibid.

59. F. Nathan Glazer and Daniel P. Moynihan, *Beyond the Melting Pot: The Negroes, Puerto Ricans, Jews, Italians, and Irish of New York City* 2nd ed. (Cambridge: Massachusetts Institute of Technology Press, 1970), 91–93.

60. James Jennings, "Introduction: The Emergence of Puerto Rican Electoral Activism in Urban America" in *Puerto Rican Politics in Urban America*, ed. James Jennings and Monte Rivera (Westport, Connecticut: Greenwood Press, 1984), 4.

61. Ibid., 5.

62. Ibid., 6.

63. Handlin, *The Newcomers*, 96.

64. Lawrence R. Chenault, *The Puerto Rican Migrant in New York* (New York: Columbia University Press, 1938), 82.

65. Maxine Seller, *To Seek America: A History of Ethnic Life in the United States* (Englewood, New Jersey: Jerome B. Ozer, 1977), 258.

66. Ibid., 262; Glazer and Moynihan, *Beyond the Melting Pot*, 108.

67. Beth Osborne Daponte, "Race and Ethnicity During an Economic Transition: The Withdrawal of Puerto Rican Women from New York City's Labour Force, 1960–1980," *Regional Studies* 30 (April 1996): 151.

68. Sherrie Baver, "Puerto Rican Politics in New York City: The Post–World War II Period" in *Puerto Rican Politics in Urban America*, ed. Jennings and Rivera, 45.

69. Ibid.

70. Maxine Howe, "Latin Politicians Focus on Registration Effort," *New York Times*, March 30, 1984, Sec. B.

71. Jennings, "Introduction" in *Puerto Rican Politics in Urban America*, ed. Jennings and Rivera, 7.

72. Ibid., 8.

73. Ibid., 4.

74. Baver, "Puerto Rican Politics in New York City" in *Puerto Rican Politics in Urban America*, ed. Jennings and Rivera, 56.

75. Joseph P. Fitzpatrick, "Puerto Rican New Yorkers 1990" *Migration World Magazine*, 23 (January–April 1995): 16.

76. James Jennings, "Puerto Rican Politics in Two Cities: New York and Boston," in *Puerto Rican Politics in Urban America*, ed. Jennings and Rivera, 92.

77. Ibid., 93.

78. James Jennings, "Conclusion: Puerto Rican Politics in Urban America—Toward Progressive Electoral Activism" in *Puerto Rican Politics in Urban America*, ed. Jennings and Rivera, 141–142.

79. Fitzpatrick, "Puerto Rican New Yorkers 1990," 16.

80. Douglas S. Massey and Kathleen M. Schnabel, "Recent Trends in Hispanic Immigration to the United States," *International Migration Review* 17 (1983), 218–219.

81. Mireya Navarro, "Recent Arrivals Quietly Change Little Havana," *New York Times*, April 6, 1997, sec. A1.

82. Ibid., 4.

83. Arva Moore Parks, *Miami: The Magic City* (Tulsa, Oklahoma: Continental Heritage Press, 1981), 154.

84. Alexandro Portes, Juan M. Clark, and Manuel Lopez, "Six Years Later, The Process of Incorporation of Cuban Exiles in the United States: 1973–1979," *Cuban Studies* 11 (July 1981): 1–24.

85. Thomas D. Boswell and James R. Curtis, *The Cuban-American Experience: Culture, Images, and Perspectives* (Totowa, New Jersey: Rowman and Allanheld, 1984), 175.

86. Dario Moreno and Christopher L. Warren, "The Cuban Community in the 1992 Presidential Election," *Harvard Journal of Hispanic Policy Annual* 6 (1992): 27.

87. Navarro, "Recent Arrivals Change Little Havana," 12.

88. "Whiff of Havana," *Economist* 280 (August 1, 1981): 33.

89. Boswell and Curtis, *The Cuban-American Experience*, 175.

90. Navarro, "Recent Arrivals Quickly Change Little Havana," 12.

91. Dale McLemore and Ricardo Romo, "The Origins and Development of the Mexican American People" in *The Mexican American Experience: An Interdisciplinary Anthology*, ed. Rodolfo O. de la Garza, Frank D. Bean, Charles Bonjean, Ricardo Romo, and Rodolfo Alvarez (Austin: University of Texas Press, 1985), 15.

92. U.S. Bureau of the Census, *General Population Statistics*, (Washington, D.C.: Department of Commerce, 1990.)

93. For histories of Mexican-Americans, see Dale McLemore and Ricardo Romo, "The Origins and Development of the Mexican American People," in *The Mexican American Experience*, ed. de la Garza, et. al.; Mario Barrera, *Race and Class in the Southwest: A Theory of Racial Inequality* (Notre Dame, Indiana: University of Notre Dame Press, 1979), Chapter 2; and Rodolfo Acuna, *Occupied America: A History of Chicano*, 2nd ed. (New York: Harper & Row, 1981).

94. Leo Grebler, Joan W. Moore, and Ralph C. Guzman, *The Mexican-American People: The Nation's Second Largest Minority* (New York: Free Press, 1970), 514.

95. Raphael J. Sonenshein, *Politics in Black and White: Race and Power in Los Angeles*, (Princeton: Princeton University Press, 1993), 247.

96. Navarro, "Recent Arrivals Quickly Change Little Havana," 12.

97. This discussion of categories of Mexican-American organizations relies on F. Chris Garcia and Rodolpho O. de la Garza, *The Chicano Political Experience: Three Perspectives* (N. Scituate, Massachusetts: Duxbury, 1977).

98. Grebler, Moore, and Guzman, *The Mexican-American People*, 513.

99. F. Chris Garcia, Rodolfo O. de la Garza, and Donald J. Torres, "Introduction" in *The Mexican American Experience*, ed. de la Garza, et al., 188.

100. Clifton McCleskey and Bruce Merrill, "Mexican-American Political Behavior in Texas," *Social Science Quarterly* 53 (March 1973): 785–798; Susan Welch, John Comer, and Michael Steinman, "Political Participation Among Mexican-Americans: An Exploratory Examination," *Social Science Quarterly* 53 (March 1973): 799–813.

101. de la Garza and Weaver, "New Participants, Old Issues" in *The Egalitarian City*, Boles, 21.

102. John A. Garcia, "The Voting Rights Act and Hispanic Political Representation in the Southwest" *Publius: The Journal of Federalism* 16 (Fall 1986): 49–66.

103. Ibid., 76–77.

104. Susan A. MacManus and Charles S. Bullock III, "Mexican-American Political Clout in Small Urban Jurisdiction: Conditions for Maximizing Influence" in *The Egalitarian City*, ed. Boles, 21.

105. Ibid., 24.

106. Garcia, "The Voting Rights Act and Hispanic Political Representation in the Southwest," 66.

107. U.S. Bureau of the Census, *1990 Census of the Population General Population Characteristics, Metropolitan Areas, Section 1*, (Washington, D.C.: U.S. Government Printing Office, November 1992), 59.

108. U.S. Bureau of the Census, *Voting Registration in the Election of November 1992* (Washington, D.C.: Department of Commerce, April 1993), 5.

109. U.S. Bureau of the Census, *Statistical Abstract of the United States, 1995* 115th ed., (Washington, D.C.: U.S. Department of Commerce, 1995), 287.

110. Sharon M. Lee and Barry Edmonston, "The Socioeconomic Status and Integration of Asian Immigrants" in *Immigration and Ethnicity*, ed. Edmonston and Passel, 103.

111. U.S. Bureau of the Census, *General Population Statistics: Current Population Survey* (Washington, DC: U.S. Government Printing Office, March 1994), 14.

112. Frank D. Bean, Jorge Chapa, Ruth R. Berg, and Kathryn Sowards, "Educational and Socioeconomic Incorporation Among Hispanic Immigrants to the United States" in *Immigration and Ethnicity*, ed. Edmonston and Passel; Douglas S. Massey and Nancy A. Denton, "Trends in the Residential Segregation of Blacks, Hispanics, and Asians: 1970–1980," *American Sociological Review* 52 (December 1987): 802–825.

113. William P. O'Hare and Judy C. Felt, *Asian Americans: America's Fastest Growing Minority Group* (Washington, D.C.: Population Reference Bureau, 1991).

114. Yen Le Espiritu, *Asian American Panethnicity: Bridging Institutions and Identities* (Philadelphia: Temple University Press, 1992), 19.

115. Ibid.

116. Ibid., 29–31.

117. Ibid., 33.

118. Sucheng Chan, *Asian Americans: An Interpretive History* (Boston: Twayne, 1991), 175.

119. Yvonne M. Lau, "Political Participation among Chicago Asian Americans" in *Asian Americans: Comparative and Global Perspectives*, ed. Shirley Hume, et al. (Pullman: Washington State University Press, 1991), 144.

120. Ibid.

121. William Wong, "Asian Americans Shake Off Stereotypes, Increase Clout as Political Activism Grows," *Los Angeles Times*, February 23, 1988. The issue of campaign contributions from Asians in the 1996 presidential election is currently being investigated by Congress.

122. Sharon M. Lee and Barry Edmonston, "The Socioeconomic Status and Integration of Asian Immigrants" in *Immigration and Ethnicity*, ed. Edmonston and Passel, 103.

123. U.S. Bureau of the Census, *Social and Economic Characteristics*, 1990 Census of the Population (Washington, D.C.: U.S. Government Printing Office, November 1993), 118.

PART II

Agenda Setting and Policy Formulation of Urban Issues

The context of the city is the milieu out of which citizen concerns and demands arise. The heterogeneity, impersonality, and interdependence of urban living provide many incentives for citizens to attempt to get their concerns on the public agenda. But for that to happen, citizens must organize and become politically active. This part of the book examines those groups that are most active in attempting to influence the urban agenda and the means they use.

Agenda Setting

The policy process begins when people recognize that a problem exists. To become a public issue, the problem must be seen as having a broad impact. A Main Street store going bankrupt is generally seen as a private problem. However, many Main Street merchants going bankrupt may be seen as a public problem requiring public action. There is no absolute standard to judge what situations lend themselves to public sector activity. The context discussed in the last section is important in determining which problems government will address.

Roger Cobb and Charles Elder were among the first to study the significance of the role of agenda setting in determining public policy outcomes.

> Whether or not a situation is considered a public problem and what the problem is, if there is one, depends upon not just facts but on beliefs and values—beliefs and values that determine what is taken to be fact. . . . Because public problems are socially constructed, a multiplicity of definitions of the problem is always possible.[1]

Many situations that might be considered public problems amenable to solution, or at least action, are never or rarely considered by government.

> The ease with which an issue can reach the public agenda, where it will be scheduled for serious consideration, is known as the *penetrability* of the political system. . . . Penetrability is determined partly by the nature of the issue, partly by the credibility of the individual or group raising the issue, and partly by characteristics of the political system itself. [Italics in original.][2]

Some issues are abhorrent in our political culture. For instance, we do not believe that government should establish policies telling us how to raise our children. Any policy in this area would be seen as challenging our basic freedoms. Yet most Americans accept the right of local government to limit working hours of children or to impose curfews, though this was not the case in the past. The value of privatism, discussed in Chapter 2, means that many Americans want to keep the public agenda limited, especially at the local level. Public policy should leave as many resources as possible in private hands and should aim at helping individuals augment those resources. As indicated in Part I, the importance of the impersonality, heterogeneity, and interdependence of urban living is that those characteristics tend to increase the number of issues on the public agenda.

As the political culture and the nature of society change, different issues may reach the public agenda. Which issues reach the public agenda is also affected by the power distribution in the political system. A major power of those who are part of the governing coalition is their ability to define the issues for public debate. They may attempt to keep certain issues off the public agenda. Even though those issues are not discussed, a decision has implicitly been made about them. The lack of discussion means that the status quo will be maintained. Some analysts call the making of decisions by refusing to discuss an issue **nondecision making**. Citizens who feel they have a problem but who do not have the resources to get that problem discussed publicly have little hope for a public solution.

> The very agenda of legitimate conflict is shaped by widely accepted and unquestioned belief systems and power distributions that predispose the decision maker to view the claims of certain groups as "reasonable" or "essential" and the claims of other groups as "questionable" or "outrageous."[3]

Those who want to get their issues on the public agenda can use symbols and strategies to "expand the scope of conflict"—that is to get the issue to the stage of discussion. To convince people of the legitimacy of the cause, proponents may link the issue to words that symbolize popular values. Symbols are a few expressive words that are used to stir emotions and paint a picture. Symbolic language is used to rally supporters or to promote quiescence.[4] For example, a new convention center or sports stadium would most likely help hotel, bar, and restaurant owners. They will seek to win support by appealing to others with symbols such as civic pride or economic development. The sports stadium will be defended because it will provide increased "family" recreational opportunities for the average citizen. Opponents of such issues may use symbols such as high taxes or the fear of a "white elephant" (that is, an expensive facility that does not attract conventioneers or sports teams) to preserve the status quo.

At any given time the public will raise more issues than government can handle. Homelessness is an example of a long-term problem that suddenly burst on the public agenda in the 1980s. Anyone living in a large city knew for a long time of areas where people slept in alleyways, on park benches, or under overpasses. These homeless people kept warm in winter by going to public libraries, "camping" on heating vents, or riding public transportation. They were often helped by such private groups as the Salvation Army. Until recently, this was not an issue for the public agenda because the homeless were defined as lazy, dirty, often alcoholic individuals who were not deserving of public sympathy or assistance.

Those seeking to get the issue on the agenda pointed out that a decrease in affordable urban housing has led to a great increase in the number of homeless. Now rather than just "shiftless bums," entire families, including children, are without shelter. In addition, many homeless are mentally ill—they are patients who have been deinstitutionalized and are unable to care for themselves. The homeless are presented as unfortunate, not undeserving. Attention has been drawn to their plight by demonstrations such as the sleep-ins in Lafayette Park, across from the White House, in which senators, representatives, and celebrities participated. Much media attention was focused on homelessness, and it was firmly on the public agenda by the end of the 1980s. Policies dealing with the homeless will be discussed in Chapter 14.

Some urban problems appear on the local government agenda, other urban problems are on the national government agenda, and some are on both or neither agenda. This is because different issues and groups have varying degrees of access to the different levels of government. On the one hand, this aids democracy because multiple access points are available. Groups can pursue their goals at the level where they have maximum strength. On the other hand, it helps to explain the often conflicting and disjointed policies designed to solve our urban problems. Different governments may enact contradictory policies.

For example, the federal government requires local governments to integrate their schools as a condition for federal aid to communities. Some communities complied by busing students, sending white students into areas where blacks predominated or black students into white areas. Many white parents with the resources to do so moved out of the community or sent their children to private schools—both resulted in increased segregation. The federal government has traditionally supported many highway programs, fostering use of the automobile; local governments have closed streets and provided low-cost public transportation to discourage auto use in congested cities.

Formulation

Once an issue has reached the public agenda, the next stage of the policy process is to develop policy proposals for governments to act on. Hence **policy formulation** can be defined as "the development of pertinent and acceptable proposed courses of action for dealing with public problems."[5] At this stage specific solutions must be attached to general problems before action can take place.

For example, economic and community development is a major problem for most American cities. Several cities, such as Sacramento, California, Pittsburgh, and Philadelphia have formulated programs aimed at attracting major league sports teams as one means of economic development. They can choose many alternative strategies. Sacramento attracted the Kings basketball team by allowing its owner to develop land that was formerly reserved for agriculture. Pittsburgh lent the Pirates baseball team more than $20 million—which must be paid back if the team ever leaves. Philadelphia kept the Eagles football team by offering rent concessions and skybox revenues.[6]

Robert Eyestone has noted that once an issue is raised, it is critical for someone or group in or out of government to provide alternatives, that is, to play the role of an "issue entrepreneur."[7] The formulation stage may be the most crucial in determining how the problem will be resolved, hence the role of the "issue entrepreneur" is key. As E.E. Schattschneider argued:

> Political conflict is not like an intercollegiate debate in which the opponents agree in advance on a definition of the issues. As a matter of fact, *the definition of alternatives is the supreme instrument of power*.[8] [Italics added.]

The definition of alternatives is important for achieving agenda status, but it is at least equally important to define the issue to maximize support at the next stage of the policy process—the stage of policy adoption. For instance, a program to fight poverty by providing young children from disadvantaged backgroups with remedial education would be more likely to be adopted than one to ensure a guaranteed minimum income. Head Start, which helps educate children who are from disadvantaged backgrounds, has been an established program for years because people care about young children and believe that early education will help get people out of poverty. The proposal by President Richard Nixon to provide a guaranteed minimum income was never adopted because it appeared to contradict the basic American value of privatism.

The next two chapters examine the groups that are most often the major contenders in influencing the government agenda and the strategies they can use. Such groups want to become part of the governing coalition or to have enough influence so that a coalition must be attentive to their demands. Chapter 5 discusses the major urban actors, highlighting the importance of major business interests. In addition, it examines the major citizen groups that will likely be active at the local level. Chapter 6 reviews the mechanisms of citizen control, discussing the importance of organization for citizen success, and looks at such participation mechanisms as elections, citizen contacting of government, protests, and public hearings.

Notes

1. Roger W. Cobb and Charles D. Elder, *Participation in American Politics: The Dynamics of Agenda-Building*, 2nd ed. (Baltimore: Johns Hopkins University Press, 1983), 23.

2. Bryan D. Jones, *Governing Urban America: A Policy Focus* (Boston: Little, Brown, 1983), 23.

3. Michael Parenti, "Power and Pluralism: A View From the Bottom," *Journal of Politics* 32 (1970): 529.

4. Murray Edelman, *The Symbolic Uses of Politics* (Urbana: University of Illinois Press, 1964).

5. Charles S. Bullock, James E. Anderson, and David W. Brady, *Public Policy in the Eighties* (Monterey, California: Brooks/Cole, 1983), 7.

6. William Fulton, "Politicians Who Chase After Sports Franchises May Get Less than They Pay For," *Governing* 1, no. 6 (March 1988): 34–40.

7. Robert Eyestone, *From Social Issues to Public Policy* (New York: John Wiley, 1978), 89.

8. E.E. Schattschneider, *The Semi-Sovereign People* (New York: Holt, Rinehart & Winston, 1960), 68.

CHAPTER 5

Urban Actors

Democracy demands that citizens play some role in making the decisions that govern them. Citizens in a democracy are not supposed to be simply passive targets of government policy; they should also participate. The policies of urban governments are always the result of participation of some citizens. The key question is the extent to which the demands that officials respond to and the policies they pursue can be representative of the interests of the whole urban population. Evidence indicates that reality falls far short of being representative of the entire population of a city.

Participation is not only important normatively as an integral component of a democratic political system, it is also important as a political resource. Citizens who want their concerns addressed by the urban political system must have resources that are valued by members of the governing coalition. In many cases, the resources derive from some form of participation. In the case of Atlanta discussed earlier, the key resource controlled by the African-American community was votes. The Atlanta case also illustrates that while it is individuals who participate, those individuals, to be effective, usually must work together in groups. One citizen alone rarely has the resources to influence the urban agenda. To understand who

might be successful in using participation to affect the urban agenda, we must understand the nature of citizen participation. What determines who participates? What is the likelihood that any individual in the city can use participation as a political resource?

Determinants of Participation

There are two categories of determinants of participation: characteristics of the individuals themselves and characteristics of the context in which the individuals live. Although these can be analytically divided for purposes of discussion, in the real world, the individual and contextual factors often interact so that certain people are likely to participate in certain situations.

Individual Determinants

Of all the individual factors that affect citizen participation, none has resulted in such consistent research results as the effect of socioeconomic status, usually measured by income, occupation, and education. Simply stated, those people of higher socioeconomic status are more likely to participate.

. . . the higher-status individual has a greater stake in politics, he has greater skills, more resources, greater awareness of political matters, he is exposed to more communications about politics, he interacts with others who participate.[1]

There are three explanations of why those of upper socioeconomic status participate more in politics: awareness, resources, and issues. One is that they are more likely to be aware of the stakes they have in politics. Their higher educational level enables them to understand the complex political process and the issues with which it deals. The second reason is that they are more likely to be successful in achieving what they want from politics. This is due, at least in part, to their greater resources. Their higher incomes, greater education, and more prestigious occupations are all resources that can be translated into political currency. Officials know this and are likely to skew policy actions to suit the needs of those who have those resources: ". . . officials operate in a stratified society. The system of stratification is a motivating factor in all that they do; it predisposes them to favor upper—over lower—strata interests."[2]

A final reason is the fact that much of the public agenda already involves issues that are of concern to upper-income people. Development issues are a common agenda item for many governments in the metropolis. Proponents, often business interests, argue for programs that are designed to bolster the local economy, for example, a new civic center or special tax provisions for a business planning to build a new office building. While some, often middle-class residents, may battle against the project because of fears about the effect on their tax rate, low-income residents, many of whom pay little or nothing in income taxes and pay property taxes indirectly—and therefore invisibly—through their rent payments, see little in the debate to interest or mobilize them.

This situation can become a vicious circle. Because those with low incomes do not get involved, officials see little need to define issues of concern to them.[3] And the low-income population has few resources to force issues that concern them onto the public agenda. Even protest, a form of political activity to which "relatively powerless" people resort, requires resources that the low-income population may lack.[4]

Another reason for the greater political activity of higher-status people is the fact that they are more likely to be targeted by political parties, interest groups, and other organizations attempting to mobilize political participation. Such high-status people are more visible to political leaders. In addition, leaders know that such people will be more likely to respond to an effort to mobilize them to political action.[5]

Although participants are more likely to come from the middle and upper classes of society, that would not be a problem if those from the middle and upper classes shared values, preferences, and interests with those in the working or lower classes. However, a recent study of participation found that participants differed from the population as a whole and the result was bias in the representation of issues.

> Whether we are considering attitudes on the economy, actual economic circumstances and needs, or opinions on government efforts to assist Blacks or Latinos, the process operates to bias participatory input in the direction of the needs and preferences of the advantaged.[6]

While the role of socioeconomic status leads to a bias in the participating public, other factors may offset that bias. The development of a group consciousness among blacks may substitute for the effect of social status and become an alternate way that citizens are mobilized for political action.[7] If individuals not only perceive themselves as a member of a group, but also believe that group to be in a subordinate position in society due to reasons beyond the control of group members, they may be especially likely to become politically active.

> The critical element in this process, however, is the translation of personal experience into collective action through evaluation of the group's relative position in society and the development of a systemic rather than a self-directed explanation for one's current status.[8]

The civil rights movement probably played a major role in the development in the African-American community of a group consciousness and a belief that their position in society was due to racial prejudice and discrimination.

> At issue was not simply a set of divisible benefits of patronage and services; rather, such questions, which had been at the core of modern urban politics since the antebellum period, were joined to questions of governance, and together they were connected to a larger analysis of black–white relations that demanded a fundamental transformation of the social structure.[9]

Contextual Determinants

Participation takes place in a context. The characteristics of the urban life-style—interdependence, heterogeneity, and impersonality—affect the incentives for participation. The interdependence of urban living may be related to a greater willingness to seek political solutions for problems or needs.

> In fact, a case can be made that, with respect to the problem with which municipal bureaucracy deals, we find a public ethic of "quality services by right" that *encourages* the translation of personal problems into political demand making.[10]

While interdependence may encourage political activity, the effect of heterogeneity on participation is not clear. Heterogeneity may discourage participation because being surrounded by those who differ may make it difficult for people to feel the sense of community that would encourage participation.[11] In addition, because participation is often a collective action, heterogeneity would make joining with others more difficult because the likelihood of conflict is greater among those who differ.

On the other hand, the recognition that one is different from one's neighbors may lead to the conclusion that political participation is necessary to protect one's own interests. The very difference of values, and the conflict that results, then becomes an impetus to participate.

> The very diversity of the neighborhood has built into it the obligation of responsibility; there would be no way to avoid self-destruction in the community other than to deal with the people who live around the place. The feeling that "I live here and I count in this community's life" would consist, not of a feeling of companionship, but of a feeling that something must be done in common to make this conflict bearable, to survive together.[12]

One study found that diversity in neighborhoods does increase participation, but only certain kinds of diversity and only among some of the residents. Specifically when a "socially advantaged minority" lives among neighbors who are less well-off, that minority is likely to become active in attempting to solve what they see as the problems of the neighborhood.[13]

The impersonality of urban living may deter socially-based participation—participation that requires cooperation among people to achieve social goals. Here again higher-status people have an advantage because such participation is more common in higher-status neighborhoods.[14]

Not only do their greater personal resources (e.g., higher levels of education and income) enhance their participation and power, but their participation is further enhanced by residence in higher status contexts where they interact with others of similar status. Thus, the effects of increased status are mutually reinforcing.[15]

Another contextual factor affecting participation is the structure of the city government. Focusing on voting as a form of participation, many studies have confirmed that those governmental systems where candidates' party identification is not listed on the ballot are less likely to have high voter turnouts than do those governments in which elections are partisan. Typical of this research is that of Albert Karnig and B. Oliver Walters who concluded: "Whatever their other advantages, nonpartisan and council–manager governments are not systems that promote citizen participation in elections."[16]

A recent study pointed to the importance of a city's political culture in affecting the perceived legitimacy of various urban participants. In a comparison of the role of neighborhood organizations in Chicago and Pittsburgh, Barbara Ferman found that in the political culture of Chicago, neighborhood organizations are viewed by the governing coalition as adversaries, while in the more cooperative and civil culture of Pittsburgh, such organizations are seen as important to civic life.[17] As a result, in Pittsburgh the governing coalition accommodated neighborhood organizations, while in Chicago the coalition strongly resisted demands from such organizations.

While grass roots organizations can succeed, business groups have particular success because of the variety of resources they command. First, individual businesses have an existing organizational structure that is staffed with people who have an interest in seeing the business prosper. Employees can clearly iden-

tify their self-interest with that of the organization. Other groups must find ways to organize and mobilize people to action. Second, money, of course, is a major help in organizing campaigns to influence government—money to hire consultants, copy writers, and speech writers; money to buy media ads. Third, the status of businesspeople and the general sense of respect that Americans have for business is another reason why business groups tend to enjoy political success. Business is so totally identified with American values that business groups in cities often are not conceived of as interest groups. Unlike neighborhood groups or ethnic groups that are seen as representing "special" or narrow interests, when business groups such as the Chamber of Commerce speak, others often perceive them to be speaking for the public good. Their requests, therefore, have greater legitimacy.

Finally, Paul Peterson argues that urban governments must rely on business because the prosperity of business affects the prosperity of the community. Local government officials pursue policies that will contribute to the economic well-being of the community. He writes: "Quite apart from any effects of economic prosperity on government revenues or local voting behavior, it is quite reasonable to posit that local governments are primarily interested in maintaining the economic vitality of the area for which they are responsible."[18] In constructing policy to achieve economic strength, officials normally look to community leaders, who are often local businesspersons, for advice because those people are believed to be "well acquainted with the problems of fostering economic growth."[19] That means that when business speaks, political leaders listen, even if they do not always obey.[20] Because of the importance of business as a participant in urban politics, this review of major participants in urban politics begins with a discussion of business.

Business

Of all the groups that are important in urban politics, it may well be that more has been written about business than any other. The question of the degree to which major economic interests control urban policy is central to the study of urban politics, and some authors identify business as the dominant participant controlling the urban political landscape. Many of those who study America's urban areas are ". . . less likely to believe that businessmen are simply another, albeit powerful, interest group" because they believe business controls local government.[21]

The metropolis needs business and will not survive without it. Residents must have jobs or they will move. Local government must have tax revenues to provide services to residents. Therefore officials and most residents will identify their interests with business interests. Intensifying the willingness to comply with business demands is the recognition that for some businesses, the local government needs business more than business needs the locality. For example, many businesses can easily exit to locations more favorable than center cities. Businesses specializing in manufacturing, which used to be the economic foundation of cities like Newark, New Jersey, or Cleveland, Ohio, have long since adopted technologies that demand sprawling physical plants rather than the vertical plants of the past. As discussed in Chapter 3, such businesses find moving out of the city especially tempting since the large amounts of land needed are less expensive in rural or suburban areas. Banks may remain in the city but make their investments elsewhere. The ability of businesses to exit the city either physically or fiscally may make public power subservient to private power.

Those who believe in the dominance of business are often referred to as **elitist** theorists. An elite is a small unrepresentative group that holds power. Referring to some theorists as elitists does not mean those theorists desire elite control, but rather that they believe that an elite is in control.[22] While the arguments of elitists vary, they tend to believe that a single upper-class elite, often referred to as a **power elite**, rules in its own interest in the community and that political and civic leaders are subordinate to the wishes of this elite. C. Wright Mills describes this elite: "The people of the higher circles may also be conceived as members of a top social stratum, as a set of groups whose members know one another, see one another socially and at business, and so, in making decisions take one another into account."[23]

Floyd Hunter conducted the first major empirical study that concluded that an elite dominated power in urban politics by examining "Regional City," which was actually Atlanta, Georgia. To determine the distribution of power in Atlanta, Hunter used a methodology known as the **reputational approach**. He compiled lists of prominent people from various areas of Atlanta's social structure: government leaders, civic leaders, business leaders, and status leaders. He then asked six "judges," who were deemed to be knowledgeable about Atlanta, to select from those lists the most influential people in the city.

Based upon overlap in the selections made by these 6 judges, Hunter produced a list of 40 people who, he claimed, composed Atlanta's power structure. Most were members of the board of directors of the same corporations. This group, according to Hunter, controlled the politics of Atlanta,[24] and therefore an elite was in power in Atlanta.

Some elite theorists claim the elite maintains its control by consciously manipulating culture and the political process. Clarence Stone rejects the argument that the elite consciously conspire to dominate politics and society. Yet he recognizes that, "Major business enterprises and other upper-strata interests seem to have an influence on local decisions not warranted by their numbers or their overt participation in political and governmental affairs."[25] This means business dominates in ways that are often invisible and behind the scenes, due to what Stone calls "systemic power."

> . . . systemic power grows out of the fact that as officeholders make decisions, they take into account: (1) economic considerations—especially the government's revenue needs; (2) associational considerations—capacities of various groups to engage in and sustain policy and other goal-oriented actions; and (3) social status and life-style considerations—especially as they bear on professional and career accomplishments.[26]

He argues that business interests are not necessarily a part of the informal governing arrangements that he refers to as **regimes**, but he believes that it is important to give business interests special consideration for two reasons: "One reason is the now well-understood need to encourage business investment in order to have an economically thriving community. A second reason is the sometimes overlooked factor that businesses control politically important resources and are rarely absent totally from the scene."[27] Members of the lower strata, meanwhile, do not have such control over important resources. They are "unlikely to succeed individually and unlikely to contribute collectively to the well-being of the whole community," and can therefore be ignored.[28] The elite dominate not because of a conspiracy or cabal, but because officeholders need them.

The existence of elite power has serious implications for the potential of popular control in cities. If an elite does dominate, then participation by other citizens would be meaningless. But not all observers agree that business interests can totally dominate urban decision making. Some have argued that business is one among many participants in urban politics and competes with other participants for political power. This is referred to as **plu-**

ralism, which is a system in which multiple groups compete for power.

Robert Dahl's classic study of New Haven, Connecticut, concluded that pluralism best describes the distribution of urban power. Dahl did not use Hunter's reputational methodology, but rather a **decision-making** approach. He focused on three major areas: the selection of mayoral candidates, urban renewal, and education. He then selected 34 important decisions that had been made in those areas over 18 years: 1941 to 1959. Dahl found that individuals who participated and had power in one area were not important in the other two areas and economic elites—the corporate boards of directors—did not dominate the decision making in all three areas. Power was shared by many groups, composing a pluralist power structure.[29]

Critiques of both Dahl's and Hunter's studies suggest that their methodologies may have predetermined their results. Hunter's critics have argued that to present people with lists and tell them to pick those with influence predisposes the respondents to choose a name, whether or not a power elite actually exists. That is, the respondents may feel they *should* produce a list for the researcher even if they know nothing about the influence of the people they are naming. Others have pointed out that Hunter's methodology actually may measure the reputation of having power, but that may not be the same as actually having power.

Dahl's critics point out that his choice of issues was a crucial determinant of what he found. Even the most ardent power-elite theorists often argue that the elite control those issues of primary importance to them and let others have their way in other areas. So, the critics said, Dahl had simply picked issues about which the power elite was not concerned.

The conflict between the two findings may not be as substantial as it appears. The power structures in the two cities studied may have differed, and thus both studies may be accurate pictures. Other researchers, using both reputational and decision-making approaches, found that having a reputation for being powerful increased the probability of participating in decision making.[30] Thus either approach may identify those in power.

In communities where a single business dominates the economy, that business can very likely exercise substantial control over local decisions. In communities where the economy is more diversified, the ability of a business "power elite" to control local politics may be limited by disagreement among business interests.

Even in an area like tax policy, different businesses may oppose each other. All businesses want to keep taxes low, but the policies to do that may differ for different businesses. For example, a firm thinking of moving into another city may seek tax exemptions to help make the move more attractive, while those firms already in the city may oppose that since such exemptions may mean higher taxes for them. Similarly, all businesses want to grow, but those businesses thinking of expanding into a new city may be opposed by businesses already in place, which would now welcome competition. Real estate agencies often favor strict zoning laws to protect the value of single-family residential areas, while developers may want more flexible laws to permit building whatever kind of housing for which there is a market at any given time.

While businesses may not control all policy in all cities, it is probable that municipal officials will implicitly grant business virtual veto power over policies that affect it. When business interests are believed to be powerful, they often can succeed in keeping issues from emerging on the policy agenda of the city or can affect the development of issues that do emerge.[31]

The power of businesses in urban politics extends beyond policies that have direct and immediate impact on them. In fact, during

the fiscal crisis in New York City in the 1970s, the price of the bailout was to surrender power to an unelected board, composed primarily of business interests. The impact of business in the governing of cities has meant that blacks, Latinos, and other minorities were systematically disadvantaged in their efforts to participate in urban elections.[32]

Businesses can, in some cases, exact concessions and accommodations from local governments. For example, General Motors presented the city of Detroit with multiple demands to facilitate the construction of a new Cadillac plant in the Poletown section of the city.

> Once the bargain between the city and the company had been struck, an air of intense crisis pervaded the decision-making process. Deadlines imposed by General Motors were inflexible, and much had to be done. . . . City officials had to acquire nearly seventeen hundred pieces of property, relocate more than thirty-five hundred residents, demolish fifteen hundred residential and commercial structures, and complete the site preparation in less than eighteen months. Moreover, the process was complicated enormously by the need to obtain financing immediately and the need to secure waivers of certain federal requirements relating to urban renewal and air quality.[33]

Despite objections of Poletown's residents to the demolition of homes and neighborhood institutions, Detroit proceeded to meet the company's demands.

It is probably too simplistic to argue that in most cities a single, monolithic business elite dominates political decision making. Yet governments in the metropolis rely upon the economic resources produced by the business community for their very existence. In his analysis of Atlanta, Clarence Stone argued: "Although the nature of business involvement extends from the direct and extensive to the indirect and limited, the economic role of businesses *and the resources they control* are too important for these enterprises to be left out completely."[34] In the governing coalitions that Stone refers to as regimes, business will normally be a vital member. The intimate connection between the strength of business and the vitality of cities can be verified by looking at what happened to cities like Youngstown, Ohio; Gary, Indiana; and Detroit, Michigan, when the dominant businesses in them collapsed or weakened. And, at least in Atlanta, Stone argues that the unity of business and its control over resources has enabled it to preempt other forces in the city and become an integral part of the ruling coalition.[35]

This is especially the case for businesses that are tied to the urban place. For those who own land in the city or whose customers are primarily residents of the city, the place itself is the source of income. Major land development companies, local media, and local utilities are examples. Such place-based businesses need the political system to pursue policies that encourage constant growth to ensure the flow of revenue. As the number of people competing for a finite supply of land increases, the value of the land increases, as will sales of local newspapers and demand for water, transportation, and other utilities.

John Logan and Harvey Molotch argue that the consensus among the members of a governing coalition on the importance of growth results in the city becoming a **"growth machine."**[36] They argue that such a growth machine will vigilantly pursue policies that will increase the value of land—its exchange value—without concern for the impact of those policies on other residents in the city—the use value of land. Important to a growth machine coalition is a political system that is willing to use its resources to help "to attract new capital and to sustain old investments."[37]

Media

The major communications media in urban areas are a special case of the role that business plays in urban politics as well as a traditional component of a growth machine coalition. The media—newspapers, radio, and television—like all private businesses need to make a profit to exist. To function, they must sell their product to consumers and advertisers. But the media also see themselves as performing at least one and perhaps two other roles in the urban area. First, they are *public informers,* responsible for ensuring important information is available to all citizens. This information is, of course, the product that they sell, but people in the media business tend to view their role as informers as a civic duty as well as part of their job.

Second, some media—especially newspapers—assume the responsibility of influencing the direction of public opinion and public policy. The role as *influencer,* of course, overlaps the informer role, as information can be an important way of influencing people. It also overlaps the media's role as a major component of the business community because the goals that the media seek are often aimed at "creating a good business climate" in the city.[38]

Media as Business. To make a profit, the American media must sell their product. For newspapers, that means, in part, selling copies of the paper. But the bulk of their money comes from selling space for advertisements. For television and radio, ads are the sole source of revenue. The necessity of selling advertising in order to exist may limit the sort of news that will be covered. For example, exposés of business shenanigans or corruption could be potentially dangerous for the media because the businesses exposed could move their advertising dollars to other media. In addition, advertisers want to buy time or space in those media that have the largest audience, thus decisions about what news will be covered as well as what programs or features will be highlighted are based, in large part, on the level of public interest. As a result, the media's roles as informant and influencer must be played out within the limits imposed by the bottom line of the balance sheet.

Because the media are businesses, they tend to be prominent boosters for projects or policies aimed at creating a good business climate. It is especially common for newspapers to be major components of local growth machines pushing for economic development projects—projects that are justified as benefiting the city as a whole but that often benefit businesses such as contracting firms, real estate agencies, and banks more than the citizens relocated during construction. The support of such projects helps the media both appear to be public-spirited and concerned about civic betterment and earn the gratitude of the businesses that will directly profit.

Media as Informer. Although limited by the imperatives of the balance sheet, people in the media, for the most part, have been socialized into a professional ethic that leads them to view themselves as protectors and defenders of the public good. Reporters usually view the news reporting function more as a way of providing information to help citizens behave rationally than as a means of making a profit. Their ability to adhere consistently to this professional ethic is limited, however.

Reporters, of course, do not control the final decisions about what appears in print or on the air. Those decisions rest with editors, publishers, or station managers who keep an eye on the balance sheet. Crusades do occur, more commonly in newspapers than on television or radio, both of which make a consistent effort to appear to be neutral. Newspaper crusades can sell papers or may produce a Pulitzer prize to enhance the paper's reputation. But crusades tend not to be designed to question the status quo, because such ques-

tions may make investors and potential investors in the city rethink their investment portfolios.

There are other limits on the media's ability to provide extensive coverage and analysis of local government. Few resources are devoted to covering local politics because such news coverage is considered too boring to attract readers or an audience. While local government should be of most interest to citizens as it is closest to them, most Americans tend to follow national political affairs more closely. So news media cover the local government primarily as a civic duty. Of course, by giving limited coverage to local government, the media contribute to the low level of interest in local government—often what is out of sight is out of mind.

Often a single reporter is assigned to the local government beat. Operating under the pressure of daily deadlines, that reporter does not have time to probe, analyze, or follow a story as it develops. In some cities, the local government assignment is given to new reporters, who are "promoted" to other beats when they have proved themselves. That means the reporters get transferred just about the time they become comfortable with and knowledgeable about the workings of local governments.

To simplify the demands of the job, reporters assigned to local government will often cultivate a symbiotic relationship with city officials. Officials clearly have an interest in what news gets reported, so they will provide the reporters with information they want released. Indeed, officials will often provide a written press release to simplify the reporter's job. Having been provided with such help from the officials, the reporter is in an awkward position to institute a muckraking campaign on corruption in government.

Reporters are also increasingly pressured by corporate owners to "substitute glitz and sensation for substance, even when reporting about governmental issues and campaigns for local office."[39] The pressure is especially intense for television news. A study of media coverage of the 1991 Philadelphia mayoral race concluded: "With no beats, little time for research, and constant pressure to come up with dramatic video and sound-bites, is it any wonder that the shallow government coverage TV reporters produce wins few accolades from focus groups?"[40] Unfortunately, research also indicates that more people are relying on local television newscasts as their major source of political news.

These limits on the media have implications for citizens. They will have less information on local government and perhaps no information that would cause them to question the status quo, a status quo that often focuses on supporting growth and economic development. The focus on the scandalous and the superficial also contributes to the political cynicism of the public and depresses interest in politics and political participation.[41]

Media as Influencer.   As suggested previously, the media vary in terms of how consciously they attempt to influence the course of events. Television and radio tend to avoid taking positions or engaging in influence attempts. Occasionally an editorial will be aired from a station manager or one of the announcers, but the norm is to portray the news as a strictly factual business. Newspapers are more likely to try to mold opinion on urban affairs.

Despite the normal avoidance of being opinion leaders, all media, TV and radio as well as newspapers, do have an influence. Over and above the question of subtle media bias—an issue that most research tends to discount[42]—the media set the agenda for public opinion. Determining which stories end up in the news affects what issues the public will be considering. The common expression is that the media may not control what you think, but they do control what you think about. Of course, while the media may set the agenda, that does not necessarily mean they can deter-

mine policy outcomes. Mead has chronicled how the persistent attempts by *The Charlotte Observer* to convince political leaders and the public that the city of Charlotte and surrounding Mecklenburg county should consolidate, kept the issue on the agenda, but did not produce consolidation.[43]

By determining what stories are covered, the media also have a substantial impact on the success or failure of various urban groups. Those groups that rely on protest are especially affected by the media's agenda-setting role. Protests depend on recruiting the support of others for success. Without media coverage, protests usually fail.

Beyond that general influence, urban newspapers tend to engage in two other kinds of influence attempts. First, as indicated before, newspapers often spearhead drives for community improvement projects that involve major construction. Second, newspapers also attempt to influence election outcomes by endorsements both of candidates for office and of ballot measures. Evidence indicates that such endorsements do have an effect, especially in those cities with nonpartisan elections and many candidates.[44] In such cities, voter confusion is at a maximum and an endorsement is a useful cue to simplify the decision process.

Challenges to Business Dominance

While John Logan and Harvey Molotch see the growth machine as the dominant form of urban coalition, they recognize that it is not universal. Other research has demonstrated variation among urban regimes. Some cities focus on **caretaker** functions, only maintaining and delivering traditional public services. A few **progressive** regimes focus not only on opposing the pressures to foster growth and economic development, but also on redistributing resources to citizens. One researcher concluded:

The political reality that economic prosperity is favored will not disappear. However, there is room to maneuver the impacts of development within those policy constraints. Growth politics, as a political reaction to competing interests, can vary.[45]

This chapter will turn to an examination of other interests that frequently compete for control over the urban agenda.

Who Participates: Citizen Activists

Obviously, the structure of participation differs in each city. Although it is impossible to cover all groups that may be active in urban politics, such as American Indians or gays and lesbians, some groups tend to be likely to become active in many cities. This discussion will focus on blacks, Latinos, and Asians; neighborhood organizations; women's groups; and unions.

Blacks, Latinos, and Asians

Chapter 4 reviewed evidence that blacks, Latinos, and Asians are becoming increasingly politically active. In the 1980s blacks, and to a lesser extent Latinos, were very successful in urban elections.[46] One study examined the extent to which blacks and Hispanics in 10 northern California cities had achieved what the authors called **political incorporation**, a term used to refer not just to the level of political activity, or even representation, but to the extent to which a group had become part of the governing coalition and had used that access to influence public policy. Although there was variation among the 10 cities, the overall conclusion was positive:

Blacks and Hispanics are no longer totally excluded from influence over government policy. They have made themselves heard, they have achieved significant incorpora-

tion, and city governments are more responsive to their interests.[47]

Recent electoral outcomes have demonstrated that getting power and keeping it are not the same thing. Many cities that elected African-American or Latino mayors in the 1980s have since chosen whites to replace them. In the 1980s the four largest American cities—New York, Los Angeles, Philadelphia, and Chicago—all had African-American mayors at some time. Each of those cities now has a white mayor. Many other cities, however, have elected African-American mayors, for example St. Louis, New Orleans, Cincinnati, Cleveland, Baltimore, Denver, and Minneapolis.

The key to any of these groups being politically successful is the creation of a coalition with others. The numbers tell the story. With the exception of Detroit (75.7 percent black) and San Antonio (55.6 percent Latino), none of the 10 largest cities has a majority of any of the ethnic groups discussed here. Bi- or multiracial coalitions have to be formed if blacks, Latinos, or Asians are to win elections.[48] The importance of such coalitions is indicated by the long-lasting success of Mayor Tom Bradley in Los Angeles as a result of a coalition between blacks and liberal whites, especially Jews. In other cities, such coalitions have either not formed or have been fleeting. It is important to consider reasons why coalitions are successful in some places but not in others.

Raphael Sonenshein argues that bi- or multiracial coalitions will be more likely to form when three conditions are present. First, coalition partners should share a liberal ideology. Second, they must have shared interests. Finally, there must be leadership among the various divisions within each community to argue for the logic of coalition.[49] He argues that these factors explain why Los Angeles could sustain a biracial coalition between 1973 and 1985, but in New York City African-Americans could not even be sure of capturing black votes. While both Los Angeles and

New York City had large numbers of liberals, Sonenshein argues that what was missing in New York were the shared interests and leadership present in Los Angeles. In New York, liberals had captured the Democratic Party and were in the governing coalition. Opening that coalition to blacks was a threat. In Los Angeles, however, blacks and liberal whites initially coalesced under the able leadership of Tom Bradley to oppose a conservative ruling elite.[50]

In general, if Sonenshein is correct, the probability of multiracial coalitions forming in today's urban areas would not seem high. As in the rest of the country, the residents of America's metropolises are becoming more conservative. Indeed, the new immigrants themselves are not necessarily liberal. Miami's Cuban population is strongly conservative, and some have argued that many Latinos have fundamentally conservative values.[51] Many of the new Latino and Asian immigrants have fled Communist regimes and oppose liberal policies.[52]

A second obstacle to forming coalitions is the absence of the sense of shared interests. As in New York City, many see the incorporation of new groups as a threat.

> In recent years our cities have become the center of intense political conflict. Most of the conflict has been associated with issues arising from the demands of some groups—especially blacks and Latins—for change, and from resistance of other groups and institutions to those pressures.[53]

That resistance often comes from the descendants of European immigrants who poured into America's cities at the turn of the nineteenth century. Many, having just barely managed to move up the social ladder to working-class or middle-class status, see the growing power of the new immigrants to the city as a special threat. While speaking specifically of blacks, Stephen Steinberg's evaluation of the conflict is relevant to some Latinos and Asians as well.

> Wherever blacks went, it seemed that one or another ethnic group occupied the stratum just above them, and therefore black efforts at self-advancement tended to arouse ethnic loyalties and provide an ethnic response. In this way a conflict that was fundamentally one between the haves and the have-nots—or more accurately, between the have-nots and those who have a little—assumed the external marks of ethnic conflict.[54]

The tension between the older ethnic groups and blacks, Latinos, and Asians has made it impossible for the Democratic Party to be the forum for building biracial or multiracial coalitions. In many cities the legacy of success of the Democratic machines in recruiting European ethnics has been a party dominated by the descendants of the early immigrants, descendants who fear the demands of the newer immigrants to America's cities.

Antagonism on the part of the older ethnic groups is only one problem the new immigrants face in forming coalitions. In cities, such as New York and Miami, with large black and Latino populations, a logical political strategy would be a coalition between the two groups, but tensions between them are often intense enough to make such coalitions impossible. In New York, blacks and Latinos will not vote for each other's candidates. In Miami, blacks strongly resent the rapid social advancement of the Cubans and the problems bilingualism causes for blacks seeking jobs. Blacks and Latinos have divergent positions on issues such as immigration and bilingual education.[55] Even community improvements, such as the siting of a new supermarket can engender conflict between the two groups as demonstrated in Box 5–1. African-Americans and Koreans have clashed in New York City, Washington, D.C., Philadelphia, Chicago, and Los Angeles.[56] In Los Angeles, as a result of Asian and Latino immigration, the propor-

BOX 5–1

Minority Tensions

The East Harlem section of New York City is one of the poorest neighborhoods in the city. It would seem to be a good thing when a major supermarket chain decided to open a large new store in the heart of the neighborhood. Supported by funds from a public–private partnership, Pathmark planned a store that would provide both inexpensive fresh groceries to residents and jobs. But the project became entangled in the complicated racial and ethnic politics of the neighborhood.

A major partner in the Pathmark project was the Abyssinian Development Corporation, which was associated with the Abyssinian Baptist Church, a major black church in the neighborhood. Many of the local grocery stores were owned by immigrants from the Dominican Republic who had worked hard to accumulate the capital to take over small stores from Puerto Ricans and then use the profit from them to buy larger stores. The Dominicans felt that after all their hard work they would be chased out of business by the new store, which was being subsidized in part by public funds.

The Dominicans began to build a political coalition to defeat the Pathmark project. One of the first members was Adam Clayton Powell IV, the son of a former African-American Congressman. Powell's mother was Puerto Rican, and he had courted the Latino vote. In addition, Powell's father had been defeated in a re-election bid by Charles Rangel, and Powell, himself, had lost to Rangel in a primary election. Rangel, who was a friend of the pastor of the Abyssinian Baptist Church, supported the Pathmark project.

Opponents of the project began to question why the Abyssinian Development Corporation was involved when the neighborhood is "... the heart of Latino Culture in New York City." This ethnic appeal led the nine members of the Puerto Rican–Hispanic Caucus on the City Council to oppose the project. One complained that "outsiders" should not be developing East Harlem. In response, some blacks counterattacked. An editorial in a weekly newspaper claimed: "Dominicans are notorious for their exploitation of Blacks."

Eventually, one of the City Council members opposing the project had a change of heart and voted for the project, fearing that opposing it would stop any future development in the area.

Source: Adapted from James Traub, "The Political Supermarket," *The New Yorker*, May 29, 1995, 41–44.

tion of blacks in the population declined from 12.4 percent to 11.2 percent between 1980 and 1990, while the proportion of Asians increased from 5.9 percent to 10.7 percent, and the number of Latinos increased 71 percent.[57] This has created greater conflict among the groups for jobs. Some fear that the growth of the new immigrant populations in some cities may result in a decline in the influence of African-Americans.[58]

One other problem facing those who would attempt to create biracial or multiracial coalitions is the diversity within each group. Blacks are divided by class, and increasingly, by ethnicity. New York City has a sizable West Indian population that does not always ally itself with African-Americans. Miami also has an increasing population of Haitians, Bahamians, and Jamaicans.[59] Puerto Ricans, Cubans, and

Mexican-Americans differ in fundamental ways, and the diversity of the Latino population is being increased by the addition of new immigrants from Central and South America. While Asians have formed many pan-Asian organizations, the population is still divided by national origin and by generational conflicts.

The increasing number of African-Americans and Latinos in office today demonstrates that political incorporation is possible. Representatives of these ethnic groups can become part of the governing coalition. Cooperation among them to achieve political power is possible. In Dade County, Florida, black and Latino leaders cooperated in a challenge to the at-large election of the county commission. That challenge was successful. In 1993, in the first election by districts, 6 Latinos and 4 blacks were elected to the 13-member commission.[60] Building the coalitions necessary to achieve incorporation into the governing coalition is difficult, however, and very much subject to local conditions.

Once achieved, the question arises of whether the incorporation of blacks, Latinos, and Asians makes a difference in the kinds of policies pursued by local governments. Analysts such as Paul Peterson argue that, given the economic limits that face all city governments, there would be much reason to believe that the incorporation of minority groups would make no difference in the policies they pursue.[61] Nonetheless, one empirical study found that the presence of African-American mayors did result in an increase in spending for social services and a decrease in other areas, but representation on the city council did not bring about the same changes.[62]

In 1984, Rufus Browning, Dale Marshall, and David Tabb concluded unequivocally that "In our ten cities political incorporation of blacks and Latinos led to increased policy responsiveness to minorities."[63] As a result, they question Peterson's conclusion that economic concerns control urban policy to such an extent that local political leaders have no discretion:

Like Peterson (1981), we acknowledge the many external, intergovernmental constraints on urban politics. However, we find that political coalitions, ideology, and conflict are significant in urban politics as in national politics, and they are necessary to any satisfactory explanation of urban responsiveness to blacks and Hispanics. Economic interests and economic competition between cities set undeniably important constraints on urban policy, but these constraints allow a great deal more room for local discretion than Peterson would have us believe—discretion that is shaped by the interests and ideologies of the changing coalitions contending for control over city government.[64]

In their more recent study, they concluded that increased incorporation of minorities has resulted in increased government employment of minorities, improved police–community relations, and increased representation of minorities on city boards and commissions.[65] But they recognized the limits of incorporation: "The painful truth is that many of the forces shaping the conditions under which the mass of low-income minority people live are not under the control of city governments, even governments run by minority regimes."[66]

It cannot be assumed that incorporation is permanent. The rise and fall of black mayors in many cities testifies to that.[67] In New York City, minority influence declined when fiscal crisis and federal cutbacks reduced funding for community programs designed to increase minority influence.[68] The intensifying fiscal plight of many other local governments may mean gains made by blacks, Latinos, and Asians will be reversed.

Neighborhood Organizations

Neighborhood organizations are a major source of fragmentation in the metropolis.

. . . diverse, fragmented citizen interests have produced a bewildering array of street-level community organizations that seek to give voice to one neighborhood demand or another. Typically they represent highly segmented and crystallized political interests: any neighborhood is likely to have scores of these small competing community organizations. . . . members of these neighborhood groups are the foot soldiers of the community in dealing with city government. They take the lead in pressing complaints and in fighting city hall.[69]

Neighborhoods are especially fertile ground for the development of political organizations. For many people, their home is their most significant investment and threats to that investment are powerful mobilizing forces. While some residents who see a potential threat may move, that option is never easy and for many is impossible. Contacts with neighbors can also have the effect of minimizing the free-rider phenomenon. The free-rider problem, discussed in Chapter 2, refers to a situation in which people who have not worked toward instituting a program still receive its benefits. The absence of anonymity in a neighborhood setting may mean pressure will be put on everyone to give their fair share to the group efforts.[70]

This does not mean that all neighborhoods can organize successfully. Indeed, many attempts at neighborhood organization have failed because disagreement among neighbors, or, more commonly, total indifference.[71] In low-income neighborhoods especially, mobilization tends to be the exception rather than the rule. Yet the number of neighborhood organizations has increased in the last three decades. One observer argued that one reason for this was an increase in the number of neighborhoods that perceived a threat. The encroachment by the new urban immigrants on neighborhoods was a major source of perceived threat. John Goering argues that "the

resistance to racial change has been and continues to be a central ingredient in the purposes of many neighborhood associations."[72]

Proposals to change the zoning of a residential area to permit commercial development are another form of threat that can mobilize urban neighborhoods. Another development that may affect the level of neighborhood organization is the process of gentrification discussed in Chapter 3. While gentrification may never involve large numbers of people, the effect of the gentrifiers on the city can be out of proportion to their number.[73] Although many city officials gleefully welcome the "gentry," seeing them as producers of increased tax revenues because the revitalization of neighborhoods raises property values, those same officials often begin to realize that more is involved in the process than a fatter city treasury. The different values and goals of the gentry and the poor, current residents of the neighborhood eventually produce conflict.

Current residents want the existing housing stock to be upgraded, without a significant increase in the cost of that housing. The gentry, on the other hand, are more likely to be worried about the investment aspects of their homes. Therefore, they will want changes that will enhance property values.[74] For example, they want density in the area to decrease—a goal that can only be accomplished if some residents move out—and eventually they will begin to look askance at long-time residents for lowering the general status of the neighborhood.

The result is an explosion in the number and activity of neighborhood organizations. An examination of gentrification in the South End of Boston demonstrated this. "The gentrification process was marked by the proliferation of opposing interest groups and by deepening divisions among their non-mobilized constituencies."[75] Another example was the mobilization of groups in the battle over attempts to slow the process of gentrification in the District of Columbia by taxing profits of real estate speculators and renovators.[76]

> On the one side were the District's real estate and financial interests, probably the largest private industry in town and a major supplier of campaign contributions in D.C. elections. On the other side were community organizations from neighborhoods most directly affected by speculation.[77]

Eventually, Ralph Nader's Tax Reform Research Group, a speculation task force, ministers, teachers, the Association of Black Social Workers, Afro-American Police Officers, and the real estate industry all got involved. Although a bill was passed that taxes short-term buying and selling of property, "compared to what it set out to do, the bill is barely half a loaf in the eyes of its original supporters."[78]

As gentrification continues, urban problems multiply. The middle class expects much—schools, parks, security, cultural facilities—and has the resources and skills to press those demands effectively. Yet, given the limits on local government revenue, response to those demands almost inevitably means less money will be available for poor residents. When that happens, low-income people will, in turn, have an incentive to mobilize for political action.

Another reason often given for the increase in neighborhood organizations is the amount of support directed to helping neighborhoods organize. In the 1960s and 1970s, programs of the federal government were aimed at helping low-income neighborhoods organize to direct their own rehabilitation. The War on Poverty conducted by the Office of Economic Opportunity (OEO) was supposed to be implemented with the maximum feasible participation of the target population. To comply, low-income neighborhoods were organized into community action agencies with a paid staff. The Model Cities program that followed also emphasized organizing the target neighborhoods and even provided some

funds to pay neighborhood residents who attended meetings. A very small percentage of the neighborhoods were actively involved in the neighborhood organizations. OEO itself only claimed that there were 1,100 community action programs in the entire country.[79]

Residents of the target neighborhoods often had no experience with political organization and had little extra time to go to meetings or plan political strategy.[80] Others have charged that some leaders of the community action agencies did not want a large membership, fearing their leadership might be challenged. One observer concluded that citizens who participated in the War on Poverty in Cincinnati "immediately began to get rid of the ladder so no other citizens could climb up."[81]

But that is looking at the glass as half empty. Viewed from another perspective, it is also half full—

> Whatever the shortcomings of the OEO effort in terms of mobilizing people, it is clear that had the effort not been made, the neighborhood movement in Cincinnati would have an even more pronounced socioeconomic bias than already is the case. The War on Poverty did at least modestly broaden a movement whose inherent tendency appears to be elitist.[82]

Another related reason offered to explain the increase in neighborhood organizations is the larger stakes that could be gained by neighborhoods. While federal funding to encourage neighborhoods declined, total federal funds going into urban areas expanded until the late 1970s. Three of the most significant federal programs for urban areas were the Community Development Block Grant program (CDBG), general revenue sharing, and Urban Development Action Grants (UDAG). These programs provided substantial funds with few guidelines for their use and also required at least some input from citizens in deciding how to best allocate the funds. The money provided an incentive to neighborhoods to organize to ensure that they got a fair share of the federal largess.[83]

The amount of federal funding for neighborhood organizations has declined. In fact, general revenue sharing and UDAG no longer exist. The current major national government program is the creation of Empowerment Zones, which are discussed in Chapter 12. That policy is aimed more at economic revitalization of poor neighborhoods than at citizen mobilization. Similarly, major foundations, such as the Ford and Rockefeller Foundations, that provide funding to solve inner city problems have emphasized economic development.[84]

Despite the decline in federal funds, Harry Boyte argues that the number of neighborhood groups has increased: he sees these groups as a true grass roots movement composed of people opposing their control by powerful economic forces. He considers neighborhood organizations to be part of a nationwide movement:

> . . . an identifiable movement was beginning to stir across the country. . . . On many fronts, Americans sought to regain some measure of power over a world in which impersonal forces threatened and destroyed with apparent indifference. Indeed, by the beginning of the 1980s, a renaissance in citizen activism was beginning to be visible at every bend.[85]

Some of the major urban neighborhood groups to which Boyte points to as part of this "backyard revolution" are the Citizens Action Program in Chicago, the Communities Organized for Public Service (COPS) in San Antonio, United Neighborhood Organization in East Los Angeles, and the Oakland Community Organization.

Others have pointed to the role of local government in establishing and providing support to neighborhood organizations. A recent study of such organizations in five cities emphasized the role of local officials, who provided a vision for creating neighborhood participation structures, remained committed to making them work, and provided them with information and access to decision making.[86] Another study, while acknowledging the role of local governments, sees the support of philanthropic organizations as a major cause of the recent expansion of neighborhood organizations.[87]

The impact of neighborhood organizations on city politics has received mixed reports. One report concluded that in Cincinnati the community councils that represent neighborhoods have been effective in influencing the city's decisions about the allocation of resources. A major reason for this success is the willingness of officials to encourage and facilitate the efforts of the community councils by involving them in the early stages of decision making and providing them with community assistance teams to help them learn how to work with the city. The biggest factor, though, was the large amount of discretionary funding available to the city, principally from CDBG program, which provided the neighborhoods with the incentive to be involved.[88]

A study of five cities with active neighborhood organizations concluded that cities that provide some resources to neighborhood organizations, whether it be staff support, budgets, or help organizing the neighborhood in the first place, are likely to have strong and active organizations that can have an impact both on politics in the city and on the attitudes of citizens. Although people of lower socioeconomic status still participated less than wealthier people, cities with strong neighborhood organizations had less socioeconomic bias in who participated. Citizens also had higher levels of trust in government. City officials, in turn, respond to the input from the organizations.

City officials respond to the neighborhood associations not simply because they gets lots of messages as to what each community wants, but because they know that the neighborhood associations are trusted by neighborhood residents.[89]

Perhaps most significant was the finding that when the city supports the neighborhood associations, the balance of power with business was altered.

Businessmen have little choice but to negotiate in good faith with the neighborhoods. In any city a neighborhood can rise up to oppose some proposed development, but what is crucial in the four citywide systems is the certainty of response by the neighborhood association. Except for the largest development projects, a developer cannot overcome neighborhood association opposition to win approval of a proposal. Business has the incentive to cooperate with neighborhood associations and to make the compromises necessary to win their support. There is really little choice.[90]

The important role of resources was also demonstrated in a study of the efforts by residents of the Tenderloin, a run-down neighborhood in San Francisco, to stop economic development in the area. The neighborhood organization was helped by the city's planning director, who used the state requirement for an Environmental Impact Report for all new developments to raise the issue of the impact of new development on low-income residents.[91] Another study found that the attitude of members of the governing coalition toward neighborhood organizations is an important determinant of their influence.[92]

Without institutional support neighborhood organizations often lack the resources to exercise meaningful power. Such organizations are often ephemeral, lacking any stable membership or leaders who are savvy in the creation and use of political power.[93] Often the neighborhood movement is too localized and fragmented to produce major change in urban policy. Although such organizations may affect the delivery of social services in a city, such change may be only "remedial and inadequate."[94] Another researcher observed that the efforts of such organizations may have negative effects by encouraging competition between racial and ethnic groups for limited resources.[95] The issue becomes a question of "What does change look like?"[96] Some see change in service delivery as a victory,[97] while others discount such change because the distribution of power and resources remains the same.[98]

Besides acting as organized interest groups to influence city policy, neighborhoods may also be important as a form of political society. "The inconveniences that arise from impersonality and diversity in big cities can inhibit the formation of close personal relationships among neighbors but also contribute to a tendency for neighborhoods to become political units."[99] These political units can help in the delivery of public services by cooperating with or augmenting the activities of cities' officials. For example, residents can help police the neighborhood by keeping track of the activities of the area's youth or assist park and recreation officials by organizing a paint and fix-up campaign for the neighborhood playground. Such activities by citizens to cooperate with government in the provision of necessary services is referred to as **co-production**. Milton Kotler discusses one neighborhood approach to co-production—the neighborhood corporation. The East Central Citizens Organization in Columbus, Ohio, established various educational programs, cooperative housing code enforcement programs, and purchased and rehabilitated homes. The organization was run by an executive council elected in a yearly neighborhood meeting. District meetings were held in subareas. Thus residents learned participatory skills while working to improve the neighborhood.[100] Box 5–2 highlights the importance of community organizations in working with the public and private sectors to improve life and conditions in poor neighborhoods.

BOX 5–2

Grassroots Urban Renewal

BALTIMORE, Md.—The Sandtown–Winchester section of Baltimore used to be home for African-Americans of various economic levels. As the barriers that enforced racial segregation started to crumble, many blacks with adequate financial resources moved away. The community became, in the words of a local minister, "a throwaway community."

Now a public–private partnership is attempting to revitalize Sandtown–Winchester by attacking its problems on many fronts. At the core of the effort is an attempt to mobilize the community at the grass roots level to help themselves. Some members of the community are paid to be "community organizers," acting as liaison between the community and the partnership that is trying to revitalize it, including the mayor, a local church, Habitat for Humanity, and the Enterprise Foundation. Other community members are asked to staff a day care center. Still others are volunteering with Habitat for Humanity to build new homes.

The ultimate goal is to convince the residents that they can improve the conditions of both the community and themselves. Rather than impose solutions on the community, as government programs of the past often did, organizers hold multiple neighborhood meetings to identify what the residents themselves see as problems and to find ways to address those problems.

Organizers need to deal with people like Deborah Gibson, a former heroin addict and mother of seven and grandmother of four, who observed: "The whole thing is survival. The whole thing is 'How can I live day by day?'" People like Ms. Gibson must be convinced that change can occur and that she can get beyond just survival by cooperating with her neighbors. She put her name on Habitat for Humanity's list for homeownership, a sign of renewed hope that the neighborhood can change and that she is willing to work to rebuild it.

Organizers know that only through community cooperation can rebuilding be successful. At the same time, hopes must not be raised too high. Only concrete results will convince people like Deborah Gibson that she can change her life.

Source: Adapted from Felicity Barringer, "Shift for Urban Renewal: Nurture the Grassroots," *New York Times*, November 29, 1992.

Community organizations can aggregate and communicate neighborhood concerns to officials, a communication process less burdensome to officials than myriad individual phone calls from irate citizens.[101] The result is a lessening of the burden on public officials.

Some portion—we cannot say how large—of the discordant business that would normally fracture the energies of urban policy makers is disposed of instead through the extemporaneous assemblies and informal executive powers of residential communities.[102]

Women's Groups

Since the 1960s, women have become important political actors at the national level. The two major political parties have made efforts to include more women in the national party conventions, women's organizations have lobbied for a variety of social and political goals, and a woman was nominated for vice-president in 1984. In 1996, not only did women play major roles in the presidential campaigns, both parties made concerted efforts to earn the votes of "soccer moms" by discussing the importance of family values. But long before women became a national political force—indeed before women even had the right to vote—they were playing a major role in local politics.

As early as the beginning of the nineteenth century, women were vital components of local voluntary associations.[103] The goal of these associations was to increase the public provisions of social services, and many of the services now taken for granted were first supplied as a result of urban reform movements spearheaded by female volunteers. For example, women's groups were crucial in the efforts to establish public education in Illinois in the mid-nineteenth century.[104] Women in New York City played a major role in attempts to provide public housing and to regulate housing construction.[105]

A primary concern of these early voluntary organizations was the equitable distribution of services. This concern still characterizes modern women's organizations and explains, in part, their increasing focus on national politics. Because of varying levels of resources, not all local governments can provide the same services. Equity requires some centralization of decision making and resource allocation.[106] Another major concern, however, is the responsiveness of policy to the needs and concerns of citizens.[107] The search for responsiveness is likely to assure that women's groups will continue to focus on the local level. Policy designed at the national level is often difficult to tailor to the individual needs of local clients. To ensure responsive policies, women need to focus on a local government as well.

A focus on local governments is compatible with the women's movement in other ways. Women's activity on the local level is more accepted. As Janet Boles observes, "Because of an association with the home and family, community politics is where women have faced fewer cultural barriers and role conflicts."[108] In addition, the rejection by feminist ideology of hierarchical structures makes grass roots activity especially likely.

Since the 1960s, the focus of women's activism on the local level has been both on changes in the delivery of services and on the provision of new or alternative public services. The major changes sought in the delivery of services included increasing the number of minority and female representatives within the social service bureaucracies and a renewed focus on the neighborhood as the basis for service delivery.

> In the 1960s, health care clinics, day care centers, after-school programs, multipurpose centers, and senior citizens centers—all based in the neighborhood and controlled by client–participants—became the new mode of urban service. The major characteristics of this new mode were neighborhood orientation, direct participation of residents in the policy process, and emphasis on equitable, responsive, and representative service.[109]

As in the nineteenth century, women's organizations focused on the expansion of local services. For example, local women's groups worked for the provision of publicly subsidized child care services. Women's groups have been in the forefront of efforts to create rape crisis centers and to change the way the criminal justice system handles rape cases. They have also worked to expand facilities and services available for battered women and for displaced homemakers.

Women's organizations also focused on changes in traditional community services. They played a major role in securing passage of Title IX of the Education Amendments Act of 1972, which established a federal mandate outlawing sex discrimination in education;

they also assured its implementation by monitoring compliance on the local level.[110] Women have also demanded alternative birthing centers in local hospitals, where a more home-like setting and "family-centered maternity care" can be provided.

The success of these efforts has varied. One researcher has found an emerging local feminist policy network in Milwaukee that concentrated on four issues: sexual assault, domestic violence, child care, and displaced homemakers. In each area the network succeeded in achieving policy changes.[111] Women have also been increasingly successful in winning election to local office. In addition, in many communities, commissions on the status of women have been formed to act as institutionalized advocates for women. As women's participation expands beyond the volunteer organizations to positions of authority, their impact may be expected to increase.

Nevertheless, women's ability to become a more potent political force is still limited. Writers have argued that the physical structure of the modern metropolis, with home very distant from work or shopping and with public transportation minimal or nonexistent, has negative consequences for women.[112] Women in households with one car who do not work outside the home are trapped at home by day. In households with more than one car, women spend their days running errands and driving children to piano lessons and Little League. In general, such women become physically and socially isolated; such isolation may make becoming politically active difficult.

Another development may also hamper the political participation of women. Women who work outside the home face severe demands on their time. Many find fitting political activity into their schedules difficult. On the other hand, such involvement outside the home may also increase the incentive for political involvement.

Unions

For the most part, the focus of union activity is not on local politics for three reasons. First, the bread and butter issues with which the unions are concerned—for example, minimum wage laws, safety precautions for employees—are controlled at the state and federal level. Second, the kind of issues that do arise at the local level may be very divisive. Joel Seidman and his co-authors illustrate this point by talking about a proposed policy of decontrolling rents in Chicago. The local steelworkers union opposed decontrol because most union members were renters. They were opposed, however, by an organized landlord group that included some active union shop stewards.[113]

> ... their success is limited by the way unions are viewed. Organized labor—even if it includes in its ranks the majority of all adult citizens in the community—is generally regarded as a "special interest" which must be represented; businessmen, on the other hand, are often regarded, not as "representing business" as a "special interest," but as serving the community as a whole. Businessmen, in Peter Clark's terms, often are viewed as "symbols of civic legitimacy." Labor leaders rarely have this symbolic quality, but must contend with whatever stigma attaches to being from a lower-class background and associated with a special interest group.[114]

While unions in general play a minimal role in city politics, John Logan and Harvey Molotch argue that union leaders have been co-opted by growth machines in many cities by the argument that growth is necessary to create jobs.[115] In addition, one kind of union has been a dominant influence on cities: municipal employees' unions. Four decades ago, municipal employee unions were virtually nonexistent. The number of unionized public employees had expanded to 48 percent in 1978;

however, the percentage had declined slightly to 43.4 percent by 1998. In some states, by law, government employees cannot unionize. In other states, such as Virginia and North Carolina, while unions are legal, it is illegal for local governments to bargain collectively with them. Although in most states it is illegal for government employees to strike, strikes have occurred nonetheless. Policemen have suddenly come down with "blue flu"; teachers have walked picket lines; garbage collectors have let refuse pile up on city streets. The essential nature of the services these people control puts them in a strong bargaining position when they threaten to withhold those services. Employee unions have another advantage. As employees of the city, they are likely to be well-informed about the processes of city decision making. That information is useful in efforts to lobby the city for increased wages and job security.

An indication of the power of municipal unions is that some have argued that a major part of New York City's financial crisis in the 1970s was due to the ability of municipal employee unions to hold the city hostage for higher wages. Yet one study of whether cities with organized and active municipal employee's unions spent more on municipal employees found no relationship.[116] The study found that in cities where employees are organized, salaries are higher than in unorganized cities, but employees are fewer in number. It appears that organized municipal employees are powerful enough to drive up their salaries, but the city responds by cutting the number of employees, therefore leaving the total amount of money spent on employees the same. This has implications for citizens. In local governments with organized municipal employees, services may suffer as the number of employees decrease with demands from unions for higher compensation.[117]

In some local governments, unions have not only been active in direct efforts to improve their salaries and/or working conditions, they have also been active in campaigning for specific candidates for mayor and council seats. For example, efforts of employee unions helped increase black voter turnout in Philadelphia in 1973.[118] In low-turnout elections, union efforts may be crucial.

Although the power of unions increased through the 1960s and early 1970s, it has now decreased. A major turning point may have occurred in San Francisco in 1976 when the mayor campaigned against the unions and won after long strikes in 1975 and 1976. In Atlanta and San Antonio, entire city departments were fired in the late 1970s. While leaders argued the public was incensed over the problems caused by employee strikes, surveys seem to, "suggest that citizens changed their views less than political leaders changed their tactics."[119] Other conditions may contribute to a decline in the power of municipal employees' unions and of unions in general. A 1977 study claimed that, "Under the dual impact of permanent recession and continuing loss of jobs, powerful labor leaders saw their memberships and treasuries shrink, and they knew that their political power—national as well as local—was ebbing away with the decline in bodies and dollars."[120]

In the 1990s, several mayors, including Edward Rendell in Philadelphia and Rudolph Giuliani in New York, took strong stands against labor union contracts that provided what they saw as unreasonable benefits. Rendell instituted a wage freeze and a cut in benefits and privatized custodial services. The unions struck, but for less than a day.[121] The popular success of Rendell probably indicates that unions will not be in a good bargaining position in the current environment of government cutbacks and privatization.

Who's In Charge Here?

For those who want urban democracy, the picture emerging here is mixed. On the one hand, there is much to cause concern. The persistent finding that higher-status residents are more likely to be active in politics raises serious questions about equal access for all citizens and about the representativeness of the issues that will constitute the urban agenda. There is substantial evidence that business interests can exercise power far out of proportion to their numbers by claiming to speak for the "public interest" in the need to establish a strong urban economic base.

Yet there is also some evidence to give hope to those who desire democracy. African-Americans, Latinos, and Asians are increasingly becoming involved in urban politics. The Census Bureau estimates that voter registration among African-Americans is 13,442,000, or 63.9 percent, and among Latinos it is 5,137,000, or 35 percent.[122] These numbers indicate the extent to which the political activity of Latinos and African-Americans is becoming focused on electoral politics. Both groups have elected representatives to office in some areas and used those positions to increase the responsiveness of city governments to their needs.[123]

In addition, some evidence points to increasing activism by neighborhood organizations. Some of this activity may have negative consequences, and many observers have deplored the degree of diffusion and fragmentation that the disparate neighborhood demands cause for policy. Also, some activism has been negative. It is often easier to stop something than to provide alternatives. In addition, activity is often motivated by the desire to keep "them" out of the neighborhood, whether the "them" are African-Americans, Latinos, Asians, whites, or yuppies. Others argue that some neighborhood organizations are positive and a necessary augmentation of the urban policy process—a form of local political society controlled by residents. While recognizing that the neighborhood movement does not offer a comprehensive plan for the future of cities, one observer believes that it has altered the terms of debate in cities:

The "neighborhood movement" has . . . established a political rhetoric of citizen participation, participatory planning, and community review which challenges the prevailing ideologies of progrowth politics. . . . No longer can government so easily engage in regressive social engineering. . . . [c]ommunity organizations and agencies provide the organizational infrastructure through which citizens at the grass roots participate in political life on a daily basis.[124]

While there may be broader participation, groups do not necessarily become powerful enough to alter the urban agenda. Contrary to business interests whose issues are seen as for the good of the public as a whole, concerns of other groups are often seen as coming from a "special interest group." Desires to allocate the resources of the city in ways to help disadvantaged citizens or to develop the human capital of the city's residents as a whole also are likely to fail because they run counter to the basic political culture of the country.

With an ideology and political culture that promote a diminished role for government (i.e., except as supporter of private sector activity), that assume a definition of economic development policy limited almost exclusively to bricks and mortar, and that employ a narrow set of policy evaluation criteria, it is hardly surprising that urban policy agendas are still dominated by a growth machine mentality.[125]

There is no clear or simple answer to the question of what the structure of power is in the metropolis now. Two models have already been discussed: elitism and pluralism. Elitists believe that a closed and unrepresentative group control urban decision making. Most frequently the elite in control is believed to be major business interests. Pluralists argue that many interests—all those who have the resources to organize—can have an impact on urban decisions and that policy results from the bargaining among those interests.

Other researchers have posited two other models: **multiple elites** and **hyperpluralism**. Multiple-elite theorists reject the idea of a single elite controlling cities by pulling strings from behind the scenes. They argue that government officials do control decision making and that multiple elites compete with each other for the right to control government offices. Citizens play little role in affecting the policies adopted by the elite, yet citizens are not completely powerless, for they control which elite is in power through elections. In this conception, citizen control through participation—other than electoral participation—is really more a myth than a reality. As Lester Milbrath wrote:

> . . . it is important to continue moral admonishment for citizens to become active in politics, not because we want or expect great masses of them to become active, but rather because the admonishment helps keep the system open and sustains the belief in the right of all to participate, which is an important norm governing the behavior of political elites.[126]

In other words, it is important to believe in the importance of citizen control, even if it does not actually occur because such belief may keep political elites wary and concerned about citizen interests. The elites are also kept accountable to citizens by the electoral connection, which enables citizens to replace one elite with a competing elite. As long as elites are worried about electoral defeat, they will attempt to produce policies the citizens want.

While this may sound idyllic, others have argued that the existence of multiple elites does not always ensure that the general public welfare is protected. Theodore Lowi has developed a conception of power in which elites do not compete in the public arena for political power; rather, they negotiate with each other and with political officials for policies. According to Lowi, "the role of government is one of ensuring access particularly to the most effectively organized, and of ratifying the agreements and adjustments worked out among the competing leaders and their claims."[127]

What Lowi is describing is a system that works according to a logrolling model in which organized interest groups effectively control the policies in areas of concern to them. Although citizens represented by effective interest groups can be successful in getting what they want from government, Lowi condemns this process, in part because of the implications for general popular control. He argues:

> Parceling out policy-making power to the most interested parties destroys political responsibility. . . . Besides making conflict-of-interest a principle of government rather than a criminal act, participatory programs shut out the public. To be more precise, programs of this sort tend to cut out all that part of the mass that is not specifically organized around values strongly salient to the goals of the program.[128]

If Lowi is correct, it would mean that business interests would control policy of direct concern to them, while other groups in the city—neighborhood organizations for example—would do the same. Each group would, in essence, be an elite in its own policy area and could control policy unhindered by others. The problem is that some more generalized public interest may be ignored by this parceling out of decision making.

Not all observers of cities believe that elites, or even multiple elites, are in control. Like those who believe in multiple elites, pluralists argue that different elites dominate different issue areas. What distinguishes pluralist thought is the belief that power is widely distributed and, more important, very open. As Robert Dahl wrote about the American political system in general: "With all its defects, it does nonetheless provide a high probability that any active and legitimate group will make itself heard effectively at some stage in the process of decision."[129]

Others take the pluralist argument one step further and argue that so many groups are making so many demands on an overstretched urban political system that no one is in control.

Urban policy makers are constantly rushing from one small crisis to another. In their reactivism they bounce from one hopeful policy response to another, constantly remake and undo decisions, and often search blindly for some solution that will work.[130]

In this situation, which Frederick Wirt defines as hyperpluralism, there is no time to balance competing demands or to establish priorities and coordinate among policies, let alone to devise rational policy responses to achieve long term goals.[131] Everyone is involved, but no one is in control. Hyperpluralism is contrary to the broader public interest because of the inability of leaders to settle conflicts among the various interests and to seek a public good separate from the demands of myriad groups.

Conclusion

The multiple models of urban power illustrate the difficulty of answering absolutely who really controls decision making in America's metropolises. Answering the question is further complicated because of the diversity among local governments. As their size, location, and economic bases differ, so too can their structure of power. The multiple models of power are not necessarily competing for universal acceptance, but are themselves indicators of the diversity. Another complicating factor is that control may differ in different policy areas, an issue that will be discussed in the last section of this book. In addition, the control exercised by the various urban groups is dependent on how active they are and what resources they have. The next chapter examines the mechanisms of citizen control.

Notes

1. Sidney Verba and Norman H. Nie, *Participation in America: Political Democracy and Social Equality* (New York: Harper & Row, 1972), 126.

2. Clarence N. Stone, "Systemic Power in Community Decision Making: A Restatement of Stratification Theory," *American Political Science Review* 74 (December 1980), 979.

3. Stephen L. Elkin, *City and Regime in the American Republic* (Chicago: University of Chicago Press, 1987), 186.

4. Frances Fox Piven and Richard A. Cloward, *Poor People's Movements: Why They Succeed, How They Fail* (New York: Pantheon, 1977).

5. Steven J. Rosenstone and John Mark Hansen, *Mobilization, Participation, and Democracy in America* (New York: Macmillan, 1993), 33.

6. Sidney Verba, Kay Lehman Schlozman, and Henry E. Brady, *Voice and Equality: Civic Volunteerism in American Politics* (Boston: Harvard University Press, 1995), 206. See also Verba and Nie, *Participation in America*, 298.

7. Verba and Nie, *Participation in America*, 151.

8. Arthus H. Miller, Patricia Gurin, and Oksana Malanchuck, "Group Consciousness and Political Participation," *American Journal of Political Science*, 25 (August 1981): 503.

9. Ira Katznelson, *City Trenches: Urban Politics and the Patterning of Class in the United States* (Chicago: University of Chicago Press, 1981), 121.

10. Elaine B. Sharp, "Citizen Demand Making in the Urban Context," *American Journal of Political Science* 28 (November 1984): 664.

11. Richard Dagger, "Metropolis, Memory, and Citizenship," *American Journal of Political Science* 25 (November 1981), 722–723.

12. Richard Sennett, *The Uses of Disorder: Personal Identity and City Life* (New York: Knopf, 1970), 114–115.

13. Matthew A. Crenson, *Neighborhood Politics* (Cambridge, Massachusetts: Harvard University Press, 1983), 186.

14. Michael W. Giles and Marilyn K. Dantico, "Political Participation and Neighborhood Social Context Revisited," *American Journal of Political Science* 26 (February 1982): 149; P. Robert Huckfeldt, "Political Participation and Neighborhood Social Context," "*American Journal of Political Science* 23 (August 1979): 579–592.

15. Giles and Dantico, "Political Participation and Neighborhood Social Context Revisited," 149.

16. Albert K. Karnig and B. Oliver Walters, "Decline in Municipal Voter Turnout: A Function of Changing Structure," *American Politics Quarterly* 11 (October 1983): 491–506; see also Rufus P. Browning, Dale Rogers Marshall, and David H. Tabb, "Minorities and Urban Electoral Change: A Longitudinal Study," *Urban Affairs Quarterly* 15 (December 1979): 215.

17. Barbara Ferman, *Challenging the Growth Machine: Neighborhood Politics in Chicago and Pittsburgh*

(Lawrence: University of Kansas Press, 1996), 140–141.

18. Paul E. Peterson, *City Limits* (Chicago: University of Chicago Press, 1981), 29.

19. Ibid, 148.

20. Stephen Elkin, *The Regime and the City* (Princeton: Princeton University Press, 1986); Clarence N. Stone, "Summing Up: Urban Regimes, Development Policy, and Political Arrangements" in *The Politics of Urban Development*, ed. Clarence N. Stone and Heywood T. Sanders (Lawrence: University Press of Kansas, 1987), 269–290.

21. Stephen L. Elkin, *City and Regime in the American Republic* (Chicago: University of Chicago Press, 1987), x.

22. Other terms have also been used to refer to the general argument concerning business control. Depending on the particular way the argument is phrased, it is referred to by some as the Marxist position or the structuralist position. This book uses the term elitist position because it is the most encompassing of the alternative terms.

23. C. Wright Mills, *The Power Elite* (London: Oxford University Press, 1956), 11.

24. Floyd Hunter, *Community Power Structure* (Chapel Hill: University of North Carolina Press, 1953).

25. Clarence Stone, "Systemic Power in Community Decision Making: A Restatement of Stratification Theory," *American Political Science Review* 74 (December 1980): 978.

26. Ibid., 984.

27. Clarence N. Stone, *Regime Politics: Governing Atlanta, 1946–1988* (Lawrence: University of Kansas Press, 1989), 7.

28. Stone, "Systemic Power in Community Decision Making", 984.

29. Dahl, *Who Governs?: Democracy and Power in an American City* (New Haven, Connecticut: Yale University Press, 1961).

30. Aaron Wildavsky, *Leadership in a Small Town* (Totowa, New Jersey: Badminster Press, 1964), 312.

31. Matthew A. Crenson, *The Un-Politics of Air Pollution* (Baltimore: Johns Hopkins Press, 1971), Chapter 4.

32. For examples of this literature, see Luis Ricardo Fraga, "Domination Through Democratic Means: Nonpartisan Slating Groups in City Electoral Politics." Paper prepared for delivery at the Annual Meeting, American Political Science Association, New Orleans, Louisiana, August 29–September 1, 1985; Chandler Davidson and George Korbel, "At-large Elections and Minority Group Representation: A Reexamination of Historical and Contemporary Evidence" in *Minority Vote Dilution*, ed. Chandler Davidson (Washington, D.C.: Howard University Press, 1984).

33. Bryan D. Jones and Lynn W. Bachelor, with Carter Wilson, *The Sustaining Hand: Community Leadership and Corporate Power* (Lawrence: University of Kansas Press, 1986), 84.

34. Clarence N. Stone, *Regime Politics*, 7.

35. Clarence N. Stone, "Preemptive Power: Floyd Hunter's 'Community Power Structure' Reconsidered," *American Journal of Political Science* 32 (February 1988): 82–104.

36. John R. Logan and Harvey L. Molotch, *Urban Fortunes: The Political Economy of Place* (Berkeley: University of California Press, 1987), Chapter 3.

37. Ibid., 66.

38. The discussion of the role of the media relies heavily on Edward C. Banfield and James Q. Wilson, *City Politics* (Cambridge, Massachusetts: Harvard University Press, 1963), Chapter 21.

39. Phyllis Kaniss, *The Media and the Mayor's Race: The Failure of Urban Political Reporting* (Bloomington: Indiana University Press, 1995), 371.

40. Ibid.

41. Ibid., 375.

42. William Schneider and I.A. Lewis, "Views on the News," *Public Opinion* 8 (August–September 1985): 9; Maura Clancey and Michael J. Robinson, "General Election Coverage: Part I," *Public Opinion* 8 (December–January 1985): 49–54, 59; Maura Clancey and Michael J. Robinson, "General Election Coverage, Part II: Wingless, Toothless, and Hopeless," *Public Opinion* 8 (February–March 1985): 43–48; Robert S. Erikson, Norman R. Luttbeg, and Kent L. Tedin, *American Public Opinion: Its Origins, Content, and Impact* (New York: Macmillan, 1988), 211–214.

43. Timothy D. Mead, "The Daily Newspaper as Political Agenda Setter: *The Charlotte Observer* and Metropolitan Reform," *State and Local Government Review* 26 (Winter 1994): 27–37.

44. Lana Stein and Arnold Fleischmann, "Newspaper and Business Endorsements in Municipal Elections: A Test of the Conventional Wisdom," *Journal of Urban Affairs* 9, no. 4 (1987): 325–336.

45. Robyne S. Turner, "Growth Politics and Downtown Development: The Economic Imperative in Sunbelt Cities," *Urban Affairs Quarterly* 28 (September 1992): 4.

46. Albert K. Karnig and Susan Welch, *Black Representation and Urban Policy* (Chicago: University of Chicago Press, 1980).

47. Rufus P. Browning, Dale Rogers Marshall, and David H. Tabb, *Protest Is Not Enough: The Struggle of Blacks and Hispanics for Equality in Urban Politics* (Berkeley: University of California Press, 1984), 242.

48. Browning, Marshall, and Tabb, *Protest is Not Enough*, 246. See also Raphael J. Sonenshein, *Politics in Black and White: Race and Power in Los Angeles* (Princeton: Princeton University Press, 1993).

49. Sonenshein, *Politics in Black and White*, 20.

50. Ibid., 231–233.

51. Earl Shorris, *The Latinos: A Biography of the People* (New York: Norton, 1992,) 425.

52. Charles P. Henry, "Urban Politics and Incorporation: The Case of Blacks, Latinos, and Asians in Three Cities" in *Blacks, Latinos, and Asians in Urban America: Status and Prospects for Politics and Activism* ed. James Jennings (Westport, Connecticut: Praeger, 1994), 23.

53. Norman I. Fainstein and Susan S. Fainstein, *Urban Political Movements* (Englewood Cliffs, New Jersey: Prentice-Hall, 1974), 2.

54. Stephen Steinberg, *The Ethnic Myth: Race, Ethnicity, and Class in America* (New York: Atheneum, 1981), 218–219.

55. Manning Marable, "Building Coalitions among Communities of Color: Beyond Racial Identity Politics" in *Blacks, Latinos, and Asians in Urban America*, ed. Jennings, 37.

56. Edward D. Chang, "New Urban Crisis: Intra-Third World Conflict" in *Asian Americans: Comparative and Global Perspectives*, ed. Shirley Hune (Pullman: Washington State University Press, 1991), 173.

57. Karen Umemota, "Blacks and Koreans in Los Angeles: The Case of LaTasha Harlins and Soon Ja Du" in *Blacks, Latinos, and Asians in Urban America*, ed. Jennings, 96.

58. Richard E. DeLeon, "Progressive Politics in the Left Coast City: San Francisco" in *Racial Politics in American Cities*, 2nd ed., ed. Rufus P. Browning, Dale Rogers Marshall, and David H. Tabb (White Plains, New York: Longman, 1997), Chapter 6.

59. Henry, "Urban Politics and Incorporation," 19.

60. Daryl Harris, "Generating Racial and Ethnic Conflict in Miami: Impact of American Foreign Policy and Domestic Racism" in *Blacks, Latinos, and Asians in Urban America*, ed. Jennings, 89.

61. Paul E. Peterson, *City Limits* (Chicago: University of Chicago Press, 1981).

62. Karnig and Welch, *Black Representation and Urban Policy*.

63. Browning, Marshall, and Tabb, *Protest Is Not Enough*, 250.

64. Ibid., 242.

65. Rufus P. Browning, Dale Rogers Marshall, and David H. Tabb, "Has Political Incorporation Been Achieved? Is It Enough?" in *Racial Politics in American Cities*, 2nd ed., ed. Browning, Marshall, and Tabb, Chapter 13.

66. Ibid., 293.

67. William E. Nelson, Jr., "Cleveland: The Rise and Fall of The New Black Politics" in *The New Black Politics: The Search for Political Power*, ed. Michael B. Preston, Linneal J. Henderson, and Paul Puryear (New York: Longman, 1982), 204.

68. John H. Mollenkopf, "New York: The Great Anomaly," *PS* 19, no. 3 (Summer 1986), 592.

69. Douglas Yates, *The Ungovernable City: The Politics of Urban Problems and Policy Making* (Cambridge, Massachusetts: MIT Press, 1978), 23–25.

70. John Clayton Thomas, "Rethinking 'Groupless' Urban Politics: A Theory of Neighborhood Mobilization." Paper prepared for delivery at the 1985 Annual Meeting of the American Political Science Association, New Orleans, Louisiana, August 28–September 1, 1985.

71. David J. O'Brien, *Neighborhood Organization and Interest Group Processes* (Princeton: Princeton University Press, 1975), 8; Paul E. Peterson, *City Limits* (Chicago: University of Chicago Press, 1981), 119–120. See also Mancur Olson, *The Logic of Collective Action* (New York: Schocken, 1968).

72. John M. Goering, "The National Neighborhood Movement: A Preliminary Analysis and Critique," *American Planning Association Journal* 45 (October 1979): 510.

73. Phillip G. Clay, *Neighborhood Renewal* (Lexington, Massachusetts: Lexington Books, 1979), 61.

74. Ibid., 21.

75. Deborah A. Auger, "The Politics of Revitalization in Gentrifying Neighborhoods: The Case of Boston's South End," *Journal of the American Association of Planners* 45 (October 1979): 519–520.

76. Carol Richards and Jonathan Rowe, "Restoring a City: Who Pays the Price?" *Working Papers for a New Society* 4 (Winter, 1977): 54–61.

77. Ibid., 56.

78. Ibid., 59.

79. John C. Donovan, *The Politics of Poverty* (New York: Pegasus, 1967), 122.

80. Kenneth Clark and Jeannette Hopkins, *A Relevant War Against Poverty: A Study of Community Action Programs and Observable Social Change* (New York: Harper Torchbooks, 1969), 88–91.

81. John Clayton Thomas, *Between Citizen and City: Neighborhood Organizations and Urban Politics in Cincinnati* (Lawrence: University of Kansas Press, 1986), 68–69.

82. Ibid., 70.

83. Ibid., 12.

84. Nicholas Lemann, "The Myth of Community Development," *The New York Times Magazine*, January 9, 1994, 30.

85. Harry C. Boyte, *Backyard Revolution: Understanding the New Citizen Movement* (Philadelphia: Temple University Press, 1980), 3. See also, Manuel Castells, *The City and the Grassroots* (Berkeley: University of California Press, 1983), 328–329.

86. Jeffrey M. Berry, Kent E. Portney, and Ken Thomson, *The Rebirth of Urban Democracy* (Washington, D.C.: The Brookings Institution, 1993), 48–50.

87. Robert J. Chaskin and Sunil Garg, "The Issue of Governance in Neighborhood-Based Initiatives," *Urban Affairs Review* 32 (May 1997): 632.

88. Thomas, *Between Citizen and City*, 159.

89. Berry, Portney, and Thompson, *The Rebirth of Urban Democracy*, 288.

90. Ibid., 287.

91. Tony Robinson, "Gentrification and Grassroots Resistance in San Francisco's Tenderloin," *Urban Affairs Review* 30 (March 1995): 492.

92. Barbara Ferman, *Challenging the Growth Machine* (Lawrence: University of Kansas Press, 1996).

93. Bryan D. Jones, "Party and Bureaucracy: The Influence of Intermediary Groups on Urban Public Service Delivery," *American Political Science Review* 75 (September 1981): 697.

94. John Mollenkopf, *The Contested City* (Princeton: Princeton University Press, 1983), 293.

95. Katznelson, *City Trenches*, 181.

96. E.E. Schattschneider, *The Semi-Sovereign People* (New York: Holt, Rinehart & Winston, 1960).

97. Thomas, *Between Citizen and City*, 159.

98. Castells, *The City and the Grassroots*, 329; Mollenkopf, *The Contested City*, 293.

99. Crenson, *Neighborhood Politics*, 298–299.

100. Milton Kotler, *Neighborhood Government: The Local Foundations of Political Life* (Indianapolis: Bobbs-Merrill, 1969), 44–50.

101. Crenson, *Neighborhood Politics*, 299.

102. Ibid., 297.

103. Barbara J. Berg, *The Remembered Gate: Origins of American Feminism: The Woman and the City* (New York: Oxford University Press, 1978).

104. Meredith Tax, *The Rising of the Women* (New York: Monthly Review Press, 1980).

105. Ronald Lawson, "Tenant Mobilization in New York," *Social Policy* 10 (March–April 1980): 30–40.

106. Local governments also may have little incentive to provide some services, especially those targeted to the low-income population. See Chapter 14 for a discussion of this. The point is made in Paul Peterson, *City Limits*.

107. Joyce Gelb and Marilyn Gittell, "Seeking Equality: The Role of Activist Women in Cities" in *The Egalitarian City: Issues of Rights, Distribution, Access, and Power*, ed. Janet K. Boles (New York: Praeger Special Studies, 1986), 93–99.

108. Janet K. Boles, "The Women's Movement and the Redesign of Urban Services." Paper prepared for delivery at the 1986 Annual Meeting of The American Political Science Association, August 28–31, 1986, 6.

109. Gelb and Gittell, "Seeking Equality," 97.

110. Joyce Gelb and Marian Lief Palley, *Women and Public Policies* (Princeton: Princeton University Press, 1982).

111. Janet K. Boles, "Local Feminist Policy Networks in the Contemporary American Interest Group System," *Policy Sciences* 27 (May–August 1994): 161–178.

112. See, for example, Boles, "The Women's Movement and the Redesign of Urban Services"; Janet K. Boles, "Making Cities Work for Women," *Urban Affairs Quarterly* 18 (June 1983): 573–580; Greta Salem, "Gender Equity and the Urban Environment" in *The Egalitarian City: Issues of Rights, Distribution, Access, and Power*, ed. Janet K. Boles, (New York: Praeger, 1986), 152–161.

113. Joel Seidman, et al. *The Worker Views His Union* (Chicago: University of Chicago Press, 1958).

114. Edward C. Banfield and James Q. Wilson, "Organized Labor in City Politics" in *Urban Government: A Reader in Administration and Politics*, rev. ed., ed. Edward C. Banfield (New York: Free Press, 1969), 492.

115. Logan and Molotch, *Urban Fortunes*, 81–82.

116. Terry Nichols Clark and Laura Crowley Ferguson, *City Money: Political Processes, Fiscal Strain, and Retrenchment* (New York: Columbia University Press, 1983), 149.

117. Ibid., 171–172.

118. Richard P. Schick and Jean J. Courturier, *Public Interest in Government Labor Relations* (Cambridge, Massachusetts: Ballinger, 1977), 51.

119. Ibid., 155.

120. Jack Newfield and Paul DeBrul, *The Abuses of Power: The Permanent Government and the Fall of New York* (New York: Viking, 1977), 232.

121. Jim Sleeper, "The End of the Rainbow: America's Changing Urban Politics," *The New Republic*, November 1993, 20–25; Jacob Weisberg, "Philadelphia Story: Rudy's Role Model," *New York*, May 2, 1994, 30–31.

122. U.S. Bureau of the Census, *Voting Registration in the Election of November 1992* (Washington, D.C.: Government Printing Office, 1993), 5.

123. Browning, et al., *Protest Is Not Enough*; Karnig and Welch, *Black Representation and Urban Policy*.

124. Mollenkopf, *The Contested City*, 294.

125. Ferman, *Challenging the Growth Machine*, 146–147.

126. Lester Milbrath, *Political Participation* (Chicago: Rand McNally, 1965), 152.

127. Theodore J. Lowi, *The End of Liberalism: Ideology, Policy and the Crisis of Public Authority* (New York: Norton, 1969), 71.

128. Ibid., 86.

129. Robert Dahl, *A Preface to Democratic Theory* (Chicago: University of Chicago Press, 1956), 150.

130. Douglas Yates, *The Ungovernable City: The Politics of Urban Problems and Policy Making* (Cambridge, Massachusetts: MIT Press, 1978), 15.

131. Frederick M. Wirt, *Power in the City: Decision-Making in San Francisco* (Berkeley: University of California Press, 1974).

CHAPTER 6

Mechanisms of Citizen Control

Few issues unite Americans more than the desirability of democracy. Despite this, apparently few Americans think very deeply about what the role of citizens should be in a democracy. Logically, if the people are to rule, they must be actively involved in the governing process. However, support for the idea of people participating in politics in any way besides voting is not nearly as widespread as the abstract belief in rule by the people. This focus on voting is congruent with the Constitution that identifies voting as a major responsibility of citizens. Yet there remains a tradition of citizens participating more directly in the decisions of government, especially at the local grass roots level.[1]

Citizens who want influence over local government policies must find a way to make their voices heard by the local governing coalition. Ultimately, citizens can be most influential if they become part of that coalition. Citizens need to participate to achieve their policy goals. The most common forms of citizen participation in government are: (1) participation in groups, (2) electoral activity, (3) individualized contacting of government officials, (4) protest activity, and (5) public hearings. The major question concerning citizen participation is what impact it has on the urban policy process.

How effective can citizens be in getting issues that concern them on the policy agenda? Can citizens affect the alternative policy options in the formulation stage? Do citizens play a meaningful role in the adoption of policies? Finally, is citizen satisfaction or dissatisfaction at the evaluation stage reflected in decisions about the future of the policy? Answering questions about the impact of participation would necessitate measuring the power citizens exercise through participating; however, social scientists have found no way to measure power empirically. Before examining the various forms of participation, it is important to understand the difficulties of measuring power.

The Problems of Measuring Power

Citizens who want to influence urban policy must influence those responsible for making that policy. That means political leaders as well as others who may be part of an informal governing coalition. The problem is how to determine if citizen participation affects those in the governing coalition. Robert Dahl has developed a definition of power which is widely cited: "A has power over B to the extent that he can get B to do something that B would not otherwise do."[2] While Dahl's definition sheds some light on the concept of power, it leaves some substantial problems unresolved for those who want to observe the exercise of citizen power. The definition requires the ability to observe behavior by B that would not nave occurred if it were not for the impact of A. But how is the observer supposed to know how B would have acted if it were not for A's influence? For example, how is it possible to know if a certain policy was enacted because of citizen demands or because political leaders wanted that policy?

Another fundamental problem arises because, in some cases, individuals can have an impact on the behavior of others without actually doing anything. Carl Friedrich calls this **anticipated reaction**.[3] For example, elected officials may make decisions designed to please their constituents without the constituents having to do anything to force the officials to act. Officials may know constituent preferences and act in accordance with those preferences, not because the constituents demanded it but because the officials anticipate a reaction if they do anything else. For example, a mayor may support tax breaks for a local development not because of specific demands, but because he knows developers may go elsewhere if not offered such incentives. In such a situation, most would agree that the developers have power over officials regardless of the absence of any observable interaction between the two groups. Clarence Stone argues that this is an important source of the influence of major economic interests in urban areas. Often they do not even have to do anything to have their concerns considered by officials. Officials anticipate their requests because of the importance of business to the urban economy.[4] Citizen demands may not be as well-known, therefore citizens need to communicate through participation.

Alternatively, officials may behave as others desire, not because of fear of future reprisal but because of philosophical agreement with them. Once again, this may be to the advantage of major economic interests. Both those interests and urban officials benefit from a strong economy, so both may agree on what policies local governments should pursue. Officials may not see how they benefit from policies for low-income residents, so such residents need to make extra efforts to convince officials to respond to their demands.

A final problem with Dahl's definition was identified by Peter Bachrach and Morton Baratz.[5] They point out that the focus is on what B *does* as a result of A. But equally important, they argue, is what B does *not* do as a result of A. The ability to stop certain actions from occurring is equal in importance as Dahl's focus on causing behavior to occur. For example, keeping issues off the agenda guarantees success to those who are opposed to them.

Dahl's definition alerts us to the fact that power is relational. It is only meaningful to talk about power in the interactions between or among individuals or groups of individuals, for example, the relations among political leaders, major economic interests, and other citizens in urban areas. The exercise of power depends on the resources and skills of those who are attempting to alter the behavior of officials and of the officials as well. Citizens will have more influence on officials who are seeking coalition partners than on those who have assembled an effective governing coalition. But power does not automatically come to those in possession of resources. Those resources must be used and they must have some impact on the behavior of others. Therefore, power is situational. Individuals may have power only at certain times or with certain people. While economic interests have advantages in attempts to influence urban policies, citizens may use their resources to demand attention from political leaders.

It is impossible to provide a simple, definitive answer to the question of whether citizens can exercise power over policy in urban areas because the answer depends on many factors in each unique circumstance. This chapter will review important resources that are needed to influence policy and the mechanisms of citizen participation.

Resources of Citizens

Citizens can use various resources to influence urban policy. The more resources citizens command, the more effective they are likely to be. However, resources can be interchangeable—that is, one can be substituted for another. The primary citizen resources are money, numbers, and expertise.

Money is a resource for some obvious and perhaps not-so-obvious reasons. Clearly, money has been used in some instances to buy power. At times, bribes and kickbacks have had a substantial effect on urban policies. But money can be used as a power resource in other ways. The wealthy are accorded a special prestige in a capitalist society that values individual success. This gives their opinions and pronouncements special legitimacy in political debates. Money can be contributed to the election campaigns of city officials, a process that at least means the contributors will be assured of the officials' rapt attention after the election. Top-level managers of major economic interests in the metropolis are likely to be wealthy.

In addition, representatives of major business interests have an easier time gaining access to officials. Access is facilitated by the fact that urban officials and business executives will often be in a situation of mutual dependence. Business may want some policy (a zoning change, for instance) for which the officials have authority. In turn, the officials know that business has an impact on the economic fate of the city and thus on their political fate.

Another way that money can be an important resource is the ease with which it can be exchanged for other resources. For example, people with money can exchange it to hire people to do such things as cleaning the house or babysitting the kids—thus freeing up time for political activity. Money can buy a car to make it easier to go to city council meetings or to get to the polls on election day.[6] Money can also contribute to maximizing the second citizen resource: the number of people who join together to attempt to influence urban policy. Those officials who owe their jobs to elections are especially sensitive to the need to listen when large numbers of urban residents agree on a policy issue. Money can help solidify support for a policy when it is used to hire public relations experts to plan a campaign to convince others of the policy's merits. Money can also buy access to media to communicate the message. Newspaper ads, TV time, radio spots, and other ways of getting the message out are costly, yet essential in some efforts to influence the opinions and actions of substantial numbers of urban residents.

While money can help in mobilizing urban residents, other resources can also help achieve the same goal. A strong leader can mobilize people without needing to rely on hired public relations experts. The effectiveness of a charismatic leader such as Dr. Martin Luther King or a committed community organizer like Saul Alinsky depended on leadership abilities, not on money.

A strong organizational structure can often be more effective in mobilizing people than a public relations campaign waged in the mass media. For that reason, the late community organizer Saul Alinsky focused his efforts at the neighborhood level and relied on existing neighborhood organizations, such as churches, to provide the nucleus for new community organizations.[7] The existing organizations were especially helpful as they already had a membership and a communication network. The advantages of an existing structure and communication network are also an important component of the success of business in urban politics.

A final resource that citizens can use is expertise. The importance of expertise rests on two sources. First, as society has become more complex, so have its problems. The value of experts—those who can claim to know more than others about a particular subject area—increases with increasing complexity. Second, because of the need of expertise, government bureaucracies have grown in size and importance. This is true for all levels of government. Bureaucrats are expected to have or to develop expertise. Because their jobs require that they be experts, they believe in using that expertise as a basis for decisions. That can create a problem for citizens who want to influence government decisions unless the citizens themselves can be seen as having comparable expertise.[8]

Virtually anyone can claim expertise in some area, but some claims are more effective than others. Presumably the poor know more than anyone else about what services they need, yet their claims of expertise in the area of poverty policy are not accorded the same legitimacy as the claims of businesspersons to be experts in, for example, tax policy.

The importance of expertise not only varies by the people in question but also by the policy area. Some policy areas are highly complex and technological, and ordinary citizens are not seen as having the expertise to contribute effectively to policy development.[9] An example would be policies regarding criteria for *how* to construct highway overpasses to ensure they will be structurally sound. Other policy areas do not require much technological competence on the part of citizens to provide policy direction. An example would be the question of *where* the overpass should be built. But as the same officials often deal with both issues as a single policy package, ordinary citizens without expertise in highway engineering often have difficulty being seen as having a legitimate voice in policy making.

In general such policy areas as transportation and sanitation are usually defined as requiring technical expertise while social service areas are usually seen as more amenable to citizen influence.[10] Officials active in the various areas do tend to differ in their willingness to involve citizens in policy development.[11] But some social service professionals see citizens as lacking adequate expertise to contribute meaningfully. For example, perhaps because of their years of education and advanced degrees, professionals in the field of education have often succeeded in defining their field as being too important and complex to permit much citizen control.[12]

Major urban economic interests are likely to have influence in the policy process because of their money and expertise. While they are not as numerous as other citizens, they can use financial resources to mobilize others on their behalf. They are aided in such efforts by the belief that business prosperity is essential for a viable community. Citizens with demands that differ from those of the business community must accumulate resources and develop strategies that ensure that they will have access to political leaders.

How Citizens Use Their Resources

While possession of one or more of the three major citizen resources is usually necessary for influencing government policy, simply having the resources does not guarantee citizen influence. The resources must be used and be used effectively. The primary value of these resources is that they can be used to gain access to policy makers. While being listened to—having access to officials—is not equivalent to success, it is a necessary prerequisite for it. Not being listened to at all leads to inevitable defeat.[13]

Although all three resources can be used to gain access to officials, the mechanisms by which they do so differ. Money confers a certain prestige and legitimacy in our society that can be used to gain the attention of officials. As indicated above, Clarence Stone has argued that major economic interests may not even have to do anything to have their concerns addressed by local officials because officials anticipate their demands.[14]

Expertise also conveys legitimacy to a request to city government. Increasingly in a complex, technological society, being able to say, "I know more about this than you," is effective in attempts to gain access. Many citizen groups use what money they have to hire their own experts to do battle with a local government's experts.

Numbers of people are harder to translate into access. It is difficult to demonstrate on a daily basis the number of people who support a particular policy request. The statement by leaders that they represent a sizable number of people may be discounted. In response, a mass demonstration could be staged or leaders could arrange to have people show up at a city council meeting waving placards. But not only is it difficult to mobilize people, such behavior is sometimes seen as vaguely illegitimate. In addition, officials may feel threatened and may react by hardening their position. Maintaining the support of large numbers of people over a long period is also difficult, especially if the potential for success appears low.[15]

In some circumstances, numbers can be translated into access. Numbers determine elections, and if a group can demonstrate that it is a major voting bloc, elected officials will be more eager to listen. Minority groups have been able to use the fact that they are an increasing proportion of the electorate in many cities as a lever to gain officials' attention. More important, they have managed to mobilize those numbers to elect their own representatives. In some instances, large numbers

of people at public hearings or city council meetings have succeeded in altering proposed policies. Such groups of demonstrators, however, are rarely seen as having the staying power to continue to be a force in the policy process and are unlikely to be given access to the governing coalition. The same can usually be said for the groups who attend protests.

Resources possessed by citizens determine which of three strategies they will use to try to influence the decisions of city officials: **persuasion, inducement,** or **constraint**.[16] Persuasion refers to changing the minds of officials by presenting a compelling argument for a different course of action. The use of inducements and constraints requires going beyond presenting an argument to adding a carrot (inducements) or using a stick (constraints) to influence a situation. With inducements, citizens offer something positive to officials in return for compliance with citizen requests. For example, citizens could promise campaign support.

The use of constraints refers to citizens threatening officials with some sort of negative consequences if officials do not comply with requests. Saul Alinsky was highly creative in devising strategies that relied on the use of constraints. For example, he advised groups to do anything—picketing, suing, demonstrating, whatever—that would embarrass, humiliate, or otherwise keep officials off-balance until they were willing to accede to the group's demands.[17]

Obviously, the strategy used should be based on a calculation of what would be most effective, and that, in turn, is dependent on the nature of the relationship between citizens and officials and the nature of the requests. Citizens who have a great deal of access to officials, who trust them and feel confident that what they are requesting from the officials will be acceptable will be wise to rely on persuasion to achieve their goals. The primary concern would be to define their requests in ways that will be most acceptable or attractive to officials. The procedure most useful in such a situation would be simply to have a representative of the group contact friendly officials and present the request in the most favorable light. Being able to speak with expertise may help in such a situation. While resources may have been expended to get to the position of being able to expect a favorable response to a request, clearly few resources are necessary once that stage is reached. Business interests are often able to participate through persuasion. Their prominence in the community gives them access to officials, and their message of economic development and growth is seen as serving the public good. They may, of course, be part of the informal governing coalition and thus have automatic access.

If citizens are less sure of a favorable response from officials, either because they have a less trusting relationship with those officials or because they fear what they are requesting cannot be packaged attractively enough to be readily accepted, they may need to use inducements to "sweeten the pot." In such a situation, it is important to have access to resources that could be exchanged for compliance. Electoral support in the form of campaign contributions, campaign workers, or a voting bloc can be strong inducements to elected officials. Such inducements may even be exchanged for access to a governing coalition. Alternatively, they may simply attract the attention of the members of the governing coalition. Many citizens have found that being part of an electoral coalition does not guarantee inclusion in a governing coalition.

Citizens who feel little hope of being successful in getting what they want from officials—again, either because of their relationship with officials or because of the nature of their requests—will have little choice but to threaten the use of negative sanctions. For example, citizens could indicate that they will mobilize their electoral support to defeat the officials in the next election, or they could threaten to use protests and demonstrations.

The latter strategy is unwise unless citizens feel it is absolutely essential. The use of constraints is potentially very costly since it may harden the position of officials and alienate other citizens who otherwise might be potential allies. In addition, the threat may not be very credible. Unless the group is very large, the threat of electoral consequences is questionable. Protests and demonstrations are hard to maintain over time, especially if there is little hope of eventual success, and officials have many ways to delay taking any action. For example, they can set up committees to study the situation or—legitimately in many cases—then can claim resource limitations make compliance impossible.[18]

The Group Basis of Participation

Participation that is aimed at altering the urban agenda, either by influencing the governing coalition or by the participants becoming part of that coalition, almost always must be by groups of people cooperating either formally or informally. While it is *individuals* who participate, rarely can an individual citizen alone have a substantial impact on the political process. Rather, it is *groups* of individuals who can increase their impact by collective behavior. As an example, Clarence Stone points out how the clout of the African-American community in Atlanta increased with the formation of the Atlanta Negro Voters League in 1949, which could present a united front to public officials and other leaders.[19] Also, groups are the targets of efforts by others to build coalitions. Political leaders looking for support for their policy agenda often target group leaders to try to achieve maximum support with a minimum of effort.[20]

Paul Peterson has argued that urban politics is "groupless" politics for three reasons. First, he mentioned that the important decisions affecting urban areas were no longer made at the urban level. Second, he argued that for many people it is easier for them to exit—to move from the city—than to try to alter policies with which they are dissatisfied. Third, he asserts that the "free-rider" problem impedes group activity. As explained before, the free-rider problem refers to the ability of people to enjoy the benefits achieved by group efforts whether or not they contributed to those efforts. Therefore, it is rational for people to sit back and let others do the work.[21]

John Clayton Thomas, referring specifically to neighborhood organizations, claimed that Peterson's argument had three errors. First, for most people, their home is their single most important investment, which gives them a stake in local politics. While policies controlled by the local government may not always be as important as those controlled by other levels of government, they may seem very important to residents of the city. Infrequent garbage collection may not rank with nuclear war in importance, but can seem very important to city residents on a hot summer day. The closeness of problems to the daily lives of city residents makes the issues of urban politics especially relevant. Second, exit is not always as easy as Peterson implies, because "transaction costs" are involved in moving. Selling the old house, finding and buying a new house in a new neighborhood, perhaps paying more interest on the new mortgage all contribute to these costs.[22] Finally, Thomas argues that the "free-rider" problem is not as important in small groups, such as those at the neighborhood level, as it is in larger, national organizations.[23] Many people join such organizations for social or ideological reasons.

Others have argued that far from being groupless, urban politics is noteworthy for the vast number of groups.

> On each political issue—decentralization or community control, the mix of low income and middle income housing, the proportion

of blacks in the city colleges, the location of a cross-Manhattan or cross-Brooklyn expressway, etc.—there are dozens of active, vocal, and conflicting organized opinions. The difficulty in governing New York—and many other cities as well—is not the 'lack of voice' of individuals in city affairs or the 'eclipse of local community,' but the babel of voices and the multiplication of claimants in the widened political arena.[24]

Although numerous, many urban organizations are often somewhat ephemeral.[25] In some cases, they are nothing more than a few activists working together temporarily, or even a single individual sending out flyers from home.

One reason for the disagreement about the role of groups may be that the term "group" has a variety of meanings. In the previous chapter, the term was used to refer generally to people who shared a common characteristic, for example women or African-Americans. Such people may or may not see any common political goals or cooperate to achieve such goals. The term is also used to refer more specifically to organizations with a structure and an identifiable list of members. Groups that do not have common political goals are unlikely to have political influence, even if they do share common characteristics. To influence the urban agenda, groups of people must be seen as sharing policy preferences and having resources to exchange with the governing coalition. While the Atlanta Negro Voters League gave voice to the concerns of African-Americans in the Atlanta of the 1940s, what gave the organization access to the governing coalition was the evidence that the African-American community as a whole, whether members of the League or not, would act as a voting bloc in city elections. The success of the community was due both to the organization of the League itself and to the broader sense of shared goals and behavior of the African-American community as a whole.

The amount of effort required of members of groups who seek political influence may vary greatly. They may simply be asked to contribute money, or they may be expected to protest a policy at the city council meeting, an activity that not only takes time and effort but also will embroil them in a conflict situation. Those groups with ample financial resources and a respected membership—for example, major economic interests—will require the least of members. The group could hire a representative to contact appropriate authorities on its behalf, or the members themselves may be able to visit informally with officials.

Successful interest groups establish close contacts not only with elected officials in government, but also with administrators who implement the policies that affect the group. The administrators and the group representatives have much in common—interests, values, expertise, and in some cases, a common professional language.[26] Group representatives can target very precise messages to the administrators, who would be more likely to respond to a request from such a group representative than from an individual citizen who may be protesting the administrators' decisions or demanding a change in policy or procedures. Indeed, even elected political officials often have difficulty changing the direction of policy when groups and administrators are in agreement, for they may lack expertise.

Other groups that lack the advantages of money or expertise will have to rely on demonstrating that large numbers of people support the groups' goals and using those numbers as an inducement—as in promising votes—to get official response or as a constraint—as in threatening a protest. Organizing large numbers of people is difficult; it takes skills in communication, knowledge of issues, understanding of the political process. It takes time to contact people and to convince them to cooperate. Success is possible, but is not readily achieved.

The resources necessary for group activity add to the disadvantages that people of low socioeconomic status have in political activity and explains the persistent status bias in who becomes active in groups and which groups are most likely to have an impact on the political process. Poor people also have problems competing in the interest group game because the condition of their lives means they have little time or energy for political activity.

> The poor, unlike the rest of us, face a daily struggle to provide the bare minimum for sheer physical survival. Because of this fact of life they are unable to afford the luxury of engaging in political activities which only *promise* to yield results in the future, even if those results might be more rewarding than results gained from short-run activities.[27]

Throughout the 1960s and early 1970s, the federal government enacted several programs intended to overcome the status bias by mobilizing the poor population, particularly the War on Poverty and the Model Cities program initiated during Lyndon Johnson's presidency. Both of these programs, which provided federal money to fight poverty, required evidence of citizen involvement in planning programs at the local level. A premise of these programs was that if the poor become politically active, they could demand the resources necessary to move themselves out of poverty.[28] In addition to these two programs aimed specifically at getting the poor actively involved in making policy, a vast number of other federal statutes of this period included requirements that local political jurisdictions prove they provided all citizens an opportunity to participate in planning programs before federal money could be used to fund those programs.

The mobilization efforts were short-lived, for local political leaders soon realized that they had everything to lose and nothing to gain from mobilizing the poor.[29] First, the increasing number of demands from the poor meant overloading a service delivery system that was already stretched to, or beyond, capacity. In addition, the War on Poverty was instituted at the same time that minority groups such as African-Americans and Latinos were increasingly focusing efforts on local, not national, politics. The result was a confrontation between political leaders and the increasingly militant poor. Pressure by local leaders on Congress led, over time, to a weakening of the participation requirements by making citizen input only advisory.

In general, evaluations of such mandated participation indicated only marginal success. In many cases those who participated in the programs had previously been active, producing little change in the distribution of participants. In addition, those among the poor population who participated were atypical.[30] They were more highly motivated and tended to be upwardly mobile. In those programs not specifically targeted to the poor, the bulk of the participants were from the middle and upper class. The major positive finding was that these programs provided some participants with training that enabled them to continue to participate effectively even after the federal programs disappeared. As a result of this newly developed indigenous leadership, some minority groups became more successful in extracting policies they desired from local governments.[31]

While the poor face substantial barriers in using an interest group strategy to influence politics, some community organizers have been successful in building grass roots organizations with political clout. Of these organizers, Saul Alinsky was one of the most successful. Alinsky used three guidelines for organizing the people at a grass roots level. First, he appealed to people on the basis of issues that had immediate, obvious concern to them. Second, he focused not on "leading" the people, but getting them to use existing organizations or to build new organizations that

they would control themselves. His goal was to develop indigenous leaders to organize himself out of a job.[32] Third, he relied on creative and dramatic tactics to publicize a group's demands.

> Using military imagery, he preached the need to keep the enemy off balance, use the establishment's rules against itself, split the opposition and appeal to its self-interest, threaten embarrassment and humiliation—in short, to do whatever was necessary to win. Demonstrate, yell, picket, sue. He once proposed that a group pressure Eastman Kodak by threatening to eat great quantities of beans and then storm the Rochester Philharmonic.[33]

Many of the organizations Alinsky helped found had a substantial impact. For instance, the Community Service Organization in the Southwest was a major political base for Mexican-Americans. The Woodlawn Organization in a southside Chicago black ghetto became a major force during the civil rights movement and later succeeded in establishing a multi-million-dollar community development corporation in the neighborhood. But Alinsky's tactics had limits. One was that his methods were aimed at mobilizing relatively small groups. His emphasis on using existing organizations such as churches or union locals meant the organization encompassed only a neighborhood. As a result, the organizations often pitted one minority group against another. For example, one of Alinsky's organizations in Chicago used its clout to keep blacks out of the neighborhood.[34]

Another problem with Alinsky's tactics was their focus on achieving limited, short-range goals. Organizations need to have some immediate success to provide their members with motivation to continue working. Ironically, however, the achievement of short-term goals may actually be a kiss of death. If an organization has achieved its goals, what reason does it have to exist? Although the achievement of a short-term goal certainly is a victory, the dissolution of the organization has ramifications for the long-term political influence of the population or its likelihood of becoming part of a governing coalition. The representatives of the population do not have time to build a reputation among officials or develop a trusting or friendly relationship with them. New organizations that emerge can more easily be ignored because officials can assume they, too, are likely to disappear quickly.

Other community organizations have tried to build broad coalitions of people to demand a redistribution of social and political resources. Rather than focusing solely on isolated groups of the poor, their goal is to ally the poor with the middle class, which is getting squeezed economically as a result of tax burdens and job insecurity.[35] For example, the Organization for a Better St. Paul organized on a citywide basis and joined with other groups to stop banks from refusing to make mortgage loans in certain neighborhoods believed to be deteriorating. This practice, known as **redlining**, made it impossible for people to buy houses in a neighborhood and, therefore, accelerated the deterioration of the area. In Washington, D.C., community groups succeeded in getting a speculation tax passed, designed to slow the process in which developers buy houses at a cheap rate and then sell them quickly at a huge profit. This practice has serious consequences for the residents of these neighborhoods. Because this speculation occurs in neighborhoods that are increasing in value, the residents who sell their homes often have no idea what the true value of their property is and sell too cheaply. Often they cannot find comparable housing with the money received from the sale. The purchaser will usually sell the property quickly at a much higher price, which contributes to raising property values in the neighborhood and leads to higher property taxes for the remaining residents.

Such efforts require lasting organizations that bring together people who are likely to be antagonistic because of racial differences. Some organizers are optimistic that such organizations can be formed and that they can be successful. They also hope that the organizations can be a catalyst for greater understanding and cooperation among racial and ethnic groups. As one community organizer observed, "We've been able to sit down and discuss things because of the issues in common without saying 'you're white, you're black, you're Mexican.'"[36] While such successes are possible, it is clearly difficult to build organizations that bridge racial, ethnic, and class differences.

Elections

Groups are important in politics, but individual participation in various forms of electoral activities is also possible. In addition to voting, citizens can participate in campaign activities by stuffing envelopes, canvassing door-to-door, or planning strategy. Of course, the ultimate form of electoral participation is to run for election. Voting in presidential elections is the most common form of political participation. Participation in local elections is substantially lower, especially, as is frequently the case, when those elections are not held concurrently with state and national elections. The percentage actually voting in local elections is typically less than 30 percent (See Table 6–1).[37]

Elections are crucial because they determine who will govern. In addition, because the granting of power is conditional, elections are supposed to keep elected officials accountable to the public. An electoral victory simply means that voters are putting the officials elected in office, but on probation for a set period. Therefore, the electoral connection is the primary means by which citizens attempt to ensure government officials will be concerned about what we think.

Electoral participation is not, however, a panacea. One major limit on the importance

TABLE 6–1

Participation in Various Election Activities

	Percentage Claiming Participation
Regularly vote in presidential elections	58%
Always vote in local elections	35%
Talk to others to influence their vote	32%
Attend a political meeting	19%
Work for a party or candidate	27%
Give money	23%

Source: National Opinion Research Center, General Social Survey, 1987. From Sidney Verba, Kay Lehman Schlozman, and Henry E. Brady, *Voice and Equality*. Copyright © 1995 by the President and Fellows of Harvard College. Reprinted by permission of Harvard University Press.

of electoral participation comes from the fact that many officials do not feel accountable to the public. The threat of electoral defeat is supposed to keep officials accountable, but a study of officials in 82 cities in the San Francisco Bay area concluded that many council members felt no compunction about voting against the majority because they did not really care if they were re-elected. Most were part-time and received low salaries in return for their public service. One of the responses shows the disdain some of these council members felt for their political futures: "I am free to do as I feel. In general it is easy to vote against the majority because I don't have any political ambitions."[38] This attitude was related to the behavior of council members.

Where the norm of volunteerism is more prevalent, councils are (a) more likely to vote against what they see as majority opinion, (b) less likely to feel under pressure from the public, (c) less likely to consider the upcoming election when choosing among policy alternatives, (d) less likely to involve constituents as part of the strategy of policy-making, (e) less likely to view political groups as having an influential part to play in city politics, (f) less likely to facilitate group access to the council, and (g)

less likely to perform services for the constituents.[39]

These attitudes may be more common among representatives at the local level of government—for example, city councils—and may be less common in large cities where salaries are high enough to encourage people to want to maintain their positions.[40] But a recent study found that most council members had little reason to fear electoral defeat.[41] Local officials who are indifferent to re-election or who believe there is little chance of electoral defeat may well be indifferent to citizens. Citizens, in turn, may rightfully see government as "remote, inaccessible, and largely unresponsive."[42]

Another major limit of electoral participation becomes obvious when the focus narrows from the role of elections in a political system to the role of an election from an individual's perspective. While the macro perspective suggests elections are crucial for keeping government accountable, an individual may feel there little is to be gained from participation in elections. Voting is an individual activity, but a single vote makes little difference. Voting tends to create political influence when groups of people are organized into identifiable **voting blocs**. Those in the bloc then may be able to claim some major impact on the outcome of the election through the aggregated votes. But, as discussed above, organizing people into such blocs is often difficult.

Because there is so little chance that a single vote will make any difference in an election, individuals may decide the costs involved in voting may not be outweighed by the benefits received.[43] While it may not take many resources to vote, the time and effort to get to the polls and perhaps to become informed about the options may still be too great if no benefits are perceived.

Individuals may also realize that a vote actually conveys no precise information to the candidates. V.O. Key once observed that voters have but two words in their vocabulary: yes and no. And, he continued, it is not always clear which word they have spoken in any given election, especially as some are saying "yes" and some are saying "no."[44] Again, the existence of a voting bloc with an identifiable spokesperson can increase the communication potential of voting because the spokesperson can define what the group expects in return for its votes.

Further complicating the process of communicating via elections is the way election campaigns are run. Public relations firms, in a common phrase, package candidates and sell them like soap. The use of such firms, with their focus on emotional appeals and image, has spread from the national level to state and local elections. When voters are limited to saying only yes or no to a public relations package, they cannot convey much information about preferences on issues.

Such doubts about the value of voting are aggravated in the urban setting. As later chapters will discuss, the political fragmentation of the urban context makes it difficult for officials in any one jurisdiction to address successfully the problems that beset their constituents. Those problems spill over the boundary lines on maps. In addition, the control exercised over urban areas by state and national governments may make the question of who is mayor seem less important than who is governor or who is president. Finally, control over major decisions is frequently shared with—or dominated by—private economic interests not subject to electoral control.

There are some specific reasons why urban residents of lower socioeconomic status have little incentive to vote. First, they are less likely to develop a sense of civic responsibility or to feel that political participation is important. Also, the search for affordable housing or the necessity of living in public housing (and thus being subject to relocation) may mean that poorer residents do not stay in one location long enough to find and maintain communication channels that would help them learn the information necessary for electoral politics. Information costs are also increased by the absence of party cues because many elections are nonpartisan at the local level.

Other government structures also affect electoral participation. Many studies have documented that minority representation in city governments is significantly decreased in cities where the council is elected in citywide at-large elections.[45] This is because although a minority in the city as a whole, a group may have a majority within a single electoral district. In addition, fewer resources are needed to run an election campaign in a district than in the city as a whole.[46] More recent research, however, has found that while African-Americans are still most equitably represented in systems with district elections, the differences in their representation in cities with different electoral systems have greatly diminished. District elections do not increase representation of Latinos, probably because they are less segregated residentially than blacks.[47]

Luis Fraga has pointed to another way that nonpartisan political systems discriminate against minorities. In nonpartisan systems, slating groups are often formed to recruit and support candidates. Examining the effect of these slating groups in Dallas, San Antonio, and Abilene, Texas, he concluded that "Extremely limited levels of ethnic, racial, and class diversity in slating group candidate backgrounds demonstrated a predominantly white, middle and upper class, business bias."[48]

In nonpartisan cities without slating groups, citizens turn to such voting cues as ethnic identity of the candidate, other background characteristics, or personality.[49] One study found that not only do neighborhoods dominated by a particular ethnic group tend to vote for candidates of the same ethnicity, but that candidates base their appeals to voters on ethnicity.[50] Such appeals to separate groups may fragment the city, making mutual accommodation among the various ethnic groups to achieve common goals more difficult.[51]

Another result of nonpartisanship is that incumbents are less likely to be defeated. Again, in the absence of a party cue, voters use name recognition as a basis for vote choice. While the success of incumbents means that officials have time to develop experience and expertise in their jobs, it also undoubtedly contributes to lessening the extent to which city officials feel they need to be accountable to the public. Elections cannot be relied upon to keep officials accountable if the officials have no need to fear electoral defeat.

In the face of these limits, it is perhaps not surprising that urban voting turnouts are low. Some researchers have argued that turnout can be increased. Case study evidence from Alabama suggests that changes in the electoral system from at-large to district elections increases African-American participation.[52]

Even if the structure itself does not change, increasing competition in city elections may increase turnout.

Turnout frequently increased in nonpartisan cities when partisan activity occurred— typically when liberal Democratic coalitions challenged incumbent Republican regimes, as in Berkeley, Oakland, and Richmond.

These electoral challenges focused attention on minority issues and resulted in increased minority representation. When new coalitions challenged incumbents, the challenge often involved an expansion of participation—an increase in voter turnout.[53]

Evidence indicates that voters who are contacted personally by a party or a candidate are more likely to vote and to take part in election campaigns.[54] That may mean that the tendency for high-status citizens to be more likely to participate is attributable, at least in part, to the tendency of parties to target such individuals and to fail to try to mobilize lower-status citizens. One study has argued that political leaders rationally allocate their limited resources to contact those people who are expected to respond. Knowing that low-income people are less likely to participate, leaders make little effort to mobilize them. Thus, the pressure that political leaders face to use their own resources most efficiently builds a class bias into their efforts to mobilize voters. In the American participatory system, class differences in mobilization typically aggravate rather than mitigate the effects of class differences in political resources. Once again, inequalities are cumulative, not dispersed.[55]

Involvement in elections could potentially be increased by party or group efforts to mobilize those citizens not currently active.

Some urban areas are showing evidence of increasing voter turnout. Chapter 5 documented the increasing activity of African-Americans, Latinos, and Asians. Elections are one form of political participation where voter numbers are the major resource. In elections, other resources such as money or communication skills are only valuable if they can be converted into numbers at the polls. Thus, elections are potentially the most democratic form of political participation because groups without economic resources may be able to compete if they are able to mobilize enough people. Of course money can be crucial in mobilization efforts. Getting citizens to the polls to vote your way is easier if you have money to print and mail campaign material, to buy TV time, and to hire people with organizational and communication skills to conduct an effective campaign. Also, the existence of electoral blocs with identifiable spokespersons may increase the importance of elections as a political strategy. The organization of such blocs and the identification of effective leaders take substantial resources.

Both African-Americans and Latinos have had significantly greater electoral success at the local level than at the state or national level. While they are a minority nationally and in most states, their concentration in some urban areas gives them a base for electoral success. But numbers alone do not assure political power. Rufus Browning, Dale Marshall, and David Tabb found that the key factor that explained the incorporation of blacks into the governing coalitions of the 10 California cities they studied was not the size of the African-American population but the degree to which they had organized to contest elections by recruiting and supporting black candidates. They found that such mobilization was less important for Latinos, due primarily to the distribution of the Latino population in the cities they studied. For both groups, the authors found the key to success lay ultimately in forming coalitions with others.

> For both groups, the size of other supportive groups in the electorate, including whites, was critical to the fruitful initiation and continuance of minority electoral mobilization, the formation of biracial and multiethnic coalitions, their victory, and therefore the inclusion of minorities in city governance. Coalition was the key to strong political incorporation, and the combination of minority and white resources was the prerequisite for successful coalition.[56]

Raphael Sonenshein argues that such a coalition was the reason for Tom Bradley's success

as the first African-American mayor of Los Angeles.[57]

Some evidence suggests that the increasing size of the African-American and Latino electorate may affect policies. One study found that cities with black mayors spent more on social services than did cities with white mayors.[58] Browning, Marshall, and Tabb concluded that the incorporation of both African-Americans and Latinos into governing coalitions resulted in a greater responsiveness of city governments to minority demands. The bottom line seems to be that while obstacles certainly exist, groups can use elections to change the structure of political power in cities and that can produce change in policies as well. Electoral coalitions of minority groups is the subject of Box 6–1.

Most electoral contests involve the choice between two candidates for office. In addition, many cities have provisions for a **recall election**. Citizens who are dissatisfied with an elected official can initiate a petition to force a recall election to determine if the candidate should be removed from office. Other kinds of electoral contests give voters direct control over policy issues. In many states policy issues can be voted on directly by voters by processes of **initiative** or **referendum**. With an initiative, citizens can require that a particular policy be put on the ballot for decision by the voters. Usually citizens must first get a certain proportion of the electorate to sign a petition indicating their support for putting the issue on the ballot. With a referendum, the legislative body is required to put a policy on the ballot for direct voter approval. At the city level, this usually means that the city council or the school board is required to seek voter support for policies.

While initiatives and referenda are procedures that have been used in many states since the Progressive Era at the turn of the nineteenth century, the effect of such direct elections is not yet clear. There is evidence that those voters who reported they had voted in

BOX 6–1

Electoral Coalitions and Racial/Ethnic Voting

When he first won election as mayor of Los Angeles in 1993, Richard Riordan was overwhelmingly supported by most white voters, although Jewish voters split their votes between him and his Democratic opponent. One-third of the Asian-Americans voted for Riordan's opponent, Michael Woo. In his successful re-election bid, Riordan received 71 percent of the Jewish vote, and two-thirds of the Asian-American vote. But what might be the most significant outcome from election 1997 was the shift in Latino votes. In 1993 only 40 percent voted for Riordan, compared to 60 percent in 1997. In his first term in office, Riordan had reached out to Latinos, forming alliances with Latino political leaders. His support of inner city schools and his close ties to the Catholic Church also helped his standing in the Latino community.

The shift of votes was especially important because for the first time the turnout of Latino voters was higher than that of African-Americans. Indeed, African-Americans constituted only 13 percent of the turnout in the 1993 election and only 19 percent voted for Riordan. African-Americans felt that Riordan was insensitive to them, pointing to the failure to renew the contract of the city's first African-American police chief.

Los Angeles was governed from 1973 until 1993 by a biracial coalition of African-Americans and liberal white voters who repeatedly elected an African-American as mayor. The 1997 election may signal the creation of a new multiracial coalition of Asian-Americans, Latinos, and whites, with African-Americans conspicuously absent. It may also be a sign of the increasing political power of Latinos as their numbers grow and as those who are immigrants become citizens. Indeed, Latino voter turnout is increasing while turnout among other groups is decreasing.

Latinos are using their numbers to become an important part of the electoral coalition in Los Angeles, and Riordan's courting of the Latino leaders between the 1993 and 1997 elections is an indicator that they may become part of the governing coalition as well. African-Americans, meanwhile, are becoming increasingly isolated from the governing coalition they had controlled for two decades.

The Los Angeles case may have implications for other cities, especially New York City. In New York, as in Los Angeles, Latinos are becoming an increasingly important voting bloc. In 1993, Rudolph Giuliani ran for mayor on a slate with Herman Badillo as comptroller. Since then Giuliani has lost some support because of a conflict with a former school chancellor who was Latino.

African-Americans, who finally managed to use their numbers to become part of the governing coalition in many cities, may be losing their control because of growing numbers of other minority groups with whom they do not always agree. Politics in many urban areas is less a politics of black and white and more of a complex mosaic.

Source: Adapted from William Schneider, "Shattering an Urban Liberal Coalition," *National Journal* (April 19, 1997): 790; Alex Castellanos, "Lessons from Los Angeles," *New York Times* (May 14, 1997): A21; Jim Sleeper, "The End of the Rainbow," *The New Republic* (November 1, 1993): 20

referenda were "more predominantly white, affluent, better-educated, and of higher subjective social class."[59] Thus, rather than making elections more democratic, such direct elections may result in a greater bias toward the interests of the "rich, well-born, and able."

Another reason such elections may result in a bias is that organized groups often become active in such elections to try to influence voters' decisions. Some analysts fear that those groups with the most money to buy newspaper space and TV and radio time for ads will be more likely to succeed in influencing the voters' choice.

Others have argued that the voters in referenda and initiative elections are more likely to vote no than yes. A study of 68 referenda on the issue of city–county consolidation over a space of three decades found that only 17 were approved by voters.[60] Also, in some states, school bond issues presented to voters for approval have a particularly dismal rate of success. Ohio is a prime example. The city of Youngstown once defeated five such school bond referenda in a row, resulting in the closure of the city's schools.

Initiative and referenda elections were intended to increase the direct control citizens can exercise over policy. As with many reforms, the results do not always meet the expectations. While the evidence is sketchy, it tends to suggest the voters in such elections are atypical of the general electorate and tend to have a preference for voting no.

Citizen-initiated Contacts

While the evidence suggests a bias in favor of those of higher socioeconomic status in most forms of political participation, such bias may possibly be counteracted by citizen-initiated contacts with government officials. Contacting usually takes few resources and permits very precise communication. It is an activity that can be effectively performed by a single individual. One study concluded that a major determinant of contacting is the perception of need,[61] while a more recent study concluded that while need motivated some contactors, others were seeking more general social goals. The latter tended to have higher socioeco-

nomic status and were less likely to be seeking policies because of their individual needs.[62]

Estimates of the percentage of people who contact local government officials have varied between 20 percent in a nationwide study to 34 percent in a study of contacting officials in Cincinnati. A study of Kansas City, Missouri, reported that 28 percent had contacted local officials.[63] The disparity in the numbers reported by various studies may be due to the way the questions were worded or interpreted by respondents.[64] Alternatively, the differences may be attributable to the unique characteristics of the areas studied.[65] In any event, contacting may be an especially common form of urban political participation. Contacting government for help contradicts some residents' feeling of responsibility to provide for themselves. In the interdependent environment of cities, it may be clearer that it is impossible for all to be individually self-reliant and, therefore, seeking government help may be more acceptable.[66]

Before concluding that contacting counteracts any bias created by other forms of participation, it is important to know something about how local governments respond to citizen-initiated contacts. A study of service delivery in Detroit identified five uniform rules that government could use to distribute routine services. One of those rules is the demand rule, meaning services are distributed in response to citizen requests. The alternative criteria are as follows: distribute services equally to all areas; distribute in proportion to need; distribute in such a way that the cost of provision of the service equals the benefit citizens receive throughout the city; and distribute according to the perceived power of citizens in various areas.[67]

The question then becomes which criterion do administrators use. Evidence indicates that the only answer to this question is "it depends." One factor that seems to affect whether urban administrators respond to citizen demands is the type of governmental structure. One study found that governments with at-large elections or with city managers are less responsive to citizens generally.[68] (The various structures of urban government will be discussed in the next chapter.) Other evidence indicates that responsiveness to citizens varies across agencies and even within individual agencies.[69] The key determinant of the variance has been identified as the extent to which issues are technical. Agencies or administrators that are responsible for technical programs want to base their actions on professional standards,[70] thus they are more likely to resist responding to citizen demands. Bureaucrats in human service agencies, however, were more likely to be responsive to citizen input.[71]

Professional or expert standards could include three of the distribution criteria identified: distributing services equally, according to need, or where the costs equal the benefits received. Professional standards would probably not lead to giving services based on the perception of the power resources possessed by citizens. Indeed, research in both Chicago and Houston has given strong support to the contention that administrators do not consider the resources of residents in determining how, when, and if to respond to requests. There was some evidence that African-American wards in Chicago tended to receive slightly more positive responses from urban bureaucrats, but the differences were slight and attributed primarily to the kind of requests made, rather than to the characteristics of those making the requests.[72]

Protests

Protest is a form of participation used by those who lack the numbers or organization to compete electorally or the money, organizational or communication skills to participate effectively in interest-group politics. The basic strategy of protest is to appeal to others to become active in support of the protesters, thus altering the balance of power.[73] Examples of protest behavior include marches, rent strikes, and nonviolent demonstrations such as picketing. A less common and more extreme form of protest is rioting.

Research indicates that protest activity is unlikely to be successful in accomplishing its goals because of the difficulty of balancing the differing demands and expectations of four constituencies: the members of the protest group; the third parties whose support is sought by the protesters; the target groups at whom the protest is aimed; and the media upon which the protesters rely for communicating protest efforts. To keep the protest group mobilized, exaggerated rhetoric and exorbitant promises are often used. Such activities may please the media because they provide a dramatic story, but they may outrage the third parties to whom the protest group is looking for support and may make the target group (government officials) dig in its heels.[74]

A case study of the efforts of a lower-class protest group to achieve a variety of concrete goals in Newark, New Jersey, illustrates the difficulty of achieving success through protest. The goals of the protesting group in the case were hardly unreasonable or threatening: enforcement of city building codes and installation of a traffic light at a busy intersection. The efforts were abysmal failures. In response, the group tried "a frontal assault at the polls" to elect an insurgent African-American to the state assembly. That effort, ". . . found itself burdened by the very sins it was trying to fight: too many years of unfulfilled pledges by too many candidates had left people immune to political promises."[75] The group failed in the election as well; their candidate polled less than 5 percent of the vote.

At times, the frustration that such failure creates has found expression in the most extreme form of protest: rioting. Chapter 4 documented the eruption of American cities in riots in the last half of the 1960s and discussed the various explanations of the riots. Charged with investigating the causes of the riots, the National Advisory Commission on Civil Disorders began by constructing certain generalizations about the patterns of violence that occurred throughout the country, while cautioning that each event was unique.

The riots, the Commission reported, began as a result of a long series of incidents and grievances that created tensions that suddenly were released in reaction to some "triggering" incident, which may itself have been minor or trivial. The Commission saw the roots of riots in legitimate grievances that blacks had with a society that consistently discriminated against them. According to the Commission, evidence for this was that the typical rioters tended to be somewhat better educated than their neighbors, underemployed, and very distrustful of the political system.[76]

Not all observers agreed with the conclusions of the Commission. Another interpretation held that the riots were due primarily to young males of lower class letting off steam. As noted in Chapter 4, the most famous spokesman for that viewpoint is Edward Banfield.[77] In the *Unheavenly City Revisited*, he concluded:

> It is naive to think that efforts to end racial injustice and to eliminate poverty, slums, and unemployment will have an appreciable effect upon the amount of rioting that will be done in the next decade or two. . . . Boys and young men of the lower classes will not cease to "raise hell" once they have adequate job opportunities, housing, schools, and so on.[78]

Claiming the riots were mainly a foray for pillage or a rampage, Banfield pointed out that almost all the arrests made were for looting, and, he noted significantly, almost half of those arrested were between the ages of 19 and 24. He argued that those buildings attacked were stores that had goods that could be consumed directly—liquor, cigarettes, TV sets, etc. Buildings that might have been seen as symbols of the white society—banks, schools, government buildings—were left alone.[79] In addition, he quoted one of the rioters as reporting later:

> This is not a riot. A lot of people have a misconception of it. This is nothing but—like the man said—pure lawlessness. People was trying to get what they could get. The police was letting them take it. They wasn't stopping it, so I said it was time for me to get some of these diamonds and watches and rings. It wasn't that I was mad at anyone or angry or trying to get back at the white man.[80]

Clearly, the quote suggests that some participants in the riots were there for fun and profit, but other research indicates that many African-Americans, whether they participated or not, saw riots as a way to communicate frustrations about their problems and to demand an end to discrimination.

Numerous empirical studies produced evidence that many in the African-American community viewed the riots as a form of political protest.[81] For example, one study was based on interviews with African-Americans in the Watts area of Los Angeles after the devastating riots there. On the basis of those interviews, the authors concluded:

> The riot participants had lost faith in the very mechanisms, generated by a white-managed system, for handling grievances. They were disenchanted with individual striving, normal administrative grievance procedures, and conventional political activity. The rioters were moving instead toward nonviolent confrontations and even violence itself. For the riot participants, the functional equivalent of conventional grievance redress mechanisms was indeed the politics of violence.[82]

The authors found no relation between class and participation in the riot, with the single exception of finding that offspring of relatively high-status, high-school-educated mothers were more likely to have participated.[83] This finding would be contrary to Banfield's theory. The Commission reported that the average riot participant, "feels strongly that he deserves a better job and that he is barred from achieving it, not because of lack of training, ability, or ambition, but because of discrimination by employers."[84] The authors of the Los Angeles study reported that attitudes—rather than social characteristics—were the best predictors of riot participation.[85] Other studies confirmed the conclusions that the average rioters were not riffraff, criminals, or outside agitators, but rather the, "cream of urban Negro youth in particular and urban Negro cities in general."[86]

Viewed from the perspective of the 1990s, both analyses appear inadequate. Despite the fact that there are still young lower-class males and there is still racial discrimination (although some of the more obvious manifestations of discrimination have disappeared), the number of riots has declined precipitously. This leads to the question—Why have the riots declined? Banfield concludes that the decline is due to the movement of inner city residents out of the center city thus, in essence, removing the critical mass necessary for rioting. But while some African-Americans are moving out, large numbers remain in the inner city. In addition, they have increasingly been joined by Latinos and new immigrants, thus leaving a substantial number of lower-class youth available for pillaging and rampaging.[87]

An alternative explanation for the decline in the number of riots can be found by asking another question: What was the impact of the riots? A 1973 study found that African-Americans and whites disagreed on the answer to that question. Most African-Americans saw the riots as "regrettable" but believed they had created sympathy among whites for their demands. Most whites saw the riots as "criminal irresponsibility" and felt themselves to be less sympathetic to blacks as a result.[88]

While contradictory, both evaluations may be, at least in part, correct. Blacks probably had produced greatly increased awareness of their demands, and in many cities more attention was paid to those demands. One empirical study reported that a sole exception to the distribution of city services in Chicago between 1967 and 1977 according to apolitical criteria was the distribution of park resources as a result of demands from the African-American community.[89] An examination of Office of Economic Opportunity (OEO) expenditures following urban riots concluded, "... *black riots had a greater direct, positive impact than any other independent variable upon total OEO expenditure increases in the latter 1960s,* as well as upon most individual poverty program increases."[90] [Italics in original.]

While many whites were sympathetic to efforts by blacks to gain equality, the riots created both anger and fear, producing "white backlash" in some cases. In such an environment, the election in the 1980s of a conservative president, Ronald Reagan, supportive of "benign neglect" of African-Americans was not surprising. Because of white backlash, blacks may have rationally calculated that further rioting would make it more difficult to achieve their social, economic, and political goals.

The evidence indicates that relatively powerless people have few means of influencing the political system, and protest as a strategy does not improve their chances of success. The hopelessness of powerless minorities presents a serious threat. American urban areas have seen other "teeming masses" pass from poverty-stricken lives in ghettos to middle- and upper-class status, but the fear is that a permanent underclass is now developing in America's central cities.[91] In some instances, the outrage that spawned the riots and protests of the 1960s has given way to total despair. The violence has turned inward in the form of drug addiction and other forms of pathological behavior. Some observers have argued that drug abuse, unwed motherhood, and crime are a form of "quiet riot."[92]

Since the 1960s many of the poor have made social and economic advances. Ironically that has worsened the lot of those left behind because it again became easier to say that poverty was due to individual failings rather than systemic factors such as discrimination. In addition, as those who succeeded moved to other locations in the city, the community was deprived of people who could act as positive role models.

Urban areas suffer from the development of an underclass. While substantial—and growing—numbers of poor people are living in rural areas, they are not as visible as the urban poor who concentrate in dense communities. Pathological behavior such as robbery, assault, and murder by some of the poor contributes to the anti-urban bias of many Americans. Perhaps more seriously, such behavior is most frequently targeted at other poor people, making their lives even more miserable. The demands on the social services and law enforcement agencies of the city are massive. The courts and prisons are overburdened. The juxtaposition of the poor and the wealthy in the dense confines of the center city leads to tension and friction.

Although rioting has not been as common a part of the urban landscape as it was in the middle of the 1960s and the early 1970s, there have been some dramatic recent examples. Rioting occurred in Los Angeles in 1992 after a jury acquitted white police officers who had been videotaped beating an African American during a routine traffic stop. The riot in Los Angeles is the subject of Box 6–2. St. Petersburg, Florida, erupted in a riot in 1996 after a police officer shot a young black man who had been stopped for speeding. The incidents are frequent enough to remind us that the tension and friction in urban

America may still make rioting a viable option for some urban dwellers.

Public Hearings

One of the most common forms of citizen participation on the local level is the use of public hearings, in which citizens are allowed a chance to express their preferences on government actions. "Sunshine laws" in most states require that public boards and agencies such as city councils and planning and zoning commissions conduct open meetings so that citizens may attend. Often city ordinances also require formal public hearings to precede final action on certain issues such as zoning changes. To comply, the appropriate public body must send out notices to affected individuals and publicize the time and place when the issue will be discussed, and citizens must be given time at those meetings to air their views.

In addition, many federal programs adopted in the 1960s and 1970s mandated that before federal grant money would be given to local governments, those governments had to permit citizens to contribute to the decision-making process. Minimal compliance with the participation requirement was often defined as the holding of a certain number of public hearings. For example, two such programs that had substantial impact on local governments were the 1974 Community Development Block Grant program and the 1976 version of General Revenue Sharing, both of which required that cities hold a minimum of two public hearings before the plans for allocating federal grants would be approved by the federal government.

Although hearings are very common, most evidence indicates that they are not a particularly effective form of participation. For example, a study that compared how cities allocated general revenue sharing money before and after the law required public hearings concluded, "No short-term or long-term effects of the hearings on so-

BOX 6-2

1992 Los Angeles Riot

The 1992 riot in Los Angeles is proof that riots are an ineffective form of political participation. The trigger for the riot was the acquittal by an all-white jury of white police officers who had been videotaped beating black motorist Rodney King. The whole city of Los Angeles was placed under a curfew during the 6-day riot in which 52 people were killed and over 16,000 were arrested. As was the case with the urban riots in the 1960s, multiple explanations were offered for the riots, demonstrating the fact that riots do not provide a mechanism for precise communication.

One study identified five major theories for the 1992 riot, all of which have some support and but no one of which can explain what was a very complex event. Some observers pointed to the looting and argued the rioting was for fun and profit. Other analysts believed the riot was a black protest of their longtime maltreatment by Los Angeles police. Pointing to the involvement by Latinos, some argued the protest was a multiethnic protest by the disadvantaged. In contradiction, others have used the attacks by blacks on Koreans as a basis for arguing the riot was a form of multi-ethnic conflict. Finally, some commentators saw the riot as evidence of the general breakdown of societal norms.

After the riot, many, especially in the black community, called for a renewed effort by the national government to address the urban crisis. That has not happened. Instead, in Los Angeles as in other American cities, an entrepreneurial mayor is looking to the business sector to rebuild the city. It appears that the major loser in the riot was the black community. Businesses started moving away from the areas where the rioting was most intense. Immigrants from many countries have rebuilt in the riot areas, and the number of black businesses has declined.

Equally serious, some observers believe that the riot hardened the fault lines separating various groups in the city. Whites opposed affirmative action policies that had primarily benefited blacks. Blacks voted for the anti-immigrant Proposition 187. Latino gangs are chasing blacks out of their traditional neighborhoods. The director of a community group in Central Los Angeles warns, "Somewhere down the line, somebody's got to stop. I see another riot comin', a civil war comin'."

Source: Adapted from David O. Sears, "Urban Rioting in Los Angeles: A Comparison of 1965 with 1992" in *The Los Angeles Riots: Lessons for the Urban Future*, ed. Mark Baldassare (Boulder, Colorado: Westview Press, 1994); Joel Kotkin, "Rebuilding Blocks," *The Washington Post National Weekly Edition*, April 28, 1997; and Wanda Coleman, "For Blacks, a Bitter Backlash," *The Washington Post National Weekly Edition*, April 28, 1997.

cial service, welfare, and health expenditures were detected, nor were any effects found on levels of spending for new and expanding capital outlays on operating programs."[93] Although the citizens themselves may become more informed about government by attending, the hearing process appeared to be "inconsequential" as a way of altering government behavior.[94]

A number of explanations can be given for the ineffectiveness of public hearings as a way for citizens to influence government policy. First, few people are likely to attend hearings. The Advisory Commission for Intergovernmental Relations reported that on average only 30 citizens per city attended the General Revenue Sharing hearings.[95] Frequently even fewer citizens show up for public hearings on such issues as zoning changes, which often address more technical and less interesting issues than how federal money should be spent. There are exceptions, of course. When citizens become aware of issues they feel will affect them directly, they can pack hearing rooms.

The representativeness of those who attend is another problem. Some in attendance are "professional participators" who seem to go to every hearing. Most others are individuals or groups who are particularly affected or interested in at least some issues under discussion. The lack of representativeness is aggravated by the pattern of who speaks at the hearings. Public hearings appear to be very democratic since anyone can attend, but many feel intimidated by such settings and are unwilling to speak. Alternatively, limitations, on time for example, may mean that only a token presentation can be made.

Another major problem with hearings is that citizens may lack, or may be seen as lacking, adequate information to make a meaningful contribution to policy making. Government officials can devote their time and their staff's time to investigating alternative proposals and developing plans—that is their job. The time and effort citizens expend, however, are above and beyond their job commitment. Under those circumstances, citizens can rarely compete with officials in knowledge about proposals.[96]

Finally, hearings are often held after the plans have been virtually finalized by government officials. Because they have devoted time and effort to the plan, officials are committed to it and often have difficulty seriously considering input from citizens, especially as citizens clearly do not know as much about the project as do officials. In addition, officials must meet funding deadlines and may avoid requests by citizens for changes because there is not adequate time to revise the plan.

A study of citizen participation in urban transportation decisions concluded:

> Often, the public is not kept well informed throughout the planning process. Therefore, instead of serving as the final step of ratification following a long exchange of information between community members and planners, the public hearing often degenerates into an arena of conflict as a result of the fact that citizens are confronted with planning and analysis decisions for the first time.[97]

Some of these problems can be ameliorated if government officials are interested in maximizing the effectiveness of public hearings. For example, the timing of the hearings can crucially affect who can attend. If hearings are scheduled during the day, many people will be unable to attend because of job commitments. People in working-class jobs (for example, factory workers, construction workers) may have greater difficulty arranging time off than corporate executives.

Holding hearings early in the planning process could maximize the potential impact of citizens. Early in the process, officials are less likely to be committed to a particular proposal and are more likely to be willing to consider alternatives proposed by citizens. Also, early involvement gives citizens time to develop some expertise, which can help them contribute more effectively to planning and also help them be seen as having greater legitimacy when they speak. An even more effective way of increasing the expertise of citizens is to make staff support available throughout the planning process so that citizens can understand the plans thoroughly and may be able to devise alternatives. Ironically, when governments respond to citizen demands to cut taxes, they often must reduce staff, making support for citizen participation less likely.

Hearings in themselves do not permit time for careful consideration of proposals, let alone time for developing alternatives. If they are the sole means of participation offered, citizens are only given a chance to vent their spleens, an exercise in futility that may result in resentment rather than an increase in trust.

The Impact of Citizen Participation

While it may be impossible to conclude definitively that citizens have power because of the difficulty measuring power, research on the effect of participation on governmental policy has produced positive findings. Numerous researchers have documented that citizen participation does alter and improve the delivery of services to the public.[98] Most studies, however, qualify this conclusion by pointing out conditions under which participation can have an impact. For example, several studies have argued that participation affects only policies that result in immediate and specific benefits to citizens—the placement of a park or a new streetlight.[99] Other studies concluded that participation had an effect in certain policy areas. One such study concluded participation had an impact on community action, health, welfare, and legal systems and no impact on urban renewal, education, environmental planning, and transportation planning.[100] Evidence shows that participation can have greater impact on stopping programs citizens oppose rather than in instituting programs they desire.[101]

One caveat must be made. Most studies have focused on the citizens who participated and asked if they got the policies they preferred, but not all citizens are identical. Participants tend to differ from nonparticipants. If the participants do manage to alter government policy to conform to their desires, the effect may well be policy that is totally incongruent with the wishes of the nonparticipant population.[102]

Those whose preferences and needs become visible to policymakers through their activity are unrepresentative of those who are more quiescent in ways that are of great political significance: although similar in their attitudes, they differ in their personal circumstances and dependence on government benefits, in their priorities for government action, and in what they say when they get involved. In terms of whose concerns are expressed, it matters who participates.[103]

One study found that in communities with a high level of consensus, participation of any kind increased the degree to which the policy priorities of political leaders and citizens were in agreement. But in nonconsensual communities, a totally different pattern emerged. When citizens in such communities participated in ways that communicated precise demands, for example by forming groups or contacting officials, officials responded to participants, but in doing so they were *less* responsive to others in the community.[104]

The impact of participation, then, is a function both of the type of community and the type of participation. The role of consensus in a community is especially significant in understanding the impact of participation in urban areas. As a community grows, it is likely to become more heterogeneous and less consensual. As a result, high levels of nonelectoral participation can be expected to mean that the nonactive citizens may be worse off than if there were no participation, because officials will be responding to vocal interests that may not represent the community as a whole. The implications are different, however, for a small, homogeneous community. This homogeneity means that even minimal participation may result in greater policy responsiveness for all. In such an environment, the nonactive citizen may have the best of all possible worlds—representation with no effort.

Several aspects of the structures of government in metropolitan areas also affect the ability of citizens to have an impact. Nonpartisan elections make it more difficult for voters to feel knowledgeable about the issue stands of candidates. At-large elections make it more difficult for minorities to elect a member of their community to office. Reliance on administrators who are not directly elected reduces citizen influence.[105] The sprawl of multiple legally autonomous governments in a metropolitan area means that for some policy areas many governments are in control simultaneously, therefore influencing one of the governments may not produce the desired results. For example, citizens concerned about air pollution will not achieve substantially cleaner air by getting clean air standards implemented in one suburb alone.

The federal role in setting local priorities has also fragmented power in some policy areas. In addition, the size and distance of the national government means citizens must mobilize greater resources to affect national policy than would be necessary for policy completely controlled at the local level. Policies controlled by special districts are less amenable to citizen control both because the districts are often invisible or confusing to citizens and because the leaders of such districts are usually appointed rather than elected.

Participation always involves some costs. It takes time to participate; opportunity costs are involved in taking time from other, perhaps more pleasurable or profitable, activities. In addition, effort is involved to get to city hall, to become informed about the issues, or to get the courage to speak at a public hearing. There is also the problem of getting embroiled in a conflict situation, which many people find uncomfortable, or of being rebuffed or defeated in the search for policy goals, which almost everyone finds uncomfortable.

Conclusion

Resources are vital in determining the success citizens are likely to have in attempting to influence urban governments. Money is important because it can be exchanged for other resources. It also gives status and prestige to its possessors. Money can make gaining access to decision makers and persuading them to alter the urban agenda easier. Numbers can be translated into influence, but to do that groups must have members with organizational skills, and an inspiring and skillful spokesperson with strong communication skills. Expertise is increasingly important as issues become increasingly complex.

In the absence of major electoral mobilization, the influence of major interest groups in the city tends to predominate. Most studies confirm that those of higher socioeconomic status, especially business groups, tend to control the chorus of interest-group demands. Only in individualized contacting do resources tend to be less important. Those contacted respond, if they respond at all, more to the kind of the request than to the kind of person making the request. But major change is unlikely to occur through such ad hoc contacts. Participation can make a difference. But it is clear that some citizens are more likely to be effective if they participate than others because of the resources they command.

Notes

1. Joshua Miller, "The Ghostly Body Politic: *The Federalist Papers* and Popular Sovereignty," *Political Theory* 16 (February 1988): 99–119.
2. Robert Dahl, "The Concept of Power," *Behavioral Science* 2 (July 1957): 201–215.
3. Carl J. Friedrich, *Constitutional Government and Democracy* (Boston: Ginn, 1950), 49.
4. Clarence N. Stone, "Systemic Power in Community Decision Making: A Restatement of Stratification Theory," *American Political Science Review* 74 (December): 978–990.
5. Peter Bachrach and Morton S. Baratz, *Power and Poverty* (New York: Oxford University Press, 1970).

6. Steven J. Rosenstone and John Mark Hansen, *Mobilization, Participation, and Democracy in America*, (New York: Macmillan, 1993), 13.

7. Saul Alinsky, *Reveille for Radicals* (New York: Random House, 1969).

8. Robert W. Kweit and Mary Grisez Kweit, "Bureaucratic Decision-Making: Impediments to Citizen Participation," *Polity* 12 (Summer 1980): 649–655.

9. Marcus Ethridge, "Agency Responses to Citizen Participation Requirements: An Analysis of the Tennessee Experience," *Midwest Review of Public Administration* 14 (June 1980): 104.

10. Joseph Falkson, *An Evaluation of Policy Related Research on Citizen Participation in Municipal Service Systems: Overview and Summary* (Washington, D.C.: TARP Institute, 1974), 27–29.

11. Ethridge, "Agency Responses to Citizen Participation Requirements," 104.

12. Marilyn Gittell, *Participants and Participation: A Study of School Policy in New York City* (New York: Praeger 1968), 50–51.

13. See for instance, E.E. Schattschneider, *The Semi-Sovereign People: A Realist's View of Democracy in America* (Holt, Rinehart & Winston, 1960); Bachrach and Baratz, *Power and Poverty*; Roger W. Cobb and Charles D. Elder, *Participation in American Politics: The Dynamics of Agenda-Building*, 2nd ed. (Baltimore: Johns Hopkins University Press, 1983).

14. Stone, "Systemic Power in Community Decision Making", 978–990.

15. See Michael Parenti, "Power and Pluralism: A View from the Bottom," *The Journal of Politics* 32 (August 1970): 501–530; Michael Lipsky, "Protest as a Political Resource," *American Political Science Review* 62 (December 1968): 1148–1157.

16. This discussion relies on William A. Gamson, *Power and Discontent* (Homewood, Illinois: Dorsey, 1968).

17. Saul Alinsky, *Rules for Radicals* (New York: Random House, 1971).

18. Parenti, "Power and Pluralism," 501–530.

19. Clarence N. Stone, *Regime Politics: Governing Atlanta* (Lawrence: The University Press of Kansas, 1989), 29.

20. Rosenstone and Hansen, *Mobilization, Participation, and Democracy in America*, 30–33.

21. Paul E. Peterson, *City Limits* (Chicago: University of Chicago Press, 1981), 119–21 and passim.

22. John Clayton Thomas, "Rethinking 'Groupless' Urban Politics: A Theory of Neighborhood Mobilization." Paper prepared for delivery at the 1985 Annual Meeting of the American Political Science Association, New Orleans, Louisiana, August 28–September 1, 1985, 4–6.

23. Ibid., 5.

24. Daniel Bell and Virginia Held, "The Community Revolution," *The Public Interest* (Summer 1969): 143.

25. Norman Fainstein and Susan Fainstein, *Urban Political Movements* (Englewood Cliffs, New Jersey: Prentice-Hall, 1974).

26. Theodore J. Lowi, *At the Pleasure of the Mayor* (New York: Free Press, 1964).

27. David J. O'Brien, *Neighborhood Organizations and Interest Group Processes* (Princeton: Princeton University Press, 1975), 20.

28. The literature on these programs is large. For a review of the origin and development of the War on Poverty, see John Donovan, *The Politics of Poverty*, 2nd ed., (Indianapolis, Indiana: Pegasus, 1973); John Mollenkopf, *The Contested City* (Princeton: Princeton University Press, 1983). For critiques, see Theodore Lowi, *The End of Liberalism: The Second American Republic* (New York: John Wiley, 1979); Daniel Patrick Moynihan, *Maximum Feasible Misunderstanding* (New York: Free Press, 1969).

29. For a good case study of the War on Poverty, see Donovan, *The Politics of Poverty*, 2nd. ed.

30. Ralph M. Kramer, *Anticipation of the Poor: Community Case Studies in the War on Poverty* (Englewood Cliffs, New Jersey: Prentice-Hall, 1969), 200; David M. Austin, "Resident Participation: Political Mobilization or Organizational Co-Optation?" *Public Administration Review* 32 (September 1972): 418.

31. Norman Fainstein and Susan S. Fainstein, "The Future of Community Control," *The American Political Science Review* 70 (September 1976): 921; Daniel P. Moynihan, "Community Action Loses" in *The New Urban Politics: Cities and the Federal Government*, ed. Douglas M. Fox (Pacific Palisades, California: Goodyear, 1972), 173; John Clayton Thomas, *Between Citizen and City: Neighborhood Organizations and Urban Politics in Cincinnati* (Lawrence: University of Kansas Press, 1986).

32. Harry C. Boyte, *The Backyard Revolution: Understanding The New Citizen Movement* (Philadelphia: Temple University Press, 1980, 50–51.

33. Ibid., 51.

34. Ibid., 52.

35. Ibid., 56–57.

36. Ibid., 62.

37. Albert Karnig and B. Oliver Walter, "Municipal Elections: Registration, Incumbent Success, and Voter Participation," *Municipal Yearbook 1977* (Washington, D.C.: International City Management Association, 1977), 70; Sidney Verba and Norman H. Nie, *Participation in America: Political Democracy and Political Equality* (New York: Harper & Row, 1972), 31.

38. Kenneth Prewitt, "Political Ambitions, Volunteerism, and Electoral Accountability" in *Public Opinion and Public Policy: Models of Political Linkage*, ed. Norman R. Luttbeg (Itasca, Illinois: F.E. Peacock, 1981), 148.

39. Ibid., 153–154.

40. Peter J. Haas, "An Exploratory Analysis of American City Council Salaries," *Urban Affairs Review* 31 (November 1995): 255.

41. Timothy Bledsoe, *Careers in City Politics: The Case for Urban Democracy* (Pittsburgh: University of Pittsburgh Press, 1993), 181.

42. Ibid., 157.

43. Anthony Downs, *An Economic Theory of Democracy* (New York: Harper & Row, 1957), Chapter 4.

44. V.O. Key, Jr., *Politics, Parties, and Pressure Groups*, 5th ed. (New York: Crowell, 1964), 544.

45. Margaret K. Latimer, "Black Political Representation in Southern Cities: Electoral Systems and Other Causal Variables," *Urban Affairs Quarterly* 15 (Sep-

tember 1979): 65–86; Albert K. Karnig and Susan Welch, "Electoral Structure and Black Representation on City Councils," *Social Science Quarterly* 63 (March 1982): 99–114; Albert Karnig, "Black Representation on City Councils: The Impact of District Elections and Socioeconomic Factors," *Urban Affairs Quarterly* 12 (December 1976): 223–242; Richard K. Engstrom and Michael D. McDonald, "The Election of Blacks to City Councils: Clarifying the Impact of Electoral Arrangements on the Seats/Population Relationship, *American Political Science Review* 75 (June 1981): 344–354; Luis Ricardo Fraga, Kenneth J. Meier, and Robert E. England, "Hispanic Americans and Educational Policy: Limits to Equal Access," *The Journal of Politics* 48 (November 1986): 850–876; Chandler Davidson and George Korbel, "At-Large Elections and Minority Group Representation: A Reexamination of Historical and Contemporary Evidence" in *Minority Group Dilution,* ed. Chandler Davidson (Washington, D.C.: Howard University Press, 1984). For an exception, see Albert Karnig and Susan Welch "Sex and Ethnic Differences in Municipal Representation," *Social Science Quarterly* 60 (December 1979): 465–481.

46. Karnig, "Black Representation on City Councils," 230.

47. Susan Welch, "The Impact of At-Large Elections on the Representation of Blacks and Hispanics," *The Journal of Politics* 52 (November 1990): 1072.

48. Luis Ricardo Fraga, "Domination Through Democratic Means: Nonpartisan Slating Groups in City Electoral Politics." Paper prepared for delivery at the 1985 Annual Meeting of the American Political Science Association, New Orleans, Louisiana, August 25–September 1, 1985 15.

49. Paul Raymond, "The American Voter in a Nonpartisan, Urban Election," *American Politics Quarterly* 20 (April 1992): 247.

50. Gerald Pomper, "Ethnic and Group Voting in Nonpartisan Municipal Elections," *Public Opinion Quarterly* 30 (Spring 1969): 79–97.

51. Ibid., 96.

52. Latimer, "Black Political Representation in Southern Cities," 65–86.

53. Rufus P. Browning, Dale Rogers Marshall, and David H. Tabb, "Minorities and Urban Electoral Change: A Longitudinal Study," *Urban Affairs Quarterly* 15 (December 1979): 215.

54. John F. Zipp, Richard Landerman, and Paul Luebke, "Political Parties and Political Participation: A Reexamination of the Standard Socioeconomic Model," *Social Forces* 60 (June 1982): 1148.

55. Rosenstone and Hansen, *Mobilization, Participation, and Democracy in America,* 241.

56. Rufus P. Browning, Dale Rogers Marshall, and David H. Tabb, *Protest Is Not Enough: The Struggle of Blacks and Hispanics for Equality in Urban Politics* (Berkeley: University of California Press, 1984), 134.

57. Raphael J. Sonenshein, *Politics in Black and White: Race and Power in Los Angeles* (Princeton: Princeton University Press, 1993).

58. Albert K. Karnig and Susan Welch, *Black Representation and Urban Policy* (Chicago: University of Chicago Press, 1980).

59. Jerome W. Clubb and Michael W. Traugott, "National Patterns of Referenda Voting: The 1968 Election" in *People and Politics in Urban Society,* ed. Harlan Hahn (Beverly Hills, California: Sage, 1972), 165.

60. Vincent L. Marano, "City-County Consolidation Reform, Regionalism, Referenda and Requiem," *Western Political Quarterly* 32 (December 1979): 411.

61. Elaine B. Sharp, "Citizen Demand-Making in the Urban Context," *American Journal of Political Science* 28 (November 1984): 662. See also Philip B. Coulter, *Political Voice: Citizen Demand for Urban Public Services* (Tuscaloosa: University of Alabama Press, 1988), 94.

62. Carol Ann Traut and Craig F. Emmert, "Citizen-Initiated Contacting: A Multivariate Analysis," *American Politics Quarterly* 21 (April 1993): 243.

63. Verba and Nie, *Participation in America,* 31; Elaine B. Sharp, *Citizen Demand-Making in the Urban Context,* (University: University of Alabama Press, 1986), 33.

64. Philip B. Coulter, "There's a Madness in the Method: Redefining Citizen Contacting of Government Officials," *Urban Affairs Quarterly* 28 (December 1992): 297–316.

65. Sharp, *Citizen Demand-Making in the Urban Context,* 35.

66. Ibid., 668.

67. Bryan D. Jones with Saadia Greenberg and Joseph Drew, *Service Delivery in the City: Citizen Demand and Bureaucratic Rules* (New York: Longman, 1980), 88–89.

68. Paul Schumacher and Russell W. Getter, "Structural Sources of Unequal Responsiveness to Group Demands in American Cities," *Western Political Quarterly* 36 (March 1983): 25.

69. Jones, et al., *Service Delivery in the City;* Marcus E. Ethridge, "Agency Responses to Citizen Participation Requirements: An Analysis of the Tennessee Experience," *Midwest Review of Public Administration,* Vol. 14 (June 1980): 104.

70. Ethridge, "Agency Responses to Citizen Participation Requirements," 104; Kenneth R. Greene, "Municipal Administrators' Receptivity to Citizens and Elected Officials' Contacts," *Public Administration Review* 42 (July–August 1982): 352; Steven M. Neuse, "Citizen Participation: Variations in Bureaucratic Attitudes," *Midwest Review of Public Administration* 14 (December 1980): 259–261.

71. Neuse, "Citizen Participation," 261.

72. Kenneth R. Mladenka, "Citizen Demands and Urban Services: The Distribution of Bureaucratic Response in Chicago and Houston," *American Journal of Political Science* 25 (November 1981): 693–714.

73. Michael Lipsky, "Protest as a Political Resource," *American Political Science Review* 62 (December 1968): 1145; James Q. Wilson, "The Strategy of Protest: Problems of Negro Civic Action," *Journal of Conflict Resolution* 3 (September 1961): 291–303.

74. Lipsky, "Protest as a Political Resource," 1157.

75. Michael Parenti, "Power and Pluralism: A View from the Bottom," *The Journal of Politics* 32 (August 1970): 501–532.

76. *Report of the National Advisory Commission on Civil Disorders* (New York: New York Times Company, 1968), 111.

77. Edward Banfield, *The Unheavenly City Revisited* (Boston: Little, Brown, 1974).

78. Ibid., 232–233.

79. Ibid., 224.

80. Ibid.

81. David O. Sears and John B. McConahay, *The Politics of Violence: The New Urban Blacks and the Watts Riot* (Boston: Houghton, Mifflin, 1973); Joe R. Feagin and Harlan Hahn, *Ghetto Revolts: The Politics of Violence in American Cities* (New York: Macmillan 1973); Joel D. Aberbach and Jack L. Walker, *Race in the City* (Boston: Little, Brown, 1973).

82. Sears and McConahay, *The Politics of Violence*, 104.

83. Ibid., 123–124.

84. *Report of the National Advisory Commission of Civil Disorders*, 129.

85. Sears and McConahay, *The Politics of Violence*, 124.

86. Feagin and Hahn, *Ghetto Revolts*, 301.

87. Banfield, *The Unheavenly City Revisited*, 232.

88. Aberbach and Walker, *Race in the City*, 61.

89. Kenneth R. Mladenka, "The Urban Bureaucracy and the Chicago Political Machine: Who Gets What and the Limits to Political Control," *American Political Science Review* 74 (December 1980): 996.

90. James W. Button, *Black Violence: Political Impact of the 1960s Riots* (Princeton: Princeton University Press, 1978), 37.

91. William Julius Wilson, "The Urban Underclass in Advanced Industrial Society" in *The New Urban Reality*, ed. Paul Peterson (Washington, D.C.: The Brookings Institution, 1985), 129–160.

92. Alex Kotlowitz, "Racial Gulf: Blacks' Hopes, Raised by '68 Kerner Report, Are Mainly Unfulfilled," *Wall Street Journal* 94 (February 26, 1988).

93. Richard L. Cole and David A. Caputo, "The Public Hearing as an Effective Citizen Participation Mechanism," *The American Political Science Review* 78 (June 1984), 415.

94. Ibid.

95. Ibid.

96. For a discussion of the problems of citizen participation in bureaucracies, see Mary Grisez Kweit and Robert W. Kweit, *Implementing Citizen Participation in a Bureaucratic Society: A Contingency Approach* (New York: Praeger, 1981).

97. Elizabeth Hanson, *An Evaluation of Policy Related Research on Citizen Participation in Municipal Service Systems: Transportation Planning* (Washington, D.C.: TARP Institute, n.d.), 108.

98. Richard L. Cole, *Citizen Participation and the Urban Policy Process* (Lexington, Massachusetts: Lexington Books, 1974), 103–104; John H. Strange, "The Impact of Citizen Participation on Public Administration," *Public Administration Review* 32 (September 1972): 457–470; Willis A. Sutton, "Differential Perceptions of Impact of a Rural Anti-Poverty Campaign," *Social Science Quarterly* 50 (December 1969): 662; Louis A. Zurcher, Jr., "The Poverty Board: Some Consequences of 'Maximum Feasible Participation'," *Journal of Social Issues* 26 (Summer 1970): 85–107; Robert K. Yin and Douglas Yates, *Street-Level Governments: Assessing Decentralization and Urban Services* (Lexington, Massachusetts: Lexington Books, 1975), 56.

99. Frances Fox Piven and Richard A. Cloward, *Regulating the Poor: The Function of Public Welfare* (New York: Pantheon, 1971), 331; John H. Strange, "Citizen Participation in Community Action and Model Cities Programs," *Public Administration Review* 32 (October 1972): 660; Richard L. Cole and David A. Caputo, *Urban Politics and Decentralization: The Case of General Revenue Sharing* (Lexington, Massachusetts: Lexington Books, 1974), 115.

100. Falkson, *An Evaluation of Policy Related Research*, 27–29.

101. Daniel A. Mazmanian and Jeanne Nienaber, *Can Organizations Change?* (Washington, D.C.: The Brookings Institution, 1979).

102. Sidney Verba, Kay Lehman Schlozman, and Henry E. Brady, *Voice and Equality: Civic Volunteerism in American Politics* (Cambridge, Massachusetts: Harvard University Press, 1995), Chapters 7 and 8.

103. Ibid, 227.

104. Verba and Nie, *Participation in America*, 325–326.

105. Cole, *Citizen Participation and the Urban Policy Process*, 57; Robert L. Lineberry and Edmund P. Fowler, "Reformism and Public Policy in American Cities," *American Political Science Review* 61 (September 1967): 715; Kweit and Kweit, *Implementing Citizen Participation*, 164.

Adoption, Implementation, and Evaluation of Urban Policy

Part I provided an overview of the urban context and its effect on the policy process. Part II discussed the major actors who attempt to influence the urban agenda and the participatory mechanisms they can use to try to get their preferred alternatives accepted as urban public policy. Part III looks at the institutions and the processes used to adopt policy and implement policy. Finally, this section looks at how these policies can be evaluated and what strategies are available to make the programs work better.

Policy Adoption

The adoption of urban policy can occur at various levels of government, as well as in various institutions. The institutional context in which policy is adopted has an influence on that policy. The national institutional context is characterized by large government composed of many different organizations with a great deal of internal specialization among those who are experts in given policy areas. These groups of specialists in the past were called **subsystems** or **subgovernments**, and traditionally operated with substantial autonomy. More recently, the term **issue net-**

work has been used to indicate that the number of participants has increased and the relationships among them are more open and fluid. The urban system is a microcosm of the national system in many respects. By virtue of their rapid growth since World War II, many local governments have increased the number of employees they hire and the vast assortment of services they provide. The requirements of many federal grants have led to the increasing specialization and professionalism of many employees.

All governments operate in a **federal** system, that is one with several levels of government. Each level of government tends to have a separation of powers among branches of government and a generally weak party system.[1] The very nature of the federal system and the intricate web of intergovernmental relations limits local government by limiting authority. Local governments are required to carry out policies created by other governments. Local governments are partners in service delivery with other levels of government. Many programs that are bought and paid for at other levels of government are implemented by the local bureaucracy. In some cases, the other levels of government provide funds for those **mandates**, but they also often necessitate the allocation of scarce local resources. This may mean that the local government cannot respond to citizen demands to put different issues on the urban policy agenda.

In addition to mandates, many other policy decisions at the local level are in direct response to policies adopted at other levels of government. For example, the recovery efforts of Grand Forks, North Dakota, after the devastating flood of 1997 occurred within the context set by resources and regulations of such federal institutions as Congress, the Federal Emergency Management Administration, the Small Business Administration, and the Army Corps of Engineers. Even during normal times, federal grant regulations and mandated standards are important parts of the policy process on the local level. The importance of decisions of other levels of government on local governments has prompted them to organize to be heard in Washington, D.C., and state capitals. This intergovernmental context limits local government autonomy and also increases its responsibilities in some policy areas.

The multiple levels of government and the separation of powers on most levels means that in many cases policy has to be adopted not once, but over and over. Policies may be the result of actions on the national, state, and local levels. Even on one level, the policy process is likely to have multiple stages. For example, normally local legislatures adopt policy proposals, but executives may be able to act unilaterally through executive orders or may have the power to veto council actions. Bureaucrats may substantially alter policy in the implementation process, filling in the holes that the legislative wording left. The judicial branch also affects policies by interpreting the wording of statutes or ruling on their constitutionality or of actions that result from them.

The policy-adoption process is generally a bargaining process because policies that are formally adopted require at least a majority vote in committee, city council, or any legislative body.[2] Indeed, proposed policies may need successive majorities as they move through the stages of the legislative process. Majoritarianism is an important symbol of legitimacy in our political culture. Because various actors representing different constituencies and different interests must band together to try to maximize their gains, bargains must be struck.

Americans generally choose to avoid conflicts where possible, and the bargaining often results in **logrolling**. (The analogy here is that in order to stay upright, lumberjacks must keep the logs on which they are standing rolling in the river. If the logs stop moving, the lumberjacks will fall off.) In political logrolling, the movement is policy change. To find common ground, each participant in the policy process must be willing to continue to alter the policy to give others what they want. As long as the cooperation continues, everyone is happy. Once someone becomes steadfastly committed to one position and refuses to move toward common ground, everyone "falls" off. Logrolling often leads to giving all participants what they want. This is one way to avoid conflict, but it may be costly to give everyone what they want. Thus as local governments many times cannot operate at a deficit, logrolling may result in higher taxes.

Unavoidable conflict may be minimized by **compromise**, in which each side is willing to trade off some issues to achieve other objectives. Unlike logrolling, where all get what they want, compromise allows all to get at least some of what they want.

In another type of bargaining, known as **persuasion**, the disputants try to convince others to support their positions. They may do this by marshalling evidence on the virtue of their position. Expertise is often a prime resource. Alternatively, disputants may try to persuade decision makers to support their position through the use of rewards, for example, votes, contributions—or the use of sanctions, for example, withheld support.

Another process for reaching decisions in the adoption process is **command**. In times of crisis, the executive can often give orders and others will quickly comply. Local governments are usually the first line of response in natural disasters such as floods, hurricanes, or tornadoes. During the Grand Forks flood, the mayor issued an emergency declaration requiring the evacuation of the whole city and most of its 50,000 inhabitants immediately complied. For the most part, though, command does not occur. The system of checks and balances gives nobody absolute power. Also, in local governments, chief executives are often quite limited in their power. The obvious exception is the city that is controlled by a strong political machine.

The participants in the policy-adoption process tend to have perspectives based on their specific backgrounds, their professional training, and the organizations to which they belong. Graham Allison has developed three models of how policy decisions are reached.[3] The "ideal" method for reaching decisions is the **rational actor model**. In this model the policy maker must first clearly determine what problem needs to be solved. He or she must then establish goals and priorities. The next step is to develop alternative means to reach the goals or ends. Subsequently the means are evaluated and finally the "best" alternative is selected. Note that this model provides the outline for this book.

As indicated in Chapter 1, while this model provides a good outline for analysis, in the real world it cannot easily be followed. Sometimes what is and what is not a problem is far from established. Many times this book made the point that an important part of the policy process is convincing others that a problem exists and that it should be addressed by public efforts. That is what is meant by the term agenda setting. Even if a particular issue is defined as a problem, deciding the cause of the problem is even more difficult. For example, while all might agree that poverty rep-

resents the problem of lack of money, some may see the real problem as lack of education, while others may see the problem as a result of a character deficiency. Even if there is agreement on what constitutes the problem, further obstacles may be encountered in obtaining all the information needed to make informed decisions. For example, how can policy makers be sure they know all means to reach desired goals? Hence, while policy makers may attempt to be rational, they may revert to other models at times.

Sometimes decision makers make decisions in a manner referred to as the **bureaucratic politics model**. This model can be described simplistically by the adage "where you stand depends upon where you sit." Each actor will develop a decision framework based upon his or her position in the organization. The president of the city council, for instance, is more likely to have a broad, citywide perspective on a problem than the councilperson who represents a specific ward. In addition the decision maker is likely to use "politics" to enhance his or her influence on the final decision.

The third model is the **organizational model**. This posits that different organizations develop decision rules (Standard Operating Procedures or SOPs) as shortcuts for defining and dealing with problem situations. Thus, members of organizations define issues in line with organizational goals. For instance, teachers in an educational institution are likely to view poverty as lack of education and attempt to develop programs to educate the poor. They would establish standard routines to deal with poor reading or poor math skills.

The members of a social welfare department may be taught to perceive poverty as caused by personal problems such as marital breakup or poor health. They might favor short-term aid to deal with the emergency as well as long-term counseling to cope with the problems. A member of the city housing authority might believe poverty results from horrible living conditions that break the will and spirit and might propose housing programs to solve the problem.

Legislators and executives who seek to build programs should be aware of the perspectives or biases inherent in organizations. Because of different perspectives, there is often a broad array of programs that may seem poorly focused and sometimes even contradictory. Sometimes policies are meant to be symbolic and are not really designed to be implemented. They may be designed merely to satisfy the proponents, without really accomplishing anything. For instance, if a neighborhood group demands more playgrounds, the government may induce a few professional basketball players to run a one-day clinic in an existing playground. This is not addressing the need for more playgrounds, but it will certainly excite neighborhood youths and perhaps satisfy their parents because at least they got some action.

Often vague policies are adopted in an effort to please as many parties as possible. This tactic defers many important decisions until the implementation stage, where decisions can be made less publicly and by experts who "know" what they are doing and can fill in the "details."

An example of bargaining in the policy-adoption stage and deferral of crucial decisions until the implementation stage occurred in attempts by East Chicago to enact an air pollution ordinance. The city attorney drafted an ordinance containing several compromises suggested by the local Chamber of Commerce. The Chamber approved the provisions of the ordinance with only two minor exceptions, and the city council passed the bill with no amendments. Yet when the air pollution inspector attempted to implement the law, local industries complained that he was "misinterpreting" it by trying to inspect pieces of industrial equipment that were not supposed to be covered. New negotiations with industry resulted in 32 pieces of equipment being exempted.[4]

Implementation and Service Delivery

Whether adopted at the local level or at a higher level of government, policy only has an impact when it is implemented. Daniel Mazmanian and Paul Sabatier discuss the crucial importance of implementation.

> Knowing the objectives set for the program by Congress, the Supreme Court, or the President usually gives only a general hint of what will actually be done by the agency responsible for carrying out the program and how successful it will be at winning the cooperation and compliance of persons affected by it. To understand what actually happens after a program is *enacted* or *formulated* is the subject of *policy implementation*. . . .[5] [Italics in original.]

Implementing programs requires three activities: (1) organization; (2) interpretation; and (3) application.[6] Some structure or organization must be established to ensure that programs will be carried out in an orderly, consistent manner. The dominant organization at the implementation stage is the bureaucracy. Bureaucrats must interpret the "legalese" of the law into some set of workable standards. Policy making continues into the implementation or service delivery phase when the bureaucracy creates administrative rules and laws that make programs operational. It also continues when the general rules are applied to specific people and places. When a general program is put together through many compromises a great deal of leeway or discretion exists when it comes to putting the policy into action.

Often programs that look good at the adoption stage run into difficulties when they are implemented. Because most policies, especially intergovernmental ones, depend on many agencies and actors both inside and outside of government, successful implementation is often elusive. In addition, many urban policy decisions are made in Washington, D.C.; when it comes to implementing them in the rest of the country, new issues and new problems arise.

Evaluation

Once services are provided, they must be examined to determine their impact and what remains to be done. This is the evaluation stage. Evaluations affect whether programs are continued, modified, or terminated because reactions to the programs affect future direction through feedback. In the past, most evaluations were ad hoc. If the public seemed happy and the program squared with our ideological orientation, it was judged successful and worthy of continuance. Many citizens have become increasingly disenchanted with government programs. Because of the scarcity of resources, a scarcity felt especially in urban areas, and controversy over the effectiveness and efficiency of government programs, it has become necessary to be more systematic in determining how to deliver services most efficiently and how to address problems most effectively. This has led to increasing demands that government programs be more systematically evaluated to determine what works and what does not.

Because of negative public evaluations of the public bureaucracy, public managers have sought new ways of delivering services; for many of those innovations they have looked to the private sector. Sometimes the public sector has shifted service delivery to the private sector, a process called **privatization**; other times, the public sector has tried to incorporate private sector management techniques such as total quality management, entreprenurial management, and re-engineering, to improve the satisfaction of urban residents, often seen as customers.

The chapters in the next part of the book examine the organizational context of urban policy adoption, implementation, and evaluation. Chapter 7 examines the various structures of government on the local level. Chapter 8 reviews the roles of urban officials. Chapter 9 describes the fragmentation of government in metropolitan areas and Chapter 10 examines the impact of other levels of government by reviewing sources of local government finances. Finally, Chapter 11 focuses on the implementation and evaluation of policies that are adopted.

Notes

1. Randall B. Ripley and Grace A. Franklin, *Congress, the Bureaucracy and Public Policy,* 4th ed. (New York: Dorsey, 1987), 6.

2. For a discussion of bargaining as a decision-making form, see Roger Davidson, *The Role of the Congressman* (New York: Pegasus, 1969).

3. Graham T. Allison, *Essence of Decision: Explaining the Cuban Missile Crisis* (Boston: Little, Brown, 1971).

4. Matthew A. Crenson, *The Un-Politics of Air Pollution: A Study of Non-Decisionmaking in the Cities* (Baltimore: Johns Hopkins University Press, 1971), 47–55.

5. Daniel A. Mazmanian and Paul A. Sabatier, *Implementation and Public Policy* (Glenview, Illinois: Scott, Foresman, 1983), 3–4.

6. Charles O. Jones, *An Introduction to the Study of Public Policy,* 3rd ed. (Monterey, California: Brooks/Cole Publishing Company, 1984), 166.

CHAPTER 7

Structures of Government

As urban areas increased in economic and social complexity, various forms of government structures were developed to adopt programs to deal with the problems that arose. Americans want government to function democratically and leaders to be accountable, but they also want to maximize government efficiency and effectiveness. These goals are not always complementary and trade-offs often must be made. Herbert Kaufman has argued that current governmental structures reflect a search for ways to meld three fundamental values: (1) representativeness, that is, elections; (2) technical, nonpartisan competence, that is, staffing based on skills rather than political connections; and (3) leadership, that is, coordinated direction that results in consistent policy.[1]

This chapter will examine the representativeness, the nonpartisan competence, and the leadership of various governmental structures. Probably there is no "best" structure of urban government. Each structure has certain built-in biases that affect who makes decisions, how they are made, and what those decisions are. Each strikes a different balance between efficiency and democracy.[2] In the following discussion, we will examine *general* forms of governmental arrangements; there are a great variety of specific forms, almost as many as local governments to try them.

New England Town Meetings

Perhaps the epitome of democratic government is the New England town meeting. In theory, the town meeting is an example of direct democracy. All eligible voters in the community meet and make all the collective decisions that affect the community, whether it is to build a new jail or to raise or lower taxes. Theoretically, there is no separate governing coalition in such a community as all citizens govern themselves. Of the core values mentioned above, a town meeting maximizes representativeness. Many Americans consider direct democracy an ideal, believing that it improves self-esteem, increases commitment to the community, and produces better policies. All members of the community working together as individuals supposedly produce the common good.[3] This fits the ideal that Jane Mansbridge calls "unitary democracy."

> People who disagree do not vote; they reason together until they agree on the best answer. . . . This democracy is consensual, based on common interest and equal respect. . . . It assumes that citizens have a single common interest. . . .[4]

Yet even in the small town, some issues lead to "adversarial democracy," in which various actors represent their self-interest rather than the common good. As communities grow and become more heterogeneous, it is harder to work together to find the common good.[5] Representative forms of government replace direct democracy. Some observers might argue that much of the impersonality and alienation in the modern city results from the separation of the governors from the governed. Separate political leaders are delegated governing responsibility; others need to influence those leaders to achieve their goals. While population size may make the town meeting impossible in larger cities, the form persists in many New England towns.

A typical town meeting might go as follows: Residents receive a copy of the agenda and time and place of the meeting a couple of weeks in advance. Informal discussions take place before the town meeting and all but the most contentious issues are ironed out. The meeting hall is far too small for all eligible voters, but ample for those who turn out. At the meeting, a moderator and a town clerk are selected to run the proceedings. Traditionally, these individuals are chosen unanimously and continue year after year. An election for selectmen (to sign papers, pay bills, and conduct any business that arises during the year) is held. Then several issues are presented and approved unanimously with minimal discussion.

Sometimes a controversial issue arises, as at a "Selby," Vermont meeting. The issue involved a 50-cent per capita fee to be paid to the Regional Planning and Development Commission. "A fellow in an Ivy League jacket, one of the few people who seemed out of place, now stood to reveal himself as the executive director of the state sponsored Regional Planning Commission."[6] He urged the town to begin plans to establish zoning that would benefit those involved in the tourist trade but hurt the small farmer.

The next ten minutes produced angry debate. Farmer Clayton Bedell argued that "there's no sense in fighting communism if your neighbor or your selectman can come in and tell you what to do with your property. What are we fighting communism for?" The lawyer responded coolly, "That's a very good and very pertinent question," and swept on to describe again, in terms understandable to a six-year-old, the advantages neighboring towns had realized from the work of the zoning commission.[7]

The debate continued; three votes were held before the Planning Commission finally lost 37 to 35.

After all the issues have run their course, the meeting adjourns until the next year. With the town meeting, citizens are the final arbiters of the local issues that concern them. For good or ill, they are in control of their lives.

Town meetings do have their critics, however. Some observers question how truly democratic the process is, and others criticize its inefficiency. Charles Adams notes both problems.

> That the town meeting should break down under the stress to which a city population must subject it is a matter of course. . . . The indications that the system is breaking down are always the same; the meetings become numerous, noisy, and unable to dispose of business. Disputed questions cannot be decided; demagogues obtain control, and the more intelligent cease to attend.[8]

Nor is it only size that makes the town meeting inefficient and undemocratic. Michael Frisch notes that political party questions, rivalries between the center of town and the outskirts, and the "pervasive antipathy to spending and taxes produced interminable squabbling about every proposal brought before the town."[9] He argues that such squabbling led to the elimination of town meetings in Springfield, Massachusetts, in the 1840s.

It can also be argued that town meetings are really no more, and perhaps less, democratic than indirect democracy. Several studies point out that participation at the town meeting is less than voting turnout in comparable communities. In New York State, small farming communities had voter turnouts ranging between 80 to 85 percent. Town meeting turnouts range from 8 to 42 percent.[10] In five New England states in 1982, attendance averaged less than 25 percent in every size group of city studied. As size of city increased, attendance at the town meeting decreased.[11]

The same class and group biases in the political process limit the participation of the lower quarter of the community in the town meeting.[12] Direct democracy also does not prevent powerful cliques from dominating the political process. Ironically, it may result in the low self-esteem, alienation, and distrust that direct democracy is supposed to prevent.

> Losing material benefits may not be as important as losing a sense of full membership in the community. Feeling excluded from consideration in the public but intimate atmosphere of a small direct democracy affects a person's self-respect. Bitterness about control by a "clique" seems intensified by the difficulty of figuring out who has influence, and why. You can't vote the rascals out if they don't hold elective office; indeed, you can't take any form of reprisal if you don't know who the rascals are. As an outsider, if you go to a town meeting, you feel manipulated by "those in the know"; if you don't go, you seem to have forfeited your right to gripe. [13]

The town meeting is an antidote to impersonality in the community. It is viable to a large extent in relatively homogenous areas where consensus can be emphasized and conflict minimized. The interdependence inherent as communities grow and become more complex usually leads to an increase in the scope of government because government must act as a coordinator among the various interests. The increased government activity makes direct democracy on every issue more cumbersome. Thus, as communities develop, the town meeting becomes a less viable form of government.

Nevertheless, methods are available for fostering direct democracy even in large, complex communities. While size often becomes a limiting factor, in most cities variations of town meetings maintain direct access for all citizens. Even a city as large as Brookline, Massachusetts (1990 population: 54,718), uses a form of "representative" town meeting.[14] In this modified town meeting, a large number of citizens are elected to conduct business. Anyone may speak on an issue, but only those who have been elected have the right to vote.

Although cities become large and heterogeneous, they are often composed of homogeneous neighborhoods where shared interests are easier to see and numbers are more manageable. "In . . . neighborhood democracies, a citizen could learn the communal virtues, partake of a 'community of values,' become a genuine participator in government, and, at the same time, learn to adopt different democratic procedures for dealing with common and conflicting interests."[15] Several cities, such as Minneapolis, Minnesota, and Dayton, Ohio, have established neighborhood-based institutions to meet and establish priorities for their neighborhoods.[16] A leading advocate of neighborhood government has suggested that the states should charter nonprofit neighborhood corporations that would be governed by town meetings.[17] As discussed in Chapter 5, one study of neighborhood organizations found that they could not only influence urban policy, but could also affect citizen attitudes.[18]

Modern technologies with interactive cable systems offer additional opportunities for increasing the number of decision makers and allowing for direct democracy. This may come in the future but many questions remain: Who decides what issues the public will decide? Can the public choose the most efficient way to get things done? And, perhaps most important, do we really want the uninformed deciding complex issues?[19]

While town meetings were popular in New England, direct democracy did not flourish in other areas of America. Some early American cities were governed by closed corporations where the governors held office for long terms and chose their own successors. Further, in cities with elected leaders, restrictions on suffrage due to sex, race, and lack of property limited participation in government. In areas where decisions were not made collectively as in the town meeting, another ideological strain, deriving from our English tradition and colonial heritage, arose—the desire to make governing difficult in order to keep the role of government limited. Modeled after the national system, separation of powers in city government became the norm by the 1820s, with a separate chief executive and a council, often bicameral. The size of the council was quite large and many could participate.[20] This form of government is called the mayor–council form.

Weak Mayor–Council System

There are a variety of forms of mayor–council systems, but they generally are classified as weak mayor and strong mayor systems, referring to the amount of power and authority vested in the mayor's office. Outside of New England, the predominant form of government until the twentieth century was the weak mayor system. Experience with British rule taught many citizens to fear centralized political power. Consequently, they established weak mayor systems in which power was widely dispersed. The concern for efficient government took a back seat to democratic control. Immediately after the Revolution, it was common for the mayor to be chosen by the council and to have few responsibilities. Direct election was introduced about 1820.

During the Jacksonian Period, demands for participation increased, coupled with the belief that the job of running a government was so simple that anyone could do it. This led to the **long ballot**, which further hamstrung the mayor. The long ballot gets its name literally because the number of elected officials is so large that the paper ballot has to be long in order to list all the offices. It was and is not uncommon for voters to select members for various boards such as park board or library board, and administrators such as attorney, assessor, and chief of police. The long ballot makes more officials directly accountable to the public, but some might question whether the general public can evaluate the competence of candidates for such technical positions.

In different cities, the types of boards as well as the number and specific administrative positions directly elected by the public may vary. Figure 7–1 and subsequent models of urban form are merely illustrative; there are many variations of these simple models. For example, one city may have a public works department, another a sanitation and streets department, and a third separate streets department and sanitation department.

As these officials are democratically elected by the public, the administrative control exercised by the mayor is clearly limited. This means that the accountability of departments to the mayor or to the public at large is also limited. The departments can act independently and coordination is difficult. The mayor's policy-making role is limited as well; in some places the mayor even lacks a veto. The council generally plays a major role in legislative matters (that is, policy making) and in administrative matters (that is, implemen-

FIGURE 7-1

Weak Mayor–Council System (Illustrative Model)

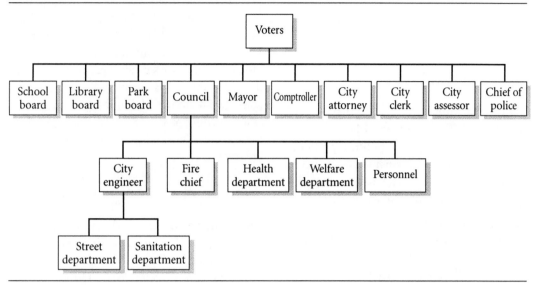

tation of those policies). The council members (sometimes called alderpersons) often sit on various boards and commissions, prepare the budget, and may appoint some administrators.

Several variations of the weak mayor system continue to exist today in many cities, mostly small ones such as Stevens Point, Wisconsin (1990 population, 23,006). This form is more common in small cities because the role of government tends to be more limited and the degree of conflict less. Although some large cities have relatively weak mayor systems—the most notable being Atlanta, Chicago, and Los Angeles—the problems that arise as cities grow usually overwhelm the system.[21] With no one in charge, getting anything done is often impossible. Any power that the mayor is able to muster is a result of the mayor's political skill rather than any formal powers granted in the city charter.[22] The mayor is forced to negotiate with various interests to develop a governing coalition. Some form of coordination is needed to assure that the system works.

In the nineteenth-century city, stronger government was necessary for specific reasons. Business needed services in order to grow. Immigrants needed help to survive. When the formal structure of government did not meet these needs, an informal structure developed known as the political machine. The machine became the governing coalition in the city. The leader of the machine acted as the political fixer or "boss" to assure that things got done. The leader may or may not have held a formal government job. While political machines developed in other cities, they were especially common in cities with weak mayors.

Most of the great nineteenth-century machines operated under this [weak mayor] plan for it encourages the boss by its very clumsiness and lack of coordination. Under this plan, the voter can scarcely determine, after the most conscientious effort, who is responsible for what, or even what functions are being performed by whom. With no clear-cut focus of answerability to the voter, the boss has a real advantage. The weak-mayor plan is most easily corrupted and bossed because of the confusing pattern of organization.[23]

Political Machines

Political machines have been criticized and romanticized. They are viewed by their proponents as merely effective political party organizations, whereas opponents view them as corrupt cliques. Fred I. Greenstein identifies four major characteristics of machines:

1. Disciplined party hierarchy.
2. Control over nominations for office to control those in office.
3. Party leadership that usually does not hold office.
4. Support base that is maintained by a mixture of material (jobs, turkeys) and nonmaterial (fellowship, recognition) rewards.[24]

There are various stereotypes of the political machine. Generally the image of the machine is a Democratic Party, in a big, old, Northeastern city, supported by lower-class ethnics (especially the Irish), and despised by businessmen because it is corrupt. Like all stereotypes, this one is an oversimplification. There were many machines outside cities (Byrd Machine in Virginia; Long Machine in Louisiana); outside the Northeast (Daley Machine in Chicago); upper class (Good Government League in San Antonio); Republican (Philadelphia); or nonethnic (Pendergast Machine in Kansas City); and supported by many businesspeople.[25] In general though, political machines depended on lower-class voters and were interested in holding power to enjoy the rewards of office (especially material as op-

posed to symbolic) rather than for ideological purposes.[26]

There are many colorful stories of the building of machines. Tammany Hall, the famous New York Machine, was founded in 1789 for fraternal and charitable purposes, much like today's service organizations. By the 1840s and 1850s, the city's leading Democrats were members of Tammany. This served as a launching pad for Boss Tweed, an Anglo-Saxon boss. Eventually, Tammany passed to the Irish.[27]

Bars were the birthplace of many machines.* As gathering places for the working class to discuss sports, politics, or be entertained, they were a natural arena to build a following. In Kansas City, Jim Pendergast used his saloon to start a political career as an alderman from the First Ward. On the council, he fought for working persons and helped in everyday matters such as posting bail for those arrested for gambling, and providing food and coal to help the poor. "Grocers, butchers, bakers and coal men had unlimited orders to see that there was no suffering among the poor of West Bottoms, and to send the bills to Jim Pendergast."[28] He opened a second saloon in the Second Ward and developed a power base there as well. His mayoral candidate won in 1900, giving him control of a great deal of **patronage**, that is, the ability to reward supporters with government jobs. As a result, he was able to put his friends in some key positions and then control crucial functions such as license inspection and policing. Power begets more power.[29]

The machine filled the leadership vacuum created by the weak mayor system.

Urban development in the nineteenth century created demands that existing institutions of city government were unable to handle. As the gap between public needs

---

*They also contributed to the perpetuation of machines. Whether illegal bars were allowed to operate and where was crucial to the German and Irish bosses of the Chicago Machine during Prohibition.

and institutional responses widened, city residents began to look beyond the governmental system to find appropriate remedies; political machines emerged to meet the expanded and diverse needs of the central city population and the urban economy.[30]

Not only did machines provide leadership, they also increased the representativeness of government by bringing new voters into the political process. The influx of poor immigrants to the city along with a system of universal suffrage, provided the machines with the votes they needed to get and stay in power. In exchange, the machine performed "welfare functions," which at that time were beyond the scope of government. They provided turkeys on holidays and acted as an employment agency for the faithful, both for municipal jobs and for jobs in the private sector.

While it is often assumed that business opposed the political machines, the machines provided "welfare" for the business community, in the form of contracts for services such as building roads or legal advice. The machines also helped business in other ways. The fragmented city government often made development quite tedious, but a nod from the boss made anything possible. Machine bosses were able to find housing for their flocks because they were able to influence the enforcement of building codes. In many machine cities, major economic interests had substantial influence on the machines' decisions.

The functions of the machine have been categorized as manifest and latent. **Manifest functions** are those duties that an organization is directly designed to carry out. The political machine's major manifest function was to get its candidates elected. This was accomplished by controlling nominations for office, supplying manpower for electioneering, and making sure that the party faithful turned out on election day.

In performing their major purposes, the machines also provided **latent functions**, that is, indirect consequences of machine activity. At a time of little formal government welfare, one latent function was the provision of welfare services. Another important latent function was socialization, or Americanization, of immigrants. New immigrants were made to feel important and part of their new homeland by machine politicians. Such immigrants often were not concerned by the boss's adage to "vote early and often." The machine offered many an avenue to respectability and upward mobility. Some advanced in the political system and thus became admired and important. Others were given job opportunities in the private sector that otherwise would have been impossible because of discrimination.

Another latent function performed by the machine was to act as a broker and provide a linkage to the system and prevent feelings of alienation and despair.[31] As we can see from the diary of George Washington Plunkett, a former ward boss in the famous Tammany Hall Machine in New York City, the boss could do many good things (Box 7–1 on page 178).

On the other hand, machines had many negative aspects. Most obvious was corruption. Plunkett distinguished between honest and dishonest graft. He made the distinction by referring to the almshouse superintendent under the white Anglo-Saxon Protestant Republican machine in Philadelphia who "stole the zinc roof off the buildin' and sold it for junk."[32] This is an example of dishonest graft. On the other hand, "If an Irishman had the political pull and the roof was much worn, he might get the city authorities to put on a new one and get the contract for himself, and buy the old roof at a bargain—but that's honest graft."[33]

Another problem with political machines was widespread election fraud. People were paid to vote in many districts using names of dead people. In Philadelphia, a machine politician proudly stated that "'These men' [signers of the Declaration of Independence] . . .

BOX 7–1

Strenuous Life of a Tammany Hall District Leader

This is a record of a day's work by Plunkett:

2:00 A.M. Aroused from sleep by the ringing of his doorbell; went to the door and found a bartender, who asked him to go to the police station and bail out a saloon-keeper who had been arrested for violating the excise law. Furnished bail and returned to bed at three o'clock.

6:00 A.M. Awakened by fire engines passing his house. Hastened to the scene of the fire, according to the custom of the Tammany district leaders, to give assistance to the fire sufferers, if needed. Met several of his election district captains who are always under orders to look out for fires, which are considered great vote-getters. Found several tenants who had been burned out, took them to a hotel, supplied them with clothes, fed them, and arranged temporary quarters for them until they could rent and furnish new apartments.

8:30 A.M. Went to the police court to look after his constituents. Found six "drunks." Secured the discharge of four by a timely word with the judge, and paid the fines of two.

9:00 A.M. Appeared in the Municipal District Court. Directed one of his district captains to act as counsel for a widow against whom dispossession proceedings had been instituted and obtained an extension of time. Paid the rent of a poor family about to be dispossessed and gave them a dollar for food.

11:00 A.M. At home again. Found four men waiting for him. One had been discharged by the Metropolitan Railway Company for neglect of duty, and wanted the district leader to fix things. Another wanted a job on the road. The third sought a place on the Subway, and the fourth, a plumber, was looking for work with the Consolidated Gas Company. The dis-

trict leader spent nearly three hours fixing things for the four men, and succeeded in each case.

3:00 P.M. Attended the funeral of an Italian as far as the ferry. Hurried back to make his appearance at the funeral of a Hebrew constituent. Went conspicuously to the front both in the Catholic church and the synagogue, and later attended the Hebrew confirmation ceremonies in the synagogue.

7:00 P.M. Went to district headquarters and presided over a meeting of election district captains. Each captain submitted a list of all the voters in his district, reported on their attitude toward Tammany, suggested who might be won over and how they could be won, told who were in need, and who were in trouble of any kind and the best way to reach them. District leader took notes and gave orders.

8:00 P.M. Went to church fair. Took chances on everything, bought ice cream for the young girls and the children. Kissed the little ones, flattered their mothers and took their fathers out for something down at the corner.

9:00 P.M. At the clubhouse again. Spent $10 on tickets for a church excursion and promised a subscription for a new church bell. Bought tickets for a baseball game to be played by two nines from his district. Listened to the complaints of a dozen pushcart peddlers who said they were persecuted by the police and assured them he would go to Police Headquarters in the morning and see about it.

10:30 P.M. Attended a Hebrew wedding reception and dance. Had previously sent a handsome wedding present to the bride.

12:00 P.M. In bed.

Source: Quoted from: William L. Riordan, *Plunkett of Tammany Hall*, ed. Terrence J. McDonald. Boston: Bedford Books of St. Martin's, 1994), 98–99.

'the fathers of American liberty, voted down here once.' 'And,' he added with a sly grin, 'they vote here yet.'"[34] Corruption had become a way of life in some cities. In one smaller city, a candidate, ". . . was accused of using money freely and offering as high as $20 per vote. Given Albany's history in this regard, the charge may have been intended more to indict Cooke as extravagant than as corrupt."[35] It seems that in Albany, it was not the vote buying per se that seemed extraordinary, only the exorbitant price paid. When necessary, the machines also used threats, intimidation, and violence.[36]

The machine was insidious in that it was generally concerned with visible individual benefits such as food or jobs, resulting in a dependency relationship rather than in policies that would enable the poor to move out of poverty. Small favors were granted to individuals, weakening the ability of the group as a whole to seek collective solutions.[37] Further, "it [the machine] socialized conservatively a generation of American working class, it inhibited the growth of a socialist party which would benefit the poor, and it helped shape the upper class reform movements which sought to save the immigrant poor both from the machine and their poverty."[38] In sum, while the poor were given benefits by the machine, they did not usually become part of the governing coalition.

In addition, machines did not always protect the lower class nor were they a consistent voice for the downtrodden. Mike Royko, in *Boss,* chronicles an attempt to integrate the neighborhood of legendary Chicago mayor Richard Daley, the father of the current mayor. It was difficult finding African-Americans willing to move into Bridgeport. "It was the kind of neighborhood they wouldn't walk through at night, and during the day it wasn't

a good idea either."[39] Finally, two African-American college students agreed to move in. After a few days of "junior sized riots" some action had to be taken.

While Daley stayed out of sight the Eleventh Ward Regular Democratic organization worked things out. While the two students were at school, the police went in the flat and carried their belongings to the corner police station. People from the neighborhood rushed in and threw the place up for grabs, smearing excrement on the walls. The real estate man who handled the move-in was summoned by the ward organization and told what to do. He listened because real estate licenses are under the control of the mayor of the city of Chicago. They told him that the two black youths were no longer tenants in the building; that two white men from the neighborhood were going to move in and were going to be given a long unbreakable lease for the apartment, and that it was all going to happen immediately. The lease was drawn up, signed, and the two white tenants moved in. The jubilant crowd joined them in the apartment for a celebration and to help clean up the mess.[40]

When the African-Americans returned, they were told they no longer lived in Bridgeport.* The owner of the building soon sold out. "Chicago has one of the nation's strictest building codes. Although rarely enforced, it provides City Hall with a powerful club over property owners."[41]

The machines can be faulted for their "tendency to put off the resolution of real social and economic issues and ignore the aspirations of newer groups."[42] It might be noted, however, "that alternative political forms have not done much better."[43] Many machines were

---

*The Bridgeport neighborhood maintains a reputation as a place where African-Americans should be careful during the day but should certainly avoid at night. The severe beating of an African-American youth by whites in 1997 buttresses this perception.

corrupt and inefficient, though perhaps no more inefficient than the weak mayor system in many cities.

Contrary to the "Robin Hood" myth of taking from the rich to give to the poor, many bosses maintained their positions by giving a pittance to the poor and a lot to business and by taking from the average taxpayer. Major economic interests in machine cities had resources that the city needed and this provided the machine an incentive to respond to their demands. For example, the Daley Machine held on to power in Chicago long after the demise of other machines by catering to the needs of business.

> The principal leaders of the opposition to Daley's election in 1955 were the city's business, banking, and civic leaders and the major newspapers that usually echoed their sentiments. . . . Daley shrewdly recognized that unless he could assuage their distrust, these groups would continue to finance challengers and undermine his legitimacy. . . . Soon after Daley took office, he wrote to some of the city's most prominent business leaders asking what the mayor could do to advance the interests of business. The result was a construction program of immense proportions in the downtown Loop that pleased bankers, real estate interests, and downtown retailers.[44]

While many people benefit from such economic development, it is necessary to consider its opportunity costs, that is, what benefits could have accrued from other uses of public power and money, in the final assessment.

After a period of romanticizing the machines, the verdict on the machines' role tends to be negative. Because political machines were able to set the agenda in cities and relied on the support of major business interests, they tended to support "bricks-and-mortar" policies at the expense of social policy. "In general, policies that benefited everyone, friend

and foe alike, had little attraction. . . . Clean air, neighborhood parks, and a vice-free city did little to create a personal following; their benefits cannot be allocated on the basis of favoritism and don't generate individual obligations to the machine."[45]

While machines did provide for the needs of the nineteenth-century immigrants and other urban residents when no other institutions existed, they did not necessarily treat all of the immigrant groups equally. The Irish machines, for example, were more likely to take care of their own before taking care of other groups such as the Poles in Chicago.[46] The pros and cons of the machine are listed in Table 7–1.

Displeasure with the machines led to urban reforms. Aimed less at representation and more at achieving neutral competence and institutionalized leadership, these reforms, along with changes in the society, have led to the marked decline of machines in all but a few places.

Several major factors contributed to the machine's decline. First, the expanding role of government into welfare provision lessened people's dependence on the machine. Second, the affluence of the society and the assimilation of many ethnics lessened the need for machines. Third, demographic changes, especially the post–World War II African-American migration, resulted in white liberal and African-American reform coalitions to challenge machines. Fourth, economic restructuring resulted in jobs moving out of the center city, changing transportation technology enabled many to move to suburbs, and shifting in the employment base (for example, from primarily industrial to more diverse business activities) disrupted machine coalitions. Fifth, the machine was undercut by the disappearance of patronage jobs or jobs to which the machine could appoint its supporters. The need for technologically sophisticated employees led to demands for merit employment and meant that fewer unskilled jobs were available to be filled by anyone with the right

TABLE 7–1

Evaluation of Machines

Pro	Con
1. Provided welfare services	1. Corrupt
2. Provided jobs	2. Inefficient
3. Acted as "ombudsman" with bureaucracy	3. Kept poor dependent
4. Helped socialize immigrants to American values	4. Supported conservative status quo
5. Offered path to upward mobility	
6. Gave psychic support	
7. Facilitated urban development	

connections. The end of the nineteenth century saw demands for civil service employment systems. Under **civil service**, agencies would be staffed on the basis of merit and administered apolitically.

A final reason for the decline of machines was the reform movement that instituted structural changes in city governments that strengthened leadership and professionalized the workforce, making the coordination function of the machines less necessary.[47] Meanwhile, the weak mayor system that had spawned machines in many places was in decline well before the demise of the machine. It continues to decline. In many places the strong mayor-council structure replaced the weak mayor system.

Strong Mayor–Council

Toward the end of the nineteenth century, most weak mayor systems evolved into strong mayor systems. Figure 7–2 (on page 182) presents a simplified illustration. However, many forms of the strong mayor system exist along a continuum of executive authority. In other words, there are numerous combinations of powers given to mayors. The classic example of the strong mayor system has the following characteristics:

1. no elected administrative officials other than the mayor;
2. mayoral control over appointment and removal of principal administrators;
3. broad mayoral veto power and perhaps a line-item veto;
4. direct election of the mayor for a four-year term; and
5. mayoral preparation and execution of the budget.

These characteristics centralize power and maximize the value of leadership, which helps achieve accountability. On the other hand, this system takes power away from the people, who no longer choose all government officials. Fulfilling the goal of neutral competence also becomes more difficult. Generally, we elect people because of their political skills, not their administrative skills, and appointments may be influenced by political considerations instead of who is most qualified for the job.

Once in office, the mayor is expected to be an astute political compromiser in order to get his or her programs approved by the council and the public. At the same time, the mayor must be an outstanding public manager. People possessing both skills are hard to find.

One method of addressing this dilemma is the use of a Chief Administrative Officer

(CAO). In many ways, this method is a bridge to a manager-type of government, which will be discussed later. Perhaps the first use of the CAO occurred in San Francisco in 1931. After World War II this idea took root in many large cities such as Philadelphia (1951) and New Orleans (1952) and in small cities such as Louisville, Kentucky (1952) and St. Cloud, Minnesota (1952).[48] The mayor in this system is free to pursue the policy role and leave the administrative "details" to the CAO. An interesting sidelight is that in Philadelphia in 1983 Wilson Goode went from CAO to mayor. Perhaps because of the complexity of the political environment in large cities, the strong mayor system is most prevalent today.

The strong mayor structure was one of the first elements in reforming the system that nourished the political machines. Machines continued in many cities, even though a strong mayor system gave a democratically elected mayor power to act. In those cities, a powerful machine controlled the mayor's office. In other cities, mayors undercut the need for machines by providing services for the lower and middle classes. The strong mayor structure was an attempt at reform, yet the end of the nineteenth century produced a confluence of forces that led to even more far-reaching reforms of urban government.

Reform Movement

For the most part, the reform movement was spearheaded by business interests and upper middle- and upper-class urbanites who sought "good government." While machines frequently pursued policies that benefited major economic interests, many business leaders wanted to reduce corruption and waste and make government more efficient. Policies that were contrary to the interests of the reformers were viewed as wasteful and inefficient. In other words, then, as now, reformers seek to alter the priorities of government in the name of

FIGURE 7–2

Strong Mayor–Council System (Illustrative Model)

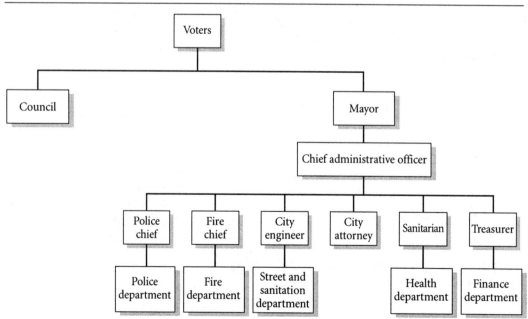

efficiency. In the late-nineteenth and early-twentieth century, four interrelated forces served as catalysts for reform. These were: (1) "Muckraking," (2) Social Reform, (3) Progressivism, and (4) Scientific Management.[49]

Muckrakers were individuals who searched for and exposed misconduct of prominent individuals and organizations, that is, they stirred up muck. *Muckrakers* and *social reformers* "were appalled by the degrading living conditions of urban lower classes, the social irresponsibility of many industrial corporations, and the open graft that seemed to characterize the relations between the business leaders and the big city political machines."[50] The muckraking journalists highlighted the excesses of the machines and their collusion with business. In 1902, Lincoln Steffens published a series of articles in *McClure's Magazine* that were later published in book form as *The Shame of the Cities* (1904). He noted among other things that new teachers in the Philadelphia school system were expected to "contribute" $120 of their first $141 to the machine that got them appointed. In Pittsburgh, $3.5-million worth of paving contracts went to the boss's firm and $33,400 went to competitors.[51]

The social reformers developed programs to improve conditions for the lower class. Some social reformers accepted the limited role of government and established private organizations to serve as alternative welfare providers so the poor did not have to depend on the machines. Jane Addams's Hull House in Chicago was a classic example of a settlement house designed to help the lower classes and socialize them to middle-class values. The problems created by heterogeneity could be mitigated if the "great unwashed" could be taught to subscribe to a homogeneous set of values.

Others sought social reform by taking over and expanding the role of urban government. Many of the social reformers were socialists; in 1911, 74 communities had elected socialists to office. One of the first social reform mayors was Seth Low in New York (1901–1903). He expanded programs for health, recreation, education, mass transit, and tenement regulation. Although his services aided the lower class, his moralism, including a strong stand on Sunday drinking, alienated them, and he served only one term.[52] As Plunkett said, reformers "are mornin' glories—looked lovely in the mornin' and withered up in a short time, while the regular machines went on flourishing forever like fine oaks."[53] Social reform mayors were elected in other cities including Cleveland, Ohio; Philadelphia; and Toledo, Ohio.

A quintessential example of a social reform mayor was Hazen Pingree of Detroit, who served from 1889 to 1897. He took on the machine, and later, corporations. He was first elected with the support of the business community, which sought to end corruption and have government run more economically and efficiently.

> Accommodations [between business and bosses] however, proved to be burdensome and unsatisfactory to the business community and to the upper third of socio-economic groups in general. They were expensive; they were wasteful; they were uncertain. Toward the end of the 19th century, therefore, business and professional men sought more direct control over municipal government in order to exercise political influence more effectively.[54]

Note that "pain in the pocketbook is always an important precipitator of reform."[55]

Once in office, Pingree vigorously attacked collusion between the former Democratic Machine and a paving contractor and greatly improved the street system, much to the pleasure of the business community. Next he attacked corruption in the construction and the furnishing of public schools and got indictments against four school board members. From there, he moved to other reforms with which business was less pleased. He challenged the high cost of ferry service, streetcars, telephone service, and even bread. He fought tax breaks for the city's elite. Pingree created public service jobs, threatened to revoke franchises, and, when all else failed, established municipal utilities. He helped organize a telephone company that had the lowest rates of any large city. While these activities were not appreciated by the business leaders, Pingree had by then achieved a working-class and middle-class coalition.[56]

These reformers who focused on social conditions did not always agree with those who wanted structural reforms, the *progressives* and the supporters of *scientific management*. The social and structural reformers disagreed over the definition of the problem and, therefore, proposed different solutions. Social reformers thought that government catered too much to business and showed little concern for the underclass. They often felt that government should play a larger role in social welfare programs.

> The social reformers were convinced that the urban utilities and large businesses that benefited from favors in franchises, taxes, and public services were the major causes of corrupt city government. They rejected the structural view that businessmen and experts were best fitted to rule the city and should dominate municipal government.[57]

Social reformers did not believe that businessmen should dominate municipal government, but believed instead in democratic participation of the masses.[58]

On the other hand, structural reformers believed that government was corrupted *because* politicians catered to the lower classes. They sought strict efficiency by depoliticizing government and improving management processes. **Progressives** sought the separation of politics and administration and attempted to devise apolitical structures. The proponents of **scientific management** wanted managers to search rationally to discover the "one best way"

that work could be performed to maximize economy and efficiency.

The structural reformers, who tended to be upper-class and upper-middle-class businessmen, sought to protect the city from excesses of the ethnics and the lower class.[59] One of the foremost was Richard Childs, son of a wealthy businessman, Yale graduate, and executive with Bon Ami Corporation, Lederle Laboratories, and American Cyanamid Corporation. As a prime mover in many reform groups such as the National Short Ballot Organization and the National Municipal League, he drew up a model charter for cities to follow.[60]

These upper-class reformers blamed the fiscal problems of the city on corruptible governments supported by "thousands of immigrants from slums and prisons of Italy and South Europe" and others from the "bogs of Ireland, the mines of Poland, the brigand caves of Italy, and from the slave camps of the South but one remove from the jungles of Africa."[61]

Progressive reformers and supporters of scientific management concentrated on eliminating the evils of the machine by advocating structural reform. They sought to weaken the political parties that spawned the machines through a series of electoral reforms and to improve the administration of government. Underlying both sets of reforms was the Progressive idea of depoliticizing government and the political process. Reformers wanted to establish civil service systems to foster neutral competence. Scientific management advocates tried to depoliticize government and increase efficiency by finding the "one best way" to do a job. Businessmen felt that "business methods" not "political methods" should be used. The efficiency ethic of the scientific management school was so strong that advocates believed, "that inequality, poverty, and even poor health and bad education were . . . the results of inefficiency in people's habits."[62] They were less concerned with representativeness than they were with technical, nonpartisan competence, and executive leadership.

Electoral Reforms

The reformers proposed a number of changes to eliminate politics in elections. For one, they advocated the **short ballot**, meaning fewer people to be chosen by election. The long ballot made it impossible for average people to judge the quality of the candidates and to hold anyone accountable after an election. Decreasing the number of directly elected officers maximizes the attainment of the goal of effective leadership, though perhaps at the cost of less representativeness.

The reformers also sought to undermine the machine through various electoral reforms aimed at weakening the party. The **direct primary, nonpartisan ballots**, and **at-large** rather than **ward** elections (that is, citywide election vs. district elections), all provided impediments to strong party control. The **direct primary** meant that all party members could participate in selecting candidates by voting in primary elections occurring before the general election. Thus the bosses could not handpick candidates in "smoke-filled rooms."

Nonpartisan ballots, in which candidates' names are listed on the election ballot without a party label, were established so that voters had the chance to select the best person regardless of party identification. The idea behind **at-large elections** is that candidates would be forced to consider the citywide collective "public interest" as opposed to the "particular, private interests" of selfish neighborhoods and groups. Of course, it also assumes that candidates know what is the public interest.

These reforms all had detrimental effects on the lower-class citizen. To the extent that the direct primary weakened party control of candidates, developing a "balanced" ticket made up of a coalition of minorities became less likely. The absence of party labels in nonpartisan elections deprived voters of access to easy information about the candidates' political orientation. In addition, parties did not provide resources to support those candidates, who themselves had limited resources. Finally, at-large elections served to dilute the votes of minorities who were concentrated in distinct neighborhoods, and, as a result, they often wound up with no representation, rather than a more or less proportional share of seats. Some cities sought to find a compromise between the two and adopted **mixed systems** where some councilors are elected at-large and others by districts.

Another part of the reformers' electoral program was introduction of recall, initiative, and referendum elections, discussed in Chapter 6. Recall provided a mechanism for removing politicians who displeased the majority of their constituents. Initiative and referenda allowed citizens to present their own policy options, or affirm or reject existing or proposed policies.

Administrative Reforms

Administrative reforms of the Progressive Era dealt another blow to the machines. Civil service was introduced to depoliticize the functioning of government. At the national level, the 1883 Pendleton Act established that administrators be chosen for their competence, not for their political connections. By 1885, a civil service system was in place in New York City, Boston, and Buffalo, New York.[63] To a greater or lesser extent, many cities followed. The belief that "to the victor belongs the spoils" went by the wayside in the quest for neutral, nonpartisan competence. This greatly weakened the rewards accessible to the machines and George Washington Plunkett of Tammany Hall spoke of the "Curse of Civil Service."[64]

More recently, courts have further limited the use of patronage. In *Elrod v. Burns*

427 U.S. 347 (1976), the U.S. Supreme Court ruled that a newly elected Cook County Sheriff could not fire even non–civil service employees strictly for partisan reasons. In *Shakman v. The Democratic Organization of Cook County* 481 F. Supp. 1315 (1979), a U.S. District Court determined that partisan considerations should not affect promotions or demotions. The U.S. Supreme Court in *Rulan v. Republican Party of Illinois* 110 S. Ct. 2729 (1990) stated that hiring, promotion, and transfer decisions based on party affiliation violated an individual's First Amendment protections.

The reformers supported concepts of scientific management and other managerial principles that, in the interest of efficiency and economy, argued for strengthened leadership capability (by centralization of authority), "departmentalization" (grouping by function), and centralized coordination of purchases.[65] These were designed to make it easier for the public to identify those responsible for specific policies and therefore to increase public accountability.

To take the politics out of such areas as education, planning, zoning, and personnel, independent boards were often established. The appointment of lay citizens to the board, it was argued, would take politics out of decision making and increase popular control. In reality, the opposite was often true. Citizens on these boards rarely represented the community at large. In general, they represented business and the middle class.

Most of the reforms provided a buffer between the average citizen and the government and depoliticized the process. Efficiency was stressed, but concern with equality was much less. Two structures were introduced that sought to improve the quality of urban government by having, as much as possible, experts run the government in a businesslike manner and make decisions in an apolitical fashion. These structures are

the commission form of government and the council–manager form.

Commission Form

The commission form of government is sometimes called the Galveston Plan because it was first conceived in Galveston, Texas, in the aftermath of a devastating hurricane in 1900. Actually the hurricane triggered structural reform that had been on the political agenda for some time. Business leaders developed a plan based on their business experience and mobilized supporters among the lower and middle classes and labor unions to lobby the state legislature. Again, this is an example of the special role of business interests in local government. The business plan called for the appointment of five commissioners. After considerable debate about democratic rights, a compromise was reached that made two of five commissioners elective offices. Legal decisions necessitated a return to a totally elective commission and the city's charter was revised two years later in 1903.[66]

The most striking difference between the commission system and the mayor–council system is the lack of separation of powers. The commissioners make up the legislative body and also serve as department heads in the executive branch. (See Figure 7–3 for an illustrative example.) For instance, one commissioner may be in charge of public safety (for example, police and fire), another responsible for public works (for example, streets and sanitation), and still another may be in charge of community development (for example, planning and housing).

One commissioner is usually elected as mayor, but the position is primarily ceremonial. Usually the mayor has no veto power. The commissioners are usually elected at-large on a nonpartisan short ballot. In many respects, the system has the failings of the weak mayor system: lack of leadership, lack of coordination, and lack of professional managers. The success in Galveston as well as the depoliticized electoral format made this structure attractive to dominant business interests around the turn of the nineteenth century. It was quickly adopted in Houston, Texas, and Des Moines, Iowa. By 1910 it was used in over 100 cities, and by 1917 over 5,000 cities had instituted it. After that time, however, it started to lose favor among reformers, who began to turn to the council–manager system. Most of the large cities that had adopted the plan have abandoned it, though it is still in use today in cities as large as Portland, Oregon. In all, about 162 (including cities with populations under 2,500) municipalities still use the commission form.[67]

In addition to the leadership problems and the lack of professional expertise of the commissioner–department heads, other problems developed that made many question the efficiency of this form of government. The commissioners became most concerned with their departments and avoided conflict by mutual noninterference—the consequence was little coordination and little accountability. In addition, the close personal ties that formed among the commissioners on the small commissions (usually five members) make it hard to say no to each other. Instead of a checks-and-balances system, conflict could be avoided by using *"logrolling,"* the practice of exchanging favors—"you vote more money for my pet projects, and I'll support your pet projects." Conflict is avoided in this way, but this is far from economical.[68]

Council–Manager Form

A more widely used creation of the reform movement is the brainchild of reformer Richard Childs: the council–manager form of government. A variation of this was first instituted in 1908 in Staunton, Virginia. By 1915, there were 49 council–manager cities. This form is now used in over 2,000 communities, mostly under 500,000 in population. Among the largest cities using it are Dallas, Texas; San Diego, California; Kansas City, Missouri; Phoenix, Arizona; and Cincinnati, Ohio. The council–manager form is especially popular in suburbs because it is well suited to the politics of consensus and the acceptance of professionalism, values that tend to characterize suburbs.[69] It has found greatest favor in the Southeast and Southwest.

The major characteristic of this system is the attempt to establish a distinct separation between politics and administration. An illustrative model is presented in Figure 7–4 (on page 187). Ideally, it maximizes the goal of de-

FIGURE 7–3

Commission System (Illustrative Model)

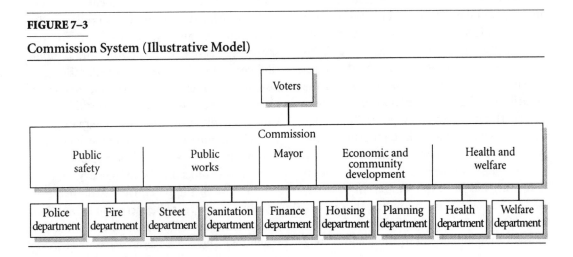

FIGURE 7–4

Council–Manager System (Illustrative Model)

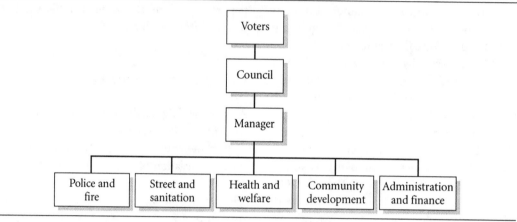

mocracy because the policy-making body, the council, is elected. In addition, the goals of effective leadership and nonpartisan competence leading to efficiency are accomplished by the appointment of a city manager to administer the policy and the creation of an extensive civil service system. The short ballot, often used in city manager government, limits election of boards and other city officials and increases the role of bureaucrats, also presumably leading to nonpartisan competence in administration.

The typical city has a small council that is elected at-large on a nonpartisan ballot. The mayor may be chosen directly by the citizenry or indirectly by the council members from among their ranks. She or he presides over the council, performs ceremonial functions, and usually lacks a veto. The manager is appointed and can be removed at any time by the council. Therefore he or she must remain in the council's good graces. The manager chooses the department heads and is generally responsible for preparing the budget, reporting to the council, and making policy recommendations.

The "ideal" of the politics–administration dichotomy has been discredited. In practice, the responsibilities of the managers can become highly political. Although some managers want to maintain a low profile and merely

administer, they may be frustrated when their professional judgment conflicts with popular demands. Other managers will take a more political role by trying to lobby and influence the public and the council to accept their policy recommendations.[70] This is discussed in more depth in Chapter 8.

James Svara, in a study of five North Carolina cities—Charlotte, Durham, Greensboro, Raleigh, and Winston-Salem—found that the relationship between council and manager varies with the nature of the task facing the government. He argues that the legislative body tends to dominate goal setting and the manager tends to control management decisions, such as hiring and employee complaints. In policy making and implementation, the responsibility is shared. When roles and responsibilities follow these delineations, conflict can be minimized. He notes, however, that some cities may deviate from the typical model, which may result in either a strong manager, a council–dominant system, council incursion into management activities, or a standoff.[71] In such cases, conflict may be more likely.

Because of the potential for conflict, it is easier for managers to be successful in homogeneous communities where value conflicts are minimized. This is one reason that council–manager structures are more common in small and mid-size cities. For very small cities, professional managers are an unnecessary expense, and large and diverse cities tend to seek the political accountability that elected mayors provide. Recently, even small and mid-size cities have re-evaluated their use of the city–manager system. Many that have chosen to remain as city–manager cities have instituted the direct election of their mayor. Now about two-thirds of city–manager cities have an elected mayor, and in 1987 the International City Management Association Model Charter included a city manager and an elected mayor as an optional form of government. An elected mayor presumably adds to the legitimacy of the leadership of the community.[72] Dallas, Texas, a large but well-administered city–manager city, considered, but rejected, a return to a strong mayor system in an effort to assure representation of an increasingly complex and diverse population.[73] Ironically, a court-ordered change from at-large to district representation had increased minority representation on the city council. The influence of those new representatives probably would have been less effective in a strong mayor system. An elected mayor would have had to respond only to a citywide constituency, while under the current system the manager had to respond only to the councilpersons representing various population groups.[74] See Box 7–2 (page 190) for a discussion of this issue.

Cincinnati also faced a challenge to its long standing city-manager system. Business interests, tired of a squabbling city council that had led to four city managers in five years, proposed a referendum to approve a strong mayor system. Issue 1, the proposal, seemed to be headed for victory until a couple of weeks before the election. "The pro-referendum forces appeared to be missing one important element in the community: human beings."[75] Procter & Gamble, headquartered in Cincinnati, contributed $60,000 and the rest of the campaign donations also came from corporations. Cincinnati has always been business-friendly, but a local newspaper columnist labeled the referendum, "a plan by the elite, for the elite," while a letter to the paper charged that "the concept is blatantly designed to ensure the elections of business-backed Republican puppets."[76] In the end, the referral was defeated, indicating that business dominance is not inevitable, especially in the electoral arena.

Two important questions need to be asked about the reform movement. The first is why have some communities adopted reforms and others not? The second is perhaps more important: What are the consequences of reform?

Distribution of Reform

All the forms of government discussed here still exist. Table 7–2 indicates the relative usage of the various governmental structures.

Several years ago Edward Banfield and James Wilson argued that there were two ethos, or sets of beliefs: private regarding and public regarding. The **private-regarding** ethos is a preference for personalized politics, oriented toward favoritism to oneself or one's group. This outlook is identified with machine politics and presumably represents the outlook of the various ethnic immigrants. The more recent neighborhood movement could also be classified as private regarding. **Public-regarding** values, on the other hand, are identified with the reform movement and are supposedly found among middle- and upper-class WASPS (White Anglo-Saxon Protestants). This group reportedly supports the common good.[77]

Based on the above, one might expect cities with large ethnic populations to exhibit less reformed government structures. A study found this not to be the case. It concluded that regionalism was more important than ethnicity in determining the amount of reform.[78] In a study of referenda, Wilson and Banfield found some support for their ethos theory, if African–Americans and Jews were included with WASPS as being public regarding.[79]

Questions were raised about this study that led Wilson and Banfield to reformulate

Which Is Best: The Strong Mayor or the Council–Manager System?

Financial World identified Dallas, Texas, the second largest city in the nation with a city manager government, as the best managed community. Despite that, Rob Gurwitt observed, "There is a good chance that Dallas will do the unthinkable: discard its city manager form of government. For the field of local administration, that would be a bit like England deciding to scrap Parliament. And it would be something more: a sign that the age of municipal reform, as it has been practiced for the better part of this century, is coming to an end." One of the reasons for considering a change was that many of the business leaders who were influential in local politics now work for out-of-town corporations or have moved to the suburbs. Some believe that this has led to a breakdown in the Chamber of Commerce consensus. Since 1991, a court-ordered change from at-large council districts to 14 wards has given representation to African-Americans and Latinos in South Dallas neighborhoods. Many of the new representatives think their constituents are not getting enough attention. At the same time, a weak Dallas economy and increasing urban ills led some to demand stronger leadership, which could be provided by a strong mayor. One commentator stated that the era of municipal reform had ended and that political responsiveness is now as important as efficiency and economy. According to Gurwitt, "it may not be possible to end poverty, house the homeless, disband gangs, repave corroding streets, find the money to revive the economy and put an end to civic squabbling. But one thing citizens clearly can do is refashion local government with the hope that someone—a mayor, an elected county executive—can assemble the political

authority to grapple better with those problems." While some champion change, others argue that it would be silly to change the system just when minorities have been given a voice. Some even believe that the Old Guard is behind the attempt to shift power from the council to a mayor. Because the mayor is elected on a citywide basis, it would give the white residents of North Dallas a larger voice in the direction of the city.

Dallas is not alone in looking at change. St. Petersburg, Florida, switched to a mayor after having a city manager form for 60 years, although the personalities of the candidates, more than the issue of change, may have affected the outcome. The acting city manager in St. Petersburg fired the police chief—who was popular in the white retiree community but unpopular among African-Americans. The dismissed chief ran for mayor, supporting a change to a strong mayor system, against the manager who supported the status quo. The chief lost but the system was changed and the former manager found himself with more power as a result of the proposal of his opponent. In addition to the personality issue, many of the neighborhoods were unhappy with expensive downtown projects and lack of public input.

Mayors are now less likely to be seen as a threat, and, as a result, sentiment may be less for adopting council–manager government structures. But the claim of strong leadership from an elected mayor may be overstated. Tercell Blodgett notes that "there are too many actors whom a mayor can not control and too little power and too few resources to compel or buy support predictably. Leadership that uses power to forge coalitions is not necessarily responsive, particularly to those

(continued on next page)

(continued)

outside the ruling coalitions." He notes that many successful mayors, who exist under the council–manager system, have been quite successful because of their personal leadership qualities—former San Antonio Mayor Henry Cisneros, for example.

Cisneros changed San Antonio from a low-income city with many problems to a thriving post-industrial city. He worked to improve K–12 and higher education, even though he had no official power in those areas. He also worked to attract tourism, biomedical, and high-tech companies to the city. Because the manager had the responsibility to run the city, Cisneros was able to serve as a spokesperson and facilitator.

In many cities, city managers are responsive to the people. Dayton, Ohio, has a very strong record of citizen participation, although it has a city–manager form of government. Blodgett says that political leadership should not be confused with merely reacting to service demands. Too often, the political leadership in strong mayor governments encourages conflict among elected officials, which, in turn, produces political gridlock. City managers can often play a facilitor role in building coalitions. In terms of management, 7 of 10 National Civic League designated All-American Cities (1992–94) and 3 of top 5 best managed cities according to *Financial World* had city–manager systems. The question of what form of government is best for individual cities and their citizens, however, remains an open one.

Source: Adapted from Rob Gurwitt, "The Lure of the Strong Mayor," *Governing* (July 1993): 36–41; and Terrell Blodgett, "Beware the Lure of the 'Strong' Mayor," *Public Management* (January 1994): 6.

their theory.[80] The public-regarding ethos became the **unitarist ethos**, which is concerned with the interests and general welfare of the community as a whole and the desire for good government. The private-regarding ethos became the **individualist ethos**, concerned with local interests, the welfare of specific individuals and groups, and concerned less with good government than with benefits received. They found only weak support for the notion that African-Americans, Jews, and WASPs tended to be unitarists, while ethnics tended to be individualists. They conclude that historically this was the case but that these distinctions have become much less important.[81]

Nonetheless, studies have led to a picture in which cities are likely to have mayoral systems and which are likely to be reformed. One study describes the typical mayoral city as heterogeneous and industrial, with a population with relatively low mobility. The cities using the commission form of government tend to be homogeneous and stable with declining populations that are low in socioeconomic status. Council–manager cities tend to be Protestant and growing, with a highly mobile and homogeneous population.[82] The town meeting type of government continues in Connecticut, New Hampshire, Vermont, Maine, and Massachusetts in cities and towns of less than 50,000.

Reformed models of government occur most frequently in homogeneous communities while heterogeneous communities, where conflict is apt to be more frequent, rely on political structures for conflict resolution. This may reflect the desire on the part of heterogeneous communities to sacrifice efficiency for representativeness or the inability to develop a consensus to change an existing system.

Cities with higher aggregate levels of education are more likely to be reformed.[83] This would indicate that the community probably contains a high proportion of middle- and upper-class people. The fact that another study revealed that council–manager government is correlated with lower percentages of foreign born is consistent with the expectation that more homogeneous communities are more likely to be reformed.[84]

The largest and smallest cities tend to have mayor–council governments.[85] As cities grow, they will probably become more heterogeneous and conflictual. Decisions based on political bargaining and compromise, which allow for some particularistic solutions, may be preferred to decisions based on neutral principles, more common in reformed governments. Small cities are likely to have mayor–council systems because they do not feel a

TABLE 7–2

Government Structures

Community Size	Number of Cities	% of Each Form	Number of Cities	% of Each Form	Number of Cities	% of Each Form
	Total over 2,500		2,500–9,999		10,000–24,999	
Mayor–council	3,310	50	2,184	57	726	44
Council–manager	2,768	41	1,284	33	757	46
Commission	155	2	76	2	52	3
Town meeting	380	6	271	7	98	6
Representative town meeting	72	1	26	1	25	2
TOTAL	**6,685**	**100**	3,841	100	1,658	101[a]
Community Size	25,000–49,999		50,000–99,999		100,000–249,999	
Mayor–council	203	31	118	35	45	35
Council–manager	402	62	216	63	81	62
Commission	18	3	3	1	3	2
Town meeting	7	1	0	0	1	1
Representative town meeting	16	2	4	1	0	0
TOTAL	646	99[a]	341	100	130	100
Community Size	250,000–499,999		500,000–999,999		Over 1,000,000	
Mayor–council	13	36	15	83	6	75
Council–manager	23	64	3	17	2	25
Commission	0	0	0	0	0	0
Town meeting	0	0	0	0	0	0
Representative town meeting	0	0	0	0	0	0
TOTAL	36	100	18	100	8	100

[a]Does not equal 100% due to rounding.

Source: Adapted from *The Municipal Year Book 1997* (Washington D.C.: International City/County Management Association, 1997), xi.

manager is necessary or they do not wish to pay for one. Also, a manager would do away with the "small town" personalism possible in smaller cities.

Reformed cities are more likely to be found in the West than the East.[86] This pattern has many possible explanations. Western cities tend to be newer and are growing. They are less hampered by the traditions of the past and are searching for an efficient way to address the problems of growth. Also, the western cities have had fewer waves of immigrants and tend to be more homogeneous. Further, progressivism played a large political role in California and its influence is still felt in that state and its neighbors.

It should be noted that although there are some patterns in government reform, like the patterns of political machines, there are many exceptions. Socioeconomic factors were tempered by politics.

> The outcome of battles between bosses and reformers was not simply a product of the urban economic and demographic shifts that often weakened machine-constituency networks. The success of political reform also depended on the reformers' ability to organize and mobilize a broad-based political coalition that would unseat ruling machines and replace them with the reform-centered governing coalitions.[87]

A study of reform movements in New York, Cleveland, and Chicago found that various ethnic groups and social classes participated in reform movements. It found that although experts were often recruited by and from business, "where and when experts were both autonomous from business and linked with reform politicians, their proposals could provide the basis for a progressive electoral coalition that cut across existing social divisions."[88] The politicians and the experts sought to maintain a coalition by providing policies that would be supported by the public. History tells us that the success of these coalitions

varied. In Chicago, the experts had the least influence; in New York City they tended to serve business interests; they were initially successful in Cleveland until the political leadership became more sympathetic to the business community.[89]

Consequences of Reform

A major question is what difference does the type of governing structure make to the governors and the governed? Is one form "better" than others? Of course, what you consider better is a function of the values you wish to maximize. Each different structure is more likely to maximize one set of values. Unreformed structures tend to emphasize representative democracy, whereas reformed structures are primarily concerned with neutral competence. Of course, these goals are not mutually exclusive. Unreformed cities may have a civil service system, which shows a concern for neutral competence. On the other hand, reformed cities have managers chosen by a directly elected council and, therefore, have representative elements.

Reform government offers a package of changes besides government structures. Reform can be seen as a continuum developed by using three variables: form of government, type of election, and type of constituency. The most reformed are council–manager systems with nonpartisan elections and at-large constituencies. The most unreformed systems are mayor–council governments with partisan elections and ward constituencies. Some cities exhibit various degrees of reform. One study indicated that reformed governments are less responsive to community cleavages over taxing and spending issues, as well as class, racial, and ethnic cleavages.[90] That study and a more recent one found that regardless of available resources, reformed governments spend less.[91] This could support the argument that reformed governments are less representative but more efficient, or at least more conservative.

The study also found that reform is a continuous variable; that is, the greater the number of reforms, the less the responsiveness.[92] The authors also argued that variables other than structure, such as ethnic or racial differences, voter turnout, and party registration, affected policy choices. In fact, other studies indicate that differences other than governmental structure are better predictors of spending levels of different city governments.[93]

There may be a regional impact on spending. Because reform governments are more likely to be found in the newer cities in the South and West, the costs of maintaining the cities' infrastructure may be less. The pattern of spending in reformed cities, however, would seem to buttress the argument that reform governments exhibit a middle-class bias. Mayor–council cities were found to have substantially higher health and welfare expenditures. The council–manager cities spent more for parks and recreation. Contrary to expectations of a middle-class bias, mayor–council cities spent slightly more on highways, but that may be the result of the impact of age of city—mayor–council cities tend to be older.[94] A recent study indicates that council–manager systems do tend to spend more money per capita on capital facilities, such as water, sewers, and roads.[95]

Reformed governments were less responsive to civil rights groups than were unreformed governments.[96] Indeed, some argue that reform government structures were adopted because they would effectively disenfranchise African-American lower-class citizens.[97] Spending on noncontroversial issues was higher in unreformed cities.[98] On controversial issues, spending was higher in reformed cities, perhaps because actions on these issues could be justified on professional grounds and there was no need to wait for a consensus. A study that compared taxing and spending in cities that had changed their governmental structure to those that had not found almost no impact in the cities with changed government structure.[99] Hence the impact of structural change is not clear, though most research supports the idea that the effect of reform is to benefit the middle and upper classes, who are concerned more with low taxes than social services.

Research has also indicated that electoral changes developing out of the reform movement have an impact. As might be expected, because reform was primarily a business and middle-class movement, these reforms tend to disadvantage the lower classes and minorities. Nonpartisan elections sought to weaken the machines by removing party cues to vote choice. Without party cues, information gathering becomes more difficult and, therefore, becomes more costly to lower-income individuals. Voting turnout declines.[100] Although nonpartisan elections were supposed to allow "anyone" to run for office, middle- and upper-class candidates find it easier to afford a campaign without party support than do those from the lower class. In some "nonpartisan" cities, such as Chicago, the parties remain active but in other places "good government" groups, dominated by middle-class interests, develop slates of candidates. Middle- and upper-class candidates are more likely to be endorsed by the "good government groups."[101] Much research has indicated that African-American candidates are slightly less successful in nonpartisan elections.[102] Nor are voting decisions more rational in nonpartisan elections. Citizens are more likely to base voting decisions on name recognition or personal characteristics rather than issue positions.[103] Voters tend to be less interested in civic affairs, less active, and less aware of issues.[104]

At-large elections also create additional problems for the lower class and minorities. They require a citywide election rather than a ward election and thus more money is needed to run. Also, while minorities may be majorities in some districts and thus be able to gain representation on city council in a ward system, the at-large system dilutes their votes. When Boston switched to the at-large election system, the first 45 councilmen elected were either Italian or Irish. Prior to the change, among the 110 councilmen elected there were, in addition to the Irish, 12 Jews, 9 Yankees, 4 Italians, and an African-American.[105] Since at-large elections are often nonpartisan, there are cumulative disadvantages for the poor and minorities.

Of course, as African-Americans gain a majority in some cities, at-large elections would increase their power, but sometimes annexation is used to dilute the voting clout of African-Americans and other minorities. A recent study indicates that African-Americans have been aided by ward or district elections; in addition, they have also increased their success in at-large elections in the last 10 years, reducing the difference in representation under the different systems.[106] This supports another study that found that African-Americans dramatically improved their success in at-large elections in the 1970s, though they are still slightly better off in district and mixed systems.[107] Neighborhood organizations have served as sources of financial and organizational support to counter the long dominance of the Chamber of Commerce and other conservative groups.[108] For Latinos, on the other hand, the effects of the various governmental structures are not as clear and vary by region.[109] Interestingly, one study found that at-large elections slightly increased the probability that females would be elected to city councils.[110] Legal issues concerning districting will be discussed in Chapter 9.

In most cities, whether manager or mayor, at least some positions are covered by a civil service system. The upshot of this is that "decision making . . . is more likely to be made on the basis of 'professional manage-ment' criteria than on narrowly 'political' grounds (or, in other words, 'bureaucratic politics' come to replace 'electoral politics' as a key arena of decision-making)."[111] Theodore Lowi has argued that the consequences of reform are that cities "are now *well run but ungoverned. . . . The legacy of Reform is the bureaucratic state. . . .* The bureaucracies—that is the professionally organized, autonomous career agencies—are the New Machines."[112] [Italics in original.] The new machines differ from the old machines in that they are organized by function (for example, housing, welfare), rather than geography (for example, precinct or neighborhood), but like the old machine, power is based on services rendered. They are similar in that they shape important policy but are run by a small self-perpetuating minority and are not easily controllable by higher authority.[113]

There is little question that the reform movement reflects a middle- and upper-class bias. The origin of reform comes from businesspeople and professionals and represents the values of economy and efficiency along with an abhorrence of corruption and particularism. Originally, reformed structures provided for citizen participation mainly by establishing blue ribbon panels made up of representatives of business and middle-class organizations.

> By weakening political structures, reform dims the public voice of the lower class. Middle and upper class groups retain a channel of expression through various civic organizations, but the lower class has need for direct political representation—for the personal link between constituent and representative.[114]

The involvement of the lower class and minorities in reformed (as well as unreformed) structures was increased as a result of federal government mandates that forced the establishment of boards to represent low-income neighborhoods. The juxtaposition of "blue ribbon" participants against those from the lower class and minority groups at times creates tension that has the potential of producing creative approaches to problem solving.

Under machines, heterogeneity and impersonalism were handled by a parceling out of rewards—both psychic and material—to all groups and dealing with problem cases on a very personal basis. Reform has accentuated the impersonality of urban living by stressing depersonalized service delivery.

As noted earlier, the various reforms resulted from the desire to achieve three, sometimes inconsistent, values. The first value was to increase representativeness through the election of top decision makers. The second value sought to maximize technical, nonpartisan competence through selection of administrators based on skill rather than political favoritism. The third value, leadership, was aimed at facilitating coordinated and consistent decisions that allow clear accountability to the public. Table 7–3 evaluates the overall impact of the reform of governmental structures according to these criteria.

Machine Politics at the End of the Century

Changes in society, as well as reform movements, have limited the prevalence and importance of political machines. Upon learning about rumors that he had passed away, Mark Twain is said to have remarked, "Reports of my death have been greatly exaggerated." The reports of the demise of machine politics may also be exaggerated. Machines may be faulty, they may work in different ways, and they may not have as much power as in the past, but there are still examples of machine-like politics in some cities.

In New York City, even in the face of the reform Koch administration, the Democratic Party organization was able to function in machine-like ways.

While still controlling access to some public and private sector jobs, elected officials associated with regular organizations have also developed great influence over how city government contracts are awarded. The rise of state and city funding of community-based organizations to deliver social services has also created a "new patronage."[115]

Koch also built alliances with various local machine leaders as part of his governing coalition.[116]

After years of disarray in Chicago after the death of Mayor Richard J. Daley (Richard I), his son Richard M. Daley (Richard II) is now the mayor and leader of the Chicago Democratic Party. While he may be unable to recapture its past glory, Richard II has pulled together an impressive coalition and enjoys strong popular support (see Box 7–3 on pages 198–199).

In Nassau County, a suburb in the New York City metropolitan area, the Republican Party has been able to use time-tested machine techniques to hold power. *Newsday* labeled it the "last political machine."[117] Although New York State subdivisions are expected to adhere to rigid state civil service requirements, *Newsday* found that Democrats held only 16 of 800 civil service jobs, and low-level jobs at that, in the town of Hempstead.[118] One way the organization assures jobs for the faithful is by hiring provisional or temporary workers, a practice learned from the old Chicago Machine. Another means is failing to publicize pending exams or creating misleading ads that make the jobs sound unattractive. A protege of the machine is U.S. Senator Alphonse D'Amato. He has used the personalistic politics of the machine to achieve success at the statewide level by making sure to get resources for his constituents and to ensure they know why they got them. He is not nicknamed Senator Pothole for nothing.[119]

The Republican Machine was damaged by publicity over the requirement that employees "kick back" one percent of their public salaries to machine coffers. "For now, Nassau's patronage army is battered and smaller than it was in its glory days, but it's still alive."[120]

Many of the current machines are not run by either party, but by the mayor, in what are called mayor-centered machines.[121] In Boston, Mayor Kevin White established "little city halls" throughout the city—ostensibly to bring government closer to the people but at the same time to build the loyalty of his employees and those receiving services.[122] Mayors have also used federal programs as a source of jobs and to dispense favors.[123]

> Favors to constituents also remain as a strategy of officeholders in search of electoral support. While reciprocal favors and personal obligations don't undergird the kind of elaborate ward-based organizations once so common in the urban communities of the nation, they remain a formidable force in contemporary politics, . . . The institution of the big city machine has faded away. Many practices associated with it linger on.[124]

Conclusion

As American cities grew, early structures for managing the city proved inadequate. Direct democracy in the form of town meetings could no longer manage change effectively and efficiently as New England municipalities developed. Other cities experimented with the weak mayor–council system, which reflected their distrust of strong executive leadership, and found it both too fragmented to make decisions and unaccountable to the public as the large number of elected officers meant that no one was in charge.

In many cities, an informal structure emerged to deal with the fragmentation of the weak mayor–council system. This was the political machine. In retrospect, it is clear that the machines performed many useful functions. They served as conduits for business in developing the city; they socialized the immigrants; and they provided jobs and acceptance to the new urbanites. On the other hand, corruption was often rampant. In addition, the

---

TABLE 7–3

Impacts of Reform

Reforms	Representativeness	Technical Nonpartisan Competence	Leadership
Government forms			
Strong mayor	High	Varies	High
Commission	High	Low	Low
Council–manager	Low	High	Varies
Election structures			
At-large	Low (disadvantages minorities)	Varies	Majoritarian
Nonpartisan	Low (hinders lower classes)	High	Low
Short ballot	Low	High	High
Administrative reforms			
Civil service	Low	High	Difficult because of careerist
Independent boards	Low	High	Diffused

BOX 7–3

The Rise and Fall—and Rise?
of the Chicago Democratic Machine

In 1931, Anton Cermak defeated Republican Big Bill Thompson for mayor of the City of Chicago. Cermak had been consolidating power as president of the Cook County Board of Commissioners since 1922. He put the machine together by uniting the Eastern European faction with the Irish faction that had been in control of the Democratic Party. With his assassination in 1933, power passed to Party Chairman Pat Nash, and Mayor Edward Kelly and the Irish regained control of the party. Nash died in 1943; Kelly remained in office until 1947 when Jacob Arvey, Chicago's only Jewish "boss" decided, in the face of scandals, that the machine should select its own reform candidate, Martin Kennelly, a businessman. Kennelly was elected mayor. He was honest and moved to expand civil service. This made the party uneasy, but because of his popularity it supported him again, over the objections of African-American Congressman William Dawson, who was upset that Kennelly allowed police raids on gamblers in the African-American community. In return for Dawson's support, the party agreed to dump Kennelly in 1955, though Kennelly was not informed of that.

In the background, Richard J. Daley had been moving up the party ranks. After his chief rival was killed in an automobile accident, Daley became chair of the Cook County Democratic Central Committee in 1953, 30 years after beginning as a precinct captain. In 1955, he received the nomination and was elected mayor. He established a reputation for Chicago as "The City that Works." He did that, and remained in power, through the use of favors and patronage, labor support—which enjoyed the overtime

pay given to assure public works projects were completed by election day—contractors who built the projects, businessmen—who benefited from liberal zoning laws and flexible tax policy—and common citizens who enjoyed good public transportation, clean and well-lit streets, and effective police and fire departments.

Daley remained in power until his death in 1976. From that time until 1989, there was considerable instability in the machine. The machine selected Michael Bilandic to replace Daley. In the primary Bilandic defeated Alderman Roman Pucinski, a Polish member of the machine and African-American State Senator Harold Washington. He easily won the mayor's race. Fate, in the form of five snowstorms in December 1978 and January 1979, brought Chicago to a halt. Snow removal, street cleaning, public transportation, and air traffic were in chaos. Bilandic alienated the African-American community by allowing Chicago Transit Authority trains to whisk white workers downtown quickly by skipping stations in African-American areas.

Jane Byrne challenged Bilandic in 1979 and defeated the machine candidate with the help of African-American voters and reformers. After winning, however, she hooked up with ethnic machine politicians and, feeling threatened by Richard J. Daley's son, Richard M., tried to retain the ethnic vote by replacing African-American appointees with whites. This issue, coupled with public strikes, resulted in turmoil.

The growing African-American population felt that it should have a larger role in the Democratic Party. The result of a coalition between the "lakefront" liberals

(continued on next page)

(continued)

and the African-American community led to the election of African-American Harold Washington in 1983 in a three-way race among Washington, Byrne, and Richard M. Daley. Washington began his term with confrontation with the ethnic machine-controlled city council. He toned down his rhetoric after re-election in 1987 and tried to rebuild a coalition. He slated a multiethnic, multicultural, gender-diverse group for county offices—Irishman, Richard M. Daley; Pole, Aurelia Pucinski; and African-American, Carol Moseley Brown. He died before a final reconciliation was achieved.

Twenty-three white ethnic alderpersons along with six African-American alderpersons selected Eugene Sawyer, an African-American, to be Washington's successor. More activist African-Americans went to court to secure an election to complete the unexpired mayoral term. Lawrence Bloom, an African-American, became the extremist candidate but, unlike Byrne or

Washington before him, his campaign fizzled. Chicagoans were obviously tired of acrimonious campaigns. Richard M. Daley ran against extremism and won the primary over Sawyer and Bloom, who split the African-American vote. African-American Timothy Evans ran against him in the election but Evans' rhetoric and "race baiting" supporters alienated the white lakefront liberals and Richard II became Mayor of Chicago in April 1989. Melvin Holli in his chapter "Daley to Daley" notes:

The city had passed through violent contractions with the death of the machine and was experiencing the birth of a new age. The city's political system, halted in its tracks for a quarter of century, was beginning to evolve again. A new age of political moderation seemed to be dawning. Low-keyed Rich Daley took 55 percent of the vote, the biggest mayoral majority since 1979 (p. 204).

Source: Adapted from Paul M. Green and Melvin Holli, eds., *Restoration 1989: Chicago Elects a New Daley* (Chicago: Lyceum Press, 1991); Mike Royko, *Boss: Richard J. Daley of Chicago* (New York: New American Library, 1971); and John M. Allswang, *Bosses, Machines, and Urban Voters*, rev. ed. (Baltimore: Johns Hopkins University Press, 1986).

machines aided the poor but kept them dependent.

The political machine fails to achieve core values that Americans seek to maximize in designing government structures. The elected leaders were usually not in charge, so it was neither democratic or accountable. Nor was it efficient. One means of alleviating the need for machines was a strong mayor system, in which an elected leader could be held accountable.

Four forces converged—the muckrakers, social reformers, progressivism, and scientific management—that suggested other reforms

aimed at weakening machines. Some wanted structural changes such as nonpartisanship to depoliticize elections. They suggested the commission form, along with civil service to increase government efficiency. These structural reformers represented business interests and sought the "efficient" provision of urban amenities such as streets, lighting, and fire protection. These reforms strengthened the electoral prospects of middle- and upper-class white, Anglo-Saxon candidates while suppressing the strength of minority ethnic and racial groups. The social reformers were more concerned with aiding the underclass and distrusted business. Their gains were relatively short-lived as structural changes were institutionalized to try to prevent machines from ever again gaining power.[125]

Reforms have been adopted by virtually all governments, though suburbs and medium-sized cities are most reformed. The increase in the importance of bureaucracy, intended to achieve government by neutral competence, has increased efficiency, but many feel it has also threatened democracy. Most believe that reform has helped middle- and upper-class urbanites at the expense of the poor.

The structure of government establishes the rules of the political game and sets the context for business or citizen control. To the extent that reformed governments succeed in taking the politics out of city government, they also succeed in limiting the ability of some residents of the city to influence urban policy. Some recent developments indicate that cities may be returning to more political structures. Cities are relying more on district elections to chose at least some members of the city council. Many cities with city managers are expanding the role of mayor to provide identifiable leadership to the city. In some cases, cities are abandoning the city manager system. Such changes have the potential of increasing responsiveness to ordinary citizens.

Notes

1. Herbert Kaufman, "Emerging Conflicts in the Doctrines of Public Administration," *American Political Science Review* 50, no. 4 (December 1956): 1057–1073.

2. Douglas Yates, *The Ungovernable City: The Politics of Urban Problems and Policy Making* (Cambridge, Massachusetts: MIT Press, 1977), 6–7 and passim.

3. See, for example, Peter Bachrach, *The Theory of Democratic Elitism* (Boston: Little, Brown, 1967); Carole Pateman, *Participation and Democratic Theory* (Cambridge, England: Cambridge University Press, 1970); Robert Pranger, *The Eclipse of Community: Power and Participation in Contemporary Politics* (New York: Holt, Rinehart & Winston, 1968); and Mary Grisez Kweit and Robert W. Kweit, *Implementing Citizen Participation in a Bureaucratic Society: A Contingency Approach* (New York: Praeger, 1981).

4. Jane J. Mansbridge, *Beyond Adversarial Democracy* (New York: Basic Books, 1980), 3.

5. Ibid.

6. Ibid., 55.

7. Ibid.

8. Charles Francis Adams, Jr., *Three Episodes of Massachusetts History* (Boston: Houghton, Mifflin, 1892) II, 965–967 in *Town Into City*, ed. Michael H. Frisch (Cambridge, Massachusetts: Harvard University Press, 1972), 72.

9. Frisch, *Town Into City*, 25.

10. Mansbridge, *Beyond Adversarial Democracy*, 48.

11. Joseph F. Zimmerman, *Participatory Democracy: Populism Revisited* (New York: Praeger, 1986), 20–21.

12. Ibid., 154.

13. Ibid., 160.

14. Charles R. Adrian and Charles Press, *Governing Urban America*, 5th ed. (New York: McGraw-Hill, 1977), 180.

15. Mansbridge, *Beyond Adversarial Democracy*, 300.

16. Rob Gurwitt, "A Government that Runs on Citizen Power," *Governing* (December 1992) 48–54.

17. Milton Kotler, *Neighborhood Government: The Local Foundations of Political Life* (Indianapolis, Indiana: Bobbs-Merrill, 1969), 44–50, 82–87.

18. Jeffrey M. Berry, Kent E. Portney, and Ken Thompson, *The Rebirth of Urban Democracy* (Washington, D.C.: The Brookings Institution, 1993).

19. See Michael Margolis, *Viable Democracy* (New York: St. Martin's Press, 1979), Chapter 7 for a discussion of these issues.

20. Edward C. Banfield and James Q. Wilson, *City Politics* (Cambridge, Massachusetts: Harvard University Press, 1965), 79.

21. Adrian and Press, *Governing Urban America*, 158.

22. Jeffery Pressman, "The Preconditions for Mayoral Leadership," *American Political Science Review* 66, no. 2 (June 1972): 511–524.

23. Ibid., 157.

24. Fred I. Greenstein, "The Changing Pattern of Urban Party Politics," *The Annals of the American Academy of Political and Social Science* 353 (May 1964): 3.

25. Robert L. Lineberry and Ira Sharkansky, *Urban Politics and Public Policy*, 3rd ed. (New York: Harper & Row, 1978), 118–120.

26. Ibid., 119.

27. Arthur Mann, "Introduction," in *Plunkett of Tammany Hall*, ed. William L. Riordan (New York: Dutton, 1968), 21.

28. Lyle Dorsett, *The Pendergast Machine* (New York: Oxford University Press, 1968), 21.

29. Ibid., passim.

30. Peter R. Gluck and Richard J. Meister, *Cities in Transition* (New York: New Viewpoints, 1979), 55.

31. Robert K. Merton, *Social Structure and Social Theory* (New York: Free Press, 1957), 60–82.

32. Ibid., 30.

33. Ibid., 30.

34. Alexander B. Callow, Jr., ed., *The Boss in America* (New York: Oxford University Press, 1976), 58.

35. Frank S. Robinson, *Machine Politics: A Study of*

Albany's O'Connells (New Brunswick, New Jersey: Transaction Books, 1977), 37.

36. See, for example, Harold F. Gosnell, *Machine Politics: Chicago Model*, 2nd ed. (Chicago: University of Chicago Press, 1968), 88.

37. Bryan Downes, *Politics, Change, and the Urban Crisis* (North Scituate, Massachusetts: Duxbury, 1976), 112.

38. Norman I. Fainstein and Susan S. Fainstein, *Urban Political Movements: The Search for Minority Power in American Cities* (Englewood Cliffs, New Jersey: Prentice-Hall, 1974), 2.

39. Mike Royko, *Boss: Richard J. Daley of Chicago* (New York: New American Library, 1971), 134.

40. Ibid., 135–6.

41. Ibid., 136.

42. John M. Allswang, *Bosses, Machines, and Urban Voters*, rev. ed. (Baltimore: Johns Hopkins University Press, 1986), 166.

43. Ibid.

44. Richard A. Keiser, "Explaining African-American Political Empowerment: Windy City Politics from 1900 to 1983," *Urban Affairs Quarterly* 29 (September 1993): 98.

45. Clarence N. Stone, "Urban Political Machines: Taking Stock," *PS: Political Science and Politics* 29 (September 1996): 448.

46. Steven P. Erie, *Rainbow's End: Irish-Americans and the Dilemmas of Urban Political Machines, 1840–1985* (Berkeley: University of California Press, 1988); and Tomasz Inglot and John P. Pelissero, "Ethnic Political Power in a Machine City: Chicago's Poles at Rainbow's End," *Urban Affairs Quarterly* 28 (June 1993): 526–543.

47. Lineberry and Sharkansky, *Urban Politics and Public Policy*, 120–121; Elmer E. Cornwell, Jr., "Bosses, Machines, and Ethnic Groups," *Annals of the American Academy of Political and Social Science* (May 1964), 27–39; Roger Lotchin, "Power and Policy: American City Politics Between the Two World Wars," in *Ethnics, Machines, and the American Urban Future*, ed. Scott Greer (Cambridge, Massachusetts: Schenkman, 1981); Lyle W. Dorsett, *Franklin D. Roosevelt and the City Bosses* (Port Washington, New York: Kennikat, 1977); Bruce Stave, *The New Deal and the Last Hurrah: Pittsburgh Machine Politics* (Pittsburgh: University of Pittsburgh Press, 1970); Greenstein, "Changing Pattern of Urban Party Politics"; Harvey Boulay and Alan DiGaetano, "Why Did Political Machines Disappear?" *Journal of Urban History* 12 (1985): 25–49; and Alan DiGaetano, "Urban Political Reform: Did It Kill the Machine?" *Journal of Urban History* 18 (November 1991): 37–68.

48. Adrian and Press, *Governing Urban America*, 162–163.

49. See William A. Schultze, *Urban and Community Politics* (North Scituate, Massachusetts: Duxbury, 1974), 203–204 and Dennis R. Judd, *The Politics of American Cities: Private Power and Public Policy*, 2nd ed. (Boston: Little, Brown, 1984), 74–79, 84–101.

50. John J. Harrigan, *Political Change in the Metropolis*, 3rd ed. (Boston: Little, Brown, 1985), 94.

51. Lincoln Steffens, *The Shame of the Cities* (New York: Hill and Wang, 1957), discussed in Gluck and Meister, *Cities in Transition*, 72.

52. Judd, *Politics of American Cities*, 74.

53. William L. Riordan, *Plunkett of Tammany Hall*, (New York: E.P. Dutton), 17.

54. Samuel P. Hays, "The Politics of Reform in Municipal Government in the Progressive Era," *Pacific Northwest Quarterly* 55 (October 1964): 167.

55. Kweit and Kweit, *Implementing Citizen Participation*, 17.

56. Melvin Holli, *Reform in Detroit: Hazen S. Pingree and Urban Politics* (New York: Oxford University Press, 1969), passim.

57. Melvin G. Holli, "Urban Reform in the Progressive Era," in *The Progressive Era*, ed. Louis L. Gould (Syracuse, New York: Syracuse University Press, 1974), 140.

58. Ibid.

59. Hays, "The Politics of Reform," 158–1589.

60. Schultze, *Urban and Community Politics*, 206–207.

61. Holli, "Urban Reform in the Progressive Era," 137.

62. Judd, *Politics of American Cities*, 101.

63. Gluck and Meister, *Cities in Transition*, 92.

64. Riordan, *Plunkett of Tammany Hall*, 11.

65. Schultze, *Urban and Community Politics*, 204.

66. Bradley Robert Rice, *Progressive Cities: The Commission Government Movement in America, 1901–1920* (Austin: University of Texas Press, 1977).

67. Adrian and Press, *Governing Urban America*, 165–166; and *The Municipal Yearbook 1994* (Washington, D.C.: International City/County Management Association, 1994), xii.

68. Rice, *Progressive Cities*, 91.

69. Ibid., 169–170.

70. Ronald O. Loveridge, *City Managers in Legislative Politics* (Indianapolis, Indiana: Bobbs-Merrill, 1971).

71. James Svara, "Dichotomy and Duality: Reconceptualizing the Relationship Between Policy and Administration in Council–Manager Cities," *Public Administration Review* 45, no. 1 (January–February 1985): 221–232.

72. Greg J. Potasel, "Abandonments of the Council Manager Plan: A New Institutionalist Perspective," *Public Administration Review* 48 (July–August 1988): 811.

73. Rob Gurwitt, "The Lure of the Strong Mayor," *Governing* (July 1993): 36–41.

74. Terrell Blodgett, "Beware the Lure of the 'Strong' Mayor," *Public Management* (January 1994): 6–11.

75. Alan Ehrenhalt, "The Unraveling of a Local Government," *Governing* (October 1995): 8.

76. Ibid.

77. Banfield and Wilson, *City Politics*, 38–44, 95–96, 101–107, 110–111. This draws on Richard Hofstadter, *The Age of Reform* (New York: Knopf, 1955).

78. Raymond E. Wolfinger and John Osgood Field, "Political Ethos and the Structure of City Governments," *American Political Science Review* 60 (June 1966): 312–324.

79. James Q. Wilson and Edward C. Banfield, "Public Regardingness as a Value Premise in Voting Behavior," *American Political Science Review* 58 (December 1964): 876–887.

80. See, for example, Wolfinger and Field, "Political Ethos," and Timothy M. Hennessy, "Problems in Concept Formation: The Ethos Theory and the Comparative Study of Urban Politics," *Midwest*

Journal of Political Science 14 (November 1970): 537–564.

81. James Q. Wilson and Edward C. Banfield, "Political Ethos Revisited," *American Political Science Review* 65 (December 1971): 1048–1062.

82. Robert R. Alford and Harry M. Scoble, "Political and Socioeconomic Characteristics of American Cities," *The Municipal Yearbook, 1965* (Chicago: International City Management Association, 1965), 82–97; see also Thomas R. Dye and Susan MacManus, "Predicting City Government Structure," *American Journal of Political Science* (May 1976): 257–271.

83. Wolfinger and Field, "Political Ethos."

84. John H. Kessel, "Governmental Structure and Political Environment," *American Political Science Review* 56 (1962): 615–620.

85. Lineberry and Sharkansky, *Urban Politics and Public Policy,* 162.

86. Wolfinger and Field, "Political Ethos."

87. DiGaetano, "Urban Political Reform," 51.

88. Kenneth Finegold, *Experts and Politicians: Reform Challenges to Machine Politics in New York, Cleveland, and Chicago* (Princeton: Princeton University Press, 1995), 171.

89. Ibid., 182.

90. Robert L. Lineberry and Edmond P. Fowler, "Reformism and Public Policies in American Cities," *American Political Science Review* 61 (September 1967): 701–716.

91. Lineberry and Fowler, "Reformism and Public Policies in American Cities," 701–716; and David Morgan and Jeffrey Brudney, "Urban Policy and the City Government Structure: Testing the Mediating Effects of Reform." Paper presented at the 1985 Annual Meeting of the American Political Science Association, August 29–September 1, 1985, New Orleans, Louisiana.

92. Ibid.

93. Terry Nichols Clark, "Community Structure, Decision Making, Budget Expenditures, and Urban Renewal in 51 American Cities," *American Sociological Review* 33 (August 1968): 576–593; Roland Liebert, "Municipal Functions, Structure, and Expenditures: A Reanalysis of Recent Research," *Social Science Quarterly* 59 (June 1974): 765–783; and Terry Nichols Clark and Lorna Crowley Ferguson, *City Money: Political Processes, Fiscal Strain, and Retrenchment* (New York: Columbia University Press, 1983), 243.

94. Naomi Bailin Wish, "The Cost and Quality of Urban Life: A Matter of Governmental Structure or Regional Variation," *Municipal Yearbook, 1986* (Washington, D.C.: International City Management Association, 1986), 17–18.

95. Samuel Nunn, "Urban Infrastructure Policies and Capital Spending in City Manager and Strong Mayor Cities," *American Journal of Public Administration* 26 (March 1996): 93–112.

96. Albert K. Karnig, "Private-Regarding Policy, Civil Rights Groups, and the Mediating Impact of Municipal Reform," *American Journal of Political Science* 19 (February 1975): 91–106.

97. J. Morgan Kousser, "The Undermining of the First Reconstruction: Lessons for the Second," in *Minority Vote Dilution,* ed. Chandler Davidson (Washington, D.C.: Howard University Press, 1984), 37–39.

98. Terry N. Clark, "Community Structure, Decision-Making, Budget Expenditures, and Urban Renewal in 51 American Communities," *American Sociological Review* 33 (August 1968): 576–593.

99. David R. Morgan and John P. Pelissero, "Urban Policy: Does Political Structure Matter?" *American Political Science Review* 74 (December 1980): 1005.

100. Robert H. Salisbury and Gordon Black, "Class and Party in Partisan and Nonpartisan Elections," *American Political Science Review* 67 (September 1963): 590; Albert K. Karnig and B. Oliver Walters, "Decline in Municipal Turnout: A Function of Changing Structure," *American Politics Quarterly* 11 (October 1983): 491–505; and Howard Hamilton, "The Municipal Voter: Voting and Nonvoting in City Elections," *American Political Science Review* 65 (December 1971): 1135–1140.

101. Luis Ricardo Fraga, "Domination Through Democratic Means: Nonpartisan Slating Groups in City Electoral Politics." Paper prepared for delivery at the 1985 Annual Meeting of the American Political Science Association, August 29–September 1, 1985, New Orleans, Louisiana, 15.

102. J. Kramer, "The Election of Blacks to City Councils: A 1970 Status Report and Prolegomenon," *Journal of Black Studies* 1 (June 1971): 443–476; D. Campbell and Joe Feagin, "Black Politics in the South: A Descriptive Analysis," *Journal of Politics* 37 (February 1975): 12–59; Theodore Robinson and Thomas Dye, "Reforms and Black Representation on City Councils," *Social Science Quarterly* 59 (June 1978): 133–141; Leonard Cole, "Electing Blacks to Municipal Office," *Urban Affairs Quarterly* 19 (September 1974): 761–782; and Albert K. Karnig and Susan Welch, *Black Representation and Urban Policy* (Chicago: University of Chicago Press, 1981).

103. Paul Raymond, "The American Voter in a Nonpartisan, Urban Election," *American Politics Quarterly* 20 (April 1992): 247–260.

104. Heywood T. Sanders, "Cities, Politics and Elections: Partisanship in Non-Partisan Elections," *The Municipal Yearbook, 1971* (Washington, D.C.: International City Management Association, 1971), 19.

105. Banfield and Wilson, *City Politics,* 95.

106. Tim R. Sass and Stephen L. Mahay, "The Voting Rights Act, District Elections, and the Success of Black Candidates in Municipal Elections," *Journal of Law and Economics* 38 (October 1995): 367–392.

107. Susan Welch, "The Impact of At-Large Elections on the Representation of Blacks and Hispanics," *Journal of Politics* 51 (November 1990): 1050–1076.

108. Susan Welch and Timothy Bledsoe, *Urban Reform and Its Consequences: A Study in Representation* (Chicago: University of Chicago Press, 1988), 52.

109. Welch, "The Impact of At-Large Elections on the Representation of Blacks and Hispanics," 1050–1076.

Earlier studies did show Hispanics to be disadvantaged. See Delbert Taebel, "Minority Representation on City Councils: The Impact of Structure on Blacks and Hispanics," *Social Science Quarterly* 59 (June 1978): 142–152 and Chandler Davidson and George Korbel, "At Large Elections and Minority Group Representation: A Re-Examination of Historical and Contemporary Evidence," *Journal of Politics* 43 (November 1981): 982–1005.

110. Albert K. Karnig and Susan Welch, "Sex and Ethnic Differences in Municipal Representation," *Social Science Quarterly* 60 (December 1979): 465–481.

111. Lineberry and Sharkansky, *Urban Politics and Public Policy,* 164.

112. Theodore J. Lowi, "Foreword to the Second Edition: Gosnell's Chicago Revisited Via Lindsay's New York," in *Machine Politics,* ed. Gosnell, ix-x.

113. Ibid., x.

114. Clarence N. Stone, Robert K. Whelan, and William J. Murin, *Urban Policy and Politics in a Bureaucratic Age* (Englewood Cliffs, New Jersey: Prentice-Hall, 1986), 118.

115. John Mollenkopf, *A Phoenix in the Ashes: The Rise and Fall of the Koch Coalition in New York City Politics* (Princeton: Princeton University Press, 1992), 80.

116. Ibid., 121–126.

117. Anne Freedman, *Patronage: An American Tradition* (Chicago: Nelson-Hall, 1994), 127–167.

118. Ibid., 141.

119. Ibid., 155.

120. Ibid., 167.

121. Alan DiGaetano, "Machine Politics in the Post-Industrial Era." Paper presented at the 1988 Annual Meeting of the Urban Affairs Association, St. Louis, Missouri, March 11, 1988.

122. Ibid.

123. Ibid.

124. Stone, "Urban Political Machines," 450.

125. James Weinstein, "Organized Business and the City Commission and Manager Movements," *The Journal of Southern History* 62 (1962): 167, 176–178; and Luis Ricardo Fraga, "Domination Through Electoral Means: Nonpartisan Slating Groups in City Electoral Politics." Paper delivered at the 1985 Annual Meeting of the American Political Science Association, New Orleans, Louisiana.

CHAPTER 8

Urban Officials

The structure of government affects the power possessed by the various urban officials and, therefore, the way they orient themselves to their jobs. Other factors also affect how the occupants of city government offices behave. For example, the financial status of the local government affects whether mayors will focus on new policy initiatives or whether their time will be consumed with dealing with fiscal crises. Officials' personal preferences also affect what they do. Many local governments face fiscal pressures, but different officials use various ways to deal with those pressures. One mayor may try to attract new business development to the area while another may emphasize bringing dollars in through tourism. The formal structure of urban government is important because it sets the context in which residents and other interests must work to influence policy, but the values and behavior of officials also substantially affect the extent to which residents can have an impact on decisions. Officials play various roles. They must decide individually how they are going to balance the various roles and which role they will emphasize.

Mayors

Americans tend to focus too many hopes and too many expectations on chief executives. At the city level, mayors are viewed as "problem-solvers-in-chief."[1] But mayors must face this expectation with varying levels of resources. As James Svara observes: "If we define executive leadership to include the initiation of proposals to deal with problems in the community and the implementation of policy through control of the bureaucracy, then such leadership is a challenge for the strong mayor, difficult for the weak mayor, and impossible for the council–manager mayor."[2]

Mayors are expected to perform three main roles.[3] First, they are supposed to be Policy Leaders, developing bold new policy initiatives to solve the problems that plague the urban scene. Thus they must be involved in the first two stages of the policy process—agenda setting and formulation of alternatives. Second, they are expected to be Financial Managers, addressing fiscal issues. This involves the twin goals of seeking new funds for the city and keeping taxes low. They need to work with others to adopt policies that will provide fiscal stability while determining the necessary mix of public services to be delivered. Finally, mayors are the Provider of Services, responsible for assuring that policies are implemented. If streets are dirty or the garbage is not collected, many believe it is the mayor's fault. Mayors must accurately evaluate the level of service and public satisfaction because negative evaluations will limit their bargaining power when new initiatives arise.

In addition to these three main roles, mayors are also expected to fulfill other functions. In some cases, they are expected to resolve the conflicts that arise within the heterogeneous mix of city residents. This responsibility can assume extreme forms. For example, during the riots of the 1960s, mayors like Carl Stokes of Cleveland and John Lindsay of New York went to the areas where the riots were in progress to talk with the people and to plead with them to "cool it." One observer refers to this as the "supreme city emergency handler role."[4]

In other cases, cities are looking for mayors who can serve as a symbol of the city, or who can project a favorable image of the city. This is the chief city ambassador role.[5] An example from the past was Edward Koch, mayor of New York City. Koch's boisterous, irreverent, sarcastic, and joyous rhetoric and behavior matched the city that elected him. In the 1990s, many mayors tend to be pragmatic, entrepreneurial leaders who match their citizens' focus on making the city work.[6] One study defined public entrepreneurs as follows: "In addition to the central feature of alertness to opportunity, we also define entrepreneurs by two other factors: their willingness to take risky action in the pursuit of the opportunities they see, and their ability to coordinate the actions of other people to fulfill their goals."[7] The study found that the major source of entrepreneurial leadership in cities came from elected officials, especially mayors.[8]

While the expectations are many, the resources available to mayors are few. To achieve

at least some of the expected goals, they should have, at a minimum, the following resources. To be policy innovators, they would need a *staff* to help devise creative solutions to problems. They would also have to have enough influence over the legislative branch of city government to get the necessary legal authority to implement new policies. That might be accomplished if the mayor could *appoint the council or its committees*. To be financial managers, mayors would need authority over the *budgetary process* as well as some leverage with the legislative branch to get approval of the budget. Given the fiscal realities of cities, mayors also need some leverage with state and national governments to pry out resources for the city. In addition they would need some way of influencing private business because it plays a major role in determining the city's economy. To be service providers, mayors would need to be in control of those who are actually out on the streets. To do that, they would need to be able to *appoint department heads*. In addition, powers that might help mayors achieve their goals are the ability to *veto* council actions, to *appoint members of boards and commissions*, to *issue executive orders*. In addition, mayors should be *directly elected* so they could claim a constituency and should be *full-time* with a *full-time salary*.

As the last chapter makes clear, mayors do not always have these legal resources. In weak mayor governments, they have few or none of the resources necessary for fulfilling their goals. While they have few resources besides the title and the ability to preside over council meetings, they may still be expected to provide leadership. They can do that only by using personal influence and setting the agenda at the council meetings. Even in cities classified as having strong mayor systems, city charters show great variety in the combination of formal powers they give to mayors. In council–manager cities, the mayor normally has no formal powers that would be considered executive.

James Svara has argued that mayors in city manager governments perform a different, but still valuable, role. Such mayors can provide "facilitative leadership," by helping the manager and council to interact successfully and by providing policy guidance.[9] In some cities with managers, the mayor has been given greater authority, for example the responsibility for proposing a budget or to make some appointments, including appointing the manager. Such assignment of responsibilities has been especially common in larger cities.

Another problem faced by many mayors, especially in smaller cities, is that the job can only be part-time because salaries are so low. A study of Oakland, California, in the 1960s concluded that the combination of the lack of staff and lack of salary meant that rather than the mayor controlling the administrators, the administrators controlled the mayor. In larger cities, the staffing and salary situations have improved. In New York City, the mayor in the 1970s could call on a staff of more than 1,000 people.[10] Mayors in larger cities such as Boston, Chicago, Houston, and Philadelphia had salaries that ranged from $100,000 to $133,004 in 1994. But in many cities with city managers, mayors are still paid little. For example, the salary of the mayor of Dallas in 1994 was $2,400, but the salary of the city manager was $134,000. Also, in small cities, regardless of the form of government, mayors have few resources to enable them to lead the city. For example, there is not a single full-time mayor in the state of North Dakota.

One review of Chicago mayors argues that they were limited not only by the absence of resources but also by constraints from three sources. First, mayors face opposition from the coalition of business interests primarily focused on growth and economic development. Second, mayors are limited by the actions of state and local government. Finally, the urban bureaucracy can present a substantial challenge to mayors, especially those seeking change.[11]

In many cases, mayors must substitute informal power resources for the legal resources they lack. For instance, Chicago has a weak mayor system, but few realized that while Richard J. Daley (the father of the current mayor) was mayor. Daley used the well-oiled Democratic Party machinery to augment his limited resources. In other instances, mayors have managed to provide leadership through what might be referred to as charisma. Douglas Yates, for instance, argued that John Lindsay's political style in New York City "was to dramatize urban problems through moralistic rhetoric and force of personality."[12] Another example might be Mayor Edward Rendell of Philadelphia who captured attention by being photographed on his hands and knees scrubbing a bathroom in city hall. Such informal power tends to be ephemeral. Mayor Rendall and Mayor William Hanna of Utica, New York, are discussed in Box 8–1 (on page 208).

Mayors can also attempt to augment their formal powers by constructing a coalition of community support. Mayors need to have two coalitions that are similar, but not identical. First, mayors need an electoral coalition to get the job in the first place. The need to find necessary votes for election is what provides the possibility of citizen influence. Citizens can trade off a bloc of votes for the expectation of influence once the candidate arrives in city hall. Once in office, mayors also need to assemble a coalition that will augment their formal powers and enable them to govern.

Groups that voted for the mayor will expect to be in the governing coalition, but because what it takes to elected is not always what it takes to govern, mayors must seek support from others as they attempt to move from candidate to mayor. For example, John Mollenkopf describes Edward Koch's calculations as candidate as he approached the final run-off election for mayor in 1977. He had to choose between a liberal strategy that would appeal to the Democratic Party base of white liberals, African-Americans, and Latinos or a

BOX 8–1

Mayoral Styles
Rendell of Philadelphia and Hanna of Utica, New York

While often lacking in formal authority, mayors are often expected to be leaders and saviors of their cities. Some current mayors are succeeding by emphasizing good management and back-to-basics policies. But some offer added flair to the job. One of the most popular and most famous of the recent crop of urban mayors is Edward Rendell of Philadelphia.

When Rendell first became mayor in January 1992, the city was in crisis. It had a $200-million deficit, had been losing factory jobs for years, and had lost one-quarter of its population since the 1970s. The new mayor dramatized the seriousness of the situation by providing a photo opportunity of himself on his hands and knees cleaning toilets in city hall. Within two years, the deficit had been eliminated without raising taxes. Rendell was credited with saving the city. (See Box 10–1 on page 256 for another view of Rendell's role in the deficit crisis.)

Rendell is serving as a model for other mayors, especially Rudolph Giuliani of New York City. As Joseph Weisberg observed, "The problem is that while Giuliani talks the talk, he lacks the personality that has made Rendell such a beloved figure. The missing element is charm, which in a politician encompasses savvy, press relations, and showmanship, in addition to actual charm." Rendell is witty and frequently obscene. He will do favors for people, such as getting Phillies' tickets for a congressman's mother. He demonstrates his concern about the city finances by performing weddings for $500, which he donates to the city. And in the end, he always shares credit for success. "By contrast Giuliani's tight-lipped, joyless demeanor makes governing look like nothing but a chore." Good management is important, but so is image.

Less known and more eccentric is Mayor Edward Hanna of Utica, New York. Hanna was first elected mayor in 1974 but was defeated in a re-election bid in 1977. During his first term in office he removed his office door to symbolize his openness to the public and fought incessantly with the city council. Recently re-elected, Hanna, like Rendell, inherited a city in crisis. State intervention was needed to forestall bankruptcy; Utica has the lowest bond rating of any city in the country. Hanna refers to sorry state of city government by saying, "Everything I've touched since the day I took office has been corrupt, stupid, and wrong."

Some think Hanna is the right man for the job as mayor now because he confronts problems head-on. Others question his priorities. He has spent money to refurbish Hanna Park, which he created in his first term and named after his father, while cutting money for police and fire services. He is pushing for the establishment of regional government, saying that he is hoping the city government will be eliminated so he will not have to finish his term.

Source: Adapted from Stephen Glass, "Philadelphia Story," *The New Republic,* May 13, 1996, 14; Jacob Weisberg, "Philadelphia Story: Rudy's Role Model," *New York,* May 2, 1994, 30–32; William Glaberson, "The Mayor Who Loves to Hate His City," *New York Times,* September 24, 1996, Sec. B.

conservative strategy to hold onto the votes of the Jewish community.

In the end, Koch sought to have it both ways by presenting himself as a "tough liberal" who could "make hard decisions and say 'no'" while also seeking support both from regular Democratic organization leaders in the Bronx and Brooklyn and from Harlem's black political establishment. This strategy was designed to capture both more liberal and more conservative Jewish voters as well as blacks and Latinos.[13]

The strategy worked. But as he took office, Koch realized he had to deal with the different expectations of the groups in his electoral coalition as well as build on to that coalition to capture resources he would need to govern.

Given these tensions within his coalition and the narrowness of his ultimate victory, Mayor Koch had to broaden, consolidate, and rationalize his base of electoral support. He had to win more votes than he lost in the process and prevent those he was causing to be dissatisfied from uniting against him. He also had to convert his electoral coalition into a governing coalition. Success at any of these tasks would feed the others: the greater his perceived electoral invincibility, the more leverage he would have over other centers of private and governmental power; the stronger his governing position, the more key institutional actors would seek to do business with him and support him at election time.[14]

Koch managed to build both electoral and governing coalitions strong enough to assure his re-election until 1989, when the strains in the electoral coalition and the contradictions between the electoral coalition and the governing coalition become unmanageable. He tried to hold on to minority voters by appealing to them on the basis of their middle-class aspirations, their fear of crime, and their ethnic identities. Meanwhile, he was also trying to build a Jewish–white-Catholic

alignment by appealing to their fear of African-Americans and Latinos. As a result, he increasingly lost African-American and Latino votes. Although he had forged strong ties with investment bankers and the corporate elite who were important in maintaining the financial solvency of the city, that support was not enough to ensure his election in 1989 after the defection of major parts of his electoral coalition.[15]

While the details are substantially different, Raphael Sonenshein describes how Mayor Bradley of Los Angeles also succeeded by first building an electoral coalition and then creating a governing coalition. Bradley won power in 1973 by appealing to Jews, liberals, African-Americans, and Latinos. Once the election was over, Bradley turned to the issue of economic development:

> Having power expanded and transformed the biracial coalition. The most far-reaching change was its incorporation of business. . . . As city hall turned toward its ambitious redevelopment plans, the coalition dramatically expanded to incorporate the economic sector.[16]

As with the Koch coalition, the addition of the economic interests to the governing coalition created strains:

> The coalition became a sort of hybrid: a progressive biracial alliance dedicated to police accountability, affirmative action, environmental planning, and antipoverty programs joined to a moderate elite alliance devoted to growth, downtown redevelopment, and the creation of a "world-class city." Bradley and his council allies were now committed to a balancing act—a situation made more ambiguous by the vast amounts of business money available to incumbents.

In general, building coalitions is easier to do when there are broad, organized groups existing in the city and harder if the community is fragmented and in conflict.[17] Clarence Stone has documented the persistence of the coalition between Atlanta's business elite and the African-American middle class. That ongoing coalition, which he called a regime, was possible because of the existing organizational base of both groups. Initially, for the business community, the primary organization was the Central Atlanta Improvement Association, and for African-Americans it was the Atlanta Negro Voters League. Over time, many other organizations also became important, including the Action Forum, the Chamber of Commerce, and the Central Atlanta Progress.[18]

On the other hand, one study of Detroit during the last days of the mayoralty of Coleman Young illustrated the problem of building a governing coalition when a city is fragmented. The study identified two different and competing coalitions, making progress in the city difficult, to say the least.

> Detroit emerges as a city with a limited and weak regime-building capacity. An incomplete and internally divided coalition pursuing a downtown revitalization strategy is being challenged by an embryonic and underfunded coalition pursuing a human-capital strategy. In contrast to the situation described in Atlanta and elsewhere of cohesive and dynamic coalitions, Detroit is a study of failed regime building. As such, it may be representative of the experience of other large cities struggling to cope with dramatic and negative social and economic changes.[19]

Despite the differences in the cities themselves and the coalitions that were formed, these examples of New York, Los Angeles, and Atlanta point to the pervasiveness of business in the governing coalitions, but also point to the fact that business support alone is not enough to make either a electoral coalition or a governing coalition successful. John Logan and Harvey Molotch argue that the common

model of urban policy is a growth machine in which major economic interests in the city will only tolerate politicians who support the focus of effort and resources on encouraging economic growth.[20] But the example of Detroit shows that business cannot always be assured of dominating a governing coalition. In San Francisco a coalition formed to oppose the pro-growth preferences of business. Richard DeLeon identified an "antiregime" which existed for a time and was able to thwart the growth machine by tying it up in "red tape."[21] The case of New York City demonstrates that electoral defeat can occur if the mayor angers too many in his electoral coalition, even if business interests are supportive.

Clearly, the influence of citizens will vary depending on their position in either the electoral or the governing coalition. Also important for citizens is the way mayors orient themselves to their jobs. A number of researchers have recognized that different mayors approach their myriad tasks in different ways with different emphases.[22] For example, one study produced a five-fold typology of mayoral roles based on what goals mayors emphasize and what resources they use to achieve their goals. They types were: ceremonial, caretaker, personality/individualist, executive, and program entrepreneur.

Ceremonial mayors focus on problems on a day-to-day basis, resulting in a "muddling through" agenda-setting style. They rely on personal appeals for network building and task accomplishment. Caretaker mayors try to influence those around them by the exchange of jobs and favors and try to direct the bureaucracy to be sure basic city services are adequately performed and specific problems are eliminated.[23]

Personality/individualist mayors rely on personal appeals to those around them and individual effort to try to make changes, rather than just maintain services as do the ceremonial and caretaker mayors. Executive mayors are also slightly more goal-oriented than the ceremonial and caretaker mayors, but differ from personality/individualist mayors by relying on exchanging favors and building coalitions in addition to personal appeals to influence those surrounding them. Executives also rely heavily on the bureaucracy to accomplish the goals they have set.[24]

Finally, program entrepreneurs differ from the other four types of mayors by specifying more long-term goals. They rely on a variety of processes, especially coalition building, to influence those around them. They also rely on individual effort, control over the bureaucracy, and "entrepreneurial" resources, or "sales skills," to accomplish their goals. Of the five types of mayors, program entrepreneurs are likely to have the greatest impact on the policy process.

One major implication of the study of mayoral types is that citizen influence would vary depending on how mayors oriented themselves to their jobs and what strategy they used to attempt to achieve their goals. For example, ceremonial mayors may well be responsive to requests for limited and short-term policies, especially if made in a personalistic way by those they know, but their lack of interest in long-term goals or coalition formation would mean they have little incentive to consider requests for major policy changes, even if accompanied by inducements.

Because of their interest in achieving long-term goals and their willingness to exchange favors and build coalitions to achieve those goals, executive and program entrepreneur mayors would be expected to be most amenable to requests from citizen groups. Their understanding of and willingness to play the political game to accomplish change should mean they would be especially amenable to offers of inducements from citizens.

While some researchers see the choice of mayoral role as individually determined, others emphasize the importance of the political and economic context of the city. This context can have an impact in two ways. First, electoral coalitions seek candidates with the particular characteristics they desire. Second, once elected, a candidate tries to meet the expectations of supporters. An example of such a model is one that argues that mayors in "normal times" will tend to be mediators among varying interest groups in their electoral coalition or advocates for the major groups in that coalition. In periods of "social upheaval," mayoral candidates will try to appeal to "emerging coalitions," and therefore will be innovators if elected.[25]

While mayors have some freedom in choosing styles in both "normal times" and in times of "social upheaval," in periods of severe financial stress, choices are almost completely in the hands of financial elites who transcend group politics, rearrange city finances, and restructure city government for the immediate future. For example, when New York City was in financial crisis in 1975, behind-the-scenes meetings—attended primarily by bankers—resulted in the creation of the Municipal Assistance Corporation (MAC) and the Emergency Financial Control Board (EFCB). One analysis concluded: "The theoretical repositories of the people's will—the mayor, Board of Estimate, the elected legislators—lost much of their authority, which shifted decisively away from the elected mayor and the Board of Estimate, to the bankers and businessmen who dominated MAC and EFCB."[26] More recently Mayor Marion Berry of Washington, D.C., was relieved of much of his authority over major policy issues as a result of both financial crisis and dismal service delivery.[27] These examples seem to indicate that financial strain minimizes citizen impact because of limits on the powers of mayors.[28]

An analysis of political fallout from New York City's fiscal crisis lends credence to the argument that citizens will have little control during times of fiscal stress. That study argues that Ed Koch revitalized the mayor's office following the financial crisis of the 1970s only by making clear "in both word and deed," that "revitalizing New York's economy is a top priority of his administration."[29] On the other hand, a study of government responses to fiscal stress in Cincinnati reported that officials kept the possible or actual responses of constituents constantly in mind in planning responses to financial stress: " . . . if complaints were received, service was restored. The possibility of protest played a greater role than the actuality of it."[30] That suggests that, in some instances, options are limited by fiscal stress, but the necessity of maintaining political support within the electoral coalition is still a factor in a mayor's decision making.

The job of mayor is obviously difficult and, for many, extremely frustrating. John Kotter and Paul Lawrence reported that of the 20 mayors they studied only three were happy.[31] In a self-analysis of his service as mayor of College Station, Texas, Gary Halter concluded:

> I did not seek reelection in 1986, in part because service on the council had ceased to be enjoyable. I found myself increasingly at odds with the elected representatives of the business community who doubled as fiscal conservatives and spoke the Reagan rhetoric and with the neighborhood advocate who opposed almost everything.[32]

The danger, of course, is that the difficulty and frustration will eventually result in people with ability being unwilling to serve—a development that may lead to "an urban crisis of unparalleled size and scope."[33]

City Councils

If mayors face frustration, evidence indicates that city council members do as well. In most cities their primary responsibility is policy adoption. They sometimes also engage in oversight of the implementation of public services. James Svara identifies four roles for council members: "representative, governor, supervisor, and judge."[34] As representatives,

council members act as spokespersons for their constituents in policy matters and respond to their requests for services or for help in solving problems. In the policy realm, council members may approach their representational responsibilities in different ways. Council members who see themselves as *delegates* believe it is their responsibility to mirror the wishes of constituents while *trustees* believe they should exercise their own judgment. The trustee role tends to predominate, probably because constituents have little knowledge of or interest in much of the business of the council.[35] But even trustees may consider constituent views in taking an independent stand.[36] As any observer of public meetings can attest, depending on the issue and on who and how many people show up, and how much noise they make, politically wise trustees may take the public counsel. This does not necessarily mean that the citizens who have appeared really speak for the wishes of the general public.

Council members may also vary in how they respond to constituent requests for particular services or for help in solving problems. While some may see that as a major part of the job, others may think that universal rules should govern the allocation of benefits in the city.[37]

Some research concludes that because many council members are only part-time and poorly paid, they view themselves as "volunteers"—and not always very eager ones at that.[38] More recent research points to the great diversity among city councils. Because they are often part-time, council members tend to be dependent on the mayor or department heads for information and guidance, but some councils are "frequently full-time, relatively well-paid legislative bodies and therefore can develop their own expertise."[39] Councils vary in, for example, staff resources, terms of office, frequency of meetings, and number of seats.[40] Many city councilors still are indifferent to the threat of electoral defeat,[41] they have little or no political ambition, and more voluntarily leave office than are defeated at the polls. In such circumstances, council members may feel little need to respond to constituency demands, thus the council would be at least somewhat insulated from the public.

At the same time, constituency pressures may become an important part of a council member's life. Citizens are increasingly likely to define issues as public and bombard council members with requests. The demands often "reflect neighborhood interests rather than broad community goals," thus diffusing the policy process.[42] One reason for this may be that many cities are changing their council electoral systems from at-large to district elections. Council members elected from districts have a clearer idea of who their constituents are and are more visible to those constituents.

Councils that are elected at-large tend to be more homogeneous, reflecting the dominant constituency in the city. Often they are white, Republican businessmen.[43] Such councils tend to be relatively consensual. Councils elected on a district basis tend to be more heterogeneous, reflecting the composition of the various city neighborhoods. Such councils tend to be more conflictual. The conflict can be aggravated by the fact that while being bombarded by citizen demands, councilors are simultaneously facing a decline in resources available as a result of cutbacks in federal aid and voter-mandated limits on taxing policies.

In some cases, time pressures and persistent citizen demands result in what some councilors call "pothole politics," which is the tendency to devote all available time to responding to individual citizen demands and complaints. This makes it difficult for council members to fulfill their roles as governors and supervisors, a situation that is frustrating to many councilors.[44] In the role of governor, the council sets goals for the city and creates policies, programs, and services to help the

city reach its goals. As supervisor, the council appoints and evaluates staff and reviews the organizational structure of the city.[45] Many observers and council members themselves believe that councils do not always perform their governor and supervisor roles effectively.

> Thus, despite the idealized view of council members as rational, detached governors and merit-minded supervisors, in actuality many are befuddled policy makers, overly engaged implementors, and nearsighted overseers who ignore their supervisory role.[46]

One factor that affects the functioning of city councils is the structure of government. In the strong mayor–council form of government, the council competes with the mayor for power. Mayors encourage councils to focus on providing services and benefits to their constituents as a way to reduce the competition, while the council attempts to find the expertise and organizational structure to compete more successfully.[47] In council–manager governments, the council is the "senior partner in the governmental process," and can define the goals of the city and direct the manager in the administration of policies to achieve the goals.[48] The role of the council is highly variable in weak mayor–council cities.[49]

Another factor that may contribute to the problem of the council fulfilling the demands of the governor and supervisor roles is the relationship between the council and administrators. Woodrow Wilson argued 100 years ago that there was a dichotomy between politics and administration with administrators being neutral implementors of policy choices made by others. The neat distinction has long been recognized as unrealistic and simplistic.

Administrators have many resources that can be used to influence substantially the policy-making process. As full-time employees, they have the luxury of developing expertise in policy areas that the part-time councilors cannot match. In addition, the role of administrators vis-à-vis councilors has expanded because administrators are believed to be more efficient. Finally, citizens often suspect councils of being controlled by special interests, while administrators are believed to be apolitical and neutral.

The extent to which administrators have moved into the policy process is indicated by a National League of Cities' survey in which council members themselves reported that staff members were almost as likely to initiate policy as were the councilors. As noted earlier, a study of five North Carolina cities with council–manager governments, found substantial intermingling of the responsibility of council members and administration at all stages of the process.[50]

While the relationship between administrator and council members is often antagonistic, it need not be. James Svara believes cooperation is possible if councils focus attention on defining broad policy goals and "do less detailed policy making, discourage the referral of implementing decisions and administrative appeals to the council, avoid picking over isolated details of administrative performance, and dispense with unnecessary errand running for constituents."[51]

In essence, Svara is proposing a reformulation of Wilson's politics/administrative dichotomy, with the council assuming primary responsibility for defining goals, the administration assuming primary responsibility for achieving the goals, and both sharing in the construction of policies to accomplish the goals. Such recommendations sound reasonable, but their implementation still is affected by the disparity in the resources of council members and the administrators. The varied responsibilities of city managers are discussed in Box 8–2.

The role of the council could be enlarged by permitting it to hire its own staff, thus providing the council with expertise to counter

that of the full-time administrators and to perform some of the errand-running required by "pothole politics." This has happened in Jacksonville, Florida, a city manager city, and in Baltimore, a strong mayor city. In addition, some councils establish committees to enable councilors to develop expertise in particular policy areas. Expertise is one reason why the role of urban bureaucrats is increasingly important.

Bureaucrats

As noted in the last chapter, Theodore Lowi has argued that urban bureaucrats have become the new urban political machines. This is in part due to the fact that these bureaucrats are dispensing the same benefits to city residents that used to be distributed by party machines. But an equally important reason for comparing bureaucracies to machines is the extent to which they centralize and monopolize power. Aside from the obvious fact that machines exist primarily to win elections and bureaucracies exist to administer public policy, the chief difference between them is that formerly machines exercised their control over geographical areas. The new urban machines exercise control over particular functional areas such as education, welfare, transportation. To emphasize the extent to which bureaucrats can dominate in those areas, Lowi refers to them as "functional fiefdoms," implying that the bureaucrats are as much in control in their areas of specialization as nobles in the Middle Ages were on the land they controlled.[52]

Some reasons for the dominance of bureaucrats have already been mentioned. As full-time employees of the city, they are able to develop expertise. In addition, despite the stereotypes, bureaucrats can appear to be more efficient than political officials—if only because the decision making is often less visible and less subject to conflicting pressures.

BOX 8–2

There Is Never a Dull Moment for City Managers

The job of a city manager is multifaceted and demanding. Brief descriptions below of some city managers and the issues they have to manage illustrate the nature of the job and the diversity of approaches that managers take.

Robert C. Bobb has been city manager in Richmond, Virginia since 1986. Like many American cities, Richmond has faced serious fiscal pressures. The state cut $11 million in aid, making it necessary for Bobb to dismiss staff and freeze salaries. Despite the fiscal crunch, he has managed so well that Standard and Poor's raised the city's rating. He is also working on economic development to increase the tax base. But financial issues are not his only concern. His portfolio includes public works, fire, police, mental health, social services, courts, and jails. He has pushed for community policing and a drug-free block program to fight crime. He admits to occasional confrontations with the city council over specific issues, such as his decision to create several user fees to permit lower tax rates, and over his management style, which he characterizes as both "participatory and autocratic."

Richard Lewis is manager of Traverse City, Michigan. He is an energetic manager who begins his work day at 7:00 A.M. He is also personable and outgoing and has been credited with improving communications in city hall. His goal is to improve service delivery in the city and make it more user-friendly. He describes his management style as "a player, the coach, and a cheerleader." Lewis has been instrumental in issues ranging from negotiations regarding development to reducing odors emanating from the sewer plant; Lewis himself says everything has been a team effort. Commissioners

credit him for a nonconfrontational style and quick grasp of the issues.

Tom Hart, city manager in Euless, Texas, believes that a good sense of humor is essential to doing the job that he describes as follows: "I get to make sure people's sewers flow and their garbage is picked up." Once, after the city's economic development director had produced a documentary video about Euless, Hart showed it to the council with an introduction from an old cartoon of Porky Pig. While he tries to have fun doing his job, he realizes it is serious. He has been fighting to stop a proposed expansion of the Dallas–Fort Worth airport because of concerns about its impact on the property values and quality of life of Euless neighborhoods. He is also pushing for a new mall to improve the city's economic base.

Michael Van Milligen tries to improve his performance as city manager of Dubuque, Iowa, by working with one of his employees one day a month. So far he has been a street laborer, billing clerk, horticulturalist, water pollution control plant operator, recycling collector, housing inspector, and police officer. He also hosts monthly coffees with employees to get to know them better. He believes that he does a better job when he knows what employees are doing and that employees will feel more comfortable sharing with him ideas about how they could do the job better. Van Milligen manages a city with 509 city employees and a $39 million budget.

Wai-Lin Lam, manager of Weslaco, Texas, has had to face one truly bizarre situation. Ms. Lam, a native of Hong Kong and a proficient pianist, once had to deal with a group claiming to be visitors from another planet who blew up a car that they believed to belong to the mayor. More tra-

(continued on next page)

(continued)

ditional issues have included convincing the commission to purchase a reservoir, reorganizing the public safety department, dealing with tax rollbacks, and firing the top three police officers. Probably all the managers described here would agree with Ms. Lam when she says of her job, "I love the challenge."

Source: Adapted from Ellen Perlman, "Managing the Details," *Public Management* 76 (April 1994): 22–24; Michelle Worobec, "A Player, Coach, and Cheerleader," *Public Management* 75 (August 1993): 21–22; Monica Stavish, "Managing with a Grin in Euless," *Public Management* 75 (December 1993): 19–21; Donnelle Eller, "Front Lines: City Manager Listens, Learns on Work Details," *Public Management* 76 (August 1994): 25–26; Nolene Hodges, "City Manager Brings a Touch of Class to Job," *Public Management* 77 (January 1995): 26–27.

Finally, bureaucrats can claim to be neutral and impartial and therefore above the squalid political wrangling among special interests that at times dominates council meetings. This image of independence and neutrality is somewhat ironic because bureaucrats try to cultivate the support of interest groups and that support contributes to their ability to dominate in particular areas. For example, once the parent–teacher association is in agreement with school administrators and faculty, who is left with credibility to question their policies?

But the ultimate source of power is bureaucrats' control over the day-to-day implementation of policy. As Wallace Sayre and Herbert Kaufman write:

> It is in execution that the bureaucrats have their most nearly complete monopoly and their greatest autonomy in affecting policy. They give shape and meaning to the official decisions, and they do so under conditions favorable to them. Here the initiative and discretion lie in their hands; others must influence them.[53]

Many studies have documented the extent to which bureaucrats can control policy by their power over implementation.[54] For example, the police have discretion in perform-

ing such ambiguous jobs as maintaining order.[55] One study found that differential attitudes of the police chiefs toward traffic tickets was the major reason for a 700 percent difference in the number of traffic tickets issued in two adjacent Massachusetts towns with similar populations.[56] Agency heads often set the tone for their organizations. Just as in the national government, at the local level elected officials often have a difficult time overseeing the appointed leadership. Likewise, appointed leadership often has a hard time controlling workers out in the field. Thus, political control of the bureaucracy is often tenuous at best.

A study of housing inspectors in Boston indicates that the discretion given them often results in apparent ad hoc decision making.[57] Another study indicated that welfare administrators are able to exercise a great deal of discretion.[58] Some jobs permit greater discretion than others, but, in general, the jobs of most "street-level bureaucrats" such as police, teachers, welfare case workers are ambiguous enough to permit—to necessitate—considerable discretion.

In such settings, the way bureaucrats define their roles can be extremely important. Research has indicated that often bureaucrats do not see themselves simply as impartial administrators of policy made elsewhere.[59] As experts and professionals, they often include, as part of their job, the attempt to influence the policy they will be in charge of implementing. Of course, the line between professional expertise and personal values can become very thin and can, in some cases, disappear altogether. Even if they do not consciously try to influence policy, administrators will often devise various decision rules, such as, "first come, first served," to attempt to simplify their jobs. These rules (discussed more systematically in Chapter 11) affect their job performance.

Many administrators have difficulty incorporating citizen influence into their concept of their jobs. Bureaucrats often believe they are expected to perform in conformance with the characteristics of the "ideal bureaucracy" as described by Max Weber.[60] This includes the belief that they should make decisions based on the expertise that they have worked so long and hard to achieve. Further, they believe they should follow professional norms—that is, how other bureaucrats think they should behave. Citizens usually lack comparable expertise or knowledge of the norms. Bureaucrats believe it is important to function according to regularized rules and procedures, whereas citizens often make demands on an impromptu, ad hoc basis. Bureaucrats believe they should apply established policy in a neutral, impersonal way; citizens want personal attention to their special problems. Yet if some are given special attention, others believe the officials are being unfair. The goal of bureaucratic organizations is efficiency, and citizen participation often results in maddening delays.[61]

The difficulty elected officials have controlling urban administrators has two important implications for urban politics. The first is that accountability to the public is questionable. Public accountability is to be achieved through oversight of administrators by officials who owe their jobs to the public. If those officials do not or cannot exercise that oversight effectively, citizen control is impossible. The second is that policy coordination becomes more difficult.

> Because of the fragmentation among the various street-level governments, there is almost no central coordination of service programs and policies although it is clear that services provided by police, welfare, and school bureaucracies, for example, are often highly interdependent.[62]

The tendency for local bureaucrats to overlap with state and federal bureaucrats in the same functional areas also limits the ability of citizens to control bureaucrats and makes policy coordination difficult at the local level. This overlap results from state or federal urban policies implemented by administrators on the local level. Often, the local administrators are looking more to specialists at other levels of government for guidance than to locally elected officials.

City Managers

One of the most difficult jobs in the urban bureaucracy is that of city manager. The manager is usually appointed by the city council; the job of the manager is to carry out the council's policies. That makes the manager the chief executive of the city. Cities with city managers also have mayors, but the mayor's formal powers are usually limited to presiding at council meetings. Often the manager is empowered to submit a city budget to the council for approval, to appoint and manage principal department heads, and to make policy recommendations to the council.

While Deil Wright reported that managers feel most comfortable in their role as administrators (that is, staffing, budgeting, and supervision) and tend to devote most of their time to such administration, he argued that managers also have policy and political roles.

A 1985 study, replicating Wright's, found that city managers devoted 50.8 percent of their time to their management role, 32.2 percent to their policy role, and 17 percent to their political role.[63] Wright concluded in his study that managers were the major policy initiators in council–manager governments.[64] Another study found "a dramatic escalation in the perceived importance of the 'policy' role of city managers."[65] Of the city managers surveyed in 1985, 55.8 percent thought their policy role (that is, controlling the council agenda, policy initiation, and formulation) was their most important role compared to 22 percent of the managers surveyed by Deil Wright in 1965. Correspondingly, only 5.8 percent of the 1985 respondents thought that their political role (that is, community leadership) was the most important role compared to 33 percent of the respondents in the Wright study.[66] By comparison, the study indicated that mayors, as might be expected, believed that their political role was most important and their management role least important. (See Table 8–1.) This illustrates that organizational structures can affect the role perceptions of the occupants of various offices.

One study indicates that the city manager's recommendations to the city council are influenced by the manager's political ideology. "City managers tend to pursue municipal goals based in part on their own personal political ideologies, despite professional norms that deny such influences."[67] Another study found that 75 percent of managers surveyed reported that they participated in policy formulation and 39 percent said they initiated policies.[68] An examination of 11 Ohio communities found that, in comparison with mayors, managers spent more time on administration and management functions and less on mission planning; it also found a substantial amount of "teamwork or collaborative governance" between mayors and managers.[69] Clearly the line between policy and administration is a thin one.

In many cities, city managers operate as policy entrepreneurs, although that role is less common for managers than for mayors. When a manager is acting as entrepreneur, it may be in cooperation with an entrepreneurial mayor.[70] On the other hand, managers and elected officials may disagree on policy. One study found managers are cautious in policy initiatives, favoring policies that have been tried successfully in other communities. Elected officials, however, "are more likely to advocate more untried ideas and to create a broader mass political base in the community that can serve as a springboard for upward electoral mobility."[71] When conflict occurs, the study identified three factors that affect the outcome: "How these conflicts play out is a function of the personalities of the actors, their ability to mobilize the different constituencies that represent their different bases of power, and the structural factors that define the relative strength of each office."[72] Once again, the importance of building public support provides citizens with opportunities to influence the policy process.

City managers must please the council to keep their jobs, but they have many opportunities to set the agenda for the council and influence the council's decisions. Managers control the day-to-day operation of the city and hire and fire department heads. Their intimate and expert knowledge of the business of the city often means that councils simply approve managers' proposals. Such control is important because, despite their appearance as neutral administrators, managers frequently exhibit biases in the ways that they view the business of the city. Managers have tended to emphasize such physical functions of city government as streets and traffic flow rather than the provision of social services. This may be because the first city managers often came from engineering backgrounds. Modern city managers must have broader perspectives, including understanding current management techniques and ways to operate with more

TABLE 8–1

Percentage of Time Spent in Different Roles for City Executives

	City Manager	Mayor
Management role	38.5%	23.1%
Policy role	55.8%	34.6%
Political role	5.8%	42.3%

Source: Adapted from Charldean Newell and David Ammons, "Role Emphases of City Manager and Other Municipal Executives," *Public Administration Review* 47 (May–June 1987): 252.

participatory structures.[73]

The position of city manager is important to citizens who want to influence city policy. Citizens themselves have no direct control over the manager; citizen control can only be exercised indirectly through the council. If the manager has been skillful in pleasing the council, citizens may be frustrated in attempts either to convince the manager to change policies or to convince the council to change the manager. On the other hand, many managers are searching for ways to involve citizens in the policy process through strategic planning and visioning exercises.[74] These techniques will be discussed in Chapter 11.

Conclusion

For citizens to have an influence on the policy process of cities, they must be able to answer the question, "Who's in charge here?" The various structures of urban government make it difficult to answer that question in a general sense. While mayors may be seen as the leaders of cities, frequently they do not possess the formal authority to be able to lead. Mayors who want to lead will usually need to look for ways to augment their formal powers. One way is to build coalitions of those who will support mayoral initiatives. First, an electoral coalition must be constructed to get to city hall, then a governing coalition must also be constructed. Mayors searching for ways to

broaden the electoral coalition will seek out those who have resources the city needs. Although cities vary, business interests have many resources that mayors seek, and they are, therefore, likely to be courted by mayors. But business does not always dominate, nor can it always protect mayors from electoral defeat. If the policy pursued by the mayor and the governing coalition is opposed by parts of the initial electoral coalition, the mayor risks electoral defeat, as Ed Koch learned in New York.

Of the other urban officials, urban administrators are the most important. While there are exceptions, most city council members are part-time and poorly paid. Their lack of expertise and time means that they are often dependent on executives—both elected and appointed—for information and guidance.

Bureaucrats who are full-time administrators of the city's business simply know more about city policy than do most councilors. Bureaucrats tend to believe their professional responsibility is to be neutral and to administer policy according to professional standards. As control slides toward bureaucrats in reformed governments, responsiveness to citizens may decline. Of course, this would not be a problem if the assumption of the reform movement that there is "one best way" were true. In that case, running a city could be turned over to the professionals and the expectation of everything functioning smoothly could be met. Unfortunately, there is seldom a "best way" for everyone.

City managers may create a special barrier to citizen influence. Hired and fired by the council, the managers must please the council, not the citizens, to keep their jobs. The council will often justify politically unpopular decisions by hiding behind the professionals. On the other hand, modern management techniques have stressed more participatory management both from within the organization and from the public.

It is also important to know the roles public officials play. While both mayors and council members are usually elected and therefore should be oriented to responding to citizen requests, their responsiveness to citizens may be limited by their relative lack of political ambition and by the pressures of responding to too many demands with too few resources. Responsiveness may be especially limited during times of fiscal stress.

Notes

1. James H. Svara, *Official Leadership in the City: Patterns of Conflict and Cooperation* (New York: Oxford University Press, 1990), 81.

2. Ibid.

3. For alternative lists of mayoral roles and styles, see Demetrios Caraley, *City Governments and Urban Problems* (Englewood Cliffs, New Jersey: Prentice-Hall, 1977); Robert Lineberry and Ira Sharkansky, *Urban Politics and Public Policy*, 3rd ed. (New York: Harper & Row, 1978); Wallace Sayre and Herbert Kaufman, *Governing New York City* (New York: Russell Sage, 1960).

4. Caraley, *City Governments and Urban Problems*, 200–208.

5. Ibid.

6. Jim Sleeper, "The End of the Rainbow? America's Changing Urban Politics," *The New Republic*, November 1, 1993, 20–25.

7. Mark Schneider and Paul Teske, with Michael Mintron, *Public Entrepreneurs: Agents for Change in American Government* (Princeton: Princeton University Press, 1995), 8.

8. Ibid., 148.

9. Svara, *Official Leadership in the City*, 106–107. See also James H. Svara, *Facilitative Leadership in Local Government: Lessons from Successful Mayors and Chairpersons* (San Francisco: Jossey-Bass, 1994); and David R. Morgan and Sheilah S. Watson, "Policy Leadership in Council–Manager Cities: Comparing Mayor and Manager," *Public Administration Review* 52 (September–October 1992): 438–446.

10. Peter Trapp, "Governors' and Mayor's Offices: The Role of the Staff," *National Civic Review* 63 (May 1964): 242–249.

11. Richard A. Keiser, "Chicago Politics, Canceled Model," *Urban Affairs Quarterly* 30 (September 1994): 179–180.

12. Douglas Yates, *The Ungovernable City: The Politics of Urban Problems and Policy Making* (Cambridge, Massachusetts: MIT Press, 1977), 149.

13. John Hull Mollenkopf, *A Phoenix in the Ashes: The Rise and Fall of the Koch Coalition in New York City Politics* (Princeton: Princeton University Press, 1992), 103.

14. Ibid., 109.

15. Ibid., 192.

16. Raphael J. Sonenshein, *Politics in Black and White: Race and Power in Los Angeles* (Princeton: Princeton University Press, 1993), 143.

17. Svara, *Official Leadership in the City*, 93.

18. Clarence N. Stone, *Regime Politics: Governing Atlanta 1946–1988* (Lawrence: University of Kansas Press, 1989).

19. Marion E. Orr and Gerry Stoker, "Urban Regimes and Leadership in Detroit," *Urban Affairs Quarterly* 30 (September 1994): 65.

20. John R. Logan and Harvey L. Molotch, *Urban Fortunes: The Political Economy of Place* (Berkeley: University of California Press), 66.

21. Richard Edward DeLeon, *Left Coast City: Progressive Politics in San Francisco 1975–1991* (Lawrence: University of Kansas Press, 1991).

22. See, for example, Wallace Sayre and Herbert Kaufman, *Governing New York City* (New York: Sage, 1960), 657–658; and Robert L. Lineberry and Ira Sharkansky, *Urban Politics and Public Policy*, 194–196; Svara, *Official Leadership in the City*, 118.

23. John P. Kotter and Paul R. Lawrence, *Mayors in Action: Five Approaches to Urban Governance* (New York: John Wiley, 1974), 112.

24. Ibid., 116.

25. Robert F. Pecorella, "The Effects of Socioeconomic Context and Group Alignments on Mayoral Style (An Outline)", Paper presented at the 1988 Annual Meeting of the Urban Affairs Association, St. Louis, Missouri, March 11, 1988.

26. Jack Newfield and Paul DuBrul, *The Abuse of Power: The Permanent Government and the Fall of New York* (New York: Viking, 1977), 178.

27. Morning Edition, National Public Radio, August 2, 1997.

28. For support, see Robert J. Wolensky and Edward J. Miller, "Everyday and Disaster Roles," *Urban Affairs Quarterly* 16 (June 1981): 483–504.

29. Martin Shefter, *Political Crisis/Fiscal Crisis: The Collapse and Revival of New York City* (New York: Basic Books, 1985), 175.

30. Charles H. Levine, Irene S. Rubin, and George G. Wolohojian, *The Politics of Retrenchment: How Local Governments Manage Fiscal Stress* (Beverly Hills: Sage, 1981), 103; see also, Irene S. Rubin, "Structural Theories and Urban Fiscal Stress," *Urban Affairs Quarterly* 20 (June 1985): 469–486.

31. Kotter and Lawrence, *Mayors in Action*, 240.

32. Svara, *Facilitative Leadership in Local Government,* 185.

33. Ibid., 243.

34. Svara, *Official Leadership in the City,* 123.

35. Ibid., 127.

36. Ibid., 133.

37. Ibid., 130–131.

38. Kenneth Prewitt, *The Recruitment of Political Leaders: A Study of Citizen Politicians* (Indianapolis, Indiana: Bobbs-Merrill, 1970), Chapter 8.

39. Peter J. Haas, "An Exploratory Analysis of American City Council Salaries," *Urban Affairs Review* 31 (November 1995): 263.

40. Timothy Bledsoe, *Careers in City Politics: The Case for Urban Democracy* (Pittsburgh: University of Pittsburgh Press, 1993), 42.

41. Ibid., 114.

42. Louise G. White, "Improving the Goal-Setting Process in Local Government," *Public Administration Reveiw* 42 (January–February 1982): 77.

43. Susan Welch and Timothy Bledsoe, *Urban Reform and Its Consequences* (Chicago: University of Chicago Press, 1988), 42.

44. Ibid.

45. Svara, *Official Leadership in the City,* 144.

46. Ibid., 153.

47. Ibid., 156–158.

48. Ibid., 158.

49. Ibid., 156.

50. James Svara, "Dichotomy and Duality: Reconceptualizing the Relationship Between Policy and Administration in Council–Manager Cities," *Public Administration Review* (January–February 1985): 221–32.

51. Ibid., 230.

52. Theodore J. Lowi, *At the Pleasure of the Mayor* (New York: Free Press, 1964). See especially Chapter 7.

53. Sayre and Kaufman, *Governing New York City,* 421.

54. Jeffrey L. Pressman and Aaron B. Wildavsky, *Implementation,* 3rd Edition (Berkeley: University of California Press, 1984); Eugene Bardach, *The Implementation Game: What Happens After a Bill Becomes a Law* (Cambridge, Massachusetts, MIT Press, 1977); and Randall B. Ripley and Grace A. Franklin, *Policy Implementation and Bureaucracy,* 2nd ed. (Chicago: Dorsey, 1986).

55. James Q. Wilson, *Varieties of Police Behavior* (Cambridge, Massachusetts: Harvard University Press,1968).

56. John A. Gardiner, "Police Enforcement of Traffic Laws: A Comparative Analysis," in *City Politics and Public Policy,* ed. James Q. Wilson (New York: John Wiley, 1968), 151–172.

57. Pietro Nivola, "Distributing A Municipal Service: A Case Study of Housing Inspection," *Journal of Politics* 40, no. 1 (February 1978): 59–81.

58. Martha Derthick, "Intercity Differences in Administration of the Public Assistance Program: The Case of Massachusetts," in *City Politics and Public Policy,* ed. Wilson, 243–266.

59. See, for example, Judith Gruber, *Controlling Bureaucracies: Dilemmas in Democratic Governance* (Berkeley: University of California Press, 1987); Anthony Downs, *Inside Bureaucracy* (Boston: Little, Brown, 1967); Charles T. Goodsell, *The Case For Bureaucracy,* 3rd ed. (Chatham, New Jersey: Chatham House, 1994); and Theodore Lowi, *The End of Liberalism: The Second Republic of the United States* (New York: Norton, 1979).

60. H.H. Gerth and C. Wright Mills, ed. and trans., *From Max Weber: Essays in Sociology,* (New York: Oxford University Press, 1958): 196–198.

61. Mary Grisez Kweit and Robert W. Kweit, *Implementing Citizen Participation in a Bureaucratic Society: A Contingency Approach* (New York: Praeger, 1981).

62. Yates, *The Ungovernable City,* 110.

63. David N. Ammons and Charldean Newell, *City Executives: Leadership Role, Work Characteristics, & Time Management* (Albany: State University of New York Press, 1990), 62.

64. Deil S. Wright, "The City-Manager as a Development Administrator," in *Comparative Urban Research,* ed. Robert T. Daland (Beverly Hills, California: Sage, 1969), 218.

65. Charldean Newell and David Ammons, "Role Emphases of City Manager and Other Municipal Executives," *Public Administration Review* 47 (May–June 1987): 246.

66. Ibid., 252.

67. Clifford J. Wirth and Michael L. Vasu, "Ideology and Decision Making for American City Managers," *Urban Affairs Quarterly* 22 (March 1987): 467–468.

68. Tari Renner, "Appointed Local Government Managers: Stability and Change," *The Municipal Yearbook* (Washington, D.C.: International City/County Management Association, 1990), 50.

69. Ibid., 24.

70. Schneider, Teske with Mintron, *Public Entrepreneurs,* 165.

71. Ibid., 167.

72. Ibid.

73. Robert T. Golembiewski and Gerald T. Gabris, "Today's City Managers: A Legacy of Success-Becoming-Failure," *Public Administration Review* 54 (November–December 1994): 525–530 and Robert T. Golembiewski and Gerald T. Gabris, "Today's City Managers: Guides for Avoiding Success-Becoming-Failure," *Public Administration Review* 55 (March–April 1995): 240–246.

74. Craig Wheeland, "Citywide Strategic Planning: An Evaluation of Rock Hill's Empowering Vision," *Public Administration Review* 53 (January–February 1993): 65–72.

CHAPTER 9

Metropolitanism

To understand the modern metropolis, it is important to realize that cities exist within a vast network of governments. Federal, state, and other local governments all play a role in influencing the policies that individual local governments can pursue. This chapter and Chapter 10 will examine the impact of intergovernmental relations on governments in the metropolis.

Vertical Relationships

As noted in Chapter 3, cities receive charters from the state and therefore are limited by conditions established by the state. Those limits were clearly stated by Judge John Dillon. Dillon's Rule, from an 1868 Iowa case, confirmed the total dependence of municipal governments on the state.[1]

> It is a general and undisputed proposition of law that a municipal corporation possesses and can exercise the following powers, and no others; first, those granted in express words; second, those necessarily or fairly implied in or incident to the powers expressly granted; third, those essential to the accomplishment of the declared objects and purposes of the corporation—not sim-

ply convenient, but indispensable. Any fair, substantial doubt concerning the existence of power is resolved by the courts against a corporation, and power is denied.[2]

As a result of Dillon's Rule, the state has vast authority to control what local governments can and cannot do. States have set out a variety of specific limitations on local government that confine their scope of activity and their ability to generate revenue. Virtually all states limit the amount of indebtedness of their communities as well as the types and levels of taxes the communities may levy. States may establish special districts, such as school districts, thus precluding general local government from acting in particular functional areas. States may set zoning regulations that supersede local rules.

All states except Alabama and Vermont have attempted to extend the authority of local government with a device known as **home rule**. Home rule is also available for counties in 37 states.[3] For the most part, home rule allows cities and counties to act in "local" matters without having to go to state legislatures for specific authority. Home rule provisions vary greatly among the states in terms of what size community is eligible and what authorities are granted. In general, local governments can amend their charters without state approval as long as the change does not affect state actions in the area. Sometimes home rule allows communities to levy new types of taxes; in other cases, it does not. Despite the name, home rule merely expands the scope of local action. Cities and counties must still work within parameters set by the state.

During much of this century, the federal government's role in urban affairs has increased as a result of fiscal concerns and federal court decisions. The ability to raise substantial amounts of money through the income tax and the desire of federal officials to appeal to the large numbers of urban voters gave the federal government both the ability and the incentive to develop a national urban policy. More recently, several changes have decreased the interest of the national government in urban areas. For one, the move of the population from center cities to the suburbs has meant that only 67 of the 435 seats (15 percent) in the House of Representatives are held by representatives from urban areas.[4] In addition, large federal deficits and anti-Washington sentiment combined to support the shift of responsibility for many policies away from Washington, in many cases turning authority over to the states. This means that less money will be flowing from the federal government to local governments.

The Personal Responsibility and Work Opportunity Reconciliation Act (PRWORA) of 1996 is a good example of an area where the federal government is transferring greater responsibility to the states. This act, discussed more thoroughly in Chapter 14, ends the 40-year national guarantee of welfare assistance to the poor and replaces it with a grant of money to states, which are encouraged to experiment to find ways to decrease poverty. Because of the concentration of the poor in center cities, the impact of this reform on those city governments will likely be substantial.

Major federal court decisions in areas such as local government management and

elections continue to influence local decisions. For example, in *Garcia v. San Antonio Metropolitan Transit Authority* 105 S. Ct. 1005 (1985), the U.S. Supreme Court ruled that state and local governments were subject to minimum wage and overtime requirements established by the federal Fair Labor Standards Act. This raised the cost of personnel to local governments and reduced flexibility in scheduling as 12-hour shifts required overtime pay.

Federal courts have also had a great influence on local government in cases dealing with the discriminatory impacts of local government elections and districts. In two cases, the Supreme Court called for "approximate equality" in the population of local districts.[5] Minorities also have challenged at-large elections, claiming that they diluted minority votes and prevented a fair representation on the city council or commission, and have won in several cities. In *City of Mobile v. Bolden* (1980), however, the Supreme Court ruled that, in the absence of proof that the at-large system was adopted or maintained to promote discrimination, the system could stand.[6] In response to this decision Congress amended the Voting Rights Act.

In *Thornburg v. Gingles* 478 U.S. 478 (1986), the Supreme Court ruled under Section 2 of the 1982 amendments to the Voting Rights Act, that if a large and relatively compact minority population lived in an area with a history of majority electoral domination, then many **majority-minority** districts should be created. In other words, the legislature could intentionally create electoral districts in which a minority would constitute a majority. More recently, the Supreme Court has not been supportive of such districts and has overturned their creation, first in *Shaw v. Reno* 61 U.S.L.W. 4818 (1993), and, in 1996, in two additional cases. The Court claimed the districts were **gerrymandered**, that is, weirdly shaped for political purposes. The conservative nature of the current Court, shown in other decisions affecting discrimination, may mean that local governments will have more latitude in this area. In June 1994 in *Holder v. Hall,* the Supreme Court refused to compel Bleckley County, Georgia, to change from a single at-large county commissioner to a five-person district commission to assure that the 20 percent of African-Americans in the county had a chance of representation. Federal courts have also been involved in other issues that affect local government such as state legislative apportionment and education.

The interactions between cities and state and federal governments are considered to be vertical relationships and will be discussed in more depth in the next chapter. These vertical relationships are important because they limit the authority of local governments, and because those governments depend on higher levels of government for fiscal resources. That fiscal dependence, in turn, further limits the flexibility of local government and the direct influence citizens can have on the local government decisions that may be dictated by higher authorities. Thus, other levels of government influence the agendas of local government, limit alternative solutions, and affect what policies are adopted. They also affect how policies are implemented.

The remainder of this chapter will focus on other governments in the metropolis that are more or less at the same level. These interactions are known as horizontal relationships.

Horizontal Relations

As cities grew, the urban population spilled over the boundaries of the original cities and, therefore, beyond the jurisdiction of the central city governments. As a result, governments in the metropolitan area proliferated, leading, in turn, to great complexity and governmental fragmentation.

On the negative side, fragmentation often separates needs from resources. Those leaving

the city tended to be economically well-off and relatively self-sufficient, while many of those left behind were dependent on public services. When the middle and upper classes leave the center city, the remaining resources are insufficient to serve those left behind. In addition, fragmentation creates a complex web of governments, making it hard for citizens to ascertain who is in charge of what. Finally, in some of these governments, officials are often appointed and virtually invisible and unaccountable to the average citizen.

However, urban fragmentation has many advantages. By dividing the metropolis into many small governments, rather than one large metropolitan government, power stays closer to the people. Thus, groups that would be a permanent minority if there were one government may be able to exercise majority control over one municipality. One school of thought, **public choice**, maintains that fragmentation allows citizens to select communities based on the amenities available. In essence, this approach views citizens making decisions about residential location as analogous to consumers choosing among various commodities in a market.

Until early in the twentieth century, fragmentation was minimal. A city's response to growth was to annex outlying areas so that the government's jurisdiction kept pace with the population. But as the century wore on, a new pattern emerged. In many places populations on the city's periphery began to incorporate, making themselves separate political jurisdictions. Suburbs were born. Soon the original city government was one among many as the growing population in the area became distributed among numerous political jurisdictions. The city was in the process of becoming a metropolis.

In addition to the municipal governments of the center city and the various suburbs, metropolitan areas also include other local governments, such as counties. Some metropolitan areas may overlap several counties.

Special districts, such as transportation districts or water districts, often span several municipalities and produce another type of local government. School districts are a distinctive type of special district. Some states also have township governments.

Governments in the Metropolis

Several years ago Robert Wood's book, *1400 Governments,* called attention to the fragmentation in the New York Metropolitan area.[7] Although that fragmentation has abated somewhat because of the consolidation of many school districts for economic reasons, there are still many governments in the nation's metropolitan areas (see Table 9–1). Of the nation's 15,834 school districts, 5,993 (37.8 percent) are in metropolitan areas. Other governments include counties, town and townships, special districts, and municipalities.

Counties exist in every state except Connecticut and Rhode Island. The structures of county government are similar to those used by city governments. The most common form is the county commission, which parallels the city commission and is used in about 80 percent of all counties.[8] Unlike city elections, which tend to be nonpartisan, about 82 percent of county commission elections are partisan.[9] Some counties have adopted the coun-

cil–administrator form, which itself is an adaptation of the council–manager form used in cities. In addition, some counties use a county executive–council model, which is similar to the mayor–council structure discussed in Chapter 7. A recent study concluded that the form of government structure has less impact on expenditures in counties than it does in cities.[10]

Counties were initially created as administrative subdivisions to aid in the distribution of state services on the local level. Traditional county functions include maintaining land records, administering elections, collecting property taxes, and providing law enforcement and judicial functions.[11] As a result of federal and state programs developed to respond to demands created by increasing urbanization, county roles have expanded to include housing, social services, health and hospitals, and environmental protection. Economic development has also become a priority among American counties.[12]

Aside from special districts, county government is the fastest growing of all local governments, and metropolitan counties have the highest growth. A study of 244 county governments in 56 of the largest metropolitan areas found that between 1972 and 1987 expenditures increased 65.6 percent and service functions increased 6.5 percent.[13]

As the responsibilities of counties ex-

TABLE 9–1

Local Governments in Metropolitan Areas in 1992

Type of Government	Total Number in United States
County	740
Town and township	5,067
Special district	13,614
School district	5,993
Municipality	7,590

Source: U.S. Bureau of the Census, *Census of Governments: 1992, Vol. 1, Government Organization,* U.S. Department of Commerce (Washington, D.C.: U.S. Government Printing Office, issued March 1994), 39.

TABLE 9–2

Special District Governments by Functional Class in 1992

Functional Class	Number of Districts in Metropolitan Areas
Single function districts	29,036
Natural resources	6,228
Fire protection	5,260
Housing and community development	3,470
Water supply	3,302
Sewerage	1,710
Cemeteries	1,628
School buildings	757
Parks and recreation	1,156
Other	2,525
Multifunctional districts	2,519
TOTAL	31,555

Source: U.S. Bureau of the Census, *Census of Governments, 1992, Vol. 1, Governmental Organization* (Washington, D.C.: U.S. Government Printing Office, 1994), 20–21.

pand, concern has grown about the adequacy of traditional county leadership.[14] As a result, county leadership is becoming more professional and more representative. The number of county commissions elected from districts rather than at-large has increased. As in city elections, the change to single-member electoral districts increases the representativeness of elected officials and more women, blacks, and younger candidates are being elected to county boards.[15]

Roles and responsibilities of counties vary greatly throughout the country. Counties tend to be unimportant in New England, but more important than city governments in some states in the South. The importance of county governments may vary for different county residents. In some areas, counties provide services primarily to residents in unincorporated sections. This often means that citizens in cities pay county taxes but receive few benefits in return.

In New England, as well as New York, New Jersey, Pennsylvania, Michigan, and Wisconsin, township governments play a larger role than do counties. Townships often have broad powers and perform functions more generally associated with municipalities. In Illinois, Indiana, Kansas, Minnesota, Missouri, Nebraska, North Dakota, Ohio, and South Dakota, the township government does very little, sometimes only road construction and maintenance. Towns and township governments exist in only 20 northeastern and north-central states.[16]

Special districts are units of local government that are generally established to perform specific functions, although sometimes they carry out several functions. Table 9–2 lists the prevalence of various functional districts.

The boundaries of special districts may be coterminous with a single municipality or may cover only a part of a community. More often, special districts are created to provide a structure for several communities to cooperate in providing a service. By establishing special districts, the general-purpose municipalities do not have to increase taxes to provide a service. For example, a water district can charge residents user fees based on the amount of water they use. The special district will impose the tax or institute user fees. This is often politically advantageous for municipalities because they can deflect blame for tax increases.

Although nothing more than a special district, school districts are counted separately by the Census Bureau because of their importance, their universality, and their number. The number declined by 1,011 between 1972 and 1982 and declined by another 555 between 1982 and 1992; 15,834 school districts remain in the United States. Of those, 14,422, or 91 percent, were independent of general-purpose government.[17] Independent school districts exist in all states except Alaska, Hawaii, Maryland, and Virginia. Hawaii has one district for the entire state; public education is a state responsibility. Independent school districts tend to be organized along the lines of the council–manager model. School board members are elected by the public. The school board then appoints a professional administrator, often a superintendent.

In the metropolitan area, the Census Bureau identifies four types of local government besides the municipality. Each of these governments contributes to complexity because it is hard for citizens to determine who is responsible for what services. If streets are not cleaned, citizens must find out if it is the responsibility of the municipal government, the county, or a special district. If they are unhappy with what their children are learning in school, they must determine if the school district is a part of the general-purpose government or an independent school district. When a citizen moves from one metropolitan area to another, he or she will likely find that the mix of service responsibilities is different.

The multiple governments in the metropolis also make citizen control difficult because problems often spill over legal boundaries into jurisdictions that citizens cannot influence. Also, some of the municipalities with the most severe problems are unable to respond to their citizenry because of limited resources. The major cause of governmental fragmentation in the metropolitan area is the proliferation of municipalities, primarily as a result of suburbanization.

Origins of Suburbia

People have been living on the fringes of cities for thousands of years. In ancient cities, the wealthy and well-born lived inside the city's protective walls and the poor and the common folk clustered outside. In America by the end of the seventeenth century, Boston had a population of approximately 7,000, and the beginning of suburbs could already be observed.[18] By the nineteenth century, when American cities were becoming more common, larger, and more important in the economy, suburbanization got into full swing. Many current neighborhoods in American cities began at that time as suburbs and were later annexed by the core city. The Boston neighborhoods of Charlestown and Roxbury were once separate communities. Advertisements once lured New Yorkers to the new suburb of Brooklyn.[19]

But the major growth in suburbs occurred in the twentieth century. In 1966, for the first time, more people lived in suburban circles than lived in the core cities themselves. The movement of people to the suburban fringes is continuing. The deconcentration of population in nearly all metropolitan areas that became evident in the 1970 census has accelerated since that time. Table 9–3 shows that the population outside of central cities has consistently increased from 1960 to 1990, while population outside the metropolitan areas consistently declined, and the center city percentage of the population remained stable.

Table 9–4 shows the changes in population distribution for selected metropolitan

TABLE 9–3

Metropolitan and Non-metropolitan Population: 1960–1990 (in Percentages)

	1960	1970	1980	1990
Inside SMSAs[a]	63.0%	68.6%	74.8%	79.5%
Central cities	32.3%	31.4%	30.0%	31.1%
Outside central cities	30.6%	37.2%	44.8%	48.4%
Outside SMSAs	37.0%	31.4%	25.2%	20.5%

[a]Standard Metropolitan Statistical Areas

Source: U.S. Bureau of the Census, *1980 Census of Population, Supplementary Reports: Standard Metropolitan Statistical Areas* (Washington, D.C.: U.S. Government Printing Office, 1984), 11; and *1990 Census of Population, Supplementary Reports: Standard Metropolitan Statistical Areas* (Washington, D.C.: U.S. Government Printing Office, 1993), 1.

TABLE 9–4

Percentage Population Change for 20 Selected Metropolitan Areas, 1980–1990

	Metropolitan Area	Center City	Outside Center City
	%	%	%
Atlanta, GA	+32.5	−7.3	+41.9
Austin, TX	+44.6	+33.9	+63.1
Baltimore, MD	+8.3	−6.0	+16.8
Boston, MA	+2.5	+1.8	+2.7
Chicago, IL	+2.3	−5.7	+9.2
Cleveland, OH	-3.3	−10.4	−0.2
Dallas, TX	+30.2	+15.6	+45.9
Denver–Boulder, CO	+13.6	−5.1	+23.4
Detroit, MI	−2.8	−13.0	+2.1
Houston, TX	+20.7	+3.1	+47.7
Los Angeles, CA	+18.5	+18.5	+18.5
Miami, FL	+19.2	+1.9	+25.7
Minneapolis–St. Paul, MN	+15.5	−0.1	+21.9
New York, NY	+3.3	+3.5	+1.7
Philadelphia, PA	+2.9	−5.6	+8.0
Portland, OR	+13.6	+17.7	+11.8
St. Louis, MO	+3.3	−8.7	+7.7
San Diego, CA	+34.2	+29.9	+38.7
San Francisco, CA	+7.7	+6.6	+8.6
Washington, DC	+21.4	+0.3	+28.1

Source: U.S. Bureau of the Census, *1980 Census of Population, Supplementary Reports: Standard Metropolitan Statistical Areas and Standard Consolidated Areas: 1980,* PC80–S1–5 (Washington, D.C., U.S. Government Printing Office, 1981); U.S. Bureau of the Census, *1990 Census of Population and Supplementary Reports: Metropolitan Areas as Defined by the Office of Management and Budget,* Vol. I (Washington, D.C., U.S. Government Printing Office, June 1993), 7, 10, 17–21, 27, 32–34, 37, 40–42, 45–46, 51–52.

areas. That table indicates that while only Cleveland, Ohio, experienced a population loss in its suburban ring from 1980–1990, many center cities lost population and many of those were older Frost Belt cities while Sun Belt cities tended to grow in population. The only exceptions were the Sun Belt cities of Atlanta, which itself dates from 1837, and Denver. The decline in oil prices between 1980 and 1990 may have affected the growth of Denver.

Not only are people moving out of center cities, they are also moving ever farther away. As George Sternlieb and James Hughes report:

> The evolution now taking place is to areas external even to the new ring city, which has been established on the circumferential highways—the last monument to the National Highway Program. This is often at radii 20 miles or more from the traditional urban core. The critical mass of services that have been established on the ring, not least among them the enclosed suburban shopping mall, provides an alternative to "downtown."[20]

Joel Garreau calls these new population concentrations on the periphery of metropolitan areas "edge cities." (See Chapter 3.) Such "cities" may not have political boundaries but do combine jobs, entertainment, and shopping, meaning that their residents do not need to rely on a central city.[21]

The great expansion of suburbia in the twentieth century can be attributed in part to technology. When people had to walk to work, suburban sprawl was unthinkable. The surge in suburbanization came with the widespread availability of automobiles. Unlike streetcars, which had set and finite routes, the automobile provided individuals access to any place in an area where there were roads. As a result, the population of the city began to spread out on the landscape like an oil slick.

But to explain the suburbanization of urban areas by technology is to beg the question. The streetcar and automobile made suburbanization *possible*, but they do not explain why people wanted to leave the city behind, even though their jobs were still there. To understand that, it is necessary to consider a variety of factors that both pushed people out of the city and lured or pulled them into the suburban fringe.

Explanations of Suburbanization

Urban areas experience intense competition for space; the cost of a scarce resource is driven up by high demand. The intense competition for space in urban areas has created high land values. The result is that except for the few very wealthy, most people in the city can afford only limited living space. The poor are jammed into incredibly cramped and often squalid housing. Many who can afford to move tolerate a long commute to work in exchange for more living area.

Of course, implicit in the discussion of such "push" factors as high density, and cramped and expensive housing are "pull" factors that would entice city residents to the suburbs. The major surge of suburbanization occurred after World War II. Because of the Great Depression and the war, housing construction had languished for 25 years. The baby boom that followed the war created an intense demand for new, moderate-cost housing for young, growing families. Developers responded to that demand—some would argue they also helped to create it—by building large housing tracts where land was cheap enough to keep the cost down and to give the young families a yard in which children could play.

The federal government aided the movement to the suburbs in two significant ways. First, the Federal Housing Administration and Veterans Administration subsidized low-interest loans that enabled many people to buy homes. Those homes were most likely to be in the suburbs because the legislation authorizing the loans and those administering them saw new single-family homes in the suburbs as a safer investment than existing homes in the city.[22] In addition to the interest rate subsidy, interest paid on mortgage loans is tax deductible, providing another subsidy to the homeowner. Second, the government provided funding to build highways that made the commute between suburbs and city as quick and direct as possible.

A move to the suburbs brings another benefit: escape from relatively close confinement with those who are poor and those who are different. Frederick Wirt, Benjamin Walter, Francine F. Rabinowitz, and Deborah Hensler wrote about the effect of the immigrants of the nineteenth century:

> As impoverished immigrants crowded into the city, older citizens became alarmed by the physical disarray that seemed to accompany their arrival. Feeling that their old, familiar city was being vandalized by immigrant hordes, many older citizens surrendered their aging flats and left the city for the suburbs.[23]

Some observers have stated that the influx of African-Americans, Latinos, and Asians in the twentieth century did not contribute to the massive migration to the suburbs of the white middle class. They argue that suburbanization could be better understood as a rush to the suburbs rather than a flight from the city.[24] This view is contrasted with others who have documented that "white flight" to the suburbs accelerates as racial minorities move into neighborhoods.[25] Others have argued that the integration of center city schools accelerated white flight.[26]

Regardless of the reason, examination of the demographics of many metropolitan areas gives clear evidence that whites did move to the suburbs in substantial numbers. Based on an examination of the 194 cities with populations 100,000 or more, Anthony Downs observes:

From 1980 to 1990 the cities gained 2 million residents, or 5 percent, half the growth rate of the nation as a whole. They lost 1.2 million white, non-Hispanic residents, 5.2 percent of their 1980 total. Thirty-eight cities lost white population, and twenty-four had declining total populations. Detroit, Newark, Gary, Miami, Hialeah, and Inglewood lost more than 43 percent of their 1980 white populations.[27]

In the past, mainly whites moved to the suburbs because the low-interest FHA mortgages mentioned above encouraged the use of restrictive covenants forbidding sale of a home to African-Americans. These were justified by the argument that such covenants would help maintain the value of the house by ensuring the area would not be racially integrated. Referring to the FHA restrictive covenants, Kenneth Jackson observed: "The lasting damage done by the national government was that it put its seal of approval on ethnic and racial discrimination and developed policies which had the result of the practical abandonment of large sections of old, industrial cities."[28] After the Supreme Court declaration in 1948 that government enforcement of such covenants was unconstitutional, the number of blacks joining the movement to the suburbs increased.

A side effect of the suburban building boom was that capital drained away from the center cities, especially as industry was also becoming suburbanized. New technology made the old multistory industrial buildings in center cities inefficient and the cost of center-city land made building replacement plants in the city extremely expensive. As a result, many industries moved to the suburbs. Indeed, John Mollenkopf reports that, "After 1946, manufacturing employment suburbanized even faster than residential population."[29] Of course, as the factories moved out, so did employees, further increasing the suburbanization of the population. Thus, as many now both lived and worked in the suburbs, they were less dependent on the central city.

Some observers argue that the pull of the suburbs was a response to a search for something much more fundamental than a large house or even a job. Robert Wood, among others, saw the move to the suburbs as an attempt to recreate the small town life of America in a world where the values of such small towns were being rapidly obliterated by the growth of cities. Wood saw the politically independent suburb as an expression of faith in the Jeffersonian idea that democracy can only flourish in small, independent settlements where a real sense of community can develop. He writes:

> The small town, the small community, this is what seems good about the suburb to most observers, what needs to be preserved, and what the large organization should not be permitted to despoil. Spontaneous collaboration, voluntary neighborliness, purposeful participation, these are the goals of real suburbanites. And all of the observers seem to cherish the hope that in the suburbs we can re-create the small communities we have lost in our industrial sprawl since the Civil War.[30]

Whether it was "push" or "pull," many people prefer to live in small communities. In 1990, one poll found that one-third of Americans wanted to live in a small town.[31] For many people the communities they choose are suburbs.[32] Further evidence of the attractiveness of suburbs for Americans is the fact that 4 in 10 central city residents were dissatisfied with their neighborhoods compared to 1 in 10 suburbanites.[33]

Life in Suburbia

There is a persistent myth about what suburbs look like. They are composed of block after block of single-family houses set in the middle of well-manicured lawns. On these lawns young children play with their dog Spot, while their mother tends the rose bushes and the father drives off to his job in the city. In some versions of this image, the houses are row upon row of identical tract houses; in some versions, the houses are large, individualized fake Tudor or Early American. But the other components are unvarying.

As with all myths, this one has a kernel of truth. After World War II, developers like the Levitts did build suburbs of identical tract houses. And there are suburbs, like Pepper Pike, Ohio, and Grosse Point, Michigan, where large, impressive houses sit well back from the street and the executives come home at night to greet their spouses and kids after a hard day in the corporate boardroom. But this myth does great damage to the diversity in suburbs.

In the myth, all suburbs are simply places where people live, although they work elsewhere. However, Leo Schnore found that only one-third of all suburbs were *dormitory* suburbs, or communities that served primarily a residential function.[34] He also identified *employing* suburbs, composed primarily of businesses and industry. People commuted to them for jobs rather than from them, as the myth portrays. A third type of suburb was *mixed;* that is, like any other city it had both business and residential areas. In a mixed suburb, one could both live and work in the same community. The only difference between such a mixed suburb and a similar-sized city or small town is its geographical proximity to the core city.

Peter Muller has developed another classification of suburbs. In the "exclusive, upper-income" suburb, the wealthy live in large homes with large lots. The "middle-class family" suburb has smaller homes and lots. A third type, working-class and poor suburbs, are often older suburban communities abandoned by the middle and upper class as they moved further away from the core city. Finally, there is the "suburban cosmopolitan" center, often the site of a college or university or a major cultural center.[35]

BOX 9–1

African-Americans in the New Jersey Suburbs

The traditional image of the suburbs as homogeneous enclaves filled with white residents becomes more inaccurate all the time. For example, one study indicates that more than 179,000 African-Americans left New York City since 1985, and many have moved to suburban communities. Many formerly all-white communities in Essex and Bergen Counties in northern New Jersey now have large African-American populations. In Teaneck in Bergen County, the black population grew by 23 percent in the last decade, primarily because of middle-class blacks leaving New York City. While the black population is growing, it is not necessarily integrating with whites. In explaining why he chose to live in the black section of Teaneck, one resident who moved from Harlem said, "I wasn't too interested in integration." What he wanted was a better school and greener spaces for his daughter.

The migration has created racial tensions in some areas. In Teaneck in 1992, a white police officer fatally shot a black teenager and was acquitted in a subsequent trial. There are also charges that the Teaneck school discriminates against black students.

But another New Jersey town in Essex County, Montclair, is attempting to forge an integrated community. One resident who moved to Montclair from Manhattan observed, "As with everything in this town involving race, no place works harder, cares more deeply, or gets better results." Evidence on how well it is succeeding is mixed. On the one hand, social events are likely to include people from both races. On the other, one student in the local high school reported: "Diversity for me means that I sit next to a black kid in homeroom. It's really an aberration when I have any meaningful contact with a black kid."

It appears that as many suburbs become increasingly heterogeneous, they need to address what inner cities have faced for decades: how to deal with the conflicts that heterogeneity creates.

Source: Adapted from Craig Horowitz, "The Upper West Side of Suburbia," *New York,* November 18, 1996, 43–49; George E. Jordan, "The Flight to the Suburbs," *Newsday,* April 4, 1995, sec. A.

Suburbs are displaying increasing diversity. One study of 1,773 suburbs in 55 metropolitan areas found that the number of predominantly white suburbs declined from 76 percent of all communities in the sample in 1980 to 64 percent in 1990. In the same period, the number of majority black suburbs increased from 3.4 percent to 4.9 percent and the number of majority Latino suburbs increased from 1.6 percent to 2.5 percent. The total number of majority Asian suburbs only increased by one, from 4 to 5. Some have argued that the suburbanization of African-Americans will reduce racial differences.[36] The impact of African-Americans on suburban New Jersey is discussed in Box 9–1. Studies have demonstrated that "blacks tend to reside in a relatively small number of suburban communities, characterized by lower wealth, worse public finances, and poorer prospects for economic growth than suburbs with small black populations."[37] That finding points to the fact that many older suburbs are beginning to face the same problems of blight and deterioration that many associate only with central cities.[38]

While there are variations *among* suburbs, suburban governments often adopt policies that attempt to ensure the homogeneity of the suburb. One such policy is **zoning**, by which a city specifies the purposes for which a particular piece of land may be used. Zoning is used to ensure a rational and aesthetically pleasing pattern of growth, yet it can also be effectively used to control who can afford to move into a particular area. This is referred to as **exclusionary zoning**. Examples of exclusionary zoning include specifying minimum lot sizes or minimum number of square feet for a house to be built on the lot. By requiring that large houses be built on large lots, the suburb ensures that only wealthy people will be able to build in that area.[*]

Many criticisms have been leveled at the creation, by government policy or otherwise, of homogeneous wealthy suburban enclaves. Perhaps the most important criticism is that these practices segregate wealthy and poor into separate legal jurisdictions. Those jurisdictions to which the poor are relegated have no way of generating financial resources necessary to provide adequate services to their residents. Because minority groups are represented disproportionately among the low-income population, this becomes, in effect, a form of ethnic or racial discrimination in the provision of government services on the local level.

The most common pattern has been for the poor to be disproportionately concentrated within the central city and the wealthy and middle class to be distributed among suburban communities. George Sternlieb and James Hughes report:

> There is a very clear linkage—the higher the family income level, the greater the propensity for the direction of migration to be from central city to suburb; conversely, the lower the income level, the greater the propensity for suburb to central city migration.[39]

As a result of that movement, the proportion of center city residents with incomes below the poverty line increased from 15 percent to 19 percent between 1970 and 1990.[40]

The core city, then, must deal with both a high demand for social services because its population is poor and low tax revenue because the poor pay few taxes. Therefore, taxpayers remaining in the city face high tax rates. Many suburbs, meanwhile, can tax their residents at low rates and still have adequate revenue to provide superior services to their residents. Alternatively, as public choice theorists suggest, residents may have chosen a suburb because of its low tax rates, even though they knew the price for low taxes would be limited services. Services not provided by the community might be supplied by the county, and county taxes are the same whether they live in the center city or the suburb. In any event, the disparity in tax rates provides more impetus to move to the suburbs.

In wealthy suburbs, residents may have little need for government services because they can afford to purchase what they want individually. For example, they may send their children to private schools and hire private guard services. Perhaps the most extreme example of this is the increasing number of private communities, most of which are constructed by private developers in unincorporated areas. The communities are run by private associations and access is restricted to all but community residents.[41]

The Advisory Commission on Intergovernmental Relations summarized the problems caused by suburbanization:

> In brief, most of America's wealth and most of America's domestic problems reside in the metropolitan areas. Why then, cannot this vast wealth be applied through vigorous social measures to meet the growing problems? Because the resources exist in one set of jurisdictions within the metro-

---

[*]Zoning and land use regulation in general are discussed in Chapter 12.

politan areas and the problems in another. Through a large part of the country this disparity between needs and resources is the disparity between the central city and its suburbs.[42]

What makes this imbalance especially galling to center-city residents is that the center-city government supports many services that the suburban residents use but do not have to pay for. Suburbanites drive on city streets to get to their jobs, visit city museums on their lunch hours, go to the theater or the sports stadium at night or on weekends.[43] But the legal fragmentation of the metropolitan area means that no single government in the area has the power to distribute services and costs on anything approaching an equitable basis.

The concentration of the poor in ghettos—be they suburbs or neighborhoods in the inner city—gives rise to various social pathologies. As Anthony Downs writes:

Thus a vicious circle of deepening poverty and despair is generated in many older urban areas. Because the lack of income flowing into such areas makes it impossible to pay for proper maintenance of housing and other physical structures regardless of who owns them, these structures become even more deteriorated and less desirable. Poor households have higher rates of both physical and mental illness than other income groups, so the incidence of these pathologies rises.[44]

Where suburban governments participate in erecting the barriers that segregate classes into homogeneous enclaves, they are, in essence, locking in the social inequalities created by the economic system. Suburbanization "not only redistributes taxable wealth, but also redistributes jobs and educational opportunities in ways that make them virtually inaccessible to minorities confined by residential segregation to part of the central city and declining

segments of the suburban ring."[45] Suburbanization creates a legal separation that assures "the best services, education, and access to new jobs are made available to affluent, virtually all-white communities that openly employ a full range of municipal powers to attract desirable jobs from the city while preventing low- and moderate-income families, or renters of any kind, from moving into the communities."[46]

Conflicts that arise between socioeconomic groups then become political because they are fought by the multiple governments in the metropolitan area. This affects the ability of citizens to exercise meaningful control over crucial policies. Some citizens are very successful in achieving their political goals. Suburban residents, often with a minimum of effort, can use the political system to encapsulate and protect themselves from the burdens caused by a large low-income population.[47] On the other hand, citizens in center cities must deal with that burden with minimal resources. The limited resources of center cities constrains the influence of citizens. The ability to participate means little if winning political power has only a minor impact on the allocation or reallocation of resources that are already stretched so thin that no extra funds exist.

To counteract these problems, Anthony Downs argues that suburbs have to be "opened up" and that people of various economic classes should be dispersed throughout the metropolitan area by increasing the amount of low-income housing in suburban communities. It should come as no surprise in this context that zoning is one of the major areas of conflict and controversy in the suburbs as zoning regulations are often used to regulate the kind of housing that can be built within a community. Suburban residents, fearing the effect low-income housing will have on property values as well as the influx of low-income residents, battle to preserve or create zoning regulations that would, in effect, make low-income housing impossible.

Politics in the Suburbs

There is an irony about politics in the suburbs. Robert Wood argued that a major pull of the suburb was the search for the values of the small town. People were searching for a sense of closeness to and control over government.

> In the suburb, according to the folklore, the school board is likely to be composed of neighbors or friends, or at least friends of friends or neighbors of neighbors. Its members do not come from another part of a large city; they are available and accessible. So are the chief of police, the water superintendent, the plumbing inspector, and the health officers. In this way, elected officials, bureaucrats, party leaders—the entire apparatus of democratic politics—are exposed to view, recognized and approached as they never are in a great metropolis.[48]

The small size and homogeneity of suburbs are supposed to enable democracy to flourish. As R.L. Bish and V. Ostrom observe: "Citizen demands can be more precisely indicated in smaller units rather than larger political units, and in political units undertaking fewer rather than more numerous 'public functions.'"[49]

What is ironic is that in many ways politics in the suburbs is like politics in small towns—not the small town of the Jeffersonian myth described by Wood but the small town described earlier in Chapter 2. While Wood and others expected participation to be greater in small communities, findings about the effect of population size on citizen participation have been contradictory. Sidney Verba and Norman Nie hypothesize that the reason for the contradiction is that size is not the important factor, but rather the degree to which

the town is identifiable as a distinct, separate community.[50] They refer to this as the "boundedness" of the community.

When Verba and Nie examined participation data from various types of communities, they initially found that the highest rates of participation were in isolated cities (those not part of a metropolitan area) and large suburbs, and the lowest rates were in isolated villages and small suburbs. But when they reexamined the data taking into account the socioeconomic characteristics of the community, they concluded:

> The small, peripheral community is not the place where participation is most inhibited. Rather, the citizens there participate more than their social characteristics would predict. It is in the suburbs where one finds citizens to be under-participators—even more than in the core cities. . . . It is in the suburbs, the communities that are the least well-bounded and that merge into urban complexes that one finds the least activity.[51]

Of course, this does not alter their initial finding that suburbs have high rates of political participation. Rather, it means that the residents of large suburbs were highly active not because of the suburban setting but because they tended to be of high socioeconomic status and such people tend to be more active in politics. It also means that the suburban context was not itself related to greater citizen activity, but to less. Their argument is that the closeness of suburbs to the core city and the degree to which residents of the suburbs rely on the core city economically, culturally, and socially reduces the extent to which residents of the suburbs develop a clear community identity.

Some evidence indicates that citizen input is even more problematical in edge cities. One study of incorporated edge cities found that they were less supportive of neighborhood participation.[52] Unincorporated edge cities have no city government to target. Some basic services are provided to residents, probably by a county government, but no central decision-making body exists to discuss public concerns of residents. Some of those residents may belong to a homeowners' association formed by a private development company. These associations are rapidly increasing in number. In their attempt to protect the property values of homes in the development, the associations often impose highly restrictive regulations, for example, governing what color the home may be painted or whether campers may be parked in the driveway, regulations that would certainly be opposed if a government attempted to impose them.[53]

Are there other possible explanations of why the suburban context may be negatively related to citizen activity? One explanation is that many suburban residents have "voted with their feet" and have less need to participate in politics.[54] Suburban communities differ in the amount and types of services they offer. By choosing among various residential locations, citizens are expressing a preference for a particular package of services. The services are chosen in an attempt to achieve a desired life-style, and, once the location is chosen, residents must merely preserve and protect the status quo by keeping the suburb as homogeneous as possible. This strategy would often make political activity superfluous as citizens and residents were already getting what they want from government.[55] When the status quo is threatened, suburbanites can be mobilized. With the NIMBY (Not In My Backyard) or LULU (Locally Unwanted Land Use) syndrome, citizens will often organize to protest undesirable land uses, such as waste dumps or prisons.

Recognizing the need for economic development to build the tax base, suburban residents have tolerated some commercial development and some county government centralization for pragmatic reasons, but when it went too far, "the electorate would raise its voice in loud protest."[56] In DuPage County, in

suburban Chicago, voters turned out their county chair, who sought to attract the White Sox and Bears, build a convention center, and expand the airport. His desire to consolidate power and expand taxation,

> unnerved municipal officials and other devotees of traditional grass-roots suburban rule. . . . Whereas the county chair viewed DuPage as the emerging metropolis of the future, the majority of his constituents clung to the suburban past. Their vision remained focused on well-maintained homes, top-notch schools, and homogeneous neighborhoods, characteristics increasingly alien to the big city.[57]

The homogeneity of suburbs provides another explanation for the generally negative relationship between the suburban context and political participation. On the one hand, heterogeneity may be related to a decrease in participation because people are often uncomfortable in interacting with others who are "different." Yet others have argued that homogeneity may also decrease citizen involvement. Discussing neighborhood politics in Baltimore, Matthew Crenson concluded:

> People convinced that they are surrounded by citizens who resemble themselves can confidently leave the affairs of their neighborhoods to others. When neighbors are pretty much alike, after all, there is little to distract them from minding their own business—in part because it does not make much difference who is minding the neighborhood's business.[58]

When the community is heterogeneous, however, citizens will have a need to become politically active to represent their interests because the neighbors cannot be relied upon to do it for them.

Suburbs are also more likely to have reform-style governments. As Chapter 6 explained, two characteristics of reform governments tend to depress participation: nonpartisanship and reliance on bureaucratic experts. Parties can function as effective mobilizers of people. In the absence of party activity, many (especially those of lower socioeconomic status) tend not to vote. The party label also provides a voting cue, which makes voting easier and therefore more likely.

Bureaucrats are shielded from "political pressures" because they are appointed, not elected, and because they can claim superior expertise. As Robert Wood argues:

> If the expert is entrusted with the really tough problems, the suburbanite has the best of all possible worlds: grassroots government run by automation. Under these circumstances, the purest theory of democracy requires no democratic action or responsibility at all.[59]

The most fundamental effect of suburbanization is the division of the metropolitan area into many separate legal jurisdictions so that residents of the area find it difficult or impossible to cooperate to solve problems.[60] Some residents do not care about certain problems. For example, the problems of the poor in center-city ghettos are, to a large extent, ignored by the inhabitants of wealthy suburbs. However, there are problems where all agree that some cooperation is necessary. Without some coordination, sewage dumped by one suburb ends up in the lake of the suburb next door. Fumes from a factory in one jurisdiction waft over the boundary to the housing development. In addition, a great deal of duplication of effort occurs, with each small suburb supplying its own fire engines, sewage treatment plant, schools, and police.

In sum, the suburban sprawl of the metropolis has been criticized as being both inegalitarian and inefficient. Thus, multiple suggestions have been made for providing coordi-

nation in the metropolis, yet few attempts to achieve that coordination have been successful.

Intergovernmental Coordination Mechanisms

Several ways of providing greater coordination in metropolitan areas have been suggested. Some of these are relatively easy to establish. Others are somewhat more difficult; still others are extremely difficult to accomplish. (A complete list of options is presented in Table 9–5.)

Suburbanization is not a new phenomenon. Colonial American cities were also ringed with small communities, but they did not face the problems of the modern metropolis because there was an easy way of ensuring coordination. **Annexation** was used to bring adjoining communities into the city. As the number of people moving to outlying areas increased, they often pressured the state legislatures to restrict the ability of cities to annex new territory. In some cases, legislatures required that only territory proposed for annexation had the right to initiate annexation proceedings. In other instances, any annexation proceedings had to be approved by majority vote in the area to be annexed.[61] As a result, annexation peaked in the early years of the twentieth century. Since then, except in the South and Southwest, cities have usually annexed only sparsely populated, unincorporated territory.

Relatively Easy Forms of Coordination

Perhaps the simplest form of intergovernmental coordination is the use of **informal cooperation**. This happens so frequently, in so many areas, that we tend to take it for granted. If a criminal crosses jurisdictions, the regular procedure is for police to cooperate. In the case of a major disaster, communities in metropolitan areas regularly help out, even if there are no formal agreements.

Another commonly used method of interlocal cooperation is the use of **interlocal service**

TABLE 9–5

Types of Intergovernmental Coordination

Relatively easy
1. Informal cooperation
2. Interlocal service agreements
3. Joint powers agreements
4. Extraterritorial powers
5. Regional councils of government (COGs)
6. Federally encouraged Single-purpose districts
7. State planning and development districts (SPDDs)
8. Contracting from private vendors

Moderately difficult
9. Local special districts
10. Transfer of functions
11. Annexation
12. Regional special districts and authorities
13. Metropolitan multipurpose districts
14. Reformed urban county

Very difficult
15. One-tier consolidation: city–county consolidation
16. Two-tier restructuring: federated structures
17. Three-tier reform: metropolitan-wide structures

Source: Adapted from David B. Walker, "Snow White and the 17 Dwarfs: From Metro Cooperation to Metropolitan Governance," *National Civic Review* 76 (January–February 1987): 16.

---

contracts. Local governments can shop for some other institution to provide the services. In some cases, the provider of the services is another municipality; in others, it is the county. The community enters into a contract with the provider to buy the services it wants. This system is often viewed as a "supermarket or cafeteria of services," because the community can select or reject services provided from other areas or choose any combination it desires. This contracting is often referred to as the Lakewood Plan because it was first used in a contract between the community of Lakewood and Los Angeles County.

In many ways, contracting for services is an ideal compromise for suburbs; it permits them to retain their autonomy and determine what mix of services they desire, while still availing themselves of the efficiency when

those services are provided on a large scale. Suburbs can shop for desired services at the cost they want to pay. Contracting for services is very popular in metropolitan areas.[62]

A third technique, which is becoming more common, is a **joint powers agreement**. Under this, two or more governments agree to work together in a specific area. For instance, rather than holding separate school board, park board, city, and county elections, the various entities may agree to set a common election date and share costs and personnel.

Extraterritorial powers are those that allow a city to control the actions of unincorporated communities outside the boundaries of the city. These powers are granted to certain cities in 35 states. The powers, which have been used extensively in the Sun Belt, are usually given to assure orderly growth as the city expands.

Another way some metropolitan areas have attempted to achieve coordination has been the use of **regional or metropolitan councils of government**, which were initially established primarily for planning purposes. City planning in America has a long history. Cities, for example Philadelphia, Boston, and Washington, D.C., were initially developed according to comprehensive city plans. The "city beautiful" movement at the beginning of the twentieth century gave impetus to planning. Metropolitan planning is an outgrowth of this city-planning function.

One problem with city planning in a metropolitan area is that each municipality can plan only for itself, yet the municipalities are necessarily interdependent because of their geographical proximity. It does not help for one suburb to zone a given area as residential if the neighboring suburb zones the area next to it as industrial. Metropolitan planning is an attempt to overcome such problems by developing comprehensive plans for the metropolitan area as a whole.

The use of metropolitan planning increased tremendously in the 1960s and 1970s, primarily because of two policies of the federal government. First, the 1965 Housing and Urban Development Act authorized funds for regional planning. Second, the 1966 Demonstration Cities and Metropolitan Development Act (Model Cities) required that programs to be funded must be approved by metropolitan review agencies before approximately 30 federal grants would be awarded. Because the guidelines for the reviews were spelled out in a circular published by the Office of Management and the Budget titled "A-95," the review process came to be called the A-95 review.

Both the provision of funds for metropolitan planning and the requirement that programs funded by federal grants be subject to a metropolitan-wide review process re-

sulted in a dramatic increase in the number of metropolitan planning commissions. Councils of government (COGs) grew until recently for three primary reasons. First, they are easy to form. All that is necessary is an agreement among the governmental units of the metropolitan region—and coordination in principle is easy to support. The difficulty often arises later, when issues take concrete form. Second, because COGs could qualify as the metropolitan review agency under the A-95 process, they were created to perform the metropolitan planning function. Even with the demise of A-95, the COGs are still a convenient way for states to conduct reviews and some federal programs, such as funds for mass transit, still require regional cooperation. Third, the National Association of Regional Councils was created to encourage the creation of COGs and to supply them with staff support.

As metropolitan planning agencies, COGs have an advantage because they are often composed of the elected officials in charge of implementing the plans. They also have limitations. For one, they generally lack the power to levy taxes. In addition, although composed of officials, the COG itself has no independent power to require compliance with its plan—it is only advisory. Finally, problems often arise in the power relations among the member governments. Most commonly each member has a single vote, but the larger members, especially the core city government, charge that this contradicts the one person–one vote principle. They want proportionate representation among the member governments. Several cities, including Cleveland, Ohio, and San Francisco, have adopted proportionate representation. The bickering among member governments is probably one reason that COGs have spent little time or effort on the major problems but have focused on noncontroversial issues for which it is easy to develop consensus. While their numbers increased, the extent to which they effectively increased coordination in metropolitan areas is doubt-ful.[63]

The A-95 review process was ended by President Ronald Reagan in 1983; it was replaced by Executive Order 12372 as part of his efforts to reduce the national government's role in urban policy. Although Executive Order 12372 gave states responsibility to establish review procedures, most adopted procedures similar to the A-95 review. In 1980, when Reagan took office, there were 632 regional councils; by 1991, their number had declined to 536.[64] The 1990 amendments to the Clean Air Act and the 1991 Intermodal Surface Transportation and Efficiency Act (ISTEA) have requirements for regional planning. In addition, there is renewed interest in using regional agencies for economic development activities. Academics have also shown a great deal of interest in regional cooperation as evidenced by several new books and articles in the area of regionalism.

Metropolitan planning did not lessen the fragmentation in metropolitan areas because the planners did not have the power to implement their plans. That power lay with elected public officials, who often had little incentive to cooperate. By following the dictates of the planners, the officials themselves would lose some autonomy. More seriously, however, the suburb itself would lose control over its development and that control is the *raison d'etre* of the suburb. In some cases, compliance with the plans so infuriated voters that officials found themselves unemployed after the next election.

While general regional planning may be declining, **federally encouraged single-purpose regional organizations** continue in some policy areas. Over the years, many federal job training, economic development, environmental, and transportation programs mandated regional cooperation. The two mentioned above, ISTEA and the 1990 Clean Air Act amendments, re-enforce the requirement for regional cooperation. Many states created **state planning and development districts** in the 1980s to replace the COGs as clearinghouses for regional review of proposals for federal government funds.

A final, easily established means of coordination in the metropolitan area is the use of **contracting with private vendors**. Similar in logic to contracting with other governments, this allows communities to realize economies of scale and save taxpayer money. Problems of accountability, however, may increase. The use of private-sector contracting is an increasingly popular management tool in metropolitan areas.

Moderately Difficult Forms of Cooperation

A very common form of cooperation is the establishment of **local special districts**. Examples of policy areas that often are controlled by special districts or authorities are schools, fire protection, transportation, water and sewers, and parks and recreation. Services that a municipality could not provide because it could not raise adequate funds or did not want to raise taxes to generate the funds can be delivered by a special district or authority. This reduces fiscal pressure on the municipality.

In general, this approach is piecemeal, doing little to affect the status quo in any substantial way. Coordination on some policies can be achieved. It is argued that coordination is possible in the policy areas concerned with **system maintenance** functions, such as water or sewage. As the population of a metropolitan area grows, some way must be found to provide safe water and sanitary disposal of waste. Dumping of inadequately treated waste in a stream may pollute the drinking water of a neighboring suburb. The urgency of the problem provides incentive to cooperate. In addition, the solutions do not usually create conflict. Deciding where the sewage treatment plant will be located may be a problem, but establishing a water and sewage district presents little threat to individual suburbs.

On the other hand, coordination of **life-style** issues such as land-use or school policies is much more problematic. Through these policies, suburbs declare their identities in a process much like "dressing for success" at the corporate level. For example, exclusive suburbs declare their exclusivity by zoning out apartment buildings and funding superior college preparatory classes in the schools. There is little desire to seek coordination across government boundaries in the establishment of such policies. To a large extent the suburb exists to achieve autonomy in those areas.[65] So suburbs use such piecemeal approaches as contracting or forming special districts for system maintenance services, but they want control over life-style policies.

Political pressure on the special districts is not inevitable, as citizens are often very confused about what districts or authorities exist, what they do, and how they are funded. The invisibility of the special districts is aided by the fact that in many cases the taxes they levy are collected by county governments. In addition, in many cases the governing boards of the districts and authorities are appointed by various elected officials. These boards can claim, as experts, to know more about the policy area than others, thus reducing oversight of their decisions. Under these circumstances, questions arise about the extent to which special districts are, or can be, held accountable to the public. While intended to provide greater coordination in a particular policy area, the multiplicity of special districts only adds to the fragmentation in metropolitan areas by dividing responsibility for policy making and implementation into multiple functional fiefdoms. The result is a confusing maze for citizens who want to know "who's in charge here?"

Rather than establish a new district or contract with another entity, a **transfer of functions** to another government may improve efficiency. For example, both suburbs and cities have developed within another political jurisdiction: the county. In some cases, the metropolitan area spills over county lines, but often the whole area is encompassed by a single county. Even though county government adds to political fragmentation, some have suggested expanding the county's powers to decrease problems of intergovernmental relations in metropolitan areas. In addition, expanding the county's role may improve efficiency in delivering services. While it may be expensive for a single community to provide a service, several communities coordinating through a county government may be able to provide the same service for all their residents at less cost. For example, the cost of fire protection could be reduced if each community did not have to invest in equipment, buildings, and crew. Economists refer to this kind of saving as an **economy of scale**.

One suggestion is to transfer specific functions from the local municipalities to the county. For instance, responsibility for water supply, garbage disposal, or fire protection could be handled by the county for all municipalities, thus providing coordination in those areas. A second suggestion is to have the county provide services and policy direction in the unincorporated parts of metropolitan areas. A third suggestion is to increase substantially the county responsibility in metropolitan areas. A charter reorganization could be used to transfer to the county government many functions that local municipalities either have problems providing adequately or that could be provided more efficiently or effectively on a metropolitan basis. This would create a metropolitan political structure with a metropolitan-wide government having responsibility for several functions and the local municipalities retaining control over others.

Another means of limiting metropolitan fragmentation and increasing coordination is the use of **annexation**, briefly mentioned above. While not generally very common, annexation continues to occur. North Carolina law allows municipalities to annex any area that is: (1) unincorporated, (2) contiguous, and (3) over two persons per acre. This law alone explains much of the population growth in North Carolina cities.[66] Annexation has also been used successfully in Texas. The Texas Municipal Annexation Act of 1963 gave cities control over subdivisions in unincorporated areas on their borders, referred to as extraterritorial jurisdiction, and also gave cities the right to annex portions of the unincorporated area without a referendum.[67] Cities such as San Antonio annexed highway rights of way, expanding their areas of extraterritorial jurisdiction. As the areas along the highways developed, the core cities annexed them without referendum.[68] In Virginia, a three-judge court rules on requests from core cities to annex territory on their borders when it begins to urbanize. Such requests are usually honored. Annexation is likely, even in states like Texas, to be increasingly opposed. Opposition by a Houston suburb to proposed annexation is seen as a "harbinger of things to come."[69]

For the most part, however, annexation does not seem to be a viable solution to the problems of metropolitan fragmentation. Annexation to the core city would force suburban residents to compete for policies necessary to achieve and preserve their life-style. In addition, if annexed, suburbanites would have to share their resources with the center city. Finally, although annexation would permit equalization of taxing throughout the metropolitan area, suburban residents would probably be taxed at a higher rate.

A frequently used solution to problems created by metropolitan fragmentation is the creation of **regional special districts or authorities** to control policy in a particular area or areas. The primary difference between authorities and special districts is in the way they are empowered to raise revenue. Special districts are usually given the power to levy taxes, while authorities can issue bonds.[70] Box 9–2 (on page 244) discusses a variety of arrangements for regional cooperation.

Regional special districts are difficult to establish. They are often set up across state lines, such as the Port Authority of New York and New Jersey. They sometimes perform only one function: for example, in the San Francisco area, the Bay Area Transportation District runs the BART rapid transit system or, in Chicago, the Chicago Metropolitan Sanitary District takes care of sanitation. Others, such as the Port Authority of New York, which controls the port, as well as bridges, bus terminal, highways, and office buildings, perform a series of related activities.

Maintaining popular control over these agencies is difficult. Perhaps an extreme example of how insulated these districts or authorities can become is given by Robert Caro's picture of Robert Moses. Moses used his position as appointed head of many public authorities in the New York area, particularly the New York Port Authority, to shape New York City and its suburbs.[71] Moses is much heralded for his accomplishments, which include bridges, highways, parks, beaches, housing, dams, and more. But by using the mantle of nonpartisan, technical competence he was able not only to bully low-income and minority citizens out of their homes but also to intimidate mayors, governors, and presidents.

Because Moses worked through an authority rather than general purpose government, he was insulated from democratic accountability.

> The official records of most public agencies are public records, but not those of public authorities since courts have held that they may be regarded as the records of private corporations, closed to scrutiny by interested citizen or reporter. . . . Public authorities are also outside and above politics, Moses said. Their decisions are made solely on the basis of the public welfare, he said. . . . They are businesslike—prudent, efficient, economical.[72]

BOX 9–2

Experiments in Regionalism

Analysts have long recognized that the governmental fragmentation of America's metropolitan areas causes serious problems. Middle-class whites and, increasingly, middle-class blacks flee the center cities and attempt to isolate themselves in suburbs. They leave behind cities where the level of poverty dooms any policies to failure. Baltimore demonstrates the impact of the migration to the suburbs. In 1950, Baltimore had a population of 950,000, or 71 percent of the 1.3 million people in the region. Currently, the population is down to 675,000, or only 27 percent of the regional population. Yet that number includes 60 percent of the poor in the region and 85 percent of the black poor.

Proposals to encourage the sharing of resources across government boundaries by creating metropolitan—or regional—level governments have often died as a result of suburban opposition. Now one analyst has argued that all governments in the metropolis have incentives to find ways to cooperate. First, some research shows that the economic health of the suburbs is dependent on the health of the center city. Second, in the global economy, it is the region that must compete rather than a single city or suburb.

Some metropolitan areas have recognized the value of cooperation and could serve as models for others. Portland, Oregon, has built on its 1972 plan to increase retail development in its downtown and has

created a popularly elected regional government with a primary goal of controlling metropolitan sprawl. Portland's metro government created an Urban Growth Boundary in a three-county area. As a result, companies are building inside the Boundary, turning investment inward and increasing property values (and, of course, the tax base). However, low-income renters are having trouble finding affordable housing. The Metro government is, therefore, considering efforts to scatter low-income housing throughout the region.

In 1967 the Minnesota state legislature created a metropolitan council for the cities of Minneapolis–St. Paul and the surrounding region. In 1971 the state passed the Fiscal Disparities Act. Forty percent of the increase in commercial and industrial property valuation is placed in a common pool that is then taxed at a uniform rate and redistributed among all the 188 municipalities in the region. The effect is to reduce the disparity in funds available to the communities.

In 1993, the Pennsylvania General Assembly approved a proposal to create an Allegheny Regional Asset District for the Pittsburgh region. The District board will administer a county-wide 1 percent sales tax, distributing half to regional parks, libraries, and other cultural facilities and half to the county and municipalities to reduce other local taxes.

Source: Adapted from David Rusk, *Cities Without Suburbs,* 2nd ed. (Washington, D.C.: The Woodrow Wilson Center Press, 1995); Neal R. Peirce, "Cities and Suburbs, Joined at the Hip," *The Washington Post Weekly Edition,* April 4–10, 1994.

Because his activity was beyond public scrutiny, Moses was able to enlist the support of the bankers, lawyers, real estate developers—

in short, those with money and influence—by paying high premiums for their services. "He made economic, not democratic, forces the forces that counted most in New York. And because he spoke for those forces, it was his voice that counted most."[73]

Moses used the apolitical facade of many authorities that he headed to give the impression that decisions were made on the basis of technical expertise, not political consideration. Those who disagreed with him were accused of being political or lacking expertise. His decisions, though, were often not value free. One project, hailed as a great technical and aesthetic success, indicates Moses's disdain for the lower class. He developed Jones Beach and built highways between it and New York City. But the highway overpasses were built too low for buses to pass under them. In an era when only the rich had cars, this ensured that the magnificent beaches and beautiful highways that looked so good to the masses were beyond their reach.[74] This illustrates how control over technical aspects of design—the height of bridges—can be used to achieve the expert's values.

The use of special districts and authorities is not inherently undemocratic. Moses, however, is a colorful and extreme example of the problem of maintaining democracy in a metropolis that relies on nonelected professionals to achieve policy coordination.

Still another attempt at coordination is the **metropolitan multipurpose district**. The multipurpose district is not widely used. The most prominent example is Seattle's METRO. Originally created to handle environmental issues, voters expanded its mandate to be responsible for mass transit. Turf battles ensued with King County and a court ruled that—because it performs more than one service function—it must abide by the same standard as general purpose government of one person–one vote for representation. As a result, its functions are being absorbed by King County.[75]

The **reformed urban county** is an attempt to provide better coordination within the county by employing a more modern government structure. As noted above, metro-

politan counties are the fastest growing type of general purpose government. As counties become more urbanized and residents increase demands for services, the commission form of government, which usually features part-time commissioners, is seen as inadequate. As a result, some counties are changing to county administrators (similar to city managers) or county executives (similar to strong mayors). In a **post-suburban era**, that is when suburbs are blending residences with commercial centers and edge cities are emerging, a reformed county government is often seen as a vehicle that can balance a desired life-style with the need for economic development.

> . . . while mouthing the glories of village life, residents of the post-suburban metropolis recognized the need for some overarching authority and supported the creation and strengthening of some unifying institutions. To some degree county government assumed a coordinating function and represented the post-suburban metropolis in its dealings with the outside world. Traditionally a unit of rural government charged with maintaining courts, repairing county roads, and operating the local jail, county government was to expand its role markedly in the post-suburban areas of the late twentieth century. Especially during the 1970s and 1980s some politicians sought to make the county into a regional supergovernment and the principal policy maker along the metropolitan fringe. They have met with limited success, but at the close of the century the county had deviated significantly from its long-standing hayseed image. . . . The county was the unit of government that helped suburbanites move into the post-suburban era without too seriously compromising their traditional ideals.[76]

This form of metropolitan cooperation is further limited by the fact that more than half of the metropolitan areas comprise more than one county.

Very Difficult Forms of Cooperation

The urbanization of metropolitan counties has led some areas to consider **one-tier or city-county consolidation**, which would result in a single government. Throughout the twentieth century considerable interest has been expressed in achieving city–county consolidation, yet few have adopted this structure. The first instance of city–county consolidation in the twentieth century occurred between Baton Rouge and East Baton Rouge Parish in 1947. It was not total consolidation, however, because the city and parish officials were both retained, although their functions were integrated. Three consolidations occurred in the 1960s. In Tennessee, Nashville and Davidson County merged in 1962 and a new government called METRO was created. In Florida, Jacksonville and Duval County merged in 1967 with the new government called City of Jacksonville; and in Indiana, Indianapolis and Marion County joined in 1969 in a new government called UNIGOV.

Several factors contributed to the success of the Nashville and Jacksonville consolidation plans. Both areas had had some obvious problems of service delivery; in addition, cities in both areas were dissatisfied with government officials, stemming from an unpopular policy and from corruption in Jacksonville. This dissatisfaction with the status quo led to a willingness to experiment with something new. Few incorporated suburbs surrounded the central cities, thus opposition to the consolidation was minimal. These cases point to a conclusion that city–county consolidation can occur only when a number of factors coalesce to create adequate political support for the consolidation and to minimize opposition.[77]

The Indiana case was also special. In most states, such major change in governing structures in a metropolitan area must be approved by a referendum vote. Indiana, though, had no long history of local home rule or referendum votes. Normally the state legislature made major urban policy. When consolidation occurred, the Republican Party controlled the mayor's office in Indianapolis, as well as the governorship and the state legislature of Indiana. That control helped local leaders push through legislation to consolidate the Indianapolis metropolitan area without the requirement of a referendum vote.[78]

Despite these successes, 51 of 68 attempts at city–county consolidation have failed over 30 years.[79] Most of the referenda took place in the Southeast; they were generally defeated because of suburban opposition. The suburbanites left the cities to escape taxes and, possibly, school integration. Center-city minorities are often opposed because of fear that their power would be diluted. Elected officials and public employees of both city and suburbs are generally against changing a government's form because their status becomes less certain and their power and their jobs are threatened. Finally, suburban newspapers opposed change in government structure because they would no longer be needed as a voice for local issues.

Conversely, city newspapers generally provide strong support of consolidation. "Good government" groups such as the League of Women Voters often are supportive, as are the Chamber of Commerce, banks, academic groups, and utilities.

Creating a **two-tier government or federated structure** would appear to be easier than total city–county consolidation. In a two-tier system, local municipalities retain control over some services and policies, so the change is not as drastic. Nevertheless, only one metropolis in the United States—Miami—has adopted this structure. Miami has had to deal with some major conflicts between the county and municipalities over questions of jurisdiction—which level of government should be responsible for what policy.[80] In addition, resource problems arose. The county was given additional responsibilities yet was denied many revenue sources by state law.[81] In 1996, the city was broke and the state was threatening to take it over. In 1998 the fiscal crisis continues.

Legal problems arise in changing the role of county government. In most cases, the state constitution has to be amended to permit a change in the functions and authority of the county government. The structure of that government also often has to be changed. Often, to fulfill demands of the expanded role of metropolitan government, the county government must include a county executive officer analogous to a city mayor or manager. One study found that the structure of county government has an impact on the scope of its functions and the size of expenditures. Counties with appointed or elected executives perform more functions than those with commission systems. Counties with elected executives spent more than twice as much per capita as commission-led structures and 75 percent more than counties with nonelected administrators.[82]

Another legal problem is that any change, once authorized by state constitutional amendment, usually must be approved by voters in the areas involved, often on a jurisdiction by jurisdiction basis.[83] Thus, the change must have substantial public approval that is often hard to generate. The real barrier, then, to any such change in the role of county governments or to the liberalization of annexation laws, is public opposition.

As if city–county cooperation is not difficult enough, special problems have to be faced in a situation where the metropolitan area spreads over more than one county. In that case, a new governmental structure with jurisdiction over the whole metro area would have to be created.

A final proposal for dealing with metropolitan fragmentation, **three-tier reform: metropolitan-wide structures**, is the most ambitious. It attempts to address problems of fragmentation in metropolitan areas covering more than one county. Its use has been lim-

ited. One example is the Twin Cities Metropolitan Council, which was created by the Minnesota state legislature in 1967. The area had been plagued for a long time by traditional metropolitan ills: fragmentation, fiscal disparities, and inadequate services. The major precipitating factor in establishing the council was a 1959 state health department study that indicated that 250,000 people in the metro area were relying on contaminated wells for water. In addition, the Federal Housing Administration refused to insure mortgages for homes without water and sewer hook-ups. This led to a consensus that some sort of coordination was necessary. Such consensus and the fact the council was created by the legislature, not by referendum, were crucial to success. The legislature's plan for a metropolitan council passed with no opposition.

The metropolitan council is composed of representatives of districts that overlap municipal boundaries, thus eliminating some of the jurisdictional battles afflicting most COGs. It can levy taxes, and it has the power to develop metropolitan plans, review municipal plans, and review grant applications from local governments. While it does not provide services itself, the Council has provided meaningful policy leadership through coordinated planning.

The metropolitan council's early record with system maintenance policies was impressive. It achieved considerable coordination in waste disposal, sewers, and regional parks. Further, it also scored successes with such life style issues as providing low- and moderate-income housing throughout the metropolitan area and by sharing hospitals between communities.[84]

Despite the successes achieved in its first 10 years, the Twin Cities Metropolitan Council has undergone considerable stress since the late 1970s. Competition between local municipalities for economic development, decreased federal funding, the increased role of the private sector, and "turf protection" by other agencies have contributed to the loss of influence of the metropolitan council.[85] In addition, proposals before the state legislature in 1993 and 1994 to provide for elected representatives to the metropolitan council, which would have increased the legitimacy of the organization, were defeated.

Some see piecemeal solutions, beginning with easy means of coordination, as a first step to achieving metropolitan government. In reality, piecemeal solutions may retard the creation of metropolitan governments.

> By isolating these services in separate agencies, the political incentives for a general forum are removed; for the "piecemeal" approach to governing the metropolis first siphons off those issues for which there is little choice but cooperation between have and have nots, suburbs and core cities. Left are those problems for which there is the least incentive to negotiate and the least amount of flexibility in bargaining—those which most divide the metropolis. . . .[86]

Global competition, however, has resulted in more regional efforts at economic development. The confirmation of a common need and a common enemy (other metropolitan areas), may increase metropolitan cooperation. In addition, a great deal of interest has been expressed in the "new regionalism." Nonetheless, two researchers have concluded that they were less optimistic about an expanded role for regional government at the end of their research than before they began.[87]

Most metropolitan areas encounter substantial obstacles in achieving coordination. People like the suburbs and are jealous of their autonomy. More Americans live in suburbs than in either center cities or small towns, and evidence indicates they are satisfied with their communities.[88] Suburbanites are much more likely than urbanites to express satisfaction in general with their community and in particular with the services provided. Polls in-

dicate that a majority of Americans do not want to live in large cities.[89] Therefore, they are unlikely to be willing to have their suburb form closer ties with the large city they chose to leave. Perhaps the attitude can best be summed up in the following:

> Local politics, played out in varying, often unique local forms, expresses the preferences of citizens and local government officials for government structure in the metropolitan areas. To date, these preferences have decidedly favored fragmentation and have been hostile toward the development of regional governance.[90]

Impact on Citizen Control

What are the effects of this metropolitan fragmentation on citizen control? Residents of wealthy suburbs would appear to have the best of all possible worlds—having both resources and neighbors with whom they share similar values about how those resources should be spent. The legal boundaries tend to lock in disparities in resources that exist in the metropolis. Instead of redistributing resources from wealthy to poor to assure minimum service standards, the fragmentation of the population into homogeneous enclaves in essence means that "them that has, gets." The wealthy, isolated in a suburb that is kept exclusive by various policies such as zoning and subdivision regulation, can assure themselves of a high level of government services because of the large tax base to which their government has access. They are the obvious beneficiaries of fragmentation.

The losers are the poor who are relegated to their own homogeneous enclaves. Especially in the Northeast and Great Lakes states, this usually means the core city and inner ring suburbs. While taxed as heavily—or more so—than the rich, the poor are condemned to a lower level of services because of the limited tax base. A concomitant of this is racial segregation because minority populations are disproportionately the poor. Limited resources mean that citizen activity in the center city can have limited effect because the government lacks the resources to respond to citizen demands.

In addition, this pattern of segregation of wealthy and poor into different legal jurisdictions sets the stage for competition among the legal jurisdictions that compose the metropolis. Each government wants to increase its tax base by enticing wealthy citizens to move in. Increasingly suburbs are also attempting to attract "the right kind" of commercial development: the clean high-technology industry or the corporate headquarters, for instance.[91] The two carrots used to attract such residents are low taxes and desirable governmental services.

The importance of developing a strong tax base means that the policy process of center cities is constrained. Responding to demands from low income residents does not add to the tax base. Officials can tell the poor that in the long run an improved tax base will benefit them, and all city residents, by ensuring resources to permit response to their demands; in the meantime, however, the poor are unlikely to succeed in getting their demands placed on equal footing on the government's agenda with those issues raised by major economic interests, which can contribute to the tax base. A side effect of the competition in the metropolis is that governments that already *have* a wealthy population can easily achieve both low taxes and quality services. Thus the disparities tend to become accentuated.

Metropolitan fragmentation also has negative effects for the ability of residents to affect policy. It does not help to agree with your neighbors in one suburb if the problem to be solved is too comprehensive for any one jurisdiction to solve. Piecemeal efforts of coordination only add to crazy quilt of political

authority in the metropolis. On top of the fragmentation caused by the creation of incorporated suburbs is added another layer of contracts for services, special districts, regional planning agencies, and COGs. It should not be surprising if citizens wonder who's in charge. Political accountability can hardly avoid suffering in such a structure.

In this "war of all against all," the losers look for help. Some recent research would seem to provide an incentive for the multiple governments in the metropolis to cooperate on problems. Several researchers have concluded that the economic health of the whole metropolis is correlated with that of the center city.[92] One study concluded:

> Cities and suburbs have a common and essential stake in their shared economies. Growing disparities between these jurisdictions erode and eventually undermine the vitality of the regional economy and, hence, the welfare of both cities and suburbs.[93]

Even if research establishes such an interdependence, overcoming resistance to metropolitan cooperation will be difficult. Many see the only hope of such coordination and redistribution as coming from other levels of government. The next chapter will examine the problems local governments face in raising revenue and providing services and the role that states and the national government play in this process.

Notes

1. *City of Clinton v. Cedar Rapids and Missouri River Railroad Co.* 24 Iowa 455, 475 (1868).
2. John Dillon, *Commentaries on the Law of Municipal Corporations,* 5th ed. (Boston: Little, Brown, 1911), vol. 1, sec. 237, 448.
3. Advisory Commission on Intergovernmental Relations, *State Laws Governing Local Government Structure and Administration* (Washington, D.C.: ACIR, 1993), 20–23.
4. Rhodes Cook, "Cities: Decidedly Democratic, Declining in Population," *Congressional Quarterly* (July 12, 1997): 1646.

5. *Avery v. Midland County* 390 U.S. 474 (1968); and *Hadley v. Junior College District of Metropolitan Kansas City, Mo.* 397 U.S. 50 (1970).

6. *City of Mobile v. Bolden* 446 U.S. 55 (1980).

7. Robert C. Wood, *1400 Governments: The Political Economy of the New York Metropolitan Region* (Cambridge, Massachusetts: Harvard University Press, 1961).

8. Richard D. Bingham, *State and Local Government in an Urban Society* (New York: Random House, 1986), 250.

9. James H. Svara, "Leadership and Professionalism in County Government," in *The American County: Frontiers of Knowledge,* ed. Donald C. Menzel (Tuscaloosa: University of Alabama Press, 1996), 110.

10. Victor S. DeSantis and Tari Renner, "Structure and Policy Expenditures in American Counties," *The American County,* 91.

11. Carol B. Lawrence and John M. DeGrove, "County Government Services," *The County Government Yearbook 1976* (Washington, D.C.: National Association of Counties and International City Managers Association, 1976), 92–95.

12. William J. Pammer, Jr., "Economic Development Strategies Among Counties" in *The American County,* 184; and Vincent L. Marando and Mavis Mann Reeves, "Counties: Evolving Local Governments, Reform, and Responsiveness," *National Civic Review* 80 (Spring 1991): 222–226.

13. Kee Ok Park, "County Government Growth and Its Impact." Paper presented at the Annual Meeting of the Midwest Political Science Association, Chicago, Illinois, April 6–9, 1995, 1.

14. Svara, "Leadership and Professionalism," and Gregory Streib, "Strengthening County Leadership," in *The American County,* 109–127, 128–145.

15. Susan A. MacManus, "County Boards, Partisanship, and Elections," in *The American County,* 53–79.

16. Bingham, *State and Local Government,* 55–56.

17. U.S. Bureau of the Census, *Census of Governments, Vol. 1, Government Organization* (Washington, D.C.: U.S. Government Printing Office, 1983), xv; and U.S. Bureau of the Census, *Census of Governments, Vol. 1, Government Organization* (Washington, D.C.: U.S. Government Printing Office, 1994), viii.

18. Frederick M. Wirt, Benjamin Walter, Francine F. Rabinowitz, and Deborah Hensler, *On the City's Rim: Politics and Policy in the City* (Lexington, Massachusetts: D.C. Heath, 1972), 5.

19. Ibid., 7–9.

20. George Sternlieb and James W. Hughes, "The Uncertain Future of the Central City," *Urban Affairs Quarterly* 18 (June 1983): 459.

21. Joel Garreau, *Edge City* (New York: Doubleday, 1988), 6–7.

22. Kenneth T. Jackson, *Crabgrass Frontier: The Suburbanization of the United States* (New York: Oxford University Press, 1985), 206–207.

23. Wirt, et al., 16.

24. Thomas M. Guterbock, "The Push Hypothesis: Minority Presence, Crime, and Urban Deconcentration," in *The Changing Face of the Suburbs,* ed. Barry Schwartz (Chicago: University of Chicago Press, 1976), 154.

25. Clarence J. Wurdock, "Neighborhood Racial Transition: A Study of the Role of White Flight," *Urban Affairs Quarterly* 17 (September 1981): 75–89.

26. James S. Coleman, S.D. Kelly and J. Moore, *Trends in School Segregation, 1968–73* (Washington, D.C.: Urban Institute, 1975).

27. Anthony Downs, *New Visions for Metropolitan America* (Washington, D.C.: The Brookings Institution, 1994), 67. See also Peter O. Muller, "Suburbanization in the 1970s: Interpreting Population, Socioeconomic and Employment Trends," in *The American Metropolitan System: Present and Future,* ed. Stanley D. Brunn and James O. Wheeler (New York: Halsted Press, 1980), 42–43.

28. Jackson, *Crabgrass Frontier,* 217.

29. John H. Mollenkopf, *The Contested City* (Princeton: Princeton University Press, 1983) 25. See also Downs, *New Visions for Metropolitan America,* 46.

30. Robert C. Wood, *Suburbia: Its People and Their Politics* (Boston: Houghton Mifflin, 1958), 16–17.

31. Sam Roberts, "Yes, a Small Town is Different," *New York Times,* August 27, 1995, Sec. E.

32. U.S. Department of Housing and Urban Development, *The 1978 Survey on the Quality of Life: Data Book* (Washington, D.C.: U.S. Government Printing Office, 1978).

33. Donald C. Dahmann, "Assessments of Neighborhood Quality in Metropolitan America," *Urban Affairs Quarterly* 20 (June 1985): 511–535.

34. Leo F. Schnore, "The Social and Economic Characteristics of American Suburbs," *The Sociological Quarterly* 4, no. 2 (Spring 1963): 122–134.

35. Peter O. Muller, *Contemporary Suburban America* (Englewood Cliffs, New Jersey: Prentice-Hall, 1981), 71–78.

36. Garreau, *Edge Cities,* 153.

37. Thomas J. Phelan and Mark Schneider, "Race, Ethnicity, and Class in American Suburbs," *Urban Affairs Review* 31, no. 5 (May 1996): 661. See also Mark Schneider and Thomas J. Phelan, "Blacks and Jobs: Never the Twain Shall Meet?" *Urban Affairs Quarterly* 26: 299–312.

38. James Barron, "In Nassau, as Inner Suburb Plans Revival," *New York Times,* April 11, 1982.

39. Sternlieb and Hughes, "The Uncertain Future of the Central City," 461. See also Downs, *New Visions for Metropolitan America,* 47–51.

40. Downs, *New Visions for Metropolitan America,* 48.

41. Timothy Egan, "Many Seek Security in Private Communities," *New York Times,* September 3, 1995.

42. Advisory Commission for Intergovernmental Relations, *Urban America and the Federal System* (Washington, D.C.: U.S. Government Printing Office, 1969), 1.

43. Anthony Downs, *Neighborhoods and Urban Development* (Washington, D.C.: The Brookings Institution, 1981), 125.

44. Anthony Downs, *Opening Up the Suburbs: An Urban Strategy for America* (New Haven: Yale University Press, 1973), 92.

45. Gary Orfield, "Ghettoization and Its Alternatives," in *The New Urban Reality,* ed. Paul E. Peterson (Washington, D.C.: The Brookings Institution, 1985), 163.

46. Ibid.

47. Mark Schneider and John R. Logan, "Fiscal Implications of Class Segregation: Inequalities in the Distribution of Public Goods and Services in Suburban Municipalities," *Urban Affairs Quarterly* 17 (September 1981): 21–36.

48. Wood, *Suburbia,* 12

49. R.L. Bish and V. Ostrom, *Understanding Urban Government: Metropolitan Reform Reconsidered* (Washington, D.C.: American Enterprise Institute, 1973), 24.

50. Sidney Verba and Norman H. Nie, *Participation in America: Political Democracy and Social Equality* (New York: Harper & Row, 1972) 233.

51. Ibid., 236–237.

52. Carmine Scavo, "Patterns of Citizen Participation in Edge and Central Cities," in *Contested Terrain: Power, Politics, and Participation in Suburbia* , ed. Marc L. Silver and Martin Melkonian (Westport, Connecticut: Greenwood Press, 1995), 129.

53. Timothy Egan, "Many Seek Security in Private Communities," *The New York Times,* September 3, 1995, A10.

54. C.M. Tiebout, "A Pure Theory of Local Expenditures," *Journal of Political Economy* 64 (October 1956): 416–424.

55. Oliver P. Williams, "Life Style Values and Political Decentralization in Metropolitan Areas," in *Community Structure and Decision-Making: Comparative Analyses* , ed. Terry N. Clark (San Francisco: Chandler Publishing Company: 1968), 432.

56. Jon C. Teaford, *Post-Suburbia: Government and Politics in the Edge Cities* (Baltimore: Johns Hopkins University Press, 1997), 7.

57. Ibid., 198–200.

58. Matthew A. Crenson, *Neighborhood Politics* (Cambridge, Massachusetts: Harvard University Press, 1983) 170.

59. Wood, *Suburbia,* 197.

60. William B. MacLeay, "Public Participation in the Emerging Suburb of Colchester, Vermont: An Observation," in *Contested Terrain,* ed. Silver and Melkonian, 114–115.

61. Advisory Commission on Intergovernmental Relations, *Governmental Structure, Organization and Planning in Metropolitan Areas* (Washington, D.C.: U.S. Government Printing Office, 1961), 22.

62. Advisory Commission on Intergovernmental Relations, *Substate Regionalism and the Federal System: The Challenge of Local Governmental Reorganization,* Report A–44, vol. III (Washington, D.C.: U.S. Government Printing Office, 1974), 67–68.

63. David C. Ranney, *Planning and Politics in the Metropolis* (Columbus, Ohio: Merrill, 1969), 104.

64. Patricia S. Atkins and Laura Wilson-Gentry, "An Etiquette for the 1990s Regional Council," *National Civic Review* 81 (1992): 466–487.

65. Oliver P. Williams, *Metropolitan Political Analysis: A Social Access Approach* (New York: Free Press, 1971), 86–93.

66. Comments to authors by Professor Tim Mead, University of North Carolina at Charlotte, in review, summer 1997.

67. Stuart A. MacCorkle, *Municipal Annexation in Texas* (Austin: University of Texas Press, 1965), 28–36.

68. Arnold Fleischman, "Sunbelt Boosterism: The Politics of Postwar Growth and Annexation in San Antonio," in *The Rise of the Sunbelt Cities,* ed. David C. Perry and Alfred J. Watkins (Beverly Hills, California: Sage, *Urban Affairs Annual Review Series* 14 (1977), 151–168.

69. Peter Muller, "Suburbanization in the 1970s," in *The American Metropolitan System,* ed. Brunn and Wheeler, 39.

70. Roscoe C. Martin, *Metropolis in Transition: Local Government Adaptation to Changing Urban Needs* (Washington, D.C.: U.S. Government Printing Office, 1963), 10.

71. Robert A. Caro, *The Power Broker: Robert Moses and the Fall of New York* (New York: Knopf, 1974).

72. Ibid., 16.

73. Ibid., 18.

74. Ibid., 318.

75. Allan D. Wallis, "Inventing Regionalism: The First Two Waves," *National Civic Review* 83 (Spring–Summer 1994): 170–171.

76. Teaford, *Post-Suburbia,* 6–7.

77. Brett W. Hawkins, *Nashville Metro: The Politics of City-County Consolidation* (Nashville, Tennessee: Vanderbilt University Press, 1966); Daniel R. Grant, "Urban and Suburban Nashville: A Case Study in Metropolitanism," *The Journal of Politics* 17 (February 1955): 82–99; William C. Havard, Jr. and Floyd C. Corty, *Rural-Urban Consolidation: The Merger of Governments in the Baton Rouge Area* (Baton Rouge: Louisiana State University Press, 1964); Melvin Mogulof, *Five Metropolitan Governments* (Washington D.C.: Urban Institute, 1973); Daniel R. Grant, "Metropolis and Professional Political Leadership: The Case of Nashville," *Annals of the American Academy of the Political and Social Science* 353 (May 1964), 72–83; John M. DeGrove, "The City of Jacksonville: Consolidation in Action," in Advisory Commission on Intergovernmental Relations, *Regional Governance: Promise and Performance–Case Studies,* Report A-41, vol. II: 17–25.

78. C. James Owen and York Willbern, *Governing Metropolitan Indianapolis: The Politics of Unigovernment* (Berkeley: University of California Press, 1985), xviii–xxxv.

79. Vincent L. Marano, "City–County Consolidation Reform, Regionalism, Referenda and Requiem," *Western Political Quarterly* 32 (December 1979): 411.

80. David R. Grant "Metro's Three Faces," *National Civic Review* 55 (June 1966): 317–324.

81. Irving G. McNayre, "Recommendations for Unified Government in Dade County," in *Government of the Metropolis: Selected Readings,* ed. Joseph F. Zimmerman (New York: Holt, Rinehart & Winston, 1968), 191–199.

82. Mark Schneider and Kee Ok Park, "Metropolitan Counties as Service Delivery Agents: The Still Forgotten Governments," *Public Administration Review* 49 (July–August 1989): 350.

83. Advisory Commission, *Governmental Structure, Organization and Planning in Metropolitan Areas*, 30–31.

84. William Johnson and John J. Harrigan, "Innovation by Increments: The Twin Cities as a Case Study in Metropolitan Reform," *Western Political Quarterly* 31 (June 1978): 208–218.

85. John J. Harrigan and William C. Johnson, "Political Stress and Metropolitan Governance: The Twin Cities Experience." Paper presented at the 1986 Annual Meeting of the American Political Science Association, Washington, D.C., August 31, 1986.

86. Oliver P. Williams, Harold Herman, Charles S. Liebman, and Thomas R. Dye, *Suburban Differences and Metropolitan Policies: A Philadelphia Story* (Philadelphia: University of Pennsylvania Press, 1965), 308.

87. Patricia Florestano and Laura Wilson-Gentry, "The Acceptability of Regionalism in Solving State and Local Problems," *Spectrum: The Journal of State Government* 67 (Summer 1994): 26.

88. Robert W. Marans and Willard Rogers, "Toward an Understanding of Community Satisfaction," in *Metropolitan America in Contemporary Perspective*, ed. Amos H. Hawley and Vincent P. Rock (New York: John Wiley, 1975), 319.

89. "Gallup Poll Finds 48% Prefer Small Towns or Rural Areas," *New York Times*, March 24, 1985. See also, U.S. Department of Housing and Urban Development, *The 1978 HUD Survey on the Quality of Community Life: A Data Book* (Washington, D.C.: U.S. Government Printing Office, 1978), 554.

90. Donald F. Norris, "Killing a COG: The Death and Reincarnation of the Baltimore Regional Council of Governments," *Journal of Urban Affairs* 16 (1994): 166.

91. Mark Schneider, "The Market for Local Economic Development: The Growth of Suburban Retail Trade, 1972–1982," *Urban Affairs Quarterly* 22 (September 1986): 24–41.

92 See, for example, L.C. Ledebur and W.R. Barnes, *Local Economies* (Washington D.C.: National League of Cities, 1994); H.V. Savitch, D. Collins, D. Sanders, and J.P. Markham, "Ties that Bind: Central Cities, Suburbs, and the New Metropolitan Region," *Economic Development Quarterly* 7, no. 4 (1993): 341–457.

93. L.C. Ledebur and W.R. Barnes, *Metropolitan Disparities and Economic Growth: City Distress and the Need for a Federal Local Growth Package* (Washington, D.C.: National League of Cities), 5. For a contrary view, see Edward W. Hill, Harold L. Wolman, and Coit Cook Ford III, "Can Suburbs Survive without Their Central Cities?" *Urban Affairs Review* 31 (November 1995): 147–274.

CHAPTER 10

Financing the City

Federal, State, and Local Roles

Fragmentation within the metropolitan area creates great difficulty for communities. The last chapter focused on *horizontal* fragmentation, that is, the multiplicity of relatively co-equal governments within the metropolitan area. This chapter will look at *vertical* fragmentation. As a result of our federal system of government, various levels—national, state, and local—have overlapping roles in the metropolitan area. Since local government is closest to the people, many believe it bears the greatest responsibility for meeting our most basic needs. Former President Reagan observed that "Americans live at the local level" and "it is at the local level that problems occur."[1]

Elaine Sharpe has argued that despite the traditional American ethic of individualism and self-reliance, many urban problems engender a belief among the citizenry in "quality services by right." This local entitlement ethic often leads to broad expectations for local government. "Rather than militating against the translation of problems into demands, this ethic encourages the politicization of problems, perhaps by heightening sensitivity to the problems of daily living."[2]

Unfortunately, local governments have limited financial resources to respond to citizen demands and limited control over what is available. As a result, conflict arises among differing interests. Budgets reflect the winners and the losers in those conflicts. City budgets establish government priorities. Authorized programs are meaningless without the money to implement them. Statements of concern are no more than rhetoric without the money to respond to the issues. Conflicts among urban interests are almost always over budget allocations. Municipal employee unions want higher salaries; business wants support for economic development; the poor want more or better jobs.

Some observers have argued that fiscal constraints and the need to maximize fiscal well-being of the community make citizen control impossible.[3] Local governments want to attract citizens and businesses that will add to their tax base. Demands from those citizens and businesses will likely be accorded a place on the government agenda. Officials often see demands from citizens who seek additional services or the redistribution of resources as a threat to the tax base, and such demands often are kept off the agenda. But political leaders also need to assemble an electoral coalition and can be forced to alter budget priorities to attract the votes of major urban groups.

Groups that want to alter the budgetary agenda must deal with the budget process, which is complex. Many decisions must be made about not only where the money will go, but also about where the money will come from. The expertise of budget specialists may mean that they exercise substantial control over budgetary issues. Such specialists are not directly accountable to the public, further complicating the citizen attempts to influence the most important decisions of local governments.

Limited Government

Local governments are formally limited by the state laws that establish their scope of activity and their access to resources. They are required to deliver some services under mandates from the state but restricted from providing others. States also limit local governments' ability to tax. A variety of incentives also encourages local governments to keep taxes low to satisfy businesses and homeowners, providing informal constraints. If tax rates are not competitive with neighboring jurisdictions, businesses and residents may flee. These limits to local resources have forced local governments to rely on state and national governments for assistance. This creates a dependency relationship that puts local government in a weak position. Resources will be made available, if the community plays by certain rules established by states and the federal government.

Traditional anti-urban bias contributes to the subordinate position of governments in the metropolis. Initially, local governments had broad authority. In Colonial America, it was relatively common for local communities to manage their own affairs. Colonial towns and colonies were virtually synonymous.[4] Following the British tradition, municipalities often regulated trade.

It was not until after the Revolutionary War that the . . . [state legislatures] began to enforce claims of sovereignty and plenary powers over matters of local concern. In the new United States, the earlier idea that local communities should be left alone as much as possible all but disappeared.[5]

The growing cities were viewed as a threat by rural residents, who feared domination by urban dwellers. The influx of newcomers to the city created increasing apprehension. The rural populace "foresaw mobs of immigrants, foreigners, Catholics, and poor people taking over the whole nation unless steps were taken to make sure cities were kept in their place."[6] The solution was to increase the control of state governments over the cities. Although the newcomers could potentially control cities because of their numbers, they lacked the numbers to control state governments. By removing power from the cities, the "rabble" was, in essence, rendered politically powerless.

This illustrates a basic principle of political power in the American system with its multilevel government. What level of government is responsible for policy has a substantial effect on determining who will win in disputes concerning that policy. Interests that could control the policy at one level of government may lose control if responsibility shifts to another level. Thus, arguments over what government level should control policy areas are frequently arguments over who should win in that policy area.[7] This chapter will examine the shift of responsibility from urban areas to the state and federal governments and the resultant decline in local government autonomy.

Numerous procedures were used to shift power from urban areas to states. For instance, states took steps to limit urban representation in state legislatures. Maine and Louisiana placed limits on the number urban legislators and cities got fewer representative than they would otherwise have been entitled to. Ten-

nessee took another tack to assure rural supremacy in the state legislature. Under the
state constitution, reapportionment was required every 10 years. Despite that mandate,
no reapportionment had occurred in 60 years
prior to the U.S. Supreme Court decision in
Baker v. Carr in 1962. Thus, between 1900 and
1960, while the cities of Tennessee grew and
the rural areas lost population, the distribution of representation remained fixed at the
1900 level. The Supreme Court, which had
previously refused to interfere with apportionment issues, ruled in *Baker v. Carr* that
federal courts have jurisdiction in matters of
malapportionment. This led to many challenges in other states that resulted in all citizens gaining more equal representation.

States (with the exception of Nebraska,
which has a unicameral, or one-house, legislature) had also followed the national legislative
model, with one house apportioned by population and the other with equal representation
for each electoral district. In *Reynolds v. Sims*
(1964), the U.S. Supreme Court held that
both state legislative houses must be apportioned on the basis of population. Chief Justice Earl Warren wrote, "Legislators represent
people, not trees or acres. Legislators are
elected by voters, not farms or cities or economic interests. . . . To the extent that a citizen's
right to vote is debased, he is that much less a
citizen. The weight of a citizen's vote cannot
be made to depend on where he lives."[8] Unfortunately for the center cities, they had already lost their population dominance to the
suburbs. Despite reapportionment, cities remained in the minority as rural–suburban
coalitions could dominate the legislature.
Thus, center cities, which were short-changed
because of malapportionment in the past, remained at a disadvantage in obtaining state
resources by the time reapportionment was
mandated.

In addition to "rigging" the state legislature to limit representation for the urban citizen, state legislatures and governors were

often directly responsible for making what
could be considered local decisions. For instance, decisions about paving streets, assigning sewer contracts, buying park land, and
running police departments were often made
at the state level.[9]

Although in the 1960s courts assisted the
urban citizen, courts at all levels of government have historically limited the role of local
government. As the last chapter pointed out,
Dillon's Rule legally established the total dependence of local government on the state.[10]
Also, the supremacy clause of the Constitution makes local government actions subject
to review by the federal court system.

In addition to the formal limits on local
governments, there are also informal limits.
The competition among municipalities limits
the range of options available to local communities. If taxes are raised or services decline, communities may lose resources to their
neighbors. People and companies "may vote
with their feet" and leave.

When those informal limits resulting from
competition are joined to formal limits on local government authority to borrow and tax,
the result is that poor communities stay poor
unless intergovernmental transfers are made.
Even rich local governments seldom have resources to meet their residents' service demands. The dependence of local governments
on other levels of government affects the allocation of resources at the local level because
the government level that transfers the funds
can determine how the monies will be used.
Local governments may only be able to use
the money to make specific expenditures and
may need to augment the funds with their
own resources. This may mean taking resources from other policy areas, thus the transferred funds are affecting the policy agenda.

Given scarce resources, Paul Peterson argues that the best interest of the city is served
by providing policies that "maintain or enhance the economic position, social prestige, or
political power of the city, taken as a whole."[11]

BOX 10–1

The Philadelphia Story

Box 8–1, in Chapter 8 (on page 208), introduced Edward Rendell, a popular mayor of Philadelphia credited with saving the city. He took office in a city with a $200-million deficit and balanced the budget within 18 months without raising taxes. The residents of the city were pleased enough to re-elect him with 70 percent of the vote. Other mayors such as Rudolph Giuliani of New York look to him as a role model.

One commentator, however, thinks that Rendell does not deserve all the credit he is getting for saving the city. In an article in the *New Republic,* Stephen Glass points out that the city's budget was balanced through state intervention that occurred before Rendell took office. The state allowed a third party to issue bonds and then lend money to the city. In addition, to allow the bonds to be issued, the city was required to impose a 1 percent sales tax. That means that although Rendell did not raise taxes, he benefited from the additional taxes imposed before he took office.

The source of Philadelphia's troubles is the loss of jobs. The city has lost 250,000 factory jobs in the last 25 years. Unfortunately, more than 50,000 jobs have been lost since Rendell became mayor.

To address the job loss, Rendell has indicated that he wants Philadelphia to become the country's number one tourist attraction. He wants the state legislature to approve riverboat gambling. Without the gambling revenue, by Rendell's own figures, the city will have a budget deficit of $58 million by 2001. The legislature, however, is unlikely to approve the gambling proposal. The odds of Philadelphia becoming the number one tourist attraction are also not good. Tourism increased 18 percent under the previous mayor but has dropped to 11 percent under Rendell.

Although Philadelphia's center city has benefited from some glitzy new development like the Liberty City Mall attached to a new Ritz Carlton Hotel, many of Philadelphia's neighborhoods are crumbling. Even once solid South Philadelphia, where generations of Italian-Americans lived, is unraveling due to the paucity of jobs.

While Rendell has given hope and inspiration to many residents, he has not eliminated the problems of urban government in the twentieth century.

Source: Adapted from Stephen Glass, "Philadelphia Story," *The New Republic,* May 13, 1996.

Over time, he argues that policies will be limited to those that can be shown to improve economic prosperity. Peterson calls these policies, which include such things as highways and urban renewal, *developmental policies.* Even with limited fiscal capacity, local government will allocate funds in these areas because they aid business and attract upper-income families.

Other policies, such as welfare, old age assistance, and programs to help the needy, he labels *redistributive policies.* Because these programs do not enhance the economic prosperity of the city as a whole, local governments are reluctant to spend their resources for them and look to other levels of government.[12] Unlike developmental policies, spending for redistributive programs is directly related to fiscal capacity. Hence poor cities allocate few resources to redistributive policies and become dependent on other levels of government.* Recent federal cutbacks in certain redistributive programs such as Aid to Families with Dependent Children (AFDC), which has been turned over to the states, will create a challenge for cities and states and the poor within them. These changes will be discussed in Chapter 14.

Martin Shefter takes Peterson's argument one step further. He argues that city politics can be seen as a "delicate juggling act," with elected officials attempting to find policies that are acceptable compromises among the major interests in the city.[13] Citizens have influence over the policy agenda because elected officials are often pushed by the search for votes to increase expenditures and spread benefits more widely among the population. But, the result is often fiscal stress, and the reaction limits the impact of citizens. When fiscal stress occurs

> . . . fiscal discipline is imposed upon the local government by the municipal bond-rating agencies and the public capital market, and by the threat that if the market closes to the city, political forces allied with local business elites may be able to wage a successful reform campaign and gain control of City Hall. Such threats provide the city's politicians and public officials with a strong incentive to reach an accord with business and to pursue fiscal policies that are acceptable both to it and to participants in the public capital market.[14]

As a result, those who control the capital and credit of the cities establish the parameters of urban policy, thus limiting the influence of other interests. The "Philadelphia Story" in Box 10–1 is an example of the impotence of local government officials in plotting their own fiscal destiny.

Evolution of Intergovernmental Relations (IGR)

Our Constitution recognizes two levels of government, national and state, with cities as creatures of the state. The federal system provides the context for intergovernmental relations. Deil Wright defines five main aspects of intergovernmental relations:

1. It involves multiple governmental units.
2. It represents officials' actions and attitudes.
3. It involves regularized interactions among officials.
4. It includes all public officials–elected and appointed.
5. It has a policy focus–the core of which is fiscal.[15]

Because of these factors, intergovernmental relations entail interdependence, complexity, and bargaining among governments and officials.[16] Over time, the interpretation of federalism has changed, resulting in increased intergovernmental cooperation and activity. The evolution of intergovernmental relations involves a series of *overlapping* epochs (see Table 10–1 on page 258) that may be categorized as: (1) dual federalism; (2) cooperative federalism; (3) creative federalism; (4) competitive federalism; and (5) new federalism. The epochs overlap because, as changes in philosophy herald a new era, vestiges of the old ideology are not immediately extinguished.

Dual Federalism (1789–1937)

Dual federalism refers to a period when there was a relatively clear delineation of authority between the national and state governments. Morton Grodzins makes an analogy to a layer cake in describing the authority of each government with each "layer" being distinct and

---

*For a discussion of policy issues see Chapters 12–14.

TABLE 10–1

Epochs of Federalism

Dual federalism	1789–1937
Cooperative federalism	1933–1962
Creative federalism	1960–1968
Competitive federalism	1965–1980
New federalism	1972–Present

separate from the others.[17] The proper scope of authority often developed out of conflict between the states and the national government. The courts firmly established national supremacy in many areas and limited state authority.

Federal supremacy was established by broadly interpreting Article I, Section 8, the "necessary and proper" clause of the Constitution, which allowed the national government to pursue policies not specifically enumerated but "necessary and proper" to accomplish the purposes expected of the national government.

In *McCulloch v. Maryland* (1819), the Supreme Court ruled that states could not tax institutions of the national government, arguing that "the power to tax is the power to destroy."[18] At the same time, it affirmed the right of the national government to establish a national bank as "necessary and proper" to regulate commerce.

The Tenth Amendment to the Constitution "reserved" certain powers to the states and the people of those states. These did not include much more extensive powers, which were "prohibited" to the states. The courts tended to interpret narrowly what was reserved to the states. Some powers reserved to the states include public education, transportation, and public safety or police powers.[19]

When states attempted to exercise their power to protect the safety of their citizens from unhealthy and exploitative conditions,

they ran into difficulty with the Supreme Court. For instance, laws establishing maximum working hours, setting minimum wages, and limiting child labor were deemed to be unconstitutional.[20] The states were thus prevented from addressing some of the major problems infecting their growing cities because the courts limited their authority. Meanwhile, the federal government chose not to act.

The relationship between states and the federal government was not entirely antagonistic during this period nor was there the complete separation between federal and state action. In reality, the relationship between the states and the national government was not as distinct as dual federalism would imply. Dual federalism underplays the significance of local and national relations during this period. As early as the Northwest Ordinance of 1787, the national government used its resources to influence state policy by providing land grants for public schools. During the early part of this period, communities often lobbied Congress for assistance with local projects.

Congress willingly responded. In 1811 President James Madison signed into law an appropriation to build a national road from Cumberland, Maryland, to Wheeling, in what was to become West Virginia. While Congress was eager to increase aid for state and local projects, Presidents Madison and James Monroe believed that this went beyond the Constitutional powers of the federal government. It was not until the 1850s that the federal government again became a willing partner. When St. Louis and Chicago were battling for supremacy in the Midwest, Chicago was aided in gaining ascendence by federal assistance in the form of a land grant to build a railroad from Chicago to the Gulf of Mexico, by mail subsidies, and by the building of federal installations.[21]

The post–Civil War era witnessed a decline in the importance of federal action for cities. The national government, an active if not visible participant in the town-building that was a feature of the antebellum period, stood on the sidelines as the modern metropolis began to emerge toward the end of the nineteenth century.[22]

The relationship between cities and the national government changed for two major reasons. First, the states asserted their authority by such actions as withdrawing city charters (Memphis, 1879) and replacing locally elected officials with state appointees (Pennsylvania, 1901). Second, the attitude toward the national government changed. In the developmental stage, cities sought outside aid to compete with other municipalities. As cities grew however, they sought to provide their own amenities. "Fat profits could be made from the provision of many municipal services; the opportunities for graft were endless."[23]

Shortly before the Great Depression, President Calvin Coolidge supported dual federalism, reaffirming the national government's desire to remain aloof from local affairs. In his 1925 State of the Union Address, Coolidge pointed out that, "the greatest solicitude should be exercised to prevent any encroachment upon the states or their various political subdivisions."[24]

There was not a neat division of powers between the state and federal governments and there were areas of cooperation. Conflicts often arose because the boundaries of government and the rights of the people were being tested. Major change in intergovernmental relations occurred during the Great Depression when severe economic stress caused many to question the limits on government imposed by the old laissez-faire economic philosophy and the antagonistic relations between state and federal governments.

Cooperative Federalism (1933–1962)

The new era of federalism that was born during the Great Depression is often labeled as cooperative federalism because it heralded an era of collaboration between levels of government. It also represented the first major step in the nationalization of urban policy.

In actuality, the idea of partnership between levels of government has roots in the land grants and even some monetary grants that occurred in the nineteenth century. Cooperation increased when several grants were created between 1914 and 1921 in areas such as highways, vocational education, and maternal and child health care.

The Great Depression solidified the shift in attitude about the role of government in society and the need for intergovernmental cooperation. No longer were just immigrants and African-Americans unable to find jobs, adequate housing, or other necessities of life. When the middle class was affected, "through no fault of their own," it was deemed legitimate for government to act. State and local governments lacked resources without national financial aid. "By late 1932, 600 urban centers had defaulted on various kinds of payments, including Detroit, Chicago and Philadelphia."[25]

Two factors allowed the national government to respond. First, the Sixteenth Amendment established the income tax, which provided resources that the national government could distribute to state and local governments through grants. Second, the Supreme Court in *U.S. v. Butler* (1936), established the broad-based power of the national government to spend for the "general welfare."

Cooperative federalism is characterized by three major initiatives: (1) the expansion of federal grant-in-aid programs, (2) the development of national planning, and (3) the use of tax credits, whereby taxes that are paid to the federal government are returned to the states for use in federally approved programs, such as unemployment compensation.[26] The federalism during this era often is referred to as a "marble cake" to indicate the mixing of functions and cooperation between the levels of government.

Creative Federalism (1960–1968)

Creative federalism is marked by a great expansion of grant-in-aid programs. In 1960, national government transfers made up 12 percent of state and local revenues. By 1968 the national share was 23 percent.[27] Prior to 1958, there were approximately 40 major grant programs costing about $4.9 billion. By 1970, there were more than 160 major programs, costing $23.9 billion.[28] In that same period, state aid to local governments increased from $8 billion to $28.9 billion.

This period is dubbed "creative" primarily because of the new initiatives and approaches that occurred. One major change was that grants went not only to general government entities but also to nonprofit groups, such as community action agencies. This was the period of the broad-based "War on Poverty" that sought coordination across many policy areas and also required citizen involvement in planning local programs. The influx of funds and programs increased local dependency, and the distribution to private groups further fragmented urban government authority.

The growing federal role changed the rules of the political game and, in so doing, affected winners and losers in the political process. Because federal mandates required that lower-class and minority interests be included in local decision making, these groups

enjoyed new power and were able to gain new material rewards. Their demands, often ignored in the past, had to be included on the urban agenda. At the national level, securing aid to minorities became a moral crusade that emphasized, at least initially, a sharing of resources and power.

Competitive Federalism (1965–1980)

Several contradictory trends emerged in the competitive federalism phase, as changes in government programs and approaches led to both tensions and programs to reduce tensions. The result was increased competition among executive leaders, program professionals, and specialists in different program areas. Three trends led to increased tensions. First, the War on Poverty attempted to foster economic opportunity by establishing community action agencies. These agencies often organized the poor, and, rather than working with the existing system to share power, they challenged the political leadership. Second, "white flight" to the suburbs led to escalating racial polarization, with African-Americans increasingly setting the agenda in the center cities and whites controlling the suburban communities. Finally, the Nixon Administration sought the elimination of many grant programs through reduced funding, consolidation, and when all else failed, **impoundment**, that is, the withholding of funds.[29]

Attempts were made to reduce tensions by fostering intergovernmental cooperation. At the local level, the federal government sought interlocal cooperation through A-95 reviews, which established a coordination requirement for communities seeking federal funds. At the state level, efforts were made to help local communities through increasing services and state aid. Washington fostered federal programs such as the Intergovernmental Personnel Act, which led to cooperative personnel exchanges between governments.[30] Also, programmatic cutbacks notwithstanding, the number of grant programs grew to 539 by 1981.[31]

These programs mitigated the competition between levels of government, but two new conflicts emerged. The first was the conflict between elected officials, or generalists, and the bureaucratic experts, or program professionals at all levels. Elected officials at all levels of government are represented by professional organizations that are called public interest groups (PIGS). Those organizations are depicted in Figure 10–1 as the three horizontal bars, one each for the national, state, and local levels of government. They are pitted against the professional bureaucrats who implement policies in specific program areas, such as welfare or higher education. Those

bureaucrats are depicted in Figure 10–1 as the vertical bars.

The generalists had problems coordinating the array of programs. Federal programs were controlled by the professionals. If governments were to participate, the elected officials had to play by rules established by the federal bureaucrats. Decisions were made outside the state and local legislatures in a variety of agencies in which few elected officials and fewer citizens could effectively participate.

The second conflict was over finances and occurred among professionals at all levels. Professionals in one policy area tried to expand the scope of their authority and resources at the expense of other professionals. If poverty was a problem, for instance, educa-

FIGURE 10–1

Picket Fence Federalism

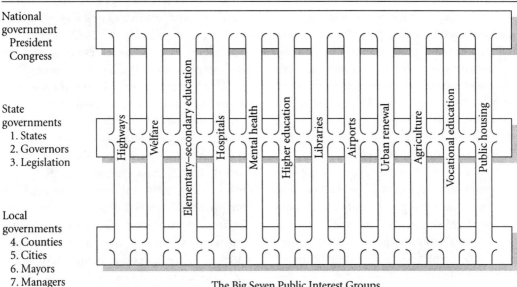

The Big Seven Public Interest Groups

1. Council of State Governments
2. National Governors' Association
3. National Conference of State Legislatures
4. National Association of County Officials
5. National League of Cities
6. U.S. Conference of Mayors
7. International City Management Association

Source: Deil S. Wright, *Understanding Intergovernmental Relations,* 3rd ed. (Pacific Grove, California: Brooks/Cole, 1988), 83.

tors would argue that expanding educational programs could decrease poverty while health professionals would point out the relationship between poverty and poor health and demand more money. These rivalries have led some to call the resultant situation as "vertical functional autocracies," or the picket fence federalism pictured in Figure 10–1. Control by administrative officials who are experts and not subject to election weakened democratic accountability.

New Federalism (1972–Present)

Aspects of competitive federalism are still with us. Federal aid to states and localities continues and the professional bureaucrats still play an important role. Nevertheless, the current era has often been labeled New Federalism. It began under President Nixon with changes in grant programs. Narrow program grants were repackaged as **block grants**, which transfer money from the national government with fewer restrictions governing how state and local governments could spend it. **Federal revenue sharing*** provided a "guaranteed" income that could be used in virtually any manner the governments desired. This period also marked a slowdown in growth of national fiscal transfers. Under President Nixon, tax collection remained centralized, but program administration was decentralized to maximize local discretion.

New Federalism under President Reagan went much further. In 1982, for the first time in 27 years, national government aid to state and local governments declined. Between 1981 and 1987 grant programs declined from 539 to 409. Some programs were eliminated entirely, while others were consolidated into 9 new block grants. The overall funding level of the block grants represented a 25 percent reduction from the previous grants-in-aid.

Reagan sought to increase state and local responsibility for raising funds and distributing resources. Rather than using federal standards, states were expected to administer programs on the basis of state goals and guidelines. States were running budget surpluses and cutting taxes at a time when the federal government was running record deficits. Thus, part of the rationale behind Reagan's New Federalism was the desire to balance the federal budget. At the same time, there was another clear ideological motive: to "shrink big government in Washington and lessen interference in people's lives. . . . Without stimulative grants-in-aid, the level of state and local activity would drop."[32] In addition, General Revenue Sharing (discussed below) was terminated in 1986. Responsibility shifted from the federal government to the states under the New Federalism, a shift that continues. Such shifting of responsibilities to lower levels of government is now called **devolution**.

A few new block grants and federal transfers have bounced back slightly since the Reagan presidency. By 1993, there were 593 federal grants, 578 categorical and 15 block grants, totaling $206.4 billion.[33] One new block grant created during the Clinton Administration was contained in the 1994 Anti-Crime Act. This bill was designed to provide money for local governments to hire more police. President Clinton had to struggle with a conservative Congress to secure funding. After the Republicans gained control of Congress in the 1994 midterm elections, control over Aid to Families with Dependent Children was transferred to the states, with the federal government providing a block grant. As the welfare package is designed to save the federal government $54.1 billion, the states will presumably have to reduce the number of welfare recipients

---

*Block grants and federal revenue sharing will be discussed in the following section.

or find additional revenues to spend on welfare.

Once again the change in the level of government responsible for providing urban services will probably have an effect on who wins and who loses. The question is whether the states have the resources or the will to help their local communities and whether those communities can help themselves. Prior to federal devolution to the states, the major regions of the country were moving toward parity in personal incomes. Since the Reagan years, a crazy-quilt pattern of disparities between and even within states has emerged.[34]

Revenues

Relationships among the various levels of government have been in flux for over 200 years. At the heart of the intergovernmental relationship is the issue of fiscal transfers. Given limited resources, local governments must depend on other levels of government to provide at least some of the revenues required to support municipal services.

Prior to Reagan's New Federalism, local governments were becoming increasingly dependent on other levels of government for financial resources because of their limited options for raising revenues. Given the fragmented system at the local level, increasing local taxes may be counterproductive because those who can afford to pay taxes can also afford to move to other jurisdictions. This outmigration may depress the local economy and consequently increase the fiscal squeeze.

Local governments have four basic sources of revenue: taxes, user charges, borrowing, and intergovernmental transfers. Figure 10–2 shows revenue trends for the last 10 years, and Table 10–2 (on page 264) summarizes revenue sources.

FIGURE 10–2

Trends in City General Revenue, 1982–1991 (in Billions)

- → Intergovern revenue
- –□– Charges & misc
- –▲– Property taxes
- –✕– Non-property taxes

Source: U.S. Bureau of the Census, *City Government Finances in 1991–92* (Washington, D.C.: U.S. Government Printing Office, 1996), 1; U.S. Bureau of the Census, *City Government Finances in 1988–89* (Washington, D.C.: U.S. Government Printing Office, 1991), 1; U.S. Bureau of the Census, *City Government Finances in 1985–86* (Washington, D.C.: U.S. Government Printing Office, 1988), 1.

Taxes

National and state governments take the "good taxes," leaving local governments to tax what is left. Before looking at specific taxes, let us consider what makes a "good tax." Three criteria are generally used in evaluating taxes: **equity, efficiency,** and **tax overlap,** or coordination. One problem governments have in establishing "good taxes" is that satisfying all these criteria with any one tax is virtually impossible.

Two principles are used to determine equity. The first is based on the **ability-to-pay,** which has two components. The first component, **horizontal equity,** means that all people in the same situation pay the same tax. For example, every family of four with an income of

TABLE 10-2

Summary of Municipal Government Revenue, 1991–92

Item	Amount (Millions of Dollars)	Percentage	Percentage Change from 1990–91
Revenue from all sources	220,048	100	+4.5
Intergovernmental revenue	48,152	28.1	+4.1
Revenue from own sources	171,896	71.9	+6.1
General revenue from own sources	123,466	56.1	+4.6
Taxes	75,486	34.3	+4.5
Charges and miscellaneous general revenue	47,980	21.8	+4.7
Utility revenue	35,168	16.0	+2.8
Liquor store revenue	292	0.1	+8.1
Insurance trust revenue	12,969	5.9	+10.9

Source: U.S. Bureau of the Census, *Government Finances; City Government Finances: 1991–92* (Washington D.C.: U.S. Government Printing Office, 1996), 1.

$30,000 should pay the same income tax. A second component, **vertical equity**, means that unequals should be treated unequally. Thus, the family of four making $50,000 should be treated differently from the same size family making $30,000. The family earning $50,000 should be able to afford to pay more and should reasonably be expected to do so. For various political and economic reasons, however, **loopholes**, or special provisions, prevent the equity criteria from being met. For example, to encourage families to send children to college, the budget deal negotiated by President Clinton and the Congress in 1997 provides for tax credits up to $1,500 for tuition and related expenses for up to two years of college for families with up to $80,000 in income.

The second principle behind equity is **benefits received**—that is, someone who receives more services than another should pay more. For instance, if you use more water than the next person, it seems fair that you should pay more. While using this principle to arrive at equity seems logical, it is often quite difficult, if only because of tradition. By this standard, a childless couple should not be expected to pay taxes for education. Those with more children in school would pay more than those with fewer. We argue, though, that everyone benefits from an educated citizenry and, therefore, all should pay whether or not they directly benefit by having their children in school. A further problem with the benefits received principle is that the poor may need more government services than the wealthy, but do not have the resources to pay for them. They receive more benefits precisely because they cannot afford to buy the services in the private market.

When arriving at a new tax or increasing an existing tax, governments consider which aspects of equity can and should be met. In addition, they consider the next criterion for evaluating taxes—efficiency. There are two kinds of efficiency: **administrative efficiency** and **economic efficiency**. Administrative efficiency refers to the ease with which a tax can be assessed and collected. From an administrative standpoint, sales taxes are quite efficient. Merchants collect the tax for government based on a table that determines the amount of tax for each purchase. To be economically efficient, a tax should not distort individuals' decisions about consumption and use. For instance, the extent to which high taxes on cigarettes and alcohol inhibit consumption make them economically inefficient or distort the allocation of resources. On the other hand, this may be what was intended. Local governments that impose taxes that encourage citizens to reduce consumption or move to other locations are creating economic inefficiency.

The final criterion in determining taxes is tax overlap or coordination. There are two problems of overlap: horizontal and vertical. **Horizontal overlap** occurs when individuals and businesses are taxed simultaneously by various jurisdictions at the same level of government. **Vertical overlap** occurs when various levels of government tax the same income base. For instance, many urban dwellers pay federal, state, and city income tax. Ideally, governments should coordinate so that the different levels tax different portions of a person's wealth. Indeed, there is a great deal of tax specialization in the United States. Although there is some overlap, the federal government relies most heavily on income taxes to raise tax revenues, states rely primarily on the sales tax, and local governments rely primarily on the property tax.

In addition, there are three tax structures: **progressive**, **regressive**, and **proportional**. A progressive tax is one where higher-income people pay a larger percentage of their incomes in tax than lower-income people. This structure is based on the ability-to-pay principle. People with more money can afford to part with more of it. It is also based on the economic concept of **marginal utility**. All money holds a high value for those who have low incomes as it all may be needed for the necessities of life. As available income rises, each additional dollar is not as crucial and, therefore, an increasing tax rate is not as onerous. The federal income tax structure is an example.

A regressive tax is the opposite; it taxes those with lower incomes at a higher percentage than those with higher incomes. For example, Social Security tax does not tax all income. Only wages are taxed and then only up to a certain level. Hence the working poor pay Social Security tax on 100 percent of their income, while the wealthy pay tax only up to a certain income limit and pay no Social Security tax on other income such as interest and investments. This is justified on the basis of benefits received because the poor receive proportionally more than they put in.

With the proportional tax, everyone pays the same proportion. Such a tax is based on horizontal equity and benefits received principles. The sales tax is an example. A $10,000 wage earner and a millionaire both pay the same tax when purchasing a $25 radio. Proponents of a flat tax want to change the federal income tax from a progressive tax to a proportional one.

Classifying a particular tax into one of the three types above can be difficult because the actual incidence of the tax may be quite different from the structure (see Table 10–3 on page 266). For example, the federal income tax, although designed to be progressive, tends to become less so as one moves up the economic ladder because of various loopholes that enable people to avoid taxation. Such loopholes are also known as **tax expenditures**, meaning that they are tax income forgone by government. As with the example of tuition tax credits mentioned above, many of these loopholes, or tax expenditures, have public purposes. Another example is the home mortgage interest deduction that helps individuals buy a house. The government is, in effect, subsidizing the interest cost, but at the same time the deduction provides many construction jobs, manufacturing and sales jobs, and helps bankers and developers. One person's loophole is another's incentive.

The tax reform adopted in 1986 increased the progressiveness of federal taxes. Some tax expenditures were scaled back. For instance, non-mortgage interest charges are now not tax de-

TABLE 10–3

Taxes

	Structure	Incidence
Federal income tax	Progressive	Only slightly progressive because of loopholes
Local income tax	Usually proportional	Generally regressive because usually taxes only wages and provides no exemptions or deductions
Sales tax	Proportional	Generally regressive though exemptions make it less so
Property tax	Proportional	Unclear

ductible. In the past, because of loopholes, those with very high incomes paid little more than some more moderate earners. The 1997 budget agreement created more tax loopholes, many aimed at those with middle and upper incomes.

Sales taxes, which are structured so that all who purchase a commodity pay the same tax, have a regressive impact. Because it taxes consumption and the poor spend a greater proportion of their income than the rich, the proportion of the poor person's income taxed is greater than that of the rich person. Some states and localities have attempted to address this problem by exempting from sales tax such things as food, clothing, and medicine. This raises questions such as whether soda is food. To get around these problems a **sales tax credit** given on income taxes may be more equitable.[35] With a sales tax credit, individuals can deduct the amount of money they have paid for sales taxes from the amount of taxes they pay on their incomes.

The last major tax is the backbone of locally raised tax revenue—the property tax. Some states tax personal property such as motor vehicles, jewelry, stocks, but administrative efficiency problems have caused personal property taxes to fall out of favor. Real property (that is, land and improvements) is what is generally meant when discussing property tax. Property is usually assessed

(valued) by an appraiser. The assessed valuation is supposed to represent the market value. Then a mill levy is charged based upon the appraisal. A mill is .001 of $1. In some states the mill levy is applied only to a portion of the total valuation.

The overall community-assessed valuation is important to government because states generally limit the mill rate. As a result, the only way tax revenues can increase is by increasing the tax base. In addition, the amount of money local governments can borrow in the form of guaranteed debt (that is, debt backed by the "full faith and credit" of the community) is based on the total community tax base.

Structurally, the property tax is proportional because all property owners pay the same mill levy. The incidence, however, has traditionally been considered to be regressive for several reasons. First, owners usually include the amount of property tax they must pay when calculating the rent they will charge. That means renters pay the taxes for owners through their rent payments, but unlike the owners the renters cannot deduct that money from their federal income taxes. In addition, the poor are often required to spend a greater proportion of their income for housing and are therefore paying taxes on a greater proportion of their total resources. They are also less likely to be owners. Further, the property tax burdens the elderly disproportionately because most of their wealth may be in their home and they may no longer be earning income.

Although the property tax affects some residents negatively, more recent studies indicate that its incidence is at least proportional, if not progressive.[36] States and localities have attempted to mitigate problems caused for the poor and elderly by property taxes with "circuit breakers" and homestead exemptions. All states and the District of Columbia have one or both of these mechanisms.[37] With a circuit breaker, if taxes exceed a certain percentage of an individual's income, the state will pay the locality the difference between the tax rate and what the person can afford. With homestead exemptions, the locality excludes a certain percentage of the valuation of the home from taxation.

Aside from the fact that the property tax may be regressive, other problems make it a less than ideal way to raise revenues. The major problem is that it fails to meet the efficiency criterion discussed above. Administrative efficiency is a problem because assessors must use judgment in determining the value of property. Assessors must be trained and must review the property and its history, and even then the true market value may only be ascertained when property is sold. Because of the difficulty of assessment, reassessment may not be done frequently on properties that are not sold. Thus, the tax burden is shifted to neighborhoods where property turnover is greatest. On the other hand, in declining neighborhoods, landowners may decide to let property be taken by the city because the value may become less than they owe in back taxes. As a result, cities have less taxes coming in and become responsible for owning "slums."

Problems of economic efficiency also arise. Because improvements to property increase its value and, therefore taxes, property owners may be discouraged from making improve-

ments. Further, as local governments compete with each other for business and affluent households, increased property taxes may make a community unattractive. Hence, the property tax becomes counterproductive.

Also, property tax often violates the ability to pay and the benefits received principles because certain "residents" are tax exempt. Government, churches, nonprofit, and education organizations pay no property taxes, yet they place a burden on local governments because they receive services such as police and fire protection. This shifts the burden to the rest of the community. This has been a major problem in places like Boston, where in 1969, 54 percent of real property was tax exempt, and in Washington, D.C., where in 1971, 50 percent of the property was tax exempt. In New York City, in 1970, 35 percent of property was tax exempt; in contrast, in 1973, only 16 percent of the property in Denver was tax exempt.[38] Jonathan Wilson, former chairman of the Council of Urban School Boards, estimated in 1991 that in center cities usually 30 percent or more of the potential tax base is exempt from taxes compared to only 3 percent in the suburbs. Further, more suburbanites benefit from tax-exempt institutions such as private colleges than do city dwellers.[39] Municipal governments will often offer tax exemptions and abatements as a lure to new businesses. This also shifts the tax burden to the other taxpayers.

If the property tax is so problematic, why do local governments rely upon it so heavily? It avoids tax overlap and, in addition, states often preclude the use of other taxes.

> The extreme dependence of local governments on the property tax rests on one ineluctable fact—lack of option. No other tax is available for productive use. Local taxation of income, sales, or business would induce shrinkage in the tax base and, therefore, bring serious injury to the locality. But real property is quite immobile. . . . Work-

ers must reside close to their work; retail outlets must locate close to consumers; manufacturing establishments, once committed, tend to stay put, since even severe property taxes are a modest part of their total costs.[40]

Even under the best conditions, increasing property taxes usually is difficult. Unlike income taxes, which are withheld from pay checks so people never see the money, or sales taxes, which are paid in increments, the property owner receives a yearly tax bill. Because taxes must be paid in a lump sum, their effect is clearly felt. The total bill often includes taxes owed various governmental entities, such as municipalities, counties, and school districts, thus making it difficult for residents to fix responsibility for "high" property taxes. It is easy to see why property taxes have triggered many grass roots efforts aimed at limiting their impact. Studies done by the U.S. Advisory Commission on Intergovernmental Relations indicate that the property tax is the most hated, that is, seen as least fair, by Americans.[41]

In 1978, Proposition 13 in California was a statewide initiated measure that reduced property taxes by 60 percent. This began a series of taxpayer revolts throughout the nation aimed at limiting property taxes and achieving general tax reform. As a result, local communities were left with less revenue, which meant they either had to cut services or find other sources of revenue, such as user fees or transfer payments from other levels of government. Some states, such as California, used state surpluses to help local communities, but those surpluses were not infinite.

In California and in other places, services have been cut back. There are shorter library hours, deferred maintenance, and closed recreation centers. Public employees have been terminated. The public service department in Oakland, California, cut its workforce by 37 percent while its budget declined by 46 per-

cent. At that level of funding, streets could be resurfaced once every 200 years. In California and in some other areas, most of the property tax savings went to business, not to the general public. The property tax limits have also necessitated user charges or fees for services such as swimming pools and zoos, and the imposition of other taxes.

Income and sales taxes are used by some localities. As of 1994, local income taxes were levied in 11 states and local sales taxes in 31.[42] In areas with this tax diversification, the property tax has decreased in significance. These taxes are not widespread, however. Other non–property taxes such as licenses and selective taxes on products such as fuel and utility services are sometimes employed, but they are also problematic. The local income tax has a very limited progressive rate and, in some cases, a flat rate. Often, deductions and exemptions are not allowed. Problems with non–property taxes can be summed up as follows:

> Because of the limited geographic jurisdiction of the governmental units, the distribution of employment and of purchasing is distorted. Decisions of workers, firms, and consumers are altered, impairing efficiency. Compliance costs are high, especially for firms that do business in many taxing jurisdictions. . . . The types of nonproperty taxes in common use do not, moreover, rate highly on grounds of equity. . . . Local levy aggravates and adds to the inequities. . . . Proponents of local nonproperty taxes have, nonetheless, one effective retort to complaints; admitting all the defects, what of the faults of alternative local taxes? Are they greater or smaller?[43]

In all, excluding borrowing, in 1991–92 local taxes accounted for 34.3 percent of local revenues (Table 10–2, on page 264). This percentage is up slightly from 32.3 percent in 1984–85.[44] The property tax has declined in importance as a revenue source for local government. Dependence on the property tax declined from 89.6 percent of tax revenue among all local governments in 1965 to 75.3 percent in 1991. In municipalities, the property tax accounts for 52.1 percent of local tax revenue. School districts receive 97.5 percent, counties receive 74 percent, townships receive 92.8 percent, and special districts receive 69.5 percent of their tax revenues from property taxes. General sales tax accounts for 27.1 percent and income taxes 13.3 percent of municipal revenues.[45] (See Figure 10–3.)

User Charges

In 1991–92 approximately 20.5 percent of local revenues came from utility charges and another 28 percent from charges, fees, and miscellaneous revenues.[46] Many cities are able to provide water, sewage treatment, even electric power because those who use them pay for them. User charges (for example, fees paid to use a service such as a swimming pool or a museum) are based on the benefits received principle. However, sometimes user charges pay for only a portion of the service; the remainder is subsidized by other revenues. Public transportation usually fits into that cat-

egory. The reasoning is that the transit system serves a public purpose and everyone benefits to some extent by lessened street congestion and pollution.

As local budgets tighten, user charges are employed more frequently. For instance, museums that once allowed free access have imposed entrance fees. Of course, as noted earlier, there are logical limits on user charges. If fees are charged for fire protection, for example, the poor may go unprotected. This, in turn, creates a threat to general public safety as fires originating in the homes of the unprotected could, if left unchecked, spread to the homes of the protected.

Public safety is a public, or collective, good. Leaving some people unprotected may endanger all. With such collective goods, user fees are impractical because to exclude some has implications for all. With museum fees, those who do not wish to pay—or even those who cannot pay—do not create any problem to the public as a whole. **Public goods** are generally defined as those with the following characteristics: (1) it is impossible to exclude individuals; (2) one person's use does not diminish the benefits to others; and (3) they are provided to all in equal quantities. These

FIGURE 10–3

Local Tax Sources, by Type of Local Government

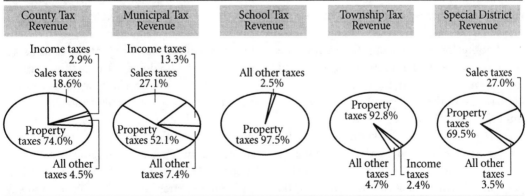

Source: U.S. Advisory Commission on Intergovernmental Relations, *Significant Features of Fiscal Federalism, 1993,* Vol. 2 (Washington, D.C., 1993), 76–77.

types of services (for example, police and fire) are generally not amenable to user fees.

In practice, distinctions between public and private goods often become the subject of political debate. Some communities do charge user fees for fire protection; thus some believe that it is possible to exclude people from that service without substantial public danger. In addition, some observers argue that excluding people from museums threatens society's cultural well being.

Borrowing

A third major source of local revenues is borrowing. Local governments incur two types of debt. The first type is known as **general obligation bonds**. These bonds are guaranteed by the "full faith and credit" of the municipality. This means that in the event of bankruptcy, bond holders would be paid first. The amount of guaranteed debt is limited by state law. Second, local governments can offer various forms of **nonguaranteed debt**, usually at higher interest rates because the risks to lenders are higher.

The interest rate that municipalities offer depends on several factors, but it is generally less than the market rate. Municipal bonds can pay a lower interest rate because federal tax policy exempts interest income from these bonds from federal taxes. Two firms, Moody's Investors Service and Standard and Poor's Corporation, rate bonds based on risk involved; in some cases, low ratings have prevented governments from marketing bonds.[47]

Another factor affecting the interest rate is the bonds' general attractiveness compared to other investments. If, for example, an individual were in the 36 percent tax bracket, any municipal bond paying an interest rate greater than 64 percent of the market rate would deliver a higher total yield than the taxable instrument. A tax-free, 6 percent municipal bond worth $100,000 would yield $6,000 annually. A taxable bond for someone in the 36 percent bracket would have to yield above 9 percent to offer an advantage (9%×$100,000=$9,000); 36 percent tax on $9,000=$3,240. Therefore, the after-tax yield would be $5,760 or $240 less than the 6 percent municipal bond. In fact, any rate higher than 5.76 percent (.09×0.64=0.576) would provide a better after-tax return.

The 1986 Tax Reform, which instituted a "minimum tax" on high-income Americans, made some of their municipal bond interest subject to taxation and has hurt the market for municipal bonds. When federal tax rates are cut, municipal bonds have to increase their yield compared to non–tax-exempt investments to remain attractive. Selling bonds is further complicated by the increasing level of debt. Bonds must be marketed to all taxpayers, not just those in the higher tax brackets. Thus, rates may have to be increased to appeal to those in lower tax brackets. The problems of and costs to local governments in raising revenues increase accordingly. Decreasing federal tax rates, while generally appealing on the surface, often shift the costs to residents in municipalities who have to raise more money to pay off bonds issued at higher interest because the differential return between taxable instruments and tax-exempt bonds has lessened. Even with higher rates, buyers may be difficult to find. Municipalities are often placed in very tenuous positions vis-à-vis the private sector. In an atypical, but by no means unique case, New York City was pushed to the edge of bankruptcy in the 1970s by the so-called "bank boycott."[48] Banks sold off their bond holdings, saturated the market, and refused to underwrite new issues to help the city meet its previous obligations.[49]

General obligation bonds are easier to market since they are guaranteed by the municipality. They are a long-term debt that is incurred primarily to finance capital improvements such as water towers, highway upgrades, and the like.

Nonguaranteed long-term debt generally takes the form of revenue bonds; that means that the bonds will be retired (paid off) by revenues generated by the project. For instance, revenue bonds for a new water treatment plant can be retired by increasing water rates until the bond holders are paid. An increasingly controversial type of municipal bonds is **industrial development bonds** (IDB). IDBs are bonds sold by a city to be used to finance private business development. The idea behind the sale of these bonds is to induce businesses to invest in the city. The city expects to benefit because new jobs will be created, and the only risk involved is that the business might not be able to pay off the bonds. This is not an inconsequential risk, as the State of Pennsylvania and the City of New Stanton found out when the Volkswagen plant they worked so hard to woo closed its doors.

Business gains from IDBs because they get loans at below-market rate because the bonds, sponsored by local governments, are tax exempt. The only sure loser is the federal treasury, which is deprived of taxes because the IDBs are tax exempt. This has led to new limits being imposed on local governments issuing these bonds and on their ability to provide tax-free interest for the investors. Now, no more than 20 percent of the funds may be used for private purposes if the bonds are to maintain their tax-free status.

Local governments also issue nonguaranteed, short-term bonds known as **Tax Anticipation Notes** (TANs), **Revenue Anticipation Notes** (RANs), and **Bond Anticipation Notes** (BANs). These are issued because taxes, intergovernmental transfers, and so on, come in at specific times of the year while governments must pay bills daily. Hence, governments borrow money to pay bills and promise to pay back the lenders when the city receives its expected income.

Because local governments are legally restricted in their ability to raise taxes—and even when they can, they are reluctant to do so—they have stepped up their borrowing,

hoping that increasing intergovernmental transfers or economic development will yield sufficient future income to pay off bond holders. This borrowing has increased the dependency of local governments on the private sector. In 1991–1992, about 33.8 percent of outstanding municipal debt was in the form of long-term "full faith and credit" bonds. An additional 63.9 percent was in long-term nonguaranteed debt, and the remaining 2.2 percent of outstanding debt came from short-term notes. This is little changed from 1984–1985.[50] Total indebtedness of all types of local governments increased from $14.2 billion in 1929 to $598.1 billion (measured in constant dollars) in 1992.[51] This is up markedly from $287.2 billion in 1984–85.[52]

Intergovernmental Transfers

As governmental fragmentation, politics, competition, and state law limit their ability to raise revenues, local governments have come to rely heavily on other levels of government for funds. In 1991–1992, 28.1 percent of revenues for municipal government came from other governments. States contributed the largest portion, 75.2 percent (up from 62.1 percent), the federal government supplied only 16.7 percent (down from 31.6 percent), and local transfers accounted for 8.1 percent.[53] As with all averages, 28.1 percent of municipal revenues masks much diversity. Some fiscally stressed cities such as Newark, New Jersey, and Buffalo, New York, rely on intergovernmental transfers for more than half their revenues. Other local governments, such as counties, school boards, and airport authorities, have even larger portions of their budgets financed through intergovernmental transfers.

Because of recent cutbacks, all types of governments have had to become slightly less dependent on other levels of government. The Advisory Commission on Intergovernmental Relations calculated a dependency index for local government. It noted that, in 1984, other levels of government contributed about 43 cents for every dollar raised locally; state governments contributed 29 cents; and the federal government another 15 cents. State aid as a share of local government revenue peaked in 1975 and federal support as a share of revenue peaked in 1978.[54]

Between 1962 and 1990, federal domestic expenditures increased from 9 percent to 15.5 percent of the Gross National Product. The majority of that growth was in programs to aid those in need, called redistributive policy. Redistributive expenditures increased 214 percent, much of them in transfer payments to state and local governments and direct payments to individuals so they would be able to support themselves. During that same 28-year period, developmental programs, those aimed at assisting state and local governments support their economic well-being, grew only 80 percent. In 1990, the federal government transferred almost twice as much money for redistributive than for developmental programs.[55]

State aid generally comes in two forms, grants-in-aid and tax sharing. **Grants-in-aid** are generally defined as monetary transfers from one level of government to another for a specified purpose with some conditions.[56] **Tax sharing**, done for administrative efficiency, was generally designed for the state to "give back" money collected in each jurisdiction. Sometimes formulas are devised to return monies based on need. In these cases, the distinction between grants-in-aid and tax sharing becomes blurred. In addition to direct financial assistance to local governments, states often reduce fiscal burdens by assuming some services and also by providing technical expertise.

Financial aid from the federal government comes in the form of grants-in-aid. Prior to 1986, the federal government also participated in General Revenue Sharing. Federal grants-in-aid can be categorized in two ways, one based on their distribution, the other on the way the money is spent.[57]

How Distributed	
Formula grant	Project grant

How Spent	
Categorical grant	Block grant

Grants from the federal government are distributed in two ways: formula grants and project grants. The allocation of money under a **formula grant** is nondiscretionary. Money is allocated to recipients on the basis of a specified formula. Governments that receive these grants usually will have to meet certain standards, and sometimes provide some of their own resources or matching funds. All block grants and about one-third of federal grants are based on formulas. The formula varies with each program but often includes such factors as unemployment rate, poverty population, tax effort, as the like. The Job Training Partnership Act and the Work Incentive Program are examples of formula grants.

Unlike formula grants, where the funds are distributed automatically, **project grants** are discretionary. State or local governments must submit project proposals to the federal government; the federal government decides whether or not to fund the project. Project grants usually, though not always, have a matching requirement, meaning that a certain percentage of the project costs (established by the law authorizing the grant) must be borne by the recipient government. For instance, a 60–40 grant means that the federal government will pay 60 percent of project costs and the state or locality pays the remaining 40 percent. A large number of project grants are available in education, such as those for literacy programs; for social services, such as services for the elderly; and for health programs, such as neighborhood health centers.

Federal grants can be spent in two ways: categorical grants and block grants. **Categorical grants** are transfers for very specific purposes, for example, Head Start or urban forestry assistance. Categorical grants-in-aid have been used by the federal government since 1787. By 1930, though, there were still only about 10 categorical grant programs.[58] The Great Depression and the post-war years led to an increase in grants, but there were still only about 132 programs in 1960.[59] Most grants were given for income maintenance and capital improvements such as highways and urban renewal. However, the number of grants increased to 379 by 1967, 109 in 1965 alone.[60] Prior to the 1960s most grants went directly to states for their use or were passed through the states to individuals and local governments or local public authorities. In the 1960s more grants went directly to cities, individuals, and nonprofit organizations. This maze of programs led to increasing criticism of the grant-in-aid process. Among the complaints were grantsmanship, distortion of budgets, coordination problems, and ignoring some problems.[61]

Grantsmanship meant that, rather than using federal funds to aid governments undergoing the most severe fiscal stress, money was going to governments that could afford professionals able to play the game. These governments were often not those with the greatest need.

Grants also distorted budgets in some communities. Sometimes projects that were not really needed were undertaken anyway because of the availability of "free" federal money. Participation in federal programs which require local matching funds, may leave little money to satisfy local needs. Coordination problems occur because the proliferation of grants creates many overlapping grants with overlapping requirements. Administration becomes a nightmare when several grants from various sources are brought together for major projects. Finally, some local problems were ignored because their problems fell outside the boundaries of federal grants or local governments lacked the resources to meet the matching requirements.

These and other problems led local governments to lobby the federal government for a broadening of grant programs and a loosening of requirements. This was congruent with the conservative ideology of Richard Nixon, who was president at that time. The result was the establishment of block grants.

Block grants, which shift the locus of power in establishing state and local priorities from the federal government to state and local governments, are transfers that allow state and local governments broad discretion in using funds within general categories. Examples include the Community Development Block Grant (CDBG) established in 1974 and the Personal Responsibility and Work Opportunity Reconciliation Act of 1996, which began the reform of the welfare system.

> The block grant approach allocates funds mostly by formula, greatly increases the discretion of recipient governments in making program choices, and simplifies the bureaucratic complexities through consolidation of several previously separate urban development-oriented categorical grants.[62]

While block grants have some administrative requirements, they have much greater flexibility. Further, matching funds are usually not required. As of 1993, there were 15 block grant programs, and 578 categorical grants.[63]

General Revenue Sharing (GRS) was the other major transfer from the federal government to local governments. Begun in 1972 under President Nixon, GRS was a strong victory for Nixon and the Public Interest Groups lobby. Two formulas were established based on factors such as poverty population, tax effort, and urbanization. Local governments had great discretion in allocating the money. This represented a great shift of power from the federal to state and local governments. Nonetheless, GRS never accounted for much more than 10 percent of federal aid. The program originally transferred money to states as well as localities but, in 1983, aid was limited to cities and counties. In 1986, the entire program was eliminated as President Reagan continued to shift authority and responsibility to states and localities, which were expected to supply more of their own funds.

Fiscal Crisis

Even during the "good times" with large intergovernmental transfers, many local governments were on the brink of disaster. Dillon's Rule set the precedent for severe legal limits on the ability of city governments to raise revenues. More recently, public initiatives have limited taxing ability. Added to this, of course, was the desire of local officials to keep taxes down and get revenues from other sources. Hope of re-election was one obvious reason, but the fiscal crisis had other, more fundamental reasons.

Local taxes have often reached their legal, if not their practical limits. The property tax revolts have already been mentioned. At a certain point, raising local taxes becomes counterproductive. If taxes go too high in relation to surrounding jurisdictions, people and business will leave. This, in turn, increases the burden on those who remain. As we have seen, those who remain in the center city tend to be less wealthy and even high tax rates yield low revenues.

Government fragmentation in metropolitan areas exacerbates fiscal woes. Individuals and firms may keep the same jobs or markets but move to escape onerous taxes, which creates a fiscal mismatch between needs and resources. Further, those who remain require and demand more services, driving up expenditures.

One observer argues that increasing activity by employee unions has driven up wage costs for local governments. In addition, high rates of inflation in the 1970s fanned the demand for higher salaries and increased other costs for local government.[64] Terry Clark and Lorna Ferguson, however, have argued that while unions have been successful in increasing the salaries of their numbers, the overall cost to the city has remained constant because the number of employees has been reduced.[65]

The population movement to the Sun Belt increased the fiscal squeeze in Frost Belt cities because they had to cope with high rates of unemployment and service demands while the tax base was eroding. Federal transfers, which went disproportionately to the Sun Belt for many years, only worsened the problem. While some Frost Belt cities, such as Boston, attracted high-tech industries, many cities faced stress because they have an old, declining industrial base. It is unlikely that the steel industry or American auto makers will ever return to the world dominance they once had. Therefore, places like Detroit, Cleveland, and Buffalo must find other economic bases if they are to grow and prosper. Most of the growth industries—computers, electronics, genetic research—have settled in the Sun Belt.

The high national debt also increased competition for funds and contributed to higher interest rates on municipal bonds. Further, the serious fiscal plight of local governments in New York City and Cleveland and Orange County, California, made it harder for other local governments to sell their bonds.

Finally, cities are also responsible for their own plight. Many cities brought themselves to the brink of disaster by employing short-term fiscal mismanagement fixes instead of long-term fiscal reform. The **expense fix** treats this year's cost as next year's so it does not appear in the current budget. The **revenue fix** treats next year's anticipated revenue as if it were this year's. The **capital fix** uses money from the capital budget (that is, the budget reserved for long-term, capital intensive, nonrecurring expenses such as fire trucks, bridges, etc.) for operating costs. The final technique is the **outright deficit fix**, in which borrowed money is used to balance the budget.[66]

These problems, coupled with lower levels of federal assistance, do not paint a bright

BOX 10–2

The Beleaguered County

Municipalities are not the only levels of government that have problems with financing. Although 48 out of 50 states have counties, not many people think much about or know much about county government. As one New York state legislator observed: "Nobody in New York says, 'I'm from Albany County.' They say, 'I'm from the town of Colonie or Bethlehem.'" Despite their relative invisibility, county governments in many states have enormous responsibilities. While there is variation among states, generally counties are responsible for property tax assessment and collection, deed recording, law enforcement, jails, courts, highways, public works, welfare and social services, health services, and agricultural and economic development.

Counties are simply administrative subdivisions of states. That means that states can delegate any responsibilities they want to county government. The result is that county governments are often responsible for the least glamorous and least visible government services. For example, in many states the county government is primarily responsible for welfare services and health care. Other local governments often have the right to cap their costs. Counties have become the government of last resort for the provision of some services. In fact, California, by law, requires that counties be "the provider of last resort for people who have no other means of support."

To make matters worse for counties, the states also control how they raise the funds necessary to pay for the services they must provide. Many states control what taxes counties can assess and the tax levels. In most cases, counties must rely on property taxes. Nor do states do much to help out county government through transfers of funds. For example, 70 percent of Jersey City's budget came from intergovernmental transfers while less than half of the revenue of the county in which it is located came from other levels of government. The county had to raise revenue itself.

The burdens on counties are increasing as other levels of government try to cut back. County governments, already primarily responsible for social services and health care in many states, will likely see that burden increase. As the national government reduces its role in welfare as a result of 1996 welfare reform legislation (see Chapter 14 for a discussion of this legislation), states are likely to delegate their new-found responsibility in this area to counties. Counties will then have to scramble to find ways to fund that responsibility.

The invisibility of counties to most people, and the fact that they are responsible for relatively mundane and unpopular duties, leaves them with little political clout to resist the shifting of responsibility or to get the resources necessary to provide the services.

Source: Adapted from Jonathan Walters, "Cry, the Beleaguered County," *Governing* 9 (August 1996): 31–37.

fiscal picture for urban America. Some states are increasing their assistance to localities to replace shrinking federal transfers, creating less budgetary flexibility. In other areas, services are being cut. These services are important because they not only provide for safety and comfort, but often are crucial for the very survival of some residents. In some cases, services are being devolved to counties. Some observers believe that the problems facing county governments are greater than those of cities. This is the subject of Box 10–2.

TABLE 10–4

Composite Ranking of Urban Distress[a]

Rank	City	Rank	City
1	Newark	6	New York
2.5	St. Louis	7.5	Boston
2.5	Cleveland	7.5	Chicago
4	Buffalo	9	New Orleans
5	Detroit	10	Cincinnati

[a]Rankings calculated from combined USAG, CBO, HUD, Treasury and Brookings Indices.

Source: Adapted from Robert W. Burchell, David Listokin, George Sternlieb, James W. Hughes, and Stephen C. Casey, "Measuring Urban Distress: A Summary of the Major Urban Hardship Indices and Resource Allocation Systems" in *Cities Under Stress,* ed. Robert W. Burchell and David Listokin (New Brunswick, New Jersey: Center for Urban Policy Research, 1981), 224.

Various studies of fiscal stress have been done. A composite ranking prepared by the Center for Urban Policy Research at Rutgers University found that 9 of the 10 most distressed cities were in the Frost Belt.[67] Newark was the most distressed city. The only southern city in the top 10 was New Orleans (see Table 10–4). A recent study notes that Frost Belt cities spend more than Sun Belt cities, which adds to their stress and hampers growth.[68] The higher costs may be due to the need to deal with greater social decay and an outmoded infrastructure, or it may be the result of political decisions to placate important factions in the community.

But whether the higher costs are justifiable or not, the higher spending in Rust Belt cities places them in a disadvantageous economic position. As change in transportation and communication undermine their quasi-monopolistic position, these cities risk continuing losses in population and economic activity. Businesses and residents will continue to be inclined to locate elsewhere.[69]

The consequences of stress are not always negative, although they are apt to hurt those at the bottom of the economic ladder. In a series entitled "Back From the Brink," the *New York Times* looked at New York City 10 years after it had teetered on the brink of bankruptcy. It concluded that New York City "is enjoying a prosperity predicted by few ten years ago, although its poorest residents are even poorer, and more numerous."[70] The route back was also at the price of the loss of local autonomy.[71] In 1997, many were again heralding the success of the New York City economy.[72]

Many services that had been criticized in 1975 were more efficient in 1985 despite cutbacks in personnel and resources. Nonetheless the fiscal crisis of the 1970s had its impact in New York City and in other cities by lowering expectations. The morale of those who remained in the city often suffered and many who lost their jobs became bitter.

Politics of Taxing[73]

Raising taxes is never easy. People expect services from government, but they prefer to shift the cost of those services to others. Nevertheless, the public will sometimes allow tax increases or support new taxes if they feel they will receive adequate benefit. One strategy used to raise taxes is **earmarking**, that is, setting aside the extra revenues for a particular purpose. One small Midwest city approved a 1 percent city sales tax because the revenues were to be set aside for infrastructure improvements, economic development, and property tax relief. The business community supported the proposal because it created an economic development fund, while the general public supported the sales tax because of the property tax cuts.

Another strategy is to raise more revenue than is needed immediately so that the excess can be distributed to various community projects. Taxes may also be more palatable if they are sold as temporary. The community may tolerate a few extra mills on property taxes if the revenue is used for a short-term project, such as building dikes to prevent future flooding. Once the project is complete, the mill levy will cease. Citizens also demand accountability. If they are being asked to finance new school construction, they are apt to want the new school to have up-to-date technologies but not extra "frills." Residents are more likely to agree to taxes if they are predictable, that is, gradual and unobtrusive. "Rather than raise one tax by a large and visible amount, politicians may raise a number of smaller taxes by a small amount so that no one group is seriously hurt and citizens feel that the burdens are being widely and equitably shared."[74]

Another technique to win approval of tax increases is to tax the politically weak, for example, a city sales tax, imposed on both residents and nonresidents, who can not vote in city elections. Another popular local tax is on hotel and motel rooms, because the people paying that tax are usually not voters in the community. Both the sales tax and the hotel and motel tax can create problems if they are too high because they may very well cause the shopper or traveler to go to another community. However, a few pennies or even dollars in sales tax will not likely affect purchases if the stores in the community are appealing. A traveler is unlikely to shop around and compare room tax rates in various communities if she

or he has chosen a city for business or pleasure.

Recipients of services and municipal employees will be more supportive of increases in taxes. Business interests will be most reluctant to raise taxes—unless they see a specific benefit.

> Interest groups are distinctly important actors in revenue politics, but their participation indicates that what kind of interest groups will be involved depends on the issue—threatened service cuts bring out service providers and recipients; tax breaks bring out specific industries and even specific companies or individuals; new taxes or shifts in the structure of taxes bring out coalitions of interest groups representing business or labor, the rich or the middle class or the poor.[75]

Expenditures

How do local governments use the money they raise? Just as a broad picture of tax revenues can be misleading because different states allow greater or lesser taxing flexibility to their local governments, a composite look at spending is somewhat distorted. Municipal government spending may be only a small percent of monies spent. For instance, in most areas school expenditures are made by special districts and therefore do not appear as an expenditure for the city government. In the Northeast, city governments are more likely to be responsible for education and for social services. It is important to keep these caveats in mind when examining Table 10–5 (on page 278), which provides a composite picture of municipal expenditures.

Utilities (water and other) accounted for 18.7 percent, followed by police and fire protection (13.9 percent), physical maintenance of highways, sewers, etc. (11.4 percent), education (8.9 percent), human resources such as welfare, hospitals and health (8.8 percent), and housing and community development (3.9 percent).[76] Figure 10–4 (on page 279) shows some general trends for the

TABLE 10–5

Summary of Municipal Government Expenditures, 1990–91

	Expenditure (in Millions)	Percent
TOTAL	$211,506	100
Police protection	19,388	9.2
Education	18,793	8.9
Highways	12,627	6.0
Sewerage	11,316	5.4
Fire protection	10,045	4.7
Interest on general debt	11,370	5.4
Public welfare	8,941	4.2
Hospitals	7,049	3.3
Parks and recreation	8,450	4.0
Housing and community development	8,286	3.9
Sanitation (other than sewerage)	6,287	3.0
General control	3,821	1.8
Financial administration	3,907	1.8
Health	2,769	1.3
All other functions	31,177	14.7
Utility expenditure	39,478	18.7
Insurance Trust expenditure	7,552	3.6
Liquor store expenditure	250	0.1

Source: Bureau of the Census, *Government Finances; City Government Finances: 1990–91* (Washington, D.C.: U.S. Department of Commerce, U.S. Government Printing Office, issued June 1993), 3.

last 10 years. City expenditures grew much more quickly than inflation in the 1960s and 1970s, but slowed down in the 1980s and 1990s. Expenditures in real dollars appear to have peaked in 1978.[77]

What determines expenditure patterns? What are the pressures to increase spending and levels of expenditures? Robert Lineberry and Ira Sharkansky discuss various factors affecting spending.[78] They identify relationships between socioeconomic variables in the community and spending:

1. *High income communities tend to spend more.* Richer communities can impose lower tax rates than their neighbors and still generate more tax revenue because

of a wealthy base. This allows them to provide better services and amenities.

2. *Manufacturing economy is related to increased expenditures because of increased tax base and demand for services.* Industrial plants generate tax revenues for the city, but at the same time they increase costs because of the need to keep streets in good repair, provide adequate water, provide secure police and fire protection, and so on.

3. *Density affects the costs of services differently.* Dense areas require increased fire protection. Density is also associated with increased costs for police and mass transit. On the other hand, education costs should be lower because of

economies of scale in school size and reduced busing costs.

4. *Growth and deterioration increase costs, but different costs are related to each.* Growing communities have high capital costs for new roads, schools, and other capital-intensive projects. In areas of deterioration, repair costs for aging water and sewer facilities and roads rise. Welfare costs may also rise because a deteriorating community may have a high unemployment rate.

5. *Higher owner occupancy leads to lower expenditures.* Home owners may oppose raising taxes because, unlike landlords who can shift the burden to renters, they are responsible for paying property taxes.

6. *Center cities spend more than suburban governments.* The heterogeneity of the city requires more policing and causes more demands for different services from museums to hospitals. The lower-income residents, who are more likely to be in the center city, often require social services. Center cities are more likely to have mayor–council systems than the suburbs and this, too, correlates with increased expenditures as mayors respond to pluralistic demands.

Lineberry and Sharkansky also examine political variables:

7. *The more states assume broad responsibilities, the less local governments spend.* If states provide many services, local governments cut back and spend less.

8. *Increased governmental aid increases local expenditures.* Grants tend to have a stimulative effect. For example, if a community were required to spend $5 million on a new water plant, it might be put off building it because of the huge increase in water rates necessary to pay for it. On the other hand, if $4 million comes in as a grant and the local share is only $1 million, the water plant might be too good a bargain to pass up.

9. *The more restrictive the debt limit, the lower the expenditures.* For legal, political, and practical reasons, local tax income is limited. Therefore, if borrowing is also restrictive, governments will have fewer funds and, thus, spend less.

10. *The current level of spending is related to the past level of spending.* Budgets tend to build on the past. Groups that have received services expect to keep receiving them. Thus, drastic funding reductions are unlikely. Communities with limited services would probably not add substantial services at any one time. Increases or decreases are likely to differ only marginally or incrementally from the past, because protocols and expectations are built up over time.

FIGURE 10–4

Trends in City General Expenditures for Selected Major Functions 1982–1991 (in Billions)

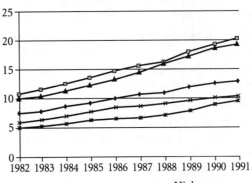

- ◆ Highways
- □ Police protection
- ▲ Education
- ✳ Fire protection
- ✳ Public welfare

Source: U.S. Bureau of the Census, *City Government Finances in 1991–92* (Washington, D.C.: U.S. Government Printing Office, 1996), 1; U.S. Bureau of the Census, *City Government Finances in 1988–89* (Washington, D.C.: U.S. Government Printing Office, 1991), 1; U.S. Bureau of Census, *City Government Finances in 1985–86* (Washington, D.C.: U.S. Government Printing Office, 1988), 1.

Other factors also affect expenditure patterns. For instance, climate affects the amount of money spent on activities such as snow removal. Resources have an impact. For example, water is more costly in Phoenix, Arizona, than in Philadelphia, Pennsylvania. The demographic profile affects budget allocations. Miami, Florida, spends more on programs for the elderly than Las Vegas, Nevada. Strong public employee unions may also result in increased spending.

In addition, local governments are expected to perform many new services. The growing concentration of the poor in the center city and the widening gap between rich and poor create new demands. Caring for the homeless seems to be a rapidly expanding job. Many local governments remember the general social unrest of the 1960s, as well as more recent outbreaks, and fear that they cannot ignore social problems, not only for humanitarian reasons but also because they want to avoid a recurrence of unrest.

While under stress on the social front, governments have attempted to step up development efforts to compete with other localities for new jobs and residents. State and local expenditures for developmental programs (transportation, safety, education, and the like) came to 10.8 percent of the GNP in 1990. At the same time expenditures on redistributive programs (welfare, health and hospitals, housing, etc.) accounted for only 3.5 percent of the GNP.

Cities are more eager to spend their own funds to attract and retain residents and businesses that will enhance the community. They are less willing to spend their own funds on programs that would attract residents needing high levels of service.[79] States and localities that depend on federal transfers to support redistributive services continue to face the specter of less federal aid. All in all, the governments in the metropolis, in general, face a severe budget crunch with no end in sight.

Politics of Spending

The budgetary problems facing governments in the metropolis have increased the political stakes of the budgetary process. Usually, the chief executive in the city submits the budget to the council, although in weak mayor cities the council or a budget branch may be responsible. There are four considerations in assembling a budget. First, and most important, the budget must be balanced because most states do not allow local governments to have a deficit. Second, the budget should at least maintain the existing level of services. Third, if possible, the budget should provide for wage increases for municipal employees. Fourth, tax increases should be avoided, "especially property-tax increases in the belief that increased property taxes cause business and industry to move from the city, reducing its tax base."[80]

The first step in preparing a budget is to estimate revenues. Intergovernmental transfers and locally raised funds must be calculated. Considerations of growth or deterioration must be made to estimate if revenues will be increasing or decreasing. Based on revenue estimates, the person responsible for budget preparation will instruct department heads to put together their funding requests subject to available resources. Department heads will likely ask for more than they can possibly get because their request is likely to be cut; therefore, they build in cushions. Department requests are then reviewed, modified, and aggregated by the budget staff, chief administrative officer, manager, or mayor and presented to the council or commission for approval. If new taxes are needed, they too must be proposed.

While this process may seem straightforward, complicating factors are many. Municipal budgets can be characterized as **fragmented, uncontrollable,** and **incremental**.[81] They are fragmented to the extent that participants involved focus on their own interests and constituency. This creates some interesting strategies that are used at all levels.[82] Agencies must present their best case by developing confidence and nurturing a clientele. For example, a housing authority would try to get the support of the tenants in public housing projects. To develop confidence, they use various techniques. For instance, "be what they think they are. Confidence is achieved by gearing one's behavior to fit in with the expectations of committee people."[83] To further increase confidence, Wildavsky suggests other strategies such as "play it straight," meaning to be truthful and "avoid surprise," meaning be prepared. The importance of clientele strategies cannot be overemphasized. Some examples of these are "find a clientele," "serve your clientele," and "expand your clientele." The budget process is fragmented because every agency is out for itself. While the budget review is designed to reduce this fragmentation, the ability of managers to make "end runs" to friendly legislators may sometimes negate attempts at coordination.

A second characteristic of budgets is that they are uncontrollable; that is, funds are already committed, either by law or by previous agreement. For instance, if the revenue estimate takes into account a federal grant that requires some matching local funds, those funds cannot be used for other purposes and are, accordingly, uncontrollable. Some expenditures that are not legally uncontrollable may be politically untouchable. Large-scale layoffs or pay cuts have great political repercussions.

Finally, budgets can be incremental, varying only slightly from previous budgets. This is because coalitions between agencies and their clients are likely to persist in their expectation of a "fair share of the pie." Agencies seek incremental gains and attempt to avoid all cuts.

Given fiscal stress, however, many cities have cut back. One observer established the following budget-cutting priorities: maintenance; equipment; operating expenses; supplies, materials, etc.; nonadministrative salaries; and administrative salaries.[84] A study of Oakland, California, found that budget analysts used the following budget-cutting rules: (1) cut increases in personnel; (2) cut all equipment that appears to be a luxury; (3) use precedent—cut what has been cut before; (4) recommend repair rather than replacement; (5) recommend study to delay major costs; (6) cut operating costs by a fixed percentage; (7) do not cut if health and safety are involved; (8) cut departments with "bad" reputations; (9) when in doubt, ask someone else; and (10) identify dubious items for the decision maker.[85]

Cutting budgets is difficult; and as the cutting priorities illustrate, people and programs are harder to cut than supplies, maintenance and the like—because people vote. Nevertheless, the general public plays only a limited role in the budgetary process. After testing three models, John Crecine concluded that budgeting does not seek an optimal solution to community problems, nor does it respond adequately to demands in the community. Budgeting is an internal bureaucratic process.[86] In sum, budgeting can be generally described as, "*insulated* from local politics and political action," and greatly affected by the availability of revenue.[87] This does not mean that individuals and groups do not try to influence budget and policy decisions, however.

Conclusion

We have seen that before the late 1970s, cities and other local governments were becoming increasingly dependent on other levels of government. With that growing dependence came a loss of authority. Charles Levine and colleagues note that "state and federal agencies added strings, mandates, and maintenance of effort requirements as conditions for receiving money." As a consequence, "there can be little doubt that one effect of fiscal stress was to reduce local autonomy."[88] If local governments cannot make choices, they cannot respond to demands of their citizens. However, decisions that affect a municipality are made far away from the people and their voices are muffled. In addition, the competition among governments in the metropolis and between and among metropolitan areas for businesses that would expand employment and tax bases imposes other constraints on local governments. Local political leaders often feel they must respond to demands of businesses that could increase the prosperity of the jurisdictions they govern. Citizen demands, especially demands from those who seek redistribution of income, are often seen as not as important as the business requests. In fact, responding to demands for redistribution may be seen as a threat to the attractiveness of the community to business. On the other hand, elected officials also need votes to stay in office, which gives citizens leverage.

In a era of federal government retrenchment, the choices that are left to the local government become more important. Determining the priorities for allocating scarce resources becomes more crucial. The question becomes not how big a piece of pie you get, but whether you get a piece at all.

Reagan's New Federalism was aimed at increasing the autonomy of local governments. But, because it provided less money, local governments were still unable to solve their problems. When the federal government refused to bail out New York City as it approached bankruptcy, the State of New York intervened. The price for the fiscal rescue was the establishment of the Emergency Financial Control Board (EFCB) with the power to oversee the city's budget. Until and unless local governments are able to raise sufficient revenues on their own, it is likely that at least in some policy areas, "whoever pays the piper will call the tune."

Budgetary decisions are perhaps the most important policy decisions because they struc-

ture all governmental action. They determine who gets what and who pays for it. Citizens clearly have an interest in those decisions. The tax revolts of the 1970s were an indication that citizens are intensely concerned about taxing and spending policies. Despite the importance of the issues and the intense citizen concern, this chapter has demonstrated that average citizens have limited impact on budgetary decisions.

One major limit on the impact of citizens is the complexity of the budgetary process. How should government resources be distributed? Personal values and ideologies complicate these decisions. More difficult still is deciding how to pay for budget appropriations. Urban tax policy is limited by state laws that specify what taxes may be imposed at the local level. In addition, federal grants-in-aid and other transfer programs alter local budget priorities through matching fund requirements and through specific guidelines governing the spending of federal money.

As with horizontal fragmentation, vertical fragmentation impedes citizen control. The answer to the pertinent question "Who's in charge here?" becomes difficult. Because of the complexity of the issues and of the intermingling of authority, the answer to the question of who is in charge is often the budgetary experts of various government levels. Those officials may attempt to make decisions according to technical criteria, but in any instance where costs and benefits are distributed, values inevitably have political consequences. To a large extent, urban politics can be seen as a competition over the distribution of costs and benefits that are the essence of budgetary decisions.

Notes

1. Ronald Reagan, "Message of the President-Elect to the National Conference of State Legislatures," December 19, 1980, cited in J. Edwin Benton, "American Federalism's First Principles and Reagan's New Federalism Policies," *Policy Studies Journal* 13 (March 1985): 570.

2. Elaine Sharpe, "Citizen-Demand Making in the Urban Context," *American Journal of Political Science* 28 (November, 1984): 668.

3. Paul E. Peterson, *City Limits* (Chicago: University of Chicago Press, 1981).

4. Richard H. Leach, *American Federalism* (New York: Norton, 1970), 3.

5. Charles R. Adrian and Charles Press, *Governing Urban America,* 5th ed. (New York: McGraw-Hill, 1977), 137.

6. Dennis R. Judd, *The Politics of American Cites: Private Power and Public Policy,* 2nd ed. (Boston: Little, Brown, 1984), 40.

7. E.E. Schattschneider, *The Semisovereign People* (New York: Holt, Rinehart & Winston, 1960), Chapter 5.

8. *Reynolds v. Sims* 377 U.S. 562, 567 (1964).

9. Judd, *The Politics of American Cities,* 41.

10. *City of Clinton v. Cedar Rapids and Missouri River Railroad Co.* 24 Iowa 455, 475 (1868).

11. Peterson, *City Limits,* 20.

12. Ibid., Chapter 3 and passim.

13. Martin Shefter, *Political Crisis/Fiscal Crisis: The Collapse and Revival of New York City* (New York: Basic Books, 1985), 9.

14. Ibid., 232.

15. Deil S. Wright, *Understanding Intergovernmental Relations* (N. Scituate, Massachusetts: Duxbury, 1978), 132.

16. Laurence J. O'Toole, Jr., "American Intergovernmental Relations: An Overview," in *American Intergovernmental Relations: Foundations, Perspectives, and Issues,* 2nd ed., ed. Laurence J. O'Toole, Jr.(Washington, D.C.: Congressional Quarterly Press, 1993).

17. Morton Grodzins, *The American System: A New View of Government in the United States,* ed. Daniel Elazar (Chicago: Rand McNally, 1966).

18. *McCulloch v. Maryland* 4 Wheaton 316 (1819).

19. James Eisenstein, Mark Kessler, Bruce A. Williams, and Jacqueline Vaughn Switzer, *The Play of Power: An Introduction to American Government* (New York: St Martin's Press, 1996), 134.

20. *Lochner v. New York* 198 U.S. 45 (1905) declared unconstitutional a law establishing maximum hours as a violation of the individual right to contract. Minimum wage legislation was thrown out in *Adkins v. Children's Hospital* 261 U.S. 525 (1923). *Hammer v. Dagenhart* 247 U.S. 251 (1918) declared a state law regulating child labor to be unconstitutional.

21. Mark I. Gelfand, *A Nation of Cities: The Federal Government and Urban America, 1933–1965* (New York: Oxford University Press, 1975), 14–15.

22. Ibid., 15.

23. Ibid., 17.

24. Fred L. Israel, ed. *State of the Union Messages of the Presidents of the United States,* vol. 4, 2669–2670, in Gelfand, *A Nation of Cities,* 22.

25. Peter R. Gluck and Richard J. Meister, *Cities in Transition* (New York: New Viewpoints, 1979), 137.

26. Ibid., 46.

27. U.S. Office of Management and Budget, *Special Analysis: Budget of the United States Government, Fiscal Year 1975* (Washington, D.C.: U.S. Government Printing Office, 1974), 210.

28. Deil S. Wright, "Intergovernmental Relations: An Analytic Overview," in *Current Issues in Public Administration,* 2nd ed., ed. Frederick I. Lane (New York: St. Martin's Press, 1982), 164.

29. Wright, *Understanding Intergovernmental Relations,* 60.

30. Ibid., 60–61.

31. Donald Kettl, *The Regulation of American Federalism* (Baton Rouge: Louisiana State University Press, 1983).

32. Robert W. Kweit, "Political Accountability Under the New Federalism." Paper presented at the 1983 Annual Meeting of the Western Political Science Association, Seattle, Washington, March, 1983, 7.

33. U.S. Advisory Commission on Intergovernmental Relations, *Characteristics of Federal Grant-In-Aid Programs to State and Local Governments: Grant Funded FY 1993* (Washington, D.C.: ACIR, 1994), iii, 6.

34. John Herbers, "A Landscape of Economic Disparities Emerges with the New Federalism," *Governing* (October 1987): 32–33.

35. James A. Maxwell and J. Richard Aronson, *Financing State and Local Government,* 3rd ed. (Washington, D.C.: The Brookings Institution, 1977), 107.

36. Henry J. Aaron, *Who Pays the Property Tax? A New View* (Washington, D.C.: The Brookings Institution, 1975).

37. Glenn W. Fisher, *The Worst Tax* (Lawrence: University of Kansas Press, 1996), 193.

38. Judd, *The Politics of American Cities,* 211.

39. Jonathan Kozol, *Savage Inequalities: Children in America's Schools* (New York: Harper Perennial, 1991), 55.

40. Maxwell and Aronson, *Financing State and Local Governments,* 136–137.

41. U.S. Advisory Commission on Intergovernmental Relations, *Changing Public Attitudes on Governments and Taxes* (Washington, D.C.: U.S. Government Printing Office, 1991), 3.

42. U.S. Advisory Commission on Intergovernmental Relations, *Significant Features of Fiscal Federalism,* 1995, vol. 1 (Washington, D.C.: ACIR, 1995), 70, 95–96.

43. Ibid., 172–173.

44. U.S. Bureau of the Census, *City Government Finances in 1984–85* (Washington, D.C.: U.S. Government Printing Office, 1986), 1; and U.S. Bureau of the Census, *City Government Finances in 1991–92* (Washington, D.C.: U.S. Government Printing Office, 1996), 1.

45. U.S. Advisory Commission on Intergovernmental Relations, *Significant Features of Fiscal Federalism,* 1993, vol. 2 (Washington, D.C.: ACIR, 1993), 76–77, 130.

46. U.S. Bureau of the Census, *City Government Finances in 1991–92* (Washington, D.C.: U.S. Government Printing Office, 1996), 1.

47. Alberta M. Sbragia, "The 1970s: A Decade of Change in Local Government Finance," in *The Municipal Money Chase: The Politics of Local Government Finance,* ed. Alberta M. Sbragia (Boulder, Colorado: Westview Press, 1983).

48. Richard S. Morris, *Bum Rap on America's Cities: The Real Causes of Urban Decay* (Englewood Cliffs, New Jersey: Prentice-Hall, 1980), 57.

49. Jack Newfield and Paul DuBrul, *The Abuse of Power: The Permanent Government and the Fall of New York* (New York: Viking, 1977), 42.

50. U.S. Bureau of the Census, *City Government Finances in 1984–85,* 2; and U.S. Bureau of the Census, *City Government Finances in 1991–92,* 2.

51. U.S. Advisory Commission on Intergovernmental Relations, *Significant Features of Fiscal Federalism, 1994,* vol. 1 (Washington, D.C.: U.S. Government Printing Office, 1994), 164.

52. U.S. Advisory Commission on Intergovernmental Relations, *Significant Features of Fiscal Federalism 1984* (Washington, D.C.: U.S. Government Printing Office, 1985), 15.

53. U.S. Bureau of the Census, *City Government Finances in 1991–92,* 1.

54. U.S. Advisory Commission on Intergovernmental Relations, *Significant Features of Fiscal Federalism 1985–86* (Washington, D.C.: ACIR, 1986), 62.

55. Paul E. Peterson, *The Price of Federalism* (Washington, D.C.: The Brookings Institution, 1995), 66.

56. Michael D. Reagan and John G. Sanzone, *The New Federalism,* 2nd ed. (New York: Oxford University Press, 1981), 54.

57. Don Cozzetto, Mary Grisez Kweit, and Robert W. Kweit, *Public Budgeting: Politics, Institutions, and Processes* (New York: Longman, 1995), 84–88; and David R. Morgan and Robert E. England, *Managing Urban America,* 4th ed. (Chatham, New Jersey: Chatham House, 1996), 25–26.

58. James L. Sundquist with David W. Davis, *Making Federalism Work* (Washington, D.C.: The Brookings Institution, 1969), 279.

59. John J. Harrigan, *Political Change in the Metropolis,* 3rd ed., (Boston: Little, Brown, 1985), 372.

60. Sundquist, *Making Federalism Work,* 2.

61. Reagan and Sanzone, *The New Federalism,* 78–80.

62. Ibid., 128.

63. U.S. Advisory Commission on Intergovernmental Relations, *Characteristics of Federal Grant-In-Aid Programs to State and Local Governments: Grant Funded FY 1993* (Washington, D.C.: ACIR, 1994), iii, 6.

64. John P. Crecine, *Governmental Problem Solving: A Computer Simulation of Municipal Budgeting* (Skokie, Illinois: Rand McNally, 1969).

65. Terry Nichols Clark and Lorna Crawley Ferguson, *City Money: Political Processes, Fiscal Strain and Retrenchment* (New York: Columbia University Press, 1983), 165.

66. S.R. Weisman, "How New York Became a Fiscal Junkie," *New York Times Magazine,* August 17, 1975, 6.

67. Robert W. Burchell, David Listokin, George Sternlieb, James W. Hughes, and Stephen C. Casey, "Measuring Urban Distress: A Summary of Major Urban Indices and Resource Allocation Systems," in *Cities Under Stress ,* ed. Robert W. Burchell and David Listokin (New Brunswick, New Jersey: Center for Urban Policy Research, 1981), 224.

68. Peterson, *The Price of Federalism,* Chapter 7.

69. Ibid., 161.

70. Martin Gottlieb, "A Decade After Cutbacks, New York Is a Different City," *New York Times,* June 30, 1985, 1.

71. Patricia Giles Leeds, "City Politics and the Market: The Case of New York City's Financing Crisis" *in The Municipal Money Chase,* ed. Alberta Sbragia.

72. Blaine Harden and Jill Dutt, "Money and Melting Pot Help Put the Town on Top," *International Herald Tribune,* May 26, 1997, 2.

73. This section draws heavily on Irene S. Rubin, *The Politics of Public Budgeting: Getting and Spending, Borrowing and Balancing,* 3rd ed. (Chatham, New Jersey: Chatham House, 1997), Chapter 2.

74. Ibid., 39.

75. Ibid., 68.

76. U.S. Bureau of the Census, *City Government Finances in 1984–85,* vi.

77. Harrigan, *Political Change in the Metropolis,* 167.

78. Robert L. Lineberry and Ira Sharkansky, *Urban Politics and Public Policy,* 3rd ed. (New York: Harper & Row, 1978), 236–242.

79. Peterson, *The Price of Federalism,* 54.

80. Crecine, *Governmental Problem Solving,* 74.

81. Lineberry and Sharkansky, *Urban Politics and Public Policy,* 243–244.

82. Aaron Wildavsky, *The Politics of the Budgetary Process,* 4th ed. (Boston: Little, Brown, 1984), Chapter 3.

83. Ibid., 74.

84. Crecine, *Governmental Problem Solving,* 189.

85. Arnold J. Meltsner, *The Politics of City Revenue* (Berkeley: University of California Press, 1961), 178.

86. Crecine, *Governmental Problem Solving,* 189.

87. Lineberry and Sharkansky, *Urban Politics and Public Policy,* 249–250.

88. Charles A. Levine, Irene Rubin, and George Wolohojian, *The Politics of Retrenchment: How Local Governments Manage Fiscal Stress* (Beverly Hills, California: Sage, 1981), 191.

CHAPTER 11

Implementation, Evaluation, and Reform

The policy process does not end when a government decides to initiate a program. That program must be implemented and decisions must be made about the success or failure of the program. Citizens have an interest in the implementation and evaluation process. The nature of the program may be substantially altered as the words of the laws are actually carried out. Citizen evaluations of programs should be used to alter or abolish programs that fail or to support those programs that succeed. Just as there are barriers to the ability of citizens to control the policy choices of local governments, there are also difficulties in influencing the implementation and evaluation stages of the policy process, as this chapter will discuss. One of the first barriers is the complexity of the implementation process.

The Complex Context for Policy Implementation

The metropolitan landscape is complex, with many governments, at many levels, with varying resources and authority trying to implement policy and provide services to residents. The state and local bureaucracy is facing challenging and exciting times as it tries to cope with increasing responsibilities, limited revenues, and a spate of new ideas on how to improve programs and the way they are delivered.

Many policies affecting local government are adopted in Washington, D.C., or in the state capital. Some programs are implemented directly by those governments. For instance, Social Security payments go directly from the federal government to individuals and provide modest income for the elderly and disabled. States also provide services to individuals and communities. In times of emergencies, such as a flood, the National Guard may be sent to communities to help sandbag dikes, police areas, and help with the cleanup afterward. Local governments also provide many services, such as police, fire, trash collection, and the like. Many other programs are administered jointly by various levels of government. As discussed previously, other levels of government often establish **mandates**, that is, requirements that local governments must meet. For example, communities must treat their water to meet federal standards. In other instances, the federal or state government provides funds or expertise to work jointly with local governments in handling local issues. For example, the national and state departments of education provide funding to local school districts and often lend expertise on curriculum issues.

Challenges in Local Service Delivery

Intergovernmental cooperation in the delivery of programs and services is often problematic. Jeffrey Pressman and Aaron Wildavsky studied the implementation of a federal job creation program administered by the Economic Development Administration (EDA) in Oakland, California. The EDA had to work through a variety of federal and state agencies dealing with such areas as health, education, labor, as well as a multiplicity of regional, county, and city agencies and private-sector firms and individual businesspersons. The authors argue that an analogy to foreign aid may help in understanding the problems of implementing programs in an intergovernmental context.[1] As is the case with foreign aid, policies are adopted in Washington, D.C., with an overly optimistic view of what the policy will accomplish and an underestimation of the problems that will occur when the policy is carried out locally. Pressman and Wildavsky note common problems: "federal grandeur, inadequate local support, and a divorce of implementation from policy."[2]

When multiple participants with varied perspectives must make multiple decisions in order to carry out a program, problems are likely to occur.[3] At the end of three years, only $3 million of the $23 million allocated to the project had been spent and few new jobs for minorities had been created. That explains the subtitle of Pressman and Wildavsky's book, *Implementation: How Great Expectations in Washington Are Dashed in Oakland; Or, Why It's Amazing Federal Programs Work at All, This Being a Saga of the Economic Development Administration as Told by Two Sympathetic Observers Who Seek to Build Morals on a Foundation of Ruined Hopes.*

Not only is intergovernmental implementation difficult because of the many governments in metropolitan areas that have to work together, but even within one government there are rivalries and different perspectives and priorities among various agencies. Even within one agency there are many actors with diverse viewpoints and goals who have to collaborate and make decisions to carry out programs. Bureaucratic organizations are structured as hierarchies. In theory, hierarchies have clear lines of authority and people in charge to provide coordination. While formal authority is at the top of the organization, the people in the field actually make many of the most important decisions in service delivery. The people at the top of the hierarchy often find it difficult to provide regular supervision of those actually carrying out a policy and, as a result, accountability at times suffers.

> The rational–comprehensive or classical model of policy implementation is simple, clear, and elegant. Democratically elected officials make unambiguous policy choices. Policies are handed over to a hierarchically structured agency. Specific instructions are formulated at the top of the pyramid and passed down the chain of command to the line personnel, who carry them out without discretion. Most observers know that this ideal is unachievable in reality.[4]

Many local services, such as law and order, education, and social welfare, are actually implemented by police officers, teachers, and social workers, individuals referred to by Michael Lipsky as "street-level bureaucrats" who exercise a great deal of discretion.[5]

Supervisors cannot effectively control street-level bureaucrats for two basic reasons. First, the street-level bureaucrats do their jobs in widely dispersed locations. The police officer in the patrol car or on the beat, the teacher in the classroom, the social worker making a home visit cannot be easily supervised. Second, generally agreed upon measures of success for such jobs are lacking. The jobs require dealing with people in settings that change constantly. It is impossible to write job descriptions for police officers, teachers, or social workers that can come close to providing them with useful guidance on the myriad complex situations they face every day.

Although supervisors may have minimal contact with them, street-level bureaucrats are in constant contact with the public. "Most citizens encounter government . . . not through letters to congressmen or by attendance at school board meetings but through their teachers and their children's teachers and through the policeman on the corner or in the patrol car."[6] Potentially, then, citizens could influence policy in the areas of crime control, education, and social services through their direct contact with the service deliverers.

There are several reasons why citizens have limited or no influence in their contacts with street-level bureaucrats. The reasons derive from the amount of job stress experienced by the bureaucrats. Their professional training and their values predispose them to want to serve people in positive ways: Police want to find ways to end criminal behavior; teachers want to educate children to enable them to succeed in life; social workers want to help individuals put their lives together. The actual conditions on the job, however, make coming close to meeting their own expectations difficult. The bureaucrats have limited resources to deal with people whose problems are often severe. The frustrations from working in a situation where failure is virtually assured lead many to find ways of coping.

Two coping mechanisms often employed by street-level bureaucrats have negative implications for the ability of citizens to have an impact. First, some bureaucrats establish routines to help them create some order and regularity in what seems to be a chaotic world. Such routines often emphasize guaranteeing each individual citizen procedural fairness by treating each equally. While that both simplifies the job and avoids any potential negative discrimination, it also probably means bureaucrats will not respond to individual needs.

Second, street-level bureaucrats may change their conceptions of their job or of the people with whom they deal to minimize their frustrations. Instead of focusing on serving the needs of citizens—needs that they often really cannot satisfy—they may scale back their expectations of their job to more manageable or "realistic" goals. For example, to ration scarce resources, they may focus their efforts only on certain aspects of the job, defining other problems as being beyond their control. This leads to an "ain't my job, man" mentality that may mean they no longer are willing to respond to individual needs. Street-level bureaucrats may also change their conception of people. Rather than being sympathetic to them, they may begin to blame people for needing assistance. Needs may be attributed to flaws in the individual rather than problems with which the bureaucrats can help. Citizens, of course, could demand that their public servants actually serve their needs. Such protest is often limited by fears of being stereotyped as a "troublemaker."

Still another limit on citizen control is the lack of a clear public consensus on what are the desired outcomes of policies. Many want zealous law enforcement because they agree with former U.S. Attorney General Edwin Meese that people who get arrested are probably guilty. Others are concerned about the rights of minorities and fear arbitrariness in law enforcement. Teachers face a similar quandary in determining public preferences. Does the public want students to learn respect for authority or should students be taught to question? Different communities have different wishes, and it is not always clear exactly what they are. Social workers are expected to control the socially unpleasant aspects of their clients' behavior while at the same time acting as their advocates.

Decision Rules and Service Delivery

Because of the ambiguity of their job, many public servants take comfort in the myth that policy implementation can be apolitical. In reality, decisions are often very political. Police who are in a position to arrest a politically prominent person, teachers who must discuss controversial social issues, or social workers who must make recommendations on clients' life-styles need to consider the political consequences of their actions. The fact that they do make policy decisions is a great concern for many who believe that it is undemocratic for unelected bureaucrats to make policy. Many ways are available to try to keep the necessary political decisions of bureaucrats in check. In fact, many federal requirements for citizen participation at the local level are rooted in the belief that citizens must play a role in implementation if democratic accountability is to be maintained.

The bureaucracy will often attempt to create the aura of being apolitical by adopting "neutral principles of administration." These principles take the form of **decision rules**, which are standards or criteria that are used to make choices.

> Professional standards . . . have an . . . advantage of appearing to be fair. Hiring qualified librarians, moving traffic and setting equal class sizes all seem reasonable and appropriate. They orient professionals to apparently worthy goals. . . . Yet somehow these benevolent norms, . . . which ought to help everyone, end up helping some more than others. . . . [These rules], like many "neutral" decision rules, are not neutral. . . . The professional norms set convenient standards for competence and quality performance while organizational norms provide a means for the agency to adjust to its environment.[7]

Bureaucrats can use five possible decision rules or premises in their exercise of discretion: power or pressure, equality, efficiency or professional norms, need, and demand.[8] *Power* is clearly a political premise. Using this rule, policies will be adopted in direct proportion to the pressure applied by the groups pushing for the policy and the political standing of that group. Bryan Jones and his colleagues argue that this premise is likely to describe the exceptional case. Most studies of service delivery support the position that the power decision rule is seldom used, but it may have important consequences in these atypical cases, such as the siting of a public housing project. Such a decision is likely to be so controversial that politicians will intervene in it.

If power is the basis for decisions, major business interests would have an advantage. Even if bureaucrats do not want to consider issues of power, they may be more likely to respond to requests by major business interests than to other citizens because they may know that if they ignore business interests, politicians may intervene.[9]

A second decision premise, *equality*, means that policies would benefit each citizen equally. The purpose here is to treat everyone in the same way. Several cities use this rule to establish trash collection. For example, each part of the city will have trash pick up once a week. Everyone is treated equally, even if some areas might need more services because of high population densities generating more trash. In principle, it is hard to argue against equality except, as the example above illustrates, equality in service provision may actually mean shortchanging areas of greatest need. Using the third premise, *efficiency*, policies would be adopted that provide the most benefits for the least cost. This rule might be used if a public transit agency needs to make cuts. It could cut the routes with the least ridership to promote efficient use of resources. This seemingly neutral principle could result in areas with low ridership losing all access to public transportation, leaving the population isolated.

A fourth premise, *need,* means that decisions would be directed to helping those with the greatest need. The policy does not treat all equally unless need is equally distributed, and the policy may not be the most efficient as more resources may be necessary to address the most serious problems. Responding to need would establish a compensatory pattern. Providing more money for schools in distressed neighborhoods is an example of this premise. A final possible standard is *demand.* The bureaucracy adopts policies for those who are most vocal in communicating their wants. Many public agencies track citizen complaints, and they then focus their energies in responding to these complaints. For example, several police departments have helped neighborhood organizations reduce prostitution and the sale of drugs by targeting problem areas identified by residents.

It is important to examine the impact of these rules and other factors on actual policy implementation or service delivery. While research has indicated bureaucrats do not frequently use power as a decision rule, conventional wisdom has embraced an **underclass hypothesis** with regard to service delivery patterns, in which those at the bottom of the socioeconomic status hierarchy are discriminated against and receive inferior services because they have less power or standing in the community. This would result from the application of the decision rule of power. An alternative hypothesis, the **ecological hypothesis**, states that certain neighborhood characteristics, such as age or density, affect service delivery patterns, an example of applying the decision rules of need or efficiency to service delivery.[10] The **decision rule hypothesis** holds that no one decision rule controls bureaucratic behavior, as different rules are applied in different situations.[11]

Patterns of Service Delivery

Four basic patterns of service delivery are possible. They are shown graphically in Figure 11–1. These patterns tend to vary by service as well as by city. Model A depicts a situation of *equity* where all neighborhoods receive roughly the same level of services regardless of their socioeconomic status. A study in Houston found that the park bureaucracy adhered rigidly to the equality standard in the allocation of resources.[12] Another study notes that, "the city of San Antonio provides remarkably equivalent allocations of [police] manpower from sector to sector. This equivalence persists whether one uses population, crime rates, or calls for service. . . . There is simply not much inequality there to be explained."[13]

FIGURE 11–1

Patterns of Service Delivery

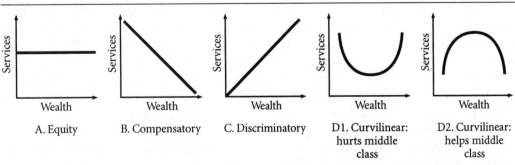

Public education resources are often allocated using a *compensatory* model (model B). Frank Levy, Arnold Meltsner, and Aaron Wildavsky, for example, found that Oakland, California (with state and federal stimuli to do so) allocated compensatory personnel and lowered class sizes in low-income and minority schools. Further, Oakland limited teacher transfers to prevent experienced teachers from moving into upper-class schools, which would continue the discriminatory allocation of teachers.[14]

There are several examples of the *discriminatory* model (model C) for the allocation of services. One of the most blatant examples was resolved by the Fifth Circuit Court of Appeals in the case of *Hawkins v. Town of Shaw*. The court found a systematic pattern of discrimination against African-American neighborhoods.[15] Almost 98 percent of the homes on unpaved streets and 97 percent of the homes without sanitary sewers were in those neighborhoods. In *Hobson v. Hansen*, the courts ordered the city of Washington, D.C., to equalize school expenditures after it was determined that although the schools were 90 percent black, the major share of the expenditures went to predominantly white schools.[16] In some instances, discrimination is not this overt and results from some of the bureaucratic decision rules discussed earlier.

Sometimes service delivery follows a *curvilinear* pattern (models D1 and D2). For instance, Robert Lineberry found the poorest level of public services in some upper-middle-class neighborhoods. This can be explained by ecological factors. The neighborhoods were receiving inferior services because they were on the outskirts of the city and were growing too rapidly for services to keep up.[17] A study in Detroit noted a curvilinear pattern that benefited middle-class residents in the enforcement of environmental ordinances. Poorer neighborhoods also needed environmental protection but lacked the skills to make demands, while upper-class neighborhoods had the skills but not the need.[18]

Most studies of service delivery conclude that there are "unpatterned inequalities." In some services and some places there are discriminatory or compensatory service delivery. The discrimination may not be overt, but rather the result of bureaucratic decision rules based on demand or ecological factors creating need. Sometimes compensatory service delivery is a response to the political skill of underprivileged groups or conditions set by other governments. For instance federal income limits may restrict some programs to the poor. At other times, compensatory delivery occurs because of decision rules based on need or professional norms. Patterns of equality will usually result from decision rules stressing equal treatment.

Curvilinear patterns may emerge because of decision rules relying on demand or need. In other words, it is unlikely in most places that one group gets a higher level of services than another in all service areas, because certain neighborhood characteristics and bureaucratic decision rules operate differently in different service areas.[19]

In sum, the decision rule of power would presumably aid urban business interests as they have power because of their impact on the economic health of a community. The rule of demand would help those citizens who were willing to press their demands on bureaucrats. The other decision rules would minimize the role of business interests and other citizens.

Evaluation and Feedback

Once the services are provided they must be examined to determine what effects they have and what remains to be done; this is the evaluation stage. Evaluation affects whether programs are continued, modified, or terminated. It is also important to evaluate the efficiency, effectiveness, responsiveness, and equity of the service delivery.

In the past, most evaluations were impressionistic and based on limited evidence. If the public seemed happy and the program squared with our ideological orientation, it was judged successful and worthy of continuance. If there were no resident complaints, it was assumed that services were being delivered in a satisfactory manner. Systematic evaluation has become more important in recent years. Many of the grants from the federal government came with mandates requiring state and local governments to evaluate the effectiveness of their programs. In addition, many residents have become increasingly disenchanted with government programs and are also critical of public servants. Because of controversy over the effectiveness and efficiency of government programs and the scarcity of resources—a scarcity felt especially in urban areas—it has become necessary to be more systematic in determining how to deliver services most efficiently and how to address problems most effectively .

Often, local governments have tried to resist or distort program evaluations. Sometimes evaluations become blatantly political. These are sometimes known as **pseudo-evaluations**, or evaluations that are not really designed to determine the effectiveness of the program. There are five types of pseudo-evaluations. The first is the *eyewash*, so-called because it is a superficial attempt to make the program look good, regardless of how it is really doing. The analogy is to "get the red out." Second is the *whitewash*, which refers to a cover-up. A third type is the *submarine*, which is used to undermine unpopular programs—only negative evidence is sought. Fourth, *posturing*, is used to create the pretense that objectives are being met. Finally, *postponing*, is an attempt to sidetrack any attempt at a serious evaluation by saying it is too soon to know if the program is working and more information is needed. Sometimes these ploys were used because agency employees were concerned that someone would discover that they were not efficient, effective, or responsive. At times these techniques were employed because of the difficulty involved in performing a legitimate evaluation.

Sometimes they were used in combination, or with more legitimate forms of evaluations, to suit political ends.

Systematic evaluation of programs is often difficult. To determine if a program is working, first it is necessary to determine what the program is supposed to do. Thus, a program like community development has many goals—better housing, more jobs, increased self-esteem—that must be prioritized and sometimes the goals conflict. As conditions and administrations change, so may the goals. Measuring achievement may be difficult. How can one measure self-esteem?

In addition, a program may have unintended consequences. For example, increasing the self-esteem of the lower class may increase demands for services, resulting in increased tensions. Programs may affect groups differently. Further, linking a specific program with specific results may be difficult. More job opportunities may be due to successful community development efforts or to changes in inflation, taxes, or interest rates.

At times some groups may try to obstruct evaluations, fearing that it may show that they are failing. For instance, bureaucrats may fear that careful scrutiny may reveal their inefficiency. They may resist comparisons with other communities or the private sector on the grounds that they are not comparable.

Table 11–1 presents an outline of the evaluation process. The process requires the

---

TABLE 11–1

The Evaluation Process

Specification
Goal setting
Research design
Measurement
Operationalization
Data collection
Analysis
Examination and interpretation

specification of how the research is to be carried out. The first step is goal setting—a complex task. Specifying clear or realistic goals can be difficult. In addition, consensus on goals may be elusive. Finally, there may also be a reluctance to be too specific because failure would then be too easy to document.

The next step is to establish a plan for gathering information. This is known as the research design. There are three basic types of research design: (1) pre-experimental, (2) quasi-experimental, and (3) experimental.[20]

Once the process is specified, analysts turn to the measurement phase, where they establish indicators of the phenomena they are observing. This sometimes involves **operationalization**, which is the specification of empirical indicators of nonobservable concepts.[21] For example, how will you recognize quality education? A major concern facing government agencies is increasing productivity. **Productivity** is maximizing the production of something with a minimum amount of resources. For example, how can students be provided with a quality public education at a minimum cost? To determine productivity, there must be measures of resources expended and the outcomes produced that are generally accepted. In the example of education, it is easy to measure the resources used by looking at the education budget. It is more difficult to measure the outcomes of education, although standardized test scores are often used.[22] After the measures are specified, data collection can begin. Finally, data must be analyzed to find and interpret their meaning. Do the data confirm or refute a program's effectiveness? Is quality education being delivered? Is the agency efficient? Once conclusions are drawn, citizens and government can know where things stand. With this information, government can be held accountable to the citizenry.

Goal Setting

Program goals and priorities are often vague. One of the sources of public dissatisfaction is that goals are often so broad and unrealistic that they can never be reached. The public wants programs that will facilitate economic development, protect the environment, end poverty, reduce crime, improve education, and so forth. Because these problems will never totally be solved, we often despair and believe nothing works and little can be done to improve a given situation. In reality, many government services work very well; others are in need of improvement. To determine what works and to develop ways to improve programs that do not, clear goals that can be measured must be established.

Increasingly, strategic planning is being used to establish goals. One type of strategic planning involves **benchmarking**, which is the establishment of reference points for success. This often involves searching for public and private organizations that are "best-in-class" and then working to meet their standards. Once the goal is set, research can begin to find the techniques that lead to success. For example, the State of Oregon and the City of Portland have been in the forefront of benchmarking in the public sector. Benchmarks are useful in goal setting.

> They take strategic planning out of the realm of abstraction, build consensus for it, and direct public and private resources to it. They focus public resources on measurable results and accountability. Typically, governments and institutions define success in terms of *inputs*: dollars spent, programs created, client contacts made. Yet additional dollars spent for, say, adult education are less telling than an increased proportion of adults who can read and comprehend a shipping order or a news report. They encourage collaboration among government agencies and public and private institutions in achieving outcomes or solving problems that are too

TABLE 11–2

Oregon Benchmarking[a]

Statewide Benchmarks	Historical		Target		
	1980	1990	1995	2000	2010
Pregnancy rate per 1,000 females age 10–17	24.0	19.6	9.8	8.0	8.0
Percentage of 11th graders who achieve specified skill levels in reading	—	83%	90%	95%	99%
Miles of assessed Oregon rivers and streams not meeting state and federal in-stream water quality standards	—	1,100	723	75	0
Real per capita income of Oregonians as a percentage of U.S. real per capita income	99%	92%	95%	100%	110%

[a]As these sample benchmarks illustrate, Oregon Benchmarks are indicators of social and economic progress. Every two years the Oregon Progress Board, a citizen panel chaired by the governor, publishes a new edition of *Oregon Benchmarks,* in effect, a report card of state progress.

Source: Adapted from *The Oregon Option Executive Summary,* n.d., http://www.econ.state.or.us/opb/OR_OPT/exec.htm.

big, complex, and stubborn to be tackled by any single organization.[23]

Table 11–2 provides a sample of the Oregon Benchmarks.

Research Design

Pre-experimental designs are the most common type of systematic evaluation because they are the easiest to do. Figure 11–2 (on page 294) presents two models: the before-and-after design and the time-trend projection.[24] The before-and-after model requires the community to take a reading of the situation, institute the program, and take another reading. If there is a change, the program is assumed to have caused that change. For instance, if a community wishes to reduce criminal behavior and it believes that a disproportionate amount of crime is committed by youths, it may implement a curfew for children under 16. To see if the plan worked, the city would note the crime rate, put

in place a curfew, and then measure the crime rate again. If the crime rate decreased, the city would probably attribute the change to the imposition of the curfew. A slightly more sophisticated model, the time trend, would take more readings to determine if there were a trend in the rate of crime, institute a curfew, and take additional readings to ascertain whether the trend had altered. More data points increase the credibility of the results.

The problem with either the before-after or the time-trend design is that there could be many confounding factors that could contribute to the findings. For instance, a lower crime rate could also be a function of a change in the weather, thus keeping teenagers indoors and out of trouble, regardless of curfews. Or, perhaps, one or two troublemakers caused most of the problems in the community, and they may have been arrested or have moved.

Quasi-experiments try to account for some, but not all, of these confounding effects

FIGURE 11–2

Pre-experimental Design

Before-and-after Design

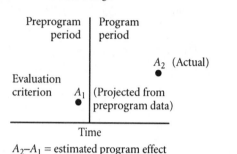

$A_2 - A_1$ = estimated program effect

Time-trend Projection Design

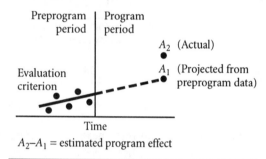

$A_2 - A_1$ = estimated program effect

success. Of course it is still impossible to account for all other explanations.

Kansas City, Missouri, undertook a quasi-experimental design to ascertain the most effective and efficient mode of policing. Three districts were established in which different levels of police activity were provided. One had no patrols—police only responded to calls. The second had patrols continued on the regular schedule; the third district significantly increased police activity. No significant differences were found in crime rates or citizen satisfaction.[25]

The use of a classic *experimental* model (Figure 11–4) is the best way to eliminate other influences. Not only is this model hard to implement in the real world, the experiment itself may affect the results. If everyone knows that a program is under a microscope, the people involved may behave differently than normal; this is known as the **Hawthorne effect**. Experiments are also difficult in the real world because participants must be chosen randomly to be part of the treatment group (those receiving the program) or the control group (those not receiving the program). Just imagine if the state or federal government said to City A that it *must* establish a

and thereby make it easier to attribute a connection between a program and the results found in a study. Quasi-experiments introduce a comparison group in addition to the experimental or treatment group that will actually receive some changed treatment (see Figure 11–3). For instance, if City A institutes a curfew and nearby City B, which is about the same size, with a similar socioeconomic profile, and similar crime problems, does not have a curfew, comparision of changes in the rate of crime in the two cities is possible. If crime goes down or rises in both cities or increases in City A but not City B, one might surmise that the curfew did not have an impact. If the rate of crime drops in City A but not City B, one might view the curfew as a

FIGURE 11–3

Quasi-experimental Design

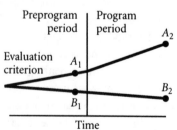

Time

Jurisdiction A has program; section B, the comparison jurisdiction, does not.

$(A_2 - A_1) - (B_2 - B_1)$ = estimated program effect

FIGURE 11–4

Experimental Design

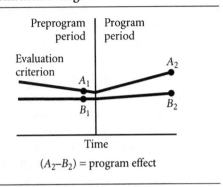

Time

$(A_2 - B_2)$ = program effect

curfew to see if it reduced crime and City B was told it could not establish a curfew, or worse yet, some teenagers in City A were randomly chosen to have a curfew and others were allowed free rein. If the program is seen as beneficial to participants, everyone wants to take part and will complain if left out. If the program is seen as punitive, nobody will want to be singled out and forced to participate.

One example of the use of an experiment examined the effect of a guaranteed income. As part of the War on Poverty, the Office of Economic Opportunity established the New Jersey Guaranteed Work Incentive Experiment. The goal was to reduce dependency and help people escape from poverty. The experiment was intricate, involving different levels of income guarantees and different deductions for earned income. The essence of the experiment was the random selection of families receiving public assistance and the assignment of them to either a control group, for whom nothing would change, or one of the experimental groups that would have various levels of income guarantees. In the face of political pressure to get quick and positive results, the study reported the program to be a success. It stated that families receiving guaranteed incomes did not cut back on their work efforts and behaved in a man-

ner similar to the control group.[26] While this report was seen as positive by then-President Nixon because he wanted to implement a Family Assistance Plan that had a guaranteed income as its centerpiece, it was greeted by skepticism by others. The Rand Corporation, which did not do the original study, reanalyzed the results. It discovered that the State of New Jersey changed its welfare rules six months into the experiment, which allowed the control group to receive many of the generous benefits of the experimental groups.[27] No wonder there was little difference in the behavior of the two groups!

Because of the controversy surrounding the New Jersey study, another experiment was commissioned. The Seattle/Denver Income Maintenance Experiment included 5,000 families and lasted 5 years. Again, participants were randomly assigned to various experimental groups or the control group. Job counseling and training were also provided. For advocates of guaranteed income, the results were disappointing. Counseling and training had no impact; work effort decreased; the longer the income guarantee, the less the work effort; and participants with income guarantees had more marital problems than the control group.

Operationalization

It is easier to develop indicators for some goals than for others. Income, hours worked, crime rates, reading scores—all are relatively easy to measure. Not all the goals of local government are that easy to measure. Often, multiple measures must be used to obtain a complete picture. A variety of indicators are used in evaluating public services and their delivery.[28] *Input measures*, which specify the amount of resources allocated to an activity, are commonly used, though they are not totally satisfying. For education, input measures would include dollars spent per student, number of books in the library, number of teachers with advanced degrees, and so forth. These data can be used to imply that there is quality in the system and show that resources are being allocated fairly and equitably. But, as noted, a clear relationship between inputs and consequences has not been established. High per-pupil expenditures may result in high levels of achievement because the money is used to keep the best teachers and provide state-of-the-art technology. Equally plausible is that high per-pupil cost is the result of inefficient and wasteful management.

Output indicators are also widely used. Output measures include such data as miles of roads repaved, number of people inoculated, tons of garbage collected. These data are more meaningful if expressed as a ratio, such as the number of people inoculated per 10,000 population or the number of miles of road repaved for every 1,000 miles of road. *Efficiency measures* are indicators that relate the amount of service output provided to the input required to produce it. Examples of efficiency measures include miles of road paved per worker-hour or number of graduates per dollars spent. These indicators can be used to compare performance over time, or to other methods of providing the service, or to other agencies or communities.

Other indicators that are used are *effectiveness or outcome measures*. These attempt to reflect the degree to which program goals are being met. One study developed multiple measures to evaluate the effectiveness of urban transportation. It measured such things as accessibility (percentage of residents within x distance from public transit), travel time (travel time between key destinations), comfort (quality of the road surface—"bumpiness"—index), safety (transportation injuries and damage), cost to users (cost per trip), environmental quality (noise along corridors), satisfaction (citizen perceptions), and monetary costs (program costs).[29] Measuring productivity requires the use of input, output, efficiency, and outcome or effectiveness measures.

Data Collection[30]

After measures are selected, data must be collected. A variety of techniques can be used to collect information. One of the most obvious methods is asking people. Interviews and questionnaires help obtain objective and subjective information about the backgrounds of program participants and the consequences of their participation by simply asking clients how many times they have used a service or how long they have to wait to receive a service (objective). Asking how satisfied clients are with the service or with the way they were treated yields a subjective reaction. Focus groups, which bring people together to try to develop discussions and elicit responses and reactions to current conditions or future proposals, are currently being used to gather a great deal of subjective information.

Program staff are a valuable source of information. Many insights into what is working and what is not can be gleaned by asking the service deliverer. Tests are often used to evaluate educational programs. Rating by experts is another means of establishing a data base. For instance, having a social work professional evaluate client attitudes toward work before and after a job training program may be one way to analyze the effectiveness of the program.

Another method of gathering data is through observation. Questions may be unneccessary if behaviors can be observed. A common and creative way of gathering data on the most popular exhibits at a museum is to look at the wear on the carpet. Another use of observation is to sit in on a public hearing and count the number of complaints presented about a specific program.

A final method of gathering data is the use of existing program records. Once the measures are identified, program records and agency files become a repository for data needed to analyze programs. It is necessary to assure that record keeping and categorization do not change over time if valid comparisons are to be made. The use of computers has made record keeping easier but also has increased the potential for breaches in the privacy of clients.

Statistical records can also be a useful source of data. An agency may be able to obtain a series of data points before a program is put into place and thus be able to chart differences that occur after program implementation.

Examination and Interpretation

Once the data are available, they must be interpreted. When using ad hoc evaluation, data are generally not gathered very systematically and the analysis is usually impressionistic. When data are systematically collected, they are generally aggregated and categorized in a meaningful way, often using statistical techniques. Sometimes simple statistics like a **frequency distribution** are adequate. An example of a frequency distribution would be counting the number of people who responded to a question concerning satisfaction with an agency's performance. For example, if 89 percent of people were satisfied and 11 percent were not satisfied with a government service, we would think that the agency was fairly successful.

Use of more sophisticated statistical techniques may provide more information from the data. For example, if we are concerned about the possibility of discrimination in the provision of a service, we may want to compare the satisfaction rates of minority groups with those of whites. If we were to find, for instance, that 98 percent of all whites were satisfied with the service but only 65 percent of minorities were satisfied, we might conclude that a problem exists. Analysts have many sophisticated statistical techniques to aid them in interpreting data and drawing conclusions. It is important to recognize that no matter how sophisticated the analysis, if any of the prior steps in the evaluation process are found wanting, the analysis could lead to improper conclusions.

Reforming Government Programs and Service Delivery

Many programs can be shown to be efficient and effective; many public servants are doing outstanding jobs. Nonetheless, conventional wisdom and ad hoc evaluation often indicate that the general public is unhappy with government. In some instances, citizen dissatisfaction with government service delivery may be due to disagreement on the decision rules that bureaucrats use. On the other hand, some of the complaints about service delivery are not really complaints about the way that the services are delivered, but reflect ideological differences about the proper role of government.

> The programs might have indeed been wasteful by some definitions, but they represented the legitimate product of the American democratic process. The danger here is that solutions billed as administrative, managerial, or technical may disguise underlying differences of policy or significant competition among disparate interests.[31]

Any flaw in service delivery will have immediate, negative consequences. "Citizens can immediately tell whether a service has been delivered: they can see whether the trash has been picked up or whether a pothole, broken traffic light, or ruptured water main has been fixed. In these cases, urban services are also distinctly tangible and visible."[32]

The public seems to judge the public sector more harshly than the private sector. While a long line in a bank may cause patrons to feel that they came at a bad time, individuals become more impatient if they go to city hall to pick up a license for their dog and they have to wait. There is a widespread perception that the public sector is less productive than the private sector. "The *image* of unproductive public service bureaucrats is an enduring and powerful one. . . . productivity is a *political* problem as well as an objective problem of management efficiency."[33] (Italics in original.)

Urban governments are under increasing pressure to improve service delivery and/or find new ways to provide those services. In addition, citizens have also frequently resisted attempts to raise taxes to pay for services that they continue to demand. Several approaches can be linked to improving productivity and quality of public services.

One standard approach to productivity improvement is structural reform, that is, revision of the form of government, consolidation of governments, or reorganization. Some cities have changed their form of government from mayor–council to council–manager because of the belief that a professional city manager will result in more efficient and effective service delivery. Some local governments transferred services to other governments, annexed new territory, or joined with other jurisdictions to increase economies of scale in service provision and to improve productivity. Internal reorganization may also increase productivity within a local government. One idea that has gained currency is merging police and fire departments into a Department of Public Safety; police and fire persons are cross-trained so they can help each other and adapt to emergency needs.

A second method of improving productivity is through technological innovation. Elaine Sharpe lists a variety of products or technological innovations that improved performance: infrared heat detection devices to help fire fighters find victims and the source of the fire even in dense smoke; special incinerators to recover energy from solid waste disposal; and mechanized refuse collection vehicles that required less people to collect garbage.[34] In Scottsdale, Arizona, for instance, the city grew in population by 50 percent over 10 years, but the number of refuse collection employees remained constant due to the use of technology.[35] Of course, computers have become so mundane that it is easy to overlook the impact they have had on improving productivity. Computers make mass mailings and record keeping easier, quicker, and more accurate. Geographical information systems (GISs) make it easy to identify the characteristics of land-use and of residents in different areas. This facilitates record keeping, planning, and service delivery.

A third strategy is management reform. A variety of management approaches have been suggested to improve the performance of service delivery by the public sector. Three of the most prominent are total quality management (TQM), reinventing government, and re-engineering. All attempt to import into the public sector techniques that were judged successful in the private sector.

Total Quality Management (TQM)

Many organizations, both public and private, have adopted the TQM philosophy with the zeal of religious converts. Others have dismissed TQM as just another passing management fad.[36] TQM may pass, but it has had a great impact in how numerous public bureaucracies function. It has been employed in places ranging from New York City to Fort Collins, Colorado, to Palm Beach County, Florida.[37] Much of the foundation for the TQM movement was laid in the 1920s and 1930s at Western Electric/Bell Labs by Walter Shewhart and his disciple, W. Edwards Deming. Joe Juran, another leader, also worked in the group founded by Shewhart. TQM can be defined as follows:

> TQM means that the organization's culture is defined by and supports the constant attainment of customer satisfaction through an integrated system of tools, techniques, and training. This involves the continuous improvement of organizational processes, resulting in high quality products and services.[38]

The orthodox TQM philosophy has several key tenets.[39] The first and most important is that the customer is the ultimate determiner of quality. Second, quality should be built into the product early in the production process rather than being added on at the end. In other words, it is easier, cheaper, and better to do it right the first time than to have to do it over again later. If a trash collector lets a lot of refuse blow away as trash is collected, he or she may be sent out to clean it up later. This entails additional gas and personnel costs, not to mention the ire of unhappy customers.

Third, eliminating variability is essential for producing high quality. TQM depends very heavily on statistical information and charts that allow tracking of outputs to make sure they fall within acceptable limits.

Fourth, quality depends on work systems, not individual efforts. Advocates of TQM believe that 15 percent of all errors may be attributed to individual failings while 85 percent of the errors are a function of work systems.[40] Because TQM requires teamwork and an organizational culture of cooperation, as opposed to competition, many proponents of orthodox TQM advocate the elimination of individual performance ratings and individual merit pay, both of which foster competition.

Fifth, quality requires continuous improvement. The environment, technologies, and customer wants are always changing and so must organizations. The focus should not be on the bottom line, because that is a short-term goal. Instead, attention should be directed toward constantly adapting inputs and processes to assure long-term excellence. In response to public pressure for increased accountability, responsiveness, and effectiveness, managers have been refining tools to better measure outputs to evaluate effective performance.

Sixth, quality improvement requires worker participation. The people performing the tasks are often in the best position to improve the process. Today's buzzword is worker empowerment. In the past, managers imposed a system on workers without seeking their input. To receive input, communications barriers need to be broken down and trust established. Problem-solving teams are established to solve problems and improve quality. These are sometimes called "quality circles," though quality circles are not intrinsic to TQM.

Implementing TQM is expensive. According to one estimate, it takes up 15 percent of staff time on a regular basis in addition to extra training time. The cost of training can run high. For example, Wilmington, North Carolina, spent $75,000 on initial training and $30,000 a year for ongoing training.[41]

Finally, quality requires organizational commitment. It requires a culture that supports using information for quality improvement, not as a way to judge or control people; employees must have the authority to carry out their duties; all members should be equitably rewarded for the success of the organization; cooperation, not competition, is necessary; job security is essential; a climate of fairness must exist; compensation should be equitable; and employees should have a stake in the organization.[42] Only under such conditions can workers remain committed to a program that demands constant improvement.

There are four main impediments to applying TQM principles in the public sector: (1) the public sector delivers services not products; (2) the real customer is not clear; (3) there are differences in the importance of inputs and processes versus results; and (4) the government culture is not conducive to consistent values.[43]

TQM was designed to improve quality and consistency of manufactured products. Delivering services is different because they are labor intensive. As a result, evaluation may be based on characteristics of the individual performing the service, rather than the service itself. A police officer who delivers a speeding ticket to a "customer" may be very efficient and courteous, but it is unlikely that the customer will appreciate the service delivered. TQM is also aimed at reducing variability. Because situations vary considerably, it is difficult to prescribe fixed processes and behaviors for service delivery. As noted above, the use of bureaucratic rules is an attempt to limit variation, but the outcomes do not always produce maximum quality.

A second problem with applying TQM in the public sector is defining the customer. The citizen in a democracy may be viewed as a customer, but he or she is also the owner. In addition, a government agency is often forced to deal with customers with competing values. Some citizens are satisfied with the performance of schools if they provide sex education while others are highly dissatisfied. Which group of citizens is the customer? Obviously both. Thus, high customer satisfaction often is not possible. In a school situation is the customer the student, his or her parents, the taxpayers of the community, or the organization that will employ the student? Still another problem is that the direct customer, in this case the student, would want access to all the latest in technologies and conveniences in school, whereas the ultimate customer, taxpayers, who may not have children in school, may want to minimize costs.

> Because government agencies must serve a wide variety of customers who have widely divergent and even contradictory demands and because the general public remains a "hidden customer" with additional, often incompatible demands, government agencies often have to deliver a service or product that reflects an uneasy compromise.[44]

A third problem is differences in the importance of output measures of success. Traditional TQM principles dictate that it is wrong to focus on short-term profits (outputs) rather than investments and improvements (inputs and processes) that will yield long-term results. In the public sector, however, managers have historically focused only on inputs (for example, how much money is in the budget) and ignored outputs. More recently, public concerns about inefficiency and ineffectiveness have led to complaints about a focus solely on inputs. As a result, governments have developed a great many results-oriented techniques, for example, merit pay to reward highly productive civil servants. Many see this as an improvement over a focus solely on trying to maximize inputs or resources, ignoring the consequences, or outputs, of government programs. Now, contrary to the dictates of TQM, the public manager must not be primarily concerned with agency budgets and procedures (inputs and processes), but must demonstrate efficiency and effectiveness (outputs).

Finally, the government culture is not well-suited to a long-term commitment to TQM. The most obvious problem is the turnover of top government managers. "In most places, when top elected or appointed officials dedicated to TQM make their departure, TQM very often goes right along with them."[45] In Hillsborough County, Florida, the county board fired the county's top management because the board viewed TQM as a threat to its power.[46] Other aspects of a culture conducive to TQM are also difficult to attain in the public sector. For example, delegating authority to go along with responsibility is often difficult. Also, a conducive culture allows employees to make mistakes. In the public sector, with media coverage, mistakes are often punished.

Nevertheless, James Swiss argues that some aspects of TQM can be reformulated to be used in the public sector. He suggests that government agencies can be improved by obtaining client feedback to be used as *one* consideration in decision making. In addition, he argues that government should track performance. It should continue its use of output measures but should also use TQM methods to evaluate processes. Quality measures would be added to quantity measures. Government agencies can and should also work for continuous improvement. Finally, mechanisms such as quality circles are a valuable way of empowering the worker.[47]

Mayor Joseph Sensenbrenner instituted TQM in Madison, Wisconsin, where it has enjoyed success. He notes that at the city garage, turnaround time went from nine days to three, that $7.15 was saved for every $1 used for preventative maintenance, and that annual savings reached $700,000.[48] See Box 11–1 (on page 302) for another example of the use of TQM in Madison. "In the right situation and trained on the right problems, Total Quality Management does seem to work. That is the good news. The bad news is that it is very hard to do well. Despite the success stories, it is no magic formula for instant government rejuvenation."[49] One commentator says that while TQM may be part of the answer to improving government performance, it is only "half a loaf," and we need to go further toward reinventing government.[50]

Reinventing Government[51]

The book *Reinventing Government: How the Entrepreneurial Spirit Is Transforming the Public Sector* by David Osborne, a journalist, and Ted Gaebler, a former city manager, revolutionized the field of public management. The book is replete with examples and success stories. The authors focus on local government, however, the federal government has attempted to use the ideas of Osborne and Gaebler. Vice President Al Gore heads the National Performance Review, which is designed to make government work better and cost less.

Osborne and Gaebler believe the old hierarchical model of bureaucracy is inadequate for modern government administration and that the search for accountability through rules and regulations has resulted in inefficiencies and red tape. They argue for giving government employees increased flexibility to

search for creative and innovative solutions to problems.

In a sense, reinventing government is based on the old idea of the separation of politics and administration. According to this idea, traced to an influential article by Woodrow Wilson, the job of the policy-making branch of government is to establish the programs and the job of the public manager is to have discretion to determine how to implement those programs effectively and efficiently. Wilson wrote, "large powers and unhampered discretion seem to me the indispensable conditions of responsibility. Public attention must be easily directed, in each case of good or bad administration, to just the man deserving of praise or blame."[52] The urban manager should be accountable to the public, not rule bound.

One author argues that public agencies are inherently less efficient than their private sector counterparts, implying government cannot be reinvented to work better and cost less.

> First, government executives are less able than their private counterparts to *define* an efficient course of action. . . . Second, public executives have weaker incentives than do private executives to *find* an efficient course of action. . . . Third, public executives have less authority than private ones to *impose* an efficient course of action. Legislatures usually refuse to give agency managers the power to hire and fire or to raise and allocate funds.[53]

Reinventing Government borrows many concepts from TQM in the search for improved performance in the public sector. It also adds additional ideas. As with TQM, it is argued that public organizations can be made better if they adhere to private management principles. Osborne and Gaebler argue that government must be based on an entrepreneurial model that "shifts economic resources out of an area of lower and into an area of higher productivity and greater yield."[54] The result is increased productivity and effectiveness. Entrepreneurial government has 10 basic principles.

BOX 11–1

The Cult of Total Quality

It may have been the oddest scene in state or local government anywhere in the country at that moment: a dozen law enforcement officers, sitting around a table on an unseasonably warm afternoon, discussing Pareto charts, fish-bone diagrams, countermeasures matrices, and assorted other teachings of a 91-year-old statistics professor whom few of them had ever heard of but who had already turned their working lives inside out.

It was a meeting of the police force in Madison, Wisconsin, convened to indoctrinate officer trainees in implementing total quality management, the system of ideas that W. Edwards Deming taught Japanese corporations in the 1950s and that he has been preaching in the United States ever since. If it sounds a little cultlike, that is because total quality management has many of the aspects of a cult: special vocabulary, intense personal relationships, and fierce dedication to its principles on the part of true believers. . . .

The process goes something like this: A labor–management "project team" is established to focus on a chosen problem. The team identifies the customer or customers who benefit from solving the problem. It gathers all relevant statistical data about how the process currently works and about all outside factors and complications affecting it (this is where the charts and diagrams come in). Then the team draws up a plan of action.

Deming developed all this to be used by industrial corporations, for which the product is a tangible object, statistical measurement is relatively simple, and the customer is easy to define. Applying it to the fuzzier world of government services is a trickier proposition. Nevertheless, governments all over the country are trying it; some, like Madison, have been into it fairly heavily for more than five years.

The way Madison applied Deming's principles to the mundane task of trash collection provides as good an example as any.

In the mid-1980s, Madison's trash collectors ("pickers," in trash jargon) were costing the city a quarter of a million dollars in workers' compensation each year. An average of almost five pickers a day were out due to on-the-job injuries.

Trash collectors blamed the injuries on new equipment—bought without their input—that cut the number of pickers on a truck from two to one. Management, meanwhile, was blaming the problem on malingering. An unhappy situation all around. "You could have scraped morale off the floor with a putty knife," says Tom Neale, who was a Madison picker at the time.

So the Madison streets division decided to unleash TQM. It set up a project team that set the goal for the project (reduce workers' compensation payments by reducing on-the-job injuries) and set about gathering data on how, why, where, and when injuries occur. The project team's findings were a complete surprise to both sides. The most important factors in injury were not equipment or malingering. They were the age of the picker and the time of year. The older the picker, the higher the injury rate. And injuries went up during the high-trash-flow seasons of spring and summer.

On the basis of the report, Madison decided to use recycling to reduce overall volumes of trash and to recruit younger pickers. The results have been impressive. In the years since, workers' compensation payments have declined by 80 percent. Days lost to injuries have been halved. Morale is way up. TQM has become the way business is done at the streets division in Madison.

Source: Jonathan Walters, "The Cult of Total Quality," *Governing* (May 1992): 38–39.

1. Focus not on providing public services but on **catalyzing** all sectors (catalytic government);
2. **Empower** citizens by pushing bureaucratic control to community control (community-owned government);
3. Promote **competition** between service providers (competitive government);
4. Let goals or **mission**, not rules and regulations, drive the government (mission-driven government);
5. Measure performance by **outcomes** not inputs (results-oriented government);
6. Redefine clients as **customers** (customer-driven government);
7. Put energies into **earning** money not spending it (enterprising government);
8. **Prevent** problems before they occur (anticipatory government);
9. **Decentralize** authority through participatory management (decentralized government);
10. Prefer **market** mechanisms to bureaucratic ones (market-driven government).[55]

The idea of **catalytic** government draws a distinction between the provision of services and the production of services.[56] It also implies that government should be more creative in the provision of public services. *Reinventing Government* presents this as the distinction between steering and rowing. Governments can make the decision that a certain service should be provided (steering) to a community, for example, schools, but it does not necessarily have to produce (rowing) the service. For instance, and the following will be discussed in a later chapter, the government can provide for education by issuing vouchers. The individual with the voucher could then choose between a variety of service producers, presumably in the public or private sector.

Osborne and Gaebler list 36 alternative forms of service delivery classified as tradi-tional, innovative, and avant-garde.[57] The traditional methods include creating rules and sanctions, regulation and deregulation, grants, subsidies, loans, and contracting. More innovative methods include public–private partnerships, public–public partnerships, vouchers, and technical assistance. Among their suggestions for avant-garde methods of service delivery are co-production or self-help, voluntary associations, and equity investments. An example of co-production would be the establishment of neighborhood watch programs to improve crime prevention as police and the public work together. In New York City, business owners were allowed to form voluntary organizations and given taxing power to fund improvements. Many city governments invest money to establish business and industrial development corporations and therefore own a share of them.   •

Another reinventing strategy is **empowering** citizens by giving them more say in the direction of programs, thereby taking some control from the bureaucracy. As may be expected, many dedicated public servants see this as another attempt at bashing the bureaucracy. Most bureaucrats feel they are working for the people and using their skills to help citizens. Nonetheless, Osborne and Gaebler state that, "the Progressive confidence in 'neutral administrations' and 'professionalism' blinded us to the consequences of taking control out of the hands of families and communities."[58] One example of citizens taking control occurred in a public housing project in Washington, D.C. Residents, fed up with drugs and crimes and all the urban ills that often accompany life in the projects, took matters into their own hands. They started tutoring students, held bake sales and raffles to raise scholarship money, and eventually moved to self-management of the project. Community organizations are often more aware of problems, have more compassion, are cheaper, and are more creative than government agencies.[59] Unfortunately, not all community projects work out as well as the Washington, D.C. example.

Competitive government is also supposed to improve service delivery. According to *Reinventing Government*, competition results in greater efficiency in both the public and private sectors, requires agencies to be more responsive to the needs of their customers, forces them be more innovative, and provides them with higher pride and morale.[60] One way of increasing competition is through **privatization**, that is, the use of the profit or nonprofit sectors to produce services currently provided by local government.[61] A number of recent studies have evaluated the efficiency of public, as opposed to private, service providers. E.S. Savas found that solid waste collection, fire protection, health care, education, and social services can often be provided more efficiently and effectively by the private sector.[62] On the other hand, Charles Goodsell examined evaluations of public–private service provision and found no pattern of private supremacy.[63] Research by Robert Stein indicates that cost savings are maximized when municipalities use a mix of direct production of services and contracting out (with both private and other public entities).[64]

Those subscribing to Savas's view would demand that government "privatize" services. If services are privatized, individuals could use the marketplace as a means of expressing their preferences. Presumably the customer could decide whether or not to buy the service and could choose among various suppliers. If services are only provided by government, control comes from complaints or pressure on the institutions of government.

Osborne and Gaebler emphasize that privatization is not the only way to increase competition. In education, open enrollment programs or free choice allow parents to send their children across school boundary lines to any public school they desire. The school that attracts the student receives per capita pay-

ment from the state. In the entrepreneurial spirit, the state of Minnesota undertook a management reform program to make state agencies compete with each other and with the private sector. From the motor pool, to central supply, to consulting services, agencies undertook market studies to find out customer needs to determine how they could compete more effectively with the private sector.[65]

The goal of reinvention is to improve efficiency by changing from rule-bound government to **mission**-driven government. Rather than focusing on means, that is, going by the book, the focus should be on ends, that is, what does the agency wish to accomplish. Obviously, some rules are necessary to provide accountability, but too often rules limit creativity and innovation. The current budgetary system in most communities results in waste, not efficiency. Generally funds are allocated for specific purposes and must be used only for those purposes even if needs are greater in another area. There is no incentive to find more economical solutions because monies could not be reallocated for other purposes. Many "reinvented" communities have loosened the reins. Visalia, California, instituted an Expenditure Control Budget to change the dynamics of budgeting. Instead of forcing local governments to spend money for a specific purpose or lose the funds, they were encouraged to save and invest money. In the past, if the police chief wanted to hire a new officer, he went to the city council for the money, which he might or might not get. Under the new system, the chief was expected to find savings in other areas so that the monies could be shifted to pay for a new officer. Mission-driven systems rather than rule-bound systems are also used to speed up and simplify the hiring process.

These more flexible systems, which create permission to fail, can obviously produce positive results. Unfortunately, they can also create big problems, as the bankruptcy of Orange County, California, highlights. Rather than raising taxes to meet the increasing costs of government, Orange County, in an entrepreneurial spirit, made risky investments to receive high returns. When the bubble burst, Orange County was bankrupt. See also the case of Visalia in Box 11–2 (on pages 306–307).

Results-oriented government focuses on **outputs** and **outcomes** rather than inputs. It requires agencies to develop measures of performance by which it can be judged. For instance, Sunnyvale, California, uses thousands of measures. It sets goals, determines the current status, sets specific objectives, and establishes performance indicators. The Parks and Recreation Department can be evaluated using such measures as the number of dead trees replaced within two months, the percentage of participants in recreation programs ranking them good or better, and the number of complaints received. Osborne and Gaebler note that "what gets measured gets done."[66] Unfortunately, this can lead to goal displacement if what is not measured, but is still important, does not get done. Results-oriented government can help to identify successful programs and those that need improvement. It can be used to reward successful individuals and organizations. As noted in the discussion of TQM, however, rewarding success is sometimes counterproductive because it may induce competition rather than cooperation.

As with TQM, **customer** satisfaction is a driving force of reinventing government. There are many ways that agencies can "listen to the voice of the customer." Some examples include citizen surveys, community surveys, customer councils, focus groups, quality guarantees, ombudsmen, and complaint-tracking systems. The West Virginia Guaranteed Work Force Program retrains employees to employer specifications; if the employers are not satisfied, there is no charge. Many high schools in Colorado and West Virginia make similar guarantees. This certainly provides an incentive for doing it

right the first time—an important component of TQM. The ombudsman is a concept that originated in Sweden and had been imported to at least 15 states, and many cities, and counties by 1988. The **ombudsman** is a contact person for citizens; he or she can help cut through red tape and help citizens with problems they have with the government. Complaint-tracking systems are put into place to discover problem areas and to see if and how long it takes to resolve problems. In Phoenix, Arizona, city council members are able to see if their constituents are getting the answers they need from city agencies.[67]

Another tenet of reinventing government is **earning** money, not just spending it. For example, the Metropolitan Milwaukee Sewage District is able to earn $7.5 million in revenue by turning sewage sludge into fertilizer. Chicago turned a $2 million cost into a $2 million source of revenue. It used to *cost* the city $24 to tow a car. Now private business *pays* the city $25 per car for the privilege. Government can also earn money by imposing fees or user charges. When refuse collection is not privatized, the public sector often charges residents to collect garbage. Governments can also make money by spending money. Studies of the Head Start Program indicate a great return on the investment of money in the program. For every $1.00 spent in delivering the program, $5.00 is saved or earned through lower welfare costs, remedial education costs, crime costs, and increased taxes paid. Investment in Welfare-to-Work programs also has long-term cost savings.[68] The Personal Responsibility and Work Opportunity Reconciliation Act of 1996 will allow states to develop innovative programs to reduce long-term welfare costs. Short-term costs, however, might have to rise if the long-term goals are to be met. States may have to provide more education and training and continue some benefits until former welfare recipients are secure in their new jobs.

BOX 11-2

Entrepreneurial Government: The Morning After

As befits a movement that encourages government to act more like the private sector, entrepreneurial government has already erected a visible legacy. If you pay attention to management trends, you might even be able to tick off some of the highlights: The huge Solano Mall in Fairfield, California, was built on land sold to its developer by the city—it gives the city a piece of its revenues; Orlando City Hall, built by a private developer in exchange for a neighboring—and lucrative—parcel of land; the concession stand that Visalia, California, erected at its softball field in exchange for a cut of the concessionaire's profits.

What you may not know is that Visalia has added a new landmark for the movement, only this time with a twist. It is a downtown Radisson Hotel. And it is the building that, for the moment at least, has put an end to entrepreneurial government in Visalia. . . .

[That building] is the city-owned Radisson Hotel, which opened at the tail end of 1990. It is the tallest building in town. From its top floor you can gaze east across the foothills to the massive wall of the Sierra Nevada, or west over the tops of the oak and sycamore trees that give Visalia a charm unusual for Central Valley cities, to the rich farmland that borders the community. As a hotel, it would be a fine addition to any city's downtown. As an economic development tool, it appears to have succeeded admirably, keeping Visalia's downtown core healthy. But as a real estate development, it's been a disaster. And as a political and management symbol, it may cast a shadow for years to come.

In the beginning, the city's contribution to the project wasn't supposed to be much more than the $4 million it cost to buy the land; so far, however, Visalia taxpayers have put in $20 million in either actual spending or debt. On its way to being built, the hotel dragged city officials into a morass of financing imbroglios that ultimately left Visalia holding the bag—ownership of the entire project rather than just the land on which it sits. It helped cost one city manager his job and, indirectly, several city council members their seats. And it has transformed the political climate in Visalia, giving civic entrepreneurialism a bad name and constricting the city's tolerance for innovation of any sort. . . .

Duckworth [the city manager after Gaebler] was a manager in Gaebler's entrepreneurial image. He, too, believed in a city government that actively sought opportunities to make money. So when Courtney [the developer] —who turned out to have a string of lawsuits dogging him from other ventures—was unable to secure a $12-million construction loan a month after he and the city had signed their lease arrangement, Duckworth agreed to have the city lend Courtney almost $3 million and to guarantee further loan payments in exchange for a share of the hotel's revenue.

But that didn't resolve the problems. Courtney proved chronically incapable of securing funding, and the city negotiated new loan guarantees in return for an even bigger cut of the prospective profits. By the time the hotel was finished in 1990 with some $1 million in cost overruns that Courtney couldn't cover, it was clear that the city would have to bail out the project or live with an empty shell sitting on prime

(continued on next page)

(continued)

downtown land. So in the spring of 1991 the city council agreed to buy the hotel, assuming debts of $12 million in addition to some $8 million it had already spent or committed.

The extent of the city's—and especially Duckworth's—involvement in the project never sat especially well with many Visalians. In fact, Duckworth had carried the entrepreneurial notion of administrative flexibility further than many citizens even knew. He had authorized payment to a local public relations firm to boost Courtney's image and payment of legal fees to help Courtney defend against lawsuits filed to stop the project. Most disturbing was the discovery, after the city bought the hotel, that in 1988 Duckworth had authorized what council members interpreted as an under-the-table payment to help Courtney qualify for a construction loan, funneled through an architect involved in the project.

Source: Rob Gurwitt, "Entrepreneurial Government: The Morning After," *Governing* 7 (May 1994): 34–35, 37–38.

Spending on new technologies and equipment often more than returns the initial cost through increased efficiencies and, sometimes, the elimination of labor costs. Another way of earning money in an enterprising organization is through sharing the savings or earnings as a means of encouraging creativity. San Antonio, Texas, hired a private law firm to collect taxes. Former Mayor Henry Cisneros said that as they get a percentage, "they have a tremendous incentive to collect taxes, and *they do things we couldn't do in terms of legal process.*"[69] [Italics added.]

Preventing problems before they become more serious and costly is a characteristic of anticipatory government. This fits with the old adage "that an ounce of prevention is worth a pound of cure." The Head Start Program mentioned above is an example. Many communities have begun recycling programs to reduce the amount of solid waste. A great number of other environmental protection programs have been implemented based on the idea that it is easier, safer, and cheaper to prevent pollution than to suffer its negative effects and have to clean up later.

Strategic planning is a tool often used to anticipate and plan for the future. The National Civic League has supervised many community visioning exercises where communities, usually with public and private cooperation, set goals for the future and develop strategies to realize those goals. "In government, one other element is necessary: a *consensus.* A government has more stakeholders than a business, and most of them vote. To change anything important, many stakeholders must agree."[70]

Osborne and Gaebler believe that political reform is needed to make anticipatory government work. They advocate regional governments as a way of planning for entire metropolitan regions. They recognize that the electoral process creates short-term incentives. From an electoral standpoint, cutting taxes is often better than spending money on programs with long-term benefits. Their hope for the future is informal civic leadership coalitions, such as BUILD in Baltimore and the Greater Indianapolis Progress Committee.

In essence, . . . [the civic leadership coalitions] act as keepers of the long-term agenda. By focusing on major issues that loom ahead, they create a forum for anticipatory thinking. By engaging as political activists and lobbyists, they then turn that agenda into government policy. Where political parties and elected leaders have failed to respond to new realities, these organizations have become virtually the only way a community can get a handle on its long-term problems.[71]

As noted earlier, the vision of these civic organizations is often the vision of the business community, which usually means a focus on their concerns.

Decentralizing government is designed to move from hierarchy toward participation and teamwork. This is another characteristic shared with TQM. One way of giving more authority to employees is through quality circles. There are other models, such as employee development programs to help employees develop talents and skills that will improve the organization, attitude surveys, employee evaluations of managers, and reward programs to honor and provide incentives to developers of innovative programs and high achievers.

Reinventing government is **market**-oriented. Too often programs and agencies fail because they are driven by politics, not markets. Programs are put into place to please constituents, not customers. Bureaucracies fight over service delivery because they are playing power games and fighting over turf rather than looking for efficiencies. New programs often create fragmented delivery systems as they are often grafted onto old programs rather than rethinking the entire idea. For these, and other reasons, Osborne and Gaebler advocate the use of market mechanisms where possible. One caveat needs to be introduced. For good or ill, public organizations will never cease to be political.

One approach to using markets is for the government to restructure the marketplace. One way to do this is to provide information to consumers so that they might make better choices in the marketplace. Another way of restructuring the marketplace is to create or augment demand for a product or service. Providing tax breaks, vouchers, or grants for day care will increase the number of day care providers because demand for the service will rise. A third way of restructuring the marketplace is to share the risk by providing loan guarantees to private developers to entice them to undertake risky projects.

Governments can also apply market-oriented thinking to regulation. They can use market-based incentives rather than commands. Workmen's compensation programs are a good example. Businesses pay a premium based upon the number and cost of injured workers. This means that it is wise for businesses to spend money to reduce accidents because that money will be returned by lower premiums, not to mention fewer hours lost and higher morale.

Many of these techniques are being used successfully. Success is often a function of the political, economic, and social setting in which these techniques are tried. Success is also tied to the effectiveness of the leaders and the competence of the followers. Increased flexibility increases creativity but sometimes creates issues of equity and accountability.

Re-engineering[72]

The latest attempt to transform local government management is called re-engineering. The short definition is "starting over."[73] Re-engineering differs from reinventing government because it is seen as revolutionary, not evolutionary. It also differs from TQM.

They both recognize the importance of processes, and they both start with the needs of the process customer and work backwards from there. However, the two programs differ fundamentally. Quality programs work within the framework of a company's existing processes and seek to enhance them by means of . . . continuous incremental improvement. . . . Reengineering . . . seeks breakthroughs, not by enhancing processes, but by discarding them and replacing them with entirely new ones.[74]

"Reengineering . . . is the **fundamental** rethinking and **radical** redesign of . . . **processes** to achieve **dramatic** improvements in critical, contemporary measures of performance, such as cost, quality, service, and speed."[75] The key terms are highlighted.

A *fundamental* rethinking involves asking the question, "why do you do what you do and why do you do it that way?" Welfare reform is an example of the federal government asking why it was providing Aid to Families with Dependent Children (AFDC). There is widespread agreement that something needs to be done about poverty, but not agreement that the federal government needs to do it. Welfare reform cast out all kinds of rules and restrictions on the way programs were to be administered by the states and localities. Thus, as responsibility for welfare is shifted, states and localities are in the position to ask why they were carrying out AFDC as they were. With many of the restrictions eliminated under the new Temporary Assistance for Needy Families (TANF) block grant, states are freer to innovate. Many conservatives are asking if the federal government needs to be providing many existing domestic programs. They believe that state and local governments could come up with more creative solutions.

The term *radical* means getting to the root. It implies a basic or fundamental change, that is, reinvention not improvement, enhancement, or modification. It requires "*discontinuous thinking*—identifying and abandoning the outdated rules and fundamental assumptions that underlie current . . . opera-

tions."[76] Many of those rules were based on outdated assumptions about technology, people, and organizational goals.

The key word *dramatic* means rejecting incremental change. Re-engineering means major change, not merely tinkering at the margins. Re-engineering is for agencies that are under siege or foresee trouble down the road. It is also undertaken by aggressive agencies that are doing fine but want to be outstanding.

The most important key word is *processes,* which can be defined as "a collection of activities that takes inputs and creates outputs that are valued by the customer."[77] This is the most difficult aspect of re-engineering because managers are used to determining what has to be done and breaking down the work to be done into simple tasks. In focusing on the separate tasks, they often lose sight of how the tasks fit together.

Michael Hammer and James Champy look at the private sector and describe how a credit corporation re-engineered its loan processing function. Executives found that the loan approval process was taking too long. They initially introduced another step, a control task, so they would be able to know where the loan request was when the people who were waiting a long time sought to find out its status. This only delayed things further. Walking through the 5 steps in the process, the managers found that the actual processing time was only 90 minutes, yet the average approval took 7 days. They discovered that the delay was caused by the movement of paperwork from office to office. Management realized that, for routine applications, many experts did not have to deal with the paperwork; yet the process was designed for those difficult cases that required extensive review. That cumbersome process delayed all transactions. As is the case with many organizations, the process fit the exceptions and not the rule. At the credit office, executives re-engineered the process so that one individual performed the entire process, with the help of sophisticated computer technology. The few complicated cases were referred to the experts. As a result, the average loan could be processed in 4 hours and the number of loans processed increased one hundredfold.[78] It is easy to see the implications of re-engineering and its applicability to many public agencies, such as a welfare agency trying to check for eligibility.

While re-engineering provides no magic formula, it does provide some guidelines. The first is that several jobs can be combined into one, as illustrated above. This results in fewer delays and expands a job's responsibilities, making it more interesting. Second, workers should be empowered to make more decisions, thus doing the job with fewer controls. Third, the steps in the process should be performed in a natural order. While a worker is moving from step one to step two of a process, she or he can also be gathering information that may not be needed until step five. Fourth, processes have multiple versions. For example, exceptions can be dealt with differently from the way standard situations are handled.

A fifth guideline is that work should be performed where it makes the most sense. For example, it is often more expensive in terms of time and personnel to route all purchases, even minor ones, through a central purchasing branch than allowing an agency to go down to the corner to buy a dozen pens, even if the pens are slightly more expensive. The sixth guideline is that the number of people who must review actions should be reduced and that leads to the seventh guideline, that the number of people who need to coordinate be minimized. As with the other management reforms, "reengineered control systems, however, more than compensate for any increase in abuse by dramatically lowering the costs and other encumbrances associated with the control itself."[79] If the work process has been streamlined so that fewer steps and individu-

als are involved, it is easier to determine if work is being properly performed. Eighth, a case manager should provide a point of contact for the customer. The role is not dissimilar to that of ombudsman. It is at least part of the job of the case manager to make sure the job gets done to the customer's satisfaction. Finally, a hybrid of centralization and decentralization should be implemented. Some functions should be decentralized, while others should be centralized. For example, neighborhood offices can be established as points of contact for citizens and can be linked to a central information system that maintains records.

Public managers continue to seek ways to improve service delivery and all these management techniques can contribute if used effectively. None, however, seem likely to be the magic bullet or the holy grail managers continue to seek. They are merely tools that can help the public bureaucracy better serve the public. William Rago's caveats on implementing TQM in the government are also applicable to the other approaches. He states that, "it is the government's environment with its political culture and the unmet needs of an unlimited supply of customers that creates real problems for the application of TQM."[80]

Implications of Management Reform

All these approaches stress customer satisfaction. While this focus may increase the responsiveness of administrators to some citizens, some fear that this can "encourage a focus on the particularistic demands of clients rather than the needs of the more important (but inattentive) customers, the general public."[81] We have seen in previous chapters that not all "clients" are equally able to present their demands. One of the responsibilities of government is to not lose sight of the common good, but the emphasis on citizens as customers may mean administrators see the common good only as client satisfaction.[82]

All of these approaches also may give business interests more influence in urban affairs. The emphasis on cooperation between the public and private spheres and the importance of urban governments acting as economic entrepreneurs blurs the line between public and private roles. Contributing to that blurring is the fact that urban officials are encouraged to accept the principles and values of business as guides to their decisions.

If urban governments need to engage in market activities to raise funds, they will become dependent on the private interests that dominate that market. That dependence gives private interests influence. For example, if governments raise revenue by investments in business stocks, those governments have an interest in supporting the economic success of those businesses. Should the business demand policies or concessions from the government, it is in the government's interest to respond positively.

While some of the principles of these techniques may lead to more active government, many also reinforce the traditional value of privatism. Under privatism, the role of government is minimized and focused on supporting the efforts of private citizens to seek economic prosperity.[83] The current push to privatize services reinforces the value of limited government. As in small towns, a limited government agenda minimizes citizen control. Similarly, the reliance on market mechanisms such as supplying vouchers for schools and housing provides support for the private entrepreneurs who will have expanded markets. In general, this intermingling of public and private roles and the minimizing of the role of government may make citizen control difficult as the activities of private business are not subject to citizen influence.

Conclusion

Delivering services in the metropolitan area is a difficult task. The fragmentation within the metropolitan area means that many government agencies at every level of government will often be required to work together to implement programs. The various actors are apt to have different concerns and priorities. Even at the same level of government or within the same agency, perspectives will differ. The complexity makes it difficult for citizens to identify responsibility for service delivery and, therefore, hinders citizen influence.

Because programs and choices can be seen in more than one way, agencies and workers within them try to rely on decision rules to justify their actions. These are reacting to power or pressure from constituents; relying on equity, that is, treating everyone equally; depending on professional norms or standards; responding to the degree of need of the constituent; or acting in response to client demands. The acceptance of the principle of responding to pressure would maximize the influence of major economic interests, while the principle of acting in response to client demands would give at least some citizens more influence. The other decision rules would lessen the influence of both business and citizen.

The patterns of service delivery resulting from decision rules are also important. There are four basic patterns. The equality model, based on the equity rule, supplies the same level of services to everyone. The outcome, however, may not be equity. The compensatory model, based on the need rule, provides more service to those with the greatest need. The discriminatory model, based on the power rule, gives more services to those with the most influence, presumably major economic interests. The curvilinear model follows the demand rule and provides service to those requesting it most. The professional rule may produce any of the four delivery patterns.

After services are implemented they are evaluated, either in an ad hoc or a systematic manner. Many evaluations are ad hoc, especially those done by the general public. They are based on gut feelings and reactions. Lately, citizens have evaluated all levels of government negatively. Systematic evaluation is a five-step process: goal setting; research design, that is, planning the method for obtaining information; operationalization, that is, finding ways to measure key variables; data collection; and analysis and interpretation.

Because programs and their delivery can always be improved, governments are searching for tools to make them more successful. Structural changes in government, discussed in previous chapters, are a way local governments try to improve productivity. A second strategy is the introduction of technological innovation. A final strategy is the use of new management techniques. Total Quality Management (TQM) is an attempt to get workers to focus on customer satisfaction and participate in improving work processes to achieve that end. Reinventing government provides a wide variety of techniques based on an entrepreneurial role for government. It, too, stresses customer satisfaction along with worker empowerment. Re-engineering shares many of the basic ideas of the other techniques but is much more radical rather than incremental.

All the methods mentioned provide means for improving government, but they must not be oversold. Public organizations exist in a political environment. Many of the management reforms suggest reducing rules and controls to speed up the process and allow more discretion and innovation to improve efficiency, effectiveness, and responsiveness. These must be balanced with the need for equity.

All the techniques may lead to increased responsiveness to the subsets of citizens who are seen as clients or customers of particular services. Some fear that this will decrease attention to the broader needs of the public. All also emphasize the importance of government acting more like a private business; such intermingling of the private and public roles may increase the influence of major private interests and decrease the role of the public.

Notes

1. Jeffrey L. Pressman and Aaron Wildavsky, *Implementation*, 3rd ed. (Berkeley: California: University of California Press, 1984), 136–142.

2. Ibid., 142.

3. Ibid., 87–124. For a discussion of different perspectives of public officials at different levels of government see Deil S. Wright, *Understanding Intergovernmental Relations* (Monterey, California: Brooks/Cole, 1977).

4. Charles J. Fox, "Biases in Public Policy Implementation Evaluation," *Policy Studies Review* 7 (Autumn 1987): 129.

5. This extended discussion of street-level bureaucratic behavior is based on Michael Lipsky, *Street-Level Bureaucracy: Dilemmas of the Individuals in Public Services* (New York: Russell Sage Foundation, 1980).

6. Lipsky, *Street-Level Bureaucracy*, 3.

7. Frank S. Levy, Arnold J. Meltsner, and Aaron Wildavsky, *Urban Outcomes* (Berkeley: University of California Press, 1974), 231–232.

8. Bryan D. Jones with Saadia Greenberg and Joseph Drew, *Service Delivery in the City: Citizen Demand and Bureaucratic Rules* (New York: Longman, 1980), 88–89; and Robert L. Lineberry and Ira Sharkansky, *Urban Politics and Public Policy*, 3rd.ed. (New York: Harper & Row, 1978), 272.

9. We wish to thank Tim Mead for this observation.

10. These are discussed in Robert L. Lineberry, *Equality and Urban Policy: The Distribution of Municipal Public Services* (Beverly Hills, California: Sage, 1977).

11. Jones, et al., *Service Delivery in the City*.

12. Kenneth R. Mladenka and Kim Quaile Hill, "The Distribution of Benefits in an Urban Environment: Parks and Libraries in Houston," *Urban Affairs Quarterly* 13 (September 1977): 88.

13. Lineberry, *Equality and Urban Policy*, 142.

14. Levy, et al., *Urban Outcomes*, 220.

15. *Hawkins v. Shaw*, 437 Federal Reporter (2nd series) 1286 (1971).

16. *Hobson v. Hansen* 327 F. Supp. 844 (1971).

17. Lineberry, *Equality and Urban Policy*, Chapter 5.

18. Jones, et al., *Service Delivery in the City*, 81.

19. See Jones, et al., *Service Delivery in the City*; Lineberry, *Equality and Urban Policy*; Levy, et al., *Urban Outcomes*; Mladenka and Hill, "The Distribution of Benefits in an Urban Environment:" George E. Autunes and Kenneth Mladenka, "The Politics of Local Services and Service Distribution," in *Toward a New Urban Politics*, ed. Louis Masotti and Robert L. Lineberry (Cambridge, Massachusetts: Ballinger, 1976), 147–169; Kenneth Mladenka, "The Urban

Bureaucracy and the Chicago Political Machine: Who Gets What and the Limits of Political Control," *American Political Science Review* 74 (December 1980): 991–998; Charles S. Benson and Peter B. Lund, *Neighborhood Distribution of Local Public Services* (Berkeley, California: Institute of Governmental Studies, 1969).

20. The classic work here is Donald T. Campbell and Julian C. Stanley, *Experimental and Quasi-Experimental Designs for Research* (Chicago: Rand McNally, 1963). Other useful works are Carol H. Weiss, *Evaluation Research: Methods of Assessing Program Effectiveness* (Englewood Cliffs, New Jersey: Prentice-Hall, 1972); Harry P. Hatry, Richard E. Winnie, and Donald M. Fisk, *Practical Program Evaluation for State and Local Government Officials* (Washington, D.C.: Urban Institute, 1973); and Susan Welch and John Comer, *Quantitative Methods for Public Administration*, 2nd ed. (Pacific Grove, California: Brooks/Cole, 1988).

21. Mary Grisez Kweit and Robert W. Kweit, *Concepts and Methods for Political Analysis* (Englewood Cliffs, New Jersey: Prentice-Hall, 1981), 355.

22. N. Joseph Cayer, "Managing Programs and Services," in *The Effective Government Manager*, 2nd ed., ed. Charldean Newell (Washington, D.C.: International City/County Management Association, 1993), 125.

23. *The Oregon Option: A Proposed Model for Results-Driven Intergovernmental Service Delivery*, http://libmail.chemek.cc.or.us/rilg/OR_OPT/contents.htm, July 25, 1994.

24. Many consider time-trend to be quasi-experimental designs. Here we will consider it to be a pre-experimental design because only the experimental group is studied. Quasi-experiments use comparison groups to contrast with the experimental group while experiments use randomly selected control groups as a contrast to the experimental group.

25. Jeffrey Henig, Robert Lineberry, and Neal Milner, "The Policy Impact of Policy Evaluation: Some Implications of the Kansas City Patrol Experiment," in *Public Law and Public Policy*, ed. John Gardiner (New York: Praeger, 1977), 226.

26. David Kershaw and Jerelyn Fair, eds., *Final Report of the New Jersey Graduated Work Incentive Experiment* (Madison, Wisconsin: Institute for Research on Poverty, 1974).

27. John F. Cogan, *Negative Income Taxation and Labor Supply: New Evidence from the New Jersey–Pennsylvania Experiment* (Santa Monica, California: Rand Corporation, 1978).

28. This section draws on David R. Morgan and Robert E. England, *Managing Urban America*, 4th ed. (Chatham, New Jersey: Chatham House, 1996), 185–196.

29. Hatry, Winnie Fisk, *Practical Program Evaluation for State and Local Government Officials*, 27.

30. This section draws on Weiss, *Evaluation Research*, 52–57.

31. John J. DiIulio, Jr., Gerald Garvey, and Donald F. Kettl, *Improving Government Performance: An Owner's Manual* (Washington, D.C.: The Brookings Institution, 1993), 9.

32. Douglas Yates, *The Ungovernable City* (Cambridge, Massachusetts: MIT Press, 1977), 18.

33. Elaine B. Sharp, *Urban Politics and Administration: From Service Delivery to Economic Development*, (New York: Longman, 1990), 51.

34. Ibid., 53.

35. Elizabeth Voisin, "Trash Pickup No Chore," *City & State* (October 1987): 30.

36. Jonathan Walters, "Management by Fad," *Governing* (September 1996): 48–52.

37. Jonathan Walters, "The Cult of Total Quality," *Governing* (May 1992): 38–42.

38. Marshall Sashkin and Kenneth J. Kiser, *Putting Total Quality Management to Work* (San Francisco: Berrett-Koehler, 1993), 39.

39. James E. Swiss, "Adapting Total Quality Management (TQM) to Government," *Public Administration Review* 52 (July–August 1992): 356–362.

40. Sashkin and Kiser, *Putting Total Quality to Work*.

41. Walters, "The Cult of Total Quality," 40.

42. Sashkin and Kiser, *Putting Total Quality to Work*, Chapter 5.

43. Swiss, "Adapting Total Quality Management," 358–359.

44. Ibid., 359.

45. Walters, "The Cult of Total Quality," 40.

46. Ibid.

47. Swiss, "Adapting Total Quality Management," 360.

48. Joseph Sensenbrenner, "Quality Comes to City Hall," *Harvard Business Review* (March–April 1991).

49. Walters, "The Cult of Total Quality," 40.

50. David Osborne, "Why Total Quality Management Is Only Half a Loaf," *Governing* (August 1992): 65.

51. This section is based on David Osborne and Ted Gaebler, *Reinventing Government: How the Entrepreneurial Spirit Is Transforming the Public Sector* (New York: Plume, 1992).

52. Woodrow Wilson, "The Study of Administration," *Political Science Quarterly* II (June 1887) in *Classics of Public Administration*, ed. Jay M. Shafritz and Albert C. Hyde (Oak Park, Illinois: Moore, 1978), 12.

53. James Q. Wilson, *Bureaucracy: What Government Agencies Do and Why They Do It* (New York: Basic Books, 1989): 349–350.

54. Osborne and Gaebler, *Reinventing Government*, xix.

55. Ibid., 19–20 and passim.

56. Ted Kolderie, "The Two Different Concepts of Privatization," *Public Administration Review* 46 (July–August 1986): 286.

57. Osborne and Gaebler, *Reinventing Government*, 30, 290–298, and Appendix A.

58. Ibid., 52.

59. Ibid., 59–70.

60. Ibid., 80–84.

61. Sharp, *Urban Politics and Administration*, 101.

62. E.S. Savas, *Privatization: The Keys to Better Government* (Chatham, New Jersey: Chatham House, 1987).

63. Charles T. Goodsell, *The Case for Bureaucracy: A Public Administration Polemic*, 3rd ed. (Chatham, New Jersey: Chatham House, 1994), 65–68.

64. Robert M. Stein, *Urban Alternatives: Public and Private Markets in the Provision of Local Services* (Pittsburgh: University of Pittsburgh Press, 1990), 187–188.

65. Michael Barzelay, with Babak J. Armajani, *Breaking Through Bureaucracy: A New Vision for Managing in Government* (Berkeley: University of California Press, 1992).

66. Osborne and Gaebler, *Reinventing Government*, 147.

67. Ibid., 177–179.

68. Ibid., 206.

69. Quoted in Ibid., 211.

70. Ibid., 233.

71. Ibid., 248.

72. This section is based primarily on Michael Hammer and James Champy, *Reengineering the Corporation: A Manifesto for Business Revolution* (New York: Harper & Row, 1993).

73. Ibid., 31.

74. Ibid., 49.

75. Ibid., 32.

76. Ibid., 3.

77. Ibid.

78. Ibid., 36–39.

79. Ibid., 58.

80. William V. Rago, "Adapting Total Quality Management (TQM) to Government: Another Point of View," *Public Administration Review* 54 (January–February 1994): 64.

81. Swiss, "Adapting Total Quality Management," 359–360.

82. Mary Grisez Kweit and Robert W. Kweit, "Ethical Responsibility for Reinvented Bureaucrats: Working for Customer-Citizens" in *Public Integrity Annual 1997*, ed. James S. Bowman and David Ensign, Lexington, Kentucky: Council of State Governments, 1997, 3–11.

83. Sam Bass Warner, Jr., *The Private City: Philadelphia in Three Periods of Its Growth* (Philadelphia: University of Pennsylvania Press, 1968), 3–4.

The overview of the stages in the urban policy process is complete. Part IV will demonstrate how that process has worked in specific policy areas.

Policy Arenas

Many typologies have been developed to differentiate public policy. Theodore Lowi classified policies into three types: regulatory, distributive, and redistributive[1] He argued that different policy "games" appear in the various arenas. Regulatory policies are designed to restrict behavior of people and businesses in order to improve living conditions for all residents. Such policies reflect local mores by establishing what is legal and what is illegal, who must go to which school, and what businesses can and cannot do. For example, regulatory policies establish whether gambling is illegal or if schools should have geographical boundaries or open enrollment. In addition, these policies might determine which private company would be given a bus route monopoly or what would be the consequences of creating air or water pollution.

Regulatory policy often results in conflict among competing groups, but policy officials often seek ways to minimize the conflict. For example, when members of the community compete for franchises, a great deal of conflict is apt to arise as only one can win and many may lose. This problem may sometimes be resolved by "distributing" the franchises more or less evenly to all applicants. In the example of controlling pollution, a high level of conflict is likely when restrictions are imposed. Once they are in place, however, an accord may be established between the implementors (bureaucrats) and the constituents to avoid conflict by limiting enforcement or modifying standards on the one hand and assuring at least token compliance on the other. Only when one side wants to change the rules or "outsiders" get involved should flare-ups be expected.

Distributive programs may be viewed as subsidies. "The recipients of distributive subsidies are not aware of each other, and there is no sense of competing for limited resources— anyone can be a potential recipient, and resources are treated as unlimited."[2] Because there is something for everyone, at least for those who are organized and accorded a place on the agenda, conflict is generally low and those involved as clients work quietly with the legislative specialists (the committees and subcommittees at the national level, especially) and the relevant bureaucracies. Policy specialists in a certain policy area tend to dominate the policy process.

Ernest Griffith was one of the first to note the importance of the interaction among policy experts, which he called whirlpools.

> . . . [H]e who would understand the prevailing pattern of our present governmental behavior, instead of studying the formal institutions or even generalizations or organs, important though all these things are, may possibly obtain a better picture of the way things really happen if he would study these "whirlpools" of special social interests and problems.[3]

Political scientists have used various terms to refer to the combination of policy specialists that dominate policy making. In addition to Griffith's term, the words "subsystems" or "subgovernments" have been used. Some referred to the combinations as an "iron triangle," with the three sides of the triangle being the affected interest groups, the legislative committee that would draft legislation, and the part of the executive bureaucracy that would implement it. More recently, the term **issue network** has often been used to acknowledge that the combination of forces working on a given policy is not as neat as a triangle and interested parties move into and out of discussions as the agenda is formed.[4]

The redistributive arena encompasses policies that deal with the reallocation of wealth or other values from one identifiable group in society to another identifiable group. As such, there are "winners" and "losers". Many policies redistribute resources from the poor to the rich. For example, tax breaks given to business are often paid for by increasing the tax burden on the average taxpayer. In general, though, the term redistributive has been used by political scientists to refer to policies that take from the haves in society and give to the have-nots. As the haves generally possess more political power than the have-nots, we would expect those policies to be limited. At the same time Americans are compassionate; and, therefore, we can expect some redistribution from wealthy to poor.

Many such issues are kept off the public agenda unless enough of the general public see a major problem. Once on the agenda, a high level of conflict ensues. This discourages action unless there are important actors championing a redistributive plan because local resources are limited and local governments strive to please the haves. Accordingly, redistributive policies generally come to local governments from other levels of government. The federal government has been reducing its role in this policy area, shifting responsibility to state and local governments.

Distributive elements are often included in redistributive programs to make them more palatable and nonconflictual. As with all simple categories created to organize complex processes, there is no clear delineation of when a redistributive policy becomes distributive. When policies viewed as redistributing benefits to the needy are modified to benefit other, non-poor members of the society, they become less redistributive and more distributive. Although designed to be redistributive, the progressive federal income tax was made more palatable to the rich by "distributing" loopholes that limit the redistributive impact. Homeowners can deduct mortgage interest, business got investment tax credits, and so forth. The 1986 tax reform, according to its proponents, eliminated many loopholes and was more redistributive. Recent budget negotiations have increased the number of loopholes, many designed to benefit middle-income voters.

Theodore Lowi's view has been criticized because many policies overlap various arenas and change in character between formulation and adoption and implementation. Paul Peterson modifies the typology to fit into the urban setting but has difficulty classifying educational issues and treats them separately. One policy area that he identifies as the most important for local politics is what he calls developmental policies.

"Developmental policies enhance the economic position of the city."[5] Peterson believes that these policies represent a community consensus on generating economic resources that can be used to improve the community's welfare. Developmental policies, as seen by Peterson, are market-driven. Because local governments are in competition for economic development that will generate income, these governments must generally keep taxes low to make the area in their jurisdiction attractive for business investment; they must also provide services and incentives so that business will choose to settle there. Peterson's analysis indicates that the ability of communities to provide redistributive programs is related to fiscal capacity. Hence, Peterson argues that developmental policies are the cornerstone of well-being for all urbanites. To be against developmental policy is akin to being against motherhood and apple pie. "They are praised by many and opposed only by those few whose partial interests stand in conflict with community interests."[6]

Other urbanists do not view developmental policies as solely the result of economic imperatives. Local officials do have the power to make choices that alter conditions in the city.[7] Local political leaders need to build a governing coalition to be successful. These coalitions often include business interests, but they do not always dominate the coalition. Other interests can be included if they control resources needed by political leaders. In addition to developmental policies, Peterson establishes two other categories: allocational policies, which are similar to Lowi's distributive policy, and redistributive policies.[8]

Peterson argues that local governments are unlikely to enact redistributive policies. The need to enact policies that contribute to the economic success of local areas means re-

sources are inadequate for redistribution. In addition, there is no local constituency with the resources to push for redistribution.[9]

This section will consider three categories of policy. Following Peterson, Chapter 12 will examine developmental policy and will discuss three areas of such policy that are key to economic well-being: planning and zoning, economic and community development, and transportation. Policies carried out in these areas often contain distributive, regulatory, and redistributive components. Following both Peterson and Lowi, Chapter 14 focuses on redistributive policy, discussing welfare policy and housing policy. Although these policies are primarily redistributive, they also have distributive and regulatory dimensions.

In addition, this section will discuss, in chapter 13, a third category of policies labeled quality-of-life issues because these issues cut to the heart of individual well-being and are of major concern to residents and to major economic interests in urban areas. Indeed, these issues are often crucial to locational decisions made by urban residents and businesses. The quality-of-life issues examined are education and crime prevention. These policy areas do not fit neatly into existing typologies. Quality-of-life issues also overlap all three of Lowi's policy categories.

At times these policies are regulatory. In urban areas the police functions, which are extremely important to the residents' quality of life, generally fit the model of regulatory policy. Police professionals stress their unique expertise to minimize conflicts, and they are successful to the extent that they internalize community expectations concerning their implementation. Schools, as the institution responsible for transmitting what are considered to be acceptable values for the society, are also, in part, regulatory.

In other ways quality-of-life programs have distributive aspects. For example, virtually all children are entitled to receive a free public education. At times, however, quality-of-life issues take on a redistributive dimension. Because education is a route of economic mobility that can determine success in life, the distribution of educational benefits, funded by the tax dollars of one group, can help others achieve a higher socioeconomic status. These redistributive aspects of education are seen most clearly when taxpayers are asked to fund such compensatory programs as bilingual education.

Each policy area—developmental, quality-of-life, and redistributive—tends to be characterized by different patterns of citizen control. The next three chapters will examine the policy process and policies in each area. They will also discuss the ability of citizens to exercise control over these policies that are so important to their lives.

In general, evidence suggests that major economic interests in urban areas do tend to dominate in developmental policy, but citizens have organized in some cities to stop development projects or the building of highways that would destroy neighborhoods. Currently, the bureaucrats charged with delivering the quality-of-life policies of education and crime control, that is, school administrators and police, tend to dominate those policies. The importance of such policies for both individual citizens and major economic interests provides the potential for broader involvement in policy making, but traditionally the bureaucrats have claimed that policy making requires their professional expertise. As Peterson argues, redistributive policies are difficult at the level of local government. At times, the federal government has created redistributive programs, both providing funds for the poor and attempting to organize them to be an effective constituency for demanding redistribution. Currently the national government is reducing its role in this area, shifting responsibility back to the states and local government. Unless a local constituency forms with an interest in redistributive policy and the resources to force such issues onto the local agenda, new initiatives in the area are unlikely. As Chapter 5 discussed, the poor themselves have great difficulty organizing to be an effective political force.

Notes

1. Theodore J. Lowi, "American Business, Public Policy, Case Studies, and Political Theory," *World Politics* 16 (July 1964): 667–715.

2. Randall B. Ripley and Grace A. Franklin, *Congress, the Bureaucracy and Public Policy,* 4th ed. (New York: Dorsey, 1987), 23–24.

3. Ernest S. Griffith, *The Impasse of Democracy* (New York: Harison-Hilton, 1938), 182.

4. Hugh Heclo, "Issue Networks and the Executive Establishments" in *The New American Political System,* ed. Anthony King (Washington, D.C.: American Enterprise Institute, 1978), 87–124.

5. Paul E. Peterson, *City Limits* (Chicago: University of Chicago Press, 1981), 41.

6. Ibid.

7. Clarence N. Stone and Heywood T. Sanders, eds., *The Politics of Urban Development* (Lawrence: University of Kansas Press), 14.

8. Peterson, *City Limits,* Chapter 3.

9. Ibid., Chapter 9.

CHAPTER 12

Developmental Policy
Land-use Regulation, Economic and Community Development, and Transportation

In 1981 Paul Peterson published an important analysis of urban politics, in which he argued that "the primary interest of cities" was "the maintenance and enhancement of their productivity."[1] He believed that goal to be so central that it dominated the urban policy-making process. "As policy alternatives are proposed, each is evaluated according to how well it will help to achieve this objective ... policy choices over time will be limited to those few which can plausibly be shown to be conducive to the community's economic prosperity."[2] He referred to these policies as **developmental**.

Since Peterson's analysis appeared, many have agreed on the importance of focusing on urban development. They have not, however, always agreed with all of Peterson's analysis or even with his definition of what constitutes a development policy. Peterson defined development policy in economic terms: Such policies provide benefits to the community greater than their costs. The primary costs involved would be taxes. Although Peterson recognized that this definition could encompass the spending of money for various community services if they could somehow lead to increased revenue, he believed that the most common

form of development policy fosters business interests. The importance of business interests normally gives them access to the governing coalitions in urban areas, thus giving them opportunity to influence policy and shape the city.

The key resource that city governments can use to maximize economic productivity is control over the use of land. City governments control tax policies that determine how much business has to pay in property taxes. City governments control zoning regulations that determine where businesses can locate and what can locate next to them. Location determines how accessible businesses are to the materials they need and to potential customers. City governments build roads that will make some parts of the city more accessible than others and put in infrastructure such as water and sewer mains that are necessary for business development.

So central is the city government's control over land use decisions that some analysts, such as Clarence Stone, have defined development policy simply as land-use policy. "Urban development *policy* can be defined as consisting of those practices fostered by public authority that contribute to the shaping of the local community through control of land use and investments in physical structure."[3] Following Stone's definition of development policy, this chapter will focus on three policy areas involving the exercise of control by cities over land use: planning and zoning, economic and community development, and transportation.

Planning and zoning decisions clearly have an impact on land use. **Land use** refers to the purpose for which land is developed, for example, housing, as opposed to shopping malls, factories, or parks. Planning involves specifying future land-use patterns; zoning is a means local communities use to enforce what they see as desirable land-use patterns. These **land-use patterns** are relationships between the different purposes for which land is developed. Although economic and community development is not as obviously a land-use policy, policies designed to develop local communities have substantial effects on the physical setting of the city. Under the rubric of community development, slums were destroyed and replaced with high-income housing, shopping malls, and office buildings. Neighborhoods are often pitted against each other and downtown interests for resources. Economic and community development is frequently defined as substituting attractive land use for the unattractive slums. Finally, transportation is a land-use policy because transportation itself requires land for highways or trolley lines, for example. But, more important, transportation will determine the relative accessibility and attractiveness of various parcels of land in the metropolitan area.

Popular Control over Land-use Policy

Peterson argued that development policy was so essential to the future of cities (determining even if there would be a future) that popular control was impossible. He concluded:

The politics of development are conditioned by the fact that these policies redound to the advantage of the city as a whole. For this reason, developmental policies are often left to be developed and implemented by autonomous agencies that operate on income generated by their own projects, free of usual political constraints. When this is not feasible, policies are developed in a consensual fashion by respected community leaders, who are often businessmen well acquainted with the problems of fostering economic growth.[4]

Others disagree with Peterson's arguments on two counts. First, Stone points out that not everyone in the city may agree that developmental policies "redound to the advantage of the city as a whole." While some residents benefit, others may be disadvantaged. In this chapter, numerous examples will be given of urban development policies that have produced severe burdens for some residents. For instance, highways helped to make the city more accessible to suburbanites, but in the process, neighborhoods and large amounts of low-income housing were destroyed. Rejecting Peterson's idea of a consensus on urban interests, Stone believes that developmental policy is produced in an atmosphere of conflict among those the proposed development will benefit and those it will harm.[5]

Second, many have disagreed that such policies are developed "free of usual political constraints." John Mollenkopf even argues that the policies have primarily been the product of the political process and that national Democratic administrations have provided the leadership. He described the action by the administrations as part political strategy and part political necessity. The strategy was to make the urban residents into Democratic voters, but he acknowledges that the demands from the urban electorate for a national urban policy could not have been ignored. "In a sense, the New Deal Democrats had little choice about using federal programs to build their political base, for a newly mobilized urban electorate forced them to do so."[6]

Stone, in turn, has argued that *local* political officials also play an important role in shaping development policies.

Local decision makers do not simply follow the imperatives that emanate from the national political economy; they must also interpret those imperatives, apply them to local conditions, and act on them within the constraints of the political arrangements they build and maintain.[7]

Local officials must build electoral coalitions that will enable them to be re-elected; therefore, maintaining a base of popular support constrains decision making. They are further limited because, in order to govern, they must rely on resources controlled by major economic interests. For example, cities need to be able to raise credit in the private financial market, and they depend on bond-rating agencies to give them a rating that would encourage private economic interests to extend credit. The importance of such private economic interests gives them special advantages in seeking access to the governing coalition that political leaders need to assemble to govern effectively.

Developmental projects help officials gain popular support and receive an adequate bond rating. Officials know that large-scale building projects are a dramatic and highly visible means of demonstrating to citizens their leadership skills and thus their qualifications for re-election. Such projects can also be pointed out to bond rating agencies as indicators of the city's economic vitality. One observer notes, "Such projects are also visible in a way that few other things that happen in cities are, and such building is taken to be a sign that much else of note is going on in the city—even if it is not."[8]

Dependence on such large-scale building projects creates a mutuality of interest between officials and the major businesses that also profit from the programs. The banks that finance the project, the construction companies that build it, the real estate agencies that rent it or sell it are examples of businesses for which urban development projects spell instant profits. Construction unions will also support the projects because of the jobs created. So will businesses such as utilities and the local media, because they may increase population size, and therefore the number of customers. The general agreement on the importance of such development leads to the creation of the city as a growth machine, as discussed in Chapter 5.[9]

This mutuality of interest means that urban officials have incentive to listen when business speaks; although listening is not always the same as obeying. There are limits on the business's ability to dominate totally the city's policy making. For one, the business community is not always in agreement on all developmental policies. In addition, protests from those who would be adversely affected by the project can delay or derail development. As will be discussed later, residents' protests have stopped many highway projects that would have destroyed urban neighborhoods.

But protests are hard to maintain for long periods. In the interim between outbreaks of opposition, officials look to groups that can provide them with the resources they need to govern. Bankers, contractors, construction unions, and real estate companies have the resources and the incentive to play a major role in determining a city's policy on aiding developmental projects.

Stone concludes that the impact of such a pattern of influence appears to be policy that produces substantial benefits for many residents but that cannot legitimately be claimed to "redound to the advantage of the city as a whole," as Peterson argued. While admitting that his argument is speculative, Stone writes:

Drawing on existing cases, I have made the argument that "prevailing coalitions" in development policy, especially ones that are executive centered and are allied with large business and financial interests, are likely to be somewhat unrepresentative of popular preferences and especially inattentive to various unorganized or weakly organized interests.[10]

This chapter will examine the three areas of land-use policy for evidence concerning the extent to which popular control can have an impact: first, the most basic land-use policy—control over planning and zoning; then economic and community development policy; and finally, transportation policies.

Planning and Land-use Regulation

Local governments often engage in planning in all these areas to facilitate orderly development. In general, **planning** is a method of guiding decision makers in making decisions and taking actions to affect the future in a consistent and rational manner, and in a way to achieve a desired goal. It is a blueprint that indicates how a community can get where it wants to go. Good planning helps a community identify future challenges and develop strategies to cope with them before they arise.

Economic planning is often part of economic development as officials try to ascertain future job trends in the community and assure that a trained work force is in place. **Transportation planning** attempts to determine future development and devise road or mass transit proposals to meet those needs. **Land-use planning** involves projecting, on the basis of the current composition of the community and expected future trends, how much land should be set aside for various purposes such as residential, commercial, industrial, and public uses. Such planning also must relate infrastructure needs, for example,

roads, water, and sewer for future development. The resulting plan addresses the future allocation of physical space.

The idea of land-use planning for urban development can be traced back as early as 3000 B.C. Many of America's Colonial cities developed according to master plans. William Penn established Philadelphia with a grid street pattern and parks at the four corners. Pierre-Charles L'Enfant designed Washington, D.C. in 1791, planning its broad boulevards and radial pattern. This public planning did not have much impact on private individuals until the twentieth century.

Owning a house on a private plot of land is so important in the American value system that it is referred to as "the American dream." It is a symbol of success—of "making it." As Sam Warner argues, today owning land "means security, credit, and the social standing that is a protection against the harassments of police, welfare, and health officials."[11] The idea that a "man's home is his castle," rooted in English common law, is firmly embedded in the constitutional protections against illegal search and seizure and against the quartering of soldiers in private homes. From this belief in the sanctity of private home and land comes the belief that land-use decisions should be made privately, leaving control over that resource substantially in private hands.[12]

When the country was sparsely populated, it made little difference to others how individual landowners used their land, and it was then that the belief in private land-use decisions became deeply rooted. As the population grew and densities increased, how others used their land became more important because their actions would have an effect on those around them. The belief in private decisions concerning land use came into conflict with the need for order and regulation. That conflict continues, even though the right of local government to exercise some control over land-use decisions has been widely accepted.

English common law, which provides the basis for property rights, also lays the groundwork for remedies when the exercise of those rights harms others. Courts are empowered to restrict use or fine landowners who impose serious discomfort or hazardous conditions on others; this is known as the **nuisance doctrine**. These unlawful conditions can range from obnoxious odors, to filthy, disease-causing conditions, to fire hazards. In fact, the first building codes in the New World (New Amsterdam, 1647) were enacted to prevent fires.[13]

> In every American city devastating fires swept whole blocks of valuable downtown districts. . . . Contaminated wells, overused and ill-tended privies, overcrowded buildings and rooms, and shiploads of undernourished and sick immigrants brought epidemic waves of cholera, typhus, and yellow fever which swept the downtown districts of the poor, seeped into hotels and public places, and frightened all classes of city dwellers.[14]

New York City passed the first comprehensive fire prevention law in 1849 and the first tenement house legislation in 1867. Much later, zoning, discussed below, was introduced as a tool to minimize the negative effects of incompatible land uses and develop positive effects by assuring synergy among uses. **Zoning** facilitates the orderly development sought in the land-use plan by regulating how space is utilized, identifying areas for residential, commercial, and industrial use and establishing usage standards, for example, density, within each of the areas.

The conflict between private decisions and public impacts has helped shape the exercise of land-use regulation in most urban areas. Although regulation exists, in most cases attempts are made to keep it minimal. When possible, market forces of the free enterprise system dominate land-use decisions. As a result, decisions by speculators often affect public expenditures and cause social inefficiencies. For example, if a speculator persuades the government to build a public facility near his or her land, the value of the land may increase. The speculator will receive positive externalities if others are willing to pay more for land located near this facility. Citizens and government officials are usually not disturbed because the project increases tax revenues. However, if government locates the facility inefficiently, such as the edge of town, and new roads must be built, the costs to the public will increase, along with their displeasure, while a private property owner reaps the benefits.

Another example involves the speculator who develops land, sells the new homes, makes profits, and moves on. The people who bought those houses are soon likely to demand increased public services such as better water pressure, parks, and schools, and the public treasury will bear the burden.

The issue of regulation most frequently becomes part of the public agenda when existing property owners enlist public assistance in protecting their private investments. Of course, there are no guarantees that zoning decisions will be consistent with the property owners' requests.

> In part, the Supreme Court held that zoning was a legitimate function of local government on the ground that it protected property owners' investments by preserving or enhancing property values. Using this logic, zoning *did* interfere with the normal functioning of the marketplace by creating an environment favorable to land investment, similar to government's role in stabilizing business transactions by enforcing laws of contract.[15]

Agenda Setting

In the beginning of the twentieth century when cities did accept the idea of establishing regulations to implement plans for the urban development, a number of conditions combined to force the idea of land-use regulation onto the government agenda. Sam Warner emphasizes two reasons why zoning achieved agenda status. One was fear of the Chinese and the other was fear of skyscrapers.[16]

As Chinese immigrants began to settle in California cities, racial prejudice reared its ugly head. In San Francisco, a group of lawyers used ingenious legal tactics to discriminate against the Chinese. Chinese laundries had become social centers to Chinese who worked as house servants. To deal with these "dens of iniquity," the San Francisco Board of Supervisors passed an ordinance declaring the Chinese laundries to be nuisances and fire hazards. Although the federal courts rejected that ordinance as discriminatory in *Yick Wo v. Hopkins, Sheriff*, 118 U.S. 356 (1886), the city of Modesto wrote an acceptable ordinance that divided the city into two zones: one zone permitted the laundries and the other did not. These restrictions spread throughout California. Los Angeles went even further, developing a more comprehensive zoning ordinance with three zones: residential, industrial, and mixed. This ordinance was a forerunner of modern zoning.

> The California precedents, when joined with the regulations of Washington, Baltimore, Indianapolis, and Boston in respect to fire precautions, building heights and strictures on construction, served to create the New York Zoning Law of 1916, the prototype statute of the nation.[17]

The second reason cited for zoning was the building of skyscrapers. In the 1880s, construction techniques were changing the face of cities. Skyscrapers (at that time up to 16 stories) were possible. In New York City, the Fifth Avenue Association, a group of retail merchants and property owners, feared invasion of tall buildings from the expanding "garment district," an area of the city specializing in clothing production. In addition, the well-heeled residents living in the area's luxurious townhouses feared a threat to their property values. The "garment district" would introduce industrial land usage and increase density, resulting in crowding and traffic problems. Finally, such expansion would also introduce many Jewish and lower-class workers into the area.

Formulation

The Fifth Avenue Association successfully lobbied the city to attempt to deal with skyscrapers. After first looking at simply building-height restrictions, the study commission developed a zoning plan "to stabilize and protect lawful investment and not injure assessed valuations or existing uses."[18] Developing such a far-reaching approach was possible for two reasons. First, private property owners participated in the process to protect their interests. Second, the zoning was designed to protect existing conditions and to use those conditions as a basis for future planning. This meant the zoning would be used to protect existing residents from "onslaughts" caused by unscrupulous developers.

Although the protection of individual landowners is congruent with the importance of private property, that focus results in protection of the status quo. By protecting existing land-use patterns, zoning made it difficult to plan for future uses or to alter uses to achieve social goals. Our traditional attitudes have produced a special irony by juxtaposing two incompatible ideals: "Our almost universal faith in private property as the anchor of personal freedom, and our recurrent recognition of private property's social, economic, and political tyrannies."[19]

Some of the effects of the "tyranny" of private property have been discussed in earlier chapters. Racial ghettos form because realtors, developers, and banks fear that property values will fall if African-Americans or Latinos move into white neighborhoods. Poor people are concentrated in one neighbor-hood, again because of the fear of declining property values if low-cost housing were built in middle- or upper-class neighborhoods and because the poor lack the resources (expertise and organization) to press the issue.

Adoption

Zoning, adopted in New York City in 1916, spread rapidly throughout the nation. One reason was New York's desire to have the idea attain cultural acceptance, thus making it more difficult for the courts to strike down the ordinance. Real estate interests strongly supported zoning because it protected land values. For reformers, who had fought for building and housing codes, zoning was an-other tool to develop minimal standards. States passed legislation allowing localities to establish zoning ordinances. Within a year, more than 20 cities had copied the New York ordinance.[20] Within a decade, the ordinance was copied by 591 cities.[21] In 1921, the U.S. Department of Commerce recognized the ac-ceptance of zoning by drafting a model stat-ute similar to New York's.

Regulation became an accepted part of the urban planning process, in part due to the ef-forts of progressive reformers seeking to re-move blight, corruption, and politics from the city. Reformers such as Jacob Riis and Lawrence Veiller, working hand-in-hand with planners, were instrumental in establishing building and housing codes. They believed that better hous-ing would lead to the acceptance of middle-class values. This environmental determinism is often reflected in planning philosophy.[22]

In addition, zoning regulations were sup-ported by powerful interests within the city that sought to preserve their preferred posi-tion and defend themselves from encroach-ment by other interests. The traditional values that created the belief that what was good for business was good for the community legiti-mized the demands for protection by groups

such as New York City's Fifth Avenue Associa-tion. The relatively small group of powerful citizens gained more support from society's haves (that is, residential property owners) to protect themselves from less desirable land uses. For example, Joe Feagin quotes an archi-tectural historian who once told a group of developers: "Zoning can protect you against the small, inefficient entrepreneur. Zoning can protect the big fellow against the marauding of little guys who have nothing at all in mind."[23] The Progressive Movement, supported by business and middle- and upper-class inter-ests, along with the social reformers, lent strength to the quest for land-use regulation.

Implementation

Challenges stemming from our traditional belief in the sanctity of private property arose when the time came to implement zoning and other regulations. The challenge came not from the masses but from the business inter-ests, primarily developers. In 1926, the case of *Village of Euclid v. Ambler Realty Co.* upheld zoning as part of the police power of the mu-nicipality.[24]

Ambler Realty brought suit against the town of Euclid, Ohio, because Ambler owned land that was zoned commercial, making it less valuable than if it were zoned for residen-tial use. Ambler Realty contended that this amounted to taking property without due process, a practice forbidden by both the Fifth and Fourteenth Amendments to the Consti-tution. The court based its decision on the nuisance doctrine and upheld restrictions placing single-family housing as the most protected land use. The court stated: "A nui-sance may be merely a right thing in the wrong place, like a pig in the parlor instead of a barnyard."[25]

The court further stated that apartment houses could destroy single-family districts and were "mere parasites." One apartment house leads to another until their size affects the "free circulation of air" and monopolizes "the rays of sun." They cause increases in noise, traffic, and business resulting in decreased safety and open space and ultimately destroy the desirability of the neighborhood. In conclusion, the court stated, "Under these circumstances, apartment houses, which in a different environment would not only be unobjectionable but highly desirable, came very close to being nuisances."[26]

Zoning today is often known as Euclidean zoning because it is based on the principles used in Euclid, Ohio. Generally speaking, a community will set aside land for various uses based on how it projects future needs. (See Figure 12–1.) Cities that have developed after zoning was established have clearer distinc-

tions and "buffer zones" between various land uses. Since many Frost Belt cities were well-developed by 1916, they have had more difficulty implementing zoning regulations. Existing land uses that violate the zoning ordinance can generally remain as "nonconforming" uses. Improvements may be forbidden so that eventually "proper" land use will occur. In the interim, however, by "grandfathering in" (that is, allowing existing uses to remain) and by preventing improvements, urban blight and decay often result.

Often zoning does not properly account for all future needs. These problems are dealt with in a number of ways. Usually a board of adjustment or similar body is empowered to grant a **variance** from the ordinance to allow

FIGURE 12–1

Typical Euclidean Zoning

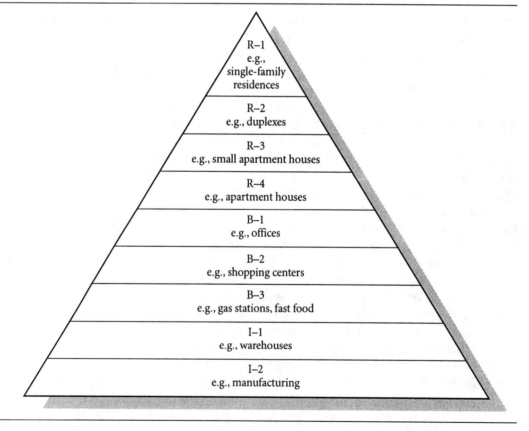

R–1
e.g.,
single-family
residences

R–2
e.g., duplexes

R–3
e.g., small apartment houses

R–4
e.g., apartment houses

B–1
e.g., offices

B–2
e.g., shopping centers

B–3
e.g., gas stations, fast food

I–1
e.g., warehouses

I–2
e.g., manufacturing

usage contrary to the ordinance, providing it will not have detrimental effects on others. For example, if a grocery store is required to have 100 parking stalls for customers based on the size of the building but the features of the land make it possible to only install 98, the developer may request a variance. The board of adjustment would have to decide if granting this request would have detrimental effects on others. This process is often criticized as a means of getting around the law. Another method of handling certain land uses is the **special use** or **conditional use permit**, which allows certain uses if owners comply with specific stipulations. For instance, home day care centers may not normally be permitted in single-family neighborhoods; however, if certain conditions are met, such as allowing no more than 6 children, having a fenced-in play area, and receiving permission from all property owners within 200 feet of the house, a conditional use permit may be granted. Finally, zoning can be changed to locate a proposed development in a certain place. If day care centers were allowed in residential areas other than the single-family zone, the day care provider may ask for a rezoning to a duplex zone rather than asking for a conditional use permit.

Classical zoning sought to segregate land usage to create homogeneous development. Several critics complained that this created a sterile environment. One such critic, Jane Jacobs, argued for mixed land use where neighborhood stores could be used as gathering and meeting places for nearby residents and parks could be used during the day by neighborhood children, at lunch by local office workers, and at night to attract people to cultural happenings.[27] Although Jacobs was often viewed as a pariah in planning circles, a new concept for zoning has evolved that follows the idea of mixed land use: **planned unit development** (PUD). In a PUD, relatively large parcels of land are "planned" to develop a mix of land uses to create an interdependent community. PUD is more flexible than Euclidian zoning and allows for more coordinated, comprehensive development and planning.

Every major city in the United States has some form of zoning. The last holdout was Houston, Texas, which only recently enacted "development controls." Although it grew without zoning, Houston differs little, from all outward appearances, from other Sun Belt cities of the same vintage. That is because order, so to speak, was retained as a result of private deed restrictions that limited land uses and thus played a role similar to zoning.

One reason for the widespread acceptance of land-use regulation was the Progressives' desire to remove politics from urban decision making. The planners tended to share the reformers' distrust of politics and politicians. Most early planners trained as engineers (like early city managers) and architects; they believed that professional standards, not political pressure, should govern urban development.

Because many believed planning was supposed to be apolitical, planning commissioners were and are usually appointed and sit for fixed terms, insulated from politics thereby. Under this system, planning commissioners are generally "respected" members of the community, who know little about planning. One study of the Charlotte–Mecklenburg Planning Commission found that people involved in development were over-represented.

Considering only the occupations most clearly associated with development interests, construction/developer, investment banker, architect, and heavy construction, 36.5 percent of the Charlotte–Mecklenburg Planning Commissioners have been affiliated with those interests. This number does not include the housewife who was the spouse of one of the largest subdivision developers or the attorney who was principally engaged in land use law or the "other" who was a real estate agent. Adding those persons to the proportion affiliated with development interests increases it to 43.8 percent.[28]

Another study raises two concerns about citizen planners' commitment to their job. First, planning directors felt that commissioners received little prestige for serving on the commission. Second, they felt that commissioners seldom had the time or desire to put in the required effort to play a meaningful role.[29]

Planning commissioners are often influenced by the planning professionals who set the agenda and provide the information. As the planners' recommendations presumably are based on nonpartisan, technical competence, commissioners tend to follow the planners' advice in the absence of public controversy. At other times, despite the intent of an unbiased independent commission, commissioners represent special interests. After all, who make better commissioners than bankers, realtors, and representatives of major industries who know the community and care about its future? At still other times, an entourage of concerned (and often ill-informed) citizens will win over the commissioners.[30]

City government often ignores the planning commission's recommendations. David Morgan discusses his participation as a planning commissioner.[31] A developer sought to rezone a tract of land near the University of Oklahoma for apartment, duplex, and single-family use. This land "abutted one of the city's nicer new single-family subdivisions."[32] The proposed development seemed to provide protection for the exclusive neighborhood, and the planning staff recommended approval. Everyone in the neighborhood, save one, signed a petition objecting to the zoning change and many attended a public hearing held by the planning commission. Most objected by using "public interest" symbols, such as increased traffic, potential drainage problems, and lack of need for more apartments. Only a couple used the "private interest" sym-

bol of declining property values. After a lengthy debate, the commission (also citizens in the community) voted 6 to 2 in favor of the zoning change and the development plan and sent their recommendations to the city council. At the council meeting the well-to-do property owners again presented their litany of complaints and this time they won. The comprehensive plan and zoning change were defeated.[33]

If the protesting citizens were not "well-to-do," the results might have been different. Another study notes that when deciding zoning matters, "local governments have been sympathetic to private developers when the latter have been pitted against 'citizen' groups."[34] The only time they listen to citizens is when the developer is seeking a zoning change to build public housing.[35]

Once a plan is adopted, the planner must implement it. He or she has several basic tools. The first is zoning (discussed earlier). A second tool is **subdivision regulation**, which usually consists of a set of rules that establish minimum lot sizes, street and utility placement, provision for open space and any special requirements for dividing large parcels of land into building-size lots. A third implementation tool for the planner is **building codes**, which are generally concerned with safety as well as aesthetics. Construction standards for insulation, supports, and building materials are established and electrical and plumbing standards are set. A fourth tool, **housing codes**, establish maintenance standards to prevent deterioration that might affect the health and safety of others. These codes are designed to prevent blight and protect the inhabitants. Still another device is the **capital improvement plan**, a means of fiscal planning that coordinates and establishes priorities for major public expenditures, for example, road construction and repair, sewers, public buildings.[36] New York City has used a variety of tools in an effort to renew Times Square as discussed in Box 12–1.

BOX 12-1

Reveille for Times Square

Times Square in New York City is world-renowned, and its tough times created an image of the city as an "ugly, dangerous, and sleazy place." West 42nd Street was the premier theater district in the early 1900s. Over the years its stature fell as its theaters became the home first to burlesque, then films, and finally X-rated and action films shown around the clock.

With the tools of planning and zoning, a combination of state, private, and non-profit groups are regenerating Times Square. A public investment of $75 million, along with $1.7 billion in private investment is expected to yield "hundreds of millions in taxes and re-establish the Times Square area as the nation's top urban entertainment district."

The city tried to encourage rebuilding by offering zoning and tax incentives. To protect the character of the entertainment district, the city added tougher design standards, "including that buildings be set back above 60 feet, incorporate Times Square–style signs and small storefronts, and offer space for theater-related activities." One observer credits the city's signage laws for making Times Square, "a much more alive place." When the sex businesses were moved off of West 42nd Street, they relocated nearby. Mayor Guiliani of New York supported a citywide zoning change that restricts "adult uses" from locating near residential areas or near each other. Gretchen Dykstra of the Times Square Business Improvement District, states that, "nothing has done more to change the image of Times Square than shutting off the red light."

Also planned is a 42nd Street trolley that would link the United Nations, Grand Central Terminal, Times Square, the bus terminal, the Convention Center, and the proposed site for a new Yankee Stadium. The future of this trolley project is in doubt. So far a Disney Store, a Virgin superstore, a microbrewery, a virtual reality arcade, clothing and gift stores, new restaurants, and new theaters have settled in the Times Square area.

Source: Adapted from Todd W. Bressi, "Reveille for Times Square," *Planning* 62 (September 1996): 4–8.

Although planners have often tried to be "value free" professionals, their job requires them to make value judgments about land use. One political scientist wrote: "The question is not whether planning will reflect politics, but whose politics it will reflect. What values and whose values will planners seek to implement?"[37] The concern about the values implicit in the planning function is one reason for current trends to integrate planning more thoroughly with the rest of the municipal government by making planning agencies responsible to the executive.[38] Anthony Catanese argues that planners must get involved in the political process because, "The local political process usually will overrule long-range and comprehensive plans based solely upon rationality principles of planning."[39] More planners are aware that in our pluralistic society, and especially in the heterogeneous urban areas, plans cannot be value-free.[40] This recognition is an outgrowth of an approach to planning known as advocacy planning, suggested by Paul Davidoff. He argued that urban development had handicapped the lower classes and that planners had traditionally been aligned with the local establishment. Davidoff believed that planners should act as advocates for poor people and develop plans that would aid them.[41]

One observer argues that advocacy planning has had a major impact on planners' conception of the public interest. The advocacy planner is more likely to assume that the community good can be discovered through pluralistic bargaining than through professional detachment.[42] Another observer, however, notes some of the limitations of advocacy planning:

> We could play at the game of citizen participation so long as the participation was limited to amelioration. We might be able to depress some highways rather than have elevated structures; we might be able to get better relocation payments for those displaced. But we could not change the program from one of building highways to redistributing the wealth of the highway corporations to the disenfranchised so that they could decide on their own programs, be they building housing, schools, hospitals, or indeed highways.[43]

The advocacy planner sought to give the havenots a chance to compete at public hearings and worked with communities to develop alternative plans.

A study of the use of advocacy planning in Minneapolis illustrates that even when the goal is less ambitious than the redistribution of wealth in society, advocacy planning does not always enable citizens to affect land-use decisions. Two Minneapolis neighborhoods attempted to stop a development plan submitted by K-Mart that required the closing of an intersection of two major streets. One neighborhood even had received a $77,000 grant to hire professional staff to develop an acceptable alternative plan. After several delays and many well-attended hearings, the issue finally was defined as "one neighborhood against the public interest." Despite attempts to show that slight modifications in K-Mart's plan could allow the intersection to remain open and that increased tax revenues would not offset the cost of city improvements, the neighborhood groups could not redefine the issue. Although the neighborhood was well-organized and also had professional expertise, it did not prevail.[44]

One commentator suggests that it may be invalid to assume that the neighborhood should always prevail:

> There is no basis for the view that citizens' groups represent "the people" or the "popular will," and developers represent simply private economic interests. Nor can one argue that citizens' groups are merely trying to make democracy work, and developers trying to undermine it.[45]

Each group will attempt to invoke the mantle of the public interest fighting a special interest. Because it is generally considered more legitimate for business or the upper and middle classes to invoke that mantle, they are more likely to prevail, although not always.

Another strategy used to give citizens more input into planning and land-use regulation is to divide a city into neighborhood planning districts and provide staff assistance. This approach is being used in several cities with over 250,000 population. Institutionalized neighborhood planning councils have been established in many cities. For example, in 1974 Atlanta adopted a city charter and a Neighborhood Planning Ordinance that grouped more than 200 neighborhoods into 24 neighborhood planning units. The participants in each unit were self-selected, elected, or appointed by citizens or citizen groups and each was assigned a staff planner, although a reorganization in 1978 limited technical resources. However, Leon S. Eplan, Commissioner of Budget and Planning, stressed that the planners worked for the city and that they were to give technical assistance, advice, and act as liaison between the neighborhood and the city.[46]

As with most attempts at citizen participation, the participants in Atlanta's planning process were atypical of the general population in terms of demographic characteristics and opinions. Home owners and those of higher status were more likely to participate and be more concerned with physical aspects of the community, such as planning and zoning, than with social issues.[47]

Nonetheless, the net impact of the neighborhood planning process in lower-income communities has been mobilization of community residents and increased influence in the zoning process. The result has apparently been a decrease in inequity of access to zoning decisions. Additionally, this access appears to offset, to some degree, deficits in personal resources and systematic biases. The formalization of citizen participation and the neighborhood planning process may be one example of what city governments *can do* to redress inequities and redistribute power.[48] [Emphasis in the original.]

Eplan acknowledged that citizen participation had "enormously improved the quality and relevance of decisions we are making."[49] Despite that, he concluded, "it is a mistake to put too much reliance on the citizens and what they have to say because the citizens tend to be a very amorphous body. They disappear, they come back, they change, and so forth."[50] This outlook is typical of many bureaucrats who are skeptical about the ability of the average citizen to understand complex, technical issues. They fear that special interests may obscure the "public interest."

An even more fundamental approach to expanding popular control over land-use decisions is the development of what Pierre Clavel refers to as Progressive cities. He identified several cities, including Santa Monica,

California; Burlington, Vermont; Cleveland, Ohio; Hartford, Connecticut; and Berkeley, California, where Progressive coalitions had succeeded in coming to power, at least temporarily. Clavel describes their goals as follows:

The main features of progressive politics . . . included attacks on the legitimacy of absentee-owned and concentrated private power on the one hand, and on nonrepresentative city councils to city bureaucracies on the other. These attacks led to programs emphasizing public planning as an alternative to private power, and to grassroots citizen participation as an alternative to council-dominated representation.[51]

For example, when Mayor Bernard Sanders took control of the Burlington, Vermont, government, he established neighborhood planning assemblies and involved the public in planning economic development projects.[52]

Clarence Stone warns, however, that such Progressive regimes have built in contradictions that tend to make them unstable and short-lived. Like all cities, they need to maintain a high level of economic development. But they also have a commitment to maintain a high level of citizen participation. Simultaneously satisfying both business interests and citizens can prove extremely difficult. Stone concludes that "in most cities a thoroughgoing progressive stance offers little hope to officeholders for a secure political future."[53]

Evaluation

Planning and land-use regulation have had a great impact on the urban residents and cities in general. Zoning laws and covenants have been used to keep "undesirables" such as Jews, African-Americans, and the poor out of some urban areas and often out of some suburban communities altogether.

Traditionally certain groups were excluded from certain areas through private restrictive covenants, which might prohibit sale to an African-American, or a Jew, or a divorced woman. Not until 1948 in *Shelley v. Kramer* did the Supreme Court hold that deed restrictions used to prevent sale or rental to minority groups could not be enforced by state action.[54] Nevertheless the Civil Rights Commission noted continuing restrictions being used to narrow access to certain communities. In 1960 in Grosse Pointe, Michigan, a wealthy Detroit suburb, homeowners and realtors collaborated to screen potential buyers.

> Fifty points was passing. However, persons "of Polish descent had to score 55 points; southern Europeans, including those of Italian, Greek, Spanish, or Lebanese origin, had to score 65 points; and those of the Jewish faith had to score 85 points. Negroes and orientals were excluded entirely."[55]

Although the Court took a firm stand on *private* actions, it has deferred greatly to local communities whose policies lead to de facto exclusion. Many communities engaged in **exclusionary zoning**, the practice of creating restrictive requirements for development that have the effect of preventing some groups from living in a community. In his book on exclusionary zoning, Michael Danielson found that 99 percent of all residentially zoned land in the New York metropolitan area was restricted to single-family housing, thus excluding apartment houses.[56] This, of course, excludes those who cannot afford to buy a house and keeps the poor where they are—primarily in the center city.

Even those who can afford to buy a modest house are effectively prevented from moving into some communities. Large lot requirements, often between two and four acres in some wealthy suburbs, are established, along with minimum floor space for dwellings to ensure only large, and therefore costly, homes will be built.

Several challenges have been mounted to exclusionary zoning. In 1971, the Second Circuit of the U.S. Court of Appeals ruled that

city officials could not prevent a black subdivision from being built in a white neighborhood.[57] In Oklahoma, a U.S. Appellate Court ruled that a community could not zone out apartments unless it could show that the intent was not to discriminate against the poor and minorities.[58]

At the same time as these two decisions, however, the U.S. Supreme Court upheld a California constitutional provision that required a referendum to approve low-income housing projects. The Court stated that the provision was not intended to be discriminatory and therefore was legal.[59] In another 1971 case, the U.S. District Court refused to hear a complaint of discriminatory zoning against Black Jack, Missouri.[60] In this case two Methodist churches sought to build 210 townhouses for moderate-income residents with subsidies from the Federal Home Administration in an unincorporated section of St. Louis County. The community was primarily upper-middle income and residents reacted negatively to the proposed project—arguing that they did not want another Pruitt–Igoe (see Chapter 14). Their response was to incorporate as a community and establish zoning to prevent the project.

Even the Justice Department joined the unsuccessful 1971 suit against Black Jack. That decision was overturned in the Court of Appeals in 1974 and upheld when the Supreme Court refused to review it in 1975. The result was that Black Jack was required to pay damages. After another suit, Black Jack agreed to allow a 135-unit project in 1982.[61] In 1975 another case gave cause for optimism in limiting exclusionary zoning. The New Jersey Supreme Court ruled that communities must accept a "fair share" of low-income housing.[62]

The hope of ending exclusionary zoning received a jolt in 1977 when the U.S. Supreme Court strongly supported local government rights in *Village of Arlington Heights v. Metropolitan Housing Development Corporation*.[63] The Court refused to strike down zoning that had prevented the construction of an integrated, subsidized housing project. The Court said that while the impact of the zoning may have been discriminatory, it would be necessary to show an *intent* to discriminate. The next year, however, in *Hills v. Gautreaux,* the U.S. Supreme Court intervened to require that communities use scattered sites throughout the metropolitan area, including the suburbs, for future housing.[64] The U.S. Department of Housing and Urban Development has also established rules tying grant eligibility to attempts to adhere to fair housing standards.

Despite this, many low-income and minority people have been prevented from escaping the center city. The city must then assume the burden of providing housing, which necessitates high service expenditures and means that the land where the housing is built is not available for development that could generate increased tax revenue.

At times local governments make laws to stifle development. For instance, in the 1960s Montgomery County, Maryland, enacted a moratorium on water and sewer extension. This effectively shifted development to Fairfax County, Virginia, which had more sympathetic development policies. It also raised the value of Montgomery County real estate because demand exceeded supply. However, because of limited development and taxpayer revolts, Montgomery County for a time faced a revenue crunch.

Several smaller cities have regulated land use to limit development in an attempt to prevent the heterogeneity and impersonality that develop as cities grow. After growing from a population of 10,000 in 1960 to 30,000 in 1972, Petaluma, California, formed several citizen advisory committees and held public hearings to develop a plan to control growth. The plan called for slowing development by limiting the issuance of building permits to 500 in subdivisions of 5 or more. The plan passed the city council and received a posi-

tive vote of 82 percent in 1973. A citizens review board was established to allocate the permits based on the quality of the proposal and the adequacy of public facilities. There was a specific provision for low-income housing. A suit was brought by some landowners and builders' associations that went to the U.S. Ninth Circuit Court of Appeals before the City of Petaluma prevailed.[65] A similar growth control ordinance had been upheld in Ramapo, New Jersey, in 1972.[66] More recently, several other communities have decided to limit their growth. Boulder, Colorado, has tried to limit residential growth; the result has been skyrocketing home prices as demand exceeds supply and increasing pollution in the area because people working in Boulder have to commute to their jobs. San Jose, California; Portland, Oregon; and Minneapolis–St. Paul, Minnesota, are other examples of cities that have decided to limit growth.[67]

Usually local communities are free to pursue their own interests and regulate land as they see fit. Despite federal incentives to encourage communities to work together in planning for the future, protection of one's life-style and property remains a major concern of metropolitan residents.[68] That is why local governments have dominated land-use regulation in the past.

One very important Supreme Court case, *First English Evangelical Lutheran Church of Glendale v. The County of Los Angeles,* has called local control into question.[69] Los Angeles County enacted an ordinance forbidding building on a flood plain. This ordinance was congruent with regulations of the federal government that make local governments ineligible to participate in federal flood insurance programs if they do not forbid building on a flood plain. However, the Supreme Court held that by restricting the use of the land the government was in fact "taking" away its utility. This was equivalent to the taking of property without just compensation and thus was in violation of the Fourteenth Amendment. Such regulations may result in the local government being forced to provide the property owner with monetary damages as a result of the impact of the regulation on the value of the property. Justice Rehnquist acknowledged that the decision would "lessen to some extent the freedom and flexibility of land use planners . . . when enacting land use regulations."[70] It also shifted the burden for establishing the impact of the regulation from the developers to the regulators and made it possible for regulation to create a severe financial burden for cities.

The "taking" doctrine is being applied in environmental protection cases where the use of land is limited because of negative environmental impacts. Eight states have passed laws requiring "takings impact analyses" before implementing environmental regulations. Bills have been introduced in 23 state legislatures, though passed in Mississippi only , to require compensation to property owners.[71] Legislation to require local government to compensate landowners for limitations on their use of their land due to environmental regulations was introduced into the 104th Congress (1994–96), but did not pass.

The "takings" issue is an example of the impact of the federal government on local land-use regulation policy. In two other areas of development policy, community development and transportation, the federal government has for a long time had a substantial impact on local government.

Economic and Community Development

Economic and community development are essential for urban areas to survive and renew themselves. The local political economy has always played a decisive role in their growth and health.

Agenda Setting

Metropolises exist in large measure to serve as marketplaces; that is, economic concerns have always been on the urban agenda. The federal government was concerned with opening transportation links between cities, but played a minor role in intraurban economic development until the Great Depression forced the issue onto the national agenda. State policies have long been aimed at economic development but as the federal role has decreased since the late 1970s, the states have been increasingly active in attracting industry to their cities.

The economic and community development agenda of urban area governments has changed over time. As Chapter 3 described, early city government saw its primary role as the support of the crafts and trades that formed the economic base of the mercantile city (the earliest form of urban settlement in America). Thus, the government established weights and measures and built public wharves.

As the industrial city emerged, the functions of city government expanded to meet the increased needs of a larger, heterogeneous population. Immigrants from the countryside and from the rest of the world poured into America's cities to find jobs in the new factories; city governments were forced to build sewer lines to stop the spread of disease from contaminated wells, establish school systems to educate children, and expand the network of streets to keep up with the burgeoning population. These new public services were not expressly for business, but business benefited indirectly. The population concentrations necessary to staff the factories could not have been sustained without the amenities provided by the urban governments. Public provision removed a burden that private business would otherwise have had to carry.

If anything, economic and community development are even more important components of the urban agenda in the metropolitan city. Technological advances have meant that neither business nor people are tied to center cities or to urban areas. The automobile freed people from the necessity of living close to jobs. Aided by the government's construction of highways and subsidizing of mortgages, people fled the city for the suburbs. Business also began to desert the city. Modern manufacturing plants require large amounts of land for the sprawl dictated by conveyor-belt technology and land is cheaper outside the center city. As a result of communications technology, many businesses no longer need to be near each other and a mobile work force frees business to decentralize even more. In the global city, decisions made abroad can place issues on the urban agenda, as competition for development involves international as well as national rivals.

Even though business is not as dependent on the urban marketplace as it once was, local governments are still just as dependent on business for economic viability. Without the jobs that business provides, the movement of people from center cities would surely accelerate. The impact of business on the value of urban land is important because local governments rely heavily on property taxes as a revenue base. Therefore, local governments focus much of their efforts on devising ways to "create a good climate for business." As people and businesses are expanding beyond the suburbs to the "exurb" and further, suburbs are increasingly joining the central cities in the competition for business. The edge cities discussed in Chapter 3 are strong competitors to the center city.

Formulation

As in the past, urban areas attempt to create a good business climate by providing services and amenities. Sewers are built and roads are paved. But city governments now go beyond providing an infrastructure for business activity. Local governments sometimes feel forced

into bidding wars with each other to keep the business they have from moving and to attract other businesses.

The bait takes a variety of forms. Communities may use municipal revenue bonds to finance industrial projects or they may develop an industrial park or provide businesses with free land. They may offer a variety of tax exemptions, for example, exempting a corporation from income taxes or from paying local sales taxes on machinery or raw material purchases. Several states have created Enterprise Zones to channel businesses to the inner city. Businesses that relocate within the zone are granted tax credits, deferrals and exemptions from state taxes and often local governments are allowed to "sweeten the pot" with further concessions. In general, local governments will try to keep taxes as low as possible as an incentive.

In addition to tax incentives, urban governments are trying other innovative techniques to bolster their economies. One approach is public–private joint ventures. Cincinnati, Ohio, for example, shares 16 percent of the profits from a hotel and office building project. Another popular device is the building of elaborate sports facilities in the hope of attracting or retaining a major league team. Seattle voters approved a multimillion dollar deal to build a new stadium for the Seattle Seahawks, who were threatening to leave the city. Detroit also is building new homes for the football Lions and baseball Tigers. The importance of leadership and public–private trust and cooperation is pointed out in Box 12–2 (on page 336), which describes the situation in Detroit.

Local governments will sometimes use land-use controls to attract business. They may limit parking space requirements, change signage limitations, or work to change zoning to make areas attractive to business investment.

In essence, local governments use public funds to subsidize private business. A study

BOX 12–2

Detroit to Have New Sports Stadiums Through Public–Private Partnerships

Sports stadiums have been a common issue on the agendas of many cities. Teams threaten to move unless new stadiums are built to accommodate more people, and more important, to have more luxury suites that can be rented by corporations. Even though there is little evidence that sports stadiums augment the finances of an urban area, cities often capitulate to team demands. This is so because of the perception that stadiums contribute to economic development as well as the fact that teams are an important component of the city's image.

In Detroit, a more cooperative arrangement between team owners and the city government is developing. The Detroit Tigers baseball team and the city government have agreed to cooperate in building a $240-million stadium in the inner city, and the Detroit Lions football team has also reached agreement with the city for a new $245-million domed stadium to be located next to the baseball stadium. In each case, the owners will pay approximately half of the cost of building the stadium.

Analysts believe these deals might not be duplicated in other cities. The owners of both Detroit teams are not only very wealthy,

they also have a firm commitment to Detroit. The Ilitch family, the owners of the Detroit Tigers, founded the Little Caesar pizza chain and has moved into real estate development. The Ford family, which still controls 40 percent of Ford Motor Company, owns the Lions. William C. Ford, who announced the stadium deal in a press conference, said, "My children and grandchildren are going to live in this area, and without a vital city center, this area is greatly diminished."

Ford also explained that the family had moved the team from Detroit to Pontiac, Michigan, in 1975 because his family had lost confidence in Detroit as a result of the race riot in 1967 and the confrontational leadership style of Mayor Coleman Young. Young has been replaced by Dennis Archer, who has strong business support.

All three of the major motor companies have made recent large investments in the city. After years of decline, Detroit appears to be reviving economically. The Detroit example illustrates the importance of local economic interests to a city's health and, as a result, the interdependence of political leaders and economic leaders in urban areas.

Source: Adapted from Keith Bradsher, "Lions Plan to Return to Downtown Detroit," *New York Times,* August 26, 1996.

conducted for the National League of Cities indicates how extensive such subsidies are. The survey of officials in 325 cities shows that 40 percent of the cities provided cash to businesses, 47 percent provided loans, 78 percent financed business projects by tax-exempt bonds, 45 percent sold land to business at reduced rates, 39 percent gave tax abatements,

30 percent provided loan guarantees, and 39 percent gave loan subsidies.[72]

Adoption and Implementation

While local officials justify such public–private partnerships as necessary for the well-being of all citizens, such policies may generate

substantial conflict from many sources because not all the interests in a community
benefit equally from the partnerships. One
source of conflict is within the business community. Urban businesses vie with each other
for larger pieces of the subsidy pie. In-place
businesses also compete with other businesses
that the community is attempting to attract.
For example, local governments may try to
lure new business with tax breaks, but expect
current businesses to continue to pay local
taxes. Local businesses may protest what they
see as unequal treatment.

Another source of conflict comes from
citizens who see social services squeezed as
business is subsidized. Money that might go
to a program such as job training for the unemployed goes instead to help a firm build an
addition to its plant. Not only must citizens
compete with business for tax money, but the
amount of tax money available is kept low because tax rates are kept at a minimum to assure a good business climate. Another source
of conflict is between the center city and the
neighborhoods. Economic development
projects usually result in gleaming new buildings in the central business district. While that
area of the city booms, many neighborhoods
continue to crumble. The author of the National League of Cities survey concludes that
economic development "is not developing a
strong indigenous business base, eliminating
physical blight, or channeling economic benefits to the poorest areas of the city."[73]

The neighborhood versus business conflict became an issue in several mayoral races.
Several insurgents such as Coleman Young in
Detroit, Richard Hatcher in Gary, Indiana,
and Frederico Pena in Denver were elected
only to find that there would be no resources
for neighborhoods if they did not play ball
with business. Coleman Young found out that
if he wanted a new General Motors plant in
Detroit, it would be located wherever G.M.
wanted it regardless of neighborhood sentiment.[74] Hatcher found massive business exo-

dus when he refused to give in to business demands.[75]

The city of Denver has been more successful in controlling the conflict.[76] As Denver
grew from "Cowtown" to "Sun Belt City," economic development focused on the downtown area. In 1983, this downtown strategy
was challenged by Frederico Pena. Although
Denver was only 18 percent Latino, Pena (a
Latino) won the mayoral election by fashion-
ing a coalition of minorities, women's groups,
gays, environmentalists, neighborhood activists, and some businesspeople. Pena had
promised to increase the influence of neighborhoods by opening up city hall.

After election, he held neighborhood
meetings, increased the staff of neighborhood
planners, and instituted a study of neighborhood traffic flows toward downtown. Pena
also reorganized city departments to facilitate
economic development. In addition, he established a 27-member panel to develop a downtown master plan. The Denver Partnership,
the downtown business development corporation, had 5 members and played a major
role. Some neighborhood groups were upset
because they had only 3 members appointed
to the panel, and because they believed that
the neighborhoods were still being slighted.

For the most part, though, Pena was fairly
successful in keeping the conflict in check because he "successfully invoked the symbols of
open and responsive government even
though he did not change the substance of development priorities."[77] He was fairly successful in selling the idea that a robust downtown
has a "trickle down" effect on neighborhoods.
In addition, in his 1985 State of the City address, Pena stressed quality-of-life issues over
economic development and announced programs such as low- and moderate-income
housing, small business loans, new parks, and
neighborhood improvements.

In many cities, the conflicts that are always incipient in economic development
policies are kept suppressed by the decision-

making mechanisms. At the urban level, decisions are often delegated to special development authorities that operate independently of the general purpose government. (See Chapter Seven for a discussion of authorities and how they limit public control.) The authorities generate their own revenue, usually from revenue bonds and user charges. The members of the authority are often appointed, in many cases by the state governor, and the appointees are most often representatives of the business and financial community. In cases where the authority's members are elected, turnout tends to be low because the public lacks both information on what the authority does and expertise to evaluate the complex tax policies that they produce. In general, use of the authority obscures urban development policies and deflects responsibility from elected officials. As a result, the public can play little role.

When the federal government became involved in economic and community development, it mandated citizen participation. That participation usually meant, however, "blue ribbon" citizen advisory boards of prominent businesspersons and developers. The first federal aid came as a result of the Great Depression and was designed to help cities eliminate blight, increase their tax base, and provide jobs. Federal aid, at that time, was focused primarily on providing housing for those who could not afford it and, in the process, on using housing programs to stimulate the construction industry, which would help provide jobs and strengthen the economy.*

After the economic crisis passed, the focus on housing began to subside. The Housing Act of 1949 first provided resources to be used for nonresidential development. In 1954 the term **urban renewal** was coined, implying that the federal aid was to be used for general urban development and not to be restricted solely to housing programs. By 1961, about

one-third of federal subsidies could be used for purposes other than housing. The national government realized that the urban renewal program, as it evolved during the 1950s and 1960s, did more to help private developers than poor people. In a 1968 report, the National Commission on Urban Problems concluded that urban renewal was a "federally financed gimmick to provide relatively cheap land for a miscellany of profitable or prestigious enterprises."[78]

In 1966 Congress passed the Demonstration Cities and Metropolitan Development Act, or Model Cities Program. The policy was billed by liberals as having a redistributive purpose. Title I of the act makes clear that liberal sponsors intended the funds to be used to help the poor:

> The purposes of this title are to provide additional financial and technical assistance to enable cities of all sizes [to implement] new and imaginative proposals and rebuild and revitalize large slums and blighted areas; to expand housing, job, and income opportunities; to reduce dependence on welfare payments; to improve educational facilities and programs; to combat disease and ill health; to reduce the incidence of crime and delinquency; to enhance recreational and cultural opportunities; to establish better access between homes and jobs; and generally to improve living in such areas.[79]

The act also required that citizens be involved in planning the allocation of money on the local level.

Despite the redistributive rhetoric, the Model Cities program became primarily a subsidy for city governments.[80] The original formulators of the program first considered focusing all resources in only one (later changed to five) cities to maximize the impact. In order to pass Congress, 63 cities were

---

*See Chapter 14 for discussion of these programs.

eventually designated for inclusion, including some small towns represented by key members of Congress. The following year there were 150 model cities. Because the money was distributed widely, there were insufficient resources in any one city to make a significant impact.

The participation requirements were also not strong enough to create substantial change. Requiring "widespread citizen participation" instead of the "maximum feasible participation" of the War on Poverty underlined the fact that citizen input was to be advisory only. As a result, the Advisory Commission on Intergovernmental Relations observed that, "city hall controlled most programs and mayors increased their powers, often at the expense of neighborhood-based citizen organizations." [81] Most citizens who became active were middle class or had previously been citizen leaders.[82]

The Housing and Community Development Act of 1974 established a block grant entitlement program for cities. The Community Development Block Grant (CDBG) consolidated seven categorical grant programs: (1) rehabilitation loans, (2) urban renewal, (3) Model Cities, (4) neighborhood facilities programs, (5) open space programs, (6) public facilities loans, and (7) water and sewer grants. These grants were allocated on a formula basis to all cities of 50,000 or more; smaller cities could compete for discretionary money, which was "earmarked" or set aside for them. Initially, the formula benefited small cities and suburbs that had not played the grantsmanship game effectively and the growing cities in the South and West. In 1977, the formula was revised to consider deterioration and population declines and therefore to help the distressed Frost Belt cities in the East and Midwest.

The Community Development program was also billed as having a redistributive focus. The act required that the benefits go primarily to low- and moderate-income residents. Many studies have established that the money was not funneled to those groups. Again, a distributive pattern with something for everyone was more likely to prevail. The citizen participation requirements under the CDBG marked another step backward from the War on Poverty. Citizens were allowed to comment before and after the application was prepared but they could be ignored; in addition, there were no provisions for technical assistance or reimbursement for costs of participation.

The idea of targeting areas of highest need returned during the Carter Administration with Urban Development Action Grants (UDAG) aimed at stimulating private investment in distressed center cities. The money could be used for commercial ventures such as malls and convention centers, which would create jobs and encourage further private investment. The grants went primarily to Frost Belt cities.

A study by Paul Dommel indicates that between 1972 and 1975 the mean increase in federal aid to eight selected Frost Belt cities was 62 percent compared to 238 percent for nine selected Sun Belt cities. With the change in the CDBG formula and UDAG grants in 1977, Dommel found a 133 percent increase for the Frost Belt cities between 1975 and 1978, compared to an 83 percent increase for the Sun Belt cities.[83]

President Reagan's major urban initiative was to request the creation of Enterprise Zones in distressed sections of cities. This proposal called for tax incentives for private firms to locate in these areas to create new jobs. This is an example of "trickle down economics." Relieving government restraint and taxes was supposed to encourage private investment by increasing the likelihood of profit. Although Congress did not pass legislation creating Enterprise Zones, it did respond to Reagan's request to cut funding for CDBG and UDAG. UDAG finally disappeared during the Bush Administration. Critics char-

acterized the Reagan policy as "a form of Social Darwinism applied to cities as it has been
previously applied, with pernicious consequences, to individuals and social classes."[84]

In 1987, Congress did pass a federal enterprise program but without substantial
commitments. Only in 1993 did Congress finally pass a law committing resources to an
enterprise zone program. The law created
nine "empowerment zones," six in urban areas
and three in rural areas. It also designated 95
"enterprise communities," 65 of which are in
urban areas. Funds from a newly created social services block grant are used to provide
the urban empowerment zones with $100
million and the enterprise communities with
$3 million. In addition, businesses with em-
ployees who live and work in the empowerment zones are eligible for a 20 percent tax
credit on the first $15,000 of wages and some
training expenses.[85]

The Community Development Block
Grants and the Enterprise Zone program are
now the cornerstones of America's federal
community development programs. As the
role of the federal government has decreased,
other actors have become increasingly important in determining development policy in urban areas. States have increased their activity,
with many establishing their own enterprise
zone programs. In addition, nonprofit groups
are becoming increasingly important both as
service providers and as a source of funds. Finally, local political leaders have become even
more important in the setting of development
policy. Mayors such as John Norquist of Milwaukee, Ed Rendell of Philadelphia, and
Stephen Goldsmith of Indianapolis have been
in the forefront of efforts to get cities to or-
chestrate their own urban recovery.[86]

Evaluation

Despite the amount of resources devoted to
economic development, it is not clear that any
of the economic and community development programs have lived up to expectations.
The constant revamping of federal policies in
this area is an indicator that no approach has
been totally successful. Although many downtowns have been revitalized, cities still have
pockets of blight. It may be that unique urban
conditions affect the impact of programs, as
several federal programs have been successful
in some cities such as Minneapolis and Philadelphia, while cities such as Detroit, Newark,
and Gary, Indiana, have had less success.

Many recent studies suggest that the role
of the political leaders in urban areas may explain some of the differences. Minneapolis
benefited from government leaders who
forged alliances with the corporate giants, like
Norwest Bank, General Mills, 3M, Dayton-
Hudson, and Northwest Airlines, that make
their headquarters in that city. On the other
hand, in Detroit the business and political
community failed to reach agreement on a
plan for the economic redevelopment in the
city. The lack of an effective governing coalition has hamstrung Detroit and is probably
also an issue in the other cities.[87] In Newark,
the government of Mayor Sharpe James has
been riddled with charges of corruption and
Prudential Insurance, the major business in
Newark, has shown little interest in joining a
coalition. The former Mayor of Gary, Richard
Hatcher was seen as antagonistic to business
and was unable to establish a successful regime.[88]

In a review of development policies in 10
communities, Michael Pagano and Ann Bowman conclude that the local government plays
a major role:

> Much of the development literature of the
> 1980s marginalizes the actions of the pub-
> lic sector, especially localities. But city gov-
> ernments are central actors. Our argument
> is that the mobilization of public capital—
> or how local officials select, package, and
> utilize the policy instruments at their dis-
> posal—is primary.[89]

Local governments rarely attempt to assess the costs and benefits of their economic development policies in any systematic way. One reason may be the difficulty of isolating the impact of an incentive program from the other factors that affect business decisions. That difficulty presumably contributes to the conflicting findings of those studies that have been done.

Many studies conclude that business incentive programs have little or no effect for two reasons. First, other factors over which governments exercise little control (for example, labor and energy costs, or population growth) are more important determinants of a business's decision of where to locate.[90] Second, businesses are not as mobile as cities assume; movement is not particularly common.[91] Other critics point out that because of the widespread competition, "the situation is roughly the same as if the federal government had required tax breaks for business everyplace."[92] As a result, Martin Gottlieb argues, "The only redirection of wealth that occurs is the shift of the tax burden to individuals."[93] For instance, in Dayton, Ohio, 34 percent of the land is now tax exempt compared to 25 percent a decade ago.

Other studies, however, have concluded that tax and expenditure policies are linked to economic growth.[94] There is some evidence that city governments may reap other benefits from the private–public partnerships beyond tax revenues. John Herbers reports that business is increasingly becoming involved in providing those services that used to be public responsibilities.

> The increase in involvement between businesses and government at the state and local levels certainly includes lobbying for direct benefits for businesses themselves. But it also extends more and more to work on behalf of social programs under which business would receive indirect benefits, especially in improving education, which

in turn would improve the quality of their work forces; to joining with public officials in public–private partnerships to achieve such purposes as urban redevelopment or crime and drug control; and to contributions to public construction projects.[95]

While local governments may receive benefits from such public–private partnerships, and business interests do so as well, serious questions remain about their impact on public accountability. The intermingling of public and private authority complicates the already complex problem of determining responsibility for policy. Beyond that, the extent to which decisions are controlled by private business limits public accountability because no direct mechanism for public control of private business exists. Finally, even the public decisions are usually obscured by the delegation of decision making to independent authorities.

On the other hand, there is evidence that citizens do play a role in development policy. The study of development policy by Pagano and Bowman cited above found that the political risk of a development project was the best predictor of the project's success.

> The more controversial the project, the more likely the project will be unsuccessful, that is, that the public will react. The public is aware of unleased office buildings, plants operating at half capacity, convention centers without events, and empty parking garages. If controversy surrounds a project's proposal, city leaders may want to think twice about committing city funds to it. Nevertheless, even in an economically troubled city, success can occur so long as it generates political support or if political controversy is muted.[96]

Two other recent studies concluded that neighborhood organizations can have an impact on economic development policies, especially if the community's political culture supports the concept of neighborhood participation and if the local government provides support to the organizations.[97]

Transportation

Transportation is intimately related to urban areas. For many of America's older cities, transportation was their initial reason for existence. The earliest American cities arose because of the concentration of people around waterways, the predominant form of transportation, especially for commercial purposes. As technology advanced, land transportation competed with waterways and spawned other cities. Railroad lines were built and cities emerged along the routes, especially at the points where multiple lines converged or ended.*

Just as transportation determined where cities would emerge, it also molded the shape of those cities. Initially, the residents clustered together in dense concentrations. Such density was inevitable because the lack of any transportation besides one's own feet—or for a wealthy few, a horse and buggy—meant that people had to live close to where they worked. Businesses clustered around the harbor, the railroad, the river; thus the population did as well.

Eventually, in some cities, the population grew to such an extent that it had to disperse. As a result, people needed rapid mass transportation to get jobs in the major business districts. As elevated rail lines, subways, and trolley lines were built, the population began to move out of the dense confines of the center city and disperse along those transportation routes.

The advent and proliferation of the automobile revolutionized both transportation and cities. No longer were people limited to living close to their jobs or close to one of the few mass transit lines. Now they could disperse in every direction and move farther and farther away from the center city—and disperse they

did. As the location of businesses drew population into the city in the past, now the dispersed population drew businesses out of the city, chasing the consumers as they drove out to their suburban homes. Shopping centers began to dot the land and downtown began to deteriorate, hit by the double whammy of competition from suburban shopping malls and the inconvenience of old downtown areas that were never designed to provide parking for seemingly limitless numbers of cars.

Urban areas began to sprawl like vast oil slicks, and, in some ways, the dispersal of jobs, shopping, entertainment, and housing was irritating to everyone involved. Commuting between job and home began to consume more and more hours. Parents had to spend more and more time transporting children to distant friends, movie theaters, and piano teachers. To some residents, however, the problem went beyond being merely irritating. The poor who could not afford cars and the handicapped or elderly who could not drive were forced into immobility in a highly mobile society.

Not only did the automobile change the shape of cities, it contributed to the increasing importance of some cities that previously had limited potential for growth because of poor transportation networks. Phoenix, Dallas, Los Angeles, to name a few, could now grow because their lack of a harbor or major river no longer mattered. Similarly, other cities declined because their access to water or a rail line was less important.

Agenda Setting

As the nation progressed from dependence on water transportation to its fascination with the automobile, government at various levels was asked for help and for transportation subsidies. The demands came from entrepreneurs who wanted to provide the transportation and reap the profits and from "boosters"

---

*The connection between transportation and the birth and growth of cities was discussed in Chapter 3.

of communities, which could grow and prosper with better transportation. Government responded positively, resulting in widespread distribution of government support for various forms of transportation.

Even before the existence of railroads, the national government was involved in providing aid for transportation. In 1806, Congress authorized surveys for a national highway to run from Cumberland, Maryland, west across the Appalachians to Ohio. But in 1816, President Monroe vetoed legislation to appropriate money to build the highway, and, for a century afterward, federal aid to highways ceased. However, the federal government provided substantial aid to other forms of transportation.

States and local governments were also active in aiding transportation, including direct grants of money, exemption from taxation, and public land grants. Most federal and state aid was focused on *interurban* transportation: connecting cities to other places in the country. Financing for *intraurban* transportation had to be raised locally. In most cases, transportation facilities were provided by private entrepreneurs. Only the largest of cities had extensive mass transit facilities. By the early years of the twentieth century, most cities relied on the electric streetcar for mass transportation, but, with few exceptions, the routes were very limited.

In the early 1900s, rural interests and automobile interests combined to form a highway lobby.[98] The goal of the lobby was to pressure the federal and state governments to build highways. It should be clear why rural people and automakers shared an interest in highways. No mass transit system could ever serve the dispersed rural population effectively, and automakers were ready to sell cars to these people as soon as roads existed on which the cars could be driven. Over time, other interests have joined with the highway lobby to pressure government for more highway construction. Some of the more prominent additions have been truckers, construction companies, building materials companies, automobile associations, bus companies, and the petroleum industry. Representatives of these affected groups established close and stable contacts with decision makers and had substantial impact on policy. This lobby, interested primarily in increasing a demand for their goods and services to boost their profits, has been the major determinant of national transportation policy.[99]

Formulation and Adoption

The Federal Aid Road Act of 1916 was an early victory for the highway lobby. The act ensured coordination in highway construction so that highways met at state lines. State highway agencies administered the federal aid, but overall coordination came from the Bureau of Public Roads, which was housed in the Department of Agriculture—an indicator of the rural bias of the legislation. Another indicator of such bias was the fact that communities with a population of 2,500 or more (that is, cities) were ordinarily ineligible for aid.

Not until the 1944 Federal Highways Act was there any large-scale provision of aid for highways in metropolitan areas. That act was primarily intended to encourage the building of an interstate highway system to connect the country's major metropolises, but 25 percent of the federally aided highways were required to be built in areas with populations of 5,000 or more. This opened the door to using federal highway funds *within* metropolitan areas.

This recognition of urban areas was hardly an unmixed blessing for cities. While some urban interests thought better highways would encourage people to travel downtown, they forgot that the roads could also be used to transport people quickly *away* from the city. As the highways were built, more and more people used them to move their households to the suburbs. As more and more people moved, demand for highways increased. As a result, in 1956, the national government passed the Federal Aid Highway Act to fund 90 percent of the cost of building the interstate highway system.

By stimulating suburban growth, these highways did little to help cities and much to hurt them. Indeed, the building of highways and the process of suburbanization became a vicious cycle with highways facilitating the movement to suburbs and the growth of suburbs creating a need for highways.[100]

Another result of the automobile revolution was the decline of mass transit. Again, this led to a vicious cycle. As more people chose to move around urban areas in their cars rather than using public transportation, ridership declined. As usage declined, the quality and quantity of mass transit also declined. Fewer riders meant transit companies and authorities no longer had the money to maintain equipment. Buses, subways, trolley cars, and other forms of public transportation became dirty and unreliable. Schedules were cut back or stations were closed. As service deteriorated, more and more people abandoned public transportation for their cars, making the financial crunch even more serious. Now, only about 17 percent of city residents and only about 10 percent of suburban residents travel on mass transit facilities.[101]

In the 1960s and 1970s, however, there was heightened concern about the reliance on the private automobile for transportation in urban areas. Several factors helped bring the issue of urban mass transit to the policy agenda. One source of concern was the growing recognition that some urban residents are seriously disadvantaged by the elimination of effective mass transit. For example, the poor have to rely upon an affordable public system of transportation because they are unable, in many cases, to afford a private car.[102] The issue of mass transit becomes increasingly acute as businesses, and therefore jobs, also moved to the suburbs. Those without cars and without the money to move to the suburbs are cut off from access to potential em-

ployment. In the 1960s, urban riots helped spotlight the problems of jobs in the ghetto and the difficulty of transporting the urban poor to suburban jobs. In addition to the poor, the elderly and the handicapped are often unable to drive, and therefore are also dependent on mass transit.

Another source of concern over the decline of mass transit was the growing awareness of environmental pollution. Cars' contribution to air pollution has been recognized since 1920. In 1965, the Motor Vehicle Air Pollution Control Act was enacted; it gave the Secretary of the U.S. Department of Health, Education, and Welfare the power to prescribe standards governing permissible auto emissions of substances that might prove harmful to humans. In response, automakers added catalytic converters to automobile engines. "By 1969, however, the 1965 Act had not produced the results that Congress had intended, because the magnitude of the technological problem had proved greater (and in the view of some observers, the auto industry's interest in solving it, less) than had been expected."[103]

In the following year, public concern over pollution was highlighted by the observance of Earth Day, including demonstrations and marches to demand the reduction of environmental pollution. Some environmental activists believed that mass transit would reduce air pollution by eliminating many trips by pollution-creating cars.

Also creating heightened interest in mass transit was the Arab oil embargo in 1973. To protest American support for Israel, the Arab oil-producing countries declared an embargo on the shipment of oil to the United States. The result was a drastic increase in the price of gas. In addition, gas shortages in this country resulted in long lines and de facto gas rationing. The United States suddenly recognized its vulnerability to Arab control of a vital commodity; new concern for energy conservation was born. Some argued that mass transit was a more energy-efficient means of transporting people than each individual driving a car.

Throughout the 1960s and 1970s, a new movement seemed to be emerging in many cities: a movement to stop the construction of highways through cities. Since the end of World War II, suburbanites had been clamoring for highways to provide easy commutes between home and job. The construction of large, limited-access highways was facilitated by federal highway acts that subsidized construction. While commuters and suburbanites benefited from this widespread distribution of transportation subsidies, others were hurt.

The construction of most of those highways meant demolishing urban neighborhoods. The neighborhoods most frequently chosen for highway routes were those in which the poor lived. By the 1960s, enough neighborhoods had been annihilated, enough people displaced, enough landmarks destroyed or overshadowed by highways that opposition was beginning to form. In 1967, the *New York Times* reported:

> Urban hostility to expressways is rising in volume and emotion and threatens in a dozen cities to delay completion of the most costly links in the Interstate Highway Program. Of the 16,400 miles of highway remaining to be built in the 41,000-mile system, scheduled to be completed in 1972, 2,296 miles will traverse cities and suburbs. So brutal has been the impact on city life of some of the completed expressways that the Federal Government has cautioned cities against hasty planning that ignores aesthetic, social and economic considerations.[104]

By 1973, the opposition to the reliance on the private car for transportation had grown enough that a mass transit lobby had emerged to counter the highway lobby. The main components of the mass transit lobby were those interests with a commitment to the center city, such as downtown businesses and the major city newspaper. Joining them were some suburban commuters. Finally, existing mass transit bureaucracies were (and are) vocal in demanding increased aid for public transportation.

Stated simply, the major policy options are to continue aiding the construction of highways, and thus subsidizing the commuters in their private cars, or to begin to devote greater financial support for the construction—or renovation—of mass transit systems. A few cities—San Francisco, Washington, D.C., Atlanta, and Buffalo—have relatively recently built subway systems. Because the costs are so high, citizens can often have a voice through referenda on bond issues that are required to support the project.

Other cities are building, or thinking of building, "light rail lines." *Light rail line* is the modern term for the old-fashioned trolley that was the backbone of urban transportation in the early years of the twentieth century. Portland, Oregon, has a light rail system that, at least initially, was hailed as a great success. Box 12–3 (on page 346) provides an alternative evaluation of the Portland experience. The advantage of light rail lines is their relatively low cost (or at least that is the claim of supporters); the disadvantage is the potential of adding to the congestion of already overcrowded city streets.

Some consideration is also being given to building elevated rail lines, a form of mass transit currently used in Chicago and to a limited degree in parts of the New York metropolitan area. Miami has built such an elevated train, referred to as an "aerial" or a "downtown-people-mover," and other cities have contemplated such a project. The problem is the cost. Others have argued that only buses provide the cheap and flexible transportation needed in cities now. A depressed neighborhood of Chicago has started an innovative use of bus transportation. North

BOX 12–3

Is Light Rail the Answer to Urban Transportation Woes?

In the 1980s, many western cities developed "light rail lines." A light rail line is the modern term for trolley lines. San Diego started the trend in 1981 by building a line between the city and the Mexican border. Other cities building such rail lines included Sacramento, San Jose, and Portland, Oregon. Light rail is touted by supporters as a relatively cheap and quick way of reducing the traffic congestion and pollution that result from commuting by car. It takes less money and less time to build a light rail line than to build a subway or elevated system. But one analysis of the Portland system questions whether it is worth the cost, even if it is less than a subway or an elevated system.

Portland completed its first line in 1986. Initial estimates indicated it could be built in 3 years for $135 million and would attract 42,500 riders a day. It took 4 years and $214 million to build and attracted only 21,000 riders per day in the first 5 years. By 1996, ridership was still only approximately 32,000 per day and operating costs were higher than expected.

The slowness of the rail line—20 miles per hour—may be one reason for poor ridership. In any event, as few people use the line, it does little to reduce either pollution or congestion because most people are still traveling by car.

Despite these problems, Portland will open a new line in 1998 and is planning other extensions. The first two lines were substantially subsidized by the federal and state governments, which together contributed 95 percent of the funding for the first line and 85 percent of the funds for the second line. Although there may be cutbacks in federal mass transit funding, Portland appears determined to continue its commitment to extending the light rail system.

The Portland case demonstrates the fact that government may not be able to lure people from their automobiles.

Source: Adapted from Robert Lindsey, "In the West, Municipal Heartstrings Go 'Zing! Zing! Zing!'" *New York Times,* November 30, 1986, sec. E; "Portland Transit: Forward into the Past," Portland Transit and Light Rail, www.teleport.com/rot/transit/html.

Lawndale is busing residents out to suburbs to help them find and commute to jobs. President Clinton has expressed support for expanding the program to other cities.

Even if mass transit facilities exist, policy makers have to figure out how to lure Americans out of their beloved cars. As one evaluator has pointed out, mass transit has numerous disadvantages when compared to the private car:

> . . . transit is not as fast, door to door; transit does not depart from one's home, nor

does it go directly to one's destination; transit is not immediately available the moment one wishes to leave, night or day; transit often cannot provide one a seat at all, much less a private, uncrowded seat; and transit offers less personal security.[105]

One option for encouraging the use of public transportation is to ban cars from urban areas. That has never been seriously considered because the business interests in the city fear that people would simply stop coming downtown and city officials fear the businesses would move out. However, a more limited version of the idea has been put in operation in some places by restricting cars from certain urban areas. Minneapolis and Denver, for instance, both transformed one of their central shopping streets into an open mall and banned all vehicles except city buses.

Another suggestion is to make automobile usage less efficient than it now is in comparison to mass transit. Some areas have established special highway lanes and bridge and tunnel entrances that enable buses to sail past lines of cars jammed into the remaining lanes. Several metropolitan areas have established car pool lanes reserved for cars with more than one person to limit the number of cars entering the city at rush hour.

A final option is to make public transportation free. Some observers have argued, however, that use of mass transit is not strongly related to the cost.[106] Others argue that decreasing transit costs would actually increase decentralization in the metropolis by making it cheaper for people to live in the suburbs.[107]

Another policy dilemma concerns who should be responsible for the provision of mass urban transportation. In 1945, 98 percent of mass transportation was privately owned and operated. The percentage of private ownership had dropped to 45 percent by 1980.[108] Congruent with the conservative philosophy of the Reagan Administration, increased private involvement in urban transportation, an example of privatization, was encouraged. In the spring of 1986, the Urban Mass Transit Administration proposed to Congress a schedule that all transit agencies applying for federal aid must follow. According to that schedule, an increasing number of competitive bids from private business interested in providing transit services would be required over a four-year period.

Some cities have already moved toward privatization. Dallas contracted out part of its bus service to Trailways Bus Company in 1984. Since then, the number of buses on the routes had to be increased because of high

ridership and the contract has been both extended and expanded to cover more routes. The goal of privatization is to increase the productivity of transit services by encouraging competition for the awarding of contracts. But for private companies to compete for a contract, they have to believe that they can make a profit by providing transit services. If no private companies want to provide the service, what should be the role of the government? Some argue that mass transportation is vital enough to citizens of metropolitan areas that it must be provided, whether by government subsidies to private businesses or directly by the government. Others argue that such services should only exist if ridership is adequate at least to cover costs, if not to provide a profit.[109]

A final problem concerns which level of government should be responsible for funding urban mass transit (assuming complete privatization is not possible). Until 1961, any governmental support for urban mass transit came from state or local governments. In 1961, the first of several national policies in support of mass transportation was enacted by Congress. By 1962, lobbying for federal support of mass transit was intensifying with the creation of the Urban Passenger Transportation Association. The United States Conference of Mayors and the National League of Cities also lobbied for federal involvement. The result was Urban Mass Transportation Act of 1964, which firmly established the idea of federal participation in transit financing.[110]

During that decade, increases in grant programs were approved and funds were also appropriated for planning, engineering, and designing mass transit projects. In addition, in 1968, administration of the federal policies was moved from the U.S. Department of Housing and Urban Development to the Urban Mass Transportation Administration, established in the newly created Department of Transportation.

Despite the growing federal involvement

in urban mass transit, the funding level remained substantially below that for highways throughout the 1960s. Several acts in the following decade significantly increased the amount of federal aid for urban transportation. The Urban Mass Transit Act of 1970 authorized $3.1 billion for local mass transit for a 5-year period. A major reason for the passage of that bill was that the highway lobby was persuaded to support it in return for the support of the mass transit lobby when highway legislation was considered. In addition, the new assistant secretary of the Department of Transportation had previously been a mayor who had led attempts by the Conference of Mayors to secure federal funding for mass transit. Thus, transit supporters were more readily received within the administration and established the kind of contacts the highway lobby had had for years.[111] In 1973, in a major change of policy, Congress authorized the diversion of funds from the Highway Trust Fund for transit projects. That act also permitted substitution of transit projects for proposed interstate highway segments.

The National Mass Transportation Act of 1974 extended federal support for urban mass transit by providing almost $11 billion for grants and loans to urban mass transit systems. Funding for mass transit was further extended in 1978 by the Surface Transportation Act, which appropriated nearly $54 billion for both highways and mass transit.

In 1982 the Transportation Assistance Act passed in the last minutes of the Ninety-seventh Congress. That act raised the gas tax five cents per gallon. The extra revenue was to be used primarily to upgrade deteriorating roads and transit systems and to finish the interstate highway system, but one cent was specifically earmarked for public transportation purposes. In addition, a new block grant program for mass transit was authorized.

After that Ronald Reagan requested that mass transit aid be cut by two-thirds and all operating aid for local transit systems be eliminated. In 1985, Congress did cut support for mass transit by 10 percent, but the aid for operating assistance was maintained at the same level. The 1982 act was reauthorized in 1987 after substantial conflicts over a variety of issues, including mass transit funding and support for various local highway projects.

The Intermodal Surface Transportation Efficiency Act (ISTEA) of 1991 is an attempt to rationalize the impacts of highways in the metropolitan area. "It requires cities and states to consider nontransportation effects of transportation planning."[112] It required that planning for the construction of highway projects include consideration of environmental impacts, the location of jobs and housing, and the use of bike lanes and footpaths. As noted earlier, it also requires intergovernmental cooperation. "The planning processes specified in the regulations associated with the act should broaden the transportation planning process so as to bring a wider range of participants into it and thus reduce the relative power of highway engineers, construction companies, and construction unions."[113]

Implementation and Evaluation

Since 1964 federal aid to urban mass transit rose from virtually nothing to over $11 billion in the 1970s; it declined in the 1980s. In the 1990s annual appropriations have hovered around $4 billion. Considering inflation and future national budget pressures, mass transportation in cities is still in trouble. New rail systems are quickly becoming prohibitively expensive. Los Angeles has completed work on a 21 mile rail line between Los Angeles and Long Beach, the first leg of a proposed county-wide rail transit system. The Long Beach line was chosen to be built first in part because it could be built relatively inexpensively because 16 of the 21 miles of the route already were a railroad right-of-way. This "relatively inexpensive" project was estimated to cost $595 million in 1985 dollars, or $690 million by the time it was completed. The cost of the METRO subway in Washington, D.C., was originally estimated at $2.1 billion, but present projections indicate the final cost will be more than $6 billion if the full system is built.

Even if a system is already in place, operating costs are substantial.

Transit is simply much more expensive than our intuitive estimates would indicate: on the average, transit costs about two-thirds *more* per passenger-mile than the private automobile (including all capital and operating costs for the car) but to be attractive to patrons it must charge them less than they would spend by car.[114]

In addition to cost, there are other problems with existing mass transit systems. Many of the older systems are deteriorating and accidents and equipment failures are becoming more common. Some of the modern systems, such as BART in San Francisco, have been unreliable because their futuristic technology did not have all the "bugs" worked out.

Another issue for mass transit is establishing a route structure. This problem is an inevitable result of the cost of building a transit system, combined with the sprawl of people in the metropolitan area. The automobile liberated people from transit lines and enabled them to disperse over larger and larger areas. As a result, it is now virtually impossible to build a new rail transit system convenient to people in metropolitan areas, especially considering the cost of building such systems.

Because of the deconcentration of people, fixed rail systems are impractical for many communities and even fixed-route buses are unattractive. Some communities have experimented with systems that attempt to bridge the gap between taxis and buses. Systems of "dial-a-ride" allow persons to receive door-to-door service, but they must share the van with

other passengers along the way. This system is often used for transportation between airports and hotels and even private residences. This form of mass transit is especially helpful to the poor, elderly, and disabled because it provides increased mobility to jobs, doctors, etc. at costs lower than taxicabs.[115]

The problems of urban mass transit contribute to and are dwarfed by one major problem: lack of riders. A 1978 study reported that only 2.5 percent of travel in urban areas occurs on mass transit facilities.[116] A 1985 study reported that, "Most trends point toward a continuing increase in the automobile's share for nearly all types of trips."[117] Many cities are rethinking the construction of rail systems. The prospect for such construction is even less rosy because of the Reagan Administration's and subsequent attempts to cut back on federal aid to urban mass transit.

While the prospect for urban mass transit may appear somewhat bleak, another development may have an impact on mass transit. Many cities are encountering increased opposition to the building of highways. In Philadelphia, plans for a freeway to replace South Street were finally abandoned (although not before the neighborhood residents and businesses were removed). After more than a decade of discussion, a proposed highway in New York City along the shore of the Hudson River was abandoned. In San Francisco, former Mayor Diane Feinstein pledged she would "become totally gray-haired in the process" if necessary to demolish the mile-long elevated freeway along San Francisco Bay.[118] Numerous other examples could be cited.

Ordinarily the highway controversy first becomes visible in informal political groups (neighborhood associations, conservation associations, businessmen's groups, civil rights groups, planning and historical associations), which seek allies in the city's political and bureaucratic structure; together they seek to influence the authoritative decisionmakers of the city.[119]

The Urban Mass Transportation Act of 1964 and the Federal Aid Highway Act of 1968 require local governments to provide for citizen input; the latter law requires fair and reasonable relocation payments for those displaced by highway construction.

When projects uproot and destroy neighborhoods, the losers are easily identifiable. Transportation links often result in reverse redistributive policy; that is, they obliterate poor neighborhoods for the benefit of the suburban commuters, which often leads to conflict.

> Because urban areas through which highways and mass transit facilities pass are generally comprised of non-white, lower-income level residents who tend to exhibit a strong sense of community, these people band together to form the citizen groups who oppose and often halt construction of the highway and mass transit facilities.[120]

In some cases, the conflict is between neighborhoods and planners and redevelopment authorities. One author discusses the futile attempt of one inner city, poor black neighborhood to convince transportation professionals in Washington, D.C., that serving their neighborhood with the new Metro would be "efficient."[121] In other cases, the battles pit neighborhood against neighborhood. In Philadelphia, a dispute over a section of Interstate 95 was a struggle between the residents of the Society Hill section of downtown Philadelphia and commuters from the northeast section of the city. The *New York Times* described the conflict:

> Every morning, from small houses with tidy lawns in Philadelphia's Northeast, columns of middle-class commuters turn onto Interstate 95 and head south along the Delaware River and into the city. That is as the highway planners of the 1950s dreamed.
>
> Every morning, too, from the renovated Colonial row houses of Society Hill, stylish young professionals and urban gentry turn out and head by foot along brick sidewalks to nearby downtown offices. That is as the pioneers of urban reclamation of the 1960s envisioned it.
>
> And with each passing morning, at the point where the Maine-to-Florida interstate runs alongside Society Hill, the two neighborhoods, rooted in the plans and dreams of different decades, have been clashing with increasing vehemence.[122]

At issue was a 2.2-mile section of the highway that was completed in March 1982. The residents of Society Hill filed a lawsuit to keep the section closed until aesthetic alterations and noise barriers were built. Meanwhile the commuters staged a parade of cars through Society Hill, honking their horns and tying up traffic to protest the delay in opening the highway.

This kind of opposition may signal a change in the role of the public in the making of transportation policy. In the past, major economic interests such as automobile manufacturers and oil companies and certain parts of the public have played a major role. Rural and automobile interests formed an effective lobby to secure federal highway funds. In the 1960s, lobbying by organizations representing cities and city governments focused attention on urban mass transit. They were helped by a growing public recognition of the problems of pollution and American dependence on foreign oil. Yet their success was due more directly to the formation of a logrolling agreement with the highway lobby. Transportation policy, then, has been most directly influenced by those citizens and businesses who have a particular interest in the policy area and who are effectively organized.

The role of the general public has been substantial, but only in an indirect way. The unwillingness of the public to desert their cars for public transportation has led many to conclude that America's mass transit policy is a failure. On the other hand, the opposition of people in many urban neighborhoods to continued destruction to provide more room for freeways has also had substantial impact in many cities. Clearly, the experts are facing a dilemma in trying to steer a course between the public's antipathy to freeway construction and reluctance to use mass transit.

Conclusion

Evidence confirms the weakness of popular control over developmental policy. Much of the policy, regardless of which level of government was responsible for initiation, was made in response to the demands of groups that would benefit directly. Land-use regulation was instituted on the local level by those who wished to protect their property values from the assumed decline brought about by "undesirables," whether offensive businesses or different groups of people. Planning and zoning commissions tend to be dominated by real estate interests and developers who are the "experts" in the issues raised. Community development policies, whether national or local in origin, tend to be designed to make cities attractive places for businesses to thrive. Transportation policy, although providing increasing aid for mass transit, has been dominated by a highway lobby composed of groups that would benefit from highway construction.

Clearly, cities need to have a strong economic base. Paul Peterson is thus correct in arguing that policies that aid business interests do benefit the entire city. But these policies also can impose substantial costs on some urban groups. Urban renewal projects that destroy low-income housing and highway projects that obliterate entire neighborhoods may make the city more hospitable to business interests, but they also harm some urban residents. Joe Feagin goes so far as to call the conflict over land use a form of class warfare:

Cities are zones of conflict between competing claims for land use, and those with less wealth and power usually lose in the competition. Development projects, large and small, benefit some people and cost others. The conflict over land use and development is a barely hidden class conflict—between those who build office towers, shopping centers, and the like and those who need better schools and better housing; between development and finance capitalists and ordinary working people.[123]

Feagin cites numerous instances in the last two decades in which citizens have protested land use and development strategies. Opposition to highway projects discussed earlier illustrates the fact that those protests have had an impact. Indeed, John Mollenkopf has argued that the action of neighborhood groups has ended any consensus that ever existed on developmental policy.

Neighborhood activism ended large-scale clearance projects, drastically revised traditional planning practices by creating citizen review and participation procedures, and created a new policy emphasis on preservation and rehabilitation. In the process, neighborhood activism led to the demise of urban renewal agencies as powerful engines of physical change. It sensitized public opinion to the defects of the "growth at any cost" mentality and the planners' assumptions that physical development can solve social problems.[124]

Mollenkopf argues that a "new social contract" is needed to determine the direction that urban development policy will take in the future. One approach is to remove the burden of providing public works from the city and shift it to the developer by using a **development impact fee,** that is, a charge to offset the public costs of private development. Because new developments either require the installation of new public facilities, such as streets

and sewers, or increase the demands on existing facilities, such as schools and parks, the
developer is charged a fee to cover necessary
improvements.[125] When voters in Loveland,
Colorado, voted down $40 million in bonds
to finance future development, the city council appointed an 18-member citizen advisory
board (equally representing citizen and development interests) to find a way for the city to
recover the costs imposed by new development. After meeting biweekly for 18 months,
the board arrived at a formula based on the
demands created on public facilities and the
cost of constructing or maintaining them.[126]

Feagin concludes that "an alternative urban future with more democracy" is needed.[127]
He suggests following the lead of Santa Monica,
California, in requiring development interests
to provide for various community needs in
return for concessions such as zoning decisions or tax abatements. Similarly, San Francisco interpreted the state's requirement for
an Environmental Impact Report prior to new
building to include consideration of negative
socioeconomic impacts and assessed private
developers for such impacts.[128]

An obvious problem with such practices is
that unless they become widespread, cities that
lacked Santa Monica's or San Francisco's appeal
might well lose in the competition for economic development. Another problem results
from a ruling of the Supreme Court in the case
of *Nollan v. California Coastal Commission.* The
Commission had required Nollan to provide
an easement allowing the public to walk across
part of his lot in return for permission for him
to build a new house on oceanfront property.
Writing for the Court, Justice Scalia said:

> When a regulation imposes restrictions on
> a developer, there must be a *substantial
> nexus or connection between that condition
> and some injury to the public interest caused
> or created by the development.* This must in
> effect be a close and precise relationship.[129]
> [Italics added.]

In effect, the impact of the *Nollan* case
would seem to make it impossible for cities to
make demands on developers unless the demands were clearly aimed at ensuring the
proposed development does not harm the
public interest. The Court stated that extracting concessions solely in return for a favorable
zoning decision was "an out and out plan of
extortion."[130] That decision removes from city
governments a power that could have been
used to force private developers to comply
with guidelines officials believed to be in the
public interest.

In *Lucas v. South Carolina Coastal Council*
(1992), the Supreme Court ruled that changes
in state legislation that rendered two beach-
front lots unbuildable constituted a taking.
Another case dealt with a request by an owner
of a plumbing supply store to expand his
parking lot. The city's Planning Commission
said it would approve if the owner agreed to
dedicate (give) a portion of that area for flood
control and the construction of a bike path. In
Dolan v. City of Tigard (1994), the Supreme
Court ruled that the request was unreasonable because there was not a "nexus" or connection between the extension of the parking
lot and the dedication request.[131]

The issue of the public versus the private
interest is still murky, but these Supreme
Court decisions make it harder for local governments to negotiate with private interests
for the common good.

Notes

1. Paul E. Peterson, *City Limits* (Chicago: University of
   Chicago Press, 1981), 15.
2. Ibid., 29–30.
3. Clarence N. Stone and Heywood T. Sanders, eds., *The
   Politics of Urban Development* (Lawrence: University
   of Kansas Press, 1987), 6.
4. Peterson, *City Limits,* 148.
5. Clarence N. Stone, "Summing Up: Urban Regimes,
   Development Policy, and Political Arrangements" in
   The Politics of Urban Development, ed. Stone and
   Sanders, 288.

6. John H. Mollenkopf, *The Contested City* (Princeton: Princeton University Press, 1983), 16.

7. Clarence N. Stone, "The Study of the Politics of Urban Development" in *The Politics of Urban Development*, ed. Stone and Sanders, 4.

8. Stephen L. Elkin, *City and Regime in the American Republic* (Chicago: University of Chicago Press, 1987), 37.

9. John R. Logan and Harvey L. Molotch, *Urban Fortunes: The Political Economy of Place* (Berkeley: University of California Press, 1987).

10. Stone, "Summing Up," 288.

11. Sam Bass Warner, Jr., *The Urban Wilderness: A History of the American City* (New York: Harper & Row, 1972), 16–17.

12. This argument follows Warner, *The Urban Wilderness*, 3–37 and passim.

13. Jerome G. Rose, *Legal Foundations of Land Use Planning* (New Brunswick, New Jersey: Center for Urban Policy Research, 1979), 62–64.

14. Warner, *The Urban Wilderness*, 202–203.

15. Dennis R. Judd, *The Politics of American Cities: Private Power and Public Policy*, 2nd ed. (Boston: Little, Brown, 1984), 182.

16. Warner, *The Urban Wilderness*, 28.

17. Ibid., 29.

18. Seymour I. Toll, *Zoned America* (New York: Grossman, 1969), 182–183.

19. Warner, *The Urban Wilderness*, 15.

20. Toll, *Zoned America*, 187.

21. Warner, *The Urban Wilderness*, 31.

22. David C. Ranney, *Planning and Politics in the Metropolis* (Columbus, Ohio: Merrill, 1969), 23.

23. Joe R. Feagin, *The Urban Real Estate Game: Playing Monopoly with Real Money* (Englewood Cliffs, New Jersey: Prentice-Hall, 1983), 186.

24. *Village of Euclid v. Ambler Realty Co.*, 272 U.S. 365 (1926).

25. Ibid., 388.

26. Ibid., 394–395.

27. Jane Jacobs, *The Death and Life of Great American Cities* (New York: Vintage Books, 1963).

28. Timothy D. Mead, "The Minions of the Developmental Regime: A Case Study." Paper presented at the Urban Affairs Association, March 13–16, 1996.

29. Francine F. Rabinowitz and J. Stanley Pottinger, "Organization for Local Planning: The Attitudes of Directors," *Journal of the American Institute of Planners* 33 (1967): 27–32.

30. One of the authors has more than seventeen years experience as a planning commissioner in a small midwestern city, which leads to this observation.

31. David R. Morgan, *Managing Urban America*, 2nd ed. (Monterey, California: Brooks/Cole, 1984), 291–292.

32. Ibid., 291.

33. Ibid., 292.

34. Clarence N. Stone, Robert K. Whelan, and William J. Murin, *Urban Policy and Politics in a Bureaucratic Age*, 2nd ed. (Englewood Cliffs, New Jersey: Prentice-Hall, 1986), 275.

35. Ibid.

36. Ranney, *Planning and Politics*, 12.

37. Norton E. Long, "Planning and Politics in Urban Development," *Journal of the American Institute of Planners* 25 (1959): 168.

38. Ranney, *Planning and Politics*, 59.

39. Anthony James Catanese, *Planners and Local Politics: Impossible Dreams* (Beverly Hills, California: Sage, 1974), 24.

40. Michael Vasu, *Politics and Planning* (Chapel Hill: University of North Carolina Press, 1979), 73.

41. Paul Davidoff, "Advocacy and Pluralism in Planning," *Journal of the American Institute of Planners* 31 (1965): 331–338.

42. Michael L. Vasu "Planning Theory and Practice in the 1980's," *Urban Affairs Quarterly* 17 (September 1981): 109–114.

43. Robert Goodman, *After the Planners* (New York: Simon & Schuster, 1971), 173.

44. Jeffrey R. Henig, *Neighborhood Mobilization: Redevelopment and Response* (New Brunswick, New Jersey: Rutgers University Press, 1982), 121.

45. Don T. Allensworth, *The Political Realities of Urban Planning* (New York: Praeger, 1975), 175.

46. Leon S. Eplan, "Atlanta: Planning, Budgeting, and Neighborhoods" in *Personality, Politics and Planning: How City Planners Work*, ed. Anthony James Catanese and W. Paul Farmer (Beverly Hills, California: Sage, 1978), 50.

47. We wish to thank John D. Hutchinson, Jr., Director, Center for Public and Urban Research, Georgia State University, for providing us with several papers he has written on planning in Atlanta, Georgia. This reference comes from John D. Hutchinson, Jr., "Citizen Representation in Neighborhood Planning," *American Planning Association Journal* 50 (Spring 1984): 183–193.

48. John D. Hutchinson, Jr., and James E. Prather, "Community Mobilization and Participation in the Zoning Process." Paper presented at the 1985 Annual Meeting of the Urban Affairs Association, 25.

49. Eplan, "Atlanta," 45.

50. Ibid., 51.

51. Pierre Clavel, *The Progressive City: Planning and Participation 1969–1984* (New Brunswick, New Jersey: Rutgers University Press, 1986), 1.

52. Ibid., 13.

53. Stone, "Summing Up," 287.

54. *Shelley v. Kramer*, 334 U.S. 1 (1948).

55. U.S. Commission of Civil Rights, *Housing* (Washington, D.C.: U.S. Government Printing Office, 1961), 126.

56. Michael Danielson, *The Politics of Exclusion* (New York: Columbia University Press, 1976), 5.

57. *Kennedy Park Homes v. City of Lackawana, New York*, 436 f 2d 108 (1971).

58. *Dailey v. City of Lawton*, 425 f 2d 108 (1971).

59. *James v. Valtierra*, 91 S. Ct. 1331 (1971).

60. This situation is discussed in Danielson, *The Politics of Exclusion*, 31–33, 84–85, 166–167, 184–186, and 321–323.

61. *New York Times,* February 25, 1982.

62. *Southern Burlington, N.A.A.C.P.* v *Township of Mount Laurel,* 67 N.J. 151 (1975).

63. *Village of Arlington Heights* v. *Metropolitan Housing Development Corporation,* 429 U.S. 252 (1977).

64. *Hills* v. *Gautreaux,* 96 S. Ct. 1538 (1976).

65. *City of Petaluma* v. *Construction Industry Association of Sonoma County,* 522 f 2d 897 (1975).

66. *Golden* v. *Planning Board of Town of Ramapo,* 285 N.E. 2d 359 (1972).

67. Daniel Sneider, "To Halt Sprawl, San Jose Draws Green Line in Sand," *Quarterly Newsletter of the American Planning Association* (December 1996): 3–4.

68. Oliver P. Williams, *Metropolitan Political Analysis* (New York: Free Press, 1971), 88–89 and passim.

69. *First Evangelical Lutheran Church of Glendale* v. *The County of Los Angeles,* 107 S. Ct. 2378 (June 9, 1987).

70. Ibid., 8.

71. John Tibbetts, "Everybody's Taking the Fifth," *Planning* (January 1995): 4–10.

72. John Herbers, "It's the New Activism as Business Primes the Government's Pump," *Governing* (July 1988): 38.

73. Ibid.

74. Bryan D. Jones and Lynn W. Bachelor, with Carter Wilson, *The Sustaining Hand: Community Leadership and Corporate Power* (Lawrence: University of Kansas Press, 1986).

75. Robert A. Catlin, "The Decline and Fall of Gary, Indiana," *Planning* 54, no. 6, (June 1988): 10–15.

76. Dennis R. Judd, *The Politics of American Cities: Private Power and Public Policy,* 3rd ed. (Glenview, Illinois: Scott, Foresman, 1988), 410–414.

77. Ibid., 413.

78. National Commission on Urban Problems, *Building the American City* (Washington, D.C.: U.S. Government Printing Office, 1968), 153, quoted in Feagin, *The Urban Real Estate Game,* 177.

79. PL 89–754.

80. Randall B. Ripley and Grace A. Franklin, *Congress, the Bureaucracy, and Public Policy,* 3rd ed. (Homewood, Illinois: Dorsey, 1984), 187.

81. U.S. Advisory Commission on Intergovernmental Relations, *Citizen Participation in the American Federal System* (Washington, D.C.: U.S. Government Printing Office, 1979), 110.

82. Joseph L. Falkson, *An Evaluation of Policy Related Research on Citizen Participation in Municipal Service Systems: Overview and Summary* (Washington, D.C.: TARP Institute, 1974), 23–27.

83. Paul R. Dommel, "Block Grants for Community Development: Decentralized Decision-Making" in *Fiscal Crisis in American Cities: The Federal Response,* ed. L. Kenneth Hubbell (Cambridge, Mass.: Ballinger, 1979).

84. Timothy Barnekoo, Daniel Rich, and Robert Warren, "The New Privatism, Federalism, and the Future of Urban Governance: National Urban Policy in the 1980s," *Journal of Urban Affairs* 3 (Fall 1981): 3.

85. Janet Hook, "Democrats Hail 'Productivity,' but Im-

86. William D. Eggers, "City Lights: America's Boldest Mayors," *Policy Review* (Summer 1993): 67; Michael Brintnall, "Future Directions for Federal Urban Policy," *Journal of Urban Affairs* 11, no. 1 (1989): 1–19.

87. Marion E. Orr and Gerry Stoker, "Urban Regimes and Leadership in Detroit," *Urban Affairs Quarterly* 30 (September 1994): 48–69.

88. Robert A. Catlin, "The Decline and Fall of Gary, Indiana," *Planning* 54 (June 1988): 10–2.

89. Michael A. Pagano and Ann O'M. Bowman, *Cityscapes and Capital: The Politics of Urban Development* (Baltimore: Johns Hopkins Press, 1995), 137. See also Robyne S. Turner, "Growth Politics and Downtown Development: The Economic Imperative in Sunbelt Cities," *Urban Affairs Quarterly* 28 (September 1992): 4; Alan DiGaetano, "Urban Political Regime Formation: A Study in Contrast," *Journal of Urban Affairs* 11, no. 3 (1989): 279; Tony Robinson, "Gentrification and Grassroots Resistance in San Francisco's Tenderloin," *Urban Affairs Review* 30 (March 1995): 507.

90. Mark Schneider, "The Market for Local Economic Development: The Growth of Suburban Retail Trade, 1972–1982," *Urban Affairs Quarterly* 22 (September 1986): 24–41; Roger Schemenner, *The Manufacturing Location Decision: Evidence from Cincinnati and New England* (Washington, D.C.: U.S. Government Printing Office, 1978).

91. U.S. Advisory Commission on Intergovernmental Relations, *State–Local Taxation and Industrial Location* (Washington, D.C.: U.S. Government Printing Office, 1967).

92. Martin Gottlieb, "States Must Try Together for Growth," *Grand Forks Herald,* August 13, 1988.

93. Ibid.

94. Catherine Armington, Candee Harris, and Marjorie Odle, "Formation and Growth in High Technology Firms: A Regional Assessment," Appendix B. Office of Technology Assessment, in *Technology Innovation and Regional Economic Development* (Washington, D.C.: U.S. Government Printing Office, 1984), 108–143; Donald A. Hicks, *Advanced Industrial Development: Restructuring, Relocation and Renewal* (Boston: Oelgeschlager, Gunn, and Hain, 1985).

95. Herbers, "It's the New Activism as Business Primes the Government's Pump," 32.

96. Pagano and Bowman, *Cityscapes and Capital,* 99.

97. Barbara Ferman, *Challenging the Growth Machine: Neighborhood Politics in Chicago and Pittsburgh* (Lawrence: University of Kansas Press, 1996); Jeffrey M. Berry, Kent E. Portney, and Ken Thomson, *The Rebirth of Urban Democracy* (Washington, D.C.: The Brookings Institution, 1993).

98. Marian Lief Palley and Howard A. Palley, *Urban America and Public Policies,* 2nd ed. (Lexington, Massachusetts: D.C. Heath, 1981), 249.

99. Allen Whitt and Glenn Yago, "Corporate Strategies and the Decline of Transit in U.S. Cities," *Urban Affairs Quarterly* 21 (1985): 37–65.

age Problems Remain," *Congressional Quarterly* 51 (December 11, 1993): 3391.

100. It should be noted that Kenneth A. Small has argued that suburbanization would have occurred regardless of the transportation policy of the federal government; nevertheless, he recognizes that such policy did contribute "significantly" to that process. See Kenneth A. Small, "Transportation and Urban Change" in *The New Urban Reality*, ed. Paul E. Peterson (Washington, D.C.: The Brookings Institution, 1985), 200, 214.

101. Small, "Transportation and Urban Change" in *The New Urban Reality*, 209.

102. John D. Kasarda, "Urban Change and Minority Opportunities" in *The New Urban Reality*, ed. Paul E. Peterson (Washington, D.C.: The Brookings Institution, 1985), 55–56.

103. Laurence E. Lynn, Jr., *Designing Public Policy: A Casebook on the Role of Policy Analysis* (Santa Monica, California: Goodyear, 1980), 327.

104. Homer Bigart, October 13, 1967, quoted in Alan Lupo, Frank Colcord, and Edmund P. Fowler, *Rites of Way: The Politics of Transportation in Boston and the U.S. City* (Boston: Little, Brown, 1971), 27.

105. Charles A. Lave, "Transportation and Energy: Some Current Myths," *Policy Analysis* 4, no. 3 (Summer 1978): 298.

106. Ibid.

107. Small, "Transportation and Urban Change," 207.

108. Wayne K. Talley, *Introduction to Transportation* (Cincinnati, Ohio: South-Western Publishing, 1983), 304.

109. Lave, "Transportation and Energy," 314.

110. This legislative history relies on Brent Sheets, "Urban Mass Transit." (unpublished manuscript.)

111. George M. Smerk, *Urban Mass Transportation: A Dozen Years of Federal Policy* (Bloomington: Indiana University Press, 1974), 76.

112. P.K. Plous, Jr., "Refreshing ISTEA," *Planning* (February 1993): 9–12.

113. John M. Levy, *Contemporary Urban Planning*, 4th ed. (Englewood Cliffs, New Jersey: Prentice-Hall, 1997), 218.

114. Lave, "Transportation and Energy," 306.

115. Small, "Transportation and Urban Change," 220–221.

116. Lave, "Transportation and Energy," 298.

117. Small, "Transportation and Urban Change," 217.

118. Robert Lindsey, "Feinstein Is Trying to Unpave the Way," *New York Times*, December 8, 1985, sect. E.

119. Frank Colcord, "The Nation" in *Rites of Way*, ed. Lupo, Colcord, and Fowler, 208.

120. Elizabeth Hanson, *An Evaluation of Policy Related Research on Citizen Participation in Municipal Service Systems: Transportation Planning* (Washington, D.C.: TARP Institute, n.d.), 41.

121. William J. Murin, *Mass Transit Policy Planning* (Lexington, Massachusetts: Lexington Books, 1971).

122. Edward Schumacher, "Two Neighborhoods Clash over Philadelphia Dreams," *New York Times*, August 10, 1979.

123. Feagin, *The Urban Real Estate Game*, 60.

124. Mollenkopf, *The Contested City*, 210.

125. Arthur C. Nelson, ed., "Symposium: Development Impact Fees," *Journal of the American Planning Association* 54, no. 1, (Winter 1988): 3–90.

126. Mark P. Barnebey, Tom MacRostie, Gary J. Schennauer, George T. Simpson, and Jan Winters, "Paying for Growth: Community Approaches to Development Impact Fees," *Journal of the American Planning Association* 54, no. 1 (Winter 1988): 23–25.

127. Feagin, *The Urban Real Estate Game*, 207.

128. Tony Robinson, "Gentrification and Grassroots Resistance in San Francisco's Tenderloin," 496–97.

129. *Nollan v. California Coastal Commission*, 107 S.Ct. 3141 (June 26, 1987).

130. Ibid.

131. Levy, *Contemporary Urban Planning*, 71.

CHAPTER 13

Quality-of-Life Issues

Education and Crime Control

This chapter will examine two policy areas that cannot be easily classified into any one of the policy types that researchers have developed. Crime control and educational policies both have distributive aspects in the sense that they are government services that are widely distributed. Obviously, crime control could also be seen as regulatory policy and certain aspects of educational policy are redistributive in impact. In some ways, both policy areas are also developmental as they help create an attractive environment for people and business. Due to the ambiguity involved, this book refers to crime control and education as quality-of-life policies, because they affect how appealing a community is to business and how satisfied citizens are with their life in the community.

Like many urban concerns, quality-of-life issues have a racial component. Nicholas Lemann argues that the huge migration of African-Americans from the South into the cities of the North interjected race as a factor in both education and crime policies:

> ... the migration hardly created a harmonious, racially synthesized country. It was disruptive; it engendered hostility. The fabric of city life in the United States changed

forever. Some of the bitterness of race relations leached into city politics. The ideal of high-quality universal education began to disappear. Street crime became an obsessive concern for the first time in decades.[1]

Nothing worries urban residents as much as crime, and with good reason. Data gathered for the Department of Justice indicate that 28 percent of urban households were victimized by crime in 1992, compared to 17 percent of rural households. In urban areas, 7 percent of households had experienced a violent crime and 20 percent had had property stolen, while the comparable numbers for rural households were 4 percent and 11 percent.[2]

Although government defines many actions as criminal behavior, most people think about crime as crime against property (that is, vandalism or theft) and crime against persons (that is, murder, assault, rape). Other kinds of criminal activity may be serious, but the crimes against our property and our person create the greatest fear. James Q. Wilson argues that such crimes are especially destructive not just to individuals, but to the whole fabric of society. He writes, " ... predatory crime, in particular crime committed by strangers on innocent victims, causes the kind of fear that drives people apart from one another and thus impedes or even prevents the formation of meaningful human communities."[3]

Education is also crucial to the quality of life because Americans have always seen education as a means to achieve the good life and the good society. In nineteenth-century America, being educated was an indicator of one's social worth. As Paul Peterson argued:

> In a society where breeding did not by itself insure social standing, education assumed a special importance. When family background meant little, the one thing that distinguished the *gentle* man from the mere businessman or merchant was the respectability that education, learning, and cultivated taste could provide.[4]

Recognizing the importance of education, immigrant parents, especially Jewish and more recently Asian immigrants, sacrificed virtually everything to send their children to school.

By the twentieth century, education was no longer as important an indicator of social status, but was valued because the skills the educated acquired enabled them to progress rapidly and successfully in their chosen vocations. Education is still valued as the route of social mobility. The educational system is also used as a means of transmitting the values of society and, in general, as a means of solving problems on the society's agenda.

Popular Control over Quality-of-Life Policies

The ability of citizens to control quality-of-life policies is crucial because these policies are so important to the urban resident's life-style. Actual citizen control has, however, been limited in both education and crime policies. This section will address some general limits on citizen control. A later section will examine the question of citizen control in more depth.

A major limit on citizen control is that those who make policy in education and crime control consider themselves professionals who have qualified for their jobs by receiving specialized training. As professionals, they can claim to know more than others about what policies are needed, a claim that is hard to refute. They can argue that only those with their background should be involved in making policy in their area of expertise. Because their status in society and in their organizations comes from their professional status and their presumed expertise, appearing to be influenced by nonexperts can be threatening.

Another major constraint is the difficulty of pinpointing authority in order to hold someone accountable for the decisions made. Both education and crime are policy areas where street-level bureaucrats—police officers and teachers—actually implement policy. As the discussion in Chapter 11 makes clear, it is very difficult for supervisors to control street-level bureaucrats because they do their jobs in widely dispersed areas and establishing precise performance standards to evaluate them is difficult.

As a result, citizen control over crime control and educational policies tends to be limited, although efforts have been made to increase that control, as will be discussed below. Citizen control is not certain, nor is the influence of major economic interests. Because both crime control and education affect the attractiveness of a community, they should be factors in its economic health. New business should want to locate in communities with good educational systems both because employees would want good schooling for their children and because the schools should guarantee a qualified work force. Also, low crime would reduce business costs for security or for replacement of losses. Therefore, businesses could be expected to want to be involved in policy making in these areas. That is not always the case.

While those business interests tend to dominate in the area of developmental policies, Clarence Stone argues that "cities differ in the extent to which their business leaders choose to confine their active involvement to development and closely related issues, or to involve themselves in a wide spectrum of issues, including questions of social policy."[5] He identifies Pittsburgh, Minneapolis, and St. Paul as cities where business does play a role in social policy and St. Louis, Atlanta, and Denver where it does not. A study of Charlotte, North Carolina, over the past 25 years found that major business leaders were intimately involved in the making of education policy because they believed that good schools were essential for economic development in the city and the surrounding county.[6]

In other areas, corporate leaders have been reluctant to support public education, especially programs that would benefit the inner city poor. They sometimes justify this by blaming the educational bureaucracy.

> City and state business associations, in Chicago as in many other cities, have lobbied for years against tax increments to finance education of low-income children. "You don't dump a lot of money into guys who haven't done well with the money they've got in the past."[7]

Other times they blame the children. "If children are seen primarily as raw material for industry, a greater investment in better raw material makes sense. Market values do not favor much investment in the poorest children."[8]

Education

The implications of providing an equal education to all as a means of ensuring equal opportunity for all are manifold. To the extent that education becomes a social leveler, conflict and controversy will inevitably surround it. Self-interest will cause some residents to resist the widespread distribution of equal education, fearing that the social advantages they enjoy will disappear.

Agenda Setting

Given the importance of education to individual and social advancement, it is not surprising that the issue of public education emerged on the governmental agenda early in the nation's history. In the period immediately following the Revolution, many leaders were adamantly opposed to the development of a permanent aristocracy. Thomas Jefferson wanted a system of government where the rulers would be chosen on the basis of their abilities rather than their family. Thus, he believed it was important to provide education to all, regardless of their social backgrounds.[9]

Another impetus for widespread education came from the expansion of suffrage. What had begun as an electorate composed only of male property holders, constituting perhaps less than 10 percent of the population, quickly expanded to include virtually all white free males as the fledgling political parties went searching for new supporters. As suffrage expanded, it was important to provide voters with an education to ensure that they would cast their votes intelligently. As Jefferson said, "If a nation expects to be ignorant and free, in a state of civilization, it expects what never was and never will be."[10]

By 1850 the principle of free public education had been accepted in every northern state, but that did not mean that public school systems actually existed.

> Immediately after the Civil War urban school systems were still fragmentary structures whose parts were scattered in ramshackle buildings under the loose direction of part-time school boards. Atlanta's system was not founded until the 1870's, Chicago's was nearly destroyed by its fire, and even as late as 1906 the San Francisco earthquake dealt the city a severe blow from which it took several years to recover.[11]

By the end of the nineteenth century, many cities had special reasons for developing free public education—they had become home to vast numbers of immigrants from other countries. As the political machines eagerly recruited these new voters, concerns arose about educating them in the culture and values of America. Many believed education would ensure that voters would understand the issues and would develop loyalty to the country.

There are two complementary explanations of the spread of compulsory public education. Some have seen the use of the educational system to socialize the immigrants as efforts by a dominant economic elite to mold the immigrants into a compliant work force. "The common school's mission was to maintain and transmit the values considered necessary to prevent political, social, or economic upheaval."[12] Paul Peterson, however, has argued that far from having education imposed on them, the immigrants and the working class eagerly sought education, recognizing the role of education in establishing their social worth. He points out:

> Working-class groups did not resist the extension of compulsory education to cover a broader age range or a longer portion of the school year. On the contrary, unions in Chicago, San Francisco, and Atlanta were among the foremost proponents of compulsory education.[13]

By 1918, every state had compulsory education.

While states and the federal government did enact some policies relevant to education in the nineteenth and early-twentieth centuries, for the most part the formulation of education policy was a local responsibility. The first public schools were established at the local level and funded at that level. The regulation of the schools was also done locally.

A recent NBC–*Wall Street Journal* poll suggests that education may move onto the national agenda. That poll indicated that 58 percent of respondents thought that fundamental changes were needed in the nation's education system and 36 percent thought that some changes are needed. Almost all respondents (93 percent) thought that the teaching of basic subjects needed improvement. While united on the need for change, the respondents were split on the policies to achieve that change.[14]

Formulation

In attempting to provide public education for everyone, local governments have encountered issues that are so complex that they spill over to other levels of government. Conflict over equal education can arise around issues of how to achieve equality. To some, equality may mean distributing the same amount of resources to everyone, as in distributive policies. But to others, equality may mean giving extra resources to those who are disadvantaged—to bring them up to an equal level. In education, this may mean giving extra resources for remedial education to those who have problems learning or who come from disadvantaged households, for bilingual education for those who do not speak English, or for busing children from poor ghetto schools to suburban schools. These policies mean redistributing resources, and some parents fear that resources will be taken from their children to provide more resources to others. They fear that equality necessitates the sacrifice of quality and that leads to opposition.[15]

No matter how equality is conceived, it is difficult to imagine how it can be achieved without some centralized control. If more is to be given to those with difficulties, it must be possible to shift resources from one area to another as needed. If all are to receive the same resources, centralized control is necessary to assure uniformity. Yet Americans have consistently feared and rejected centralized control over educational systems.

This fear seems to arise from the belief that the schools are transmitters of basic val-

ues to students. Actually, research on socialization indicates that schools are much better
at reinforcing values transmitted by the family
than at conveying a totally different value system.[16] Nevertheless, parents have vigorously
supported local control over public school
systems and strenuously opposed any attempt
to centralize that control. In fact, many advocate "neighborhood schools" to prevent the
redistributive effects of centralized schools.[17]

Yet such localized control makes equality
of education impossible. In transmitting the
values of the local community, often the
schools reinforce inequalities rather than creating equality. For example, in some south-
western school districts, Latinos have been
discouraged from taking anything but vocational courses because of the community's expectations (hopes?) that they could not succeed in more difficult classes. In one amazing
case, the son of a prominent businessman was
given the responsibility of marching the Latino
students out of class because it was considered important for him to learn how to manage them![18]

Other research has indicated that in some
places the parents' fear that schools may
transform their children is so strong that they
wanted to keep the education mediocre.[19]
Thus, not only would children be unlikely to
learn new values, they also would be unlikely
to be able to get jobs that would allow them,
or require them, to move away.

Finally, another way that local control
makes equality impossible is the fact that local
control implies local financing. Based on the
assumption that "he who pays the piper calls
the tune," the bulk of the financing of school
systems comes from local taxes. Because residents tend to be segregated on the basis of socioeconomic status, some local school districts have a great deal of money to allocate to
schools and others have very little. This tendency is especially pronounced in highly fragmented metropolitan areas.[20] To the extent
that the availability of financial resources is

important in determining the quality of education (a point to be discussed later), the reliance on local funding also reinforces inequality rather than increasing equality.

The same belief that the schools control
the transmission of society's basic values that
leads to demands for locally controlled schools
also leads to the demand that schools solve
society's problems. If racial segregation is a
problem, then school children should be bused
to achieve racial balance in the schools and,
presumably, to eliminate the prejudice that
leads to discrimination and segregation. If
teenage pregnancies are a problem, then
schools should teach sex education and, in
some instances, provide birth control. School
authorities debate if, and at what age, schools
should address issues such as AIDS and other
sexually transmitted diseases.

In homogeneous communities, the question of what values should be taught can be
resolved relatively easily. In urban areas where
schools controlled by one school board must
deal with children from different ethnic groups,
different religions, different languages, and different social classes, establishing a consensus
on desirable values is much harder. Thus, urban school systems are frequently the subject
of conflict among varying groups in the city
and often find maintaining an image of neutral, professional competence difficult.

Ironically, schools are not always successful in transmitting the values they hope to
transmit. The values present in the schools are
the values of the staff. Teachers and administrators tend to be middle-class professionals.
When they deal with the children of other
middle-class professionals they are not *transmitting* values so much as they are reinforcing
the values children are learning at home. When
the middle-class professionals deal with the
children of the poor, however, their success in
changing values is limited. Many poor children see no need to learn subjects being taught
in schools as they cannot imagine how those
things are relevant for the world in which they

live and they cannot imagine living under different circumstances.[21]

In sum, the educational system is valued as a means of individual and societal improvement, however, it is also feared for the power that such improvement implies, and it is looked down upon because it does not always accomplish what is expected.

Although educational policy has traditionally been a local issue, there has been some national and state involvement. As early as 1785, the Land Ordinance required that land in each township in the Northwest Territories (roughly what are now the states of Ohio, Indiana, Illinois, Michigan, and Wisconsin) be reserved "for the maintenance of public schools." The local government could decide where to locate the school or could even sell the land to raise money for schools. In 1862 the Morrill Act gave states a grant of land if they established agricultural and mechanical colleges. In 1917, the Smith–Hughes Act provided federal money to states to establish vocational education programs in schools. And in 1944, the Serviceman's Readjustment Act (G.I. Bill of Rights) provided veterans returning from World War II with money to attend college. Federally guaranteed student loans are available for higher education expenses. The 1997 federal budget agreement allowed up to $1,000 (rising over four years to $2,500) in interest on those loans to be deducted from adjusted gross income for tax purposes and provided for tax credits of up to $1,500 for tuition and related expenses for the first two years of college.

Some states were also involved in education from the earliest years of the country. New York, the first state with educational policy on its agenda, created a Board of Regents in 1784 to oversee its schools. By 1861, 28 of the 34 states in the union had a state education official whose goal was to create some uniformity in school policies. All states now distribute at least some money to local school districts. These payments are designed to ensure a minimal level of resources to provide an adequate education and are usually distributed based on a student per capita basis.

Other than these limited intrusions by states and the national government, education has remained primarily a local issue and responsibility. In the 1950s, three major issues beyond the control of the local community forced education onto both the state and national agenda.

The first issue was racial integration. In 1954, the Supreme Court in *Brown v. Board of Education of Topeka, Kansas* declared that schools segregated on the basis of race were in violation of the equal protection clause of the Constitution. This started a continuing effort to integrate public schools.

The second was the launching of an orbiting satellite, Sputnik, by the Soviet Union. The realization that the Soviets were ahead of us in developing space technology outraged Americans. The focus of their anger became the school system that, it was feared, was not providing adequate training in math and science. The result was the 1958 National Defense Education Act, which, in effect, represented the first major attempt to provide substantial federal aid to higher education.

Meanwhile, while not as dramatic as the *Brown* decision or the Sputnik launching, another factor was pushing education onto state and federal agendas. With local control of education came local responsibility for funding. Because local areas are limited in the taxes they can impose, schools in most areas were funded primarily by local property taxes. The pattern of residential segregation by income level (that is, the wealthy live in one place and the poor in another) meant that great disparities existed in the amount of money various school districts could spend on education.

The property tax is based on some percentage of market value of the taxable property. This means that very expensive properties can be taxed at very low rates and still generate substantial money while it takes a much higher tax rate on less valuable properties to generate the same amount, or even less. Thus, people in poor school districts may be paying taxes at a much higher rate than those in wealthier areas, and the district may still have less money to spend. A further irony results from the fact that local property taxes are deductible on federal income taxes, so the more a homeowner pays to maintain quality schools, and the higher the tax bracket, the larger the subsidy in reduced federal taxes.

Several court cases developed out of challenges by poor and minority parents in school districts that could spend less per pupil than other districts despite having higher tax rates. In two cases, *Serrano v. Priest* in California and *San Antonio Independent School District v. Rodriguez* in Texas, courts declared the disparities that resulted due to the local tax base to be a form of unconstitutional discrimination. The Supreme Court reversed the *Rodriguez* decision in 1973, arguing that education . . "is not among the rights afforded explicit protection under our Federal Constitution."[22] This precluded further federal judicial action in the area of fiscal disparities.

The combination of the *Brown* ruling, the Sputnik launching, and legal challenges to funding disparities forced education onto the national legislative agenda and led to the development of new initiatives. Various public opinion polls in the 1950s and early 1960s indicated widespread support for federal aid to education.[23] In addition, numerous groups supported increased federal aid, including the National Education Association, the American Federation of Teachers, the AFL-CIO, and various other liberal, African-American, women's, and service organizations. Yet many other groups were opposed, including the American Farm Bureau Federation, chambers of commerce, the National Association of

Manufacturers, and various patriotic groups such as the Daughters of the American Revolution.

In the 1960s, improved education was tied to solving the problems of poverty. This approach linked education with questions of redistributing society's resources and, as a result, embroiled education in substantial conflict. Opponents to increased national support for education argued that such aid would bring increased federal control and that parents would lose control over what their children were taught as increasing federal regulation accompanied federal money. Federal control was seen as intrinsically bad and a threat to individual liberty and state's rights.

Underlying the basic debate were a number of other issues that made resolution of the conflict difficult. One particularly thorny issue was the question of whether federal aid should go to religious schools as well as to public schools. A proposal by President John F. Kennedy (a Roman Catholic) to supply federal aid only to nonsectarian schools was defeated when urban Catholics joined conservatives and southern Democrats to vote against it.

Another underlying issue was race. Although the Supreme Court had declared segregated schools unconstitutional in 1954, segregation was still the norm in many schools. A study estimated that if southern states desegregated at the same rate they did between 1954 and 1961, it would take 3,180 years to desegregate southern schools.[24] Southerners worried that segregated schools would not be able to receive aid. Indeed, throughout the 1950s, Adam Clayton Powell, the African-American chairman of the Education and Labor Committee in the House of Representatives, amended federal education aid bills to prohibit money for segregated schools. These amendments produced a coalition between conservatives and southern Democrats that always succeeded in defeating the legislation on the House floor.

Adoption

While looking to other levels of government for fiscal assistance, local boards of education still set much school policy dealing with curriculum, class size, teacher salaries, and the like. Of course, increasing reliance on higher levels of government often means more interference in local prerogatives in areas such as minimum standards and racial integration.

Local decisions are made by school boards, which are discussed briefly in Chapter 9. School boards are usually elected, although in some areas they are appointed by the mayor, council, or city manager. In most communities, the board is autonomous and responsible for raising its own revenue. In some places, it is a department of the city or county government and relies on the city or county for its revenue. Traditionally, prominent businessmen and professionals were members of the school board and minorities and lower classes were excluded.

In many ways, independent school boards are analogous to reformed governmental structures. They developed around the same time out of a value system that sought to make administration apolitical. Elwood P. Cubberley, a respected educator, was highly influential. He believed that board members should be elected—not political appointees of the mayor. To further depoliticize boards and to make sure "good" members were elected, school board elections were frequently nonpartisan and at-large. Such elections often resulted in an under-representation of both minorities on the school boards and of minority teachers in the school system.

The "typical" board member is a male middle-aged, white Republican, who is highly educated, has a prestigious occupation and high income, and is a long-time community resident. Further, most board members have little aspiration to higher office and therefore have little reason to respond to public demands.[25] In addition, voter turnout for school board elections tends to be low. Recently, the Christian Coalition has targeted school board elections as a way of accomplishing such goals as requiring prayer in the school and the teaching of creationism. In some places where the Christian Coalition has been successful in elections, its agenda has embroiled the board in controversy.[26]

The under-representation of minorities on school boards has an impact on school policy, resulting in policies that tend to discriminate against minority students.[27] One study found that African-American students may face discrimination even if they are attending school with white students. Blacks are more frequently assigned to "slow" classes while whites are assigned to classes for gifted children. The study also found that African-American representation on school boards is positively related to hiring African-American administrators, which leads to the hiring of more black teachers. This, in turn, depresses the bias in class assignment.[28] The study recommends replacing at-large elections for school board with ward elections to increase the representation of African-Americans.[29]

While the board sets school policy, it usually relies on school administrators for professional advice. The administrators tend to believe that school policy is too important to be left to amateurs. Because they lack time and expertise, board members frequently defer to the experts.

> As school districts have become larger and the process and organization of schooling has [sic] become more complex, school boards have had to turn more and more of the actual administration and policy-making for the schools over to trained educators. Moreover, school boards composed of laypersons serving on a part-time basis have found themselves increasingly dependent on the full-time professional school administrators for advice, recommendations, and information about the school and educa-

tion in general. As a result, boards have become inclined to defer to the expertise of their administrative staff. And, at the same time, they have been told, time and again, that they *should* do so because this will produce the "best," most professional, scientifically sound educational decisions.[30]

This deference helps to defuse conflict and preserve the image of the schools as professional and "above politics." However, many citizens believe that education professionals are rigid and unresponsive. Many urban administrators are trained educators, not managers, and concern may be expressed about their leadership skills. In light of this perception, it is interesting that both Washington, D.C., and Seattle, Washington, have hired retired generals to run their schools. One middle-class mother in Seattle thought the city's decision to look outside the education bureaucracy to hire John Sanford was a great idea. "He may not know how to teach reading, . . . but he knows it's the most important thing schools do. That's where we need to start."[31]

Adherence to professional norms is much easier when they can be adapted to community values. More conflict exists between school boards and superintendents in large heterogeneous urban school districts than in suburban or small town districts, and there is also more conflict on the board itself. Because of the divisiveness on urban boards, they are less likely to prevail over the superintendent.[32] Conflicts are less likely on general administrative issues than on emotional issues such as sex education, creationism, or censorship. These issues are likely to involve citizens in the community, but the involvement tends to be focused solely on the single issue and is fleeting.

One citizen group that has a more general and long-term involvement with educational policy is the parent–teacher association (PTA). While parents are often active in PTAs, it is of-

ten argued that the PTAs exist primarily to co-opt parents to the educational policy of the professionals.[33] **Co-optation** is the process of absorbing people into the leadership structure who will help provide stability and avert threats to the status quo. The professionals may have to adapt to the PTA members' wishes but, generally, parents are satisfied merely to be players in the game. As a result, these organizations tend to defer to the experts and basically act as boosters and fund raisers for the schools rather than as lobbyists seeking to change the policies of school boards or superintendents.

The American PTA is rarely anything more than a coffee and cookies organization based on vague good will and gullibility. It is chiefly useful to the administration for raising money for special projects and persuading parents who are interested enough to attend meetings that the local schools are in the front ranks of American education.[34]

Writing in 1969, Maurice Berube and Marilyn Gittell observed: "In most American cities, the public has little to say about how their schools are run; urban school systems, dominated by professionals, remain isolated and unaccountable to their public."[35] The authors were hopeful that people, especially the poor, who tended to have the least control over their neighborhood schools, would effectively demand control and tailor the schools to their needs. Little has actually changed in the ensuing years.

Teachers also have been involved in attempting to influence school policy. Unionization by the majority of the nation's teachers has increased their political clout. They often negotiate such items as salaries, grievances, maximum class hours, and maximum class sizes. The teachers' unions have been especially effective with issues such as seniority and transfer clauses.[36] Even in states where collective bargaining is prohibited, for example, North Carolina and Virginia, teachers' organizations have been able to influence educational policy.

The rising militancy of unions has created fiscal problems for school districts. Urban teachers, because of their heterogeneous clientele and often dangerous working conditions, have gone on strike to receive higher wages. Cities face losing their best teachers to suburban school districts that generally are able to pay more and provide better teaching conditions.[37] The alternative would be to raise the wages of city teachers, which would probably necessitate tax hikes.[38] This, of course, produces a vicious cycle because it provides impetus for more flight from the city and makes providing the educational quality to prevent further flight more difficult.

Teachers' organizations are also active in lobbying other levels of government. Frederick Wirt and Michael Kirst argue that: "the unions' long-run influence . . . may come more from influencing decisions at state and federal levels that then percolate down to the local school system."[39] These organizations were active lobbyists in attempts to secure increased federal funding for education. The powerful lobby arm of the National Education Association and of the American Federation of Teachers were especially active in support of the Elementary and Secondary Education Act of 1965 (ESEA).

ESEA is significant because it substantially increased the involvement of the national government in providing aid to the nation's elementary and secondary schools. The breakthrough was possible because of many factors. First, the 1964 Civil Rights Act had prohibited the use of federal funds for any program that discriminated against African-Americans, which meant that federal aid could not go to segregated schools and, therefore, the racial issue was no longer relevant. Second, the bill was structured so that the aid would be targeted to specific programs rather than providing general aid to the schools. This substantially defused the re-

ligious issue because aid could go to children in parochial schools. The line was thin, but the argument was that the aid went to students, not to schools, and therefore parochial students could qualify. This resulted in minimizing conflicts and distributed benefits widely.

Another reason for ESEA's success was the general political climate in 1965. President John Kennedy had been assassinated in 1963 and a tremendous outpouring of support and sympathy accompanied President Lyndon Johnson's efforts to enact Kennedy's programs. Michael Harrington's book, *The Other America*, also swayed public opinion in Johnson's direction.[40] The 1950s was a decade of remarkable prosperity for most Americans, but in 1962 Harrington stunned a self-satisfied nation by painting a grim picture of the scope of poverty in America. That contributed to public support for Johnson's declaration of the War on Poverty.

Federal aid to education was justified as a way of fighting that war because aid was to be targeted to low-income children. In fact, although it was initially discussed as an antipoverty program, the federal aid from ESEA went to about 95 percent of the nation's school districts.[41] The fact that it would be so widely distributed helped create support for the program among legislators.

As the Congress and the president were wrestling over federal aid to education, the courts were continuing to address two issues relevant to the question of how to achieve equality in schools. One was the continuing problem of segregated schools; the other was the effect of fiscal disparities among various school districts. Although the congressional debates resulted in a policy that widely distributed education aid, the implications of court rulings often had redistributional overtones.

Implementation

In 1954, the Supreme Court had clearly ruled that it was unconstitutional to segregate schools by law. Yet, because of the presence of segregation in housing, this meant that many schools were all white or all black simply because they existed in all-white or all-black neighborhoods. The proposed remedy was to bus children out of their neighborhoods to achieve racial balance.

Busing generated immense controversy both because of the volatile issue of race relations and because of the strong belief in and support of the neighborhood school and local control over schools. In addition, some parents in white schools feared the quality of their children's education would decline and both black and white parents were concerned with safety. In its 1970 term, the Supreme Court attempted to deal with the constitutionality of busing to achieve racial balance. Although the decision was unanimous, it was reportedly the result of massive compromise and bargaining among the justices.[42] The Supreme Court upheld a ruling by a U.S. District Court judge that required schools in Charlotte, North Carolina, and surrounding Mecklenburg County to desegregate. The judge had ordered that each school must have the same proportion of blacks and whites as the proportion in the total school population. Thus, each school was to be 71 percent white and 29 percent black. To achieve that, school attendance zones were altered and 13,000 students were bused. This ruling legitimated mandatory busing as a means of achieving racial integration.

In *Swann v. Charlotte–Mecklenburg Board of Education,* the Supreme Court upheld the District Court's ruling, by saying that "the very limited use made of mathematical ratios [of blacks and whites in schools] was within the . . . discretion of the District Court." Yet the Supreme Court also said the Constitution did not require racial balancing in schools.[43]

That left the issue unsettled. Two years later, an evenly divided Supreme Court overturned the ruling by District Judge Robert R. Merhige, Jr., requiring Richmond, Virginia's, school district, which was 70 percent black, to merge with two adjacent suburbs that were 90 percent white.[44] The Supreme Court later overturned a similar Detroit busing order, arguing that the suburbs had played no role in segregating Detroit schools and therefore should not be forced to participate in resolving the problem.[45]

The Richmond and Detroit cases made it clear busing between city and suburban school districts could not be required. The lesson to white parents in the city who did not want their children to attend schools with African-Americans was obvious—move to the suburbs. How much "white flight" has been caused by the question of school integration is not clear.[46] But the fear of white flight may be influential, regardless of whether it occurs. In Chicago, a school board member cast the deciding vote for a segregated attendance plan, arguing, "In my mind [it] is the only way we can prevent exodus from the city."[47]

Fear of white flight brought the busing issue back to the federal courts again in 1986 and has raised questions about the enduring quality of the *Swann v. Charlotte-Mecklenburg* decision. In 1970, Norfolk, Virginia, was found to be operating a dual educational system based on race. The federal courts required the city to develop a plan for integrating schools. After the *Swann* decision, the courts began to require a desegregation plan that included mandatory busing. By 1975, the federal court determined that Norfolk had complied and had established a unitary system, free of racial discrimination. Declining white enrollments made integration impossible, thus Norfolk decided to end mandatory crosstown busing for elementary school students. In *Riddick v. School Board of City of Norfolk* (1986), the U.S. Court of Appeals ruled that Norfolk was rightly concerned with the white exodus from public schools and that the decision to end mandatory busing was not based on discriminatory intent, but on the desire to keep enough whites in the school system to prevent resegregation.[48]

Another area of court involvement is the issue of resource disparities. Inequalities exist throughout the educational system in the United States. Nationally in 1991–92, the average per pupil expenditure for public school students in grades K–12 was $5,621. Per-pupil spending was highest in New Jersey, which spent $9,711—the state contributed $4,060 and $5,277 was raised locally. Federal aid accounts for the additional $374 per pupil. At the bottom of the list was Mississippi which spent $3,355 per pupil—$1,805 coming from the state, $1,000 from the locality, and the remainder from federal aid. The amount various states contribute to education differs greatly, with poorer states often contributing much less to education than wealthier states. In 1991–92, the average state per-pupil contribution to education was $2,661. New Hampshire contributed the least, spending $487 on each child in school while Alaska, with $6,073, contributed the most.[49]

Disparities also exist among school districts within states, again with wealthier districts, such as those in affluent suburbs, contributing more to education than is possible in poorer districts, such as many of those in the inner city. In North Carolina, local units are not required to supplement state allocations and some counties do not. Because urban counties have been adding to state funds and some rural counties have not, there has been a flow of teachers to the urban counties.[50]

As noted earlier, local funding disparities have been challenged in court. The New Jersey Supreme Court in 1973 ordered the state to establish an income tax to equalize educational funding. After three years of legislative inaction, the court closed down all schools until the legislature finally passed the income tax. Inequities still existed in 1985. Administrative Law Judge Stephen L. Lefelt argued that the state justifies disparate conditions "as the need to protect against further diminishment of local control," but went on to note that the state has been willing to take control of urban districts that it judged to be poorly managed.[51] Opponents argued that no additional funds should be provided to urban districts until they could prove that they would be disbursed "wisely."

> No testimony . . . , has been provided to affirm "that high-spending districts are spending [money] wisely." Under the defendants' argument, "wealthy districts can continue to spend as much money as they wish. Poor districts will go on pretty much as they have. . . . If money is inadequate to improve education, the residents of poor districts should at least have an equal opportunity to be disappointed by its failure."[52]

The need for state equalization was upheld by the New Jersey Supreme Court again in 1990.[53] This helps to explain why, in 1991–92, state aid was quite high. Since that time, Christine Todd Whitman became governor on a pledge to cut state taxes. She followed through on her promise and one result was relatively less state funds transferred to local government for education.

In a 1971 case in California, petitioners noted that Beverly Hills residents paid $2.38 on each $100 of taxable property while residents of nearby Baldwin Park paid $5.48 on each $100. But Beverly Hills could afford to spend $1,282 for each pupil in school, while Baldwin Park could only spend $579 because the value of the Baldwin Park property was much less.[54] The California Supreme Court ruled on the basis of the state constitution that this was unequal protection, in effect requiring some form of statewide tax equalization. As a result, the California legislature increased its share of funding to lessen the disadvantage of poorer districts.

In Texas, a Federal District Court ruled that it is necessary to develop a means of financing education that does not discriminate against poor districts. As previously noted, the United States Supreme Court struck down the federal decision in Texas, leaving remedies to the states.[55]

Disparities also arise within school districts. With regard to intra-district disparities, Federal District Court Judge Skelly Wright ordered in *Hobson v. Hansen* (1967) the equalization of expenditures across all schools.[56] The case arose because most of the money in the Washington, D.C., school system went to schools in white neighborhoods despite the fact that the school system was 90 percent black. Jonathan Kozol found vast disparities in several urban school systems. He noted, for example, that District 10 comprising much of the Bronx in New York City could be viewed as two districts: Riverdale, mostly affluent and white, and the rest, mostly poor and heavily nonwhite. Riverdale got the best teachers, smaller class sizes, more library books and computers per student, and nicer surroundings. Kozol believes that these disparities result from class and racial discrimination.

> Some of the most stunning inequity, . . . derives from allocations granted by state legislators to school districts where they have political allies. The poorest districts in the city get approximately 90 cents from these legislative grants, while the richest districts are given $14 for each pupil.[57]

There is unwillingness to spend more money in the poorest districts because of fears it would be "wasted on poor children. This message 'trickles down to districts, schools, and classrooms.' Children hear and understand this theme—they are poor investments—and behave accordingly."[58]

The courts have not addressed the issue of disparities between states, but that was, in part, the goal of the Elementary and Secondary Education Act. Passage of the act was facilitated by tying it to the War on Poverty. Aid was to be targeted to low-income students. Yet initial audits of the money spent indicated that local school districts were using the money as a form of general aid to purchase whatever they wanted: football jerseys, swimming pools, etc.[59] In other words, the money was being distributed widely among many students rather than being targeted to poorer students. As initially implemented, the program was more distributive than redistributive. Pressure from civil rights groups and other organizations succeeded in getting the implementing agency, the Office of Education, to issue specific guidelines that established eligibility for receiving the funds. Recent evaluations indicate greater success in using the money to upgrade the education of low-income students. On the other hand, since 1980, federal funding for elementary and secondary education has dropped from 9.1 percent to 5.6 percent of the total funds spent on education.[60]

One other issue is relevant to the goal of educational equality: community control. On the one hand, community control of schools at the level of the local school district has contributed to inequality because local control has been tied to local financing. The solution appears to be to provide greater centralization of education to equalize resources available to all. On the other hand, some minority parents have argued that inequalities in schools are the result of too much centralization, that decisions by citywide school boards and state departments of education have produced an educational policy that discriminates against the schools attended by poor and minority populations. They demand more decentralization of control to give parents a better chance to make sure that their children receive an education they desire.

An attempt to respond to those requests for greater community control failed in New York in 1969. Dissatisfied parents in the depressed Brooklyn neighborhoods of Ocean

Hill and Brownsville had formed an alternative school board to protest the conditions in their schools. Initially, the United Federation of Teachers, the teachers' union, supported the parents because the union thought the parents would support the teachers' goals. As both parents and union sought to increase their control over the schools, they were on an unavoidable collision course.[61]

New York Mayor John Lindsay designated the Ocean Hill–Brownsville school district as one of three pilot projects in school decentralization. The three projects were to test a proposal to give locally elected school boards final control over such crucial aspects of school policy as budget, curriculum, and personnel. School professionals opposed the plan; as it went into effect in Ocean Hill–Brownsville, some observers thought the professionals were intentionally trying to sabotage the experiment. In May 1968, the local school board transferred 19 professionals out of the Ocean Hill–Brownsville district for alleged sabotage. The teachers' union went on strike for the remainder of the school year. The Ocean Hill–Brownsville confrontation effectively ended the school decentralization plan and the increase in local community control over urban schools that decentralization was intended to achieve.[62] New York City now has 32 community school districts, and the boards in each district are advisory only.[63] The confrontation underscored the power that school professionals can exercise over school policy.

The Ocean Hill–Brownsville controversy also illustrated how education can become embroiled in conflict when it is seen as raising issues relevant to the redistribution of power or social resources. Community control in Ocean Hill–Brownsville would have given the poor residents of that neighborhood both greater power over educational policy and potentially greater success in using the educational system to increase their children's social mobility. The issue of who should run the lo-

cal schools is still contentious. Box 13–1 discusses the ongoing struggle in New York City.

Evaluation

Since the Supreme Court's 1954 decision, schools have been in the middle of debates over how to achieve equality, yet a consensus has not been reached. Does equality mean simply eliminating legal segregation of schools or does it mean busing children to achieve equal racial ratios in each school? Does equality mean distributing resources to each school district simply on a proportional basis, with each district receiving a set amount for each student? Or does equality mean giving more resources to those districts with larger numbers of disadvantaged students? Must schools provide bilingual education to children who speak no English?

While debates over such issues have often been bitter, ironically the Coleman Report found that the amount of money spent in a school district was not related to student achievement. The best predictors of student achievement were the socioeconomic background of the students themselves and of their fellow students.[64] Presumably, socioeconomic status is related to life experiences and attitudes that make children more capable of benefiting from the educational environment. Others have argued that the methodology of the Coleman study predetermined his conclusions. Coleman controlled for the effect of race, which meant that he examined the effect of school expenditures separately for white and black schools. He never *compared* the expenditures for white and black schools, a comparison that might have resulted in expenditures appearing to have a substantial effect on achievement.[65] Kozol documents that many urban schools, especially inner city schools, suffer from a shortage of qualified teachers because of salaries and conditions in the schools. They lack adequate supplies; in many instances, teachers buy everything from

BOX 13–1

Who Should Control the Local Schools?

It is a case of déjà vu all over again. The first edition of this book had a box reporting on the efforts of the new chancellor of New York City schools to gain control of the decentralized school system. Since passage of the Decentralization Act in 1969, much of the control over the city's schools has been exercised by the 32 9-member elected community school boards. The boards were created in response to demands, especially from residents in minority neighborhoods, to give neighborhoods more control over their schools. The boards were given a budget and were in control of some curriculum issues and the hiring of teachers.

While more minority teachers were hired under the decentralized school board system, there were complaints they were "mired in patronage and politics." Because few people participated in the board elections, teachers' organizations such as the United Federation of Teachers and local political organizations were guaranteed control. In 1988, an estimated 28 percent of board members were school employees. The new chancellor was trying to find a way to involve more parents and to bar school employees from serving on the boards.

In 1996, the boards remain unchanged, but not unchallenged. There were still charges of patronage and mismanagement and the majority Democrats in the New York State Assembly wanted to abolish the community school boards. Republican Governor George Pataki and the Republican-controlled State Senate wanted to retain them but to abolish the city's central Board of Education and give the mayor more control over its budget and the choice of the chancellor.

Negotiators were proposing a compromise that would remove the community boards' control over budgets and hiring and leave them solely as advisors. But no one could agree on who should control budgetary and hiring decisions. The Democrats in the Assembly wanted to transfer powers to governance councils composed of parents, teachers, and administrators. The governor and Senate were proposing giving at least some of the power to the chancellor.

Source: Adapted from Joseph Berger, "Green Tries to Get a Grip on City's Decentralized Schools," *New York Times,* July 3, 1988, sec. E; Clifford J. Levy, "Efforts to Alter Education Board Stall in Albany," *New York Times,* July 9, 1996.

paper and books to VCRs with their own money. Classes are overcrowded. Counseling is inadequate. Students lack access to science equipment. Buildings are literally falling down. In contrast, wealthy suburbs have well-paid teachers, computers, and libraries with many volumes, and provide multiple counselors to help students plan for college.[66]

More recently, former U.S. Education Secretary William Bennett argued that the amount of money spent does not determine the quality of education. He stated "you cannot buy your way to better performance."[67] Still, many people behave as if money does matter. Many middle-class families "scrimp and save" to buy homes in areas with good schools and many upper-class families send their children to expensive private schools. If money does affect the quality of education, it is hard to imagine that the students in inner-city schools can compete with those in better-funded urban or suburban schools.

One measure of the perceived quality of the urban public school systems can be seen in the fact that in 1989 the president of the Chicago School Board, a former teacher and administrator, and Mayor Richard Daley, Jr., did not send their school-age children to public schools.[68] President Bill Clinton's daughter Chelsea did not attend Washington, D.C., public schools. Many African-American leaders agree that urban public education is failing. The National Association for the Advancement of Colored People (NAACP), which had supported litigation in *Brown v. Board,* is now more concerned with improving school performance than with integration. That seems to indicate that some think separate but equal may be a more effective strategy than the current system which is clearly unequal and often separate.

Added to these debates are two other trends affecting schools. One is a declining confidence in American schools. Continuous decline in Scholastic Aptitude Test (SAT) scores from the mid-1960s to the 1990s was evidence of the problems of American public schools.[69] In addition, business, increasingly challenged by competition from other countries, worried that the schools were not producing employees with the skills necessary to compete in a complex and technologically sophisticated marketplace.[70] The Department of Education commissioned a study that reported that the American education system was mediocre at best and the result was that the United States had become "A Nation at Risk." That report stated, "If an unfriendly foreign power had attempted to impose on America the mediocre educational performance that exists today, we might have viewed it as an act of war. As it stands, we have allowed this to happen to ourselves."[71]

At the same time, the school system has been caught, along with social services in this country, by the reluctance of Americans to raise taxes and the imperative that the national budget deficit be brought under control.

Some cuts in educational aid were made at the start of the Reagan presidency, but in 1984 Congress reversed the budget cuts and passed a record high budget.[72] In 1986, Guaranteed Student Loan funding was cut by restricting eligibility, requiring recipients to pay interest on the loan while they were in school, and reducing subsidies to state agencies that guaranteed the loans. In efforts to reduce the huge budget deficit and balance the budget, education funding came under close scrutiny.

The combination of lack of confidence in the schools and budget crunches have contributed to a rash of proposals and experiments in educational reform. One proposal is a "back to the basics" movement, the goal of which is to focus the efforts of the schools on basic education (reading, writing, and arithmetic) and to cut out the "frills." While few dispute the importance of basic education, debates abound over exactly what are frills. One person's frill is another's quality education. At one stage the Philadelphia School Board attempted to cut out football as a frill, only to be forced to capitulate and fund football and cut other programs. Among the areas that have been targets are foreign language instruction and art and music classes. Also put in possible danger by such cuts are remedial education courses and bilingual courses for those students, especially Latinos, for whom English is a second language.

Proclaiming himself the education president, George Bush called a summit conference of the nation's governors in 1989 to develop national education goals. Called the Goals 2000 program, the resulting recommendations led to the Neighborhood Schools Improvement Act of 1992; it, however, failed to pass Congress. President Clinton, who had participated in the 1989 summit meeting as governor of Arkansas, submitted his own version of reform to Congress, and signed it into law in 1994. It basically provided federal money to help states meet national educational guidelines.

Goals 2000 has proven to be very controversial. Initial controversy focused on so-called Opportunity-to-Learn standards, which required that states provide qualified teachers and current textbooks. Republicans feared that such standards would produce a spate of lawsuits from parents. Other provisions of the law established eight national education goals toward which states that participated in the program should work. Examples of the goals include achieving a 90 percent graduation rate, encouraging more parental involvement, and establishing national curriculum standards. Conservatives thought that the program was a stalking horse for more national intrusion into local school systems. After the Republicans took control of Congress in 1995, they rewrote parts of the law to reduce the federal role, leaving the program subject to charges that it is now "hollow, and that it is doing little to enhance education standards."[73]

Some cities have experimented with privatizing their school systems. Baltimore contracted with Education Alternatives, Inc., to run some of its schools, but ended its contract early. Evaluations had indicated that the privatized schools spent $18 million more than comparable schools in the city, and test scores of students in the privatized schools went down while scores of students in the other schools went up.

Chicago passed a School Reform Act in 1988 that attempted to give local schools more autonomy. It provides for each school to be governed by a Local School Council (LSC) composed of two elected community residents, six elected parents, two teachers elected by the staff, and the principal. The LSC appoints the principal for renewable four-year terms and develops the school improvement plan with targets for student achievement. Evaluations of the reform were cautiously optimistic, but there are fears now that fiscal crisis is jeopardizing its possible success. In 1995, the Illinois legislature gave the mayor control over the schools for the next four years.[74]

Many variations of suggestions have been made about ways to provide students and their parents with greater choice of schools. Currently, most children are automatically assigned to a school based on residence. Many argue that if students and their parents could choose which school the students would attend, schools would have an incentive to attract students. Because of the resulting competition, the schools would work to improve the quality of education.

The State of Minnesota has allowed elementary and secondary students to attend school outside their districts. The district that the child selects gets the money the state would have allocated to the district in which the child lives. Milwaukee, Wisconsin, has a voucher program which pays the expenses of students who want to attend private schools.

Other districts have established magnet schools that offer special programs and are given extra resources; an average of 20 percent of high school students in large urban districts attend magnet schools.[75] One aim of the magnet schools is to keep upper- and middle-class students in the public school system. They do not necessarily lead to more integration and often result in a diversion of resources from poor schools to support the magnet programs. Magnet schools, then, may create a two-tiered system. "The *Chicago Tribune* has called the magnet system, 'a private school system . . . operated in the public schools.'"[76]

Kozol presents an example of the bias often associated with magnet schools. In Chicago, Dearborn Park is a redevelopment area attractive to urban, white professionals. Nearby is a public housing project, Hilliard Homes. Dearborn Park parents requested and got the school board to build a new elementary school. However, they did not want the children from the Hilliard Homes to attend. They used their political clout with the Board of Education to allow their children to enroll in the school from kindergarten but the Hilliard children had to wait until third grade—by which time they are likely to be be-hind the more advantaged children. The school for the first three grades was a "'a tem-porary branch school' in 'a small, prefabri-cated metal building surrounded on three sides by junkyards'"[77]

> The parents from Dearborn Park insist that, if the school is attended by the children from the projects—these are the children who have lived there all along—the stan-dards of the school will fall. The school, moreover, has a special "fine arts" magnet program; middle-class children, drawn to the schools from other sections of Chicago, are admitted. So the effort to keep out the kids who live right in the neighborhood points out class and racial factors. The city, it is noted, had refused to build a new school for the project children when they were the only children in the neighborhood. Now that a new school has been built, they find themselves excluded.[78]

Perhaps the most sweeping proposal for school choice comes from John Chubb and Terry Moe. They argue for complete renova-tion of the school system to minimize the role of the education bureaucracy that they claim dooms schools to failure because of the sti-fling centralized rules and regulations. In their plan, the state would establish minimal criteria for what constitutes a public school. Any school, whether currently public or pri-vate, could apply to the state and, if it met the criteria, it could be chartered as a public school. The district would set up a Choice Of-fice and include in it a Parent Information Center to help parents choose which school best meets their child's needs. Once parents choose, the Choice Office would provide funding to the school selected.[79] As of 1994, 9 states and 100 schools were experimenting with charter schools.[80]

Some doubt if any form of choice will make a difference. Less than 1 percent of stu-dents have taken advantage of Minnesota's statewide choice plan. On the other hand, some see choice as a way to provide a quality education to poor children in the inner city.[81] Ninety-three percent of students who partici-pate in the Milwaukee voucher program are African-American or Latino. The failure of the current school system to meet the needs of African-Americans and Latinos is indicated by the fact that their drop-out rates are higher than those of either whites or Asians.[82] Wilbur Rich points out that the poor education of Af-rican-Americans not only cripples individu-als, but also makes it difficult for black mayors to succeed. Because investors and developers seek a well-educated workforce, they may be unwilling to move into areas with large num-bers of African-Americans because of fears about their level of education. Since black mayors often preside over cities with a large number of African-Americans, they may find it difficult to lure businesses into the city to spur economic development. Their failure to improve the economic fortunes of the city can be detrimental to their political future.[83]

For the most part, these educational trends are national in scope and affect rural as well as urban schools. The problems, however, seem to be exaggerated in cities. The role of schools as socializers and equalizers seems es-pecially important and especially difficult in the heterogeneous mix of the urban society. The clash of cultures and values is inevitable and intense in the crush of metropolitan America. The urban school system handles children of people with vastly differing values and life goals, experiences, and abilities. To prepare them all for the future is the task we give our urban schools. That they have diffi-culty fulfilling our expectations is hardly sur-prising.

Crime Control

The criminal justice system has two major goals, to prevent crime from occurring without trampling on the liberties of those who have no intention of committing a crime and to assure that the guilty are punished. The problem is how police can have enough control to stop crime without controlling the innocent as well.

Once a crime has been committed, society has an interest in punishing those who are guilty. The problem is to apprehend the person who is guilty, and leave the innocent in peace. Nor do we worry only about the rights of the innocent. Our society wants to protect the rights of the guilty as well. The term "due process" refers to a set of procedural and substantive safeguards established by our society to ensure that, in the attempt to control crime, the government does not itself act in criminal ways. Some of the components of due process safeguards will be discussed later.

Clearly, the criminal justice system operates in a difficult environment. Lines must constantly be drawn—lines balancing our desire for freedom from police intrusion with our desire for prevention of crime, lines balancing the rights of the accused with the rights of the victim and of society as a whole. The context of crime control policy has become even more complicated recently. Starting in the 1960s, the incidence of predatory crimes against both people and property increased substantially. The number of offenses known to police more than doubled between 1960 and 1970.[84] Crime rates continued to climb steadily until the early 1980s. With this rise came increased fear about crime and additional pressure on the criminal justice system to prevent crime or punish the guilty.

Much of the increase in crime occurred in urban areas—especially in the largest cities. In 1973, Herbert Jacob found a close relationship between city size and murder rates and car thefts.[85] He concluded, "Not all cities bear an equal share of the crime burden. Large cities have more crime.... [T]he incidence of these crimes per 100,000 population is much higher in the largest cities than in smaller ones."[86] In a later study he noted that the rate of violent crime had increased more steeply in cities with declining populations, while property crimes increased at similar rates regardless of whether the city was growing or declining.[87]

Table 13–1 shows that most violent crimes still occur in metropolitan areas. The overall incidence of crime has declined in the 1990s. For example, in New York City the number of homicides has dropped 50 percent since 1990. In 1996, the number dropped below 1,000 for the first time since 1968.[88] Department of Justice data show that nationwide violent crime declined by 9 percent in 1995.[89] Despite the drop, surveys have revealed that residents' fear

TABLE 13–1

Violent Crimes by Area, 1995

United States	**1,799,000**
Metropolitan areas[a]	1,619,000
Other cities	105,000
Rural areas	75,000

[a]A city of at least 50,000 or more inhabitants or urbanized area of 50,000 and a metropolitan population of at least 100,000 (75,000 in New England).

Source: U.S. Federal Bureau of Investigation U.S. Bureau of the Census, *Statistical Abstract of the United States: 1997,* 117th ed. (Washington, D.C.: U.S. Government Printing Office, 1997), 201.

of crime has remained relatively stable since the early 1980s.[90] Indeed, in 1996 a *Washington Post* poll indicated that crime was the second in a list of top 20 worries. (Education ranked first.[91]) Some reasons why the level of fear has not changed even though crime has declined will be discussed in the agenda-setting section below.

The urban setting is conducive to crime for many reasons. The conditions of urban living—impersonality, heterogeneity, and interdependence—contribute to a context in which crime is more likely. The impersonality of urban areas means that people are less likely to be acquainted with potential victims or witnesses. Robbing a stranger is presumably easier than robbing a friend. The personalism of small towns makes it easy to identify those who engage in criminal activity, as Box 13–2 illustrates.

Heterogeneity also contributes to a setting conducive to crime. Criminal behavior is anything the government says it is. This means that the definition of what is a crime is a product of the political process and, in many ways, is a reflection of the values of those with political power. There may or may not be consensus on those values. While few would question a law forbidding one person from murdering another, many did question the constitutional amendment making it illegal to sell or consume alcoholic beverages. Many examples can be given of laws such as Prohibition that many believe to be misguided. In addition, examples can be given of laws that virtually all of us would think are silly. North Dakota, for instance, still has a law giving municipalities the authority to license, tax, and regulate runners for stage coaches! Crime control becomes more difficult when there is no agreement on the laws to be enforced.

Small communities, which exert pressure on residents to conform, are likely to have greater agreement about what is acceptable behavior and what is not.[92] In urban areas,

such agreement is less likely. If you disagree that smoking marijuana or committing adultery should be crimes, a metropolis is large enough to ensure that you can find others who agree with you. In such an environment, where diversity and disagreements are obvious, laws may seem to be less absolute.

Heterogeneity contributes to crime in another way. While extremes of wealth exist in small towns, those extremes are often not as obvious as they are in urban areas. The pressure for conformity in small towns makes the ostentatious display of either wealth or poverty unacceptable. Those constraints are not present in large communities and conspicuous displays of both extreme wealth and extreme poverty are likely to co-exist in close proximity. In such an environment, the temptations to the poor are more flagrantly flaunted and may contribute to more people yielding.

Interdependence also makes crime more likely. Interdependence results in more areas of our lives being regulated. Farmers can legally throw garbage out their kitchen windows if they so desire; city dwellers cannot. As more aspects of our lives are regulated by laws, more opportunities for us to break those laws arise.

The conditions that give rise to urban crime have serious consequences for all urban residents. Many wealthy urban residents have walled themselves up in luxurious fortresses. Once they have achieved personal safety, they often become indifferent to the problems of crime. In addition, the problem of personal security is shifted from the citizenry to the authorities. This exacerbates the problem of preventing crime.

An apathetic, detached citizenry far too often limits its participation to bitter criticism of police for not accomplishing work which rightly must be undertaken by the citizenry itself. The well-off citizen, by isolating himself in a secure fortress, by restricting his

BOX 13-2

Out of Place in a Small Town

McHENRY, North Dakota—A lone gunman robbed the Security State Bank here Friday, making off with an undisclosed amount of money.

Foster County Sheriff John Statema said a man entered the bank at about 10:30 A.M. Friday. The teller was alone at the time. The man brandished a handgun and told the teller she wouldn't be hurt if she cooperated. The teller allowed him to take an amount of money and the thief fled in a gray, 1985 Volkswagen Golf, license number DEC229. . . .

Statema described the suspect as a white man with grayish-brown hair, a beard and mustache. He was about 5 feet 10 inches tall and had a pot belly. He covered his face with a handkerchief during the robbery. . . .

Half a dozen investigators studied tire tracks, took fingerprints and interviewed witnesses for about four hours Friday.

Other officers staked out country roads and checked abandoned farmsteads around McHenry. A truck driver reported seeing a small gray car speeding south toward Jamestown on N.D. Highway 20 shortly after the robbery.

Several people around the town of 90 noticed the robber hanging around town Friday morning.

Darlis Short, manager of McHenry Cafe, said she saw the suspect drive up and down the gravel main street past the cafe, post office, bar, grocery store, and bank. Eventually he drove the car back to the center of town and backed it up to the curb in front of the bank. He continued to loiter on foot, apparently watching the bank from outside the senior citizen center across the street.

Short was so suspicious of the man that she mentioned him to the bank teller when she went in to make a deposit at 10:15. She noted his license plate.

"It was easy to remember—December 229. And it had a Dickinson State sticker in the rear window and Richardson Taylor [High School] on the license plate cover," Short said.

Wayne Bergan noticed the man, too. He said the man looked suspicious and he could almost tell he was going to do something funny.

"If another cow comes in, the whole herd knows it," he said.

Grocer John Aarestad saw the man walking slowly up and down the street until finally picking up his pace. Aarestad's small store is next to the bank.

Soon afterward he saw the Volkswagen drive away "with quite a bit of speed."

Mayor Marvin Miska found out about the robbery when he took his wife in to do some banking. The note on the door said the bank was closed till further notice. Later he stood on the sidewalk, watching the investigators work.

"This put us on the map, but it's a hell of a way to be put on. We've got more cars in town now than any day of the week, except taco night, Wednesday night," he said.

Miska said he felt sorry for the teller, a local woman and active community leader. She wasn't hurt in the robbery, but she was shaken.

The teller's husband was one of the first on the scene, arriving just before the sheriff. The bar manager across the street called him after she saw the stranger run out the door. He said his wife was surprisingly calm when he arrived.

"She was holding strong, but I'm afraid it will hit her tonight," he said.

Note: The car used in the holdup was stolen and when it was discovered in Montana a few days later, the police arrested the suspect.

Source: Jaime DeLage, "McHenry Bank Robbed," *Grand Forks Herald,* August 2, 1997, sec. A.

own ventures into the streets, and by demanding that authority assume all responsibility for ensuring the safety of streets, has effectively set the stage for the defeat of his own demands. The street, without the continued presence of the citizen, will never function safely for him.[93]

The poor, who are less able to control their own immediate environments, are more likely to become the victims of crime.

If crime is preponderantly an urban phenomenon, the search for crime control and for justice is also. Regardless of what level of government passes the laws, the local government must enforce them, even if little support for such laws is evident.

Agenda Setting

Colonists in pre–Revolutionary America followed the British tradition of having local volunteer police services because the British feared that a permanent police force could begin to function as a standing army and become despotic. Some cities paid taxes for a night watchman. Others elected constables who were paid from the fines they levied.[94] Only in southern cities, concerned by the threat of uprisings of the slave populations, were efforts made to provide a substantial police force.

By the 1830s, changes in northern cities necessitated better police services. Immigrants had begun arriving, increasing both the size and heterogeneity of America's cities. Both Boston and Philadelphia experienced anti-foreign, anti-Catholic, anti-black riots in the 1830s and 1840s. Well-publicized homicides added to urban residents' fears about order and safety. Citizens demanded more effective crime control procedures. As a result, major cities began to establish police forces. By the 1870s, all major American cities had police forces.

Crime has been a common item on the national political agenda since 1964.[95] Despite the fact that crime control is primarily a local government responsibility, some research has indicated that crime has not been so prominent on the local political agenda.[96] One analyst has concluded that national politicians have used the crime issue both to win votes and to avoid dealing with issues necessitating difficult decisions about allocating resources in society.[97] Who can argue with a politician who expresses concern about crime? Many other observers have pointed to the role of the media in keeping crime on the national agenda.[98] Television viewers in major metropolitan areas probably would not realize that crime rates have been declining while they watch stories of horrible crimes night after night. The tendency for national politicians to talk about crime and for the media to focus on crime keep the fear of crime high even though crime rates have been declining during the 1990s.

Formulation

The early police forces were appointed and were, therefore, part of the political patronage system. Thus, they rotated with the party in power and individuals were involved in politics to preserve their jobs. In some cities, the police chief and sometimes the whole police force were elected. Major concerns about police corruption had arisen by the twentieth century. Police in many cities had shown a remarkable consistency in forming profitable relationships with those they were supposed to be controlling—prostitutes, gamblers, bootleggers, and others.

Some states attempted to eliminate corruption by bringing the police under state control. Such efforts never lasted long. In other areas, urban police boards composed of citizens were established to insulate the police from politics and, therefore, presumably from corruption. In the early years of the twentieth century, the idea of dealing with corruption by establishing professional police forces under the control of a professional police administrator began to spread. The efforts to control police corruption and to professionalize the police force continue to be major concerns of many cities to this day.

What normally brings crime control to the governmental agenda is a visible increase in the kind of crime that scares people. Crime has tended to rise and fall in cycles. When crime is on the increase, crime control becomes a central concern. That is what happened in the 1960s, when the rates of violent crimes and crimes against property began to skyrocket.[99] For example, there were 6.9 murders per 100,000 people in 1946. By 1962 the number had declined to 4.5 per 100,000. By 1972, the number had climbed to 9.4, the highest it had been since 1936.[100] In 1973, James Wilson reported:

If the murder rate holds constant at today's level, then a child born in 1974 in Detroit and living there all his life has a one in thirty-five chance of being murdered. And if the murder rate continues to increase at its present pace, his chances of meeting a felonious end increase to one in fourteen. At current levels, Barnett points out, a typical baby born and remaining in a large American city is more likely to die of murder than an American soldier in World War II was to die in combat.[101]

Nor was murder the only crime to escalate. In 1946 the robbery rate was 59.4 per 100,000. By 1959 the rate had declined to 51.2. But by 1968 the robbery rate had zoomed to 131 and continued to rise to 225.1 per 100,000 in 1986.[102] Car thefts were at an all-time low in 1949 when 107.7 cars per 100,000 were stolen. By 1960 the rate had increased to 181.6, and it continued to climb. Table 13–2 shows crime rates for selected cities.

TABLE 13–2

Crime Rates by Type, for Selected Cities, 1993[a]

	Violent Crime				Property Crime		
	Murder	Forcible Rape	Robbery	Aggravated Assault	Burglary	Larceny Theft	Motor Vehicle Theft
Baltimore, MD	48.2	91.1	1,689	1,166	2,442	5,655	1,449
Chicago, IL	30.3	n/a	1,262	1,425	1,637	4,350	1,450
Dallas, TX	30.4	95.9	712	905	2,012	5,197	1,675
Detroit, MI	56.8	n/a	1,332	1,274	2,264	4,198	2,751
Indianapolis, IN	8.0	136.9	543	968	2,020	3,808	1,384
Los Angeles, CA	30.5	50.3	1,090	1,204	1,425	3,378	1,695
Memphis, TN	32.0	117.1	867	618	2,474	3,786	2,147
New York, NY	26.5	38.4	1,171	854	1,350	3,200	1,531
Philadelphia, PA	28.1	50.3	739	437	969	2,512	1,525
Phoeniz, AZ	15.2	42.7	331	757	1,984	4,655	1,498
San Antonio, TX	22.3	56.1	302	302	1,813	6,219	1,197
San Diego, CA	11.5	34.1	401	714	1,257	3,262	1,665
San Francisco, CA	17.5	49.0	1,148	600	1,515	4,693	1,501
Washington, D.C.	78.5	56.1	1,230	1,558	1,995	5,444	1,395

[a]Numbers are crimes known to police per 100,000 population as of July 1.

Source: U.S. Bureau of the Census, *Statistical Abstract of the United States 1995,* 115th ed. (Washington D.C.: U.S. Government Printing Office, 1995), 201.

These figures are numbing enough, but it is even more amazing to realize that many crimes are never included in the crime statistics. The differences between reported and actual crime can be estimated by comparing the official crime rates to public opinion polls that ask respondents whether they or members of their families have been victims of a crime. Victimization studies show that official crime rates often underestimate the actual amount of crime.[103] The extent of the inaccuracy is often a function of the type of crime. For instance, car thefts are usually reported for purposes of collecting insurance, so those rates tend to be fairly accurate. Rapes, however, are often not reported or prosecuted because the victims do not want to go through a process that will constantly remind them of an experience they want to forget and because, at least in the past, people in the criminal justice system have tended to blame the victim.

Victimization studies show that some cities keep accurate data on crime rates while others do not. For instance, Minneapolis tends to have an official crime rate that is roughly one-quarter as large as the crime rate reported in surveys. Newark, on the other hand, tends to keep very accurate official records. Thus, when Robert Lineberry and Ira Sharkansky looked at official crime rates, Minneapolis ranked twenty-third out of twenty-six major cities, but, based on survey reports of victimization, Minneapolis had the highest crime rate. Using official crime rates for the same year, Newark ranked third in the amount of crime, but using survey results Newark was twenty-third out of twenty-six.[104]

Crime rates also vary within cities. To maintain the reputable image of certain neighborhoods, cars will be listed as "missing" rather than stolen. Finally, crime rates can vary in some cities over time. There is evidence that crime rates have been manipulated up and down in some cities before elections to help the campaigns of specific candidates.[105]

In some ways the fear of crime is as important as the actual crime rate. As noted above, fear of crime is more widespread than is crime itself.[106] Those who are most fearful are women, urban residents, the elderly, and those with incomes less than $6,000.[107] Interestingly, there is only a weak relationship between having been a victim of a criminal act and the fear of crime.[108] Some evidence, however, shows that indicators of neighborhood deterioration—litter, grafitti, etc.—are related to a fear of crime.[109]

In addition to increases in crimes against property and people, the 1960s and early 1970s were also times of other challenges to public order. Many black urban ghettos erupted in riots. In 1968, following the assassination of civil rights leader Dr. Martin Luther King, stores two blocks from the White House were burned. National Guard troops were stationed in front of the Capitol. To publicize their opposition to America's involvement in Viet Nam, protestors staged various marches and demonstrations. Some of the protests erupted into violence.

People demanded increasing efforts to restore and maintain public order. "Law and order" became an important symbol on the political agenda. Richard Nixon made redressing the balance between the rights of society and the rights of criminals a theme of his 1968 and 1972 presidential campaigns. The issue was the key to the mayoral campaigns in several cities. In Philadelphia, Police Commissioner Frank Rizzo was elected mayor in 1971 primarily on the issue of law and order.

> Crime as an issue in the 1971 campaign was reflective of national concern. However, *candidate* Rizzo, professional policeman, could speak with special expertise and alarm, since major Crime Index offenses in Philadelphia had risen more than 25 percent in a year. Once it was Mayor Rizzo . . . , the mayor's office again stressed the distinction of having the lowest rate of crime in the 10 largest

cities in the United States. Of course, since the local police department is the source of such crime statistics, there had been intimation that the figures were tailored, first to alert the citizenry during the campaign and then to give the mayor an aura of success thereafter.[110]

As noted above, the appeal of the law and order theme for an aspiring politician should be clear. It is impossible to be against law and order in principle. In addition, emphasizing that theme may mean the support of the police. While long removed from direct political involvement, the police have still been vital political forces in several cities. Police cars carrying signs opposing Mayor Carl Stokes of Cleveland may have played a role in his defeat in a re-election bid. Police forces clearly were crucial to the election of Frank Rizzo in Philadelphia and of Charles Stenvig in Minneapolis. Police rallied against Mayor David Dinkins in New York City in 1993.

The problem with relying on the law and order issue is fulfilling promises after the election is over. While there is consensus on the desirability of reducing crime, there is no consensus on how to do it. One position holds that getting at the root causes of crime, which are believed to be racial discrimination, poverty, unemployment, poor education, and a variety of other social ills, is important. Wilson summarized that viewpoint

... if, by any chance, crime was actually increasing, it was the result of a failure to invest enough tax money in federal programs aimed at unemployment and poverty; and third, to the extent crime might occur even after such investments, the proper strategy was to rehabilitate offenders in therapeutic facilities located in the community rather than in prisons.[111]

On the other side are those who believe that crime rises because society is not tough enough on criminals. Wilson has described *that* position as follows:

The conservative position was that crime was destroying American society, but that this could be prevented by 'supporting your local police' (bumper stickers with such sentiments were thoughtfully provided as a low-cost way of implementing that support), impeaching Chief Justice Earl Warren and reversing the Supreme Court rules that were 'handcuffing' the police, appointing a 'get-tough' attorney general, and reviving the death penalty.[112]

In addition to these two extreme positions of attacking poverty or getting tough with criminals, there are other suggestions for dealing with crime. Wilson himself argues that one approach is to "change the risks of robbery and the rewards of alternative sources of income ... " for potential thieves.[113] He suggests trying to decrease teenage unemployment, as teenagers are the most likely to engage in robbery, and to increase the certainty that if caught stealing the culprit will receive a jail sentence. Others have found that the certainty of punishment has a greater deterrent effect on crime than the severity of the sentence.[114] Many states have established mandatory sentencing laws such as California's requirement of life imprisonment after an individual has committed three felonies.

Edward Banfield has argued that crime can be reduced by "raising the costs of crime or by raising the benefits of noncrime."[115] To do this he also suggests attacking the employment problem for youths and increasing the certainty of immediate punishment. In addition, he suggests giving poor youths old cars to lower car thefts and introducing them to activities such as parachute jumping to provide them other sources of excitement besides crime.[116]

Other researchers have argued that police should alter the way they go about deterring crime. One idea is for police to become more visible in the community. Sometimes this means having police frequently drive through a community in marked patrol cars rather than simply responding to calls for assistance. This strategy is referred to as "proactive patrolling." Sometimes this means assigning teams of police to specific neighborhoods with instructions to get to know the people, to investigate and to follow-up on crimes, and even to help people in the community in their contacts with social service agencies. This is referred to as "community policing."[117] One study of community policing in Houston and Newark found positive results.

> Community Policing, as implemented in Houston and Newark, showed some success at responding to neighborhood disorder. All of the programs (particularly those in Houston) involved organizational decentralization, and placed considerable responsibility for problem-solving in the hands of officers on the street. The Community Policing teams in both cities found distinct ways of reaching out for community input and support—through foot patrol, by walking door-to-door, distributing newsletters, holding meetings, allying themselves with local organizations, and opening highly visible and approachable neighborhood offices. In almost every instance, disorder went down and satisfaction with the area and with the police went up.[118]

New York City incorporated some principles of community policing in the reforms it instituted in the 1990s; the result has been a dramatic drop in crime. Indeed, one study concludes that New York's reduction in crime accounts for over 60 percent of the crime reduction nationwide.[119] The city made several changes with the ultimate goal of shifting the focus of police efforts from responding to crime to crime prevention. The police now focus on the kind of crime that signals neighborhood disorder—graffiti, panhandling, drug dealing—based on the belief that they not only breed fear among residents but also accelerate decline and breed more crime.[120]

To implement this new focus, precinct commanders were given more resources and more authority to address situations in the local neighborhoods for which they are responsible.[121]

This approach to reducing crime was first suggested by James Q. Wilson and George Kelling. They argue that crime increases in areas of general disorder, for example, garbage on the street, broken windows, generally unruly people. In such areas, people retreat into their own homes and leave the public area open to criminals. Wilson and Kelling suggested that the police should work with the community to determine what it sees as instances of disorder and attack those problems.[122] Because indicators of disorder contribute to increased fear of crime, attacking neighborhood disorganization should also decrease that fear.

Other observers have argued that police must go on the attack against crime. To do this, they may become more vigilant in arresting prostitutes or drug dealers. They may stake out stores likely to be robbed or perform "street stops" to question suspicious-looking people. Or they may dress as derelicts, old women, or other apparently vulnerable people to lure potential criminals into criminal acts that then result in arrest.

Another suggestion is simply to make it more difficult to commit certain kinds of crimes. Banfield has suggested that citizens and merchants should follow a strategy of "hardening the target." By that he means designing buildings with glass-enclosed outside stairways, eliminating windows on ground floors, installing burglar alarms, using timers to turn on lights, locking doors and windows, and similar actions that would make committing crime more difficult.[123] The evidence is mixed on the effectiveness of these strategies.

Newman proposes another strategy to take back the streets, focusing on such changes in urban design as low-rise public housing to foster control of children, entryways accessible from the street rather than secluded inner courtyards for ease of public surveillance, and semi-public areas to allow neighbors to develop a territorial bond. Through changes in building and spatial configurations, Newman believes citizens and communities can regain control of their environment.[124]

Adoption

At the national level, the War on Poverty was aimed at what Wilson termed the "liberal position": crime is a product of poverty and unemployment. Although the War on Poverty was not defined as a policy to attack crime, many of its programs were aimed at what some saw as the root causes of crime. In the 1960s and 1970s, both the Manpower Development and Training Act and the Comprehensive Employment and Training Act focused on increasing adult employment. The Neighborhood Youth Corps and Job Corps program attacked unemployment among the young. The Head Start program was designed to increase the ability of poor children to achieve in school and therefore to learn skills to help them find employment when they graduated. Head Start also provided breakfasts and hot lunches. If children were well-fed, their attention spans would be longer. They would also be healthier and therefore miss less school. These policies were redistributive because of their efforts to direct social resources to the poor.

Several other federal programs were also aimed at social conditions in poor neighborhoods. Housing programs and neighborhood renewal programs such as Model Cities or the Housing and Community Development Act were intended to provide safe, sanitary, and decent housing for all residents. Some proponents hoped that by having poor people help eliminate blight in their neighborhoods, the despair and hopelessness that could lead to crime would also be eliminated.

In addition to adopting programs to attack poverty as a possible cause of crime, the federal government also adopted a program to respond to the demands of conservatives to support local police. The Omnibus Crime Control and Safe Streets Act of 1968 was designed to help local areas fight crime more effectively. The act created a Law Enforcement Assistance Administration (LEAA) to provide federal assistance to local areas in devising law enforcement systems. In addition, it provided grants to local areas both for developing comprehensive law enforcement plans and for carrying out those plans. Finally, the act also created a National Institute of Law Enforcement and Criminal Justice to encourage research into ways of improving the fight against crime.

While the president and Congress together were devising programs to attack poverty (as a root cause of crime) and to support local police in the 1960s and 1970s, the United States Supreme Court was producing rulings to protect the rights of those suspected or accused of crime. Some of the Court's rulings have been particularly controversial. One of the earliest was the 1961 case of *Mapp v. Ohio* involving the question of the Fourth Amendment guarantee against unreasonable searches and seizures.[125] The Court has ruled that, with few exceptions, prior to making a search, a police officer is required to obtain a search warrant from an officer of the court. That search warrant must be based on the ability of police officers to give specific descriptions of what is to be searched and for what they are searching.[126] The Supreme Court had long ago ruled that any evidence produced by an illegal search would not be admissible as evidence in a *federal* court. This is referred to as the **exclusionary rule**. In 1961, the Court broadened the exclusionary rule by ruling that any illegally obtained evidence could not be used in state courts.

Even more controversial than the extension of the exclusionary rule were decisions concerning the right to counsel. In 1964 in *Escobedo v. Illinois*, the Court ruled that individuals must be given the right to consult a lawyer as soon as they become the prime suspect in a police investigation. As the majority opinion of the Court reads, when "the process shifts from investigatory to accusatory— when its focus is on the accused and its purpose is to elicit a confession—our adversary system begins to operate, and, under the circumstances here, the accused must be permitted to consult with his lawyer."[127]

Police throughout the country were dismayed at the ruling. Two years later, when the Supreme Court *expanded* the *Escobedo* ruling the outcry was bitter. In 1966 in *Miranda v. Arizona,* the Court ruled that *any suspect in custody* has a right to legal counsel.[128] Specifically, the Court required that before questioning an arrested suspect, police must tell the suspect that:

1. The suspect has the right to stay silent.
2. Anything the suspect says may be used against him or her in court.
3. The suspect has the right to have an attorney present before any questioning begins.
4. If the suspect wants an attorney but cannot afford one, an attorney will be provided at no charge.
5. If the arrested suspect agrees to be questioned after being told his or her rights, he or she must reach that decision "knowingly and intelligently" and can shut off the questions at any time.

While the outcry over the Supreme Court's rulings was escalating, many cities were responding to increasing crime rates by spending more money on police. The number of police officers, however, did not drastically change during this period. The number of officers relative to the population increased only marginally.[129] In addition, the increased money did not result in police engaging in different activities. The increased expenditures had little effect on arrests or increasing focus on violent crime on the part of police.[130]

More recently, the federal government again become a major player in the making of policy on crime at the local level. In 1988, presidential candidate George Bush (Republican) benefited from an advertisement showing a criminal circulating through a revolving door, symbolizing the prison furlough program in the home state of his opponent, Democratic Governor Michael Dukakis. In 1992, Democratic candidate Bill Clinton also embraced the crime issue. When elected, he pushed for the passage of legislation that combined elements of both the liberal and conservative approaches to reducing crime.

The 1994 Crime Control Law Enforcement Act included $6.9 billion for crime prevention programs such as after-school sports leagues and job training programs and $8.8 billion for community policing and the hiring of new police officers. It also expanded the death penalty to more than 60 crimes and mandated life imprisonment without parole for those convicted of three violent felonies.[131] Some local law enforcement officials resent what they see as intrusion by the federal government in a policy area that is primarily local. The district attorney of Staten Island, New York, complained: "The problem [of crime] is local, local, local." In his view, the role of the federal government should simply be to provide local governments with money to fight crime as they see fit.[132]

Implementation

At the local level, urban police implement most crime control policies. Citizens tend to think of police as simply having the responsibility to catch and arrest people who break laws. Yet police themselves, and those who study them, agree that law enforcement is only one aspect of the job of the police—and a relatively minor one. The International Association of Chiefs of Police estimates that only about 10 percent of police work is devoted to solving crimes and apprehending criminals.

A more common function is providing various services to the community. Some of this is relatively ad hoc—finding lost children, helping injured people. In some communities the service is part of the organizational mission of the police force. For example, some police departments run programs to get children off the streets and involved in clubs or athletic contests.

A final function of police forces is keeping the peace, or what Wilson calls order maintenance.[133] Stopping a violent fight between a husband and wife or stopping a drunk from picking fights with other patrons at a bar are examples of the peacekeeping function. In such ambiguous circumstances, police, like all street-level bureaucrats, must exercise a substantial amount of discretion to find ways of "handling the situation."[134]

Law enforcement is also complicated by ambiguity. In real life, the police have to define the fuzzy lines that society draws between rights of society and rights of those who are suspected or accused of crime. Many of the suggestions for ways of decreasing crime increase ambiguities. Community policing would make police responsible for general social services. How much time should police spend helping people deal with the social service bureaucracy as opposed to tracking down the cocaine distributor in the area? Expecting the police to address the signs of general disorder in the neighborhood means that the police need to be sensitive to the general neighborhood culture to know what is seen as disorder and what is acceptable behavior. For the police on the street, another set of rights become equally important: the right to protect and defend themselves in a job that constantly has the potential of being dangerous.

While New York's experiment with a version of community policing has been successful, there have been mixed evaulations of the experience in Houston. As reported earlier, a 1990 study reported success. A later study concluded Houston's experience to be a failure. Resistance from police who felt they were

asked to do too much was a major cause. During Houston's experiment, both crime and the fear of crime escalated.[135]

As with all street-level bureaucrats, police have a tremendous amount of discretion in how they do their jobs. While the courts have ruled that police must normally have a warrant to search people or places, the courts have also said that searches can be conducted if they are "incidental" to a legal arrest or if the officer has "probable cause" to believe that a crime is being committed or if the suspect is armed and dangerous. What is "incidental" to a legal arrest? What is "probable cause"?

Equally problematic for the police is the question of what laws should be enforced and how stringent that enforcement should be. The Supreme Court has upheld the right of states to have laws forbidding certain sexual acts, even if the acts are performed in private by consenting adults. Many states have laws forbidding these acts and the Court's decision paves the way for the enforcement of those laws. (See Box 13–3 on page 386.) It is the police, of course, who are charged with the enforcement. How are the police to get evidence to get a search warrant to see if the citizens are engaged in those illegal activities in the privacy of their own homes?

There are many laws that we do not really want enforced fully. Some laws we want enforced only on some people, or in some areas. (There are often different standards of law enforcement used in poor neighborhoods or in African-American or Latino neighborhoods than in wealthy or white neighborhoods.) We never want our own transgressions of the law to be prosecuted. In this highly ambiguous environment, the police have few absolute guidelines to aid them.

As the police wrestle with these problems, little control can be exercised over them. As Herbert Jacob observed:

> Control of the police is perhaps more difficult than for other organizations because most of the patrolman's work is unobserved

BOX 13–3

The Case Of The Peeping Cop

Atlanta Police Officer K.R. Torick issued a summons to Michael Hardwick for drinking in public outside a gay bar on July 5, 1982. Hardwick became confused about when he was supposed to appear in court to answer the complaint. When Hardwick did not appear on schedule, Officer Torick entered Hardwick's apartment without permission or a warrant. Hardwick was not home at the time but upon returning realized he had missed his court appearance. Upon calling the court he was told not to worry because an arrest warrant would not be issued for 48 hours and that he could pay the fine the next morning. Hardwick paid the fine and was assured that no war-

rant would be issued. About three weeks later, Officer Torick appeared again at Hardwick's apartment with an invalid arrest warrant. He entered the apartment and proceeded to Hardwick's bedroom where, it has been reported, the door was ajar and Officer Torick witnessed Hardwick engaging in a sexual act with another man. Hardwick and his companion, DeWitt, were arrested for sodomy under a Georgia statute. Hardwick, along with a married couple, "the Does" filed suit to challenge the constitutionality of the law.

On June 30, 1986, in *Bowers v. Hardwick* 106 S.Ct. 2841, the Supreme Court upheld the law.

Source: Joel D. Joseph, *Black Mondays: Worst Decisions of the Supreme Court* (Bethesda, Maryland: National Press, 1987).

and leaves few traces. He and his partner ride in their patrol car and respond to radio dispatches. No supervisor can observe what they do between radio calls; no supervisor can see what they do when they respond to a call.[136]

This is not always a problem: "In better-off white communities, the police do support the community—they do what the people in power who dominate the community want them to do—and the community, naturally, supports the police."[137] Of course urban areas tend to be heterogeneous, so community values are harder to discover. When police satisfy middle-class white values they often displease minority and lower-class segments of the population. Special racial tensions can arise when white police officers are assigned to minority neighborhoods.

The difficulty of adapting to neighborhood culture can be illustrated by the expectations concerning police control of gang activity. Gangs regularly engage in criminal behavior and gang violence contributes to the sense of danger and random violence that pervades many sections of American cities. But gangs also are a way that neighborhoods try to protect themselves from those they believe would prey on them. That means that many communities are ambivalent about gang activity.

When residents feel they are losing control of their neighborhood to gangs, they will support the authorities' efforts to counteract gang activity. However, if the authorities' efforts make residents feel they are losing control of their community to the authorities, they will criticize the authorities' zealousness and appear to be siding with the gangs.[138]

Police, as most regulators, believe in their own expertise and also feel that they should be insulated from political pressures. They do recognize, though, that their jobs may be easier with limited citizen involvement.

> The task of administering a police agency, especially in a large city, would become all but impossible if detailed operating policies on all aspects of police functioning were subject to approval by numerous citizen groups at the neighborhood level. . . . [But] more direct involvement of citizens may contribute to better policies, to better day-to-day relations with the community, and to increased understanding of police functioning.[139]

The success and acceptance of citizen involvement varies according to place, time, and the nature of the public role. The public has been involved in several ways: crime prevention, regulating discretion, reviewing complaints, and community control. Citizen involvement is seen as most legitimate in the area of crime prevention. The National Advisory Commission on Criminal Justice Standards and Goals recommended that:

> Every police agency should immediately establish programs that encourage members of the public to take an active role in preventing crime, that provide information leading to arrests and conviction of criminal offenders, that facilitate the identification and recovery of stolen property, and increase liaison with private industry in security efforts.[140]

Several jurisdictions have established such programs. Buffalo, New York, established a "Community Radio Watch" in which vehicles equipped with two-way radios report crimes or suspicious activities to the police. Several cities have participated in "Operation Identification" where citizens are educated in crime prevention techniques such as marking their valuables for identification or watching businesses and homes and alerting police to any unusual activity. In the Laurelton neighborhood of Queens, New York, a "Safety Patrol" was established where volunteers ride around the neighborhood and report any problems to police.[141]

These activities are a form of co-production where citizens work with police to provide crime prevention; they have generally been well-received. One crime prevention program that has been less well received by the police is the "Guardian Angels," which operates as a vigilante group. It originated in New York City but has spread to several cities. These groups "patrol" high crime areas to deter crime and to apprehend criminals. One study indicated that while this group had public support, there was also a sense of uneasiness. The police are ambivalent. They split almost 50–50 on support for the Guardian Angels, but they overwhelmingly agree that only the police should fight crime.[142]

A second type of citizen participation is designed to regulate discretion by involving citizens in establishing standard policies and practices. As a result of the unrest in the 1960s, several communities established citizen committees to advise police. The National Crime Commission concluded that: "membership generally includes only those people who agree with the police or otherwise do not cause trouble." David Riley interprets that to mean " . . . businessmen, civic organization leaders, and others whose stake in the community is obvious; it does not mean the very people who should be advising and talking to police, namely the youth and the poor with whom the police have the most contact on the beat."[143] The police are willing to try to serve certain masters in the community but others are not viewed as legitimate.

That attitude colors the police reaction to a third form of civilian involvement—civilian review boards. In the 1960s, the urban riots and political protests were attacks on state authority and the police were often seen as symbols of that state.

The police saw much of the criticism directed at them coming from groups and individuals against whom they were required to take action—alleged criminal offenders and disruptive protesters. They feared that the proposed review mechanisms would be used by these groups to retaliate against them. Officers in agencies which did not engage in the practices most commonly criticized resented the wholesale distrust implied both in the criticism directed at them and in the proposals that were made. They were offended by the notion that their actions would be judged by individuals removed from the situations that confronted them.[144]

A civilian review board established in New York City was disbanded in 1966 after a referendum rejected the concept. This referendum vote was accompanied by a great deal of political activity by the police and had a strong racist undercurrent.[145] In Philadelphia, a civilian review board was established in 1958 and disbanded in 1967 because of lack of mayoral support.[146]

However, some cities do have civilian involvement in complaints against the police. Berkeley, California, has provided citizens with an important institutional role in affecting government decisions. The Berkeley Police Review Commission is composed of nine citizen commissioners appointed by the city council. The Commission reviews police activity and makes recommendations to the council and city manager; it also investigates, holds public hearings, and reports on complaints, although its role is strictly advisory.[147] Rufus Browning, Dale Marshall, and David Tabb note that the establishment of police review boards is more closely related to the degree of power held by African-Americans in the community than any other factor.[148]

The fourth and most expansive citizen involvement comes in proposals for community control of police. The most ambitious program

was the Pilot District Project in Washington, D.C., implemented in the late 1960s and early 1970s. Financed by a $1.4-million grant from the Office of Economic Opportunity and additional money from the Law Enforcement Assistance Administration (LEAA), the plan called for: (1) community advisory committees that represented ghetto residents; (2) decentralized service centers; (3) paid youth patrols made up of ghetto youth; and (4) use of civilians from the project area to perform clerical tasks. The project was fraught with difficulties. Conflict concerning the power to be exercised by the Citizen's Advisory Board was constant. In addition, African-Americans felt that the project was attempting to create a spy network. Whites were suspicious of the project because they feared "ghetto control."[149] It was disbanded after five years.

One study identified four reasons for the program failure: (1) neither the mayor or the police chief forced the police to cooperate with citizens; (2) police received more intensive training than citizens and were paid quite differently—$3.00 per hour for civilians compared to $7.00 per hour for police; (3) stable leadership was lacking; and (4) too much responsibility was given to citizens who lacked administrative and technical skills.[150]

Herman Goldstein mentions a general problem with community control in large cities.

The residents of neighborhoods within large cities would in all probability realize a higher degree of satisfaction if police services were under their direct control, but this might be at the cost of a deterioration in the quality of the service a person traveling through the neighborhood would receive. The challenge in the larger cities is trying to achieve some of the benefits of neighborhood-oriented policing without sacrificing the commitment that the larger jurisdiction must maintain toward providing a high level of services to all citizens moving between areas. . . .[151]

For a variety of reasons, citizen participation, except in crime prevention programs, has had a limited impact. A general reason is the nature of the regulatory function. The regulators expect to make decisions insulated from political pressures and based on technical, professional expertise that the general citizenry lacks. The police enforce community norms that generally represent middle-class and business values. When the middle class came into contact with police as a result of the political activities related to the Viet Nam War, there was a flurry of activity to establish participatory mechanisms. In general, though, serious police contacts tend to be with the lower classes and criminal elements whose inputs are anathema to the typical police officer. With citizen involvement as a limited check on police behavior, much of the behavior will depend on the attitudes of police professionals.

Wilson believes that the police are sensitive to the dominant political culture in a city.[152] He has categorized police behavior into three dominant styles. In the **watchman** style, the police emphasize the function of peacekeeping. In their attempts to maintain order, they often ignore what they consider to be minor offenses, such as certain traffic violations, or handle offenses informally with a warning.[153] Wilson argues this style is most likely to occur in cities led by politicians who appeal to a lower-class and working-class constituency that desires a low-tax, low-service government.[154]

The second style is **legalistic**, in which police emphasize the law enforcement aspect of their jobs. According to Wilson, "A legalistic department will issue traffic tickets at a high rate, detain and arrest a high proportion of juvenile offenders, act vigorously against illicit enterprises, and make a large number of misdemeanor arrests even when, as with petty larceny, the public order has not been breached."[155] This style is most likely to occur in communities with reformed governments and professional city managers.

Finally, in the **service style**, the police intervene frequently (unlike in the watchman style) but are not likely to intervene formally (unlike the legalistic style). This style is most common in homogeneous communities that agree about the importance of maintaining public order but do not demand a legalistic approach. As Wilson says, "In these places, the police see their chief responsibility as protecting a common definition of public order against minor occasional threats posed by unruly teenagers and 'outsiders' (tramps, derelicts, visiting college boys)."[156]

The fact that police styles differ in different communities does not mean, according to Wilson, that the public directly control the police. Rather, the police adapt to the dominant values in their communities.

> . . . The police are in all cases keenly sensitive to their political environment without in all cases being governed by it. By *sensitive* is meant they are alert to, and concerned about, what is said about them publicly, who is in authority over them, how their material and career interests are satisfied, and how complaints about them are handled.[157]

The criminal justice system is part of the political process, and many urban interests spend much time, effort, and money to persuade the police and others to make decisions favorable to them. But Jacob points out that in an adversarial process, a decision beneficial for one interest often hurts another.

> When the police clear a sidewalk on a hot summer night, they do a favor to some residents but the loiterers feel harassed. What is order for one group may be considered oppression by others; what is considered just by one person may be perceived as exploitation by another. Thus, the quest for justice resembles the quest for many other government services. It engenders conflict in which the benefit of one person is often

obtained at the cost of another. Everyone seeks to be a winner, and no one wishes to be among the losers.[158]

Rhetoric about crime and justice is common in party platforms and campaign speeches, but parties and elections are not where decisions about crime and justice are made. Rather, as Jacob points out, the decisions are made as a result of pressure by interest groups. He writes, " . . . interest groups vie for advantageous treatment by currying the favor of the police, by vigorously bargaining in attorneys' offices and court hallways, and by energetically pushing litigation through trial courts to appellate tribunals."[159]

In addition to the environmental pressures placed on the police, much attention has been paid to the impact of personality on the role of the police professional. Some have argued that those who choose to become police officers possess an authoritarian personality.[160] Individuals with authoritarian personalities have several identifying characteristics, such as a rigid adherence to conventional values and a strong opposition to anything that appears to differ from those values. They are cynical about other people and about the condition of the world. They tend to be superstitious, to employ stereotypes when thinking of people, and to think about the world in terms of a simplistic confrontation of good versus evil. Finally, they tend to be aggressive.[161]

While agreeing that police often do exhibit characteristics similar to those of authoritarian people, Arthur Niederhoffer argues that it is not because authoritarians are likely to join the police forces. Rather, he argues that the conditions police encounter on the job predispose them to develop these characteristics.[162] By the nature of their job, police come into contact with people who would hardly inspire an optimistic view of human nature. Even people who would normally be considered respectable are often not at their best when dealing with police. Of course, those citizens who encounter police with authoritarian attitudes may not be particularly concerned with what causes the police to behave as they do.

Police do tend to rely on stereotypes. When attempting to determine how to allocate their time and attention in controlling crime, police need to develop cues to help them predict how others will behave. They focus on the young, the "different," the African-American, the Latino. Over time, many police begin to see themselves as poorly paid, unvalued defenders of "good" against an evil world.

What makes this tendency of police to exhibit authoritarian characteristics most serious is that, "The system places the most authoritarian men where they have the most opportunity to demonstrate authoritarianism."[163] This occurrence is due to several factors at work in the process of assigning police. For one, people with higher educational levels tend to be less authoritarian, but they also tend to do better on promotion tests and are moved off the street quickly. In addition, police administrators will send the "toughest" cops into the toughest areas, where they are given freer rein to use force. Finally, those police officers who are less comfortable with being aggressive and using force may seek assignment in areas where those attributes are less necessary. They may seek assignments where they devote most of their time to service rather than to law enforcement or order maintenance. This means that the most aggressive, cynical police are left on the streets to deal with people. Those police are the ones who are likely to be least tolerant of the ambiguities involved in law enforcement and order maintenance.

If the ambiguities of the job are frustrating to police, so is the fact that they are only one component of the criminal justice system. The police are charged only with apprehending criminals. Those accused of crime are then turned over to others; the police have minimal control over what happens next. Defense lawyers will try to find ways of clearing the accused. Prosecuting attorneys will often be willing to compromise on charges against the accused in the interest of moving the case out of an already overcrowded court. This process of defense and prosecuting lawyers cooperating to clear the case quickly is referred to as **plea bargaining**. Usually, defendants are convinced to plead guilty to a lesser charge, therefore receiving a lesser penalty than if they were tried and found guilty of the offense for which they were arrested. Once the defendant agrees to plead guilty to some crime, a trial is not necessary.

Bureau of Justice statistics for 1979 indicate that 45 out of 100 felony arrests ended in guilty pleas. Five additional cases were brought to trial with 4 being found guilty and 1 acquitted. The remaining 50 cases were dropped or dismissed.[164] Hence, half the people arrested walked away without a trial. Ninety percent of the others pleaded guilty, often to lesser charges. Eighty percent of the small group brought to trial were convicted. Imagine how frustrated police would become when they see people whom they had arrested for a serious crime getting off completely or with a lesser penalty.

Even if a case goes to court, there is no guarantee the police will believe justice has been done. Juries can hand down what police see as illogical verdicts. Judges have leeway in sentencing, and the sentencing often reflects a bias for or against certain people. For example, one study found that African-Americans were more likely than whites to be sentenced to prison in state larceny cases and that juveniles and women are likely to receive lighter sentences than men or older people.[165]

In general, the whole criminal justice system leaves a great amount of room for discretion—from the actions of the cop on the beat to the sentence of the presiding judge. This discretion means that justice is affected by the dominant values in the city and by the power of the contending interests. Table 13–3 shows that the degree of plea bargaining varies considerably between jurisdictions. Those jurisdictions with low proportions of guilty pleas are more selective in screening arrests, less likely to reduce serious charges, and more likely to impose stiff sentences.[166]

Evaluation

Crime rates are declining, as reported above. It is not clear that crime control efforts are the cause of the decline. Many observers believe

---

TABLE 13–3

Prevalence of Plea Bargaining in Selected Cities

City	Percent of Plea Bargains to Trial	City	Percent of Plea Bargains to Trial
Geneva, IL	97%	Lansing, MI	88%
Manhattan, NY	96%	Tallahassee, FL	86%
Littleton, CO	95%	Washington, D.C.	80%
Golden, CO	94%	New Orleans, LA	75%
Colorado Springs, CO	92%	Portland, OR	75%
St. Louis, MO	90%		
Salt Lake City, UT	89%	**Mean**	92%

Source: Calculated from U.S. Department of Justice, "The Prevalence of Guilty Pleas," *Bureau of Justice Statistics Special Report* (December, 1984).

that crime may be due more to social and demographic conditions or to individual psychology than to any procedure of police or courts.[167] Others, reviewing the success New York City has had with its reform of police practices, have concluded that police practices can make a difference.[168] But much about crime is unknown. While crimes are committed disproportionately by young males in poorer sections of urban areas, clearly not all young males in those areas become criminals. Why some become criminals and some do not is not known. And, of course, many who are not young, urban, or male also commit crimes. As Wilson concludes, "some persons will shun crime even if we do nothing to deter them, while others will seek it out even if we do everything to reform them."[169]

Despite the overall decrease in crime, urban dwellers still are reminded daily of the danger of their environment. The media duly report the day's most spectacular transgressions. The physical environment often is scarred with graffiti indicating the turf of the dominant gang in the area. Innocent people are often caught in the gunfire of rival gangs. Regardless of the continuing decline in crime rates, crime remains a potent political issue. Both parties want to be seen as being tough on crime.

Conclusion

Both education and crime control are crucial policy areas for urban residents. Schools are related to individual success and advancement because they provide children with the skills necessary to get jobs and to excel. So important is education that parents will often decide where to live based on the quality of schools. Therefore, schools have contributed to white flight from the center cities. Schools are also charged with transmitting the values that are believed to be crucial for maintaining

our civilization. Controlling crime is also essential for the maintenance of a civilized society. No policy area intrudes so totally on urban residents' lives than the concern for minimizing crimes against persons. Both education and crime control have implications for major economic interests as well. Businesses want a safe environment and an educated work force.

Education and crime control are connected. The failure of the educational system contributes to the burdens of the criminal justice system. Kozol cites statistics from the New York Department of Corrections indicating that 90 percent of the male inmates in the city's jails are school dropouts.[170]

While these education and crime control policies are important to citizens and to major economic interests, control of either is limited by the street-level bureaucrats, who rightfully view themselves as experts and professionals. Teachers and police resist the oversight of their actions by the general public who are seen as lacking the knowledge to produce meaningful input. In general, attempts to establish community control of schools or police forces have failed.

Indirectly, both the school and the police try to remain sensitive to the dominant values of the community, but that task is harder in the heterogeneity of the metropolis than in more homogeneous communities. What constitutes a quality education is conceptualized differently by parents who want their children to be prepared to go to college as opposed to those parents who want their children to be able to find a job. Similarly, what constitutes the "peace" that police officers are to enforce differs among people from different cultural and class origins.

The street-level bureaucrats' jobs produce stress. Often, they cope in ways that erect barriers between the bureaucrats and their "clients," who are the citizens whom they are to serve and with whom they must deal constantly. The discretion necessary on the job prevents supervisors from controlling these coping mechanisms.

At times issues in these areas do elicit widespread citizen concern. Worries about the quality of American education in the 1950s and 1960s and fears about the rising crime rates in the 1960s and 1970s resulted in national attention being given to both education and crime control. Policies were enacted and money was appropriated, but bureaucrats' control in these areas was not substantially altered.

Efforts are likely to continue to increase the effect of citizens on policies in crime control and education. As business continues to face global competition, more major economic interests may feel it is important to address these quality-of-life issues to ensure a qualified pool of potential employees and a safe environment. Business interests have been involved in these policies in some places. For example, major economic interests have played a major role in education policy in Charlotte, North Carolina.[171] But their control in these areas is not as universal as it is in the developmental policies discussed in Chapter 12.

One reason why economic interests may have an incentive to become more involved in the future is that these policy areas are related to questions of development. Referring to proposals for economic revitalization in a depressed area of New York City, Andrew Cuomo, the Secretary of Housing and Urban Development, observed:

It's misleading to say, once IBM moves to the South Bronx everything's going to be rosy. One, IBM isn't going to the South Bronx, because the other cost of doing business outweighs the tax incentives. Also, if IBM did show up, the people in the zone aren't in a position to show up. They need training, and services like day care—a comprehensive strategy.[172]

Crime would contribute to the costs of doing business in an area such as the South Bronx and the poor quality of the schools in the area is a reason why the citizens would not be qualified for jobs in a high-tech company such as IBM. In the future, major economic interests that want urban revitalization may push to include the issues of education and crime control on the local agenda more frequently. One study of Detroit did find the core of a governing coalition devoted to "human capital," that is helping residents develop to their full capacity, rather than on the development of the downtown.[173] If the governing coalition did focus on these quality-of-life issues, the dominance of the professional bureaucrats would likely decrease.

Notes

1. Nicholas Lemann, *The Promised Land: The Great Black Migration and How It Changed America* (New York: Vintage Books, 1991), 200.

2. U.S. Department of Justice, Bureau of Justice Statistics, *Crime and the Nation's Households, 1992* (Washington, D.C.: Department of Justice, Office of Justice Programs, 1993).

3. James Q. Wilson, *Thinking About Crime*, rev. ed. (New York: Vintage Books, 1985), 5.

4. Paul E. Peterson, "Urban Politics and Changing Schools: A Competitive View" in *Schools in Cities: Consensus and Conflict in American Educational History*, ed. Ronald K. Goodnow and Diane Revitch (New York: Holmes and Meier, 1983), 229.

5. Clarence N. Stone, "The Politics of Urban School Reform: Civic Capacity, Social Capital, and the Intergroup Context." Paper presented at the Annual Meeting of the American Political Science Association, San Francisco, California, August 29–September 1, 1996, Appendix B, 12.

6. Stephen Samuel Smith, "Hugh Governs? Regime and Education Policy in Charlotte, North Carolina," *Journal of Urban Affairs* 19 (1997): 247–274.

7. Jonathan Kozol, *Savage Inequalities: Children in America's Schools* (New York: Harper Perennial, 1991), 80.

8. Ibid., 75.

9. Clarke E. Cochran, Lawrence C. Mayer, T. R. Carr, and N. Joseph Cayer, *American Public Policy: An Introduction*, 2nd ed. (New York: St. Martin's Press, 1986), 265.

10. Ibid., 264.

11. Peterson, "Urban Politics and Changing Schools," 223.

12. Colin Greer, *The Great School Legend* (New York: Penguin, 1977), 74.

13. Peterson, "Urban Politics and Changing Schools," 232.

14. Gary A. Ferguson, "Searching for Consensus in Education Reform," *Public Perspective* 8 (June–July 1997): 49.

15. Edward Morgan, "Technocratic vs. Democratic Options for Educational Policy," *Policy Studies Review* 3 (1984): 263–278.

16. Robert Weissberg, *Political Learning, Political Choice and Democratic Citizenship* (Englewood Cliffs, New Jersey: Prentice-Hall, 1974), 30.

17. Tim Mead made this comment in correspondence with authors.

18. Maxine Seller, *To Seek America: A History of Ethnic Life in the United States* (Englewood, New Jersey: Jerome B. Ozer, 1977), 251.

19. Peter Binzen, *Whitetown USA* (New York: Vintage Books, 1970), 31, 104–105.

20. Paul E. Peterson, *City Limits* (Chicago: University of Chicago Press, 1981), Chapter 5, especially 94–99.

21. Douglas G. Glasgow, *The Black Underclass: Poverty, Unemployment, and Entrapment of Ghetto Youth* (San Francisco: Jossey-Bass, 1980), 60.

22. *San Antonio Independent School District et al. v. Rodriguez,* 411 U.S. 1 (1973).

23. V.O. Key, *Public Opinion and American Democracy* (New York: Knopf, 1967), 88.

24. Donald R. Matthews and James W. Prothro, "Stateways vs. Folkways: Critical Factors in Southern Reactions to *Brown v. Board of Education*" in *Essays on the American Constitution,* ed. G. Dietze (Englewood Cliffs, New Jersey: Prentice-Hall, 1964), 144.

25. L. Harmon Ziegler, M. Kent Jennings, with G. Wayne Peak, *Governing American Schools: Political Interaction in Local School Districts* (N. Scituate, Massachusetts: Duxbury, 1974), 39–42.

26. Hans Johnson, "School Board Crusade," *Church and State* 48 (July–August, 1995): 9; Rob Boston, "Failed Crusade," *Church and State* 47 (November 1994): 9; John B. Judis, "Into the Wilderness," *The New Republic* 213 (October 2, 1995): 4.

27. See Luis Ricardo Fraga, Kenneth J. Meier, and Robert E. England, "Hispanic Americans and Educational Policy: Limits to Equal Access," *The Journal of Politics* 48 (November 1986): 850–876; Kenneth J. Meier and Robert E. England, "Black Representation and Educational Policy: Are They Related?" *American Political Science Review* 78 (1984): 392–403.

28. Kenneth J. Meier, Joseph Stewart, Jr., and Robert E. England, *Race, Class, and Education: The Politics of Second-Generation Discrimination* (Madison: University of Wisconsin Press, 1989), 5–6.

29. Ibid., 142.

30. William L. Boyd, "School Board–Administrative Staff Relationships" in *Understanding School Boards: Problems and Prospects,* ed. Peter J. Cistone (Lexington, Massachusetts: D.C. Heath, 1976), 104.

31. Rene Sanchez, "A Battle Cry on Education," *Washington Post National Weekly Edition,* May 19, 1997.

32. Ziegler and Jennings, *Governing American Schools,* Part III.

33. Leslie W. Kindred, Don Bagin, and Donald R. Gallagher, *School and Community Relations,* 3rd ed. (Englewood Cliffs, New Jersey: Prentice-Hall, 1984), 143.

34. James Koerner, *Who Controls American Education?* (Boston: Beacon, 1968), 26.

35. Maurice Berube and Marilyn Gittell, eds., *Confrontation at Ocean Hill–Brownsville: The New York School Strikes of 1968* (New York: Praeger, 1969), 4.

36. Frederick M. Wirt and Michael W. Kirst, *Schools in Conflict* (Berkeley, California: McCutchan, 1982), 150–151.

37. Susan M. Johnson, "Teacher Unions in Schools: Authority and Accommodation," *Harvard Educational Review* 53 (1983): 309–326; and Kozol, *Savage Inequalities.*

38. Peterson, *City Limits,* Chapter 5.

39. Wirt and Kirst, *Schools in Conflict,* 151.

40. Michael Harrington, *The Other America: Poverty in the United States* (Baltimore: Penguin, 1962).

41. Cochran, et al., *American Public Policy,* 270.

42. Bob Woodward and Scott Armstrong, *The Brethren: Inside the Supreme Court* (New York: Avon Books, 1979), 107–128.

43. *Swann v. Charlotte–Mecklenburg Board of Education,* 402 U.S. 1 (1971).

44. *Bradley v. State Board of Education of the Commonwealth of Virginia,* 411 U.S. 913.

45. *Milliken v. Bradley,* 418 U.S. 717 (1974).

46. Christine H. Rossell, "School Desegregation and White Flight," *Political Science Quarterly* 90 (Winter 1975–76): 688.

47. Paul Peterson, *School Politics: Chicago Style* (Chicago: University of Chicago Press, 1976), 175.

48. *Riddick v. School Board of City of Norfolk,* 784 F. 2nd 521 (4th Cir. 1986), cert. denied 107 S. Ct. 420 (1986). The Fifth Circuit upheld the right of Austin, Texas, to end mandatory busing (*Overton v. Austin Independent School District,* 87–1576) but the Tenth Circuit ruled that before Oklahoma City could discontinue mandatory busing it would have to prove that discrimination would not be revived (*Dowell v. Board of Education of Oklahoma City Public Schools,* 795 F. 2d 1516 [1986], cert. denied 107 S. Ct. 420 [1986]). By refusing certiorari the U.S. Supreme Court has let contradictory decisions stand, hence the matter of mandatory busing is not settled.

49. U.S. Department of Commerce, *1992 Census of Governments: Government Finances, Public Education* GC92(4)-1 (Washington, D.C.: U.S. Government Printing Office, 1995), 24.

50. Tim Mead in comments to the authors.

51. Kozol, *Savage Inequalities,* 168–169.

52. Ibid., 169.

53. *Abbott v. Burke,* 119 N.J. 287 (1990).

54. *Serrano v. Priest,* 96 California Reporter 601 (1971).

55. *San Antonio Independent School District et al. v. Rodriguez,* 411 U.S. 1 (1973).

56. *Hobson v. Hansen,* 269 F. Supp. 401, 517 (1969).

57. Kozol, *Savage Inequalities,* 98.

58. Ibid., 99.

59. James E. Anderson, David W. Brady, Charles S. Bullock III, and Joseph Stewart, Jr., *Public Policy and Politics in America,* 2nd ed. (Monterey, California: Brooks/Cole, 1984), 207.

60. Margaret Sims, "Public Schools: Chance or Choice?," *Black Enterprise* 23 (May 1993): 49.

61. Berube and Gittell, *Confrontation at Ocean Hill–Brownsville,* 14.

62. Ibid., 14–15.

63. Joseph F. Zimmerman, *Participatory Democracy: Populism Revisited* (New York: Praeger, 1986), 154.

64. James S. Coleman, *Equality of Educational Opportunity* (Washington, D.C.: U.S. Government Printing Office, 1966).

65. William Ryan, *Blaming the Victim* (New York: Pantheon, 1971), 46–47.

66. Kozol, *Savage Inequalities,* passim.

67. Response of Secretary William Bennett, *Chicago Tribune,* March 24, 1988, quoted in Kozol, *Savage Inequalities,* 78.

68. Ibid., 53.

69. John E. Chubb and Terry M. Moe, *Politics, Markets and America's Schools* (Washington, D.C.: The Brookings Institution, 1990), 8.

70. Ibid., 9.

71. National Commission on Excellence in Education, *A Nation At Risk: The Imperatives for Educational Reform* (Washington, D.C.: U.S. Government Printing Office, 1983), 5.

72. Janet Hook, "Hill Boosted School Spending: Several Reagan Cuts Reversed," *Congressional Quarterly Weekly Report* 42 (1984): 2991–2997.

73. Jeffrey L. Katz, "Goals 2000 Under Siege Again in House Labor-HHS Bill," *Congressional Quarterly* 54 (August 10, 1996): 2253–2254.

74. Joel F. Handler, *Down from Bureaucracy: The Ambiguity of Privatization and Empowerment* (Princeton: Princeton University Press, 1996), 199–209.

75. Valerie Martinez, R. Kenneth Godwin, Frank R. Kemerer, and Laura Perna, "The Consequences of School Choice: Who Leaves and Who Stays in the Inner City," *Social Science Quarterly* 76 (September 1995): 487.

76. Kozol, *Savage Inequalities,* 59.

77. Ibid., 61.

78. Ibid., 60–61.

79. Chubb and Moe, *Politics, Markets, and America's Schools,* 219–224.

80. Daniel McGroarty, "Education's Long March: The Choice Revolution Shifts to the States," *Policy Review* (Summer 1994): 53.

81. Ibid.

82. Garland Thompson, "School Dropouts: Despite Progress, Minority Rates Still Exceed Whites," *Black Issues in Higher Education* 12 (June 15, 1995): 24.

83. Wilbur Rich, *Black Mayors and School Politics: The Failure of Reform in Detroit, Gary, and Newark* (New York: Garland, 1996), 197–198.

84. Herbert Jacob, *Urban Justice: Law and Order in American Cities* (Englewood Cliffs, New Jersey: Prentice-Hall, 1973), 23.

85. Ibid.

86. Ibid.

87. Herbert Jacob, "Policy Responses to Crime" in *The New Urban Reality,* ed. Paul E. Peterson (Washington, D.C.: The Brookings Institution, 1985), 228–230.

88. Jon Marcus, "Cities See Fewer Murders in '96," *Grand Forks Herald,* January 1, 1997, sec. A.

89. Rebecca Carr, "A Debate over Punishment and Prevention," *Congressional Quarterly* 54 (October 5, 1996): 2810.

90. Terance D. Miethe, "Fear and Withdrawal from Urban Life" in *Reactions to Crime and Violence,* ed. Wesley Skogan (Thousand Oaks, California: Sage, 1995), 18.

91. Ibid.

92. Arthur J. Vidich and Joseph Bensman, *Small Town in Mass Society: Class, Power, and Religion in a Rural Community* (Garden City, New York: Doubleday, 1960), 39; Jacob, *Urban Justice,* 139.

93. Oscar Newman, *Defensible Space* (New York: Macmillan, 1972), 14–15.

94. For histories of urban police forces in the United States, see James F. Richardson, *Urban Police in the United States* (Port Washington, New York: National University Publications, 1974); and William J. Boop and Donald O. Schultz, *A Short History of American Law Enforcement* (Springfield, Illinois: Charles C. Thomas, 1972).

95. Stuart A. Scheingold, "Politics, Public Policy, and Street Crime" in *Reactions to Crime and Violence,* ed. Wesley Skogan, 164.

96. Ibid.

97. Ibid.

98. Jeffrey D. Alderman, "Leading the Public: The Media's Focus on Crime Shaped Sentiment," *Public Perspective* 5 (March–April 1994): 26; Vincent F. Sacco, "Media Constructions of Crime" in *Reactions to Crime and Violence,* ed. Skogan, 141–154.

99. Ted Robert Gurr, "Crime Trends in Modern Democracies Since 1945," *International Annals of Criminology* 16 (1977): 41–85; *Crime in City Politics,* ed. Anne Heinz, Herbert Jacob, and Robert L. Lineberry (New York: Longman, 1983), 5.

100. James Q. Wilson, *Thinking About Crime* (New York: Vintage Books, 1977), 6.

101. Ibid., 19.

102. *Crime in the United States* (Washington, D.C.: U.S. Department of Justice, 1986), 16.

103. Richard W. Dodge, Harold Lentzner, and Frederick Shenk, "Crime in the United States: A Report on the National Crime Survey" in *Sample Surveys of the Victims of Crime,* ed. Wesley G. Skogan (Cambridge, Massachusetts: Ballinger, 1976).

104. Robert L. Lineberry and Ira Sharkansky, *Urban Politics and Public Policy*, 3rd. ed. (New York: Harper & Row, 1978), 282. More recent data are not available as the Federal Victimization Survey is no longer broken down by city.

105. Heinz, et al., *Crime in City Politics*, 15.

106. Wesley G. Skogan and Michael G. Maxfield, *Coping with Crime* (Beverly Hills, California: Sage, 1981), 60–63.

107. Terance D. Miethe, "Fear and Withdrawal from Urban Life" in *Reactions to Crime and Violence*, ed. Skogan, 19.

108. Ibid., 19–20.

109. Ibid., 21. See also Wesley G. Skogan, *Disorder and Decline: Crime and Spiral of Decay in American Neighborhoods* (Berkeley: University of California Press, 1990).

110. Peter C. Buffum and Rita Sagi, "Philadelphia: Politics of Reform and Retreat" in *Crime in City Politics*, ed. Anne Heinz, et al., 132.

111. James Q. Wilson, *Thinking About Crime*, rev. ed. (New York: Vintage Books, 1985), 3.

112. Ibid.

113. James Q. Wilson, *Thinking About Crime*, 1st ed., (New York: Basic Books, 1975), 199.

114. Gordon Tullock, "The Deterrence of Crime," *The Public Interest* (Summer 1974): 103–111.

115. Edward C. Banfield, *The Unheavenly City Revisited* (Boston: Little, Brown, 1974), 196.

116. Our thanks to Timothy D. Mead for pointing out that there would be interesting legal questions raised if a youth were killed in a jump taken at the urging of the mayor!

117. Wilson, *Thinking About Crime*, 1st ed., Chapter 5.

118. Wesley G. Skogan, *Disorder and Decline*, 162–163.

119. Eli B. Silverman, "Crime in New York: A Success Story," *The Public Perspective* 8 (June–July 1997): 3.

120. Ibid., 4.

121. Ibid.

122. James Q. Wilson and George Kelling, "Broken Windows," *The Atlantic Monthly* (March 1982): 29–38.

123. Banfield, *The Unheavenly City Revisited*, 204.

124. Newman, *Defensible Space*, 204 and passim.

125. *Mapp* v. *Ohio*, 367 U.S. 643 (1961).

126. For a review of cases in this area, see Henry J. Abraham, *Freedom and the Court: Civil Rights and Liberties in the United States*, 4th ed. (New York: Oxford University Press, 1982), 137–138.

127. *Escobedo* v. *Illinois*, 387 U.S. 478 (1964).

128. *Miranda* v. *Arizona*, 384 U.S. 436 (1966).

129. Heinz, et al., *Crime in City Politics*, 13–14.

130. Ibid., 15.

131. *Congressional Quarterly* 52 (August 27, 1994): 2503; Carr, "A Debate over Punishment and Prevention," 2811.

132. Carr, "A Debate over Punishment and Prevention," 2811.

133. James Q. Wilson, *Varieties of Police Behavior* (Cambridge, Massachusetts: Harvard University Press, 1968), 18.

134. Ibid., 31.

135. Mike Dorning, "Community-based Policing: Houston's Community Policing Program Is an Example of an Approach that Didn't Work," *Grand Forks Herald*, March 6, 1994, sec. A.

136. Jacob, *Urban Justice*, 27.

137. David P. Riley, "Should Communities Control Their Police?" in *Policing America*, ed. Anthony Platt and Lynn Cooper (Englewood Cliffs, New Jersey: Prentice-Hall, 1974), 195.

138. Martin Sanchez Jankowski, *Islands in the Street: Gangs and American Urban Society* (Berkeley: University of California Press, 1991), 318.

139. Herman Goldstein, *Policing a Free Society* (Cambridge, Massachusetts: Ballinger, 1977), 121.

140. National Advisory Commission on Criminal Justice Standards and Goals, *Police* (Washington, D.C.: U.S. Government Printing Office, 1973), 66.

141. Thomas A. Johnson, Gordon E. Misner, and Lee P. Brown, *The Police and Society: An Environment for Collaboration and Confrontation* (Englewood Cliffs, New Jersey: Prentice-Hall, 1981), 47.

142. Brian B. Ostrowe and Rosanne DiBiase, "Citizen Involvement as a Crime Deterrent: A Study of Public Attitudes Toward an Unsanctioned Civilian Patrol Group," *Journal of Police Science and Administration* 11 (June 1983): 185–193.

143. Riley, "Should Communities Control Their Police?," 193.

144. Goldstein, *Policing a Free Society*, 158.

145. David W. Abbott, Louis H. Gold, and Edward T. Rogowsky, *Police, Politics and Race* (New York: American Jewish Committee, 1969).

146. Richard J. Terrill, "Complaint Procedures: Variations on the Theme of Citizen Participation," *Journal of Police Science and Administration* 10 (December 1982): 401.

147. Ibid., 403–404.

148. Rufus P. Browning, Dale Rogers Marshall, and David H. Tabb, *Protest Is Not Enough: The Struggle of Blacks and Hispanics for Equality in Urban Politics* (Berkeley: University of California Press, 1984), 154.

149. Johnson, et al., *The Police and Society*, 277.

150. Ibid., 278.

151. Goldstein, *Policing a Free Society*, 148.

152. Wilson, *Varieties of Police Behavior*, 230.

153. Ibid., 140.

154. Ibid., 236–237.

155. Ibid., 172.

156. Ibid., 200.

157. Ibid., 230.

158. Jacob, *Urban Justice*, 3.

159. Ibid.

160. David Rapaport, *Diagnostic Psychological Testing*, vol. 1 (Chicago: Yearbook Publishers, 1949), 29, cited in Arthur Niederhoffer, *Behind the Shield: The Police in Urban Society* (Garden City, New York: Anchor Books, 1967), 109–110.

161. T. W. Adorno, Else Frenkel-Brunswik, Daniel J. Levinson, and R. Nevitt Sanford, *The Authoritarian Personality* (New York: Harper, 1950).

162. Niederhoffer, *Behind the Shield,* 138.

163. Ibid., 137.

164. U.S. Department of Justice, "The Prevalence of Guilty Pleas," *Bureau of Justice Statistics Special Report,* (December 1984): 1.

165. Stuart S. Nagel, "Tipped Scales of American Justice," *Transaction* (May–June, 1966), 3–9.

166. U.S. Department of Justice, "The Prevalence of Guilty Pleas," 4.

167. M. Gottfredson and T. Hirschi, *A General Theory of Crime* (Stanford, California: Stanford University Press, 1990), 270.

168. Silverman, "Crime in New York," 5.

169. Wilson, *Thinking About Crime,* 1st ed., 235.

170. Kozol, *Savage Inequalities,* 118.

171. Smith, "Hugh Governs?," 247–274.

172. Nicholas Lemann, "The Myth of Community Development," *New York Times Magazine,* January 9, 1994.

173. Marion E. Orr and Gerry Stoker, "Urban Regimes and Leadership in Detroit," *Urban Affairs Quarterly* 30 (September 1994): 48–73.

CHAPTER 14

Redistributive Policy

Welfare and Housing

Although the Bible warns us that "the poor ye shall have always with ye," Americans in the twentieth century find it hard to understand how poverty can exist in the midst of affluence. This chapter examines the policies that have been designed to address the problems of poverty. Such policies are often referred to as redistributive because it is assumed that their purpose is to take from the haves to give to the have-nots.

In fact, few of these policies actually redistribute much from rich to poor. Opposition from many citizens to the idea of redistributing resources means that policies that may initially be designed as redistributive are often transformed to distribute benefits for many groups in the process of securing adoption. Some observers even argue that such policies may be aimed as much at silencing or even regulating the poor as at finding solutions to the problem of poverty.[1]

Poverty is not uniquely an urban phenomenon, but nowhere does the contrast between the rich and the poor appear so stark as in cities where both exist so close together. In addition, the characteristics of urban living make the problems of poverty especially acute. In small towns, poverty may be understood as a result of hardships beyond the con-trol of individuals. The impersonality of the city, however, makes it easier to "blame an anonymous victim" of poverty. There is less likely to be personal empathy or a feeling that there but for fortune go I.

Interdependence in the city also makes more likely the conditions of squalor that will affect everyone. The sharp contrasts between rich and poor make urban poverty much more visible and, in this sense, much more uncomfortable—not only to the poverty population itself but to others who must observe and confront these inequities.

Table 14–1 (on page 400), which provides a breakdown of the poverty population, shows that poverty has increased in the metropolitan areas since 1987 while declining in rural areas. One in 5 persons in the center city compared to 1 in 10 people in the suburbs are below the poverty line.

The poverty line was set at an income less than $15,029 for a family of four in 1994. In that year, O'Hare found that about two-thirds of the poor are white, but are only 11 percent of the white population. About one-third (31 percent) of the African-American and Latino populations are classified as poor. Of those living in female-headed households, 39 percent are below the poverty line. The young are disproportionately likely to be poor. More than 1 in 5 (22 percent) under the age of 18 are poor, compared to 12 percent for those over 18. The percentage of elderly who are poor has declined from 15.3 percent in 1981 to 12 percent in 1994, the same percentage as in the 18-to-64 age range.[2]

Despite the acuteness of the problem of urban poverty, local governments are seriously constrained in finding solutions. The fiscal limitation caused by changes in the job structure, the dual migration of the haves to the suburbs and the have-nots to the inner city, and metropolitan fragmentation that limits the scope and effectiveness of city taxes

have made it impossible for cities alone to meet the needs of the underclass. Local governments are also constrained because the more resources they divert to redistributive problems, the less attractive the city becomes to the middle and upper classes and to large corporations on which the city depends for economic health.[3] Accordingly, many programs addressing poverty result from federal incentives.

Since the Great Depression, the federal government has accepted the responsibility of providing a "safety net" to help the urban poor. Many federal programs were adopted in the 1930s and 1960s as a result of large Democratic

TABLE 14–1

Distribution of Poverty in America

| | Percentage of Poverty Population by Selected Groups | | Percentage of Group below Poverty Line | |
	1987	1992	1987	1992
	%	%	%	%
Race				
White	65.8	66.5	10.4	11.6
Black	29.5	28.8	32.4	33.3
Hispanic	16.8	18.0	28.0	29.3
Family Status				
Female-headed, no husband present	52.2	52.4	34.2	34.9
Male-headed, with or without wife present	47.8	47.6	12.0	15.6
Age				
Under 18	39.9	39.6	20.3	21.9
Over 65	11.1	10.8	12.5	12.9
Place of Residence				
Metropolitan area	72.0	74.2	12.5	13.9
Central city	42.7	42.4	18.6	20.5
Outside metropolitan area	28.0	25.8	16.9	16.8

Source: U.S. Bureau of the Census, Current Population Reports, *Poverty in the United States: 1987* (Washington, D.C.: U.S. Government Printing Office, 1989), 22, 24, 27; U.S. Bureau of the Census, Current Population Reports, *Poverty in the United States: 1992* (Washington, D.C.: U.S. Government Printing Office, 1993), 2–4, 6, 39–42.

majorities in Congress and strong executive support. Extensive redistributive policy was implemented during the Great Depression, when President Franklin D. Roosevelt took a strong leadership role, aided by the economic crisis that made such policy seem more legitimate to many Americans. In the 1960s, another skillful president, Lyndon Johnson, declared War on Poverty. Democratic political leaders pushed for such policies as a way of trying to build their national electoral coalition by capturing the votes of urban residents.[4] The movement of population out of the center cities to the suburbs and beyond decreased the constituency for national initiatives in redistributive policy. In 1997, only one of six districts in the House of Representatives is urban. Even Democratic presidential candidates have to take policy stands appealing to people outside major urban areas.[5]

Federal dollars have certainly helped the financially strapped local governments to feed, clothe, and house the poor, but there have also been costs. Dependence on federal funding limits the freedom of action for local governments because the standards and policies are set in Washington, D.C. These programs have also caused local bureaucracies to burgeon. Local citizens can have great difficulty influencing these programs because decisions are made from afar and implemented by nonelected experts.

Perhaps more seriously, the impact of many War on Poverty programs increased the level of conflict in many American cities. The conflict, in turn, increased the movement of investment capital outside the city to the suburbs[6] and resulted in a backlash that led, in the 1980s, to a federal retrenchment in efforts to find a solution to poverty. When the Republican Party gained a majority in Congress in 1994, the federal government began to remove the federal safety net for the poor. Major changes were made in both welfare and housing policy, the impacts of which still are not known. After more than half a century of federal involvement, urban poverty is as intractable as ever and the solution appears even more elusive. Increasingly, the federal government is transferring responsibility to state and local governments. The necessity for local governments to enact policies attractive to major economic interests make it unlikely that policies at that level will be developed to respond to the needs of the poor. Unless the poor mobilize to create an effective voting bloc for elections, local political leaders will be unlikely to give their demands a place on the public agenda.

Public Control over Redistributive Policy

In other policy areas, the general public plays a minimal role in altering policy. Those citizens who have a special interest in and who are likely to benefit more from the choice of one policy option over another tend to play a major role in land-use policy. Street-level bureaucrats tend to dominate the quality-of-life issues of education and crime control. As experts and professionals, they resist efforts by nonexperts to control them.

In the area of redistributive policy, the pattern of citizen control is reversed. Those who potentially may benefit from the poverty policy—the poor themselves—have little say in decision making. Nevertheless, general public values concerning poverty are important in the development of policy. The political culture of the United States affects the extent to which poverty is viewed as a public problem and the role government should play in addressing the problem. Those who think that poverty is due to individual weaknesses, such as lack of incentive or laziness, also believe that involvement by government to provide the poor with benefits will only aggravate the problem. Governmental programs will, it is argued, decrease incentives even further and reward laziness.[7]

Others argue that the poor cannot compete successfully as a result of societal failures, rather than individual ones. They point to changing economic conditions or racial prejudice as making it difficult for many to find jobs with salaries adequate to lift them from poverty. They believe society has a responsibility to provide aid.[8]

Of the two explanations of poverty, the individualist one tends to predominate. The belief in individualism and capitalism, which the colonists brought from England, has had a major impact on American thinking. Our Protestant heritage also affected our definition of the poverty problem. "In the early church, the poor as a group were deemed to be of the highest moral status and the rich were demoted to second-class spiritual status."[9] However, Protestant theology held a different attitude toward the poor—it equated poverty with laziness and vice.

The first poor laws, established in England in 1531, required a "means test" to determine who would be eligible to beg. Unlicensed beggars could be fined and whipped. In 1536, local governments had to assume responsibility for caring for the poor. In 1572, the first distinction between the "impotent or deserving poor" and the "vagrants or undeserving poor" was made.[10]

The American colonists borrowed the tradition of local authority over poverty-based issues and many of the punitive provisions of the Elizabethan Poor Laws.

> The colonists granted their local governments the responsibility to provide assistance to the poor. They also gave their officials the power to establish residence requirements for relief eligibility and to aid only the "worthy poor," who in a period where unemployment was not a problem were defined to be the old, the sick, and women and children who had lost the male breadwinner. Anyone else could be excluded, because, "[i]ndustry and thrift were

considered critical and poverty considered a lack of both."[11]

These beliefs are still held by many. A 1975 study found that Americans believed that poverty was more likely to be caused by individual failings than by forces beyond the control of the poor. The four most frequently mentioned explanations of poverty essentially "blame the victim" for his or her plight. These explanations were: (1) lack of thrift and proper money management; (2) lack of effort; (3) lack of talent or ability; and (4) loose morals and drunkenness. After these causes, other causes, beyond the individual's control, were mentioned: (1) sickness and physical handicaps; (2) low wages; (3) failure of society to provide good schools for many Americans; (4) prejudice and discrimination against African-Americans; (5) failure of private industry to provide enough jobs; (6) being taken advantage of by the rich and; (7) bad luck.[12]

These beliefs determine the extent to which poverty is seen as society's problem, and therefore a legitimate issue on the public agenda, and what kind of assistance programs will be tolerated. The urban economic context also affects the problem of poverty and our way of dealing with it. The private enterprise doctrine equates private property with individual dignity and liberty, which leads to an acceptance of the legitimacy of wealth and a reluctance to abridge any prerogatives of the rich to protect the poor.

Our unwillingness to interfere with private prerogatives has three important consequences. First, by considering intervention illegitimate, "there will always be a gap between the needs of the poor and assistance. . . . Mostly, aid will institutionalize poverty, keeping the poor in a state of destitution."[13] Second, welfare is not accepted as legitimate. More but inadequate programs are established because society creates a disjointed, overlapping, contradictory set of responses rather than a coherent program. Finally, intervention that aids the upper and middle class is disguised. In other words, aid to the poor is seen as undeserved and is given grudgingly, whereas tax deductions are not seen for what they really are—redistribution from poor to rich. The justification for these tax deductions is that they will help stimulate investment and business (a goal that is considered to be in the public interest), while helping the poor is seen as helping a special interest group.

Although other special interests are accorded access to policy making in areas where their interests are at stake, the poor often are not. Chapter 5 discussed the reasons why it is difficult to organize the poor into a political constituency with enough clout to force their issues onto the agenda. The poor are usually spending their whole time and effort simply to survive. In addition to lacking the time for political participation, they lack the necessary organizational and communication skills. And they certainly lack the money to hire others with those skills. Although in many locations their number should make them a potential political force, their inability to organize makes it easy for the governing coalition to ignore their concerns.

Welfare Policy

Programs for the poor have evolved and been defined according to four distinct orientations. These orientations can be seen as: punitive, alleviative, preventative, and curative.[14] **Punitive** policies were designed to punish or at least demean the poor. **Alleviative** policies would provide immediate assistance to aid those who fell into poverty through no fault of their own. **Preventative** programs were instituted so that people could be protected from falling into poverty as a result of circumstances beyond their control. **Curative** programs were designed to work to remove the causes of poverty. A community's values

affect its choice of policy options. Because the poor are the only ones to benefit from the redistribution of resources, poverty policy normally lacks a powerful constituency. Those who see themselves as potentially subsidizing the poor often oppose the policies, while the potential beneficiaries lack the resources to effectively make their demands known.

The recipients of punitive, alleviative, and preventative policies have very little input in policy formation. But curative policy, defined through the participation mandates of the War on Poverty, enabled citizens in poor neighborhoods to have an impact.

Agenda Setting

Until the 1930s, most solutions to poverty were framed in punitive terms. Frances Piven and Richard Cloward describe the development of solutions in early America.

> The doctrine of self help through work which distinguishes nineteenth century capitalism flourished in its purest and fiercest form in the United States. By contrast with other countries, where some residue remained of earlier Christian teachings that poverty was a blessing that should inspire charity in the rich and meekness in the poor, poverty in the United States came to be regarded as "the obvious consequence of sloth and sinfulness. . . . " The very notion of a relief system seemed blasphemous.[15]

The notion that poverty was a local matter resulted in a patchwork of local arrangements varying from giving food, to indentured service (that is, requiring the poor to work for private business), to incarceration in almshouses. In the early nineteenth century, "indoor relief" or almshouses dominated. By the Civil War, however, almshouses had fallen into disfavor because of high operating costs and sanitation problems.[16] Many cities instituted assistance programs for the poor in their own homes. Known as "outdoor" relief, this type of welfare was not nearly as degrading. But the aid during this period was meager, due to resource constraints of local governments, which had sole responsibility for providing assistance, and to the prevalent attitude that the poor required little more than subsistence.

One attempt to place the problem on the national agenda prior to the 1930s failed when President Franklin Pierce vetoed a bill that would have provided land grants for state mental hospitals. In his veto message he emphasized the local responsibility for the welfare function.[17]

Formulation

The national economic turmoil caused by the Great Depression changed attitudes about why people were poor and who was responsible for aiding the poor. When the middle class faced poverty, the issue was redefined and moved from the local to the national agenda. Local governments were incapable of providing welfare services to all the needy, and the crisis situation forced welfare first onto the state and, later, onto the national agenda.

Widespread unemployment meant that not only the lazy were out of work. A large group of unemployed middle class presented a political force that could not be ignored. As relief was losing its negative connotations, the formulations proposed were no longer punitive. Instead the policies were designed to be alleviative, that is, to provide short-term assistance to tide people over when economic or personal emergencies occured. Aid to Families with Dependent Children was an example. If something happened to the breadwinner, the federal government, through the states, helped the spouse to care for the children until they were able to take care of themselves. In addition, preventative, insurance-type programs were instituted so that people would put money aside during the good times in return for assistance when it was needed. Social Security is an example—people pay in while they are young and can expect a payback when they retire. While this was initially supposed to serve only as a supplement, many believe that Social Security alone should keep them out of poverty in old age.

Roosevelt's New Deal brought national involvement in a broad array of former state and local responsibilities as many local governments faced bankruptcy in the face of demands. The most far-reaching legislation was the Social Security Act of 1935, which established a partnership between the federal government and the states to provide assistance to the "deserving poor." Programs were established for the elderly (Old Age Assistance), the blind (Aid to the Blind), and dependent children (Aid to Dependent Children, later changed to Aid to Families with Dependent Children).

In addition, the act established a social insurance component, designed as a preventative program. Its best-known legacy is the Old Age and Survivors Insurance, or later, the Old Age, Survivors and Disability Insurance, which provided direct payments to retirees, widows or widowers, and dependent children of eligible participants. This insurance program eased the pressure on local governments. In keeping with our middle-class ideology, working Americans were required to pay premiums, supplemented by their employers, to provide for a secure future. This program is not redistributive because the unemployed did not pay in and therefore were not covered. Also, although payments are somewhat redistributive, the allocations are not sufficient to sustain those who have paid in little and lack other resources.

Other alleviative programs also developed during the Great Depression. One was unemployment insurance, which emerged as a federal–state partnership and continues today to help the "deserving" unemployed. The

Federal Emergency Relief Administration was established to reduce unemployment by providing grants to states to create jobs. Although ostensibly aimed primarily at urban unemployment, rural areas actually benefited as much as did cities.[18]

The public assistance aspects of New Deal programs were viewed as temporary. Once the economy improved, the alleviative programs were expected to be unnecessary. Hence the end of the Great Depression marked the end of any belief in the legitimacy of being poor. Preventative social insurance programs, however, became accepted and were incrementally expanded. For instance, Aid to the Permanently and Totally Disabled was added to Social Security in 1950.

During the presidential campaign in 1960, John Kennedy was struck by the poverty in the hills of West Virginia. After he was elected president he read Michael Harrington's *The Other America*, which documented the extent of poverty and discrimination in the United States and concluded that America contained two nations:

> Millions and tens of millions enjoy the highest standard of life the world has ever known. . . . At the same time the United States contains an underdeveloped nation. . . . Its inhabitants do not suffer the extreme deprivation of the peasants of Asia or the tribesmen of Africa, yet the mechanism of the misery is similar. They are beyond history, beyond progress, sunk in a paralyzing, maiming routine. The new nations, however, have one advantage: poverty is so general and so extreme that it is the passion of the entire society to obliterate it. . . . But this country seems to be caught in a paradox. Because its poverty is not so deadly, because so many are enjoying a decent standard of life, there are indifference and blindness to the plight of the poor.[19]

President Kennedy resolved to put the problem of poverty back on the federal agenda. Although he was assassinated before substantial action could be taken, President Johnson picked up the gauntlet. He had two goals: He wished to finish the legacy of the New Deal and he wanted a major initiative he could call his own. On January 5, 1964, President Johnson announced, "I shall shortly present to Congress a program designed to attack the roots of poverty in our cities and rural areas. . . . "[20] This War on Poverty was not to be merely alleviative or preventative but curative.

Rather than piecemeal formulations, Johnson's Great Society programs attacked the multiple causes of poverty through a variety of programs aimed at education, job training, self-help, and political empowerment. The Economic Opportunity Act of 1964 (EOA), sought to help low-income children through Head Start, a preschool program that attempted to provide poor children with a background similar to middle-class children when entering school. For other youths, EOA established job programs like the Neighborhood Youth Corps and the Job Corps and provided work–study funds to help the poor go to college.

The War on Poverty package contained several job programs for adults. A major one was the Manpower Development and Training Act aimed at teaching new skills to facilitate employment and higher pay. This program evolved into the Comprehensive Employment and Training Act (CETA), which provided federal reimbursement for private businesses to train new employees and created public service jobs. In 1982, CETA ended with the passage of the Job Training Partnership Act (JTPA). The JTPA eliminated public service jobs that had helped local government by providing training and a short-term subsidized work force. It also shifted administrative power from the local to the state level. This program relies strongly on the private sector to provide jobs and training. Some commentators feared the JTPA would shift the focus of job training away from the most disadvantaged. "The new program will serve both fewer people and people who are less disadvantaged because of the proclivity of private employers to 'cream' for the most employable of the eligible populations."[21]

Another major component of the War on Poverty, perhaps the Achilles heel of the program, was community action. The Economic Opportunity Act of 1964 specified that programs should be carried out with "maximum feasible participation" of the target population. This provision was based on the assumption that part of the problem of being poor was a sense of helplessness and powerlessness to affect one's life and the political system.

In 1968, urban conflict reached a crescendo. Protest over America's involvement in Vietnam combined with the urban riots and the newly organizing urban neighborhoods to produce what many saw as a fundamental challenge to social control and stability in America's cities. Richard Nixon rode the tide of fear and resentment, among other things, to the White House by basing his presidential election campaign on appeals to the white, blue collar, ethnic voters who had previously formed the backbone of the New Deal coalition.

Because the War on Poverty was believed to have caused the conflicts in the cities and to have mobilized constituents who would be likely to support Democratic candidates, one of Nixon's major goals was to terminate or cut back on the Great Society.[22] This began a trend that is still continuing—retrenchment. Funding was cut or, if Congress refused the cuts, impounded. Categorical grant programs were replaced by block grants that were distributed broadly rather than being targeted to the urban poor.

During the Nixon presidency, one major new initiative was proposed—a Negative In-

come Tax or Family Assistance Plan. The idea was to eliminate the costly and "bloated" welfare bureaucracy and develop a national welfare system using tax returns. Those above the poverty line would pay taxes; those below would receive income transfers. The plan cut bureaucracy, thus it had conservative support. Because it was less demeaning than existing programs and removed much of the burden on local government by federalizing and equalizing welfare payments, it had liberal support.

Despite its appeal, the negative income tax never developed enough support for adoption. Conservatives wanted low-level support lest the poor choose not to work. Liberals felt that those low levels would leave the poor worse off than they already were.

More retrenchment occurred during the Carter presidency. President Jimmy Carter initially proposed to return to the urban policies of his Democratic predecessors. He asked for a 25 percent increase in aid for urban areas.[23] Carter promised a "comprehensive urban policy" but could not deliver. As inflation weakened the economy, Carter began to cut back on aid for urban areas.

The Reagan approach was to return to the locality its traditional role in welfare. A basic premise of Ronald Reagan's philosophy was that government aid is not the solution to problems, but the cause of problems. In his 1982 State of the Union message, President Reagan argued that because of the "jungle" of federal grants-in-aid to states and localities, the national government had become pervasive, intrusive, unmanageable, ineffective, costly, and unaccountable. Reagan suggested, "Let's solve this problem with a single, bold stroke: the return of some $47 billion in Federal programs to state and local government, together with the means to finance them and a transition period of nearly 10 years to avoid unnecessary disruption."[24]

A central part of the proposal was that the national government would assume all responsibility for Medicaid while states would take all responsibility for Aid for Families with Dependent Children and food stamps. Reagan argued that "this will make welfare less costly and more responsive to genuine need because it'll be designed and administered closer to the grass roots and the people it serves." Of course, the federal government would be involved initially to fill the void created by the inability or unwillingness of localities to provide services. The transfer that Reagan sought came to fruition with the passage of the Personal Responsibility and Work Opportunity Reconciliation Act of 1996, which will be discussed below.

In 1992, Bill Clinton campaigned for the presidency on the promise "to end welfare as we know it." As governor of Arkansas he had supported the passage of the Family Support Act of 1988, which sought to strengthen child support enforcement, required states to offer a wide range of education and job training options, required the provision of child care, transportation, and work expenses, mandated the payment of transitional Medicaid, and established "workfare" or a work requirement. In 1994 he suggested that there be a time limit on welfare, though it need not be enforced as long as recipients played by the rules and sought work when possible.[25]

Adoption

During the Great Depression, state and local governments were unable to provide for the welfare of their citizens. President Roosevelt's New Deal began a 60-year tradition of federal provision of basic welfare services. The tenor of the time, strong presidential leadership, and Democratic majorities helped nationalize welfare policy.

A compromise to secure passage of the Social Security Act of 1935 resulted in the removal of a provision that required states to provide income to the needy at a level "compatible with health and decency." This action gave rise to a lingering problem—the varying levels of support provided in different cities and states. The result may be that the poor move to areas with higher benefits, in effect penalizing localities for being compassionate by increasing their costs.[26] Although there were federal standards, significant latitude was given to the states and allowed "southern states to operate autonomously from central government authority and deprive African-Americans of the social rights extended to other citizens."[27]

In the initial formulation of the Social Security Act, a program of national health insurance was discussed but was discarded because it was not a priority at the time and was seen as too far-reaching to achieve legislative support. It is interesting that national health insurance was recently back on the agenda and again failed to win legislative acceptance. Some state legislatures have taken the lead in this area.

The second flurry of activity, the Great Society and War on Poverty of Lyndon Johnson, received support for reasons similar to the support of the New Deal. The Equal Opportunity Act of 1964, which established the War on Poverty programs, passed easily because of presidential leadership and because both houses of Congress contained large, liberal Democratic majorities. Further, the interest groups representing local government supported the influx of federal dollars to deal with the urban poor. Because of the high level of initial support, some problems that were to plague implementation were overlooked. While the New Deal was born out of an economic depression, the War on Poverty was created during a time of affluence and optimism. After World War II, the country was relatively affluent and therefore the "few" needy were left to state and local programs. John Kenneth Galbraith argued that our affluent society had led us to ignore the consequences of poverty and inequality in our midst:

Poverty—grim, degrading and ineluctable—is not remarkable in India. For few the fate is otherwise. But in the United States the survival of poverty is remarkable. We ignore it because we share with all societies at all times the capacity for not seeing what we do not wish to see. . . . In our own day it enables us to travel in comfort through south Chicago and the South. But while our failure to notice can be explained it cannot be excused. "Poverty," Pitt explained, "is no disgrace but it is damned annoying." In the contemporary United States it is not annoying but it is a disgrace.[28]

While President Kennedy raised the conscience of America, President Johnson used the emotional capital provided by the Kennedy assassination to achieve his goal of finishing the promise of the New Deal. Johnson had grown up poor in Texas and saw how important federal aid was to the poor and to local government.

The federal government came to the aid of state and local governments again in 1974 under President Nixon. Over one thousand categorical federal programs with aid to states and localities for the deserving poor (the blind, disabled, etc.), were combined under Supplemental Security Income (SSI). The federal government took over funding for these programs and established a national standard. Most states supplement this grant.

By the late 1970s Congress and the American public was becoming disenchanted with the programs aimed at what many saw as the "undeserving" poor. Despite all the money spent, poverty had not been wiped out. It should be noted that the cost of the Vietnam War prevented the War on Poverty from receiving all the funding that was initially planned. Programs that had been seen as temporary, such as AFDC, had become a way of life for some and, in some cases, three generations were on welfare.

Due to tough times and a relatively conservative outlook, President Jimmy Carter began to reduce federal support for addressing social problems. "Despite criticism from mayors, urban policy analysts, and unions that Carter had abandoned his commitment to the cities and was jeopardizing his chances for reelection, the administration persisted."[29] Congress responded by cutting even more than Carter requested. Such cuts were early indicators of the developing conservative trend in the country.

President Ronald Reagan's conservative ideology resulted in more initiatives to limit the role of the federal government and to empower the states and the people to make choices. Reagan's plan for the transfer of functions, discussed above, was never approved by Congress. The states were leery, to put it mildly, of proposals to increase their responsibilities in the social welfare field, while a sagging economy was both decreasing their financial stability and increasing the number of people who needed financial assistance. In addition, many state officials saw the swap of programs as a Trojan horse proposal, hiding within it a cutback of federal funds. While the administration argued that increasing efficiency made possible from the implementation of programs on the state level would more than compensate for the reduction in funds, the states remained unconvinced.

At the end of the Reagan presidency and with the leadership of Democrat Senator Pat Moynihan, the Congress passed the Family Support Act of 1988, mentioned above. This major overhaul of the welfare system sought to "cure" causes of poverty by focusing on education and training programs while providing interim support in the form of child care, food stamps, and other programs to allow the poor to move in an orderly manner to self-sufficiency. Immediate reduction of benefits when people rose above an established income level had been a disincentive for getting off welfare. Often, the poor were better off on welfare than if working full-time. This new program attempted to deal with that. The act passed the House by 347–53 and the Senate by 96–1.[30]

The job-related provisions of the act were not fully implemented during the Bush Administration primarily because a recession prevented states from supplying their share. President Clinton sought to build incrementally on the act.[31] During his first two years as president, Clinton focused his efforts on overhauling health care. Health care is closely related to the problems of poverty; medical insurance is becoming increasingly expensive and, therefore, most of the poor are uninsured. Many of the poor decided to stay on welfare rather than take a job without health benefits that might raise their income just enough to make them ineligible for Medicaid.

The defeat of Clinton's health proposal was followed by the capture of both houses of Congress by the Republicans in 1994. Most of the freshmen Republicans were conservatives and had campaigned on the basis of a 10-point Contract with America. The Contract included, among other things, promises to address what was seen as an ineffective and perhaps damaging welfare system. Many were charging that the welfare system, which was designed to help people in temporary periods of distress, was instead becoming a way of life.[32] In addition, charges were made that many were defrauding the system. Ronald Reagan had instilled in many people's minds the image of "welfare queens" driving Cadillacs. The Congressional Republicans drafted a bill, called the Personal Responsibility Act, that proposed radical changes in the welfare system, ending for the first time since the 1930s a government guarantee of income to the poor. The bill passed Congress but was twice vetoed by Clinton at the end of 1995.

While Clinton sought to change the Family Support Act, he felt that the proposal was too harsh and would hurt children.

In 1996, the National Governors' Association resurrected the idea of welfare reform at its February meeting. Clinton, facing an election for a second term, was eager to portray himself as a "New Democrat" and indicated that he was willing to consider ending the guarantee of a welfare check, but wanted to continue guaranteed health care through Medicaid. In July, the Republicans dropped the proposed change in Medicaid from the bill, and Clinton signed it.

The thrust of the legislation is essentially what the Republican Contract with America had proposed. The most substantial change was requiring welfare recipients to work within two years of receiving welfare and limiting benefits to five years over the space of a person's lifetime. In addition, the federal government will send states money for welfare in the form of block grants, giving the states control over determining both eligibility standards and benefit levels. Legal immigrants would not be eligible for most types of assistance,* nor would those convicted of welfare fraud or drug abuse. Unwed pregnant teenagers will only be eligible if they attend high school or an alternative training program and live with an adult supervisor.[33] This bill ended welfare as an **entitlement**, which is a guarantee that eligible persons would receive benefits. It does provide more funds for day care and allows some people to continue to receive Medicaid.[34]

Implementation

New Deal programs were provided directly to individuals, for example, Social Security, or through states and local authorities, for ex-

---

*The budget compromise of 1997 restored eligibility for cash benefits to disabled legal immigrants, whether disabled now or if they become so in the future.

ample, Aid to Families with Dependent Children (AFDC). Most welfare programs are administered at the local level by county social service agencies or more recently by private, often not-for-profit, vendors. Many of the New Deal programs were designed to instigate state and local action through the use of subsidies. The results are highly variable as the implementation of AFDC indicates. In 1994, Alaska offered the highest monthly benefit, $920 for a family of three. This compares with Mississippi, which provided the lowest benefit, $120 per month to a three-person family. Fourteen states, mostly in the South, provided less than $300 a month in benefits to a three-person family.[35] Funding disparities affect local governments. In about half the states, cities or counties had no responsibility for funding welfare. In those states with local contributions, the amount varied widely. In some cities, the local share was minimal. For example, in Baltimore, it was less than 10 percent. In cities like New York, the local contribution exceeded 25 percent.

The War on Poverty programs attempted to involve the poor in their implementation. There are numerous commentaries but most seem to agree that no one really knew what the mandate for "maximum feasible participation" meant. Attempts to implement this policy threatened and frightened local officials.

As E.E. Schattschneider has stated, the mobilization of previously inactive citizens can be a revolutionary event.

> The whole balance of power in the political system could be overturned by a massive invasion of the political system, and nothing tangible protects the system against the flood. All that is necessary to produce the most painless revolution in history, the first revolution ever legalized in advance, is to have a sufficient number of people do something not much more difficult than to walk across the street on election day.[36]

In essence, requiring citizen participation was supposed to incorporate new ideas and interests. The shock waves struck quickly when the program was implemented. John F. Shelley, the Democratic mayor of San Francisco, stated that the Office of Economic Opportunity was "undermining the integrity of local government by organizing the poor into militant, politically active groups."[37] The community action aspects of the War on Poverty created political difficulties not only for that program but for other initiatives that were part of President Johnson's Great Society initiative.

J. David Greenstone and Paul Peterson looked at the impacts of citizen participation on implementation of the poverty program in New York City, Chicago, Philadelphia, and Los Angeles. They found that the stronger the political machine, as in Chicago, the more the distribution of the material benefits, but the less distribution of power to the poor. The reformed cities were more likely to redistribute power, but less successful in distributing other resources. They write that the increase in citizen involvement "insofar as it broadens influence over policy formation and invokes the amateur's enthusiasm, inevitably leads to confusion, delay, inefficiency, and perhaps, even to outright corruption."[38]

The success at involving the poor in designing and implementing programs was spotty at best. Involving the poor did, however, provide a basis for neighborhood organization and help to develop a cadre of leaders who have continued to influence the policy process.[39] As African-American and Latino neighborhoods began to organize to demand increased power in the city, conflicts with existing political forces became inevitable. The escalating conflict provided the context for a conservative countermovement.

African-American ghettoization and participation in community action, often at the expense of white ethnics, led to reduced political support for urban programs. Job training and affirmative action programs that forced African-Americans into jobs changed indifference to hostility among blue collar workers who had traditionally supported the Democratic Party.[40] The Republican Party took advantage of the concerns of middle-class Americans and their antipathy toward the welfare state to capture the White House in every election between 1968 and 1992, with the exception of 1976, when Jimmy Carter was elected.

In addition to increased tensions, sky-rocketing costs of health and welfare programs undermined support for them. While Democratic presidents could use redistributive programs as a way of capturing urban votes, Republican presidents have no such incentive. President Reagan, a Republican, cut back spending in redistributive programs by making major changes in eligibility guidelines. During the 1981 federal budget process, changes were made in four entitlement programs: Aid for Families with Dependent Children (AFDC), Medicaid, food stamps, and Child Nutrition. For example, in the AFDC program, the following changes were made:

1. States were permitted to require aid recipients to work in return for the aid;
2. The amount of money that aid recipients could earn before aid payments were reduced was decreased;
3. No one earning more than the state-established level of need would be eligible for aid;
4. Strikers, students older than 18, and women in the first 6 months of their first pregnancy could not receive payments;
5. Part of a stepparent's income was to be considered as support for a stepchild;
6. Recipients were required to report their income each month, with the previous month's income used to determine the coming month's aid.

Changes such as these derived from the Reagan Administration's philosophy that accepting welfare is debilitating because it creates a dependency relationship. The goal was to keep as many people as possible off the welfare rolls.[41] Many people became ineligible as a result of these changes. While the impact of these stricter standards under Reagan varied somewhat in the states, Richard Nathan and his colleagues concluded that "most of the cuts in federal spending for AFDC were ratified by states."[42] They found similar results in other entitlement programs: Food Stamps, Child Nutrition, Refugee Assistance, and, to a lesser degree, Medicaid. The impact of these cuts on city and county governments was to increase demands for local services. An area in which such increase in demand was most intense was child nutrition, and the Nathan, et al., study showed that no local jurisdiction made up for federal cuts.[43]

Reagan also reduced federal regulation of states and localities by consolidating categorical grants (which come with substantial regulatory strings) into block grants (which have fewer regulatory strings). The 1981 Omnibus Budget Reconciliation Act provided for the consolidation of 54 categorical grants into 9 block grants. The block grants give state governments more discretion. Many observers have argued, and research has substantiated the argument, that the movement of responsibility for social welfare policy to the state level means that such policies will not achieve the redistribution of resources.[44]

The Nathan, Dolittle, and Associates study concluded that the, "most pronounced effects of the Reagan program have been on people, especially the working poor."[45] The working poor are an enduring problem. In 1994, 20 percent of the poor aged 22–64 worked 50 or more weeks during the year. Forty-eight percent of this age group worked at least part of the year.[46] Low wages, not necessarily lack of effort, are responsible for a large percentage of the working poor.

The minimum wage was raised to $4.75 an hour in 1996 and raised again to $5.15 an hour on September 1, 1997. Currently, a minimum-wage worker at a full-time, 40-hour-per-week job earns $10,712 a year. Opponents of the increase in the minimum wage argued that it would hurt the very people it was designed to help. Small businesses might be forced to close, thus reducing available jobs. In general, business might not be willing to hire unskilled workers for the higher wage, thus reducing the job market for those with little education. Proponents argued that those who are willing to work full-time should make enough to stay out of poverty. They also pointed out that two-thirds of the workers earning a minimum wage are over 20 years old and are their family's sole source of income.[47]

Before the minimum wage was increased in 1996, it was at a forty-year low in terms of buying power. That is at least a partial explanation for why the number of poor, which had declined as a result of the Great Society programs, was again on the increase. John Schwarz reports, "The period after 1979 constitutes the first sharp rise in net poverty in America for any extended period since prior to 1950."[48]

Although the dollar figures have changed over the years, the following example shows the dilemma facing the low-wage worker. The *New York Times* reported the quandary facing a typical mother with two children in Pennsylvania in 1987. Without working, she would receive $7,670 in AFDC, food stamps, and Medicaid benefits. If she earned $8,000 a year (which was above the minimum wage) and had to pay taxes, as well as day care and other work-related expenses, her disposable income would be only $6,908—$762 less. Although she would still be receiving food stamps as part of that income, she would no longer have Medicaid protection.[49]

One of the aims of the Personal Responsibility and Work Opportunity Reconciliation Act of 1996 (PRWOR) was to remove the disincentive structure built into the welfare system and put people to work. Prior to the passage of this act, 43 states had received waivers from the federal government giving them more leeway in implementing welfare policies.[50] Block grants under PRWOR allow states considerable latitude in how they implement welfare reform. The law does not dictate how state and local governments get people off welfare, but it does require that the poor be off welfare within two years and that they do not receive more than five years in benefits over their lifetimes, with limited exceptions.

Evaluation

One problem in evaluating the success of poverty programs results from the controversy over the definition of poverty. The poverty index is based upon the amount of money needed for minimal subsistence. In the 1950s, a Department of Agriculture survey established that the poor spend about one-third of their income on food. The poverty line, then, becomes three times the cost of a subsistence diet. Some have argued that the poor now allocate much less of their income to food and hence this figure is too low. Others argue that the value of assistance programs like food stamps and housing subsidies should be added to monetary income to determine who is poor.

Using the poverty index, approximately 22 percent of the population was poor in 1959. By 1969, only 12 percent of the population was classified as poor.[51] Poverty was at an all-time low in 1973 at 11.1 percent.[52] In 1979, the rate was 11.7 percent but with the value of in-kind transfers such as food stamps added to income, the number remaining below the poverty line was reduced to 6.8 percent.[53] After remaining under 12 percent in the 1970s, poverty rates increased in the 1980s and 1990s, peaking in 1983 at 15.2 percent.[54] This was the result of a recession and cutbacks in welfare eligibility. The major cuts have occurred in the alleviative and curative redistributive programs such as AFDC, Food Stamps, Medicaid, Job Training, and the like. In 1995 the poverty rate was 13.8 percent, which was reduced to 10.3 percent after transfers were factored in.[55] The gap between actual poverty and poverty after transfers have been considered has narrowed due to cutbacks, so more of the poor are worse off.

Federal government cuts have been a response to the popular belief that federal programs have interfered with local prerogatives and have become too costly. While Americans are compassionate toward "the deserving poor," they are suspicious about welfare. In that context, it is instructive to examine distribution of money in welfare programs. The budget for the 1997 fiscal year projected spending $30.5 billion for Supplemental Security Income, the program that provides payments to low-income elderly or blind or disabled persons, and $18 billion for Aid for Families with Dependent Children. In fiscal 1997, $368.1 billion (including a 2.8 percent increase for inflation) went to Social Security payments to the elderly, a program that has widespread support due, in part, to the fact that the money goes to all elderly whether they are rich or poor and many feel entitled because they contributed to the program.

Concern about welfare cheaters is widespread. President Reagan liked to tell the story of a Chicago welfare queen with "80 names, 30 addresses, 12 Social Security cards and a tax-free income of over $150,000."[56] Despite the ubiquitous anecdotes and the general image of a system riddled with fraud, most studies find less than 10 percent of recipients are cheaters. In a report on food stamps, Jean Mayer states:

> The fact is that less than 5 percent of total spending goes to ineligible recipients or is overissued. The rate of fraud is much lower

than with income tax returns. Incidentally, the major frauds have been perpetrated not by poor recipients, but by crooked caseworkers in collusion with disreputable retailers and hard-core criminals.[57]

A more serious concern is that poverty is becoming intractable for certain groups, and no one really knows why. These groups—female-headed families, the elderly, and minorities—tend to be concentrated in urban areas. Many believe that poverty continues because of an inherent flaw in the poor. Several authors write of a "culture of poverty."[58] The basic argument is that the poor differ from the rest of society, not only in economic terms but also in terms of values and beliefs. These pathological attitudes doom the poor and governmental programs aimed at ending poverty. Edward Banfield describes the lower class as lacking the ability to plan for the future:

> The lower-class individual lives from moment to moment. . . . Impulse governs his behavior either because he cannot discipline himself to sacrifice a present for a future satisfaction or because he has no sense of the future. . . . Whatever he cannot use immediately he considers valueless. His bodily needs (especially for sex) and his taste for "action" takes precedence over everything else—and certainly over any work routine.[59]

Other researchers have argued that the behavior of the poor is not based upon deviant beliefs but instead constitute an adaptation to their life circumstances. "People respond to the situations—and opportunities—available to them and change their behavior accordingly."[60] William Julius Wilson states that while individuals make their own choices regarding conduct, "decisions and actions occur within a context of constraints and opportunities that are drastically different from those present in middle-class society."[61] He hypothesizes that economically marginal people will act in mainstream ways if they are part of stable neighborhoods but will behave pathologically in ghetto neighborhoods. "Ghetto related practices involving overt emphasis on sexuality, idleness, and public drinking, 'do not go free of denunciation' in the inner-city ghetto neighborhood," but the lack of middle-class social organization and role models makes such behavior more likely.[62]

Studies indicate that the poor do possess similar values as mainstream society.[63] One such study of black street corner society notes that

> ... the streetcorner man does not appear as a carrier of an independent cultural tradition. His behavior appears not so much as a way of realizing the distinctive goals and values of his own subculture, or of conforming to his models, but rather as his way of trying to achieve many of the goals and values of the larger society, failing to do this, and of concealing this failure from others and from himself as best he can.[64]

Whether the causes of poverty lie within the poor themselves or result from structural conditions in the society, the cutbacks at the federal level mean that the burden for redistribution falls to the states and localities. Localities are ill-equipped to provide redistributive programs. The need of the governments in the metropolis to remain economically viable means that demands for redistributive policies, which only drain local coffers, will be ignored. The dominance of economic concerns often keep demands for redistributive policies off the agenda at the local level.

> The politics of redistribution at the local level is thus an arena where certain kinds of citizen needs and preferences seldom become demands; an arena where demands, when voiced, do not gain much support; and an arena where redistributive questions, even when posed as major political

issues, are treated by a variety of strategies designed to forestall, delay, and preclude their implementation.[65]

At a minimum, the movement away from federal contributions and standards creates concerns about the inequities among localities. Many worry that the PRWOR will lead states and localities to race to the bottom. That is, they may believe that if they are less generous in supporting the poor than their neighbors, the poor will leave and the community will be more attractive to taxpayers. It is noted in Box 14–1 that some states reduced welfare benefits even prior to the 1996 Act.

Many believe that the existing welfare system has failed. Charles Murray argued that the welfare state faltered because it was too compassionate toward the poor and eliminated the stigma attached to welfare. By removing individual responsibility and acknowledging social inequities, the welfare system made it easier for people not to work. Further, rules and regulations in federal programs made staying at home more profitable than seeking employment.[66] Mead argues that traditional programs and liberal empathy toward the poor led the poor to reject work and become dependent.

> A combination of resistance to low wages, pessimism about long-term prospects, the isolation of the ghetto, and group memories of a harsher past cause many to turn aside from the chances to work that exist. Thus, the poor remain economically passive in a society where other low-skilled people find abundant opportunity.[67]

The Temporary Aid to Needy Families (TANF), which replaced AFDC under the PRWOR Act, began on July 1, 1997, so the long-term impact is unclear. Republicans and those Democrats who voted for it hope that the strong work requirement and support programs will succeed in getting people off welfare rolls.

BOX 14-1

The Race to the Bottom?

One possible unintended consequence of the new welfare reform legislation is a "race to the bottom" among states. In the past, the national government established the qualifications for welfare and provided states the bulk of the money for welfare spending. Under the 1996 reform, states would receive a fixed amount of money in a block grant. For the most part, states will determine how to spend that money. In the past, states that cut welfare benefits lost some federal aid. In the new system, states would receive their full share of federal funding even if they cut state welfare spending to 75 percent. In addition, the law created an additional fund for states with growing populations and low welfare benefits per recipient.

Critics argue that these provisions will entice states into reducing the amount of state money going to welfare. They believe that with a fixed amount of money from the federal government, states will want to discourage the poor from moving in and perhaps encourage their own poverty population to move out. The way to do that is to lower benefits below those of neighboring states. Supporters of the law deny that states would take such action, but even before the law was signed there was evidence that some northeastern states were already in a negative competition. In December 1995, Governor George Pataki of New York proposed reducing welfare benefits for a woman with two children from $577 a month to $424 to be equivalent to New Jersey's level. He also wanted to adopt New Jersey's cap on additional welfare benefits for women who have additional children while they are on welfare. There was concern that Governor Christine Todd Whitman of New Jersey would reduce her state's benefits in response because the lower cost of living in New Jersey might lure New York's poor.

Meanwhile, when Massachusetts limited welfare benefits to 24 months, Connecticut instituted a 21-month limit and cut benefits from $581 to $543 a month for a family of three. Connecticut was considering lowering benefits even further in response to New York's lower rates.

Source: Adapted from Jacob Weisberg, "How Low Can You Go," *New York*, January 15, 1996, 20–21.

The hope is that the "workfare" aspect of welfare reform will force people to accept jobs. In the process, they should develop greater self-confidence. After reviewing state workfare initiatives, Mead concluded that while it does not substantially improve earnings, nor lower welfare roles, it does substantially increase work activity. He speculates that "if participation in workfare is stringently enforced, the passive nature of welfare may finally change."[68] Wisconsin has been a model for many other states in workfare policy. Between 1989 and 1993, Wisconsin decreased its welfare rolls by 3 percent while the national caseload had increased by 29 percent.[69]

Initially states were strong supporters of welfare reform because it increased their control. Now some concern is beginning to be expressed. Prior compulsory training programs and work requirements have not saved money or moved mothers off welfare rolls.[70] This is because "single mothers do not turn to welfare because they are pathologically dependent on handouts or unusually reluctant to work—they do so because they cannot get jobs that pay better than welfare."[71] Neither the Family Support Act of 1988 nor the Personal Responsibility Act of 1996 changed these facts. One study found that a welfare family of three typically consumed goods and services worth $12,000 per year and that work expenses would add $4,000 to that.

> If they [welfare mothers] earned $6 an hour, which is a bit more than those with regular jobs actually earned, they would have to work 2,667 hours a year. If they worked every week and took no vacation, they would have to put in fifty-one hours per week (50 percent more than the average American works) to maintain their current standard of living. If they were unemployed 10 percent of the time, they would have to put in fifty-seven hours during the weeks they worked.[72]

Critics of the latest welfare reform point out that jobs for low-skilled workers are decreasing and that those jobs do not pay enough to keep people above the poverty line. Peter Edelman argues that in cities like Chicago; Youngstown, Ohio; or Newark, to name a few, there are not enough appropriate private sector jobs, even at a time when the national unemployment rate is below 5 percent.[73]

A program to find jobs for people on welfare in Kansas City, Missouri, had only 1,409 of 15,562 finding jobs over 2 years; currently only 730 are still employed. In Chicago, a program in the Cabrini–Green housing project succeeded in putting 54 percent into full-time jobs over a 5-year period. "This is a remarkable (and unusual) success rate, but it also shows how unrealistic is a structure that offers only a 20 percent exception to the five-year time limit."[74]

Under current policy, the federal government will continue to aid the deserving poor, but only on a temporary basis through block grants to the states. Policy increasingly relies on the market or state and local government to assist the rest. Unfortunately for local governments, the economic upturn for the majority of Americans has left many groups untouched, especially minorities, female heads of household, and high school dropouts. As a consequence, local governments cannot expect the problems of poverty to go away. Poverty is a multifaceted problem—the lack of income affects the self-image and the health of the poor. In addition, a large poverty population and inadequate local government resources have resulted in severe housing problems.

Housing Policy

Housing as a redistributive concern—that is, as a means of the better-off helping the lower class—was initially a private concern. Slum living was viewed as an insidious cancer attacking the moral foundations of the poor. Many believed that the physical environment was the key to the urban problem. "Thus it was presumed that an improvement in the physical environment would lead to an improvement in all the social and economic problems besetting urban communities."[75]

Social reformers made the first attempts at improving housing conditions during the latter part of the nineteenth century. Again drawing on programs from England, reformers and foundations attempted to develop model tenements based on the principle of "limited dividends."[76] The developers agreed to limit their rate of return to a very low level, often between 4 and 6 percent and to return excess profits to manage and maintain the housing.

The idea of limited dividend housing was taken over first by cities and later by states.[77] Other early state and local efforts in housing policy were regulatory in nature. For example, the almshouse, which provided shelter, was also a means of controlling the poor. The fear of epidemics and fires resulted in local regulation of housing through building codes.*

Agenda Setting and Formulation

As in many other policy areas, the Great Depression catapulted housing issues from the state and local agendas to the national agenda. Federal aid in housing took two basic tacks, only one of which had a redistributive goal. One set of policies was designed to encourage home ownership. This began in 1934 with the establishment of Federal Housing Administration (FHA)–guaranteed mortgages. The primary motivation for this program was the desire to stimulate the construction and banking industries to help move the country out of the Great Depression. In reality, this program helped the middle class escape to the suburbs, thus leading to increasing blight and erosion of the tax base of the cities. More recently, programs including those of the FHA have attempted to help low- and moderate-income residents become home owners within the city.

A second set of policies was clearly redistributive and was designed to assist low-income families to rent "safe, sanitary, and decent" housing. These programs established subsidies to local public authorities (LPAs) to build and maintain public housing. The LPAs were designed as a means of keeping politics out of housing, another legacy of the reform tradition. The programs also subsidized the private sector to encourage it to provide affordable housing. More recently, attempts have been made to subsidize rents directly, thus allowing residents a broader choice of where to live.

For a brief period in the 1980s and 1990s, the issue of those with no housing, the homeless, was on the national agenda. As the homeless became more visible on urban streets, celebrities staged a "Grate American Sleep-out," spending a night on the streets of Washington, D.C. (The use of *grate* was a pun, since many of the homeless attempt to keep themselves warm on cold nights by positioning themselves over heating grates.) The issue of homelessness was legitimized for three basic reasons. First, much of the increase in so-called street people was attributed to deinstitutionalization of the mentally disabled. As society changes its definition of and responsibility for those with mental illness, more people with questionable abilities were put back into society. Many are incapable of coping with or mastering the rules of society and, hence, maintain a hand-to-mouth existence. Because it is not sloth but mental incapacity that dooms them, they are viewed as deserving poor. Second, the economic downturn in the early 1980s increased unemployment, foreclosures, and destitution. These factors, too, were beyond the control of the individual. Third, these individuals tend to be meek, mild, and pathetic, not angry and militant. Consequently, they aroused middle-class sympathies.[78]

In 1987, a $443-million Homeless Aid bill became law. Among its provisions, the bill supplied grants to build more shelters and a housing assistance program aimed at people with mental or physical disabilities, families with children, and the elderly. In addition, it provided funding for various social services such as medical care, education, and job training for the homeless and made it easier for them to qualify for other federal aid programs such as food stamps.

Since that time there has been less sympathy for the homeless. They have become more pervasive and tiresome to the middle- and upper-class urban dwellers. The homeless have also, at times become more aggressive and dangerous. In addition, because of the

---

*Discussed in Chapter 12 on land-use policy.

concern in the 1990s for cutting back on government and cutting the size of the deficit no new Federal initiatives have been made to address the issues of housing and homelessness. Referring to the housing appropriations bill passed in 1996, one critic has observed:

> With one obscure sentence, the Federal Government has essentially conceded defeat in its decades-long drive to make housing affordable to low-income Americans. Even in an era of Government retreats this one stands out, both for its importance and its odd election-year invisibility. No one seems to have noticed, least of all the candidates. But two decades of rising rents and falling wages have created record numbers of people, *including working people,* who can't afford to pay the rent.[79]

Adoption and Implementation: Home Ownership Programs

The Great Depression seriously affected the construction industry. With a tenuous economy and troubled banks, it was impossible for the private sector to initiate any major construction initiatives. FHA-insured mortgage loans spurred construction activity and provided necessary housing. That program continues today.

The goal was distributive, although it could be argued that it had redistributive implications. In 1934 the FHA established loan guarantees to encourage banks and savings and loan institutions to make more mortgage money available, thus stimulating the economy and improving housing conditions. Without these guarantees, buyers were often required to make large down payments and repay the principal in a lump sum within a relatively short time (usually 5 to 10 years) or face default. With the federal government assuming all the risk, banks were willing to accept smaller down payments, longer terms, and a gradual paydown of principal, but not lower interest rates.

This program opened many more opportunities for the middle class to own homes. It also provided construction jobs and protected banks, which were facing difficulty in the Great Depression. If the middle class could afford new housing, then their former homes would "filter down" to the working class, and the poor could move to housing left behind by the working class, although that housing was often in bad shape by the time it filtered down.

The implementation of FHA loan guarantees has created problems for urban areas in general and the poor specifically. The FHA did not lend money directly to consumers, but encouraged lending by creating guarantees for the private sector. The conservative nature of the agency led it to define an "economically sound" decision as favoring new construction over rehabilitation, building in the suburbs as opposed to inner cities, and in white neighborhoods as opposed to minority or racially mixed neighborhoods.

The practice of refusing to make or guarantee loans in older, urban neighborhoods, known as **redlining** because red lines were drawn around areas of "high risk," created a self-fulfilling prophecy. As an area aged, or filtered down, money was needed to refurbish it. However, money was not made available because the lenders believed this area would decline in value. The lack of resources assured deterioration. The FHA criterion of "economic soundness," which greatly limited its utility in the inner city, was not modified until 1967. Further, since FHA guaranteed loans did not significantly lower interest rates, the poor could not consider buying homes. Over the years, the FHA program has greatly hurt the inner city's viability and helped suburban development.

The Housing Act of 1968 gave the poor a significant chance to own their own homes. Following the idea that home ownership would stabilize neighborhoods and create pride that would help to prevent deterioration, Section 235 of that act originally was designed to allow families earning between $3,000 and $7,000 to purchase homes valued at up to $20,000. Families were required to make down payments as low as $200 and use up to 20 percent of their incomes in mortgage payments. The FHA guaranteed the loans and the federal government provided a subsidy to make up the difference between the market interest rate (at that time between 6.5 percent and 7 percent) and what the family could afford. This certainly appears to be a redistributive program, thus it is intriguing to note that this program and a rent supplement program "were largely the work of the most powerful Washington lobbying group in the housing and urban development field, the National Association of Home Builders, and a broadly based organization of large and small home builders, mortgage bankers, and some land speculators and realtors."[80]

From the beginning, this program was fraught with implementation problems. The major difficulty arose because of inadequate governmental oversight and dishonesty on the part of realtors, developers, and FHA appraisers. Oftentimes developers only made superficial repairs to dilapidated housing. FHA appraisers then gave high appraisals. The unsuspecting poor often sank their meager savings into a house only to find it needed additional and costly repairs. They often found maintaining such homes impossible and had to walk away. Banks were cavalier about screening applicants as the loans were guaranteed, and even some of those who purchased good housing could not meet the payments. Thus, after properties were foreclosed, the Department of Housing and Urban Development (HUD) became a major owner of slum properties. In 1975 HUD spent an estimated $410,970 a day watching over 57,000 empty houses.[81]

These empty homes encouraged vandalism; copper pipes and anything of value were scavenged. Further, the houses also became a haven for drug addicts, resulting in further deterioration of neighborhoods that Section 235 programs were supposed to renew. In 1976 and 1980 standards were changed to require participants to have more income and make larger down payments, and to limit the federal subsidy to a 3 percent mortgage write-down. As a result, subsidies have declined markedly under this program.

Another means of fostering home ownership in decaying neighborhoods, Urban Homesteading, has been tried with mixed success. Wilmington, Delaware, and Baltimore, Maryland, were in the forefront of this program, which sold abandoned houses for a nominal fee (sometimes $1) to people who would renovate them and live in them. In 1974 the federal government agreed to give foreclosed properties to local governments to be used in homesteading programs. In 1976 HUD established a demonstration program in 22 cities in partnership with communities and private lenders. Because of the cost of renovation and the skills needed, the poor were often precluded from participation. In some communities, however, neighborhood corporations worked together to rehabilitate and create better housing conditions for the lower class. At times urban homesteading was "too successful" and property values and desirability became so great in "gentrified" neighborhoods that the poor were pushed out.

These home ownership programs have helped many Americans achieve their dreams, have helped the construction, realty, and banking industries as well as the general economy, but the number of poor who benefited was minimal. On the other hand, rental housing programs such as public housing and rent subsidies, and urban renewal, while not without some serious defects, have provided many benefits to a great number of low-income urbanites.

Adoption and Implementation: Rental Housing Programs

Public housing and rent subsidy programs also began early in the New Deal. The first forays into low-income housing by the federal government can hardly be seen as primarily redistributive. Harold Wolman notes that

> ... much of the concern about easily visible slums was not about the deprivations suffered by their inhabitants, but rather about the affront to aesthetic sensibilities caused by these blights on the urban landscape. ... It is not surprising, therefore, that the first slum clearance and public housing program, initiated in 1933, was administered by the Public Works Administration.[82]

The highest priority was to address the devastating unemployment caused by the Great Depression by creating construction jobs. Next came furnishing "safe, sanitary, and decent" housing for those unable to afford adequate private housing, eradicating slums, demonstrating the utility of large-scale community planning, and encouraging states to facilitate public housing projects.[83] These projects encountered problems that continue to plague urban redevelopment efforts. Because land values were so high, rents in new housing often doubled, thus pricing out the former residents. "This situation in which the slum dweller does not reap the benefits of slum clearance remains a perennial feature of such programs."[84]

The Public Works Program was followed by the Housing Act of 1937. This legislation was significant for many reasons. First and foremost, it established permanent ties between the federal government and municipalities, bypassing the states except for state-enabling legislation needed to create local public authorities to administer the housing programs. This also led to increased federal control in local areas, much to the chagrin of local administrators.[85]

President Franklin D. Roosevelt put the issue of housing on the national agenda in his 1937 inaugural address when he stated that "one-third of a nation is ill-nourished, ill-clothed, and ill-housed." Congress readily approved the request for funds for housing because the building materials industries saw housing construction as a way of stimulating their business. Other groups, such as real estate and savings and loan interest groups that would oppose such public support for housing in the future, were silent in 1937. The reason for their quiescence was that they "were still too depression-shocked to offer any effective opposition."[86]

This program greatly expanded the government's role into what had been the private domain. The Housing Act of 1937 established the United States Housing Administration (USHA) with the purpose of providing local public housing authorities with long-term, low-interest loans to build low-income housing. It also provided capital grants and operational subsidies. The real estate lobby did not stay on the sidelines for long. The National Association of Realty Boards sought to protect its own interests.

> With the federal Treasury now opened up for the battle on the slums, realtors saw an opportunity to go beyond the slow-moving process of rehabilitation into the much more challenging but also potentially more lucrative field of clearance and rebuilding. First, however, a way would have to be found to channel federal funds away from the "socialistic" housing program and into subsidies for private enterprise. ... Fearful that low income, non-taxpaying projects would monopolize the best sites, realtors saw destruction of the USHA as an essential prerequisite to the successful prosecution of their battle to preserve the "private city."[87]

The unwillingness of the private sector to provide for the poor led to federal intervention. Because the profits from housing the poor were so low, private investors sought other building projects, leaving the responsibility to house the poor to the federal government. However, when the private sector mobilized and unemployment abated, Congress rethought the federal role in housing and turned down a 1939 USHA request for more money.

Not until 1949 did the federal government take additional steps to help house the lower class. Skillful handling of the public and subsidized housing issue by President Harry Truman helped to get it back on the agenda.[88] The Housing Act of 1949 was an amalgam of provisions aimed at pleasing various constituencies. Title I provided subsidies to the private sector to create low- and moderate-income housing. This provision pleased the conservatives by ensuring the private sector a role in redevelopment and also pleased realtors, developers, and commercial interests. Title III of the act contained a public housing provision that pleased the liberals.

Jewel Bellush and Murray Hausknecht argue, however, that the public housing provision was subordinate to the primary goal of the program, which was aiding private development.

> Thus Title I helps clear slums by helping private entrepreneurs, but Title I does nothing about the reverse side of the coin—standard housing for the displaced slum dweller. In 1937 public housing was seen, in part at least, as a means of alleviating the distress of the slum dweller. In 1949 . . . public housing is justified . . . for those displaced by private projects who cannot find housing at rents they can afford. In sum, the emphasis shifts from the social and economic situation of the slum resident to the needs of private enterprise.[89]

The essential goal of the act was to help local communities to clear blighted areas that the private sector would not approach. Once an area was declared blighted, the federal government would contribute two-thirds of the difference between the cost of acquisition, clearance, rebuilding the infrastructure (sewers, streets, etc.), and relocating tenants, and the price that the city could get for the cleared land from a private developer. For instance, if the costs of a project were $15 million and the land was sold for $3 million, the federal government would pay two-thirds of the difference, or $8 million. The local government absorbs $4 million, which will presumably be repaid through higher property taxes, and the developer receives a $12-million subsidy.

The conflict between the two goals of the 1949 act—housing the poor and developing the city—was felt most intensely by urban politicians and administrators who "found themselves engaged in the tricky job of satisfying ill-housed voters and profit seeking private developers."[90]

The 1949 Housing Act had sought to develop 810,000 subsidized units in 6 years. However, 5 years after its passage, only 60 cities had progressed to the land acquisition stage.[91] In a 20-year period (1934–1954), only 400,000 units were actually built. At that rate slum clearance would have taken over 200 years.[92] This illustrates one problem with involving the private sector in building low-income housing—too little profitability.

The Housing Act of 1954 brought several important provisions. First, it coined the term **urban renewal**. The use of that term was to indicate that more resources would be directed to rehabilitation and conservation than destruction. Second, and especially significant with respect to low-income housing, the act dropped the insistence that new construction be primarily residential. Ten percent of federal grants could be used for nonresidential construction, which began an incremental shift. By

1961, 30 percent could be used for nonresidential purposes. This tied housing programs to a broader concept of community development. Third, the Housing Act of 1954 established a Workable Program requirement, which called for comprehensive analysis and planning as well as "citizen participation." Wolman notes that:

> More than any of the other provisions of the program, . . . [the citizen participation requirement] has been honored more in the breach than in the observance. Most attempts at citizen participation have been more ritual approval of plans presented to the citizens. Furthermore, Workable Program citizen committees historically have had very few low-income members.[93]

On the positive side, urban renewal improved the economic vitality of cities by obliterating slums and increasing the tax base. Many cities can point to commercial revitalization such as Nicollet Mall in Minneapolis and public and cultural projects such as Lincoln Center in New York City. Urban renewal allowed for the expansion of hospitals and universities, such as the University of Pennsylvania in Philadelphia. It increased the availability of middle- and upper-income housing and, in general, improved the overall appearance of many cities. Indeed, it can be argued that the urban renewal program can be more appropriately understood as an economic development program than a welfare program.[94]

Further substantiation for this interpretation can be found in an examination of the impact of urban renewal on the lower class. The Housing Acts led to the destruction of neighborhoods that represented security and a way of life to many low- and moderate-income people.[95] In addition, as a study of Newark points out, the most blighted areas were often ignored because there was little private interest in redeveloping in the middle of a slum. More interest was shown in old, deteriorating properties on the fringe of the commercial districts to be used for luxury housing or business development.[96] Urban renewal also was seen as a way of removing minority groups, especially African-Americans. Martin Anderson estimates that two-thirds of those uprooted by urban renewal were black or Puerto Rican.[97]

While local housing authorities were responsible for helping residents to move from the slums to "safe, sanitary, and decent" housing that was affordable, clearly if such housing had existed people would have left the slums before their homes were destroyed. Some families moved from one urban renewal area to another. Small businesses that depended on good will built up in the neighborhood over a number of years could not easily re-establish themselves in other parts of the city. Many never reopened.

Because of the private sector's general lack of interest in providing low-income housing, much of the housing for low-income people was public housing. While this provided improved housing at affordable rents to many, it, too, experienced problems derived from restrictions on income, siting, cost and design, and administration.[98]

One problem with public housing is that it has often excluded the poorest of the poor. The intent of the 1949 Housing Act was to help the "deserving poor." Requirements were established to screen out the chronically poor and potential troublemakers.[99] Further, **income restrictions** became a disincentive to some because if they earned too much they would be evicted; any increase in income might not cover the higher rentals required on the private market. Those who were upwardly mobile and made more money eventually were forced to move out. Thus, those who could have served as role models were not around to provide inspiration to others.

A second major problem was **siting restrictions**. Any attempts to build public housing projects outside the slum were fiercely resisted. Zoning restrictions have made it almost impossible to build public housing in many suburbs.* Major concerns were a fear of crime and vandalism and a decline in property values if low-income minorities moved in. Low-income groups are often different in terms of dress, speech, and language. Fear of large concentrations of low-income people has been aggravated by the failures of some public housing projects. The classic example is Pruitt-Igoe in St. Louis, which consisted of thirty-three 11-story buildings housing about 10,000 people. First occupied in 1954, it was demolished in 1974 because people refused to live in it. Crime and vandalism were rampant, encouraged by poor design such as elevators that stopped only on the fourth, seventh, and tenth floors, forcing residents to walk up and down stairs to reach their apartments and exposing them to opportunistic criminals.

While Pruitt-Igoe may have been the worst, it is not atypical. Former Mayor Jane Bryne of Chicago once created a great deal of publicity by moving into Cabrini-Green housing, notorious for its conditions. Quickly, and relatively quietly, she left.

HUD tried to encourage smaller, scatter-site projects to achieve greater racial, social, and economic integration. In 1972 at HUD's encouragement, the New York Housing Authority, backed by Mayor John Lindsay, announced a plan to build a low-income housing project in the middle-class neighborhood of Forest Hills in Queens. The plan called for three 24-story buildings housing 842 low-income families.[100] After much discussion with the community, a compromise was worked out by an unknown lawyer and college professor, Mario Cuomo, who later became governor of New York. The compromise called for three, 12-story buildings for 432 families with a certain percentage set aside for the elderly poor.[101]

Scatter-site housing frequently results in controversy. Nevertheless, a 1984 study in 87 cities indicated some success with scatter-site housing programs.[102] In *Hills v. Gautreaux*, the Supreme Court intervened to desegregate public housing. The Court ordered that sites be selected for future subsidized housing in white neighborhoods and even in the suburbs.[103]

The third major problem with public housing is **poor design due to cost restrictions**. Because land in the center of large cities is expensive, high-rise projects are the norm. This complicates supervision of children because mothers are unable to do their household chores and easily watch and control their children outside. Thus children could more easily become involved in crime and vandalism. The bias against making the poor too comfortable, lest they lose incentive to be "productive" members of society, meant little attention was given to "frills" like green spaces and playgrounds. There was also little attention given to safety features such as good security and lighting. Buildings tend to lack anything distinctive that would encourage any pride. Recently, however, colorful murals painted by residents, often reflecting their cultural heritage, have been used to improve the surroundings.

During the first Clinton Administration, Secretary of Housing and Urban Development Henry Cisneros supported programs to create smaller, mixed-income housing projects. In an effort to redesign public housing, he presided over the destruction of 22,000 units of the worst public housing and replaced them with smaller units mixing the poor with working class residents. The problem is that such projects reduce the number of affordable housing units and contribute to the housing shortage.[104]

The fourth problem is **administrative restrictions** used to "regulate the poor." Those

---

*See Chapter 12.

who might not fit "middle-class" standards could be eliminated. In some projects, relinquishing one's independence was the price of living in public housing. Residents are required to keep lawns mowed, use green plastic trash bags, refrain from keeping pets, and so on. It can be argued that, rather than an insidious plot to make the poor "just like us," these regulations are the necessary accommodation to urban living. Nonetheless, the regulations often went beyond the minimum necessary to maintain civility.

Dissatisfaction with public housing, on the part of both liberals and conservatives, led to new initiatives. In the Housing Act of 1968, Section 236 provided for rent subsidies. Section 236 participants were required to spend up to 25 percent of their income (depending on family size) for rent and HUD would pay the difference up to what had been determined to be the fair market rate. This gives the poor a broader range of housing choice, encourages dispersion into various parts of the city— thereby reducing segregation—and removes people from the unsavory environment that often characterizes public housing. Developers are able to expand their market to those who could not previously afford fair market rents.

Section 8 of the Housing and Community Development Act of 1974 has become the major rent supplement program, providing more flexibility with respect to income restrictions, rents, and apartment choice. The federal government provides subsidies to local housing authorities to make up the difference between 25 percent of a person's income (changed to 30 percent in 1981) and the total rent. This encourages developers to produce low- and moderate-income housing. Initially the subsidies could be used for new construction and rehabilitation, but the new construction component was ended in 1984. Low-income applicants may receive certificates providing rent supplements in any apartment that qualifies—the subsidies are not limited to specific apartment complexes or buildings.

The Section 8 program has been quite successful in aiding racial and economic integration. In fiscal 1975 and 1976 many Section 8 apartments were located in predominantly white areas with little low-income housing.[105] On the other hand, this program has been very costly, and there is not enough assistance for all who qualify. The available funds never served more than about 25 percent of the eligible population.[106] In addition, HUD sometimes establishes the "fair market rate" below actual rents in metropolitan areas, especially for large apartments needed by large families. Finally, this program has been more effective in helping the elderly or "deserving poor" because realtors and landlords have less aversion to them.[107]

Problems with the Section 8 program have been the focus of scrutiny by Congress. Because of the automatic escalation in the rent subsidies of residents in Section 8 housing, HUD is, in some instances, paying landlords more for housing than they could get in the private market. Congress has forbidden HUD to pay more than 20 percent above the "fair market rent" in renewing the contracts with landlords. The problem? Landlords need the rents they have been charging or they will not be able to pay their mortgages, which are insured by the government.

Evaluation

Despite the spate of programs to help make "safe, sanitary, and decent" housing available to the poor, finding low-income housing is becoming an even greater problem than it has been in the recent past. One observer estimates that 15 million households qualify for housing assistance from the federal government but only 4.5 million actually receive help.[108] The 1997 federal budget provided no funds to increase the number who could receive federal housing assistance. Many people, some working full-time, pay as much as 70 percent of their income for housing. Although the minimum wage has recently increased, the stock of cheap housing has decreased due to destruction and gentrification. The poor must devote large portions of their income to housing, living just a lay-off away from joining the ranks of the homeless. Even if the poor manage to maintain a home, one study found a relation between high rent burdens and malnourishment of children.[109]

The 104th Congress that commenced in January 1995 targeted the Department of Housing and Urban Development for elimination. The battle over funding for HUD was one of the issues that led to the government shutdown in late 1995 and early 1996. Funding was only approved seven months into the 1996 fiscal year. In the budget for fiscal year 1997, Congress made substantial cuts in HUD appropriations, especially in housing programs. Most of the cuts were in rent subsidies for low-income people. In addition, Congress appropriated funds for experimenting with the handling of the troubled Section 8 program. The goal was to find a way to lower mortgage costs, thus permitting lower rents to be charged. The appropriation also consolidated several programs into block grants aimed at giving local housing authorities more control and removed the requirement that each unit of public housing destroyed must be replaced.[110]

HUD is now spending almost $2.5 billion a year just maintaining existing public housing projects. It is spending another $550 million demolishing the worst of the old projects and building smaller, mixed-income developments. Looming in the future is a crisis in the Section 8 program. When it began in the 1970s, Section 8 was financed by long-term contracts that are now expiring. The cost of renewing the contracts could consume the whole HUD budget. Concern about financing has led to the decision to prohibit any expansion of the program in the future. As the number of poor increases, the stock of affordable housing decreases, and the support of government shrinks, it seems inevitable that the number of homeless will increase.

Estimates of the number who are homeless vary widely. Getting firm numbers is difficult because many people without homes may be living with relatives and friends at least part of the time. They may or may not use shelters, preferring in some cases to live on the streets. They may move in and out of the homeless ranks as their employment status fluctuates. In 1984, HUD estimated the number of homeless to be between 250,000 and 350,000. The 1990 census calculated that 600,000 people were homeless. A 1994 Clinton Administration task force estimated that 7,000,000 Americans were homeless at some time during the second half of the 1980s.[111]

Christopher Jencks has identified four "promising explanations" for an increase in homelessness. Two were noted above: the deinstitutionalization of the mentally ill and the decline in the availability of cheap housing. A third explanation is the widespread availability of crack, a form of cocaine that is very cheap. Use of the drug can make a person with marginal job skills unemployable. Also, while cheap, buying crack could drain money that might otherwise go to rent. Finally, long-term joblessness has increased because the demand for unskilled workers decreased while the supply of such workers did not. Also, women without skills were less likely to marry than in the past, although they continued to have children.[112]

If correct, two of these explanations—the use of drugs and the bearing of children out of wedlock—leave some of the causes of homelessness within the control of the homeless themselves. But other explanations point to changes over which individuals have little control. Structural changes in the job market or destruction of affordable housing to find more profitable uses of valuable urban land are outside individuals' control. Nevertheless, the federal government has reduced its commitment to finding safe, decent, and affordable housing even for those who work full-time jobs. The impact of homelessness is depicted in Box 14–2 (on page 426).

BOX 14–2

Children Are the Hardest Hit as Nation's Homeless Population Continues to Grow

By Marsha King

SEATTLE, Washington. . . Lori Sherill—a beautiful, bright, soft-spoken child—is still bothered by memories of those first weeks in the shelter and of leaving her best friend, Crystal, back home.

"I felt sad. I never cried because I knew I was going to see Crystal again. But I wasn't sure. I can remember all the things we did. All the songs we sang. All the jokes," she says quietly.

But she was excited about her new school in Seattle. Until her classmates chased her from the bus stop to the shelter and threw a raw egg in her hair, ruining her new permanent.

She has two chums now, but says others still tease her about where she lives. they taunt: "You guys live in a shelter and you guys are on welfare."

"And we are not on welfare," she insists.

Mother Anne sees to that. Last week, after 2 1/2 months at Broadview Shelter, she accumulated enough money to move the close-knit family into a $150-a-month transitional apartment. Broadview is one of a few shelters that operate a transitional apartment program—a sort of way station—before the move to total independence. The rent comes from Anne's 11 P.M.-to-6 A.M. job making Winchell's doughnuts for $3.75 an hour and selling blood twice a week for $8.

The place is meager—one bedroom, a bath, a living room with stove, a refrigerator and sink against the wall and three beds and one dresser for five people. There is no television, no living-room furniture and few toys. But there are two roses in a cheap vase on the table and a pretty calendar tacked to the wall. It's a step up from living at the shelter.

The system has two ways to put a roof over the head of a homeless family in Seattle: finding space in one of the area's 15 family shelters or finding an agency to "voucher" them into a low-income motel. Instead of maintaining their own shelters, several agencies such as Traveler's Aid and the Fremont Public Association buy hotel space. About 500 beds (101 in motels through voucher programs) serve homeless families in Seattle.

The hotels are not the Westin. "They end up in the hotels that are already run-down because those are the only ones that will take shelter clients," explains a worker with the Seattle Indian Center. She says reluctant motel managers complain that many homeless families drink and fight on the premises.

Still, Seattle's family-shelter system is more progressive than those in many cities—including New York, where families may be warehoused with hundreds of others in huge rooms. Locally, people usually are housed in private apartments or with others in small rooms. And though programs vary from shelter to shelter, many do provide counseling and on-site referral health care. A few offer modest programs for youngsters. . . .

If that sounds like rock bottom, many families never make it into the system.

Where do they go?

"We don't know where they are. They are literally invisible if not in the shelter system," says [Marty] Curry of [Seattle's] Community Development [Department].

Others—the police, street people, shelter workers—say the uncounted homeless double or triple up with friends, live out of cars on suburban side streets, camp out in parks, ride Metro buses all night or hole up comunally in low-income hotels. . . .

Source: *The Seattle Times,* May 31, 1987. Reprinted by permission.

Many bitter commentaries critique society's refusal to seek solutions. Jonathan Kozol has warned that attitudes toward the homeless are changing: "So from pity we graduate to weariness; from weariness to impatience; from impatience to annoyance; from annoyance to dislike and sometimes to contempt."[113] Such feelings, he fears, are too easily translated into public policy. Jason DeParle points out the irony of doing so little about low-income housing at the same time that the society subsidizes housing for middle- and upper-class citizens.

> The death of affordable housing—what a strange notion in a nation as spectacularly housed as this one. Overall, the United States shelters more people in better-quality homes than any country in the world. (Ask the Japanese.) And it does so by offering the middle- and upper- classes exactly what it tells the poor it can no longer afford: generous Government subsidies. The $66 billion a year the Federal Government spends on mortgage-interest and property tax deductions is about four times as much as it spends on low-income housing. More than two-thirds of it goes for families with incomes above $75,000.[114]

In some areas, local governments aided by private foundations are attempting to fill the void left by the national government. In Chicago, National Housing Services (NHS), a nonprofit group, is working on finding money to help residents buy homes. The premise is that home ownership gives residents a stake in the neighborhood that will motivate them to do other things to improve it. A private bank has provided NHS with a revolving loan fund that is repackaged into small loans with low interest rates that people of modest means can afford. In addition to money, NHS also provides community members with the organizational skills to demand their fair share of city services. One Chicago neighborhood chased out drug dealers by constantly demanding that the city maintain a streetlight and increase police patrols.[115]

One estimate indicates that approximately 2,000 nonprofit housing groups in the country like NHS have built or renovated more than 450,000 units in the past decade.[116] Such groups package government money along with contributions from corporations and foundations.

While these organizations have been successful in many urban neighborhoods, they cannot mount the kind of broad-based efforts to deal in a comprehensive way with the problems of housing. An indicator that no one expects any level of government to mount such as effort is the fact that one commentator wrote: "Inner-city neighborhoods won't come back big time until big-time private business perceives them to be profit centers."[117] Some are optimistic that will happen because, although the profit margin on loans for affordable housing is low, the volume is greater than with the luxury housing market.[118] Still, such efforts will leave out those who cannot afford even a low-interest loan.

Conclusion

The general public has had little direct role in shaping redistributive policy, but general attitudes about poverty have shaped that policy. Americans are ambivalent about policy that is designed to redistribute resources from the haves to the have-nots. The commitment of Americans to the superiority of a capitalist economic system and to the belief in "the American dream" of progressing from rags to riches as a result of hard work leads many Americans to conclude that poverty is the individual's fault rather than a consequence of social factors. For those who believe that the source of poverty is individual failure, the idea of government assistance to the poor seems not only useless but damaging because the aid will only remove incentives for the poor to better themselves. Programs to aid the poor do exist, however, because Americans have compassion for those labeled "the deserving poor" (the old, the young, the mentally and physically disabled).

Local governments had traditionally been responsible for aiding the poor. Federal involvement began during the Great Depression when large numbers of people who suddenly were poor created a constituency for national poverty programs. Nonetheless, the policies that were adopted then still distinguished between the deserving poor and the unworthy. Efforts by the national government at that time were designed to alleviate some of the hardship until the economy rebounded and to provide aid to such groups of deserving poor as the elderly, the temporarily unemployed, the blind, and children.

As the economy improved, demands, even tolerance, for redistributive programs waned. Housing assistance began to be diverted from providing the poor "safe, sanitary, and decent" housing to improving the appearance of the city. That meant removing slums and blight and, ironically, reducing the housing stock for the poor. Those citizens who had not enjoyed the same economic improvement as many Americans—those who were still poor—found themselves competing for government aid with realtors and developers.

For a brief period, the federal government tried to wage war on poverty. The goal was not to create interim measures or provide patchwork aid, but to eliminate the causes of poverty. Included were job training programs and educational enhancement programs for the children of the poor. The War on Poverty was short-lived, however. Part of the problem was that another war was being fought at the same time, and gradually that war—the one in Vietnam—took precedence over every-

thing else. Another part of the problem was the belief that the programs simply were not working. Race was also an issue.

> The community action programs that might have provided a precedent for extensive intervention in the inner cities and prevented the spiral of decline so painfully visible to observers on all sides of the political spectrum became instead embroiled in the task of extending political rights to African Americans. That proved their undoing. Rather than responding to the need for jobs, housing, and social services . . . , the nation turned its back on cities.[119]

But a major part of the problem with the War on Poverty was the effort by community action agencies to mobilize the poor into an effective political force to make increased demands on local government. Local officials felt threatened. Other interest groups in the metropolis resented the competition for resources. The backlash has resulted in a substantial narrowing of national efforts to deal with poverty.

In 1980, the President's Commission for a National Agenda for the Eighties observed that cities, especially old cities, were being "transformed." In the process, the Commission noted that some residents of those cities may be "consigned to become a nearly permanent urban underclass."[120] The Commission concluded that the national government could not and should not interfere.[121] The welfare reform of the 1990s and the reduction in efforts to provide citizens with decent, safe, and affordable housing are congruent with that recommendation.

The responsibility for dealing with poverty is therefore moving back to the state and local levels. Historically, local governments have been more comfortable with programs aimed at economic development than with programs serving the poor. Programs that help business are viewed as serving the public interest because aid is seen as producing more jobs and a strengthened tax base. Housing programs have been most successful when they were aimed at stimulating the construction, banking, and real estate interests rather than at providing low-cost, decent housing for the poor. Local governments fear that if they respond to demands from their poor constituents, they will have to raise taxes, and that, they believe, will result in the flight of business and the middle and upper class from the city.

Although bankers participate in banking policy and farmers participate in agricultural policy, the poor have traditionally had little role in welfare policy. The notable exception was the War on Poverty. Still, the poor never achieved the legitimacy of other groups in our society. Defense contractors, for instance, can renegotiate contracts, but the poor cannot negotiate food stamps. The programmatic impact of the participation stimulated by the War on Poverty was limited, but the legacy of training local leadership did have some effect. Many citizens who first got involved in government through the War on Poverty programs went on to elected and appointed positions at all levels of government. This illustrates again that mobilization and participation are essential for political power.

The poor are limited in political power. They have numbers, but numbers mean little unless people can be mobilized. Their demands, even if articulated, have been defined as coming from a "special interest," and one that could be damaging to the city, while the demands of business are defined as in the "public interest." General public attitudes tend to agree that the poor are not only a special interest group, but one that is not deserving because poverty is seen by most as an individual failing. While many would like to see poverty disappear, they are unwilling to have their money in the form of taxes be used for that goal. Failure to mobilize to get their concerns on the public agenda means that the de-

mands of the poor are rarely addressed in the policy process.

Notes

1. Frances Fox Piven and Richard A. Cloward, *Regulating the Poor: The Functions of Public Welfare* (New York: Vintage Books, 1971).

2. William P. O'Hare, *A New Look at Poverty in America*, Population Bulletin 51, no. 2 (Washington D.C.: Population Resource Bureau, September, 1996), 14, 17.

3. Paul E. Peterson, *City Limits* (Chicago: University of Chicago Press, 1981), Chapter 9.

4. John H. Mollenkopf, *The Contested City* (Princeton: Princeton University Press, 1983).

5. Rhodes Cook, "Cities: Decidedly Democratic, Declining in Population," *Congressional Quarterly* 55 (July 12, 1997): 1645–1653.

6. Mollenkopf, *The Contested City*, 16–17.

7. Charles Murray, *Losing Ground: America's Social Policy 1950–1980*, (New York: Basic Books, 1984).

8. Piven and Cloward, *Regulating the Poor*.

9. Chaim I. Waxman, *The Stigma of Poverty*, 2nd ed. (New York: Pergamon Press, 1983), 75.

10. Ibid., 78.

11. Marian Lief Palley and Howard A. Palley, *Urban America and Public Policies*, 2nd ed. (Lexington, Massachusetts: D.C. Heath, 1981), 120.

12. Joe R. Feagin, *Subordinating the Poor: Welfare and American Beliefs* (Englewood Cliffs, New Jersey: Prentice-Hall, 1975), 97.

13. Harrell R. Rodgers, Jr., *Poverty Amid Plenty: A Political and Economic Analysis* (Reading, Massachusetts: Addison-Wesley, 1979), 46.

14. These classifications are used by Thomas R. Dye, *Understanding Public Policy*, 5th ed. (Englewood Cliffs, New Jersey: Prentice-Hall, 1984), 114–133; James E. Anderson, David W. Brady, Charles S. Bullock III, and Joseph Stewart, Jr., *Public Policy and Politics in America*, 2nd ed. (Monterey, California: Brooks/Cole, 1984), 136–164.

15. Piven and Cloward, *Regulating the Poor*, 46.

16. Palley and Palley, *Urban America and Public Policy*, 2nd ed., 121.

17. Ibid., 122.

18. Mark A. Gelfand, *A Nation of Cities: The Federal Government and Urban America, 1933–1965* (New York: Oxford University Press, 1975), 43.

19. Michael Harrington, *The Other America: Poverty in the United States* (Baltimore: Penguin, 1962), 155.

20. James C. Donovan, *The Politics of Poverty*, 2nd ed. (Indianapolis, Indiana: Pegasus, 1973), 26.

21. D. Lee Bawden and John L. Palmer, "Social Policy: Challenging the Welfare State" in *The Reagan Record: An Assessment of America's Changing Domestic Priorities*, ed. John L. Palmer and Isabel V. Sawhill (Cambridge, Massachusetts: Ballinger, 1984), 211–212.

22. Mollenkopf, *The Contested City,* 122–126.

23. Ibid., 274.

24. President Ronald Reagan, State of the Union Address, January 30, 1982, *Congressional Quarterly* 40 (January 30, 1982): 178.

25. Peter Edelman, "The Worst Thing Bill Clinton Has Done," *Atlantic Monthly,* March 1997, 44.

26. Terry N. Clark and Lorna C. Ferguson, *City Money: Political Processes, Fiscal Strain, and Retrenchment* (New York: Columbia University Press, 1983), 214–216; see also Richard J. Cebula, "Local Government Policies and Migration," *Public Choice* 19 (Fall 1974): 85–93.

27. Jill Quadagno, *The Color of Welfare: How Racism Undermined the War on Poverty* (New York: Oxford University Press, 1994), 190.

28. John Kenneth Galbraith, *The Affluent Society* (New York: Mentor, 1958), 252.

29. Ibid., 275.

30. Julie Rovner, "Congress Clears Overhaul of Welfare System," *Congressional Quarterly* 46 (October 1, 1988): 2699.

31. Edelman, "The Worst Thing Bill Clinton Has Done," 44.

32. James G. Gimpel, *Fulfilling the Contract: The First Hundred Days* (Boston: Allyn and Bacon, 1996), 79.

33. Jeffrey Katz, "Welfare Overhaul Law," *Congressional Quarterly Weekly Report* 54 (September 21, 1996): 2696–2708.

34. O'Hare, *A New Look at Poverty in America,* 40.

35. Ibid., 36–39.

36. E.E. Schattschneider, *The Semi-Sovereign People: A Realist's View of Democracy in America* (New York: Holt, Rinehart & Winston, 1960), 98–99.

37. Donovan, *The Politics of Poverty,* 55.

38. J. David Greenstone and Paul E. Peterson, *Race and Authority in Urban Politics: Community Participation and the War on Poverty,* (New York: Russell Sage Foundation, 1973), 220.

39. Daniel P. Moynihan, *Maximum Feasible Misunderstanding: Community Actions in the War on Poverty* (New York: Free Press, 1969), 129.

40. Quadagno, *The Color of Welfare,* 11.

41. Richard P. Nathan, Fred C. Doolittle, and Associates, *The Consequences of Cuts: The Effects of the Reagan Domestic Programs on State and Local Government* (Princeton, New Jersey: Princeton Urban and Regional Research Center, 1983), 3.

42. Ibid., 29.

43. Ibid., 101.

44. Nancy Beer and John R. Lago, *The Dynamics and Directions of New Jersey Medicaid* (Princeton, New Jersey: Princeton Urban and Regional Research Center, 1987); Catherine Lovell, "Deregulation of State and Local Government," *Policy Studies Journal* 13 (March 1985), 607–615; David R. Morgan and Robert E. England, "The Small Cities Block Grant Program: An Assessment of Programmatic Change Under State Control," *Public Administration Review* 44 (November–December 1984), 477–482; Osbin L. Ervin, "The State–Local Partnership and National

Objectives: An Examination of the CDBG Small Cities Program, *Policy Studies Journal* 13 (March 1985): 634–642.

45. Nathan, et al. *The Consequences of Cuts,* 6.

46. O'Hare, *A New Look at Poverty in America,* 10.

47. "Raise the Minimum Wage?", *U.S. News and World Report,* April 29, 1996, 34.

48. John E. Schwarz, *America's Hidden Success: A Reassessment of Public Policy From Kennedy to Reagan,* rev. (New York: Norton, 1988), 153.

49. "The Worth of Work," *New York Times,* April 12, 1987, sec. E.

50. National Public Radio, June 30, 1997.

51. James E. Anderson, et al., *Public Policy and Politics in America,* 2nd ed., 166.

52. O'Hare, *A New Look at Poverty in America,* 14–15.

53. Anderson, et al., *Public Policy and Politics in America,* 2nd ed., 152.

54. O'Hare, *A New Look at Poverty in America,* 15.

55. Eleanor Baugher and Leatha Lamison-White, *Poverty in the United States: 1995* (Washington, D.C.: U.S. Bureau of the Census, Current Population Reports, Series P60–194, U.S. Government Printing Office, 1996,) xii.

56. Thomas Byrne Edsall and Mary D. Edsall, *Chain Reaction: The Impact of Race, Rights, and Taxes on American Politics* (New York: Norton, 1991), 148.

57. Jean Mayer, "The Food Stamp Dilemma," *Washington Post,* February 19, 1982, sec. E3.

58. See for example, Oscar Lewis, *Five Families: Mexican Case Studies in the Culture of Poverty* (New York: Basic Books, 1959); Oscar Lewis, "The Culture of Poverty" in *On Understanding Poverty: Perspectives from the Social Sciences,* ed. Daniel Patrick Moynihan (New York: Basic Books, 1968): 187–220; Edward Banfield, *The Unheavenly City Revisited,* (Prospect, Illinois: Waveland Press, 1974).

59. Banfield, *The Unheavenly City Revisited,* 61.

60. Herbert Gans, "Culture and Class in the Study of Poverty" in *On Understanding Poverty,* ed. Daniel P. Moynihan, 206.

61. William Julius Wilson, *When Work Disappears: The World of the New Urban Poor* (New York: Knopf, 1996), 55.

62. Ibid., 71.

63. Lee Rainwater, "The Problem of Lower-Class Culture and Poverty War Strategy" in ibid., 229–2259; Robert E. Lane, *Political Ideology* (New York: Free Press, 1965).

64. Elliot Liebow, *Tally's Corner* (Boston: Little, Brown, 1967), 222.

65. Peterson, *City Limits,* 182.

66. Murray, *Losing Ground.*

67. Lawrence M. Mead, *The New Politics of Poverty: The Nonworking Poor in America* (New York: Basic Books, 1992), 12.

68. Ibid., 183.

69. "Reformers All," *The Economist,* February 4, 1995, 24.

70. Kathryn Edin and Christopher Jencks, "Welfare" in *Rethinking Social Policy: Race, Poverty and the*

Underclass, ed. Christopher Jencks (New York: Harper Collins, 1992), 204.

71. Ibid.

72. Ibid., 226–227.

73. Edelman, "The Worst Thing Bill Clinton Has Done," 52.

74. Ibid., 53.

75. David C. Ranney, *Planning and Politics in the Metropolis* (Columbus, Ohio: Merrill, 1969), 4.

76. Palley and Palley, *Urban America and Public Policy,* 188.

77. Ibid., 188–189.

78. Mark J. Stern, "The Emergence of the Homeless as a Public Problem," *Social Service Review* 58 (June 1984): 294.

79. Jason DeParle, "Slamming the Door," *New York Times Magazine,* October 20, 1996.

80. Chester W. Hartman, *Housing and Social Policy* (Englewood Cliffs, New Jersey: Prentice-Hall, 1975), 137.

81. Palley and Palley, *Urban America and Public Policy,* 200.

82. Harold Wolman, *Politics of Federal Housing,* (New York: Dodd, Mead & Company, 1971), 28–29.

83. Harold Ickes, cited by Jewel Bellush and Murray Hausknecht, "Urban Renewal: An Historic Overview" in *Urban Renewal: People Politics, and Planning,* ed. Jewel Bellush and Murray Hausknecht (Garden City, New Jersey: Anchor Books, 1967), 7.

84. Bellush and Hausknecht, "Urban Renewal," in Ibid., 8.

85. Ibid.

86. Charles Abrams, "The Future of Housing" in *Urban Renewal,* ed. Bellush and Hausknecht, 40.

87. Gelfand, *A Nation of Cities,* 115.

88. Leonard Freedman, *Public Housing: The Politics of Poverty* (New York: Holt, Rinehart, & Winston, 1969), 102.

89. Bellush and Hausknecht, "Urban Renewal."

90. Gelfand, *A Nation of Cities,* 155.

91. Wolman, *Politics of Federal Housing,* 38.

92. Bellush and Hausknecht, "Urban Renewal," 14.

93. Wolman, *Politics of Federal Housing,* 41.

94. The authors wish to thank Luis Ricardo Fraga for this observation.

95. Herbert J. Gans, *The Urban Villagers: Group and Class in the Life of Italian-Americans* (New York: Free Press, 1962); Marc Fried, "Grieving for a Lost Home: Psychological Costs of Relocation" in *The Urban Condition,* ed. Leonard Duhl (New York: Basic Books, 1963), 151–171.

96. Harold Kaplan, *Urban Renewal Politics* (New York: Columbia University Press, 1963).

97. Martin Anderson, *The Federal Bulldozer* (Cambridge, Massachusetts: MIT Press, 1964), 65.

98. Freedman, *Public Housing,* 105–122.

99. Ibid., 106.

100. Mario Cuomo, *Forest Hills Diary: The Crisis of Low-Income Housing* (New York: Vintage Books, 1974), 23.

101. Ibid., 192.

102. *New York Times,* September 30, 1984.

103. *Hills* v. *Gautreaux,* 96 S. Ct. 1538 (1976).

104. DeParle, "Slamming the Door," 54.

105. Palley and Palley, *Urban American and Public Policy,* 372.

106. Palmer and Sawhill, *Reagan Record,* 372.

107. Keitha D. Lawrence, "Section 8 Housing : In the Case of Efficiency and Effectiveness." Unpublished paper, 1985.

108. DeParle, "Slamming the Door," 52.

109. Ibid., 57.

110. Jon Healey, "VA–HUD Spending Bill Clears with Bipartisan Support," *Congressional Quarterly* 54 (September 28, 1996): 2762–2764.

111. John Diamond, "Homeless Over Here, *Grand Forks Herald,* November 10, 1996, sec. 4a.

112. Christopher Jencks, *The Homeless* (Cambridge, Massachusetts: Harvard University Press, 1994).

113. Jonathan Kozol, *Rachel and Her Children: Homeless Families in America* (New York: Fawcett Columbine, 1988), 183.

114. DeParle, "Slamming the Door," 53. See also Elliot Liebow, *Tell Them Who I Am: The Lives of Homeless Women* (New York: Free Press, 1993); Michael J. Dear and Jennifer R. Wolch, *Landscapes of Despair: From Deinstitutionalization to Homelessness* (Princeton: Princeton University Press, 1987).

115. Rochelle E. Stanfield, "Home, Sweet Home," *National Journal* (September 14, 1996): 1949.

116. DeParle, "Slamming the Door," 94.

117. Stanfield, "Home, Sweet Home," 1950.

118. Ibid.

119. Quadagno, *The Color of Welfare,* 196–197.

120. President's Commission for a National Agenda for the Eighties, *A National Agenda for the Eighties* (Washington, D.C.: U.S. Government Printing Office, 1980), 69.

121. Ibid., 66.

CHAPTER 15

Epilogue

"The mobs of great cities," observed Thomas Jefferson, "add just so much to pure government as sores do to the strength of the human body."[1] Many contemporary observers of America's metropolitan areas feel that Jefferson was right. In 1967, Robert Dahl commented on the failure of Americans to come to grips with an urban society.

> City building is one of the most obvious incapacities of Americans. We Americans have become an urban people without having developed an urban civilization. Though we live in cities, we do not know how to build cities. . . . We seem to lack the innate grasp of the essential elements of the good city. . . .[2]

In many ways, causes for despair have increased since 1967. There is fear that for the first time a permanent underclass is developing in America and its members—many of them African-American, or Latino, or female heads of household, or dependent youth—are making inner cities their home. In addition, increasing numbers of homeless are eking out an existence on city streets, finding it difficult to qualify for even minimal social benefits because they have no permanent address. The national welfare reform promises to "end welfare as we know it," but no one is sure what its impact will be.

Faced with increasing demands, governments in the metropolis have suffered fiscal crisis. Tax revolts at the state and local levels have limited their ability to raise revenues. In the 1980s the Reagan Administration substantially cut back on federal income transfers to urban areas and the people who live in them. Current concern for the size of the federal deficit and debt has led to further retrenchment in federal programs to help the nation's metropolises and their citizens. Fiscal problems are exacerbated by the continuing migration of the middle and upper classes to ever more distant suburbs. As people move out, their dependence on—and support for—center cities lessens. Edge cities develop that provide jobs, shopping, and entertainment to residents, who then have no need to travel to the center city in the metropolis. New gated communities enable those who can afford them privacy and protection from those who differ. As the populations of the center cities decline, the density decreases. Vacant buildings blight neighborhoods and become targets for arsonists or hovels for the homeless or worse.

This fiscal stress—at times being extreme enough to bring cities such as New York and

Philadelphia to the brink of bankruptcy—has led some observers to despair of the ability of citizens or of the political process to determine the future of urban America. Many of the resources that local governments need to succeed are privately controlled. Reliance of local governments on major economic interests derives from the fundamental need to encourage economic development. Given the dependence of governments in the metropolis on major economic interests, some worry that the political process has little latitude in altering policy. The question of citizen impact on that process is, therefore, moot.

While economic interests have advantages in urban politics because of their control of resources important to the health of cities, the role of political leaders and citizens should not and can not be dismissed. Citizen control of urban policy through an accountable political process is essential for democracy. Three-quarters of Americans live in urban areas. If they can not exercise control over the important decisions in the metropolis, we must question America's right to be called a democracy.

Politics does matter. As Robert Dahl argued, "the policies of city hall and the totality of city agencies and activities are so important to our lives that to participate in the decisions of the city means, or anyway can mean, participating in shaping not merely the trivial but some of the most vital aspects of our environment."[3] Research has demonstrated that the political process sets the direction for urban development.[4] Political leaders have authority to guide and to constrain major economic interests. While political leaders will normally listen to the demands of those interests, they can use their planning and zoning powers to influence and to alter what private landowners do.

Citizens also matter. Major economic interests control resources that urban officials need, but so do citizens. Political leaders need an electoral coalition to gain and retain office.

Citizen votes are necessary for that coalition. Organized blocs of citizens can exchange their electoral numbers with officials for policy initiatives. Organized neighborhoods can bargain with developers for input into construction decisions.

Citizens can play a meaningful role in the creation and implementation of policy that affects their lives in American urban areas. But there are substantial limits on their ability to do so. This last chapter will review those limits as well as the evidence of success.

Limits on Citizen Control

Clearly, there are limits on citizen control. Economic pressure on local governments cannot be discounted. Both officials and citizens value economic development and major development projects are indicators of urban success.[5] That creates popular pressure on political leaders to respond favorably to the demands of developers and other major businesses. The irony is that citizens themselves aid in creating the mutuality of interests between the political leaders and major economic interests. The tendency for all to see business demands as representing the public interest limits citizens' ability to control urban policy in other areas by reducing the resources available once business demands are satisfied.

There are other limits on citizen control. In city after city, middle-class progressive reformers succeeded in implementing a variety of changes in government structure aimed at undercutting the power of party machines. Urban officials were required to run on nonpartisan ballots. Candidates for city council were required to run in citywide elections rather than from wards. In some places, mayors and councils were replaced with commissions. In other places, an unelected city manager was vested with responsibilities for day-to-day operations.

The power of machines declined, but as a consequence so did citizen participation. Research has consistently indicated that in reformed governments citizens participate less and have less impact.[6] The effect is particularly devastating for minorities, who have little or no hope of success when forced to run on a citywide basis, and for the lower class, who depend more on party labels for voting cues. These structures effectively dilute the impact of minority voting.

The fragmentation of metropolitan areas also affects participation, especially for minorities and the lower class. A variety of factors entice residents out of center cities. High land costs in the city, distaste for the density of urban living, fear of crime, desire to leave the polyglot mixture of the city to live with people like oneself all contribute to push people out of the center city and pull them into suburbs and edge cities. Past federal policies that subsidized mortgages for suburban homes and built highways between center cities and suburban developments contributed to population shifts. In turn, the suburb offers ownership of a single-family home—the American dream—and a unique package of government services. Businesses also move out in search of cheap land, meaning that residents in the suburbs and edge cities no longer need to be dependent on the center city for jobs.

By choosing among the suburban communities that ring the city, citizens can vote with their feet for the package of services they desire. Once the choice is made, the only purpose of further political activity is to maintain what is in place. Some suburbs adopt a variety of zoning regulations designed to control building, thus ensuring the "right kind" of people and businesses move in. Those citizens who can afford to move to the suburb of their choice have the best of all worlds. They need to exert little effort to have the government policies they prefer. Being surrounded by people like themselves means that there is widespread agreement and therefore little necessity to fight with their neighbors for the policies they want.

For those without such resources, the impact of suburbanization is grim. Suburbanization divides the metropolis into a patchwork quilt of separate legal jurisdictions. Because of efforts by some suburbs to ensure residents will be from high-income segments of the population, the poor are left disproportionately in the center city or in a few fringe suburbs. In the center cities, the poor are often African-American and Latino, and they are often confined to ghettos.

The people living within these ghettos often manifest many pathologies, for example, crime, drug addiction, and illegitimacy, that create dependency and despair. Residents are locked into the ghetto because of their poverty and because of racial discrimination in society. The educational system is often inadequate or is seen as irrelevant.[7] The effects of discrimination in housing and employment are even more acute because of the movement of jobs to the suburbs. As the poor are dependent on sometimes nonexistent public transportation to reach those jobs, the picture for employment is bleak.

The governments of the center city and a few suburbs face a population with a great need for social services and little capacity to pay taxes, while many suburbs have a wealthy population with little need for government services. Legal jurisdictions with a large percentage of low-income residents have to tax them at high rates and still have little money to serve the demands of the population. Jurisdictions with a predominantly wealthy population can tax at low rates and still have ample funds to provide desired services. The inequity is clear. Those who are wealthy pay a lower percentage of their income in taxes and get good services; the poor pay a high percentage of their income in taxes and get poor services. The political fragmentation makes an equitable distribution of costs and benefits impossible, regardless of how much the poor participate in local politics.

Another effect of the legal fragmentation of the metropolis is the difficulty addressing problems that transcend the legal divisions. Transportation would be chaotic without some attempt to coordinate highways and bus lines. Attempts to improve air and water quality also depend on coordination among the various governments, as do many other metropolitan problems and policies. Citizens have difficulty exercising control because action by just one jurisdiction can not solve the problem.

Governments in the metropolis have proven to be very creative in devising ways to coordinate on specific policies without reducing their autonomy over other areas. Suburbs contract with other governments for specific services. Special districts such as regional transportation authorities are formed. Officials from the various governments meet on a regular basis in councils of government to discuss common problems. These devices provide partial coordination, but add to that already confusing jumble of governments in the metropolis. Answering the question "Who's in charge here?" becomes difficult and this complicates the job of citizens who want to alter policy.

If the fragmentation of legal authority in the metropolis complicates the job of the citizen, so does the nationalization of policy. Local governments are legally creatures of the state and have always been subject to control by state governments. Even in states that provide home rule for local governments, states determine which governments are eligible for home rule and precisely what policies can be controlled under a home rule charter. The twentieth century has been characterized by even greater external control over urban policies because of power flowing from state governments to the federal government. The limited capacity of local government to raise adequate revenues to finance vital services has

spurred the federal government to transfer funds. Many transfers come in the form of grants that require matching funds and specify guidelines for how the funds are to be spent. The need to find matching funds can skew fiscal priorities; the guidelines can, in effect, dictate policy.

The result has often been a local government that marched to a tune piped in Washington. Citizens who wish to alter policy, then, must look beyond city hall, and even beyond the statehouse, to Congress, the president, and the Washington bureaucracy. This further adds to the difficulty citizens have finding the answer to the question "Who is in charge?" Recent devolution of government programs from the national to the state level may make this problem less serious, but may also mean that less money will be available to address urban problems. That, in turn, may increase the reliance of local governments on major economic interests.

Evidence of Citizen Control

While the limits on citizen control are formidable, they do not preclude the possibility of citizens exercising control. The environment of the metropolis does create barriers to effective citizen control, but it also creates incentives and opportunities. The heterogeneity and interdependence of cities result in conflict that provides the incentive for participation. The impersonality makes expression of disagreement and conflict acceptable. While cities may produce barriers to participation, so do small towns, which are often viewed nostalgically as the bastions of democracy. The personalism of small towns (and the suburbs that mimic them) creates a pressure for repressing conflict that arises. Evidence suggests that small towns are often dominated by small cliques.[8] Nor is the environment less hospitable now than in the eras of the mercantile city and industrial city, in which the definition of governmental power was so small that few issues were considered appropriate for the public agenda.

While involvement of the federal government in many ways complicated citizen control, it actually facilitated citizen action in other ways. The influx of money into the metropolis provided citizens with the incentive to participate in decisions governing the allocations of that money. Many of the programs required, as one of the strings attached to the grants, that citizens be given some opportunity to participate in allocation decisions. Although some of this mandated participation was nothing more than symbolism, in other cases (most notably the War on Poverty and Model Cities programs) an indigenous leadership emerged within previously inactive neighborhoods.[9] These neighborhoods still tend to be more active than other neighborhoods with otherwise similar populations.

Often the impetus for the national programs came from groups in the city, African-Americans for example, and local officials who felt that involvement by the national government was the only way to break the control of state legislatures or local power structures that have historically been unresponsive. The devolution mentioned above may be a threat to the advances made by urban minorities.

A major reason for qualifying the positive response to a question about the role of citizens in urban policy is the consistent finding that not all citizens can or do have an equal impact. Citizens can use a variety of mechanisms to try to control urban politics. They can become involved in electoral activity in ways ranging from running for office to turning out to vote. They can organize interest groups or mobilize a protest or demonstration. They can contact a government official about a specific problem or vent their spleens at a public hearing. The available evidence indicates these tactics vary in how successful they are likely to be and what resources are necessary.

Simply attending a hearing demands little of a citizen besides the effort of finding out where and when the meeting is being held. Unfortunately, the hearing probably will not change anything. Contacting officials also requires few resources besides the knowledge of whom to contact, and evidence indicates officials do respond to such contacts. However, the contacts and the responses tend to focus on specific requests for service—clean my street, put a new swing set in my neighborhood park—and are not likely to result in major policy alterations. Of course, citizens may not want major policy changes.

A single vote in an election also requires little effort, but in itself has little potential of success. A bloc of votes, however, can determine the outcome of an election and major changes in the public agenda can be produced by the electoral mobilization of groups of people. The dependence of political leaders on the resources controlled by major economic interests means that those interests will be likely partners in the governing coalition. While participation in an electoral coalition does not guarantee access to the governing coalition, an effective voting bloc may be included and can at least force its issue concerns onto the public agenda.

Regardless of electoral mechanisms such as at-large elections, African-Americans are becoming an increasingly powerful force in many cities as they make up an increasingly large proportion of the urban electorate. Latinos are also potent political forces in cities such as Miami and San Antonio. Asians are also becoming a more important political force as the newer immigrants are naturalized. The catch is that mobilizing large numbers of voters takes resources: money to buy media time, communication skills to get out a compelling message, volunteers to get out the vote.

Finally, interest groups have been shown to be effective if they have resources. Groups must be seen as cohesive forces and have effective leaders to speak for them. Being seen as having expertise or legitimacy also helps. Money can help groups be successful because it can be used to hire people to represent them to political leaders, to plan efforts to mobilize the membership, and to demonstrate cohesiveness. Money also helps groups appear legitimate.

Of the three main resources that citizens can use to alter urban policy—money, expertise, and numbers—money is usually the easiest to use because it can be exchanged for other resources. It can be used to hire experts or to plan campaigns to communicate the group's message effectively. In addition, because our society values individual achievement, money is used as an indicator of success and accords those who possess it special legitimacy. Numbers, however, are difficult to use. Proving widespread support for a policy may necessitate actually mobilizing to demonstrate, or write letters, or vote. That, in turn, requires other resources: communications, volunteers, and good leaders. Organization is also necessary to mobilize numbers into a visible voting bloc.

Considering the resources that are necessary to alter policy helps explain the persistent finding that those people with high socioeconomic status are more likely to be politically active and successful. There is ample evidence that officials need to respond to requests from major economic interests with an urgency not accorded to other urban residents. The dependence of the city on major businesses is an important factor in this relationship.[10] But the electoral defeat of Mayor Ed Koch in New York City demonstrates that the support of major economic interests in itself is not sufficient for success. As Koch pursued policies that alienated the African-Americans and Latinos who were initially part of his electoral coalition, he eventually lost their support and the 1989 election, despite his support for economic development.[11]

Evidence indicates that bias is not inevitable. As William Gamson observed in referring to the political process: "Entry is not prohibited for those with the gumption, the persistence, and the skill to pursue it long enough."[12] Some community organizers like Saul Alinsky have been successful in mobilizing low-income populations. The Great Society programs, along with the civil rights movement of the 1960s and the voting rights acts of the last three decades, played a major role in mobilizing African-Americans for electoral activity. Some evidence indicates that this mobilization, in turn, has had the effect of increasing the political activity of Latinos.[13]

One observer claimed a grass roots "backyard revolution" was occurring throughout America, including the neighborhoods of America's cities.[14] Manuel Castells saw this neighborhood movement as a social movement that could eventually lead to citizens taking control of governments in the metropolis. He concluded, "At last, citizens will make cities."[15] While the neighborhood movement alone may not determine the future of America's cities, John Mollenkopf believes it has effectively ended the previous consensus on development policies and could provide the raw material from which a new consensus on urban policy could be forged.[16] Recent research has shown that when neighborhood organizations are supported by the city, they can be effective ways for citizens to affect decisions in the city, even in some cases in opposition to major economic interests.[17]

The movement of some middle- and upper-class residents into redeveloping urban neighborhoods will also increase citizen activity at the neighborhood level. The "gentry" will demand amenities to protect the rising property values of the neighborhood. The incumbent residents will organize to protect themselves from displacement. Although some of the participation efforts will have a negative focus, for example, keeping people out of the neighborhood, the intensity of the conflict will very probably involve people in efforts to influence urban redevelopment policies. Such attempts at influence at least provide a possibility of finding solutions that consider the needs of the low-income residents of gentrifying neighborhoods as well as the gentry. Even fiscal stress can increase the role of citizens in the search for new and creative solutions to urban problems. For example, there is likely to be increasing reliance on citizens in the co-production of public services such as crime protection. In addition, there may be more reliance on citizens to find solutions to urban problems.

Yet bias persists. The middle and upper classes are more active in politics, at all levels of American government, including the metropolis, than are members of the lower class. There are many reasons for this disparity, not the least of which is the fact that participation takes resources that low-income people lack. These different levels of political activity have an impact on the policies that structure metropolitan life.

Citizen Control of Public Policy

For the most part, the policies examined in this book tend to reflect the values and preferences of middle- and upper-class urban residents who are most likely to be active in politics. Land-use policies, like planning and zoning, community development, and transportation tend to be dominated by those interests that will reap benefits from the policies. Developers, real estate corporations, and contractors join government officials to create "progrowth coalitions" that urge the city to foster development.[18] Some argue that the pressure to encourage growth in the city results in a "growth machine."[19]

Such a pattern is not inevitable, however. Citizens have organized to stop development.[20] Organized neighborhoods have forced developers to work with them in planning.[21] One analysis of economic development in Boston noted: "However much developers might advocate purely market-driven development, the current political climate dictates otherwise, and citizen participation has become inextricably woven into the normal development process."[22]

An increasingly common urban conflict has developed over efforts by low-income neighborhoods to halt the construction of highways that threaten the viability of the neighborhood. In the past, construction of such highways had been viewed as a distributional policy because all potentially could use them, yet the construction actually benefited the suburban commuters at the expense of poor neighborhoods (the most frequent sites for such highways). The success of protests against the building of highways is the basis of Mollenkopf's argument that the mobilization of urban neighborhoods, in part due to the efforts of the Great Society programs, has ended consensus on development policies.[23]

Quality-of-life policies, such as education and crime control, tend to be dominated by professionals in charge of implementing policy at the grass roots level. The public at large has played little role in the creation or implementation of these policies, despite the salience of education and crime control to urban residents. In some instances, blue ribbon panels of selected citizens on community boards or police commissions or citizens advisory boards do play a major role. In some areas, police are encouraging a broader policy role by neighborhoods because they recognize the importance of neighborhood cooperation in the co-production of police services. By watching for crime and providing police with the information to help apprehend criminals, neighborhood residents can lighten the burdens of the police. Further, general public values of the dominant community affect educational and crime control policies. Often the political leadership and major economic interests also have minor roles in quality-of-life policies.

General public values are also important in the making of redistributive policy. The widespread belief that poverty is due to individual failure means that support for redistributive policy is limited. Although redistributive policy is supposedly aimed at shifting resources from the middle and upper classes to the lower class, the lower class plays little role in policy formulation.

Most initiatives for urban redistributive policy have originated at the national level as Democratic political leaders attempted to form an electoral coalition at that level by initiating policies to appeal to center city voters. While those policies did have some effect on redistributing societal resources, in most cases the major thrust was eventually altered so that the middle and upper classes also received benefits These alterations were a result of pressure from interest groups representing the middle and upper classes. In other words, many policies that were initially designed to redistribute resources eventually became distributive.

Backlash to the redistributional aspects of the policies enabled Republicans to capture the White House and Congress and cut back on social welfare programs. The shifting of population out of center city to suburbs and edge cities has led Democrats to realize that to be successful they must appeal to constituencies in addition to those in central cities. The "New Democrat" Bill Clinton won election in 1992 by promising to "end welfare as we know it." The welfare reform bill passed in 1996 fulfilled that promise. The changes in both welfare and housing policies at the national level threaten to reduce even further efforts to aid those at the bottom of the economic ladder. As federal financial transfers decrease, political leaders at the local level may become even more dependent on the resources that major economic interests control.

Conclusion

America's metropolises are a clear illustration that individuals in rational pursuit of their own self-interest can produce undesirable social outcomes. As Thomas Schelling observes, "How well each does for himself in adapting to his social environment is not the same thing as how satisfactory a social environment they collectively create for themselves."[24]

Individuals are moving out of cities because they want to live in areas that are greener, safer, less crowded, and cleaner. Factories are moving out because their sprawling plants demand space, and land costs less outside the city. High-technology industry moves in because it needs the close access to communication channels to keep on the cutting edge of its industry. Minorities move to the center city because it has traditionally been the land of opportunity. Each is rationally pursuing reasonable goals, but the result is that the poor and unskilled are trapped in a center city, which has few jobs for which they are qualified. As the concentration of the poor, who are frequently African-American and Latino, becomes greater, more of those with the resources to do so flee to the suburbs and edge cities, partly because of racial prejudice and partly because of fear—of declining property values, of crime, of poor schools.

Individual values do not always result in satisfactory social environments. Thus, solutions to urban problems must be found by pursuing collective goals rather than individual ones. Harlan Hahn and Charles Levine argue:

[T]he solution of many community problems such as crime, mental health, and education may depend more upon initiatives taken by private citizens than upon programs provided by governmental agencies. This perspective could focus increased attention on the extent to which public resources can be used to support the development of social networks and a "sense of community" in modern cities.[25]

If this is to occur, there must be a re-evaluation of the traditional individualistic value system and a greater willingness to focus efforts of both citizens and government on the attainment of collective goals for the good of the metropolis as a whole. Such a community-based definition of public good is contrary to the basic ethic of urban privatism and to our country's history and tradition. However, without such a conception of public good, many suggestions for addressing metropolitan problems will not be implemented. Gary Orfield, for example, has suggested school desegregation and fair housing enforcement throughout the metropolitan area as a way of dealing with the concentration of poor unskilled minorities in center cities.[26] William Julius Wilson wants increased public spending to improve conditions in the ghettos.[27] Anthony Downs has argued for more centralized metropolitan governments to help in coordination and equalization.[28]

The possibility of new initiatives seems remote in a period when fiscal retrenchment at the national level has become inevitable because of efforts to control the budget deficit. But national policy is cyclical. The current period of retrenchment followed substantial efforts in the 1960s and 1970s to solve the urban crisis. There is a possibility that national leadership could again focus on making America's cities not just deserts where we exist, but places where we want to live.

The likelihood of that happening will be increased by clear evidence that urban citizens are a political force that can not be ignored. Greater political activity of African-Americans, Latinos, and Asians is a major part of that effort. Their increasing political activity can give those groups substantial control over urban governments, as the climbing number of African-American and Latino city officials demonstrates. Success would be more likely if those groups could form coalitions with others. Biracial coalitions are possible, as the regime in Atlanta and the Bradley coalition in Los Angeles demonstrate.[29] But diversity among and within the groups makes coalition formation difficult. In addition, gaining control of many local governments may be a hollow victory for citizens because of the constraints on those governments.

Citizen involvement does not guarantee acceptance or development of policy that all would agree is good. Citizen activity is motivated in large part by self-interest, but that is precisely why it is important for all citizens to have access to the political process. One group's view of public good—even if that group is business—is not everyone's view. It is in this sense that Stephen Elkin talks about democracy increasing the "social intelligence" of the political system. Citizens are by no means always rational or reasoned, but neither are those who speak for other interests.[30]

Efforts to balance the national budget deficit mean there is little likelihood of any massive increase in federal aid for urban America. That is why, as Hahn and Levine observe, much of the initiative for rebuilding urban areas must come from the citizens themselves and from their political leaders. The challenge of transforming our metropolises is enormous. It is a challenge of democracy. Despite his grim view of America's cities, Robert Dahl believes it is a challenge we must not avoid:

> One advantage of the city as a unit for democratic government is, then, that it confronts us with a task worthy of our best efforts because of its urgency, its importance, its challenge, the extent of our failure up to now, and its promise, and the promise of the good life lived jointly with fellow citizens.[31]

Notes

1. Thomas Jefferson, *Works of Thomas Jefferson*, quoted in *The Intellectual Versus the City*, ed. Morton and Lucia White (New York: New American Library, 1964), 25–26.

2. Robert A. Dahl, "The City in the Future of Democracy" in *Readings in Urban Politics: Past, Present, and Future*, ed. Harlan Hahn and Charles H. Levine (New York: Longman, 1984), 384.

3. Ibid.

4. See, for example, Michael A. Pagano and Ann O.M. Bowman, *Cityscapes and Capital: The Politics of Urban Development* (Baltimore: Johns Hopkins University Press, 1995).

5. Paul E. Peterson, *City Limits* (Chicago: University of Chicago Press, 1981).

6. See, for example, Robert H. Salisbury and Gordon Black, "Class and Party in Partisan and Nonpartisan Elections," *American Political Science Review* 67 (September 1963), 584–592; Albert K Karnig and B. Oliver Walters, "Decline in Municipal Turnout: A Function of Changing Structure," *American Politics Quarterly* (October 1983), 491–505; Howard Hamilton, "The Municipal Voter: Voting and Nonvoting in City Elections," *American Political Science Review* 65 (December 1971), 1135–1140; Mary Grisez Kweit and Robert W. Kweit, *Implementing Citizen Participation in a Bureaucratic Society: A Contingency Approach* (New York: Praeger, 1981).

7. John D. Kasarda, "Urban Change and Minority Opportunities" in *The New Urban Reality*, ed. Paul E. Peterson (Washington, D.C.: The Brookings Institution, 1985), 57–58.

8. Arthur J. Vidich and Joseph Bensman, *Small Town in Mass Society: Class, Power, and Religion in a Rural Community* (Garden City, New York: Doubleday, 1960).

9. John Clayton Thomas, *Between Citizen and City: Neighborhood Organizations and Politics in Cincinnati* (Lawrence: University of Kansas Press, 1986).

10. Clarence N. Stone, "Systemic Power in Community Decision Making: A Restatement of Stratification Theory," *American Political Science Review* 74 (December 1980): 978–990; Stephen L. Elkins, *City and Regime in the American Republic* (Chicago: University of Chicago Press, 1987); Peterson, *City Limits*.

11. John Hull Mollenkopf, *A Phoenix in the Ashes: The Rise and Fall of the Koch Coalition in New York City Politics* (Princeton: Princeton University Press, 1992).

12. William A. Gamson, *The Strategy of Social Protest* (Homewood, Illinois: Dorsey, 1975), 143.

13. Rufus P. Browning, Dale Rogers Marshall, and David H. Tabb, *Protest Is Not Enough: The Struggle of Blacks and Hispanics for Equality in Urban Politics* (Berkeley: University of California Press, 1984).

14. Harry C. Boyte, *The Backyard Revolution: Understanding the New Citizen Movement* (Philadelphia: Temple University Press, 1980).

15. Manuel Castells, *The City and the Grassroots* (Berkeley: University of California Press, 1983), 336.

16. John Mollenkopf, *The Contested City* (Princeton: Princeton University Press, 1983).

17. Jeffrey M. Berry, Kent E. Portney, and Ken Thomson, *The Rebirth of Urban Democracy* (Washington, D.C.: The Brookings Institution, 1993); Barbara Ferman, *Challenging the Growth Machine: Neighborhood Politics in Chicago and Pittsburgh* (Lawrence: University of Kansas Press, 1996); Tony Robinson, "Gentrification and Grassroots Resistance in San Francisco's Tenderloin," *Urban Affairs Review* 30 (March 1995): 483–513.

18. Mollenkopf, *The Contested City*.

19. John R. Logan and Harvey L. Molotch, *Urban Fortunes: The Political Economy of Place* (Berkeley: University of California Press, 1987).

20. Robinson, "Gentrification and Grassroots Resistance in San Francisco's Tenderloin," 483–513.

21. Berry, Portney, and Thomson, *The Rebirth of Urban Democracy*; Ferman, *Challenging the Growth Machine*.

22. Janice K. Tulloss, "Citizen Participation in Boston's Development Policy: The Political Economy of Participation," *Urban Affairs Review* 30 (March 1995): 525.

23. Mollenkopf, *The Contested City*.

24. Thomas C. Schelling, *Micromotives and Macrobehavior* (New York: Norton, 1978), 19.

25. Harlan Hahn and Charles H. Levine, "Preface" in *Readings in Urban Politics: Past, Present, and Future*, 2nd ed., ed. Harlan Hahn and Charles H. Levine (New York: Longman, 1984), viii.

26. Gary Orfield, "Ghettoization and Its Alternatives" in *The New Urban Reality*, ed. Paul E. Peterson, 161–193.

27. William Julius Wilson, "The Urban Underclass in Advanced Industrial Society" in Ibid., 129–160.

28. Anthony Downs, *New Visions for Metropolitan America* (Washington, D.C.: The Brookings Institution, 1994), 161–162.

29. Clarence Stone, *Regime Politics: Governing Atlanta 1946–1988* (Lawrence: University of Kansas Press, 1989); Raphael J. Sonenshein, *Politics in Black and White: Race and Power in Los Angeles* (Princeton: Princeton University Press, 1993).

30. Stephen L. Elkin, *City and Regime in the American Republic* (Chicago: University of Chicago Press, 1987), 169.

31. Dahl, "The City in the Future of Democracy," 388.

Glossary

ability-to-pay Belief that those who have more money should contribute more to the coffers of society.

administrative efficiency Ease with which a tax can be assessed and collected.

administrative restrictions Bureaucratic rules and regulations that are often intrusive and are used to assure "acceptable" behavior.

agenda setting Stage of the policy process where issues or problems are raised in the hope that they will receive consideration by political actors.

alleviative policies Social programs, usually perceived as short-term, that are designed to reduce suffering of people who experience misfortunes not of their own making.

annexation Expanding the boundaries of a municipality to include other communities.

anomie Sense of normlessness or lack of direction.

anticipated reaction Individuals behaving in a certain way because of expectations of how others will behave.

at-large elections Elections in which the candidates are voted on in a city-wide election rather than in subdivisions of a city.

balancing the ticket Selecting representatives of various ethnic or racial groups to run together for the purpose of building a coalition of support from voters of all the represented groups.

benchmarking Strategic planning that involves the establishment of reference points for success.

benefits received Services received by individuals that are sometimes used as a basis for allocating costs.

block grants Transfers of money from one level of government to another with relatively few restrictions on how the money can be spent.

bond anticipation notes (BANs) Non-guaranteed, short-term bonds issued by local governments.

bosses Leaders who controlled the hierarchically structured political party organizations often called "machines."

budgetary process Procedures used to allocate financial resources among competing program areas.

443

building codes   Regulations generally concerned with safety and aesthetics. Examples include construction standards for insulation, supports, and building materials and electrical and plumbing standards.

bureaucratic politics model   Form of decision making in which participants take issue stands as the result of their position in an organization.

capital fix   Using money from the capital budget (that is, the budget reserved for long-term, capital-intensive, nonrecurring expenses such as fire trucks, bridges, etc.) for operating costs.

capital improvement plan   Means of long-term planning that coordinates and establishes priorities for major public works expenditures.

caretaker regime   Limited government that maintains and delivers only traditional public services.

categorical grants   Intergovernmental monetary transfers for very specific purposes.

central business district (CBD)   Main downtown area of retail, commercial, and service activities.

centralization   Stage of the ecological process at which different areas become focal points for different activities.

civil service   System of staffing government agencies on the basis of merit.

command   Form of decision making in which the decision maker has the power to issue an order and expect compliance.

commuter zone   Area ringing the city in the concentric circle model of urban development. The area is usually referred to as suburbs.

compromise   Situation in which each side is willing to trade off some issues to achieve other objectives.

concentration   Stage of the ecological process at which various people and business are attracted to settle in one location.

conservative view [of causes of disorder]   Viewing violence as pathological behavior engaged in by deviant people, who are spurred to action by outside agitators seeking to disrupt American society.

constraint   Negative consequences that citizens can threaten if governmental officials do not comply with citizen requests.

contracting with private vendors   Instead of government actually producing a good or service for citizens, it makes an agreement for the provision of the good or service by a nongovernment entity.

co-optation   Process of absorbing people into the leadership structure who otherwise could threaten the status quo as a way to attempt to assure stability.

co-production   Activities of citizens to cooperate with government in the provision of necessary services.

culture   Basic long-term beliefs and values held by a people.

curative policies   Social programs designed to work to remove the causes, not just the symptoms, of poverty.

decentralization   In the ecological process, the stage at which businesses move parts of their operations away from the center.

decentralizing   Moving authority from a central leadership to a broader number of people. It is designed to move from strict hierarchy to participation and teamwork.

decision-making approach   Method of ascertaining who holds power by looking at who the actors are in various policy areas.

decision rule hypothesis Holds that no one decision rule controls bureaucratic behavior, as different rules are applied in different situations.

decision rules Standards or criteria that are used to make choices.

development impact fee Charge to offset the public costs of private development.

developmental [policy] Programs designed to enhance a community's economic prosperity.

devolution Shifting of responsibilities to lower levels of government or to the private sector.

direct primary All party members participate in selecting candidates by voting in primary elections occurring before the general election. This was designed to prevent the bosses from selecting their hand-picked candidates in "smoke-filled rooms."

dispersion Stage of the ecological process in which individuals and businesses begin to move away from the original settlement because of changes in density and land values.

earmarking Setting aside revenues for a particular purpose.

ecological hypothesis States that certain neighborhood characteristics, such as age or density, affect service delivery patterns.

economic planning Often part of economic development as officials try to ascertain future job trends in the community and assure that a trained work force is in place to qualify for the jobs.

economic setting Economic make-up of the community.

economically efficient tax One that does not distort individuals' decisions concerning consumption and use.

economy of scale Cost savings generated by changing the scope of an activity. For example, in providing services that engender high equipment costs, it is often more efficient for several communities to work together in supplying the service rather than each buying its own equipment.

efficiency Maximizing the amount of outputs from a set amount of input.

elitist theorists Those who believe that a small unrepresentative group holds power in a community. Many in local government believe that business leaders make up the elite. Referring to some theorists as elitists does not mean those theorists desire elite control, but rather that they believe that an elite is in control.

entitlement Guarantee that persons who meet certain criteria will receive benefits.

equity There are various concepts of equity but the basic idea is that of fairness.

ethnic politics Political strategies designed to gain support of groups defined by their national origin.

evaluation Last stage of the policy process in which programs are assessed to determine their effectiveness.

exclusionary rule Ruling by the Supreme Court that any evidence produced by an illegal search is not admissible as evidence.

exclusionary zoning Practice of creating restrictive requirements for development that have the effect of preventing some groups from living in a community.

expense fix Treats this year's cost as next year's so it does not appear in the current budget.

externality Cost or benefit that is not reflected in (or is external to) market transactions.

extraterritorial powers   Powers that allow a city to control the actions of unincorporated communities outside the boundaries of the city. The powers are usually given to assure orderly growth as the city expands.

federal revenue sharing   Revenue transferred from the federal government to local and state governments; it provided a "guaranteed" income that could be used in virtually any manner the governments desired.

federal system   Nation with more than one level of government, each having some unique responsibilities that are guaranteed. The United States has a central national government and separate state governments.

filtering down   As housing ages those who can afford to, move, and their housing then becomes accessible to those of lesser means.

formula grant   Money allocated to recipients on the basis of a specified formula; it is usually nondiscretionary.

fragmented budgets   Budgets in which everyone involved focuses on their own interests and constituency.

free rider   Citizens who shirk political activity because they believe others will bear the burden and all will share in any benefits that result.

general obligation bonds   Type of debt that is guaranteed by the "full faith and credit" of the government entity issuing the bond. In the event of bankruptcy, bondholders are paid first. The amount of guaranteed debt is limited by state law.

gentrification   Term derived from the word "gentry," meaning gentlemen or aristocracy. It is used to refer to the upgrading of deteriorating neighborhoods by the upper and middle class.

gerrymander   To draw electoral districts' boundaries specifically to help particular groups maximize their chances of success in elections.

ghetto   Section of a city that is usually run down and inhabited by minority groups.

governing coalition   Group of individuals who have the resources to control decisions in the community.

grants-in-aid   Monetary transfers from one level of government to another for a specified purpose with some conditions.

growth machine   Members of a governing coalition who vigilantly pursue policies that will increase the value of land, without concern for the impact of those policies on other residents in the city.

Hawthorne effect   Situation in which an experiment may affect the results. For example, if everyone knows that a program is under a microscope, the people involved may behave differently than they do normally.

heterogeneity   Characteristic of urban living resulting from the intermingling of residents with diverse characteristics.

historical setting   Impact of past development on the present.

home rule   Provisions that allow cities and counties to act in "local" matters without having to go to state legislatures for specific authority. The provisions vary greatly among the states in terms of what size community is eligible and what authorities are granted.

homogeneity   Characteristic of small town life where most people share a common background.

horizontal equity   All people in the same situation pay the same tax.

housing codes Codes which establish maintenance standards to prevent deterioration that might affect the health and safety of others.

human ecology Processes that determine the settlement and spatial distribution of people and institutions over time.

hyperpluralism Model in which it is not possible to balance competing demands or to establish priorities and coordinate among policies, let alone to devise rational policy responses to achieve long-term goals. Everyone is involved, but no one is in control.

impersonality Characteristic of urban living whereby individuals do not establish close connections because most people are strangers.

impoundment Withholding of funds that have been appropriated for a specific purpose.

incremental budgets Budgets that vary only slightly from previous budgets.

individualist ethos Concern more for the welfare of the individual and the provision of specific benefits for individuals and groups than for the more general public good.

individualistic political culture Belief that government actions should encourage private initiative.

inducements Positive offering to officials in return for compliance with citizen requests. For example, citizens could promise campaign support.

industrial development bonds (IDBs) Bonds sold by a city to be used to finance private business development.

informal cooperation Agreement between governments to help each other under certain conditions; for example, if there is a large fire neighboring communities would send in their fire equipment.

initiative Provision in which citizens petition government to require that a particular policy be put on the ballot for decision by the voters.

interdependence Characteristic of urban areas resulting from the complexity of the community which necessitates that individuals rely on other people.

interlocal service contracts Local governments entering into a contract with a provider (counties, other municipalities) to buy needed services. This system is often viewed as a "supermarket or cafeteria of services," because the community can select or reject services provided from other areas or choose any combination it desires.

invasion Stage of the ecological process in which new groups or land uses move into an already established area.

issue network Fluid relationships among many interests trying to influence policy formation in a given area.

joint powers agreement Technique in which two or more governments agree to work together in a specific area. For instance, rather than holding separate school board, park board, city, and county elections, the various entities may agree to set a common election date and share costs and personnel.

land use Purpose for which land is developed.

land-use patterns Relationships between the different purposes for which land is developed.

land-use planning Projecting on the basis of the current composition of the community and expected future trends how much, and where, land should be set aside for various purposes, such as residential, commercial, industrial, and public uses.

latent functions Unanticipated consequences of an organization's activity.

legalistic style of policing Police emphasize the law enforcement aspect of their jobs.

liberal view of causes of disorder Seeing violence as the result of social conditions.

life style Dominant characteristics of the social component of communities.

local special districts Governmental entities created to deliver specific services, for example, schools, fire protection, transportation, water and sewers, and parks and recreation.

logrolling Practice of exchanging favors— "You vote more money for my pet projects, and I'll support your pet projects."

long ballot The number of elected officials is so large that the paper ballot has to be long in order to hold all the offices.

loopholes, tax Special provisions in the tax code that lower the tax obligation for those who qualify; also known as tax expenditures.

majority-minority electoral districts Districts created to ensure that a minority group in the larger society constitutes a majority in the district.

mandates Requirements established at one level of government that other levels of government must meet, whether or not they create costs for the government to comply.

manifest functions Duties that an organization is directly designed to carry out.

marginal utility Economic concept that examines the satisfaction gained from the last unit of a good or service obtained. It is usually assumed that the first units hold more value than the last; for example, you would give greater value to

the first ice cream cone you received than the tenth.

mercantile city Cities in Colonial America in which government regulated and promoted commerce.

metropolis Urban area with a large population and many local governments, including cities, suburbs, counties, and others.

metropolitan area *See* **metropolis.**

metropolitan multi-purpose district Special district that performs more than one service function.

mixed systems System in which some councilors are elected at-large and others by districts.

moralistic political culture Belief that the local government has a responsibility for the economic and social life of the community.

muckrakers The name given to individuals who searched for and exposed misconduct of prominent individuals and organizations in the late nineteenth century.

multiple elites Model in which theorists reject the idea of a single elite controlling cities by pulling strings from behind the scenes. They argue that government officials do control the decision making and that multiple elites compete with each other for the right to control government offices. Citizens play little role in affecting the policies adopted by the elite, yet citizens are not completely powerless for they control which elite is in power through elections.

nondecision making Making of decisions implicitly by refusing to discuss an issue.

nonguaranteed debt Bonds issued by governments not backed by "full faith and credit" but by revenues brought in by the activity for which the bonds were issued.

nonpartisan ballot   Election ballot in which candidates' names are listed without a party label. These were established so that voters would select the best person regardless of party affiliation.

ombudsman   Contact person for citizens to help them with their problems with the government.

one-tier or city-county consolidation   Structure of government that combines two levels of government into a single government.

operationalization   Specification of empirical, that is, observable, indicators of unobservable concepts.

organizational model of decision-making   Posits that different organizations develop decision rules (Standard Operating Procedures or SOPs) as shortcuts for defining and dealing with problem situations.

outright deficit fix   Using borrowed money to balance the budget.

patronage   Reward of supporters with government jobs or other material benefits.

penetrability   Degree to which issues can be placed on the agenda for consideration by the political system.

personalism   Characteristic of small towns whereby individuals establish close connections because most know each other.

persuasion   Type of bargaining in which the disputants try to convince others to support their positions by presenting a compelling argument for a course of action.

planned unit development (PUD)   Land development in which relatively large parcels of land are "planned" so as to develop a mix of land uses to create an interdependent community.

planning   Method of guiding decisionmakers in making decisions and taking actions to affect the future in a consistent and rational manner and in a way that helps achieve a desired goal.

plea bargaining   Defense and prosecuting lawyers cooperate to strike a deal for the defendant that ensures punishment of a defendant for a lesser crime rather than going to trial on more serious charges and possibly ending up with no conviction.

pluralism   System in which multiple groups compete for power.

pluralistic power structure   Structure in which power is distributed among many—plural—sources.

policy   What governments say and do about a particular issue.

policy adoption   Stage of the policy process in which a choice is made among competing policies.

policy agenda   Combination of issues that are the focus of public debate and decision.

policy evaluation   Stage of the policy process in which the impact of a policy is examined to determine whether it addresses the problem that initially triggered the process.

policy formulation   Stage of the policy process in which proposed solutions are developed to address a social problem.

policy implementation   Stage of the policy process in which an adopted policy is put into effect.

political culture   Fundamental attitudes about the proper role of government in society and of the citizens who are part of society.

political economy   Interrelationship between economic factors and government policy.

political efficacy Feeling that one's actions can have an impact on the political system.

political incorporation Extent to which a group has become part of the governing coalition and has used that access to influence public policy.

political machines Very strong party organizations that develop a loyal following by distributing tangible material benefits such as jobs to potential supporters, along with symbolic rewards such as recognition.

positive externality Those not part of a transaction reap benefits from it.

post-suburban era Period when a new pattern of development blends the characteristics of suburbia with characteristics of the central city in "edge cities." These communities combine major shopping, job, and entertainment centers near typical suburban residential development.

power elite Single upper-class group that rules in its own interest in the community. Political and civic leaders are subordinate to the elites' wishes.

preventative policies Social programs instituted so that people can be protected from falling into poverty as the result of circumstances beyond their control.

privatism Belief that government should play a passive role in cities and act primarily to support the decisions of private actors.

privatization Process by which the public sector shifts the delivery of a service to the private sector.

private-regarding Preference for personalized politics, with favoritism to oneself or one's group.

problem formation Recognition that a problem exists that the public sector might address.

productivity Efficiency with which outputs are produced in relationship to inputs used, or the ratio of output to input.

progressive [regimes] Governing coalitions that focus not only on opposing the pressures to foster growth and economic development, but also on redistributing resources to citizens.

Progressives Reformers at the turn of the nineteenth century who sought the separation of politics and administration and attempted to devise apolitical structures.

progressive tax Tax in which higher-income people pay a larger percentage of their incomes in tax than lower-income people. This form of tax is based on the ability-to-pay principle.

project grants Discretionary monetary transfers between government for specific projects.

proportional tax Tax in which everyone pays the same proportion; for example, all pay 6 percent on a purchase. Such a tax is based on horizontal equity and benefits-received principles.

pseudo-evaluations Evaluations, performed with a political agenda in mind, that are not really designed to determine the effectiveness of the program.

public choice School of thought maintaining that fragmentation allows citizens to select communities based on the amenities available, similar to allowing consumer choice in the marketplace.

public goods Goods from which it is impossible to exclude individuals. One person's use does not diminish the benefits to others, and they are provided to all in equal quantities.

public interest Belief that there is a common good that is greater than individual interests.

public opinion Beliefs held by the general population about current issues.

public-regarding Values that supposedly support the common good.

punitive policies Social programs designed to punish or at least demean the poor.

rational actor model Model in which the policy maker must first clearly determine what problem needs to be solved before establishing goals and priorities. The next step is to develop alternative means to reach the goals or ends. Means are evaluated. Finally the "best" alternative is selected.

radical view [of causes of disorder] considered the urban riots as rebellion against a political and economic system that left African-Americans in a position of subjugation.

recall election Election to determine whether a candidate should be removed from office.

redlining Practice in which banks refuse to make mortgage loans in certain neighborhoods believed to be deteriorating. This practice makes it impossible for people to buy or repair houses in a neighborhood and, therefore, accelerate the deterioration of the area.

referendum Election in which citizens vote to sustain or repeal a law previously approved by a legislative body.

reformed urban county Attempt to provide better coordination within the county by strengthening the leadership structure with a county administrator or county executive.

regimes Relatively stable group interacting regularly in the making of governing decisions.

regional or **metropolitan council of government** Council established for the purpose of developing comprehensive plans for the metropolitan area as a whole.

regional special districts or **authorities** Entities created to control policy in a particular area or areas. They have the authority to issue bonds.

regressive tax Tax in which lower-income individuals pay a higher percentage of their income than those with higher incomes.

reputational approach for studying power Methodology that entails compiling lists of prominent people from various areas of social structure—government leaders, civic leaders, business leaders, and status leaders—and asking "judges" to choose the most influential people in the city from those lists.

revenue anticipation notes (RANs) Non-guaranteed short-term debt that will be paid when expected receipts are collected.

revenue fix treats next year's anticipated revenue as if it were this year's.

sales tax credit A credit granted to taxpayers enabling them to deduct the amount of money paid for sales taxes from their income taxes.

scientific management School of management that believed that through time and motion studies the "one best way" to manage could be found that would maximize economy and efficiency.

segregation Stage of the ecological process of spatial patterning in which separate areas have specialized uses. This term is also used to refer to areas that are differentiated by racial, socioeconomic, age, ethnic, or other, uniqueness.

service style of policing   Police intervene frequently (unlike the watchman style) but are not likely to intervene formally (unlike the legalistic style).

short ballot   Ballot with few people who had to be chosen by election.

siting restrictions   Use of pressure and zoning regulations to prevent public housing projects in specific locations.

social reformers   Opponents of machine politics who tried to institute policies to help the lower classes who were being exploited by the machines.

social setting   Social make-up of a community.

spatial setting   Characteristics and influence of geographical location.

special use or **conditional use permit**   Permit that allows certain land uses if owners comply with specific stipulations.

subdivision regulation   Usually a set of rules that establish minimum lot sizes, street and utility placement, provision for open space, and any special requirements for dividing large parcels of land into building-size lots.

subsystems or **subgovernments**   Groups of individuals inside and outside of government with expertise and interest in certain policy areas who regularly work together to further their general interests.

succession   Stage of the ecological process in which the land use or groups in an area are different from those originally established when the area was first developed.

system maintenance   Keeping the existing infrastructure in good repair.

tax anticipation notes (TANs)   Non-guaranteed short-term debt that will be paid when taxes owed are collected.

tax expenditure   Tax income forgone by government. *See also* **loopholes.**

tax overlap   Two governments collecting revenue on the same base, for example, when both the national government and state governments tax income.

tax sharing   Taxes collected by one level of government are given to another. Most commonly state governments "give back" money collected in local jurisdictions. Tax sharing is used to make the tax collection more efficient.

three-tier reform, metropolitan-wide structure   Intricate governmental structure that provides strong mechanisms for regional cooperation.

traditionalist political culture   Set of beliefs that sees the role of government as limited and led by socially prominent people.

transfer of functions   Shifting service delivery from one level of government to another.

transportation planning   Attempting to determine future development trends and then planning to develop road or mass transit proposals to meet future needs.

two-tier system or **federated structure**   System in which a local municipality retains control over some services and policies, while the county or another local government retains control over other services and policies.

uncontrollable budgets   Budgets in which funds are already committed, either by law or by previous agreement.

underclass hypothesis   States that service delivery patterns are affected by socioeconomic status. Those at the bottom of the socioeconomic status hierarchy appear to be discriminated against and receive inferior services because they have less power or standing in the community.

unitarist ethos Concern for the interests and general welfare of the community as a whole along with a desire for good government.

urban renewal Federal aid to be used for urban redevelopment. It usually involved purchase of blighted slum areas with federal funds and local development through the public or private sectors.

vertical equity Criterion for apportioning taxes that holds that unequals should be taxed unequally.

voting blocs Identifiable groups that can communicate citizen demands to government through aggregated votes.

watchman style, of policing Police emphasize the function of peacekeeping. In their attempts to maintain order, they often ignore what they consider to be minor offenses.

zero-sum conflict Resources going to others are resources that will not come to you. That is, if there are winners, there must be losers, with the final total balancing out to zero.

zone of better residences Generally the area of the city in the concentric zone model of urban development, containing moderately expensive homes, that spans the boundaries of city and suburb.

zone of transition Area of the city in the concentric zone model of urban development that is composed of areas on the fringes of the downtown that have become run down.

zone of workers' homes Blue-collar neighborhood in the city in the concentric zone model of urban development that is between the zone of transition and higher-class suburban development.

zoning Policy by which a city specifies the purposes for which a particular piece of land may be used. Zoning facilitates the orderly development sought in the land use plan by regulating how space is utilized, identifying areas for residential, commercial, and industrial use, and establishing usage standards.

Index

('b' indicates boxed material; 'i' indicates an illustration; 'n' indicates a note; 't' indicates a table)